# FILM AND THE AMERICAN LEFT

# FILM AND THE AMERICAN LEFT

## A Research Guide

M. KEITH BOOKER

**GREENWOOD PRESS**
Westport, Connecticut • London

**Library of Congress Cataloging-in-Publication Data**

Booker, M. Keith.
    Film and the American left : a research guide / M. Keith Booker.
      p. cm.
    Includes bibliographical references and index.
    ISBN 0–313–30980–9 (alk. paper)
    1. Motion pictures—Political aspects—United States.  2. Working
class in motion pictures.  I. Title.
    PN1995.9.P6B66   1999
    791.43′658—dc21       99–11268

British Library Cataloguing in Publication Data is available.

Library of Congress Catalog Card Number: 99–11268
ISBN: 0–313–30980–9

First published in 1999

Greenwood Press, 88 Post Road West, Westport, CT 06881
An imprint of Greenwood Publishing Group, Inc.
www.greenwood.com

Printed in the United States of America

The paper used in this book complies with the
Permanent Paper Standard issued by the National
Information Standards Organization (Z39.48–1984).

10 9 8 7 6 5 4 3 2 1

For Dubravka

# CONTENTS

# PREFACE

The following is a reference work intended to provide a useful starting point for students and scholars interested in the cultural production of the American Left, a phenomenon that has been largely ignored in mainstream accounts of American cultural history but that is coming more and more to be recognized as a crucial element of American culture in the twentieth century. This volume joins the author's earlier *The Modern British Novel of the Left* (Greenwood Press, 1998) and *The Modern American Novel of the Left* (Greenwood Press, 1999), which catalog the production of novels by leftist writers in Britain and the United States. The current volume includes detailed discussions of more than 260 films that have either addressed ideas and issues of concern to the American Left or at least included central contributions from writers, directors, and actors with leftist inclinations or associations.

The discussions of individual films in this volume focus on the engagement of the films with leftist ideas and concerns. "Leftist" is defined here in the broad sense of a quest for economic, social, and political justice for all people, regardless of their class, ethnicity, or gender. "Leftist" here also implies a suspicion, inspired by the Marxist tradition of social critique, that capitalism is fundamentally incompatible with this quest for justice. As such, this volume seeks to demonstrate the extent to which a leftist critique of capitalism has informed the production of the American film industry. The focus is on mainstream Hollywood films, although a number of documentaries and other independent films are also included, especially when their leftist messages are particularly strong or when they demonstrate important historical trends in American filmmaking.

There are, of course, a number of ironies and difficulties inherent in this project. For one thing, any attempt to tease out the presence of leftist ideas in films that are in general not overtly leftist places the investigator in a position weirdly reminiscent of that of the House Un-American Activities Committee (HUAC) of the late 1940s and 1950s, which seemed almost desperate to detect a sinister communist influence behind even the most seemingly innocent film motifs. In the present volume, however, the presence of leftist ideas is considered a positive virtue. Meanwhile, this volume also pays significant attention to the suppression of leftist ideas and to the extent to which American filmmakers have felt it necessary (partly because of pressures such as those brought to bear in the HUAC investigations) to suppress leftist ideas, or at least to express leftist concerns in extremely oblique and muted ways.

Michael Denning's *The Cultural Front* (1996) has been an especially valuable forerunner to this effort. Denning's argument that the legacy of the proletarian culture of the 1930s has in fact remained far more influential in subsequent American culture is important and largely convincing. However, Denning points out that the most important evidence of this influence is found not in literature, but in popular culture, particularly film. Indeed, film has long been a part of American leftist culture, from the early working-class silents, to the work of Orson Welles, the "Hollywood Ten," and other leftists (many of them members of the Communist Party) in the middle part of the century, to the countercultural films of the 1960s and 1970s, to the recent political films of new filmmakers such as John Sayles and Oliver Stone. On the other hand, the relationship between film and the American Left has been a complex one. For one thing, there have been far more antileftist films than leftist ones; for another, most leftist filmmakers have been forced by the exigencies of the American film industry to work within constraints that are highly inimical to the expression of genuinely leftist political ideas.

The films to be included in this guide come from a number of categories. For example, many of the earliest films discussed are silents made by working-class directors, often with the financial support of labor unions. American industrial capitalism and American organized labor, a response to the growing exploitation of workers by the new capitalism, both came into full force at the beginning of the twentieth century. Film arose at approximately the same time, so it is not surprising that both labor and capital would employ the new medium as a tool in their efforts to popularize their positions. Indeed, as Steven Ross has argued in his important recent book, *Working-Class Hollywood* (1998), film became a crucial part of American working-class culture even as early as the first decade of the century and continued so until the political repression associated with World War I put a virtual halt to the making of such films (and to radical organized labor activity in general). Even pioneer silent filmmaker D. W. Griffith, although often remembered for his racist politics in films such as *The Birth of a Nation*, had certain working-class loyalties and made numerous early films of protest against the exploitation of workers by emergent American capitalism. And, of course, Charlie Chaplin (essentially exiled from America in the 1950s because of his leftist politics), consistently lampooned the rich and showed sympathy for the poor, even in his earliest films, though it was not until the sequence of films beginning with *Modern Times* (1936) and extending through *The Great Dictator* (1940) and *A King in New York* (1957) that his leftist political position became overt in his films. Given the participation of such important figures as Griffith and Chaplin, it is clear that early working-class film was central not only to the evolution of leftist culture but to the evolution of the cinema itself.

The 1920s saw the beginnings of the reemergence of working-class film, though this phenomenon was quickly cut short by the rise to dominance of Hollywood and the Hollywood style in American film. Nevertheless, films with working-class themes continued to be made and even experienced something of a resurgence in the 1930s, as can be seen by the fact that left-leaning documentaries, such as Pare Lorentz's *The Plow that Broke the Plains* (1936) and *The River* (1937), were made under the sponsorship of the U.S. government as part of the New Deal. Independent leftist film companies produced a number of important documentaries in the 1930s as well, and even commercial Hollywood films were forced to pay attention to the social and economic conditions brought about by the Depression of that decade.

The Depression also played a central role in the dramatic increase in production of proletarian novels in the 1930s, and many of these novels were eventually made into films, though often in diluted form. By the beginning of the 1940s, the major political emphasis in films of the Left was antifascism, in accord with the policies of the Popular Front alliance against fascism. Political films through the 1940s were dominated by such themes, and the war years brought leftist filmmakers, with their strong antifascist experience and credentials, to the forefront in Hollywood. The HUAC purges and subsequent blacklists brought this prominence to a quick end, and Hollywood political films of the postwar years tended to be virulently anticommunist—though some of these anticommunist films are so ludicrous that one is tempted to suspect a sly attempt to undermine anticommunism by demonstrating the hatred, hysteria, and irrationality that lay at its heart.

Meanwhile, in the late 1940s and early 1950s, the genre of the film noir, often regarded as the quintessential American film form, had risen to prominence in American film. A close look at this genre, however, shows that many of its leading practitioners (Welles is an obvious example) had ties to the political Left. Moreover, recent readings of the film noir by Denning and other scholars (such as Mike Davis) have emphasized the subtle anticapitalist message that seems to be inscribed in the genre as a whole, even if there is generally no accompanying suggestion that socialism or other noncapitalist systems might provide a preferable alternative.

Although the political climate of the 1950s made it impossible to make overtly leftist films in Hollywood, subtly leftist films continued to be made. Moreover, leftist filmmakers, blacklisted and exiled from Hollywood, made a few independent, overtly leftist films, of which Herbert Biberman's *Salt of the Earth* (1954) is the leading example. Meanwhile, leftist films dealing with American themes, such as *A King in New York* or the British films of Joseph Losey, continued to be made abroad. Then, in the 1960s, the blacklist was broken with films such as *Spartacus* (1960, written by Dalton Trumbo, one of the Hollywood Ten), and a whole new kind of oppositional political films, in tune with the climate of the time, began to be made, even by mainstream Hollywood studios. Formerly blacklisted director Martin Ritt made a particularly large number of working-class films in the 1960s and subsequent decades, while emergent directors such as Stanley Kubrick, John Sayles, and Oliver Stone treated numerous political themes, including labor activism, Vietnam, American imperialism, racism, and the Culture Industry.

Together, these films indicate the existence of a rich, though complex, relationship between film and the American Left throughout the twentieth century. This guide seeks to track that tradition. In that spirit, it is arranged chronologically, rather than in the alphabetical arrangement typical of reference works. Within years, films are arranged alphabetically by title. In addition, to facilitate location of films by title, an alphabetical list of the films discussed is included in Appendix 1. Appendix 2 includes a list of the films arranged by director. To facilitate further research, a selected bibliography is included at the end of the discussion of each individual film.

# SUMMARIES OF
# SELECTED FILMS

*THE STRIKE* (PATHÉ, 1904). Modern consumer capitalism and motion picture arose almost simultaneously in America at the beginning of the twentieth century. It is no surprise, then, that emergent capitalism is one of the central subjects of early silent films. But early films also often deal with the concomitant attempts of the working class to resist the increasingly exploitative practices of the new system. *The Strike*, a silent short made for American distribution by the French company Pathé Frères, an early leader in the industry, is a good example of this phenomenon. It centers on a strike by workers in a factory where the abusive owner's continuing refusal to meet their just demands eventually leads to a violent confrontation in which several striking workers are shot dead by the factory's security force. The mother of one of the dead strikers then avenges herself by killing the factory owner. She is arrested and brought to trial but released after the owner's son, recognizing the evils of his father's ways, pleads on her behalf. This conciliatory attitude then leads to a resolution of the earlier difficulties as the son, now in charge of the factory, agrees to install more equitable management practices. The film is thus ultimately liberal, rather than radical, attributing the exploitation of workers to bad management rather than to the capitalist system. Nevertheless, it is a good illustration of the extent to which working-class concerns were represented in the genre of film from the very beginning. *Selected bibliography:* Musser.

*THE MINING DISTRICT* (PATHÉ, 1905). Like the even earlier *The Strike* (1904), *The Mining District* is an example of the films made for American distribution by the French firm Pathé Frères in the first part of the twentieth century. *The Mining District* includes scenes of a man and his son laboring in a coal mine, making clear the harshness of the conditions under which they are forced to work. Moreover, these conditions are unsafe, as becomes clear when an explosion occurs in the mine, killing the son. The film then ends with a shot of the bereaved father weeping over the body of his fallen son. Sentimental and simplistic though it may be, *The Mining District* is clear in its sympathy for the depicted miners and equally clear in its suggestion that their lives are made more difficult (and more dangerous) by the practices imposed upon them by the mining company in its ruthless quest for profits. *Selected bibliography:* Musser.

**THE BANK DEFAULTER (LUBIN, 1906).** As Charles Musser notes, *The Bank Defaulter* is essentially a reworking of Edison's 1905 production, *The Kleptomaniac* (479). However, the later film, produced by the upstart Lubin Company, is much more radical in its "explicitly subversive view of society" (479). In particular, *The Bank Defaulter* frequently cuts back and forth between scenes from the life of its wealthy, but evil, banker and scenes from the lives of his poor, but virtuous, working-class depositors. Moreover, the film makes it clear that the wealth of the banker is obtained through exploitation of his poor depositors. The banker is, on the surface, a paradigm of respectability, attending church regularly and doting on his family. He is soon revealed, however, as an adulterer and thief, who flees with a large sum of money stolen from his depositors. The latter are plunged into poverty due to the loss of their savings. The banker is apprehended and taken to trial, but, in a clear comment on the class inequality of American justice, he is acquitted of the crime and released—just after a poor woman, one of his ruined depositors, has been shown being convicted of stealing a loaf of bread to avoid starvation. Somewhat sensational and simplistic, *The Bank Defaulter* with its depiction of the American justice system as a prop for upper-class immorality at the expense of the poor, well illustrates the tendency of early Lubin films to play to working-class audiences. *Selected bibliography:* Musser.

**THE MILL GIRL (VITAGRAPH, 1907).** *The Mill Girl* was one of a number of films in the first two decades of this century to emphasize the fact that, while workers in general were being exploited under the emergent system of American industrial capitalism, women often came in for special forms of harassment. In the film, a girl working in a textile mill is subjected to the unwanted sexual advances of the mill owner. The young man she loves, who also works in the mill, comes to her rescue and knocks down the owner, who then decides to seek revenge by hiring two thugs to beat up the man. However, the thugs turn out to be no match for the worker, with his superior strength and intelligence. The boss then fires the worker and returns to his sexual harassment of the girl but is interrupted when a fire breaks out in the mill. The girl is endangered by the fire, but is saved when her lover returns to rescue her.

As Steven Ross notes, the number of working women in America doubled between 1890 and 1910, and *The Mill Girl* was one of a number of films that responded to this social phenomenon (51). Moreover, if the content of the film reflects changes in American society, the form of the film reflects changes in film itself. As Eileen Bowser notes, the film, as a melodrama, was unusual for its time, although melodrama would soon become the dominant mode in American cinema (60). Moreover, the film features an unusually large number of different shots and unusual camera angles that help to call attention to the most significant action and to link sequences of shots together in ways that were soon adopted by other filmmakers. Made by Vitagraph, one of the leading early film companies, *The Mill Girl* illustrates the centrality of working-class themes to the early American cinema. *Selected bibliography:* Bowser; Ross.

*THE UNWRITTEN LAW* (LUBIN, 1907). Called by Charles Musser "the most controversial film produced prior to the establishment of the Board of Censorship in 1909," *The Unwritten Law* (subtitled "A Thrilling Drama Based on the Thaw-White Tragedy") is a sensational film account of murder and sexual adventure among the decadent rich (479). The film is based on the 1906 shooting of famed architect Stanford White by millionaire Harry K. Thaw after Thaw's discovery that White had seduced Thaw's wife, model Evelyn Nesbitt, some years before their marriage. This same incident would later become the basis of an important part of the plot of E. L. Doctorow's novel *Ragtime* (1974, film adaptation 1981). It still remains one of the most sensational media events of the twentieth century. The film appeared while the case was very much in the news; indeed, Thaw (who was ultimately acquitted on the grounds of insanity after his first trial ended in a hung jury) was still in the midst of his first trial at the time. The film is clearly an attempt to cash in on the notoriety of the case and the widespread media attention it had received—attention that, among other things, ultimately made Nesbitt the first major sex symbol of American media culture. But the film also capitalized on the widespread belief that the rich were decadent and immoral and would stoop to virtually anything in the pursuit of pleasure.

The film is largely supportive of Thaw, arguing, as the title indicates, for the existence of an unwritten law that allows husbands to defend their conjugal rights by any means necessary. In particular, the film tends to verify Thaw's suspicions and justify his reaction by showing Nesbitt as she goes to White's home, where he stupefies her with drugged wine, rendering her defenseless so he can have his way with her. Such scenes made the film a big hit with audiences around the country, though it was banned in numerous locations, presumably because of its scandalous subject matter. However, its sharp, class-based critique of the immorality of the rich (typical of the Lubin films of the time) no doubt contributed to the opposition to the film. *Selected bibliography:* Bowser; Musser.

*THE SONG OF THE SHIRT:* **DIR. D. W. GRIFFITH (1908).** One of nearly 500 short films produced by director D. W. Griffith for Biograph between 1908 and 1913, *The Song of the Shirt* is a central example of Griffith's early working-class cinema, constructed around a Manichean opposition between the evil of the exploitative rich and the virtue of the oppressed poor. Some of the film's most striking visual images involve stark contrasts between the poverty in which the poor must live and the luxurious surroundings of the rich. It opens, for example, with a scene in the meager flat where a poor seamstress (played by Florence Lawrence) lives and does piece work (her sewing machine stands in the center of the room) to try to support herself and her mortally ill sister, who shares the flat. In the next scenes, Lawrence's character has to suffer insults and abuse simply to get piece work from a local factory, while the owner of the factory is shown carousing in a fancy restaurant with first one woman and then two women. The factory's inspector then declares Lawrence's work inferior and refuses to pay for it, increasing her desperation, while the owner continues his debauchery in alternate scenes. As the film comes to a close, Lawrence's sister, unable to obtain medical care because of the lack of money, suffers a melodramatic death, while Lawrence tears her hair in grief.

As Steven Ross notes, Griffith's representation of poverty in this and other early films is a bit sanitized and unrealistic. Florence's flat, for example, is impeccably neat and clean, despite her poverty and over-work, contributing to a representation of the poor as "middle-class people without money" (50). Griffith's sympathy for the poor thus seems contingent upon their willingness to accept middle-class values, and it certainly presents no fundamental challenge to the capitalist system. Nevertheless, Griffith's representation of the rich as idle and decadent and of the poor as respectable and hard-working did a great deal to challenge contemporary notions that the rich become rich because of their talent and hard work, while the poor become poor because of their laziness and moral degeneracy. *Screenplay:* D. W. Griffith and Frank E. Woods. *Selected bibliography:* Gunning; Jesionowski; Ross.

*A CORNER IN WHEAT:* **DIR. D. W. GRIFFITH (1909).** Based on Frank Norris's novel *The Pit* (1903), *A Corner of Wheat* is a fourteen-minute short that attempts to capture, in condensed form, the gist of Norris's story of unscrupulous speculation in the wheat market. Employing Griffith's characteristic technique of alternating contrasts, the film constantly switches back and forth between scenes focusing on poor workers, who are actually responsible for the production of wheat, and rich investors, who make most of the profits from this production. The film begins with a shot of farmers sowing wheat in a field, then immediately switches to a shot of wealthy speculator W. J. Hammond, who is concocting a plan to corner the world market in wheat. We next see a shot of the commodities exchange, where Hammond's manipulations trigger a frenzy of trading in wheat. The result is a dramatic rise in wheat prices, resulting in huge profits for Hammond, whom we next see celebrating at a lavish banquet. By contrast, in the next scene, set in a baker's shop, the price of bread has risen so high that the kinds of poor workers who actually produce the wheat can no longer afford to buy bread.

After a series of cuts back and forth between the banquet and the bakery, the next scene features a visit by Hammond and some of his cronies to a wheat processing facility to see his investments in operation. While there, he receives a communication informing him that he has now gained control of the entire world's supply of wheat. Excited, he accidentally falls into a grain elevator and is smothered to death as tons of grain pour in on top of him. As the film ends, he is dragged out of the grain, crushed and suffocated by the object of his own greed. The final shot then shows a farmer again planting wheat, as the cycle of production goes on. *A Corner in Wheat* is probably Griffith's best known critique of class inequality in America. The film leaves no doubt that justice has been served through Hammond's death, and it makes clear the contrast between the evil rich and the suffering, but virtuous poor, a contrast that is typical of early Griffith films. There is, however, no suggestion in the film, or in any other Griffith film, that these class differences might be resolved by socialist means. *Screenplay:* D. W. Griffith and Frank E. Woods. *Selected bibliography:* Bowser; Davison; Gunning; Jesionowski; Ross.

*THE LONG STRIKE* (ESSANAY, 1911). Charles Musser identifies such films as *The Long Strike*, *The Girl Strike Leader* (1910), *The High Road* (1915), and *Her Bitter Cup* (1916), as important for their "compelling portraits of women labor leaders who led their comrades, male and female, on strike" (74). In *The Long Strike*, the haughty son of a factory owner (a stock character in early working-class films), takes over as a strike looms. He nearly falls victim to an attack by the strikers but is saved by the intervention of the daughter of one of the strikers. A cross-class romance for the two appears to be on horison, but the young woman instead opts to remain true to her class and to reject the owner's son in favor of a suitor from the working class.

*The Long Strike* is notable for its refusal of the notion that any working-class woman would jump at the chance to be courted by an upper-class man. Also important is its general depiction of workers as adult human beings rather than as children dependent on their paternal bosses or dehumanized animals snarling viciously in response to their bosses' commands. On the other hand, the film seems to assume without question that strikers tend to resort to violence, thus accepting a standard (but inaccurate) antilabor cliché of the time. The film thus led some contemporary reviewers to suggest that strikes should be avoided as the subjects of future films for fear that such depictions might ignite the pre-existing tendencies of strikers toward violence. *Selected bibliography:* Bowser; Musser.

*A MARTYR TO HIS CAUSE* (SEELY, 1911). On October 1, 1910, the downtown printing plant of the *Los Angeles Times* (a notoriously antilabor paper) was rocked by two explosions that, together with the subsequent fire, caused massive damage to the building and led to the deaths of twenty-one men. Six months later, John McNamara, secretary-treasurer of the International Association of Bridge and Structural Iron Workers Union (BSIW) was arrested and charged with the bombing, along with his younger brother, James. The subsequent trial, in which Clarence Darrow was brought in by Samuel Gompers to defend the brothers, became one of the most important in U.S. labor history. Bill Haywood, the IWW leader, called for a national general strike on the first day of the trial, and Labor Day of 1911 was widely observed as "McNamara Day" as crowds gathered around the country to declare their belief in the innocent of the McNamara brothers. The two brothers, confronted by substantial evidence against them, eventually pled guilty in late November 1911, James to bombing the *Times* plant and John as an accessory to the separate bombing of a local factory. Darrow alienated many socialists by encouraging the guilty plea. In the meantime, he himself was charged with attempting to bribe a juror in the case, but was acquitted after offering an eloquent defense in his own behalf.

Made by the W. H. Seely Company with funds supplied by the American Federation of Labor's (AFL's) McNamara Legal Defense Committee, *A Martyr to His Cause* was part of a major effort mounted by the BSIW to portray the McNamaras as innocent victims of an anti-union conspiracy. It was America's first feature-length worker-made film (Ross 93). Focusing on John McNamara, the film seeks to create a sympathetic image by showing various scenes from his life that portray him as a ordinary, decent citizen who loves his family and works hard to make a better life for them. The film also focuses on the questionable tactics used by the authorities in the investigation of the crime and on the illegal techniques used to arrest John at a union meeting in Indianapolis and then bring him to Los Angeles without a proper extradition procedure. Finally, it plays to the emotions of audiences by featuring sentimental scenes such as the McNamaras' mother weeping over the fate of her sons. Although playing to relatively conservative values in its portrayal of John McNamara as a solid citizen, *A Martyr to His Cause* is radical in its defense of union activity and in its presentation of the legal system as part of a criminal antilabor conspiracy. It played to large audiences after its September 1911, release, but its run came to an abrupt end after the November confessions. As Ross notes, the film was a good example of the strategy of worker-filmmakers of "wrapping explicit political messages in the popular garb of narrative melodramas filled with romance and action" (92). *Selected bibliography:* Adamic; Buhle, Buhle, and Georgakis; Ross.

*CHILDREN WHO LABOR:* **DIR. ASHLEY MILLER (1912).** *Children Who Labor* appeared in the midst of a national debate over the exploitative use of child labor in the new industries of emergent American capitalism in the early twentieth century. The film was produced by the Edison Company in cooperation with the Child Labor Committee as part of a national campaign to gain support for new child labor legislation that was being considered at the time. It appeals for sympathy primarily through melodramatic scenes of suffering children trudging into a hellish factory to work, pleading as they enter to a huge allegorical figure of Uncle Sam to rescue them from their plight. Clouds in the darkened skies over the factory form the word "GREED," suggesting the reason for their plight. Unfortunately, Uncle Sam ignores their pleas, as does the heartless factory owner, Mr. Hanscomb, who is interested only in increasing his profits by employing cheap child labor. Then follows an unlikely series of events in which Hanscomb's daughter falls off a train and is taken in by a poor immigrant family, essentially becoming their adopted daughter. She is soon forced to go to work in her real father's factory, where she collapses from exhaustion but is eventually recognized and reunited with her father. The latter now realizes the error of his former ways and decides henceforth to employ only adult labor. The happy children, freed from labor, can now return to school, though the film ends with another scene of more suffering child workers vainly begging Uncle Sam for help, warning that the problem is far from solved.

Presumably designed to support government intervention in the child labor problem, *Children Who Labor* identifies enlightened bosses like Mr. Hanscomb after the reunion with his daughter as the true solution to the problem. The politics of the film are thus ultimately moderate, despite the tone of moral outrage. As Steven Ross points out, "neither this nor other films dealing with factory exploitation or the horrors of tenement life ever ask why these conditions arose or challenge the capitalsit system that created them or the government that sustained them" (54). *Children Who Labor* is a testament to the early recognition of the potential political power of film, but it also demonstrates the difficulty of making truly radical political statements in the emergent medium. *Selected bibliography:* Bowser; Ross.

*BY MAN'S LAW:* **DIR. WILLIAM CHRISTY CABANNE (1913).** In a rather transparent reference to John D. Rockefeller's Standard Oil Company, *By Man's Law* features an evil oil magnate who takes control of the industry by ruthlessly gobbling up his competitors, then uses his newfound monopoly power to cut costs and increase profits to the detriment of his workers. He meanwhile manipulates the police to support his policies and help keep his workers in line. His actions cause numerous workers to lose their jobs, and one of them, a young working girl, nearly falls victim to white slavers as the result of her unemployment. The film's delineation of the human cost (especially to the working class) of the greedy and unscrupulous practices of robber barons such as Rockefeller is quite clear, though not necessarily radical, especially as its critique of the oil monopoly is not inconsistent with the policies of the U.S. government at the time. Ironically, the film was made by Biograph, a company that was itself part of a trust then under attack by the federal government. Still, the film was judged controversial enough to be banned by local authorities in several cities. *Selected bibliography:* Bowser; Ross.

*FROM DUSK TO DAWN:* **DIR. FRANK E. WOLFE (1913).** A ninety-minute feature made with professional actors and production personnel, *From Dusk to Dawn* (also known as *Capital Versus Labor*) was one of the most sophisticated (and successful) of the numerous films about working-class subjects made in Hollywood in the first two decades of this century. Made with the cooperation of the Socialist Party in Los Angeles, the film's plot line centers on a romance between two working-class characters, iron molder Dan Grayson and laundress Carlena Wayne. But this romance develops against a background of labor activism and leftist politics. Some of the film's most powerful images involve scenes of poverty in the squalid urban slums in which workers much live, combined with scenes of the stifling and unsafe conditions under which they must work. These scenes are made all the more powerful by their accuracy, many of them having been taken from actual documentary footage. Employing a technique frequently used by writers such as Émile Zola (and used earlier in film by D. W. Griffith), Wolfe also enhances the power of his images of the hardships and poverty of workers by cutting back and forth between these images and scenes of the luxury enjoyed by the decadent rich who have gained their wealth through exploitation of the poor workers.

The plot of the film involves the gradual evolution of the love between Dan and Carlena as they become centrally involved in a battle of factory workers against their exploitative employers. Fired for leading their fellow workers in a demand for higher wages and safer working conditions (after an explosion in the factory kills Carlena's brother), the two become the focus of a strike as their fellow workers, in a show of working-class solidarity, go out to protest the firings. Countering conservative films at the time (which tended to depict strikers as demented fiends gathering in violent mobs), the film shows the strikers as orderly, reasonable, and well organized. They also remains staunchly committed to their cause, despite attacks by hired thugs and police and the arrest of Dan and Carlena under a hastily passed anti-picketing law. The strikers remain firm even with their leaders in jail, and the strike is eventually won. Propelled by this victory, Dan subsequently goes into politics and runs for governor on the ticket of the Socialist Party. Fearful of a Socialist victory in the election, the capitalists attempt to frame Dan on conspiracy charges, but Dan is successfully defended in court by Clarence Darrow (played by himself) and acquitted. Buoyed by strong working-class support, Dan is elected governor. The Socialists take control of the state senate as well and begin to implement their program, though in a reasonable and moderate way. The film then culminates as a new age of social justice dawns with the two lovers in each other's arms, having found personal happiness through their contributions to collective struggle.

*From Dusk to Dawn* is an important film both for its open endorsement of socialism as a solution to America's early-twentieth-century social ills and for its innovative cinematic techniques, particularly in its mixture of documentary and fictional footage. Heartily endorsed by union and socialist newspapers, the film was a great commercial success, playing to large and enthusiastic audiences. Forward-looking both in its treatment of class and in its treatment of gender, it shows workers as strong and honorable people, while showing women as strong and equal partners of men in the battle for justice. As Steven Ross puts it, "the film provided viewers with a blueprint for change and demonstrated how, by abandoning individualism in favor of collective action, wage earners could succeed in transforming production and politics" (95). *Screenplay:* Frank E. Wolfe. *Selected bibliography:* Ross.

**WHY? (ÉCLAIR, 1913).** One of the more radical works of the early political cinema, *Why?* is uncompromising in its presentation of the corruption and decadence of the upper classes and in its suggestion of a workers' revolution as the inevitable response. The film is clear in its anger at the conditions of working-class life, conveyed in an early dream sequence showing needless deaths suffered by railway workers and featuring oppressed seamstresses who are forced to use their own blood to produce red thread for the consumption of the rich. The protagonist is a fiery immigrant who leads his fellow workers in a rebellion against their corrupt bosses, and the film's central scenes involve pitched battles between workers and capitalists over issues such as child labor, corporate greed, and class inequality. In one highly allegorical scene, which

Kay Sloan says could have been "scripted by Marx himself," the capitalists, when shot, transform into sacks of gold (36). The film's violence culminates in the destruction of Manhattan, the capital of capitalism, as the workers set fire to the Woolworth Building, the flames soon spreading through the city.

The seeming celebration of violent rebellion in *Why?* caused an outcry of protest from critics and potential censors, who argued that the new medium needed to be reined in before it led to an actual rebellion. As Frederic C. Howe, chairman of the National Board of Censorship of Motion Pictures, put it, such films "tended to excite class feeling ... [and] to bring discredit upon the agencies of the government" in ways that could potentially lead to a time when (horror of horrors!) film might become "the daily press of industrial groups, of classes, of Socialism, syndicalism, and radical opinion" (cited in Sloan 36–37). *Why?*, of course, was unusual in its seeming call for revolutionary violence, and political film in America, especially after the rise of Hollywood, would ultimately prove to be more of a vehicle for bourgeois reform than for proletarian revolution. *Selected bibliography:* Ross; Sloan.

*THE JUNGLE:* **DIR. AUGUSTUS THOMAS (1914).** Written and directed by prominent playwright Augustus Thomas (himself a former labor activist), *The Jungle* is a screen adaptation of Upton Sinclair's famous 1906 novel of capitalist exploitation and working-class resistance. The film, like the book, focuses on Lithuanian immigrant Jurgis Rudkis (played by well-known actor George Nash), who comes to America with his family in search of a better life but finds only brutal exploitation and poverty. The film, like the book, emphasizes the inhuman and unhealthy conditions encountered by Jurgis as he works in Chicago's meatpacking plants and lives in Chicago's squalid working-class slums. Relative to the book, however, the film pays less attention to the living and working conditions of Chicago's workers and more to the attempts of those workers to improve those conditions and obtain social justice. Jurgis becomes involved early on in labor activism as he and his fellow workers are forced by exploitative employers to go on strike, only to find that, as strikers, however peaceful and reasoned their efforts, they are subject to brutal attacks by police, representing the interests of capital. Meanwhile, Jurgis winds up in prison after he revenges himself on a foreman who coerces Jurgis's wife, Ona (Gail Kane), into sleeping with him. By the time Jurgis is released, Ona and their son have died.

Jurgis wanders about on the verge of despair, then stumbles into a socialist meeting, where he discovers a ray of hope for a better life in the uplifting words of a speaker there. This speaker, played by Sinclair himself, inspires Jurgis to become a socialist and to devote himself to work for the coming better world. As the film ends, Jurgis is working in a rural socialist utopian community, with the implication that this community might serve as a model for the institution of socialism on a broader basis. Generally praised by the leftist press and often excoriated by mainstream critics, the film version of *The Jungle* made less of an impact than the original novel but received significant attention. The film was rereleased in an expanded and updated version by Labor Film Services in 1922 as part of an upsurge of interest in labor-oriented films in the early 1920s. *Screenplay:* Augustus Thomas and Benjamin S. Kutler. *Selected bibliography:* Barrett; Brownlow; Ross.

*WHAT IS TO BE DONE?:* **DIR. JOSEPH LEON WEISS (1914).** Borrowing its title from Nikolai Chernyshevky's nineteenth-century socialist utopian novel, one of the most widely read works of leftist literature worldwide in the early years of the twentieth century, *What Is to Be Done?* was directly inspired by events surrounding the Ludlow Massacre, one of the most famous events in American labor history. In that event, a 1913 miners' strike against the Colorado Fuel and Iron Company eventually led to a deadly assault by the National Guard on a tent village occupied by the strikers and their families in 1914. The massacre drew a great deal of national attention to the plights of workers and to complicity between the government and exploitative employers in banding together against workers. It was the basis of Upton Sinclair's fine 1917 novel *King Coal*.

*What Is to Be Done?* does not dramatize the Ludlow strike directly, but instead addresses the issues raised by that strike. It actually focuses on a factory strike, carefully delineating the brutal conditions and low pay endured by the workers there, while presenting their lives within a broad social context. For example, scenes of factory work and of the strike are supplemented by scenes showing the poverty and squalor in which the workers and their families are forced to live. Interestingly, the film focuses on a woman character, Louis Laffayette, a stenographer in the factory, who becomes a leader in the strike. Meanwhile, in an apparent bid to add entertainment value and keep audience interest, Weiss also has her become involved in a cross-class romance with the liberal son of the factory's owner.

In the film's crucial scenes, Louise addresses representatives of the factory owner, explaining the grievances that have led to the threat of a strike. Her speech is then intercut with scenes, in a variety of settings, that establish the validity of these grievances. In one such scene, the son of a working-class family dies because they cannot afford medicine for him. In another scene (reminiscent of the Triangle Fire), a lecherous foreman accidentally starts a fire in a sweatshop while sexually harassing the seamstresses there. Other scenes show hungry men and women in bread lines and the mourning families of men killed in a mine explosion.

But Louise's arguments fall on deaf ears, and the factory's employees are indeed forced to strike. The remainder of the film shows the progress of the strike, in which the company begins to employ violence against the strikers, hiring thugs who beat up picketers and kill one of the union leaders. But, reminded of the recent tragedy at Ludlow (which is reviewed in detail at this point in the film), the factory owner relents and agrees to the strikers' demands. In the end, however, the workers gain little as the owner and his capitalist allies simply raise prices of the necessities required by the workers to offset the pay increase won in the strike. The film closes as the workers, near despair in the face of such capitalist collusion, look heavenward and ask the question that provides the film's title.

Given the reference to Chernyshevsky, the film potentially implies that the solution lies in the kind of socialist utopia envisioned in the Russian novel. However, the film otherwise does little to suggest alternatives to capitalism, leaving open the interpretation that the best solution to the workers' woes lies in more enlightened management of the current system. Still, that such films could be made at all demonstrated the extent to which the exploitation of labor and labor's response to that exploitation were on the public mind in the years just prior to World War I. Meanwhile, *What Is to Be Done?* was remarkable for its time in featuring a strong female protagonist. *Screenplay:* Joseph Leon Weiss. *Selected bibliography:* Long; Ross.

*THE FLOORWALKER:* DIR. CHARLES CHAPLIN (1916). The first film made by Chaplin under a lucrative new $10,000 per week contract with Mutual Studios, *The Floorwalker* centrally addresses the emergent consumer capitalism that was a distinguishing feature of American society at the time. As William Leach points out in *Land of Desire*, the rise of large department stores in urban centers was one of the central markers of the transformation of American capitalism in the first decades of this century. *The Floorwalker*, set in such a department store, acknowledges this phenomenon. Moreover, the film shows an appreciation for many of the social issues involved in this phenomenon. For example, like so many Chaplin films, it shows a clear appreciation of the class differences that underlay the rise of consumer capitalism.

In the fancy department store of the film, Chaplin, as the Tramp, clearly represents the masses of common people who cannot, by and large, afford to shop in such stores. Indeed, he becomes an object of suspicion the minute he enters the store, drawing the immediate attention of the shop assistant (Albert Austin), whom he subsequently, and predictably, torments with his antics. In the meantime, with the assistant distracted by the Tramp, the wealthy patrons of the store go on a shoplifting binge, pocketing expensive items left and right and thus suggesting the basic greediness and dishonesty of the rich. In addition, much of the plot of the film involves the efforts of the store manager (Eric Campbell) and his assistant (Lloyd Bacon) to abscond with the money from the store's safe, suggesting the dishonesty of businessmen. However, the Tramp, a lookalike for the assistant manager, with whom he for a time comically exchanges identities, inadvertently foils their efforts. By the end of the film, all is well, and the two robbers have been apprehended by detectives. The more wealthy shoplifters, however, get away with their loot, suggesting a common complaint about capitalism—that the richer one is, the more likely one is to get away with crime. *Screenplay:* Vincent Bryan and Charles Chaplin. *Selected bibliography:* Huff (*Early Work*); Leach; McDonald; Ross.

*INTOLERANCE:* **DIR. D. W. GRIFFITH (1916).** *Intolerance* was Griffith's followup to the groundbreaking *The Birth of a Nation* (1915), the film that clearly established Griffith as America's foremost maker of films. The blatant racism of *Birth of a Nation* was, however, something of a scandal even in 1915, and many have seen the follow-up film as a sort of atonement—or at least as an answer to the critics of the earlier film. *Intolerance* is an elaborate and impressive (if sometimes plodding) spectacle that dramatically pushed the envelope of filmmaking technique. However, it was not a commercial success, as audiences apparently found it too long, complex, and elaborate for their tastes. The complexity of the film lies primarily in its structure, which consists of four interlaced narratives, one set in ancient Babylon, one in Judaea in the time of Christ, one in sixteenth-century France, and one in America of the film's present day. All four narratives, we are told by an introductory title, are designed to demonstrate the age-long battle between hatred and intolerance, on the one hand, and love and charity on the other.

Charity is the key word, and the film's principal narrative is the one set in the current day, focusing on the Jenkins Mill and various characters associated with it. The mill owner, Mr. Jenkins (played by Sam de Grasse and probably modeled after John D. Rockefeller), is described in an intertitle as an "autocratic industrial overlord," and he is clearly willing to stoop to any means to extract more labor from his workers at less cost. The workers, meanwhile, are represented by an unnamed allegorical "Boy" (Robert Harron) and "Girl" (also known as "The Dear One," played by Mae Marsh) and their families. The workers suffer greatly from Jenkins' exploitation, living in squalor while he lives in fabulous and ornate wealth. In this sense, *Intolerance* directly continues the themes of earlier Griffith class-conflict films such as *The Song of the Shirt* (1908) and *A Corner in Wheat* (1909).

However, the film gains a significant dimension through the introduction of Jenkins's sister, Mary (Vera Lewis), who decides to devote herself to charitable work to help "uplift" the poor. It soon becomes clear, however, that Mary and her allies (described in various intertitles as "meddlers," "modern Pharisees," "hypocrites," and "vestal virgins of uplift") are nothing more than a pack of interfering old biddies who seek to compensate for their own sexual frustrations by forcing their own priggish morals on the poor, thus ensuring that the poor will not enjoy pleasures that the uplifters lack. Mary convinces her brother to fund the Jenkins Foundation on the grounds that it will help to keep the workers in line. However, she extracts so many contributions from him that he decides to cut wages in order to compensate for the cost, leading to a bitter and violent strike in which the Boy's father is killed by company security guards.

The Boy, unable to find work after his participation in the strike, turns to petty crime to make ends meet, working for a local gangster known as the "Musketeer of the Slums" (Walter Long). Meanwhile, he meets the Girl and begins to court her, marrying her after her own father dies. He resolves to go straight and to be a good husband, but the Musketeer, resenting the move, frames him for a crime and has him sent to prison. The Girl gives birth to a baby while the Boy is in prison, after which ladies of the Jenkins Foundation wrongfully accuse her of being an unfit mother, then seize the baby and place it in their institution. After the boy gets out of prison, the Musketeer begins to court the Girl, eventually leading to a scene in which his jealous girlfriend, "The Friendless One" (Miriam Cooper), shoots him to death. The Boy is accused of the crime and seems on the verge of execution despite his innocence, providing a powerful statement against capital punishment, which an intertitle describes as "a murder for a murder." But then the real killer confesses and the Boy, already on the gallows, gets a last-minute pardon from the governor. He is reunited with his wife and child, and all, presumably, will live happily ever after.

The other three narratives are blatant examples of what Georg Lukács, in *The Historical Novel*, criticizes as "modernization," the projection of contemrpoary psychology, attitudes, and motivations onto the past. Yet this is, in a way, largely the point of the historical segments, which are not meant to stand alone, but to reinforce this main one, aligning Mary Jenkins and the other women of the Jenkins Foundation with notorious villains throughout the ages. In the Babylonian segments, an evil priest (Tully Marshall), infuriated by the religious tolerance of Prince Belshazzar (Alfred Paget), conspires with the rival Persians to take control of Babylon. An innocent but courageous "Mountain Girl" (played by Constance Talmadge, with enough flair that she actually becomes the dominant character in these segments) tries to save Belshazzar and Babylon, but to no avail. These rather Orientalist segments, which feature the film's most spectacular sets, rival the main narrative in impact; they were re-edited and issued as a separate feature, *The Fall of Babylon*, in 1919. (At that time, the contemporary story was also released separately, as *The Mother and the Law*, as Griffith sought to recoup his financial losses from the full film.) The other two historical narratives relate, respectively, the undoing of Christ (Howard Gaye) by the intolerance of rivals such as the Pharisees and the persecution and massacre of the Protestant Huguenots by Catholics in sixteenth-century France.

These three background narratives make Griffith's critique of charitable "uplift" in the contemporary narrative particularly strong. Griffith's understanding of charity in the film is reminiscent of leftist works such as Bertolt Brecht's play, *St. Joan of the Stockyards* (1932). As one intertitle puts it, the Jenkins Foundation is designed to enable the rich to "advertise themselves" at the expense of the poor, while at the same time stabilizing the social conditions that ensure the continuation of economic disparities between the rich and the poor. Given that such "uplift" projects were rampant at the time the film was produced, *Intolerance* had a special pertinence at the time it was first released. Its critique of charity, however, remains relevant today, as do its criticisms of capital punishment and economic inequality. Meanwhile, the technical aspects of *Intolerance* made the film one of the most influential of all time in terms of its impact on other directors, perhaps most notably Sergei Eisenstein. *Screenplay:* D. W. Griffith. *Selected bibliography:* Brownlow; Drew; Everson (*American Silent Film*); Gunning; Huff (Intolerance); Kepley; Leondopoulos; Lukács; Rogin ("The Great Mother").

*THE RINK:* **DIR. CHARLES CHAPLIN (1916).** *The Rink* is largely a work of physical comedy built around Chaplin's legendary roller-skating skills, a routine first developed in his music-hall days and later featured prominently in *Modern Times* (1936). But *The Rink* is also centrally concerned with class-based social commentary. Chaplin, as the Tramp, is a comically inept waiter (again foreshadowing *Modern Times*) who competes for the hand of a young woman (Edna Purviance) with the wealthy Mr. Stout (Eric Campbell). Stout's fancy clothing, pompous attitude, and large girth identify him as wealthy. Meanwhile, the fact that Stout is married suggests a bourgeois tendency toward adultery, a tendency pointed out most famously in *The Communist Manifesto*. Indeed, the equally rotund Mrs. Stout (played by a man, Henry Bergman) is also involved in an adulterous relationship with Edna's father (James T. Kelley). Predictably, the Tramp wins Edna away from Stout, largely through his demonstration of superior skating skills, though it is also the case that the Tramp must pose as Sir Cecil Seltzer in order to win over the bourgeois Edna, who appears greatly impressed by anything associated with the European aristocracy.

The film culminates when Edna hosts an elite skating party attended by a variety of wealthy invitees. The Stouts are surprised to meet each other there (with separate dates), and the party soon degenerates into a comic farce in which the Tramp becomes involved in a comic on-skate fracas with both Stouts, until police, typically taking the side of the upper classes, arrive to pursue him about the arena. But, in an obvious fantasy of the reversal of class power, the Tramp's wealthy pursuers are no match for him on skates. Eventually, he skates out of the rink pursued by police and wealthy party-goers. He grabs the back of a passing car and is towed away to safety, once again getting away with his transgressions against class boundaries. *Screenplay:* Charles Chaplin. *Selected bibliography:* Huff (*Early Work*); McDonald; Ross.

*THE CONTRAST:* DIR. GUY HEDLUND (1921). Angered by the use of motion pictures to convey antilabor propaganda, Joseph Cannon, field director of the Labor Film Service, sought to counter such propaganda with more positive (and more realistic) representations of the cause of organized labor. One of the products of this project was *The Contrast*, which deals with a West Virginia coal strike, and which would prove to be the biggest success of the films produced by the Labor Film Service, though it often had to be shown in secret because of official efforts to suppress it as inflammatory.

The Contrast was inspired by the labor strife that disrupted life in the mountains of West Virginia at the beginning of the 1920s, culminating in the Battle of Blair Mountain, a crucial historical event in which thousands of Appalachian coal miners, in the summer of 1921, took up arms to oppose the increasingly brutal and corrupt practices through which they were being exploited by the mining companies and oppressed by the allies of the companies who were running the local governments of the area. In the battle, the miners were defeated by a combined force of sheriff's deputies, company thugs, and the U.S. Army, sent in by President Calvin Coolidge to help quell the rebellion and prevent it from spreading among the poor and oppressed of other areas of the country. These events would later form the basis of Denise Giardina's 1987 novel, *Storming Heaven*. These same events also provided the subject for a number of Hollywood productions, which generally distorted the events in order to make the striking miners appear at fault. *The Contrast* responds to these productions, presenting the events from the perspective of the miners.

As the title indicates, the film is structured around contrasts between the workers and their bosses, in terms of both the conditions in which they live and work and the relative morality of the two. For example, the film features scenes in which a pampered dog belonging to a rich family eats better than a child of a coal miner. Meanwhile, the violent attacks on the strikers that were so central to the turmoil in West Virginia are central to the film, which portrays the strikers as peaceful and law-abiding victims of antistrike violence. However, the film ends more positively than did the historical events that inspired it, showing the workers winning their demands through their determination and solidarity. *The Contrast* stands as one of the more radical of the labor films produced in the first decades of this century, both in its negative depiction of the mine owners and in its clear attempt to rally workers to take action to resist the kind of exploitation that is shown in the film. *Screenplay:* John W. Slayton. *Selected bibliography:* Brownlow; Ross.

*THE NEW DISCIPLE:* **DIR. OLLIE SELLERS (1921).** *The New Disciple*, a prolabor film that was the first feature to be produced by the union-dominated Federation Film Corporation, is a leading example of the resurgence in working-class cinema after the years of World War I and the subsequent Red Scare had virtually extinguished such production. It was, in fact, the most widely distributed labor film of the time, being seen by at least a million viewers in its first year of release (Ross 167). Technically, *The New Disciple* drew upon the latest developments in film technology and looked very much like a typical Hollywood production. Thematically, however, the film differs strongly from the typical Hollywood fare of the time, which was anti-Bolshevik, antiradical, and antilabor. Indeed, it makes a strong plea for the cause of organized labor, arguing that only organized workers can restore the American economy to proper working order after the imbalances produced by wartime profiteering and the associated antilabor practices of American business.

The film begins in the appropriately named small town of Harmony, where benevolent factory owner Peter Fanning (played by Alfred Allen) gets on well with his workers and where Fanning's daughter, Mary (Norris Johnson) is involved in a romance with John McPherson (Pell Trenton), the son of one of the factory workers. The outbreak of war and the subsequent availability of huge profits to the unscrupulous turns the formerly benevolent Fanning into a greedy exploiter. McPherson, meanwhile, goes off to fight in the war, then returns to find that Fanning's exploitative policies during the war have shattered the former harmony of the town, leading to a crisis in relations between the classes. As the workers organize to defend themselves against Fanning's abuses, Fanning falls under the influence of a spy from a competing company that hopes to use the tensions to drive Fanning out of business. At the instigation of this spy, Fanning rejects his workers' reasonable demands and institutes a lockout, raising tensions still higher. Fanning tries everything to beat the workers into submission, causing great hardship for them and their families. But the workers and their families remain resolute, and Fanning is eventually driven into bankruptcy. The day is saved, however, when the workers, with the help of local farmers, institute a cooperative to buy the factory and put it back into production, saving their jobs and the town. Fanning, realizing the error of his ways, rescinds his order that Mary should stay away from McPherson, and the two lovers are reunited.

The message of *The New Disciple* is that factories are best owned and run by the workers rather than by bosses who might be tempted to employ exploitative practices in the quest for greater profits. But this potentially radical message is tempered somewhat by the film's efforts to present the demands and actions of the workers as reasonable and moderate. It is the war profiteers, such as Fanning, whose behavior is extreme; meanwhile, the worker takeover of the factory (which occurs by peaceful and legal means) simply restores order and tranquility to the once-peaceful town. In this way, the film not only countered the anti-labor stereotypes of crazed strikers that were being promulgated in mainstram Hollywood films, but also reached out to middle-class viewers in its attempt to popularize the cause of organized labor. *Screenplay:* William Piggott. *Selected bibliography:* Brownlow; Ross.

*LABOR'S REWARD:* **AMERICAN FEDERATION OF LABOR (1925).** Produced by the American Federation of Labor (AFL) as part of its "union label" campaign of the mid-1920s, *Labor's Reward* is addressed to consumers (including union members themselves), urging them to buy products made by union labor. It begins by showing scenes of slavery in antiquity, with the clear implication that modern workers, without the support of unions, would find themselves working in very similar conditions. As the film moves forward in history to a more modern setting, it focuses on Mary, a harassed worker who is rescued from oppression when she helps organize a union to stand up for her rights. The film specifically contrasts the lives of union and nonunion workers, implying that the purchase of products made by nonunion labor merely serves to perpetuate the sweatshop conditions under which such workers labor and the squalor and poverty in which they live.

Though politically moderate (as one would expect from an AFL production), *Labor's Reward* still encountered significant opposition and was seldom shown in mainstream movie houses. However, the film was, for its time, unusually progressive in its treatment of gender, with its focus on the woman worker Mary and in its presentation of her as a leader in the subsequent movement toward unionization. Granted, the film did find it necessary to portray Mary's actions within the framework of a love story between her and a fellow worker, Tom. However, it is Mary who educates Tom in the virtues of buying union, rather than the other way around. *Selected bibliography:* Brownlow; Ross.

*THE PASSAIC TEXTILE STRIKE:* **DIR. SAM RUSSACK (1926).** Described by Kevin Brownlow as consisting mostly of an extended news-reel," *The Passaic Textile Strike* documents events surrounding the historic 1926 strike at six textile mills in Passaic, New Jersey. The strike was of particular importance because it was the first large-scale strike in the United States to have been led primarily by the Communist Party. Ultimately, however, leadership in the strike was assumed by the moderate United Textile Workers Union (affiliated with the AFL), which negotiated a settlement in which the striking workers actually gained very little.

The film version of these events begins with a fictional prologue in which a family of Polish immigrants comes to America seeking opportunity, but finds only poverty and oppression. The prologue sets the stage for the strike by showing in naturalistic fashion the squalid living conditions of the workers and the inflexible attitudes of a boss, Mr. Mulius, in dealing with them. The remainder of the film, which features numerous actual participants in the strike, then portrays scenes from the strike itself, some apparently reenacted, most obviously filmed as they occurred. These include positive scenes of union meetings, picket lines, and relief efforts in support of the strikers, plus vivid shots (apparently filmed from neighboring rooftops as they occurred) of vicious police attacks on the peaceful strikers. These powerful scenes are supplemented by Margaret Larkin's extensive subtitles. The action of the film ends in September, 1926, as the United Textile Workers are taking over the strike.

Noting the film's consistent emphasis on groups rather than individuals, Brownlow, whose own anticommunist bias is quite clear, characterizes the film as "a 'mass film' in true Communist style, the first such film ever to be made in America" (498). The more objective Steven Ross, however, finds the film's documentary footage "powerful" and "remarkable," especially when contrasted to the representations of labor-capital confrontations in mainstream Hollywood cinema of the time (162). *The Passaic Textile Strike* is historically important for a variety of reasons, including its avowedly radical stance, its on-the-scene documentation of an important event in U.S. labor history, and its status as the only one of the early American labor films to have been preserved essentially intact. *Screenplay:* Margaret Larkin. *Selected bibliography:* Brownlow; Goldberg; Albert Weisbord (*Passaic*); Ross.

*THE CROWD:* **DIR. KING VIDOR (1928).** One of the last great works of the silent cinema, *The Crowd* is an extended study of the mass society brought about by modern consumer capitalism in the United States. It begins as its protagonist, John Sims (played by James Murray), is born on the fatidic date of July 4, 1900. It then quickly traces John's childhood to age twelve in an idyllic small American town. Encouraged by his father, who has had high hopes for him from the very beginning, John dreams of accomplishing great things. His father then suddenly dies, injecting a note of brute reality into John's life. The film then skips to 1921, when John moves to New York, still dreaming of great things and with high hopes of distinguishing himself from the millions of other New York inhabitants.

The early scenes of New York, with its teeming crowds and traffic-laden streets, are especially effective as visions of mass modernity. Also effective are the shots of John's new workplace after he gets a job as a clerk for the Atlas Insurance Company. In scenes reminiscent of Fritz Lang's *Metropolis*, we see masses of workers being herded in and out of the building like sheep, while John sits working in a huge room, one of hundreds of identical clerks doing identical work at row after row of identical desks. John, however, is not discouraged, but remains hopeful of setting himself apart from the throng. He studies nights with an eye toward advancement, but then, through his fun-loving fellow worker, Bert (played by Bert Roach), meets Mary (Eleanor Boardman), a young woman who immediately catches his fancy. The two are soon wed and head for Niagara Falls for their honeymoon, fantasizing about their future life in a fine suburban house.

Reality, however, is more mundane. When they return to New York, they live in a tiny flat beside an elevated train line. Their lives are re-duced to tedium, as John continues to plod away at his mind-numbing job, while Mary attempts to make a home for them in the cheap flat, which gradually deteriorates into an increasing state of disrepair. Ten-sions grow in the relationship as well, but a potential breakup is averted when Mary becomes pregnant and gives birth to a son, Junior. An inter-title then informs us that, for the next five years, there are virtually no events in their lives to distinguish one day from another, though Mary does give birth to a daughter and John does receive a paltry raise in his salary. He continues to do the same job, however, while his friend Bert receives a promotion, apparently through flattering "the bosses."

A significant event finally occurs when John wins $500 in an adver-tising slogan writing contest. However, this brief moment of light in their drab lives is extinguished quickly when their daughter is hit by a truck while rushing across the street to celebrate her father's winning of the prize. Distraught over his daughter's death and frustrated by years of tedium, John suddenly quits his job but then finds that it is difficult to find another. Offered a job by Mary's two interchangeable brothers (played by Daniel G. Tomlinson and Dell Henderson), John refuses, wishing to remain his own man. He comes near to suicide, but is saved by the devotion of his son. Finally, he manages to get a job wearing a clown suit and juggling balls while carrying a signboard advertising a diner. But even this demeaning job is to John a hopeful development. He rushes home to give Mary the happy news, only to find that she is preparing to move out of their flat to go live with her brothers. He convinces her to stay, however, and the three members of the reunited family celebrate by attending a vaudeville show. In the last scene, they laugh at the antics of the clowns on the stage as the camera recedes into the distance, revealing hundreds of other spectators similarly laughing at the same events.

*The Crowd,* with its realistic depiction of the everyday lives of ordinary people, was a very unusual American film for its day. Moreover, like much of Vidor's work, *The Crowd* is clearly critical of many of the developments in American society in the early twentieth century, while remaining rather ambiguous about its own ideological stance. For example, the film's critique of the mind-numbing routinization of John's life, reminiscent of the cultural criticism of Max Weber, is obvious. However, "the crowd" in the film is consistently depicted as the enemy of the individual, and the film could easily be interpreted as elevating the desires of the individual over the demands of mass society. But the film can also be seen as critical of the individualist ideology of capitalism, which sets up this false opposition between the individual and the group, while encouraging John to dream dreams that can never be realized within the constraints of the capitalist system. *Screenplay:* King Vidor, John V. A. Weaver, and Joe Farnum. *Selected bibliography:* Bush; Durgnat and Simmon; Hansen; Rhodes; Vidor; Weber.

*THE MINERS' STRIKE:* **DIR. SAM BURKE (1928).** Though Kevin Brownlow reports that there is no record of *The Miners' Strike* ever having been completed (507), Steven Ross, relying on contemporary descriptions of the film reported in the *Daily Worker,* summarizes the completed film in some detail (221–22). Set in the coalfields of Ohio and Pennsylvania, where labor disputes had left more than 150,000 miners on strike for sixteen months, the film, made in cooperation with the communist-led national Miners' Relief Committee, details the events surrounding this strike in a documentary fashion reminiscent of newsreels. The film features actual scenes of miners digging coal in deep subterranean mines. It also documents actual mining disasters that had recently killed hundreds of nonunion miners, while showing scenes of the poverty in which actual miners and their families were forced to live. It thus introduced audiences to the brutal hardships faced by the miners, rebutting claims by the mining companies that reports of such hardships had been greatly exaggerated.

Ross notes that the editing of *The Miners' Strike* is reminiscent of the work of Soviet filmmaker Sergei Eisenstein in its collage-like juxtaposition of alternate scenes showing the hardships of the miners faced at home and in the workplace. The film thus "showed in stark visual terms the adverse effects capitalist exploitation had upon the lives of working-class families" (Ross 221). On the other hand, the miners and their families are not merely passive victims, but are also shown resisting exploitation in mass displays of solidarity and in battles against mine guards and scabs. The effectiveness of such scenes can perhaps be judged from the fact that the film, however accurate it might have been in depicting the conditions and events it documents, was banned in Chicago for ridiculing the upper classes and for inciting the lower classes to riot (Ross 222). *Selected bibliography:* Irving Bernstein; Brownlow; Ross.

*THE GASTONIA TEXTILE STRIKE:* **DIR. SAM BRODY (1929).** The bitterly fought, communist-led 1929 strike at the Loray Mill in Gastonia, North Carolina, was to become one of the central events in U.S. labor history, memorialized in no less than six leftist novels in the years after the strike. These novels include Mary Heaton Vorse's *Strike!* (1930), Grace Lumpkin's *To Make My Bread* (1932), Sherwood Anderson's *Beyond Desire* (1932), Fielding Burke's *Call Home the Heart* (1932), Myra Page's *Gathering Storm* (1932), and William Rollins's *The Shadow Before* (1934). Even before these novels, however, the strike had been documented on film. *The Gastonia Textile Strike*, filmed by a crew sent to Gastonia during the strike by the Workers' International Relief (WIR). In Gastonia, cameraman Sam Brody recorded, in newsreel style, numerous scenes from the strike, eventually producing a brief one-reel film for public distribution as part of an effort to raise funds to support the strikers. The film includes graphic scenes of the poverty, hardship, and disease that were the everyday lot of the mill workers, thus establishing the justice of their demands for better pay and better living conditions. It also shows scenes of vicious attacks on picketers by police and National Guardsman, as well as capturing on film the destruction of the union's headquarters by an armed mob. It thus documents, in an immediate way unavailable to the Gastonia novels, the actual texture of the strike. However, filmed in medias res, it does not record the end of the strike, which was largely unsuccessful for the strikers, many of whose leaders were convicted on questionable criminal charges and forced to flee to the Soviet Union for political asylum. *Selected bibliography:* Beal; Cook; Draper; Reilly; Ross; Vera Buch Weisbord.

*ALL QUIET ON THE WESTERN FRONT:* **DIR. LEWIS MILESTONE (1930).** Based on Erich Maria Remarque's classic 1929 antiwar novel of the same title, *All Quiet on the Western Front* details the horror and brutality of World War I trench warfare from the point of view of a number of young German soldiers. In so doing, the film, like the book, not only comments on the gruesome nature of modern combat, but also makes a number of telling remarks about the senselessness of war in general, while condemning the patriotic rhetoric that allows old men to send young men off to kill and die in the defense of empty platitudes. The film is extremely effective in achieving all of these goals, mixing powerful scenes of combat with poignant scenes that emphasize the humanity of the soldiers and satirical scenes that emphasize the stupidity of those who have sent them off to war. One of the earliest major sound films, *All Quiet on the Western Front* remains one of the most powerful antiwar films ever made.

The film begins in the first year of World War I, as patriotic fervor runs high in Germany. One of the first characters we see is the mild-mannered postman, Himmelstoss, who proudly announces that, as a member of the reserves, he will be going off to join the war the next day. The scene then shifts to a schoolroom in a gymnasium, where Professor Kantorek (Arnold Lucy), a pompous schoolmaster, extols the glories of war, inspiring several of his students immediately to leave to join the army. The remainder of the film focuses on these new recruits, who include Paul Baumer (played by Lew Ayres), Franz Kemmerick (Ben Alexander), and Albert Kropp (William Bakewell). The next segment involves their training under the direction of Himmelstoss, whom they are surprised to find transformed by army life into a brutal and sadistic taskmaster. Himmelstoss seems to take great pleasure in tormenting the trainees, though they manage to survive and even get a measure of revenge on the last night in training camp by waylaying a drunken Himmelstoss, caning his bare ass with their swords, and dumping him into the mud.

The bulk of the film then focuses on the experience of the new soldiers in actual combat, which turns out to bear very little resemblance to the glorious visions of Kantorek. Indeed, as they disembark from the troop train in the French town where they will join their new units, they are immediately bombarded by French shells, and one of them is killed. The young soldiers get another rude awakening when they join the veterans in their unit, a cynical, battle-hardened group of men who have already become well aware of the true nature of war. Among other things, the men have no food, though the almost Rabelaisian Sergeant Katczinsky (Louis Wolheim) soon solves that problem, at least temporarily, when he arrives with a freshly killed pig slung over his shoulder. But even the vivacious "Kat" is a cynic who greets the new recruits by shaking his head in wonder that boys could be stupid enough to leave school to join the army.

The boys are soon introduced to actual combat, spending their time waiting interminably in claustrophobic, rat-infested underground bunkers, ducking bullets in trenches filled with mud and stagnant water, and charging across open fields into enemy fire. The battle scenes are impressively realistic and involve a number of inspired shots and technical innovations. These scenes make clear the confusion and senselessness of the conflict, while showing the huge human cost associated with battles over meaningless pieces of devastated land. One by one the boys are killed or maimed, eventually leaving only Paul. In late 1917, Paul is seriously wounded and nearly dies in a field hospital, after which he is granted a leave to return to his hometown to complete his convalescence. What he sees there horrifies him. Kantorek is still spouting his patriotic nonsense to a new generation of impressionable students; old men, including Paul's father, still discuss the war as if it were a glorious game; and everyone ignores Paul's attempts to explain what the war is really like.

Frustrated, Paul is almost glad to get back to the front, where, at least, everyone shares his understanding of the true nature of the war. However, most of his old comrades are gone, and the ranks are being constantly replenished with new teenage recruits, just as Paul once had been. He does locate Kat, who is again out scrounging for food in the countryside. Kat is wounded in the shin by a bomb from a plane as they talk, and Paul hoists his old mentor onto his shoulders to carry him back to camp, at one point being staggered by the near-miss of another bomb. It is only when Paul gets back to camp that he discovers that Kat has been killed by shrapnel from the second bomb. Soon afterward, Paul is killed in battle, and the film ends with a haunting epilogue in which ghostly versions of the original recruits march across the screen, looking accusingly back into the camera, against a background of a battleground that has been converted into a graveyard.

A huge commercial and critical success, the antiwar message of *All Quiet on the Western Front* accorded well with the mood of America in 1930. The film fails to capture the historical significance of World War 1 as the moment when the new capitalist order destroyed Europe's old feudal regimes once and for all, a notion that is well captured in Jean Renoir's 1937 classic *Grand Illusion*. Moreover, in depicting World War I as essentially meaningless, *All Quiet on the Western Front* fails to capture the view of many on the Left that the war, however unnecessary, was a carefully crafted capitalist exercise designed to produce profits for war industries, to convert the growing tide of international working-class solidarity into patriotic hatred for workers from other countries, and to justify the brutal suppression of "subversive" political movements within individual countries, including the United States. Still, the film accords well with the American Left's essential suspicion of the war. Indeed, though the soldiers in the film are German, they are played by American actors who speak a distinctively American idiom and otherwise make no effort to appear as anything other than American. This tactic may have been designed partly to increase the identification of American audiences with the soldiers, but it also effectively makes the point that American soldiers and German soldiers were fundamentally similar, with the same hopes, dreams, and desires, all of which were shattered by the war.

*All Quiet on the Western Front* won Academy Awards for best picture and best director. The film was remade as a television movie in 1979, but the original remains far more powerful and effective. A 1937 sequel, *The Road Back* (directed by James Whale and also based on a novel by Remarque), described the efforts of returning German soldiers to readjust to civilian society after the war. *Screenplay:* Del Andrews, Maxwell Anderson, and George Abbott. *Selected bibliography:* DeBauche; Isenberg; Schatz (*Genius*); Thompson ("*All Quiet*").

*LITTLE CAESAR:* **DIR. MERVYN LeROY (1931).** Though a bit dated, *Little Caesar* is historically important as the first of the cycle of gangster films (other important entries included *Public Enemy* and *Scarface*) that brought new energies into the American cinema at the beginning of the 1930s. A huge box-office success, the film also propelled its lead actor, Edward G. Robinson, to major stardom, while at the same time generating considerable controversy. Robinson plays Rico Bandello (a.k.a. Little Caesar), a small-time hood who gradually rises, through ruthlessness, dedication, and hard work, in the hierarchy of crime, eventually becoming a top mob boss. In the end, however, Rico's fall is even more precipitous than his rise. Fingered for the murder of the city crime commissioner, Rico goes into hiding and ends up a penniless drunk in a flophouse. He is then shot down by police after he calls the station to protest their negative portrayal of him in the press, allowing them to trace the call and track him down.

At first glance, *Little Caesar* would appear to be a fairly straightforward crime-doesn't-pay drama. On the other hand, the film pays far more attention to Rico's rise than to his rather artificially presented fall. Moreover, Rico is clearly modeled after Al Capone (via a novel by W. R. Burnett), and the film's base in reality makes potentially damning comments about the nature of American society. Not only does the film call attention to the level of crime and violence that prevailed in America at the time, but the focus on the ruthless killer Rico as the protagonist was perceived by many as generating sympathy for criminals. In addition, Rico's career, before his sudden fall, is only a slight modification of the standard successful American business career. Indeed, as Andrew Bergman points out, Rico seems to achieve his success through close adherence to the step-by-step program mapped out by Andrew Carnegie in his 1917 how-to guide, "The Road to Business Success" (7–10). Not only does Rico work hard, but he concentrates strictly on business, particularly avoiding women and alcohol, both of which, nevertheless, eventually become crucial to his downfall. Recognizing this connection obviously calls attention to the ruthless competitiveness required of successful businessmen, but it also makes a mockery of the American dream, suggesting that, especially in the Depression, Carnegie's simplistic program will work only for criminals.

Rico's rise and fall have other implications as well. For one thing, despite his essential alienation from all those around him, Rico has success only when he is supported by his gang; his fall occurs when he is at last left on his own. The film, like many gangster films, can thus be taken as a celebration of the group over the individual, in opposition to the standard glorification of the individual in American culture. Further, as Rico rises to the top, his fall is foreshadowed by the fact that he is clearly getting out of his element in terms of class. Thus, when he visits the Big Boy (whom he will ultimately supplant as leader of the local mob), Rico is almost overwhelmed by the trappings of wealth and culture with which the Big Boy has surrounded himself. Told that a painting he admires cost $15,000, Rico is awed—and assumes that the high price must have been due to the picture's gold frame. Almost totally without education or bourgeois refinements, Rico may be able to supplant the suave Big Boy through violence and force of will, but he is not likely to be able to sustain the position very long. In this sense, the film is open to varying interpretations. On the one hand, it could be seen as a warning that one should not attempt to rise above one's class. On the other, it could be taken as a criticism of the rigidity of a class structure that makes such a rise so difficult. In either case, however, *Little Caesar* calls attention to the reality of class, as opposed to most American popular culture, which tends to seek to efface the existence of class altogether. *Screenplay:* Robert N. Lee, Francis Edwards Faragoh, and Robert Lord. *Selected bibliography:* Bergman; Brill ("Gangster"); Munby; Roddick; Roffman and Purdy.

*PUBLIC ENEMY:* **WILLIAM WELLMAN (1931).** Along with such films as *Little Caesar* (1931) and *Scarface* (1932), *Public Enemy* helped to establish the gangster film as a major genre of early-Depression American cinema, expressing as it did so many anxieties of the era. As Robert Sklar notes, "Gangster films set the character of the first golden age of Depression-era movies. ... Hollywood's gangsters stood at the very center of their society's disorder—they were created by it, took their revenge on it, and ended finally as its victims" (179). *Public Enemy* is particularly notable for its direct presentation of the brutal realities of gangster life, and its star, James Cagney, set the standard for subsequent screen gangsters. Like the other gangster films of its time, *Public Enemy* makes it clear that gangsterism arises out of a Depression-era economic situation that leaves few legal opportunities for social and economic advancement. The film also directs trenchant criticisms at the phenomenon of Prohibition, which it sees as a major spur to the growth of organized crime through the 1920s and into the early 1930s.

*Public Enemy* begins in 1909, as boyhood friends Tom Powers and Matt Doyle grow up in an impoverished Chicago Irish neighborhood. Tom in particular already shows a penchant for troublemaking, a penchant that is only enhanced by the beatings administered to him by his father. But it is clearly the poverty of their environment (reinforced by hints of ethnic exclusion due to their Irishness) that eventually leads both Tom and Matt to crime. The film then skips to 1915, as Tom and Matt (now played, as in the remainder of the film, by Cagney and Edward Woods) turn to more serious crimes as young adults. They are recruited by Putty Nose (Murray Kinnell), a local fence and small-time crime boss, to participate in the robbery of a fur warehouse. The robbery goes badly, and police are drawn to the scene when a panicky Tom fires his gun at a stuffed bear in the warehouse; Tom and Matt escape, but one of their cohorts is killed. A policeman is killed as well, and the two have to go into hiding after Putty Nose, who had promised to provide protection for them, disappears.

The film then moves to 1917, as Tom's virtuous (and rather sanctimonious) brother, Mike (Donald Cook), joins the army and prepares to go off to fight in World War I. Tom and Matt, the heat now off from the warehouse robbery, continue their life of crime, while also becoming friends of saloon owner Paddy Ryan (Robert Emmett O'Connor). By 1920, Prohibition has forced the basically honest Ryan to turn to crime, and Tom and Matt go along with him. Ryan sets them up to work as muscle for gangster Nails Nathan (Leslie Fenton) in his bootlegging operation. For a while, the two have successful careers as gangsters. They also extract revenge by killing Putty Nose. Money is plentiful, and Matt falls in love with and marries Mamie (Joan Bondell), a woman he picks up in a club. The radically alienated Tom, however, has less successful relationships, eventually taking up with the seductive, but cold, Gwen Allen (Jean Harlow). Mike, in an understated bit of social critique, returns from the war a shadow of his former self, finding few opportunities waiting for him. He passionately disapproves of Tom's criminal activities, while Tom has nothing but contempt for Mike's determined (but largely fruitless) attempts to better himself through honest hard work.

Events take a sudden turn when Nathan dies in a freak accident, killed when he falls from his horse and is kicked in the head. Showing the mindlessness of their penchant for violence, Tom and Matt kill the horse in revenge. Meanwhile, Nathan's death triggers a power struggle in the local bootlegging business, leading to a gang war between the mobs of Ryan and his rival, Schemer Burns. After Matt is killed by Burns's mob, Tom conducts a one-man assault on Burns's headquarters. He himself is badly wounded but is hospitalized and seems to be gradually recovering, swathed in bandages. Then, Burns's mob kidnaps him from the hospital and, in a particularly chilling scene, deliver his bound and bandaged corpse to his family's doorstep. As Mike opens the door, the corpse falls into the living room, bringing an end to Tom's illustrious career. **Screenplay:** Kubec Glasmon, John Bright, and Harvey Thew. *Selected bibliography:* Bergman; Bookbinder; Brill ("Gangster"); Jowett; Langman; McCarty (*Hollywood Gangland*); Munby; Roddick; Sklar (*Movie-Made America*).

*I AM A FUGITIVE FROM A CHAIN GANG:* DIR. MERVYN LeROY **(1932).** One of the earliest and most memorable of the "social problem" dramas of the 1930s, *I Am a Fugitive from a Chain Gang* is a scathing indictment of the penal system in post-World War I Georgia and, by extension, in the United States as a whole. Indeed, the state of Georgia is never mentioned by name, but the implied setting was clear enough that the film was banned in Georgia. Based upon the autobiographical writings of former Georgia chain-gang escapee Robert Elliott Burns (who remained at large during the making and distribution of the film), *I Am a Fugitive from a Chain Gang* presents, with uncompromising realism, the victimization of its protagonist, James Allen (convincingly played by Paul Muni), by the justice and penal systems. Forced at gunpoint to participate in the robbery of five dollars from a humble hamburger stand, he is unjustly convicted and sentenced to ten years at hard labor, during which he is so brutalized that he decides he must try to escape in order to save not only his human dignity, but his very life. The unflinching representation of these conditions is effective enough that the film received an Academy Award nomination for best picture, while at the same time becoming one of the defining works in the genre of the prison film, which had become popular in the two years immediately preceding the making of *I Am a Fugitive.*

The social implications of the film are broadened by its presentation of Allen as a multiple victim of society's injustices, and it is clear that, while the Georgia prison is an especially egregious case, Allen suffers from carceral conditions wherever he turns in American society. Returning from army service in World War I, with decorations and high hopes, he finds no opportunities open to him except his old job as a factory shipping clerk. Finding it difficult to readjust to this drab routine, he goes on the road, looking for work at which he can put his army training in engineering to good use. However, he is unable to find anything as he travels from one town to another, from New England, to New Orleans, to Wisconsin. That he is not alone is indicated in one scene, in which he attempts to pawn his war medals in St. Louis, but discovers that the pawnbroker already has a display case full of such medals. Indeed, Allen is very much a typical figure; as Roffman and Pudy put it, the story of Allen becomes "a mini-history of America from 1918 to the Depression, the country's descent mirrored through the downfall of war veteran Allen" (79).

Then comes the robbery and his imprisonment, signaling, as Andrew Bergman indicates, that "the forces that continually disrupt Allen's life are invisible but all-powerful: implied were a decaying economy and a rigid, depersonalized legal structure" (94). Given such forces, Allen finds that his problems continue, even after he escapes and ostensibly becomes a respectable member of society. With the boom of the 1920s in full swing, he manages, calling himself "Allen James," to get a job as a laborer for a Chicago construction firm, working his way up until he becomes the company's general field superintendent. Along the way, his landlady (Helen Vinson), whose advances he has spurned, discovers his identity and forces him to marry her in return for her silence. The marriage is a disaster; when he finally falls in love with another woman, Marie (Glenda Farrell) and demands a divorce. In response, his wife identifies him to the authorities. When they try to return him to the chain gang, his case gains considerable public attention, leading to the promise of a pardon if he will voluntarily return for a token sentence of ninety days of clerical work. He agrees to the deal, only to find that he is instead sent back to the chain gang and that his pardon is continually delayed. After more than a year, Allen again escapes, this time into an America torn by the Depression and thus offering him even fewer opportunities than before. As the film ends, he continues to be a fugitive, living as a petty criminal on the margins of society, devoid of any hope of re-establishing a successful mainstream life. As the film ends, he contacts Marie, who asks him how he lives. "I steal," he says.

In its ending, *I Am a Fugitive from a Chain Gang* avoids the tendency of Hollywood's social problem dramas to soften their critique of American society with uplifting conclusions. Indeed, Roffman and Purdy call this pessimistic ending, which drew considerable criticism at the time, "Hollywood's angriest statement on the Depression" (80). Tino Balio calls the ending "the starkest of any social problem film of the period" (282). To this extent, the film is one of the most radical to be produced in Hollywood during the Depression. The film, however, is reformist, rather than revolutionary, in its politics; it does little to suggest that a fundamental change in the American system is required to cure the ills it documents. Moreover, in its emphasis on the suffering of its protagonist (enhanced by Muni's impressive performance), it does nothing to challenge the individualist basis of American capitalism. *Screenplay:* Howard J. Green, Brown Holmes, and Sheridan Gibney. *Selected bibliography:* Balio; Bergman; Roddick; Roffman and Purdy.

*SCARFACE:* DIR. HOWARD HAWKS (1932). *Scarface* joins such films as *Little Caesar* (1931) and *Public Enemy* (1931) as the central examples of the early-Depression American gangster film. The film begins with an on-screen announcement that it is intended as an indictment of "gang rule" and as a demand that the government end its "indifference" and do more to quell the rising tide of gangsterism in America. Meanwhile, Paul Muni plays the title character, Tony Camonte (clearly based on Al Capone), as a particularly ruthless and brutish killer. Yet the aplomb of Muni's performance wins for Camonte a certain sympathy, as does the fact that, despite the prologue, he seems ultimately overmatched by the forces of official power that are arrayed against him. As Robert Sklar notes, the protagonists of films such as *Public Enemy* and *Scarface* became heroes to Depression audiences who could vicariously enjoy their violent power, while identifying with their ultimate helplessness: "If a disordered society led an individual to lawlessness, his strength could not compare with the deviousness and force available to a lawless society" (181). The film's makers, incidentally, seem to have been perfectly well aware of this phenomenon. In one scene, a newspaper publisher is criticized by a citizens' delegation for publicizing Camonte's exploits and thus making him a hero. Camonte responds that the good citizens and their police should put their efforts into stopping crime in the first place rather than into censoring press reports of that crime.

The tone of *Scarface* is set in the first scene, as Camonte, seen only in silhouette, shoots down mob boss Big Louis Costillo (Harry Vejar), for whom he was supposedly working as a bodyguard. Camonte then walks away, whistling, completely unaffected by the deed. It soon becomes clear that Camonte killed Costillo at the behest of Costillo's chief lieutenant, Johnny Lovo (played by Osgood Perkins and based on Johnny Torrio, one of the architects of organized crime in America). Lovo quickly takes over all of Costillo's former operations on the South Side of Chicago, installing a new, more efficient, and more businesslike regime. Camonte, who becomes Lovo's chief enforcer, continually refers to his activities as "business," and it is obviously possible to read the film's presentation of the brutal competition for profits among rival gangsters as an allegory of capitalism.

If Lovo's gang operates like a corporation, then Camonte, aided by his own right-hand man, Guino Rinaldo (George Raft), operates very much like the ambitious junior executive willing to do anything to rise to the top of the corporate hierarchy. In this sense, *Scarface* and the other early-Depression films are reminiscent of the more explicit parallels between capitalism and organized crime in Bertolt Brecht's then-recent *Threepenny Opera* (1928, still in its first run in Berlin until 1933), in which the protagonist, Macheath (a.k.a. Mack the Knife), is a gangster who dreams of becoming a respectable banker. Brecht, meanwhile, was influenced by reports of gangland activity in Chicago, which always functioned for him as the prototypical capitalist city.

In any case, Camonte's ambitions go beyond Lovo's plans, especially after Lovo orders Camonte not to try to move into the North Side, which is dominated by the O'Hara gang. Tensions also arise between Camonte and Lovo when the former meets, and is obvious drawn to, the latter's mistress, Poppy (Karen Morley), the prototypical cool blonde gun moll. Following his own ambitions rather than Lovo's orders, Camonte sends Rinaldo to assassinate O'Hara, triggering a gang war between O'Hara's gang, now led by his old lieutenant, Gaffney (Boris Karloff), and Lovo's gang, despite Lovo's efforts to avert escalation. Camonte finally kills Gaffney, thus seemingly winning the war, but then Camonte is almost killed in a subsequent, obviously well-planned, attack. Deducing that the would-be killers were hired by Lovo, Camonte has Rinaldo kill Lovo, then goes to claim Poppy as his trophy.

Camonte seems to be riding high, but, when he returns after a month in Florida, he finds a city administration newly dedicated to ending his reign of terror. He also finds that his eighteen-year-old sister, Cesca (Ann Dvorak), is now living with Rinaldo. Camonte has furiously fought throughout the film to keep Cesca pure, with a zeal the incestuous implications of which are rather clear. It thus comes as no surprise that he brutally guns down his old friend Rinaldo, as a horrified Cesca looks on. Camonte is then stunned to learn from the tearful Cesca that she and Rinaldo were in love and had been married the day before. Camonte staggers back to his house, a veritable fortress with steel doors and shutters, in a state of shock. Cesca awaits him, planning to kill him, but is unable to go through with it. Meanwhile, a large detachment of police shows up and lays siege to the house, which Camonte and Cesca defend together, until she is shot and killed. Overcome by fumes from a gas grenade, Camonte staggers downstairs and is gunned down as well as he tries to escape, dying in the street just beneath his favorite sign, an advertisement for Cook's Tours reading "THE WORLD IS YOURS."

Among other things, *Scarface* is a virtual catalog of gangster history. In addition to its central reliance on the career of Al Capone as a model, the film builds a number of well-known specific events into its plot, including scenes based on the shooting of "Big Jim" Colosimo in a phone booth, the Saint Valentine's Day massacre, and the assassination of "Legs" Diamond in his hospital room. *Scarface* was the springboard to major film careers for both Muni and Raft and was the only one of the early-Depression gangster films to be named to *Film Daily*'s list of the year's Ten Best films. It was also, despite its success, the last of the major gangster films of its era, as Production Code restrictions against glorification, or even explicit presentation, of crime made such films harder and harder to make. The 1932 version of *Scarface* was the basis for the

1983 film (directed by Brian DePalma and written by Oliver Stone) of the same title. *Screenplay:* Ben Hecht. *Selected bibliography:* Bookbinder; Brill ("Gangster"); Hagemann; Langman; McCarty (*Hollywood Gangland*); Munby.

*DUCK SOUP:* **DIR. LEO McCAREY (1933).** Characterized by Robert Sklar as being "as thorough a satire of politics and patriotism as any film before *Dr. Strangelove*," *Duck Soup* is considered by many to be the zenith of the film career of the Marx Brothers (182). Like all Marx Brothers films, the plot of *Duck Soup* is minimal (and silly), really just a pretext for the brothers to perform their typical absurdist vaudevillian shtick. On the other hand, the film's wacky humor is not pointless, but is aimed directly at a number of the sacred cows of American society. In this, it is reminiscent of absurdist political comedies such as Alfred Jarry's 1896 play, *Ubu Roi*. As the film begins, the presumably European mythical kingdom of Freedonia is in dire financial straits, just as the United States, at the time was mired in the Depression. The government seeks to borrow twenty million dollars from a wealthy widow, Mrs. Teasdale (played by frequent Marx Brothers foil Margaret Dumont), in order to keep the government in operation. But, frustrated with the government's ongoing mismanagement, Mrs. Teasdale agrees to make the loan only on the condition that reformer Rufus T. Firefly (Groucho Marx), on whom she has a crush, be placed in charge of the government.

The arrangement is accepted, with predictably zany consequences. Firefly, in what could be read as a parody of the fascist governments then rising to power in Europe, immediately institutes a new series of laws that makes almost everything illegal, though it is also clear that he is not particularly interested in enforcing those laws. What he is interested in is creating mayhem, which he does to great effect. Though not romantically interested in Mrs. Teasdale, whom he continually insults in typical Grouchoesque fashion, the competitive Firefly begins to pay court to her when he realizes that she is being courted by Trentino, the ambassador from neighboring Sylvania. Trentino, it turns out, hopes to marry Mrs. Teasdale as part of a plot to seize control of the Freedonian government. He also employs two spies, Chicolini (Chico Marx) and Pinky (Harpo Marx) to keep tabs on Firefly, leading to some of the classic comic scenes of American film. In a clear parody of capitalist competition, Chicolini and Pinky, posing as peanut vendors, cannot resist tormenting a nearby lemonade vendor (Edgar Kennedy), even though by rights peanut vendors and lemonade vendors should be natural allies. The film's most famous moment occurs when all three brothers dress as a nightshirt-clad Groucho, leading to the classic mirror scene, perhaps the most famous of all Marx Brothers routines.

Firefly, meanwhile, hatches a plan to send Trentino scurrying back to Sylvania by insulting him. In the ensuing comic melee, both men get insulted, and war is declared between the two countries. As war approaches, the Freedonians launch into a gleeful frenzy of patriotic and militaristic fervor, accompanied by parodic musical numbers including the famous "All God's chillun got guns" segment. These scenes might again be read as a mockery of fascist posturing, but they hit extraordinarily close to home and are highly reminiscent not only of American movie musicals but of American celebrations of patriotism. In fact, the film openly associates Freedonia specifically with the United States in a number of ways. The very name of the country suggests the emphasis on freedom in American political rhetoric, and we also learn that Firefly claims to belong to an old family that "came over on the Mayflower." Meanwhile, baseball seems to be the favorite national pastime (something that would occur in no European country), and Firefly dons a series of quintessentially American costumes during the course of the war, appearing in sequential scenes, without explanatory transition, as a Civil War officer, a boy scout leader, a frontiersman with coonskin cap, and a band leader.

The war begins in a very American way when Firefly sends Pinky, who, along with Chicolini has now switched sides, on a midnight ride, à la Paul Revere, to alert the locals. Unfortunately, the ride is derailed by Pinky's inability to resist stopping to accost the women he sees through windows along the way. The rest of the war is similarly absurd. The Freedonians, despite their patriotic zeal, are no match for the better-organized Sylvanian forces, which lay seige to Mrs. Teasdale's home, where she and the four Marx Brothers (including Zeppo, who plays Firefly's secretary, Bob Roland) have taken refuge. All appears lost until Trentino gets his head stuck in a door as he charges into the house, forcing him to surrender as the Marxes pelt him with fruit. As the film ends, Mrs. Teasdale launches into a patriotic victory song, causing them to pelt her as well.

*Duck Soup* should not be taken as a critique of the newly installed Roosevelt administration, which the brothers, especially Groucho, openly supported throughout the 1930s. It is, however, a powerful critique of patriotism, militarism, and the undue influence of the rich on government decisions. Indeed, the Marx Brothers, who actively worked for the unionization of the film industry through the 1930s, frequently lampooned the rich in their work. Because of the comic absurdity of their work (and their box-office success), they were able to get away with things that more "serious" filmmakers could not. It also helped that their satire had a rather light touch. Thus, Gerald Weales notes that their subversive humor was accepted not only because of its "sheer madness," but because they used satire "lightly, echoing the popular consensus"

(77). Nevertheless, after *Duck* Soup, the Marx Brothers moved to MGM, where they were substantially reined in by conservative producer Irving Thalberg, leading to a marked decrease in the pointedness of their satire and the quality of their films. *Screenplay:* Bert Kalmar, Harry Ruby, Nat Perrin, and Arthur Sheekman. *Selected bibliography:* Balio; Bergan; Eyles; Gehring; Sklar; Weales.

*GOLD DIGGERS OF 1933:* DIR. MERVYN LeROY (1933). *Gold Diggers of 1933* is a definitive example of the 1930s movie musical. Sprinkled with music throughout, the film is dominated by three lavish musical production numbers, all choreographed by the legendary Busby Berkeley, who also makes a cameo appearance in the film. As with all such musicals, the plot is simple and formulaic, though this plot does address the economic difficulties caused by the collapse of the American economy in the Great Depression. As the film begins, the New York stage scene is among the casualties of the Depression, and we are introduced to three roommates, unemployed showgirls, whose most recent show has been canceled due to lack of financing. These showgirls (Polly Parker, Trixie Lorraine, and Carol King, played by Ruby Keeler, Aline MacMahon, and Joan Blondell, respectively) are struggling to find a way to make ends meet, thus setting the stage for the evolution of the plot.

Opportunity seems to knock when they learn that producer Barney Hopkins (Ned Sparks) is about to launch a new show, in which they will all be able to get parts. The show is all ready to go, except for one thing: Hopkins has no financing whatsoever. However, Brad Roberts (Dick Powell), a songwriter who lives in the same building as the showgirls, offers to save the day by putting up $15,000 to allow the show to go on. Trixie and Carol are skeptical, wondering how someone in Brad's position could possibly get so much money, but Polly, who is in love with Brad, has absolute faith in him. He does indeed produce the cash, and the show does go on, featuring Brad's music and with Polly, at Brad's insistence, in a starring role. Moreover, at the last minute, Gordon (Clarence Nordstrom), her costar, develops a bad back, and the reluctant Brad has to go on in his place.

Spotted on the stage, Brad is soon identified as Robert Treat Bradford, scion of an old Boston family, who has been living incognito in New York to pursue his dream of being a songwriter, a dream of which his family staunchly disapproves. His older brother, J. Lawrence Bradford (Warren William), arrives in town with the family lawyer, Faneuil Hall Peabody (Guy Kibbee), to try to put a stop to such foolishness, especially after he learns that his young brother plans to marry Polly, whom Lawrence regards as a "cheap and vulgar" showgirl. Considerable comic confusion ensues, as the showgirls deflate the pretensions of the pompous Lawrence, with his class-based notions of superiority. In the end, however, class is transcended. Brad marries Polly, Peabody marries Trixie, and Lawrence marries Carol. All, presumably, will live happily ever after.

Meanwhile, the show goes on, which is the real point of the film. The production numbers also provide important thematic material. The central production number, "Pettin' in the Park," spiced with risqué hints of sexuality and nudity, simply reinforces the romantic comedy theme of the plot. But the opening and closing numbers provide the film's most striking engagement with the economic realities of the Depression. The film begins with an elaborate performance of "We're in the Money," featuring Ginger Rogers (as showgirl Fay Fortune, singing largely, and weirdly, in Pig Latin) leading a chorus of showgirls clad in scanty costumes made of strategically placed sparkling coins (but, of course, with discreet body suits underneath). This number, so out of tune with the realities if the time, proves to be merely a dress rehearsal for a soon-to-open show. It ends suddenly, however, as reality (in the form of the sheriff and deputies) bursts in. The sheriff closes the show and confiscates the props and costumes toward the payment of the show's debts, leaving the showgirls out of work and initiating the plot of the film. (On the other hand, the success of *Gold Diggers of 1933* and other musicals helped to put a staggering Warner Brothers back in the money, making the opening sequence oddly appropriate.)

The film then closes with a counterpoint to this number, the memorable "Forgotten Man" sequence. Here, the performers, led by Carol, wear costumes simulating poverty and sing of the hardships of the Depression, with an emphasis (inspired by the 1932 Bonus Army march on Washington) on the failure of America to live up to the promises made to the soldiers who fought in World War I. Particularly striking is a sequence showing a troop of soldiers proudly marching off to war, then staggering back, wounded and bleeding, then standing in line at a soup kitchen. The film ends, without commentary, as the number closes, but the implications of the sequence are powerful, especially when read against the opening sequence and the romantic resolution of the plot, both of which this last number tends to undermine. It would be a mistake to make too much of the implications of this number within the context of a film clearly designed for pure entertainment, just as the film's potentially interesting allegorization of gender roles (men supply money, women supply nubile bodies) is certainly not meant as an intentional challenge to conventional figurations of gender. Still, the "Forgotten Man" sequence provides one of the central examples of the attempts by Warner Brothers films in the 1930s to comment on the social problems of the time—in carefully packaged ways and without suggesting radical solutions. *Screenplay:* Erwin Gelsey, James Seymour, David Boehm, and

Ben Markson. *Selected bibliography:* Bergman; McElvaine; Mellencamp; Rubin.

*HEROES FOR SALE:* **DIR. WILLIAM WELLMAN (1933).** Very much a Depression-era work, *Heroes for Sale* presents a great deal of the landscape of Depression America within the framework of a relatively brief (seventy-three minutes) film. The protagonist is Tom Holmes (Richard Barthelmess), a typical 1930s forgotten man, a stock figure in the Warner Brothers social dramas of that decade. Holmes is a World War I veteran who finds, on returning home to America, that the country has little to offer him in return for his service. He has already become a morphine addict during treatment for his war wounds, while a bravery medal he earned in the course of acquiring the wounds has been awarded instead to the cowardly son of a rich banker. Back in America, Holmes goes to work for that banker but is fired and imprisoned after he embezzles funds to support his morphine habit. After he is released, he wanders from town to town in search of opportunity but receives little sympathy from those he meets, who are more concerned with their own problems.

Eventually, Holmes travels to Chicago, where he becomes involved with Ruth Loring (Loretta Young), providing the film with a romantic subplot. Ruth helps him get a job in a small laundry run by the kindly Mr. Gibson (Grant Mitchell). Soon, he meets European inventor Max Brinker (Robert H. Barrat), who has developed a revolutionary new kind of laundry machine. Max rails against the wealthy and appears to be a socialist, but changes his tune when his invention begins to make him rich, when he begins to rail against the poor. Holmes, meanwhile, becomes Brinker's partner in Consolidated Laundries, which takes over and automates Gibson's laundry, making it hugely profitable. In the last part of the film, Holmes becomes the central figure in the laundry company's attempts to suppress protests by workers who, displaced by Brinker's invention, have been stirred to violence by communist agitators. The workers are presented as misguided in their turn to violence in their protests, though the film also suggests that many of their grievances are valid and result from exploitative practices by their employers.

*Heroes for Sale* is a typical example of the attempts by Hollywood, in the midst of the Depression, to acknowledge the pressing social issues of the day, while at the same time counseling patience and suggesting that America's difficult social and economic problems would be solved in due time. As Andrew Bergman puts it, the film "had faith in capitalism but none in capitalists" (99). The film is strongly supportive of the New Deal, reserving its most trenchant criticisms for social conditions and policies that prevailed in America during the years before Roosevelt took office. Roosevelt, in fact, takes office shortly before the film ends, and Holmes, in his final speech, refers to Roosevelt's inaugural address as evidence of better times to come. Giuliana Muscio notes that Warner Brothers even attempted to get permission to use footage of Roosevelt in the film, though the permission was denied on the grounds that if one film used Roosevelt they would all want to use him (99). However, Jack Warner remained a close associate of Roosevelt, a fact to which some have attributed the leeway government censors allowed Warner Brothers in their social problem films of the 1930s. *Screenplay:* Robert Lord and Wilson Mizner. *Selected bibliography:* Bergman; Muscio; Roffman and Purdy; Thompson; Wellman.

*MR. MOTORBOAT'S LAST STAND:* **DIR. THEODORE HUFF AND JOHN FLOREY (1933).** An experimental short film made by amateur filmmakers Theodore Huff and John Florey, *Mr. Motroboat's Last Stand* allegorizes the capitalist rat race in ways that clearly attribute the poverty and hardship of the Great Depression to the heartlessness of capitalist competition and inherent instability of the capitalist system. Though now little known, it was effective enough in doing so to win the Amateur Cinema League's annual film contest. An ironic comedy, the film satirizes the inability of the capitalist system to deal with the crisis posed by the Depression. It focuses on an unemployed black man who lives in a junkyard, fantasizing about better times. *Mr. Motorboat's Last Ride* follows his fantasies as he imagines the junked car in which
he lives to be a luxurious limousine, taking him to work on Wall Street. Unfortunately, even in fantasy, life under capitalism offers little security. Having risen to the top, the hero falls with the crash of 1929, returning him to the reality of poverty. The film uses the junkheap as an allegory of the capitalist system, which tosses aside individuals who are no longer needed in the ruthless quest for greater profits. Indeed, most of the film's images are highly allegorical, causing Jan-Christopher Horak to compare it to medieval morality plays (399). *Screenplay:* Theodore Huff and John Florey. *Selected bibliography:* Horak.

*WILD BOYS OF THE ROAD:* **DIR. WILLIAM WELLMAN (1933).** Modeled to some extent on the 1931 Soviet film, *The Road to Life* (based on A. S. Makarenko's classic socialist realist novel of the same title), *Wild Boys of the Road* presents a broad and reasonably realistic panorama of America's social problems during the Depression. Following on the heels of Wellman's earlier *Heroes for Sale*, *Wild Boys* is one of the finest examples of the Warner Brothers social problem films of the 1930s. The film features two high-school boys, Eddie and Tommy (played by Frankie Darro and Edwin Phillips, respectively), who begin the film living comfortable middle-class lives (complete with picket fences, apple pie, and high-school dances) with their California parents. When the Depression hits, and their fathers lose their jobs, the boys go off in search of opportunity, hopping rides on freight trains, joining other "wild boys [and girls] of the road" as they go. Along the way, they are run out of one town after another, and Tommy has his leg crushed when he falls in the path of a train while fleeing railroad detectives in a train yard.

The group runs afoul of the law when they kill a railroad detective who forces them off a train and rapes one of the girls (played by Rochelle Hudson) in a freight car. They make their way to Cleveland, where (with official permission) they use leftover sewer pipe and other supplies to set up a "sewer city." They then fight off police, who attempt to evict them after local merchants complain that the sewer city might be a breeding ground for crime. When the gang is eventually driven out with fire hoses, they again hit the road and move on to New York, where they settle in a garbage dump. Eddie, duped by some thieves, becomes involved in a theft ring and is arrested. Fortunately, he comes before the wise and compassionate Judge White (Robert Barrat). After Eddie makes an impassioned speech on behalf of himself and those like him, Judge White (who bears more than a passing resemblance to President Roosevelt) acknowledges his understanding that times are hard but assures the young man that, with the New Deal kicking into gear, things will get better soon. He dismisses the case and promises to see to it that Eddie and his friends find jobs. The film is thus ultimately reassuring in its expression of faith in the ability of the government to deal with America's economic crisis, though it depicts that crisis in unusually direct terms. In this and in its seeming endorsement of violent resistance (as when the boys battle railroad detectives), the film drew considerable criticism at the time. *Screenplay:* Earl Baldwin. *Selected bibliography:* Bergman; Muscio; Roffman and Purdy; Thompson; Wellman.

*THE BLACK CAT:* **DIR. EDGAR G. ULMER (1934).** Paul Buhle identifies *The Black Cat* as perhaps the leading contribution of leftist filmmakers to the genre of the horror movie. Noting director Ulmer's leftist sympathies, Buhle also notes that Ulmer interpreted the film as "an effort to convey the moral bankruptcy of capital" (108). Meanwhile, Ulmer produced an early classic of the horror genre as a whole, among other things featuring the first on-screen pairing of horror legends Boris Karloff— characterized by Buhle as a "one of Hollywood's first ardent unionists and a doughty anti-fascist" — and Bela Lugosi—who, Buhle notes, would later become one of Hollywood's "most important anti-fascists," a leader of the Hungarian Democratic Front, a wartime Popular Front organization (107).

The plot of *The Black Cat*, loosely based on a story by Edgar Allan Poe, is fairly simple, and the film (as is typical of the horror genre) depends more on its brooding atmosphere of supernatural threat than on clever plot developments. The story begins as two American newlyweds, Peter and Joan Alison (played by David Manners and Jacqueline Wells), ride the Orient Express on their way to a honeymoon in Budapest. On the train, they meet Hungarian psychiatrist Vitus Verdegast (Lugosi) and learn that Verdegast is only now making his way back home after having been captured in World War I and placed in a famously horrible prison, where he has inexplicably been held ever since. The Alisons agree to stop off at Visegrad, just short of Budapest, and accompany Verdegast on a visit to the home of his old acquaintance, the prominent Austrian architect Hjalmar Poelzig (Karloff).

Poelzig's home, an ultramodern Bauhaus mansion, is the film's dominant image. Its crisp, horizontal lines and high-tech furnishings provide a model of modern efficiency and of the accomplishments of modern technology, but its shining surfaces nevertheless exude an air of doom that makes the visitors decidedly uneasy. Among other things, the ominous titular black cat roams about the mansion amid dialogue that recounts medieval visions of black cats as the embodiment of evil. The cat has a particularly strong effect on Verdegast, who has a phobia of cats. His fears are well placed. As the plot develops, it turns out that the modernist mansion is merely a whited sephulcher that hides considerable ruin and corruption. It is constructed on the ruins of an old fort, the dungeons and subterranean passages of which still exist beneath the house—and which are apparently haunted by the ghosts of the thousands of Austro-Hungarian soldiers who died there in World War I after having been betrayed to the Russians by their commander, Poelzig.

Verdegast had been at the fort as well and was captured as a result of Poelzig's treachery. He has, in fact, returned for revenge against his old commander, though he learns only after arriving that Poelzig, after Verdegast's capture, had married Verdegast's young wife, Karen. It turns out, however, that Karen died soon after the marriage and that Poelzig is now married to her (and Verdegast's) daughter, also named Karen (Lucille Lund), the spitting image of her mother. When we first see Poelzig, in fact, he is arising from bed, the partly nude body of his sleeping wife beside him. This first scene sets the tone for the note of sexuality that pervades Poelzig's characterization. We soon discover, for example, that he still has the perfectly preserved body of the original Karen stored in a glass case in the subterranean portion of his mansion. Moreover, he has the bodies of other beautiful young women stored in similar cases.

Poelzig soon targets Joan as his next specimen, and it becomes obvious that the stored bodies are the result of unspeakable rites performed by Poelzig and a local Satanic cult, which he heads. When the current Karen learns that her father, whom she had thought dead, has arrived, Poelzig murders her. He then imprisons Peter in a dungeon and goes forward with plans to make Joan his next ritual victim. Verdegast, however, helps Joan escape, while Peter manages to free himself from the dungeon. Peter shoots Verdegast, not realizing that he is trying to help. Then he and Joan flee the mansion, while the dying Verdegast triggers a self-destruct mechanism that blows up the entire mansion.

Poelzig is a prototype of the evil scientist, who would become such a stock figure in the horror genre. Moreover, as a scientist whose surface devotion to reason and technology conceals his deeper devotion to forces of darkness, he might even be read as a figure of German Nazism, which would make *The Black Cat* the ultimate prematurely antifascist film. Polezig's house reinforces these interpretations, and, in any case, both Poelzig and his mansion can be taken as reminders that the humanist surface of capitalism and the European Enlightenment potentially conceals a dark interior of violence and domination, much in the mode described by Max Horkheimer and Theodor Adorno. *Screenplay:* Edgar G. Ulmer and Peter Ruric. *Selected bibliography:* Buhle; Horkheimer and Adorno.

*MASSACRE:* **DIR. ALAN CROSLAND (1934).** Although primarily an entertainment-oriented action picture, *Massacre* nevertheless participates in a movement toward more treatment of social issues in 1930s films, while showing a sympathy toward the plight of Native Americans that at least goes beyond the woeful stereotyping that was typical of most Hollywood films at least until the 1960s. The protagonist of the film is a Sioux, Joe Thunder Horse (played rather unconvincingly by Richard Barthelmess), who returns to his old reservation to visit his dying father after years of absence. Thunder Horse has been working as a key performer in a wild west act at the Chicago Century of Progress exhibition. Already growing disgusted at his role as a stage Indian, he is appalled at the conditions he finds on the reservation and at the treatment meted out to the Sioux by Indian agent Elihu Quissenberry (Dudley Diggs) and his minions. Thunder Horse decides to embrace his identity as a Native American, attempting to reestablish contact with his true cultural heritage rather than the commodified travesty of that culture he has been performing in Chicago.

This commitment leads him to active resistance (supplying the action for the film), which includes the killing of a white Indian Affairs officer (played by Sidney Toler), who has raped Thunder Horse's sister. Thunder Horse is arrested and summarily convicted in a sham trial, but he escapes. Amid a budding rebellion, he realizes that the only real hope for improved conditions is enlightened support from the government, so he heads for Washington to file a complaint with the Indian Affairs Commissioner. With the New Deal in full swing (and fully endorsed by the film), this commissioner is sympathetic and promises support but warns Thunder Horse that unspecified "powerful interests" (apparently capitalists seeking to profit from timber, oil, and other resources that rightly belong to the Native Americans) are arrayed against them both in the fight for justice. In the final analysis, the violent revolt is calmed, Quissenberry is sent to prison, and Thunder Horse ends up working for the New Deal government.

In its portrayal of Thunder Horse, *Massacre* clearly attempts a sensitive understanding of the difficult cultural position of Native Americans in the early 1930s. At the same time, its emphasis on this single protagonist often makes his problems appear more existential than cultural, tending to obscure the real issues that are involved. Granted, the ultimate suggestion that Native Americans should not revolt but rely on the federal government to defend their rights is problematic, to say the least. Still, the assumption that intervention on behalf of the weak and oppressed is obviously an appropriate role for the federal government is indicative of the political idealism of the 1930s and perhaps continues to hold lessons at the end of the century. Moreover, the film's indignation at the treatment of Native Americans is real and represents a significant step forward in the portrayal of Native Americans on film. The film is also ahead of its time in its suggestion of the stereotyping faced by Thunder Horse, especially from white women, who seem to regard him as an exotic stud. *Massacre* was based on a story by screenwriter Block and Robert Gessner, author of the 1933 novel, *Broken Arrow*, which offers a far more nuanced treatment of the plight of Native Americans in modern America. *Screenplay:* Ralph Block and Sheridan Gibney. *Selected bibliography:* Bergman; Roddick; Roffman and Purdy.

*NEW EARTH:* **DIR. JORIS IVENS (1934).** Although made by a Dutch director and focusing primarily on Dutch efforts to reclaim land from the Zuiderzee, *New Earth* is an excellent example of the leftist films that brought new energies to American filmmaking in the 1930s. Indeed, director Ivens contributed significantly to American leftist film during the decade. Not only were films like *New Earth* greatly influential for American documentary makers, but Ivens came to America and made such films as *The Spanish Earth* (1937) and *The Power and the Land* (1940). Named as a communist in the 1951 House Un-American Activities Committee (HUAC) hearings, Ivens left America never to return. In the 1950s and 1960s, he worked largely in the communist world, including Eastern Europe, North Vietnam, and Cuba. He continued to make films almost until his death in 1989.

Most of *New Earth* consists of documentary footage recording the actual work of land reclamation, yet Ivens manages to convert this seemingly mundane material into what William Alexander calls a "great film." Citting the "gripping" quality of Ivens's narrative of the land reclamation work, Alexander notes that the film was impressive enough to win Ivens an invitation to the Soviet Union, where master fimmakers such as V. I. Pudovkin felt that they could learn much from him (117). Alexander goes on to call the film's climactic scene, the final closing of the dike, "one of the most striking sequences in all of film" (118). *New Earth* manages to convey with drama and suspense the sheer immensity and audacity of the land reclamation project, presenting it as an almost allegorical example of the ability of human beings, working together in large numbers and driven by dedication to a common goal, to overcome almost any obstacle and to build a better world for themselves. The potential political implications of this presentation are clear. Meanwhile, the last quarter of the film takes an explicitly political turn as indignant crowds, whose anger is matched by the film's own, march to protest the exploitation of the newly reclaimed land by a capitalist order that destroys excess food supplies in order to drive up prices, even as thousands go hungry. *Screenplay:* Joris Ivens. *Selected bibliography:* Alexander; Meyers and Leyda; Rotha.

*OUR DAILY BREAD:* **DIR. KING VIDOR (1934).** A sound-film sequel to Vidor's earlier silent-film classic, *The Crowd* (1928), *Our Daily Bread* traces the continuing attempts of John and Mary Sims (now played by Tom Keene and Karen Morley) to make ends meet as the Depression makes their already hard lives all the harder. With John unemployed, they ask Mary's prosperous Uncle Anthony to help him get a job. Anthony responds with an offer to let them work an abandoned farm to which he has the title and which is so worthless the bank has not even bothered to foreclose on it. In a motif partly inspired by President Roosevelt's proposal for the establishment of subsistence homesteads, they agree and move to the dilapidated, but promising, farm to try to make a new life. Unfortunately, John knows virtually nothing about farming, and he makes little headway despite his best efforts. Then a car carrying a Swedish farmer and his family on their way to California breaks down on the road by the farm. John suggests that the farmer, Chris (John Qualen), stay and help him work the farm rather than moving on to California. Chris agrees, and things soon begin to look up on the farm, though John and Chris still need more help to work the land effectively.

Having had great success with Chris, John decides to advertise the same deal to other homeless unfortunates in the area, and before he knows it, dozens of families join them, creating a collective farm, described by John as "a sort of cooperative community." The new arrivals pool their resources and skills, creating a cooperative economy based on the sharing of labor and the bartering of both goods and services. They decide to establish no further system of government other than simply designating John their leader. For a time, all goes well, minor disputes are easily settled, and soon the crops (mostly corn) begin to grow. John looks at the newly sprouted plants and feels a surge of confidence and a sense of accomplishment. "There's nothing for people to worry about," he tells Mary, "not when they've got the earth. It's like a mother."

Trouble brews momentarily when the sheriff arrives to announce that the bank has decided to auction off the land after all, but this problem is quickly solved when the members of the community intimidate other potential bidders into silence, then buy the farm themselves for $1.85. However, more serious trouble looms when the farmers realize that they do have the resources to acquire food to tide them over until the crops come in. Louie (Addison Richards), a leading member of the community, saves the day when he turns himself in to the sheriff so that the farmers can collect the $500 reward that has been placed on his head. The suggestion that the good of the community outweighs the good of any particular individual is clear.

In the meantime, the farmers are joined by Sally (Barbara Pepper), a sexy blonde from the city, who arrives in her car with her "unconscious" father. When the farmers go to give aid to the old man, they discover that he is dead. Sally, rather undisturbed by her father's death, decides to stay on at the farm for a while. She soon begins a flirtation with John, who is clearly attracted. When a serious drought begins to destroy the crops, all looks hopeless. Out of frustration and a sense of failure, John agrees to run away with Sally and abandon the entire project. As they drive away from the farm, however, he spots a previously undiscovered stream flowing with water two miles from the fields. He sends Sally on her way and runs back to the farm to alert the farmers about the water.

In the film's most impressive scenes (and some of the most impressive utopian scenes of collective action in all of American film), the farmers band together, working day and night to dig an irrigation ditch from the stream to their fields. Working so closely together that their effort seems almost like a well-choreographed dance, they succeed in diverting the stream, bringing desperately needed water to the crops and saving the farm. As the film ends, John and Mary are reunited, while the farmers and their families cavort joyously in celebration of the success of their collective effort to save the crops and their cooperative community.

Although made on a shoestring budget because MGM's right-wing production chief Irving Thalberg became horrified by the film's obvious socialistic implications, *Our Daily Bread* remains one of the most moving and vivid images of the Depression to have been recorded on film. The farm clearly enacts the Marxist notion of "from each according to his ability to each according to his needs," and it was bashed by the Hearst papers and other elements of the right-wing press as communistic and un-American. From this point of view, it did not help that the film drew obvious inspiration from Yuli Rayzman's 1930 Soviet film, *The Earth Thirsts*. Yet the film's political message, like that of most Vidor films (and

many populist films), is mixed. The film may suggest socialist cooperation as the key to surviving the Depression, but its nostalgic, back-to-the-
land message carries potentially reactionary implications. In any case,
this "socialist" farm must still survive amid a larger capitalist economy,
which makes its solution to the economic problems of the Depression
highly questionable. Moreover, this utopian community is thoroughly
male-dominated, with wives playing secondary and supporting roles,
while the only woman in the film who is not safely circumscribed within
marriage is the evil Sally. The community is also all white; it contains a
variety of European nationalities (and even one Jewish family), but there
are no black, or even brown, faces in sight. *Screenplay:* King Vidor,
Elizabeth Hill, and Joseph L. Mankiewicz. *Selected bibliography:* Bergman; Durgnat and Simmon; James Tice Moore; Roffman and Purdy;
Vidor.

*PIE IN THE SKY:* DIR. RALPH STEINER (1934). *Pie in the Sky* is a
highly polemical send-up of the promises by organized religion that
those who patiently bear suffering in this world will be rewarded in the
next. The title of the film is taken from a recurring phrase in the well-
known song "The Preacher and the Slave," by the IWW labor activist and
poet Joe Hill, first published by the IWW in its *Little Red Song Book* in
1909. Hill's song lampoons the false promises of a better future life
offered by Christianity as a way of discouraging political action in the
present, and the film does much the same. In it, two working-class protagonists struggle through capitalist society (represented in the film by a
garbage dump), hoping to find food, but finding instead empty slogans
and platitudes, served up by various figures of authority representing
church, state, and charity organizations. Unable to live on slogans, the
protagonists eventually die of starvation, then go to heaven, from there
leading the film's audience in a parodic sing-along that makes abundantly clear the film's contempt for the use of spiritual promises as a
substitute for the basic necessities of material life. *Pie in the* Sky was
produced by a left-wing group associated with New York's Group
Theater, which, organized by Harold Clurman in the early 1930s, featured actors such as John Garfield and produced plays by such rising
playwrights (and soon to be successful screenwriters) as John Howard
Lawson and Clifford Odets. A young Elia Kazan and his wife, Molly Day
Thatcher, were also major participants in the making of *Pie in the Sky*.
They had also been involved with the Group Theater and with the
Theater of Action, an overlapping leftist theater group. The film shows
the clear influences of the backgrounds of its participants in activist
theater. Indeed, as Brian Neve suggests, the film appears very much like
"a series of improvisations that came out of the street theater skits of the

Theater of Action" (11). *Selected bibliography:* Alexander; Clurman; Horak; Neve (*Film*).

*VIVA VILLA!:* **DIR. JACK CONWAY (1934).** A highly fictionalized, and expurgated, account of the career of famed Mexican revolutionary leader Pancho Villa, *Viva Villa!* is clearly a film concerned more with entertainment than historical accuracy or the delivery of any sort of political message. Indeed, the film begins with an announcement, in on-screen text, that identifies it as fiction and disavows all claim to be a work of history. Nominated for four Academy Awards, including best picture, the film was a great success and was considered a prestige production for its studio, MGM. Still, in 1934, the story of poor peasants battling for economic justice could not help having some political reverberations, even though the film focuses not on the larger issues surrounding the Mexican Revolution, but on Villa as an individual, attempting to make him a colorful, Rabelaisian figure whose appeal lies not in ideology but in his simple sincerity and robust zest for life.

The film begins with Villa is a boy, as the peons of his village learn that the government is confiscating their land. Led by Villa's father, they go to the local aristocracy to protest the confiscation, in response to which the elder Villa is brutally whipped to death in front of his people, including his son. The body is then hanged from a tree as a warning to others who would challenge the authority of the aristocracy, described as being a vestige of Spanish colonial rule in Mexico. The young Villa then takes to the hills, where, as he grows older, he gradually develops a reputation as a Robin Hood-like bandit leader, taking revenge on the rich for their oppression of the poor. When the Mexican Revolution begins, Villa (played as an adult by Wallace Beery) becomes a follower of Francisco Madero (Henry B. Walthall), in whose service he attempts to develop greater military discipline, transforming his gang of bandits into an effective army. Villa sweeps to a series of impressive military victories in northern Mexico, as Madero's chief general, the haughty Pascal (Joseph Schildkraut), jealously looks on. The dictator Diaz is deposed, and Madero is elected the new president of Mexico.

Villa, the revolution presumably complete, returns to his village, but the ambitious Pascal, knowing Villa's devotion to Madero, continues to regard him as a potential threat to his own desire for greater power. When Villa turns to bank robbery (in an effort to get his own money out of the bank), he is arrested. Pascal personally oversees his conviction and sentence of death. Villa begs for mercy, knowing that his death will mean the end of Madero, and mercy in fact arrives in the form of a pardon from Madero, delivered on the condition that Villa leave the country. With Villa in Texas, Pascal quickly kills Madero and takes power. Villa then returns, reorganizes his army, and begins a furious campaign of vengeance, eventually sweeping Pascal from office and then (in an entirely fictional episode) executing him by covering him with honey and staking him out for the ants to eat.

Villa becomes president of Mexico but is unable to cope with the frustrating bureaucratic demands of the office. He again retires quietly to his village and is not seen until some time later as he returns on a visit to Mexico City. There, Villa encounters his old friend, Johnny Sykes (Stuart Erwin), a newspaperman who had reported on many of his earlier exploits. As the two old friends reminisce, Villa is cut down by assassins' bullets, fired from across the street by three men, led by Don Felipe (Donald Cook), an aristocrat whose sister had earlier been accidentally killed by Villa's men. As Villa dies in the street, he urges Sykes to make up some good last words for him because he is himself too inarticulate. When Sykes responds by supplying a plea for absolution from his sins, the surprised Villa dies, asking "What did I do wrong?"

Beery plays Villa almost as a sort of idiot savant, a childish and simple figure who is unable to control his temper or libido or to understand the intricacies of government and diplomacy, yet who is somehow a brilliant military strategist and charismatic leader. Still, the film seems to want to be sympathetic to Villa despite its Orientalist portrait of him, a portrait that helps to make clear that such a leader is to be admired only in a primitive setting like Mexico and is not to be taken as a model for political action in the United States. Meanwhile, the film elides all mention of Villa's troubles with the United States, most particularly the 1916 invasion of Mexico by an expeditionary force led by General Pershing in an unsuccessful attempt to apprehend Villa for his alleged involvement in the killing of some Americans in Chihuahua and a raid on a border town in New Mexico. The film omits numerous aspects of the Mexican political situation as well. For example, there is no mention of other important leaders of the revolution, such as Emiliano Zapata, presumably in order to avoid diluting the focus on Villa. More importantly, there is no mention of the role of the Catholic Church in perpetuating the power of the Mexican aristocracy or in opposing the subsequent revolution. *Screenplay:* Ben Hecht. *Selected bibliography:* Guzmán; Friedrich Katz; Mistron; Pinchon; Reed (*Insurgent Mexico*); Christopher P. Wilson.

*FURY:* DIR. FRITZ LANG (1936). *Fury,* one of the best-known films of famed director Lang, presents a dark vision of middle America, employing themes and techniques that clearly anticipate the later development of the film noir. The film, which revolves around an apparent lynching, reveals a hidden violent core at the heart of life in a supposedly idyllic small middle-American town. Moreover, given the timing of the film and Lang's status as an exile in flight from the Nazis in Europe, there are unspoken suggestions of parallels between the dark impulses revealed in the film's small-town Americans and the kinds of impulses that made fascism possible in Europe. At the same time, the film also points out the long history of lynching in America, while questioning the reliability of the American legal system, which ultimately convicts twenty people of the murder of a man who is actually still alive.

*Fury* begins as two young lovers in Chicago, Joe Wilson and Katherine Grant (played by Spencer Tracy and Sylvia Sidney), window shop and dream of their future life together. Katherine, a teacher, soon takes a job in another city, where she will make more money and thus make more rapid progress toward saving for their future. The honest and hardworking Wilson stays behind and builds his savings as well, meanwhile excoriating his brothers, Charlie and Tom, when they become involved in criminal activities. Eventually, Wilson reaches the point where he believes he can afford marriage. He buys a car and sets out on the road to fetch Katherine and begin to fulfill their American dream. On the way, however, he is stopped in the small town of Strand and eventually arrested on suspicion of involvement in a recent kidnapping there. Word of the arrest spreads rapidly through the town's well-developed gossip system. Lang presents a sinister vision of small-town America as the locals, driven by secret murderous impulses and seemingly ignorant of the Bill of Rights and other principles of American justice, become more and more incensed over the crime. Eventually, an ugly lynch mob gathers outside the jail. In some of the films most expressionist scenes, the camera focuses on the gleefully malevolent faces of the respectable citiznes who make up the mob. The town sheriff (Edward Ellis) struggles valiantly to defend his prisoner and manages to prevent the mob from getting to Joe's cell. Unable to get to their intended victim, the mob sets fire to and then dynamites the jail, burning it to the ground and presumably killing the prisoner, who is still locked in his cell. Meanwhile, the real kidnappers are apprehended, and it becomes clear that Joe had been innocent all along.

It turns out, however, that Joe had escaped when the dynamite blew open his cell door. He goes into hiding, appearing only to his brothers and urging them to pursue the prosecution of the mob's leaders for his murder. The second half of the film is essentially a courtroom drama detailing the trial of the twenty-two citizens of Strand who are indicted for the killing. Other citizens of the town falsely testify, providing alibis for the defendants, but to no avail because the entire event had been captured by newsreel cameras. The only hope of the defense is that Joe's body has not been found, raising questions about whether he is really dead. But Katherine, who had rushed to Strand to try to come to Joe's aid, testifies to having seen him through the window of his cell as it was engulfed in flames, sealing the case. In the meantime, she discovers that Joe is still alive and begs him to come forward. Obsessed with revenge and with his former idealism destroyed by his ordeal, he ignores her pleas to reveal himself. Overwrought with guilt, Katherine breaks off their engagement but keeps Joe's secret. Ultimately, twenty of the accused are convicted of murder and will presumably face death sentences, but Joe experiences a change of heart and reveals himself in the courtroom as the verdicts are being read. He is reunited with Katherine in a conventional Hollywood happy ending, but ominous echoes still remain from the earlier events depicted in the film. *Screenplay:* Bartlett Cormack and Fritz Lang. *Selected bibliography:* Bogdanovich; Humphries; McGilligan; Ott; Roffman and Purdy; Velde.

*THE GENERAL DIED AT DAWN:* DIR. LEWIS MILESTONE (1936). *The General Died at Dawn* is primarily an entertainment film, combining an exotic (and somewhat Orientalist, in Edward Said's sense) adventure story with some genuinely snappy dialogue by screenwriter Clifford Odets. But Odets also manages to work in a few political statements, mostly in the explanations of the American protagonist, O'Hara (Gary Cooper), concerning his work on the behalf of Chinese insurgents who are battling against the regional warlord, General Yang (played by all-purpose Hollywood foreigner Akim Tamiroff). In the film, O'Hara agrees to take some money for the rebels to Shanghai, where it can be used to purchase arms and ammunition for the battle against Yang. On the way, he is captured, and the money falls into the hands of Peter Perrie (Porter Hall), a sniveling American working for Yang. O'Hara escapes and makes his way to Shanghai, where he kills Perrie. Then O'Hara is again captured by Yang, along with the rebel leader, Mr. Wu (Dudley Digges), and Perrie's beautiful daughter, Judy Perrie (Madeleine Carroll), who has fallen in love with O'Hara.

The prisoners are taken aboard Yang's junk, which also contains Yang, his personal guard, and Brighton (William Frawley), an American arms dealer. Also aboard is Yang's German military advisor (Hans Fürberg), whose presence helps to link the evil Yang with European fascism, thus aligning the battle against Yang with the battle against fascism in Europe. Indeed, when O'Hara suggests that he is helping the Chinese insurgents because it is only natural for Americans to fight against oppression and for democracy anywhere in the world, his speech can be taken as a plea for support for the Spanish Republicans in the civil war just under way in Spain at the time of the release of the film. On the other hand, Yang is also a rather stereotypical Oriental despot, treated almost as a god by his slavishly devoted followers.

Eventually, Yang is accidentally, and fatally, stabbed by Brighton. Before he dies, however, the general orders his guards to commit mass suicide as a demonstration of their loyalty to them. Wu and the Americans, however, are released after O'Hara cleverly convinces Yang that their testimony will be needed so that the rest of the world can learn of this final impressive act of devotion to Yang on the part of his guards. O'Hara the Westerner thus outsmarts the Oriental Yang, whose quest for personal glory overwhelms his judgment. In addition, the film carefully avoids any mention of Mao Zedong and the Chinese communists, though it is clear that the insurgents whom O'Hara supports could in reality be no one other than communists. This recognition adds additional force to the film's leftist political message, despite its occasional forays into Orientalist stereotyping. *Screenplay:* Clifford Odets. *Selected bibliography:* Roffman and Purdy; Said.

*MODERN TIMES:* **DIR. CHARLES CHAPLIN (1936).** *Modern Times,* which is in a sense both Chaplin's final silent film and his first sound film, is one of the classic landmarks of American film, both because of its place in the evolution of film technology and because of its crucial commentary on the place of technology within the modern world as a whole. In some ways, *Modern Times* is a dystopian work that describes the potential horrors of mechanization and industrialization in a mode reminiscent of earlier films such as Fritz Lang's *Metropolis* (1926), while suggesting the political oppression that might accompany growing technologization in a mode that anticipates later works such as George Orwell's *Nineteen Eighty-four* (1949). Yet Chaplin's Tramp, carried over from the earlier silent films, remains his lovable self, and *Modern Times* conducts its social critique in a charmingly comic mode that is entirely lacking in most dystopian works. Moreover, Chaplin's film is quite specifically set in the midst of the Depression of the 1930s and thus has a direct contemporary topicality that sets it apart from most dystopian satire, which may involve a critique of contemporary society but which typically does so through a mode of defamiliarization achieved through settings in times or places distant from those being commented upon.

*Modern Times* begins with a symbolic shot of a giant clock face, followed by suggestive parallel shots of a herd of sheep and a stream of workers going into a modern factory to begin their shift. The film then continues as the Tramp works on a Taylorized factory assembly line, surrounded by huge, menacing machinery while he repetitively tightens nuts in a mechanical fashion that threatens to reduce even the Tramp, that ultimately human figure, to a machine. Some of the film's most striking scenes occur during these early moments as the Tramp struggles to keep up with the ever-increasing speed of the conveyors on the line. One of the film's most comic, but also most telling, comments on the dangers of technology occurs when the Tramp is used to test the new "Bellows Feeding Machine," which is designed automatically to supply workers with food while they stay at work on the line, thus eliminating the need for lunch breaks. Predictably, the machine goes berserk, pummeling the Tramp and leaving him covered with food. These early scenes are also important because of their introduction of sound. It is significant that the first recorded human voice to appear in a Chaplin film is the voice of the plant's president giving commands over an Orwellian telescreen through which he, Big Brother-like, can keep the entire plant under surveillance. Throughout the film, mechanically reproduced human voices are associated with oppressive authority, while the Tramp continues speechless, his status as a silent-film character lost in a sound film further establishing his alienation within modern society.

In another strikingly self-reflexive moment, the Tramp falls onto the conveyor and is drawn into the plant machinery, winding through a series of gears in manner that is unmistakably similar to film being threaded through a projector, suggesting Chaplin's own sense that, as a filmmaker, he is being overwhelmed by a modern technology that, among other things, forces him to begin using sound in order to survive in the film business. The Tramp emerges from the gears apparently deranged, then runs amok in the plant and finally has to be taken away in an ambulance. The film then cuts to his later release from a mental hospital, and we see none of his treatment there, though we can surmise, especially from later events in the film, that the hospital is a rather carceral institution, in the mode described by Michel Foucault in *Discipline and Punish*.

Altthough presumably cured, the Tramp is also now unemployed, and he emerges into a Depression world in which jobs are indeed hard to find. On the street, the Tramp picks up a red warning flag that falls off the back of a lumber truck, then waves the flag to try to get the driver's attention. At this moment, a group of marching workers comes around the corner, carrying signs that demand their economic rights. The police attack and mistake the flag-waving Tramp, because of his red flag, for the communist leader of the workers' demonstration. They therefore take him off to jail, in a commentary on political oppression that is made all the more powerful because it seems perfectly natural within the context of the film that such a communist leader would be jailed, the rhetoric of American political freedom notwithstanding. We soon learn, meanwhile, that the Tramp will get on well in the jail (while strikes and riots rage outside), which is no more carceral than the factory and the hospital to which he is already accustomed. Indeed, scenes of regimentation of the behavior of prisoners in the jail are obviously designed to parallel that of the workers in the earlier factory.

After the Tramp is taken to jail, we are introduced to the film's other major character, the Gamin, fetchingly played by Paulette Goddard. With her mother dead and her father unemployed, she is engaged in stealing bananas to help feed herself, her father, and her two younger sisters, though she shares her bounty with other neighborhood children as well.

Soon afterward, her father is killed in street violence; the Gamin and her sisters are sent to an orphanage (another of the film's carceral institutions), though the Gamin escapes back onto the streets, where she again begins to steal food. The Tramp, meanwhile, has been released as a reward for foiling a jail break while high on an inadvertent dose of cocaine, thus suggesting that no one in his right mind would act in support of modern carceral authority. Having already lost one job, the Tramp is determined to return to jail, and he spends the next segment of the film flagrantly breaking the law (in an obvious fantasy of freedom from the restraints of modern bourgeois regimentation and routinization) in an attempt to return to jail. In this case, he attempts to take the blame for the Gamin's theft of a loaf of bread, though a witness foils his attempt by identifying the Gamin as the thief.

The Tramp next goes into a restaurant and eats an elaborate meal for which he cannot pay, again flagrantly breaking the law, but tellingly doing so in a Depression-situated way that involves a quest for food. He is indeed arrested and taken away in a paddy wagon, where he is joined by the Gamin. The two then escape together after the wagon is involved in an accident. Observing a scene of suburban tranquillity, the two dream of someday having a nice home together. The Tramp resumes his search for work toward that end and soon lands a position as a night watchman in a department store. He invites the Gamin to join him inside during his shift, and the two frolic among the abundant commodities that stock the store awaiting purchase by well-to-do customers, in powerful contrast to the poverty that reigns on the streets outside. Their night in the store includes, among other things, a famous scene of Chaplinesque physical comedy (reminiscent of scenes from Chaplin's 1916 film, *The Rink*) in which the Tramp roller-skates blindfolded in the toy department, repeatedly veering dangerously near the edge of a balcony where the safety railing has been removed for repairs. When some hungry workers break into the store looking for food, the Tramp joins them. He is discovered the next morning sleeping off his revels and is again sent to jail.

When he is released, the Gamin excitedly greets him, announcing that she has found a home for them. They then go together to an abandoned shack that contrasts sharply with their earlier dreams of bourgeois suburban bliss. Hoping for a real home, the Tramp again gets work, this time helping to repair the machinery in his former factory, now about to reopen after an extended shutdown. After a few comic misadventures in the plant, he again finds himself unemployed as the workers decide to go out on strike. As he leaves the plant, he becomes inadvertently involved in an altercation with police (presented, without comment, as an oppressive body opposed to working-class collective action). He is once again taken to jail, and the cyclic nature of his modern life continues.

As the Tramp serves still another jail term, the Gamin is observed dancing in the street to the music of a carousel; she is then hired to perform in a café that features live entertainment. A success as an entertainer, the Gamin is able to get the Tramp a job in the café as well, working as a singing waiter. Predictably, the Tramp is a comic disaster as a waiter. He fares better as a singer, however. Unable to remember his lines, he sings a nonsense song, "Titina," simply making up gibberish as he goes along, accompanied by a hilarious comic dance. The Tramp's first words on film are thus sung, not spoken, and they make no sense, suggesting that his virtues as a performer do not lie in verbal communication. Just as things are looking up, juvenile authorities show up to take the Gamin back to the orphanage, and the two have to make an abrupt escape. The film ends the next morning as they walk together, smiling happily despite their recent disappointments, down the middle of a road that extends out of sight into the distance.

This apparent romance ending does not resolve any of the social and economic problems that arise in the film, and there is evidence that Chaplin changed the ending to avoid making an explicit statement about the need to take political action to resolve those problems (Maland 146). On the other hand, the ending as it stands suggests that these problems are not easily solved, especially by lone individuals like the Tramp. Meanwhile, the ending may be richer than it appears, as much a parody of a romance resolution as a resolution proper. The Tramp and the Gamin walk off together not into the sunset, per convention, but into the sunrise, suggesting that they are going not into the future but against the grain of history, into the past, where they, as silent-film characters, properly belong. Chaplin thus reluctantly acknowledges the ascendance of modern sound-film technology, while at the same time associating that technology with growing regimentation that makes life in modern times increasingly carceral, imposing bourgeois values that make it impossible for free spirits like the Tramp (who can neither conform to the rules of modern work-oriented capitalism nor cooperate in collective action to oppose capitalist exploitation) to continue to survive. The film's political statement is potentially powerful, even if Chaplin never overtly expresses his own political position in the film, apparently remaining ambivalent about the ability of art to work significant social change. The film received considerable positive critical reception on the Left, as when Kyle Crichton, writing in *New Masses*, noted that "I came away stunned at the thought that such a film had been made, and was being distributed. ... To anyone who has studied the set-up, financial and ideological, of Hollywood, *Modern Times* is not so much a fine motion picture as an historical event." Given the institutional restraints of Hollywood, *Modern Times* is indeed a striking political statement and one that remains surprisingly relevant even today. *Screenplay:* Charles Chaplin. *Selected bibliography:* Crichton; Foucault; Jaffe; Maland (*Chaplin*).

*THE PLOW THAT BROKE THE PLAINS:* **DIR. PARE LORENTZ (1936)**. Lorentz's documentaries of the 1930s, supported by government funds and widely distributed despite opposition from the film industry, which claimed the government was infringing on their territory, are among the leading cultural documents of the decade. Perhaps the single best-known example of Lorentz's work is *The Plow that Broke the Plains*, which presents, in monumental style, a history of the American Great Plains, that vast strip of 400 million acres of grassland stretching from the Texas panhandle to Canada. The film begins with a prologue of on-screen text describing the location, extent, and climate of the plains, then (without irony or apology) announcing that "By 1880 we had cleared the Indian, and with him, the buffalo, from the Great Plains." It is at this point, in the mode of colonialist historiography, that, according to the film, the history of the region begins. "First came the cattle," announces narrator Thomas Chalmers early in the film; he then describes the region as a "cattleman's paradise." But the real heroes of the film are the farmers who came after the cattlemen, and the heart of the film is dedicated to the efforts of these farmers, with the help of modern technology, to tame the often harsh conditions they found on the plains.

Much of the film is devoted to scenes from this battle, as legions of tractors and other agricultural machines march triumphantly across the plains, announcing the ability of modern American technology to conquer nature. Among other things, the heroic farmers are credited with having played a major role in the Allied victory in World War I by supplying wheat to the troops and the civilian population during the war. The 1920s are then quickly described as an era of land boom and wheat boom, with a veiled suggestion that the plains are being unwisely exploited through capitalist greed. Then come the droughts of the 1930s, and the plains are reduced to a dustbowl, the farmers battling valiantly but vainly to maintain their farms in the face of this natural calamity. As the film ends, the farmers are shown gradually abandoning the now arid plains and heading west, a "great army of the highway," seeking opportunity in California. In a sense, then, *The Plow that Broke the Plains* serves as a sort of predecessor to such later works as *The Grapes of Wrath*, though the documentary does not deal with conditions met by the farmers in California. It is, however, clearly intended as an appeal for sympathy for the migrating farmers, who are depicted as good, hardworking Americans whose poverty arises from causes outside their control. *Screenplay:* Pare Lorentz. *Selected bibliography:* Alexander; Denning; Muscio; Snyder; Charles Wolfe.

*THESE THREE:* DIR. WILLIAM WYLER (1936). The screenplay for *These Three* was adapted by Lillian Hellman from her own play, *The Children's Hour*. However, the film, by order of the Hays Office, is a significantly bowdlerized version of the play. In particular, while the play deals centrally (and sympathetically) with the topic of lesbianism, that topic is missing from the film altogether. In the film, college friends Martha Dobie and Karen Wright (played by Miriam Hopkins and Merle Oberon) run an exclusive private boarding school attended by Mary Tilford (played by Bonita Granville, who won an Oscar nomination for best supporting actress for the role), a mean-spirited girl whose behavior draws the censure of Martha and Karen. In a bid for revenge, Mary (falsely) tells her grandmother that Martha has been carrying on a sexual relationship on school grounds with Dr. Joseph Cardin (Joel McCrea), who is Karen's boyfriend. (These rumors replace the rumors of lesbianism that were spread in the play, though there is a still a certain erotic charge to the relationship between Martha and Karen on screen). Mary manages to blackmail another girl, Rosalie Wells (Marcia Mae Jones), into corroborating her story, and Mary's horrified grandmother (Alma Kruger) spreads the scandal, advising parents to remove their children from the school. Martha, Karen, and Joe respond by filing a libel suit against the grandmother, and the truth eventually comes out. The rumors, however, have destroyed both the school, which is forced to close, and the friendship between Martha and Karen. Joe loses his post at a local hospital and moves to Vienna, where Karen eventually joins him.

Paul Buhle, in his attempt to suggest a typology of the American film of the Left, concludes that "a particular kind of woman's film in the hands of Lillian Hellman" constitutes an entire subgenre unto itself (107). He sees *These Three* as perhaps the most important example of this subgenre, especially because of Hellman's ability to project a vague sympathy for lesbianism despite the rigid censorial strictures under which she was working. Hellman would, of course, go on to become a major figure of the Hollywood Left and a major target of the HUAC investigations of Hollywood, as recounted in her memoir, *Scoundrel Time*. In 1961, Wyler and Hellman collaborated on a remake of the film (under the title *The Children's Hour*) that changing standards allowed to be much more faithful to the original play. *Screenplay:* Lillian Hellman. *Selected bibliography:* Buhle; Dick (*Hellman*); Erhart; Hellman (*Scoundrel Time*); Titus.

*DEAD END:* DIR. WILLIAM WYLER (1937). Perhaps the most important of the slum dramas to be produced by Hollywood in the late 1930s, *Dead End* focuses on New York's East End, not only calling attention to the poverty in the slums there, but vividly depicting class difference by showing a luxury high-rise apartment building that has been placed smack in the middle of the slums in order to give its wealthy inhabitants a view of the river. The striking contrast between the apartment building and the surrounding streets and tenements is the dominant image of the film, present in nearly every scene. In a motif with obvious implications, a uniformed doorman (Ward Bond), backed up by police, acts as a guard, constantly sweeping trash from the doorsteps of the apartment building, while beating the slum dwellers, regarded as human trash, away from the building's doors. Such reminders of class difference are also emphasized in the plot of the film, but *Dead End*, like the Sidney Kingsley play on which it was based, relies primarily on an exploration of the social and economic conditions in the slums for its effect.

What there is of a plot focuses on several adult characters who themselves grew up in the slum. One of them, Babyface Martin (Humphrey Bogart, in one of his earliest roles), is now a notorious killer who has returned to the neighborhood, disguised by plastic surgery, to visit his mother (Marjorie Main) and his old girlfriend, Francie (Claire Trevor). He finds, however, that his faded and worn-out mother wants nothing to do with her infamous son. And he wants nothing to do with Francie after he discovers that she has turned to prostitution as a means of surviving under the brutal economic conditions that prevail in the slums of Depression-era New York. Martin is also rebuffed by Dave Connell (Joel McCrea), a boyhood friend, who has worked and struggled to get through college and is now an architect. Unfortunately, economic conditions have made it impossible for Dave, however honest and hardworking, to realize his dream of replacing the local tenements with decent housing; he himself remains unemployed and mired in poverty, stuck in the slum despite his education.

Dave is romantically involved with Kay Burton (Wendy Barrie), a formerly poor woman who is now the mistress of one of the rich inhabitants of the apartment building. But Kay, now accustomed to the good life, is so appalled by the slum that Dave eventually realizes the two of them could never share a life together. Meanwhile, the virtuous Drina (Sylvia Sidney) lives in the slum with Tommy (Billy Halop), her younger brother. She works hard to make a better life for herself and her brother, but her low-paying job offers little hope for escape from the slums. Indeed, throughout the film, she and the other employees of the unspecified company where she works are on strike for better wages. This strike is entirely peripheral to the plot, but its suggestion of collective action to oppose the exploitative conditions that lead to poverty even for hardworking individuals is potentially important. In addition, official attempts to suppress the strike (Drina is at one point clubbed by a policeman in an attack on the picket line) provide a reminder that society puts far more resources into perpetuating poverty than into ending it.

In the course of the film, Martin attempts to murder Dave to prevent him from revealing his identity to the police. Dave, however, survives the attack and ends up killing Martin, who dies in a dark and filthy alley with $20,000 in his pockets, a reminder that crime ultimately does not pay. Dave then finally notices Drina, who has long admired him, and the two appear headed for a life together as the film closes. But the real focus of the film is not on these adult characters but on the gang of juvenile delinquents who inhabit the slum and who are gradually driven into crime by the conditions they encounter there. This gang, led by Tommy, Spit (Leo Gorcey), and Dippy (Huntz Hall), provides a striking enactment of life in slum and was effective enough that its members would go on to star in a whole series of films over the next few years, first as the Dead End Kids, then as the East End Kids, then as the Bowery Boys.

The central point of *Dead End* is that these boys have little hope of escaping from the slum, except perhaps via the rout taken by Martin. Martin, we are told, was "smart and brave and decent" as a boy, driven into criminal depravity by the social conditions under which he grew up. Tommy seems headed in the same direction. After one scene, in which the gang beats up a snotty rich boy (Charles Peck) from the apartment building, Tommy is apprehended by the boy's father, Mr. Griswold (Minor Watson), whom he stabs, wounding slightly, in order to escape. Tommy then becomes the object of a manhunt. Finally, trying to do the right thing, Tommy gives himself up, but the pompous Griswold, brother of a powerful judge, refuses to be merciful, insisting on pressing charges and seeing to it that Tommy goes to reform school, depicted in the film as a preparatory school for crime. As the film ends, Tommy is taken away by a policeman, though Dave resolves to use his reward money from killing Martin to hire a lawyer to try to win leniency for the boy. The camera then pans upward from the slum to the Manhattan skyscrapers, filled with corporate offices, that tower over it.

While this ending suggests some possibility of a better future, that future is by no means assured, and *Dead End* has the virtue of eschewing the simple resolutions typical of Hollywood film. One need only compare the 1938 follow-up, *Angels with Dirty Faces*, which also features the Dead End Kids but which ends optimistically, and unrealistically, with them successfully reconciled to society, primarily through the good offices of a kindly priest. In its focus on the dehumanizing effects of poverty in the East Side slums, in its contrast of this poverty with the luxurious lifestyles of the idle rich, and in its insistence that virtue and hard work alone are insufficient to lift individuals out of poverty, *Dead End* makes some of the most potentially powerful political statements of Hollywood film in the late 1930s. Granted, most of the film's specific political points are not explicitly stated but are left for the audience to fill in, but the process is a rather simple one. The implication that the poor are victims of brutal social conditions rather than simply lazy or immoral was especially clear in the midst of the Depression. The plight of the film's women, who must choose among the literal prostitution of Francie, the figurative prostitution of Kay, and futile drudgery of Drina (leading ιο the exhaustion of Mrs. Martin), adds an important element of commentary on gender, but the injustice of class inequality remains the unmistakable focus of the film's social commentary. *Screenplay:* Lillian Hellman. *Selected bibliography:* Bergman; Clarens; Roffman and Purdy.

*THE GOOD EARTH:* **DIR. SIDNEY FRANKLIN (1937).** *The Good Earth* is a successful, if somewhat romanticized and sentimentalized, screen adaptation of Pearl Buck's 1931 Pulitzer Prize-winning novel of the same title. Both book and film focus on the tribulations of a Chinese peasant family, though the book makes it more clear that these tribulations are due largely to an outmoded social system that was badly in need of radical transformation. This transformation, of course, would ultimately be achieved only by the establishment of communist rule in China in 1949, though Mao Zedong and the communists had already begun their long struggle when the book was written in 1931. The film puts little emphasis on such historical developments, instead focusing on the private problems of its central family. Nevertheless, in its reasonably sympathetic treatment of its Chinese protagonists, the film differed from the kind of Orientalist stereotypes that were typical of American culture at the time.

The film's central character is poor farmer Wang Lung, played by Paul Muni, who does not look very Chinese but nevertheless delivers an effective performance. The film begins on Wang's wedding day, as he awakes with great anticipation of acquiring a new wife to help with the farm work and to produce sons. He then goes to a nearby rich estate, where his bride, whom he has never seen, works as a kitchen slave. He purchases the young woman, O-lan (Luise Rainer), from the estate and takes her home with him. Wang clearly regards O-lan as his subordinate, rather than his equal, but he treats her far better than she had been treated on the estate. The two work diligently together on the farm, which prospers to the point that they are able to purchase several new tracts of land, greatly expanding their holdings. In the meantime, O-lan gives birth to two sons and (to the great disappointment of Wang) a daughter.

A terrible drought brings an end to the family's prosperity, and they are eventually forced to migrate to the south so Wang can seek work in a city there, though their primary income comes from O-lan and the children begging in the streets. The situation seems hopeless, until the Manchu dynasty falls in the revolution of 1912, leading to chaos in the city where the family is living. Unfortunately, the film does essentially nothing to explain the basis of the revolution or to describe the actual political situation in China at the time. By sheer chance, O-lan finds a bag of jewels left in the aftermath of the looting of a rich estate, giving the family the resources to return to the north and rebuild their farm, which soon grows into a rich estate in its own right. Wang, meanwhile, becomes overly enamoured of his new wealth, becoming estranged from the land he once loved. He also becomes enamoured of Lotus (Tilly Losch), a beautiful young dancer, whom he takes as his second wife, which introduces considerable discord into the family.

All of Wang's wealth is then threatened when a massive plague of locusts approaches the area. In an impressive scene that pushed contemporary filmmaking technology to its limit, Wang leads the local farmers in a heroic battle against the insects, not only saving most of their harvest, but also re-establishing his connection with the land and with his fellow farmers. Soon afterward, the long-suffering O-lan falls ill and dies. Too late, Wang realizes her true value. After a sentimental death scene, he decides to sell his mansion and return to the land. *Screenplay:* Talbot Jennings, Tess Slesinger, Frances Marion, and Claudine West. *Selected bibliography:* Balio; Hoban; Roffman and Purdy.

*HEART OF SPAIN:* DIR. HERBERT KLINE (1937). *Heart of Spain* presents the Spanish Civil War from the point of view of a director with a strong background of participation in American leftist culture—and who was, in fact, in Spain covering the civil war for the communist cultural journal *New Masses.* The film began, at the suggestion of Canadian doctor Norman Bethune (whose career would become the subject of the 1990 biopic, *Dr. Bethune*), as an educational documentary designed to raise money for the Loyalist medical service. It was to focus on Bethune's new techniques for transfusion and blood preservation. Director Kline and cameraman Geza Karpathi (a still photographer) had no previous filmmaking experience, but they managed to convert this mundane subject into a powerful piece of political footage. Filming in hospitals and on the front, they documented the medical techniques they saw there in a powerful and immediate way that made clear the human dimension of the civil war. Then, helped by experienced leftist fimmakers Leo Hurwitz, Paul Strand, and Ben Maddow, they managed to edit their raw footage to produce a film that went far beyond the original medical documentary to produce a moving document of the war as a whole. The film was then released as the first film from the newly formed leftist independent film company Frontier Films.

William Alexander believes that *Heart of Spain* may have been the finest film produced by Frontier Films, although he admits that *People of the Cumberland* and *Native Land* would vie for that honor as well (162). In any case, the final product captures both the horror of war and the idealist dedication of the Spanish Loyalists to the fight against fascism. Indeed, the film manages to crystallize in a few brief sequences the terms of the war, with Franco and the fascists, fighting to protect the interests of their wealthy supporters, on the one side and the heroic Spanish masses, fighting for freedom, on the other. It also makes clear and urgent its appeal for American help to the Loyalist side. As Alexander notes, it is natural to compare *Heart of Spain* to the better known *The Spanish Earth*, but the film that *Heart of Spain* resembles most as a documentary film is actually Joris Ivens's *New Earth*, which was a powerful and direct influence, with its vision of committed films as arising from "the mature and deeply human testimony of a particular group of artists" (166). *Heart of Spain* received a special award of merit from the Spanish Loyalist government. **Screenplay:** Herbert Kline and Ben Maddow. **Selected bibliography:** Alexander; Kline.

*MARKED WOMAN:* **DIR. LLOYD BACON (1937).** *Marked Woman* is an excellent example of the modified gangster films that were produced in Hollywood in the late 1930s in an attempt to overcome complaints that earlier gangster films (*Little Caesar, Public Enemy, Scarface*) tended to make heroes of their gangster protagonists. *Marked Woman* is based on the career of New York mob kingpin Charles "Lucky" Luciano, represented in the film as Johnny Vanning (played by Eduardo Cianelli). But the central figures of the film are Mary Dwight (Bette Davis), a prostitute who works for Vanning but who eventually testifies against him, and crusading district attorney David Graham (Humphrey Bogart), based on Thomas E. Dewey. The focus is thus shifted from Vanning and his criminal empire to the virtuous and courageous souls who participate in the destruction of that empire.

As the film begins, Vanning has just taken over a club where Mary and her fellow prostitutes work euphemistically as "hostesses," using the club as a home base for their prostitution activities. Vanning, in fact, is taking over New York's entire network of organized prostitution, thus warning Mary and her fellow workers that they can either accept the terms he offers them or find themselves unable to work anywhere in the city. They grudgingly accept his terms, and the club seems to be operating smoothly until one of Mary's clients, Ralph Krawford (Damian O'Flynn), runs up a big gambling debt at the club, which he pays with a bad check. On Mary's advice, Krawford decides to skip town, but Vanning's thugs catch up to him and murder him before he can leave. Graham, seeing the murder as a long-awaited opportunity to get to Vanning, traces the dead man to Mary, then coerces her into testifying against Vanning, who is brought up on murder charges along with several of his associates. What Graham does not know, however, is that Mary is working under the instructions of Vanning's attorney, Gordon (John Litel). As a result, her testimony falls flat at the trial, and all of the defendants are acquitted.

Mary goes back to work for Vanning, but another disruption occurs when her innocent younger sister, Betty Strauber (Jane Bryan), comes to New York for a visit. Mary (who has changed her last name to Dwight to avoid besmirching the family honor through her unsavory occupation) is putting Betty through college, supposedly by working as a model. When Betty discovers the true nature of Mary's work, she is shocked and responds by beginning to hang out with Vanning's crowd herself. When she resists the advances of one of Vanning's associates at a party, Vanning accosts her, inadvertently knocking her down the stairs and killing her. Mary eventually learns what happened and again goes to Graham, this time to testify in earnest. Vanning's thugs attempt to intimidate her, beating her badly and leaving her face scarred. But she testifies nevertheless, along with four of her fellow workers. Their joint testimony leads to the conviction of Vanning, who is given a sentence of thirty to fifty years, with the judge's admonition that, if anything should happen to any of the witnesses, Vanning will be certain to serve the maximum sentence. As the film ends, Mary and her fellow witnesses walk away together into the fog and into their future, which remains uncertain: they may be relatively safe from Vanning's violent revenge, but they are also unemployed in the midst of the Depression.

*Marked Woman* thus ends on a potentially troubling note that makes it anything but a simple affirmation of the triumph of law and order. Meanwhile, the film's open sympathy for the prostitutes as workers exploited by an unscrupulous boss suggests the hypocrisy of a society that would reject them as disreputable, while opening endorsing the exploitation in more respectable occupations that had driven them into prostitution in the first place. This comment on the treatment of women workers under capitalism is reinforced by the fact that Vanning, after taking over as the city's prostitution kingpin, does everything possible to institute more efficient and businesslike practices. By thus suggesting that prostitutes are just another form of exploited labor, the film potentially suggests the economic commodification of all workers under capitalism, as well as the sexual objectification of all women under patriarchy. Indeed, as Charles Eckert has noted, the film, in its opposition between Vanning and the prostitutes, can be read as a story of class conflict, albeit in a rather muted and indirect form. *Screenplay:* Robert Rossen and Abem Finkel. *Selected bibliography:* Clarens; Eckert; Haralovich; Thomas Price.

**THE RIVER: DIR. PARE LORENTZ (1937).** Produced by the Farm Security Administration, *The River* purports to be the story of the Mississippi River and the gigantic system of continental drainage that feeds it. The documentary presents a great deal of historical and geographical information about the river. The real focus, however, is on the people who live in the Mississippi Valley. It features numerous scenes of life in the valley, focusing especially on scenes of work, most of it related to the river in one way or another. Men are shown logging, working in steel mills, farming, building levees, and loading boats and ships. The film, narrated by Thomas Chalmers in the rhythmic prose-poem style typical of Lorentz's 1930s documentaries, emphasizes the magnitude and grandeur of the river but also the danger of it. It shows the people of the valley achieving great things with the help of the river, but also battling against the sometimes mighty obstacles that the river poses. Much of the film, in fact, is devoted to flood scenes and to the devastation caused by various floods in the history of the river, culminating in the major floods of 1937.

Ultimately, *The River* is a propaganda film devoted to the promotion of the extensive federal programs underway in 1937 to tame the river and to bring greater prosperity to the impoverished Southeast. The film emphasizes the growing poverty of the valley, especially of its farmers, then turns to a description of the recent accomplishments of the Tennessee Valley Authority (TVA) and the Army Corps of Engineers in building huge dams that both control flooding in the river system and promote economic and industrial development in the region through the generation of cheap and plentiful hydroelectricity. It includes extensive scenes of the construction of the massive dams of the TVA and further scenes of these huge monuments to progress in actual operation. It also outlines the reforestation and soil conservation programs of the Civilian Conservation Corps (CCC), ending with a confident vision of the future. Ultimately, *The River* is a paean to industrialization, modernization, electrification, and central planning, a celebration of the achievements of modern American technology, through the management of the federal government, to master the daunting challenges posed by nature to human domination of the North American continent. As such, it has much in common with the Soviet "propaganda" films of the 1930s. *Screenplay:* Pare Lorentz. *Selected Bibliography:* Alexander; Denning; Muscio; Rollins ("Ideology"); Snyder; Charles Wolfe.

*THE SPANISH EARTH:* **DIR. JORIS IVENS (1937).** Produced by Contemporary Historians, Inc., an independent group of American leftists that was formed specifically to make and distribute the film, *The Spanish Earth* was one of the central attempts by the cultural Left in America to drum up support for the Republican cause in the Spanish Civil War. Members of the group included John Dos Passos, Lillian Hellman, Helen van Dongen, Ernest Hemingway, Archibald MacLeish, Clifford Odets, Dorothy Parker, and Herman Shumlin. At the end of 1936, they commissioned Joris Ivens to direct the film and sent him to Spain on a shoestring budget with the intention of making a fictional film based on a scenario provided by the group. When Ivens arrived at Fuentedueña, the Spanish village where the film was to be shot, he realized that the village was far too heavily involved in the fight against Franco and his fascists to allow the shooting of a fictional film there. Instead, he began, accompanied by Hemingway and cameraman Johnny Ferno, to film the villagers as they participated in the struggle, supplementing this footage with similar scenes shot in Madrid. The result was a fifty-two-minute documentary that seeks to capture the hardships, sacrifice, and nobility of the Spanish people, as well as their courage and determination in the struggle against fascism.

Designed to gain the sympathy of American viewers and to encourage those who saw the film to donate money to the Republican cause, *The Spanish Earth* carefully avoids any potentially controversial political issues, hoping to avoid the appearance of being leftist propaganda. It thus eschews ideology in favor of an attempt to convey the humanity and reality of the Spanish peasants and workers who were carrying on the desperate fight against the forces of Franco and the large German and Italian fascist armies that supported him. The word "fascist" is even avoided, with Franco's forces simply referred to as "rebels." The original version of the film, previewed in a special showing at the White House on July 7, 1937, among other places, was narrated by Orson Welles, but several of the members of Contemporary Historians felt that Welles's rich, melodious tones were inappropriate for the gritty realism of the film. In the final released version, Hemingway, who had written the narration, also reads it.

The film opens with a panoramic view of the Spanish landscape, then shifts to shots of the peasants of Fuenteduena going about their daily lives, a large part of which involves producing food to send north to Republican Madrid along the Valencia Road. Indeed, the film emphasizes the importance of this supply route to the defense of Madrid, declaring that, in order to be victorious, the "rebels" would have to cut this road. Much of the activity in Fuenteduena involves work on a new irrigation project which will enable the people there to increase the output of crops from their arid land. Meanwhile, scenes of this work are intercut with scenes of Republican forces going into battle and with scenes from Madrid, where the Republican defenders have long been holding out against a prolonged fascist siege. Many of the shots of Madrid emphasize the damage done by fascist shelling of the city, including not only substantial structural damage to buildings, but also significant civilian casualties. There are also brief shots of some of the leading figures among the Republicans, including Enrique Lister, Carlos, José Diaz, Dolores Ibarruri, and the German writer Gustav Regler, but there is no mention of the substantial support being given the Republicans by the Soviet Union. The film ends with coverage of an important battle in which the Republican forces successful defend the Valencia Road against a fascist assault, thus assuring that supplies will still be able to reach Madrid from Fuentedueña and the other villages that remain loyal to the Republican government.

Powerful despite its attempts at political neutrality, *The Spanish Earth* is widely regarded as one of the greatest nonfiction films of the 1930s. On the other hand, the effectiveness of the film is limited its evasion of politics and its failure to provide any real background or explanation for the war. All we see is that the Republicans are good and noble people fighting to defend their country against "rebels," but the film does nothing to indicate why it is so important that the rebels be defeated, except perhaps to show that they are willing to bombard a city filled with civilians in the interest of their own cause. The film drew a positive response from President Roosevelt but did not convince him to alter his policy of nonintervention in Spain. It did, however, raise a significant amount of money, much of it at private showings, though the film did eventually go into distribution, showing at over 400 theaters in sixty American cities. All of the profits went to aid the Spanish Republicans, much of it for the purchase of ambulance chasses to be sent to Spain for use by the Republican forces. *Screenplay:* Ernest Hemingway. *Selected bibliography:* Alexander; Barnouw; Barsam; Coleman; Ivens; Meyers and Leyda; Michalczyk; Waugh ("'Men'"); Waugh ("Water").

*YOU ONLY LIVE ONCE:* **DIR. FRITZ LANG (1937).** Possibly inspired by the careers of Bonnie and Clyde, *You Only Live Once* narrates the travails of a young couple, Eddie Taylor and Joan Graham (Henry Fonda and Sylvia Sidney), who dream of a quiet life together only to find that public forces destroy their private hopes of domestic bliss. Joan, who works as a secretary to public defender Stephen Whitney (Barton MacLane), has had a long relationship with Eddie, a basically decent man who has nevertheless run afoul of the law on numerous occasions. As the film opens, he is just being released from prison after his third term there, all for felonies. Joan greets him, and they are soon married. When they go on their honeymoon, however, they are quickly reminded of the burden of his past, when the proprietor of a country inn asks them to leave his establishment because of Eddie's record. Meanwhile, the two newlyweds observe a pair of croaking frogs, while Eddie, in a moment of rather heavy-handed symbolism, delivers the ominous news that frogs cannot survive the death of a mate, so that mated pairs of frogs tend to die together.

Soon afterward, as the couple makes plans to buy a house, Eddie is fired fi om his new job as a truck driver, supposedly because he is once late for work, but really because his boss is uncomfortable employing an ex-con. From this point forward, things only go from bad to worse for the couple. Not realizing that Eddie has been fired from his job, Joan moves into their new house in advance, assuming he will make the necessary down payment. With this added financial pressure, Eddie grows increasingly desperate but continues to find it impossible to find another job. Only his old gang, planning a new series of robberies, offers him employment. Then, a bank robbery occurs in which six guards are killed. Circumstantial evidence points to Joe's involvement, though he shows up at the house soon afterward, frantic and disheveled, and swears to Joan that he is innocent. She believes him and, trusting the system, urges him to turn himself in. They debate the point, delaying his escape, while police meanwhile surround the house and apprehend him.

Eddie is quickly convicted and sentenced to death, shocking Joan, who had not believed that such a thing could happen to an innocent man. Then follows an almost preposterously unlikely series of events, during which Eddie acquires a gun and tries to escape from the prison, holding a doctor as hostage. Suddenly, word arrives that he has been proved innocent and pardoned. Eddie, however, believes the news is a trick and refuses to believe it. He ends up shooting and killing Father Dolan, the prison chaplain, who tries to prevent his escape and convince him that he is in the clear. Eddie then escapes. He and Joan, now pregnant, head north, hoping to escape to Canada. On the way, Joan has her baby and hands it over to her sister for safe keeping until she and Eddie can establish themselves in Canada. Eddie and Joan commit minor robberies to get gas and food as they head north, while others commit thefts that are blamed on the couple. Wildly exaggerated rumors sweep through the media, depicting their trip as a spectacular crime spree. For Lang, however, the American populace has little sympathy for outcasts and losers. Eddie and Joan do not become media idols, but are objects of fear and hatred everywhere they go. Eventually, they are tracked down, due to a tip delivered by a concerned citizen, and shot and killed by police. The potentially powerful ending then turns ludicrous, as Eddie dies, hearing Father Dolan (whose interference, after all, contributed in a central way to Eddie's eventual death) calling for him to join him in heaven.

More a grim parable than a realistic narrative, *You Only Live Once* is somewhat marred by the silly ending and by the unlikely nature of so many of the developments in the plot. Still, the film is reasonably engaging and contains a great deal of social commentary. Of the latter, the most obvious criticisms are directed at the legal system, depicted as carceral very much in the sense later discussed by Michel Foucault in *Discipline and Punish*. The film also places a great deal of emphasis on economic pressures. Given that Joe's downfall can be traced directly to the loss of his truck-driving job, the film makes a powerful point about the way in which, under a capitalist system with virtually no social safety nets, individuals can be destroyed at the whim of an unsympathetic boss. The film also has its interesting moments, the most effective of which is probably the sequence, after the bank robbery, in which the film makes it unclear whether Eddie really participated in the robbery. Then, when he is proved innocent, the audience realizes that it had suspected him partly because of his past, mimicking the characters in the film who refuse to give Eddie a fresh start. *Screenplay:* Gene Towne and Graham Barker. *Selected bibliography:* Bergman; Clarens; Foucault; Roffman and Purdy.

*BLOCKADE:* **DIR. WILLIAM DIETERLE (1938).** Scripted by leftist screenwriter John Howard Lawson, *Blockade* is the only Hollywood film to present the Spanish Civil War from a genuinely leftist perspective. At that, the politics of the film are extremely muted as it seeks to convey its message in moderate tones and within the framework of a relatively conventional spy story. Lawson later expressed his frustration at the strict limitations placed on the film in terms of its political stance (Carr 76). Nevertheless, the film caused considerable controversy, especially among right-wing supporters of the Spanish fascists, when it was released.

*Blockade* opens in 1936 with a picturesque shot of the peaceful Spanish countryside. The protagonist, Marco (Henry Fonda), unloading fertilizer from an ox-cart, expresses to his sidekick Luis (Leo Carillo) his love for Spanish nature, but also his belief that modern technology (such as that embodied in the fertilizer) can sometimes be used to help nature along. Marco's peaceful reflections are broken, however, as an automobile driven by a beautiful blonde, Norma (Madeleine Carroll), crashes into his ox-cart. Marco and Luis help get her and her disabled car to the town of Castelmare, and Marco is clearly smitten with her.

The sudden destructive impact of Norma's modern auto on Marco's traditional ox-cart sets the stage for much of the rest of the film; the civil war itself, which breaks out soon after this initial scene, is depicted as just such an intrusion of modern violence into the idyllic life of the Spanish peasant. As the war proceeds, Marco becomes a dedicated fighter for the Republican side and is soon promoted to lieutenant for his bravery. Assigned to counterespionage duty, Marco soon becomes involved in a complicated plot that sees him kill Norma's father, Basil (Vladimir Sokoloff) and then arrest Norma, mistakenly thinking she is a spy for the fascists. Norma is soon released but, under pressure from the sleazy international munitions dealer André Gallinet (John Halliday), is soon forced to work for the fascists in reality. In this capacity, she helps reinforce the fascist blockade of Castelmare but then repents and confesses to Marco when she sees the effect of this blockade on the starving women and children of the town. Using the information provided by Norma, Marco and the Republicans outwit the fascists and manage to slip a food ship past the blockade, saving the people of the city from starvation. Marco and Norma are reunited as lovers, and Marco tops off the film with a final call to action on behalf of the Republicans, speaking directly into the camera and asking "Where is the conscience of the world?"

Clearly designed, despite its moderation, to create outrage (and hopefully to produce support for American intervention on the Republican side), *Blockade* was generally cheered by leftist groups. It was, meanwhile, strongly opposed by the Knights of Columbus and other Catholic groups that supported the Spanish fascists. Among other things, attempts by such groups to suppress the film made it the center of a number of debates concerning film censorship in America in the late 1930s. Later, it was used against Lawson as part of the HUAC investigation that eventually led to his imprisonment, along with other members of the Hollywood Ten, for his political beliefs. *Screenplay:* John Howard Lawson. *Selected bibliography:* Carr; Dick (*Radical Innocence*); Roffman and Purdy; Valleau.

*PEOPLE OF THE CUMBERLAND:* **DIR. ELIA KAZAN, ROBERT STEBBINS (SIDNEY MEYERS), AND JAY LEYDA (1938).** *People of the Cumberland* was produced by Frontier Films, an independent production company formed in 1937 by a group of leftists aligned with the Popular Front. Indeed, Michael Denning describes the film as "perhaps the most successful independent Popular Front film of the period," though one might also argue that *The Spanish Earth* (1937) deserves that distinction (72). To make the film, Frontier sent a crew to Monteagle, Tennessee (near Chattanooga), where southern leftists Myles Horton and Donald West had been running the Highlander Folk School since 1930. The school had become an important center for southern labor organizers and would later make an important contribution to the emerging civil rights movement, having taught such students as Rosa Parks, Fannie Lou Hamer, and Stokely Carmichael (Denning 72). The school also provided the center for *People of the Cumberland*, which focuses on the school and its work. The makers of the film also used the school as a home base for their own work while in Tennessee. In the process, cameraman Ralph Steiner captured striking documentary footage of Southern poverty, but without condescension and with an accompanying acknowledgement of some of the positive aspects of Southern highland folk culture. The film thus anticipates such works as James Agee's and Walker Evans's *Let Us Now Praise Famous Men*, though the documentary footage is supplemented by footage (supplemented by fictional dramatic segments) that emphasizes the role of Highlander School in contributing to the organization of southern labor. The boundaries between the documentary and fictional segments are sometimes blurred, and the filmmakers often step into the frame, as it were, as they are heard asking questions to which workers then respond. The film includes voiceover commentary written by Erskine Caldwell and Ben Maddow. Kazan later cited his work on the film in his notorious HUAC testimony as his only participation in a "subversive" group after leaving the Communist Party in 1936. Oddly enough, however, the film seems to promote Americanism more than communism, and William Alexander rightly notes the film's "surprising' degree of "american patriotism" (176). *Screenplay:* Elia Kazan; Robert Stebbins (Sidney Meyers), Ben Maddow, and Erskine Caldwell. *Selected bibliography:* Alexander; Barnouw; Denning; Winston; Charles Wolfe.

## THE CITY: DIR. RALPH STEINER AND WILLARD VAN DYKE (1939). Sponsored by the Institute of City Planners and funded by a grant from the Carnegie Foundation (with a secondary grant from the Rockefeller Foundation), *The City* was the first project undertaken by Steiner and Van Dyke after their break with Frontier Films in early 1938. The final film carefully avoids overt political statement, thus showing the impact of the film's capitalist sponsors, who had serious wrangles with the filmmakers in the course of the making of the film. Yet the film still manages to make a powerful comment about the negative impact of capitalist modernization and industrial development on American cities, while also arguing forcefully that the human and environmental devastation brought about by capitalist development are entirely unnecessary and could easily be overcome by careful central planning, as opposed to laissez faire development.

The film begins with scenes set in an idyllic rural community of the kind that might be presumably found in America at the end of the eighteenth century before the Industrial Revolution. Life in this utopian community is quiet, peaceful, and well balanced, informed by cooperation among the residents and harmony between the residents and their natural surroundings. The film then suddenly cuts to the dystopian scene of a modern steel mill, with shots of fire and molten metal that are clearly intended as images of hell. A sudden increase in the cadence of the narrative indicates the jolting increase in the pace of life that has been brought about by industrialization, while scenes of the squalid conditions in which the plant's workers live, in the shadow of the monstrous mill, choking on its smoke, indicate the human cost of this industrial development. "Who built this place?" the narrator (Morris Carnovsky) asks. "There must be something else. Why can't we have it?"

The irony, of course, is that "this place," clearly suggestive of the steel mill regions of Pennsylvania's Monongahela Valley, was largely built by the Carnegie Corporation, a fact that was not lost on the film's nervous sponsors. The film carefully avoids issues such as treatment of the workers in the plant, but its indictment of the steel industry is rather clear. The scene then shifts to Manhattan, with shots of skyscrapers filled with workers busily engaged in office work at row after row of identical desks, in a buzz of activity that the film's imagery clearly associates with bee hives, a frequent image in dystopian fiction. Other scenes show bustling traffic (and accidents) and crowds scurrying about on the streets, frantically rushing from one place to another but with no real final goal in sight. Even recreation turns out to be a fast-paced and highly regimented activity, as long lines of identical cars sit in traffic jams, struggling to make it to the beach for a few moments of recreation that are hardly more restful than work in the city. The New York scenes are more satirical and less overtly hellish than the Pittsburgh ones. They are, in fact, often quite humorous, as in the scene where customers at an automated lunch counter frantically devour machine-prepared food, almost in the mode of the "Bellows Feeding Machine" of Chaplin's *Modern Times*. Nevertheless, the indictment of the kind of life brought about in the city by the growth of modern consumer capitalism remains clear in these New York scenes.

Having established these negative visions of the modern city, the film then shifts to the scene of a utopian alternative, depicting a new kind of city, smaller and closer to nature, one that combines the productivity of capitalist cities with the harmony and tranquility of precapitalist villages. Carefully planned for beauty, cleanliness, and efficiency, these new cities, with safe streets and quiet neighborhoods, allow their residents once again to live in harmony with nature. All is driven by clean, inexpensive hydroelectric power. Factories and laboratories are clean and quiet, pleasant places to work, yet also carefully separated from residential neighborhoods. Work in both the home and the factory is made easier by the latest technology, freeing up much time that had formerly been given over to labor for the pursuit of recreation and culture. The emphasis is on community, and here "playgrounds, schools, libraries are meant for everyone, not just the few who get the breaks." The film then ends with the declaration that this new kind of city is already within our reach, already available as an alternative to the crime and noise and pollution of the conventional modern city. "You take your choice," says the narrator. "Each one is real. Each one is possible."

While *The City* again carefully avoids politics in its description of this utopian city, the emphasis on planning, community, and release from labor through technology could have come straight out of Marx. On the other hand, many in the audience are likely not to recognize this, and the lack of explicit commentary among other things leaves the audience with no guidance concerning exactly what steps need to be taken to make the choice proposed by the film. Moreover, the attempt to associate many aspects of life in this utopian city directly with life in the film's initial agrarian community could even be interpreted as a reactionary vision.

The lack of commentary also tends to make the film seem at times like a standard Chamber of Commerce promotion of the glories and capabilities of American technological know-how. Indeed, the film's central exposure occurred during its regular showings at the 1939 World's Fair, during which it was screened more than 500 times and where for many it was seen simply as part of a celebration of the promise of modern technology. *Screenplay:* Lewis Mumford (narration), Pare Lorentz, and Henwar Rodakiewicz. *Selected bibliography:* Alexander; Barnouw; Barsam; Engle; Medhurst and Benson.

*CONFESSIONS OF A NAZI SPY:* DIR. ANATOLE LITVAK (1939). Produced over the objections of the Production Code Administration, *Confessions of a Nazi Spy* is an anti-Nazi propaganda film that was the first American film openly to depict the German Nazi regime as a threat to the United States. Produced in semi-documentary style (and based on the book *The Nazi Spy Conspiracy in America* by former FBI agent Leon G. Turrou), the film details the efforts of the FBI to counter the activities of German spies in America in the 1930s. The film, on which Turrou served as a technical advisor, describes the efforts of agent Ed Renard (played by Edward G. Robinson and based on Turrou) to ferret out a German spy ring that is operating under the auspices of the German-American Bund. The film, released at a time when many in America were still hoping to avoid war with Germany, received considerable criticism, including an official protest from the German government. At the same time, it became the prototype of a spate of anti-Nazi films that were produced in America once the Americans entered the war.

Renard learns of the existence of the Nazi spy ring in America after intercepting a communication from Nazis operating in Great Britain. He sets out to track them down and soon succeeds in extracting a confession from Kurt Schneider (Francis Lederer), a gullible German-American worker who has been duped into working for the ring by its leaders, the nefarious German intellectual Dr. Kassel (Paul Lukas), and the evil sadist Franz Schlagel (George Sanders). Nazi agents kidnap Kassel and spirit him back to Germany, apparently to be executed for his failure in America. The rest of the ring is rounded up, but the film ends with Renard's recognition that the fight has just begun.

At one point in the film, Renard goes so far as to declare that the Germans seem to be operating as if they are already at war with the United States, and *Confessions of a Nazi Spy* punctuates its detective-story plot with pointed attacks on the Nazi regime as oppressive and imperialistic, though the antisemitism of the Nazis is omitted from the critique. The three central Nazi figures, the fanatic intellectual, the evil sadist, and the gullible dupe, established most the central stereotypes of Nazis that would reappear in the numerous anti-Nazi films of the 1940s. *Screen-*

*play:* Milton Krims and John Wexley. *Selected bibliography:* Balio; Roffman and Purdy; Shindler.

*THE GOLDEN BOY:* DIR. ROUBEN MAMOULIAN (1939). Based on Clifford Odets's leftist play of the same title, *The Golden Boy* is the forerunner of classic anticapitalist boxing dramas such as *Body and Soul* (1947), *Champion* (1949), and *The Set-Up* (1949). Like these later films, *The Golden Boy* figures the fight game as a microcosm of capitalism in which individuals battle ruthlessly for financial gain, while those who do the real work are constantly exploited by those who do little more than put up working capital. *The Golden Boy* adds a particular wrinkle, however, in its contrast between the world of boxing (i.e., business) and the world of music (i.e., art). It focuses on Joe Bonaparte (William Holden), a young Italian American who has struggled almost all his life to pursue his dream of being a concert violinist, with the strong support of his immigrant father (played by Lee J. Cobb), a grocer. Mr. Bonaparte is willing to make any sacrifice necessary to further his son's musical ambitions, but Joe finally tires of accepting these sacrifices and decides to try to make something of himself on his own. To this end, he begins a career as a prizefighter, much to the horror of his father. Through much of the rest of the film, Joe's dream of being an artist functions as a utopian alternative to the debased world of boxing.

Struggling manager Tom Moody (Adolphe Menjou), using his own girlfriend, Lorna Moon (Barbara Stanwyck), as a lure, finally convinces Joe to overcome his doubts and devote himself to fighting. Once he does so, he wins a series of bouts, quickly rising through the middleweight ranks. Impatient to move up even more quickly, Joe aligns himself with gangster Eddie Fuseli (Joseph Calleia), who gradually nudges Moody out of the picture altogether. Fuseli gets Joe a big bout in Madison Square Garden against "Chocolate Drop" (James D. Green), the top contender for the title. Joe wins the fight by a knockout, though breaking his own hand in the process. Later, he learns later that Chocolate Drop has died from injuries received in the fight. Lorna, who has remained loyal to Moody despite falling in love with Joe, rushes to Joe's side, knowing he will be distraught over the death of his opponent. Joe announces to Fuseli that he is through with fighting, then returns with Lorna to his father's home, announcing that he is back to stay. Family, art, and authenticity thus triumph over greed, gangsters, and opportunism, though the ending has a rather artificial ring to it. Indeed, by contrast, the Odets play ends much more darkly as Joe and Lorna are killed in an essentially suicidal car crash. Nevertheless, many of Odets's points about the difficulty of getting ahead in capitalist society without becoming ruthless or dishonest are still made in the film, despite the happy ending.

*Screenplay:* Lewis Meltzer, Daniel Taradash, Sarah Y. Mason, and Victor Heerman. *Selected bibliography:* Recchia ("Setting").

*JUAREZ:* DIR. WILLIAM DIETERLE (1939). *Juarez* was, by a good margin, the most expensive of the prestige biopics — others included *The Story of Louis Pasteur* (1936) and *The Life of Émile Zola* (1937) — through which Warner Brothers sought to shore up its reputation in the second half of the 1930s. All three of these films feature Paul Muni in the title role, though in *Juarez* he is actually on-screen a fairly small amount of time. He plays Benito Juarez as thoughtful and spiritual, with such understatement that he seems on the verge of nodding off to sleep at any moment. Far more dynamic is John Garfield, as Juarez's lieutenant Porfirio Diaz, while Brian Aherne, who won an Academy Award nomination for best supporting actor for his portrayal of the Emperor Maximilian von Hapsburg, is really the central figure in the film. Indeed, the film, as a biography of Juarez, suffers substantially from its focus on the thoughts and deeds of the aristocrat, perhaps assuming that such a figure would be more interesting to American audiences than Juarez, the poor Indian who rose to become president of Mexico. The de-emphasis on Juarez may have also had something to do with warnings from Catholic clergy against heroicizing a figure that the Church regarded as a great villain, given his policy of redistributing some of the Church's vast wealth and lands among the poor peons of Mexico (Roddick 195). In any case, the emphasis on Maximilian and his wife, Carlotta, has an identifiable source in the fact that the film began as an adaptation of Bertita Harding's romantic novel about the couple, *The Phantom Crown*, with much of the Juarez material added later.

The film opens in Paris in 1863, as Louis Napoleon Bonaparte (Claude Rains), the dictator made famous as a bumbling tyrant in Marx's *Eighteenth Brumaire*, ponders the next move in his attempt to add Mexico to his empire, an attempt that has been made possible by the American Civil War but that now seems in jeopardy as the union forces gradually gain the upper hand in that war. Fearing that the United States will soon be in a position to enforce the Monroe Doctrine and to drive out the French armies that have been attempting to conquer Mexico for the past two years, Louis Napoleon, egged on by his wife, the Empress Eugenie (Gale Sondergaard), conceives a plan to install Maximilian as a puppet emperor, negating the Monroe Doctrine by having Maximilian called to rule Mexico by a plebiscite. The vote, of course, is rigged, though Maximilian is unaware of that fact, arriving in Mexico with Carlotta (Bette Davis) expecting an enthusiastic greeting. Instead, the new emperor and empress find that the people of Mexico remain largely loyal to Juarez, the legally elected president of the country and the leader of the forces who have been battling the French armies for the past two years.

Maximilian has virtually no understanding of the Mexican situation, and, though he means well and has liberal inclinations, every move he makes seems to get him into more trouble and to further alienate the Mexican people. Eventually, the French armies that support his rule are withdrawn at the demand of the United States, which meanwhile supplies arms and money to Juarez's forces in their ongoing battle against Maximilian. Carlotta goes to Paris in a vain attempt to convince Louis Napoleon to resume his support, giving Davis an opportunity to perform some acting histrionics as Carlotta suffers a mental breakdown after Napoleon's refusal to help. Maximilian, meanwhile, is captured by Juarez's forces, going nobly to his death by firing squad. The film ends as Juarez views Maximilian's body and asks for his forgiveness.

Anyone seeking to learn about Juarez, or about Mexican history in general, will get relatively little help from this film. Indeed, the characterization of Juarez relies mainly on a continual series of parallels between the Mexican president and his contemporary, Abraham Lincoln. Juarez even wanders through the film dressed in a Lincolnesque stovepipe hat. Meanwhile, the politics of the film hardly seem radical, consisting primarily of support for democracy (defined by Juarez as the opportunity of the people to choose their own government) and treating the aristocrat Maximilian in an extremely positive light. However, *Juarez* had numerous implications for the political situation of the time. For one thing, Juarez was widely regarded as an important predecessor of Mexican President Lázaro Cárdenas, who held office from 1934 to 1940, pursuing a dedicated leftist program that, among other things, continued many of the land reform projects begun by Juarez. Moreover, it is rather obvious that the film, especially in its portrayal of Louis Napoleon as a sinister (though sometimes ridiculous) dictator, comments on the rise of fascist dictators such as Hitler and Mussolini in Europe. One scene, in which the French ruler converses with the American ambassador while preposterously perched atop a life-size wooden horse, is worthy of Chaplin's *The Great Dictator*. More specifically, there are a number of subtle suggestions that we are to read the film as an oblique commentary on the Spanish Civil War. Director Dieterle had, after all, recently completed the film *Blocakde*, which is explicitly about the Spanish conflict. From this point of view, Louis Napoleon's French armies play the role of the German and Italian armies that invaded Spain, while Juarez's forces (referred to several times in the film as "republicans") represent the Loyalist forces. The depiction of American aid as saving Juarez can then be taken as a suggestion that American intervention might have led to a different outcome in Spain. *Screenplay:* John Huston, Wolfgang Reinhardt, and Aeneas MacKenzie. *Selected bibliography:* Balio; Roddick; Vanderwood (*Juarez*).

*THE GRAPES OF WRATH:* DIR. JOHN FORD (1940). *The Grapes of Wrath* enjoys the unusual status in American cultural history of being a screen adaptation of one of the classics of American literature that is itself one of the classics of American cinema. Indeed, the ongoing prominence of the book (despite its overtly radical, even revolutionary, political message) can be at least partly attributed to the commercial and critical success of the film, which was nominated for Academy Awards in almost every major category (including best picture, best screenplay, and best actor, for Henry Fonda), winning the award for best director and best supporting actress (Jane Darwell). The film is actually a relatively faithful adaptation of the book, with a couple of notable exceptions, including the excision of the book's controversial ending, a scene of solidarity among the poor in which the Joad daughter, Rosasharn, whose baby has just died, offers her breast to a starving man so he can derive sustenance from her milk, which would otherwise go to waste. George Bluestone has pointed out the way in which the film gained acceptability by muting much of the book's overt political message. Similarly, Robert Sklar has argued that the film, whatever its images of the suffering poor, is "carefully constructed to stay within the bounds of essential Amreican cultural and political beliefs. And Robert Ray is even more skeptical, finding that the film proposes that "political problems can only be solved by messianic, individualistic leaders," while portraying "workers as powerless, lazy, and fearful" (18). though Leslie Gossage's recent argument that one should nevertheless not ignore the radical potential that resides even in the film is an important one. In particular, the film remains a powerful portrayal of the sufferings of the poor in Depression-era America, complete with an acknowledgement that this suffering is exacerbated by the greed of the rich.

The film, like the book, begins as Tom Joad (played by Fonda) returns from a prison sentence unjustly received when he killed a man in self-defense, setting the stage for a thorough indictment of the current social and economic system that runs throughout the book. On the way back to the family farm in Oklahoma, Tom runs into the Christlike Jim Casy (John Carradine), an ex-preacher who will serve as a sort of mentor for Tom with his trenchant observations about morality, society, and life in general. When Tom arrives at the farm, he finds that his family is preparing to move to California in search of work, having been driven off their land not by drought, but by the large farming corporations that are gradually taking over the area and instituting large-scale mechanized farming methods. When the Joads finally arrive (after a long and difficult journey) at the promised land of California, they find that, contrary to what they had been led to believe, jobs there are quite scarce. Indeed, ruthless fruit and vegetable growers have propagated a false vision of California as a land of plenty in order to lure an excess of workers to the area so that wages can remain low as desperate migrants compete for scarce jobs. Meanwhile, the legal system and the media are mobilized to protect the growers and to keep the pickers in a position of weakness, defeating their efforts to achieve justice.

*The Grapes of Wrath* presents a dreary picture of the lives of the Joads and their fellow migrant farmers. But the film, like the book, does occasionally suggest that there is hope for a better future. One of the central messages of Steinbeck's novel involves the potential power of collective action to improve the lives of exploited workers, and at least some of this message is preserved in the film. For example, the film reproduces the book's presentation of the government-sponsored Weedpatch Camp as a sort of utopian enclave, where the poor band together under their own leadership, make their own rules, and live together in peace and harmony. The camp is nothing more than an example of working socialism, and the fact that the camp is sponsored by the United States government potentially makes it even more subversive as an image, suggesting a call for centralized government planning and management of resources, perhaps along the lines of the Soviet Union. The camp is even administered by a central committee, the Soviet undertones of which seem clear.

The film's ending, in which Ma Joad (played by Darwell) envisions a better future when the perseverance of the poor will at last pay off, is also hopeful, if less striking than the ending of the book. Similarly, the film contains some suggestions of the value of working-class collective action, though the film shows less faith in the masses and more faith in strong individual leaders than does the book. The film's most famous image of working-class perseverance (and one of the most famous scenes in American film history) occurs as Tom bids goodbye to his mother before leaving to go on the run from the forces of the law, which have already murdered Casy. Tom vows to devote himself to the fight for justice, telling Ma Joad in a famous scene that, while she may never again see him in the flesh, he will be symbolically present wherever there is injustice or resistance to it. "I'll be there," he tells her. "Wherever there's a fight so hungry people can eat, ... whenever there's a cop beating a guy, I'll be there." The first volume of Ford's "poor folks" trilogy (which continued with *How Green Was My Valley* and *Tobacco Road,* both released in 1941), *The Grapes of Wrath* is by far the best and most important film of the three, both for its deft use of imagery and narrative and for its genuine sympathy with those who have suffered from the abuses of capitalism in one of its darkest hours. *Screenplay:* Nunnally Johnson. *Selected bibliography:* Bluestone; Gallagher; Gossage; Robert Ray; Sklar; Sobchack.

**THE GREAT DICTATOR: DIR. CHARLES CHAPLIN (1940).** In what may be the single most memorable example of the anti-Nazi films of the

1940s, Chaplin delivers a tour de force comic performance in the role of Adenoid Hynkel, dictator of Tomainia. In a mode reminiscent of such comic works as Bertolt Brecht's *The Resistible Rise of Arturo Ui*, Hynkel/Hitler is presented as a ridiculous figure, a farcical buffoon driven by megalomanical fantasies of world domination but dedicated to no particular ideology other than his own aggrandizement. Chaplin, in what is essentially a reprise of his Little Tramp character, also plays the role of a modest Jewish barber, who is a victim of Hynkel's antisemitic persecution. The barber, along with his feisty companion, the Jewish washerwoman Hannah (played by Paulette Goddard), is the film's sympathetic center, but it is Chaplin's Hynkel that dominates the film and provides both its most hilarious comedy and its most powerful political satire. Some of Hynkel's most effective comic moments involve pantomime reminiscent of Chaplin's silent film days, such as the famous sequence in which he performs a dreamy ballet of world domination in which he balances a balloon/globe. But Chaplin also makes extremely effective comic use of the spoken word in his portrayal of Hynkel, especially in Hynkel's ranting pseudo-German speeches to adoring crowds of onlookers.

The film begins with an extended comic sequence, also reminiscent of Chaplin's earlier silent films, involving the barber's experiences in the Tomainian army in World War I. This sequence ends when the barber is injured in a plane crash, leading to his hospitalization and the total loss of his memory. He remains institutionalized into the 1930s, as Hynkel rises to power in Tomainia. The barber then wanders away from the hospital and returns to his old shop in a Jewish ghetto now being terrorized by Hynkel's storm troopers. The barber becomes romantically involved with Hannah, with whom he battles against storm troopers. He is eventually taken away to a prison camp, while Hannah and Mr. Jaeckel (Maurice Moscovich), a kindly neighbor, migrate to the neighboring country of Osterlich, where they will presumably be free from antisemitic persecution. The barber soon escapes from the prison camp by disguising himself in a Tomainian uniform. A predictable confusion of identities then occurs as Hynkel, out of uniform while duck hunting, is mistaken for the escaped barber and arrested. The uniformed barber, meanwhile, is mistaken for Hynkel and thrust into the command of a Tomainian invasion of Osterlich, which the real Hynkel has arranged after an extended comic negotiation with his counterpart Benzino Napoloni (played with great comic effect by Jack Oakie), dictator of Bacteria, who had also hoped to invade Osterlich.

The film then culminates in its most controversial scene, in which the ersatz Hynkel is asked to make one of his patented speeches to cap the victorious invasion. His response provides a positive alternative to the hatefulness and greed of the bumbling Hynkel and his unscrupulous followers when he makes a speech that pleads for peace, tolerance, and humanity, calling for an end to aggression and persecution. In a line reminiscent of the themes of his earlier film, *Modern Times*, he excoriates the new generation of "machine men with machine minds and machine hearts," calling for the people to end the reign of such men and to fight to free the world of national barriers. Then, addressing himself to the distant Hannah, who clearly hears him (whether by radio or telepathy is unclear), he envisions the coming of a kinder world, which he describes, in words similar to those often used in the utopian rhetoric of the Soviet Union, as "the glorious future." While the principal political orientation of the film is simply one of contempt for Hitler and his fascist followers, there are other clear indications of the film's specifically leftist politics as well, as when the class divisions of the societies it depicts are suggested by opening credits that group the cast under the opposed categories of "People of the Palace" and "People of the Ghetto."

As Charles Maland points out, the barber's final speech was controversial both because it violated many of the established dramatic conventions of popular film and because it aligned Chaplin so clearly with the progressive politics that had come to characterize the Popular Front in the late 1930s (179). Indeed, Maland notes that, though *The Great Dictator* as a whole was viewed by enthusiastic audiences and was a great financial success, it garnered mixed reviews and led to a politicization of Chaplin's image that was ultimately the beginning of a substantial decline in his popularity as an American film star. The film nevertheless won substantial recognition, including Academy Award nominations for best picture, best screenplay, best Score, best actor (Chaplin), and best supporting actor (Oakie). It stands as an important historical document and as one of the central classics of American political film. *Screenplay:* Charles Chaplin. *Selected bibliography:* Jaffe; Maland (*Chaplin*).

*THE HOUSE OF THE SEVEN GABLES:* DIR. JOE MAY (1940). To an extent, *The House of The Seven Gables* is a straightforward, though simplified, adaptation of Nathaniel Hawthorne's 1851 novel. As in the book, the film focuses on the Pyncheons, an old New England family who live in the haunted house of the title, a curse having been placed on the family as a result of the thieving activities of an ancestor in the days of the Salem Witch Trials. It focuses on two brothers, Clifford and Jaffrey Pyncheon (played by Vincent Price and George Sanders, respectively), the latest generation of the family. The main action begins when Clifford decides to sell the house in order to help save the family from financial difficulties caused by bad investments recommended to their father by Jaffrey. Jaffrey, however, opposes the sale, believing that a large sum of gold and the deed to a vast tract of land supposedly given the family by Charles II are hidden somewhere in the house. When the father becomes upset and dies of a pulmonary hemorrhage (as dictated by the curse), the evil Jaffrey wrongfully accuses the virtuous Clifford of murder so that he cannot sell the house. Clifford is convicted and sentenced to life in prison. However, Jaffrey finds to his chagrin that, in order to avoid creditors, the house had already been placed in the name of Clifford's fiancée and cousin, Hepzibah Pyncheon (Margaret Lindsay).

Hepzibah locks herself in the house and lives essentially as a hermit, though continuing the fight to get Clifford released from prison. Eventually, she decides to take in boarders to make ends meet, though no one wants to live in the presumably haunted house. In the meantime, Jaffrey becomes a prominent lawyer and businessman. While in prison, Clifford meets Matthew Maunde (Dick Foran), a radical abolitionist who is briefly jailed for his political activities. Maunde is the descendent of the man who originally placed the curse on the Pyncheons, but he and Clifford immediately become friends—both are modern men who do not believe in curses. When Maunde is released, he takes up residence as a boarder in the Pyncheon house, calling himself Matthew Holgrave. Eventually, Clifford's sentence is commuted (in the significant year of 1848, when popular revolutions were sweeping across Europe). He returns from prison and sets about, with the help of Maunde/Holgrave, trying to clear his name. Eventually, Jaffrey signs a statement clearing Clifford of the murder of their father, then also dies of a pulmonary hemorrhage. Clifford and Hepzibah are married, as are Maunde/Holgrave and Phoebe Pyncheon (Nan Grey) another cousin. All appear on the road to long, happy lives, free of the curse.

In the course of telling this story, leftist screenwriter Lester Cole (later to become a member of the Hollywood Ten and thus experience his own witch trial) manages to preserve the critique of American materialism that was already there in Hawthorne, while injecting a more radical element of his own. One can, for example, detect Cole's voice in the scene in which Clifford sarcastically toasts his ancestors for their treacherous and rapacious activities in pursuit of wealth and power. Cole also introduces a significant antislavery theme through his characterization of activist Maunde/Holgrave, substantially radicalized relative to his original in Hawthorne. In his 1971 memoir, *Hollywood Red*, Cole recalled *The House of the Seven Gables* as one of his favorite films and marveled that no one had complained of his revisions of Hawthorne (172–73). *Screenplay:* Lester Cole. *Selected bibliography:* Cole; Dick (*Radical Innocence*).

*MEN AND DUST:* **DIR. SHELDON DICK (1940).** One of the greatest problems faced by the leftist filmmakers of the 1930s was the woeful lack of funding for their projects. Funding, however, was less of a problem for Sheldon Dick, the wealthy son of mimeograph magnate A. B. Dick.

Something of a rebel against his family background, Dick had for some time been involved with the culture of the Left when, in 1939 he traveled to the mines of the tri-state region of Kansas, Missouri, and Oklahoma, and was appalled by the conditions he observed there among the miners. The result was *Men and Dust*, an experimental documentary Dick made (and financed) to express his concern and to call attention to the plight of the miners and their families.

Noting the impoverished and unhealthy conditions in which the miners and their families live, *Men and Dust* emphasizes the outrage that such conditions should occur in "the richest country in the world," as the opening narration notes. The film begins with conventional scenes of American productivity to dramatize the country's overall wealth and fertility then suddenly shifts to a stark shot of a gray and ravaged, heavily quarried landscape. *Men and Dust* continually employs such sudden shifts in scenery, as well as in narrative voice, disrupting the absorption of the viewer in any given scene and producing a sense of outrage that is more intellectual than emotional. William Alexander, who greatly admires the film, accurately describes this technique as "Brechtian" (289). For Alexander, "it is this constant, mind-jogging change of stance, and this constant refusal of evasion, that make *Men and Dust* so affecting and powerful a film" (292). The film, no matter how self-conscious its technique, never loses sight of the reality of the miners' lives. It is also clear in its support for the efforts of the International Union of Mine, Mill, and Smelter Workers to improve the lives of the miners and their families. Dick and his wife, Lee, a former actress, produced the film through their company, Lee Dick, Inc., which eventually became Dial Films after the success of *Men and Dust*. *Selected bibliography:* Alexander.

*THE PHILADELPHIA STORY:* **DIR. GEORGE CUKOR (1940).** *The Philadelphia Story* was written by leftist screenwriter Donald Ogden Stewart , who in the late 1930s became president of the pro-Soviet Anti-Nazi League, and who in 1947 would be driven out of the country because of his political beliefs. Stewart, in fact, won an Academy Award for his screenplay. However, the film, a romantic comedy of life among the upper classes, shows few overt signs of Stewart's political orientation. For one thing, he was merely adapting the screenplay from Philip Barry's play. Still, the film serves as a sign of the extent to which leftist screenwriters (of whom there were many) were unable to convey their political beliefs in the Hollywood films of the years prior to World War II. The film does, however, have its subtly suggestive moments, and it is perhaps not for nothing that Paul Buhle has called Stewart "a master of subtext, ridiculing bourgeois life without any direct or slashing attacks" (110).

*The Philadelphia Story* is essentially a vehicle for its three stars, Katharine Hepburn (who starred in the play on Broadway), Cary Grant, and James Stewart, and as such it was highly successful. Stewart (no relation to the screenwriter) was given a best-actor Academy Award for his performance, while Hepburn and director Cukor received nominations. The plot is typical "screwball" romantic comedy fare. Wealthy heiress Tracy Lord (Hepburn) is about to be remarried two years after her divorce from her first husband, C. K. Dexter Haven (Grant). Scandal magazine publisher Sidney Kidd (played by Henry Daniell) gets wind of the wedding and decides to send reporter Macaulay "Mike" Connor (Stewart) and photographer Elizabeth Imbrie (Ruth Hussey) to cover the event. However, the wealthy Lords shun publicity, especially of the kind associated with Kidd's *Spy* magazine, apparently a sort of forerunner of the *National Enquirer*. Kidd, however, has compromising information concerning Tracy's father, Seth Lord (John Halliday), and a dancer in New York. In return for the suppression of this information, Dexter, who has been in South America since the divorce, returns and agrees to help Connor and Imbrie get a story on the wedding. After learning the situation, Tracy agrees to cooperate as well.

Tracy's fiancé is George Kittredge (John Howard), a former coal miner who has somehow worked his way up to become general manager of Quaker State Coal and who now has political ambitions. Kittredge, it is clear, does not really fit in with Tracy, who apparently only admires him for his successful upward mobility. When we first see him, he has just purchased a new riding outfit, on which Tracy immediately smears dirt because it looks too new, thus signaling his recent acquisition of wealth. When he was a coal miner, he tells her, the great trick was to get clean. Now, as general manager, he is apparently required to look slightly soiled. It then turns out that he does not know how to ride, having presumably not been given riding lessons in his working-class childhood. We are not, however, asked by the film either to admire or sympathize with the upstart Kittredge. Though the only one of the major characters who has ever actually accomplished anything in his life, he is treated negatively throughout the film, coming off as a sort of *nouveau riche* stuffed shirt who wears his newfound wealth far more pompously and less comfortably than the Lords or Haven, who are to the manor born. The treatment of Kittredge, who clearly could have been made a much more interesting and sympathetic character, might be interpreted as a sign of contempt for the lower classes, but it might also be interpreted as a critique of those who have risen from the working class and then forgotten their origins. Kittredge is, after all, the film's only legitimately bourgeois character, whatever his origins, and his negative treatment could be interpreted as a subtle subtextual critique of bourgeois pretentiousness.

Predictably, the old romantic sparks between Tracy and Dexter (who, we are repeatedly reminded, "grew up together") are re-ignited by his return. Connor, apparently unaware that Imbrie is in love with him, also becomes romantically attracted to Tracy, though the film does suggest important differences in their class backgrounds (he is a petty bourgeois intellectual, the son of schoolteachers, who has published a single, very arty novel). Eventually, Tracy and Connor become involved in a drunken revel the night before the planned wedding. And, though we are assured that nothing sexual occurred (the chivalrous Connor recognized that she was drunk and felt that there are "rules against" taking advantage of such a situation), this revel leads to the breakup of the engagement between Tracy and Kittredge, who stalks off with a surprisingly direct expression of class anger. He tells Tracy that he has had it with "you and your whole rotten class. You're on the way out, the lot of you. And good riddance." Connor then asks Tracy to marry him, but she declines, ostensibly out of sympathy for Imbrie's feelings. She then opts to continue the wedding ceremony, which is already underway, but to marry Dexter instead of Kittredge. In the meantime, Dexter has acquired compromising information on Kidd that forces the publisher to squelch both of his stories on the Lords.

Presumably, this is a happy ending, Tracy and Dexter having been meant for each other all along. However, the film does not explore the implications of Tracy's rejection of two suitors from lower classes in order to marry the wealthy, but profligate, Dexter. In the meantime, Kittredge's class-based outburst is passed over as arising from the bitterness of a spurned suitor, and thus seems to be dismissed as another example of Kittredge's lack of breeding. In any case, coming from Kittredge, the remark about the demise of the Lords' class is not a prediction of a coming proletarian revolution, but simply a reminder that the real movers and shakers of capitalist America are bourgeoisie like himself, not the old, and idle, rich. Kittredge's remark is thus a reminder, as is *The Communist Manifesto*, that the bourgeoisie, in the course of history, supplanted the aristocracy as the ruling class. If that is the case, they can presumably be supplanted in turn. Perhaps it was remarkable that such a line got into an MGM comedy from 1940 at all. *Screenplay:* Donald Ogden Stewart. *Selected bibliography:* Bernardoni; Buhle; Levy; Phillips.

*POWER AND THE LAND:* **DIR. JORIS IVENS (1940).** Produced by the United States Film Service for the Department of Agriculture's Rural Electrification Administration, *Power and the Land* is a relatively straightforward argument for the value and desirability of rural electrification. The film is set on an actual Ohio family dairy farm, where Bill and Hazel Parkinson live and work with their children. Most of the scenes are enacted by the Parkinsons on Ivens's instructions, but the director intentionally left these instructions vague so that the Parkinsons would essentially perform the tasks being filmed just as they normally would. During most of the film, the farm is without electricity, which makes many tasks unnecessarily arduous and time-consuming, while also making it difficult to prevent spoilage in the milk. The family does the best they can, working hard together to support themselves and to help supply milk to the American people. "Everybody has to help," announces the narrator. "When you're a farmer, that's the first thing you learn."

The scene then suddenly shifts as electricity comes to the farm. With farm work and house work now automated, life is suddenly easier on the farm, as well as more productive. America gets more milk, and the Parkinsons get more time together for leisure and family activities. This electricity is brought in by a farmers' cooperative with the help of the federal government, and Ivens envisioned the film as a celebration of such cooperative efforts and as a biting critique of the refusal of privately owned power companies, concerned more with making profits than providing service to deserving farmers such as the Parkinsons. However, the film's government sponsors, already under pressure from Congress, rejected Ivens's criticisms of private enterprise, insisting that he stick to a demonstration of the value of electricity to farmers, thus encouraging them to participate in cooperatives of the type depicted in the film. The result is a film almost devoid of leftist political comment, except for vague gestures such as that noting the importance of cooperative effort on the farm. It does, however, capture the Parkinsons in a mode that is representative of Iven's characteristic feel for the humanity and dignity of common people. *Screenplay:* Stephen Vincent Benét. *Selected bibliography:* Alexander; Barsam; Ivens; Charles Wolfe.

*CITIZEN KANE:* **DIR. ORSON WELLES (1941).** Often found at the top of lists of "all-time great films," *Citizen Kane* is undoubtedly the most important film by a man widely regarded as America's most important film director. Michael Denning argues that Welles is "the American Brecht, the single most important Popular Front artist in theater, radio, and film, both politically and aesthetically. ... Welles is our Shakespeare" (362–63). And Denning is not alone in his admiration for Welles's work. For example, Thomas Schatz calls *Citizen Kane* "easily the most innovative and controversial picture in prewar Hollywood," noting also the unusual extent to which the film bears the creative stamp of its director (90). Welles's innovative use of a variety of narrative strategies and of imaginative camera angles and techniques such as deep-focus cinematography (in which both the foreground and the background are entirely in focus) made *Citizen Kane* one of the most technically influential films in Hollywood history. His use of newspaper magnate William Randolph Hearst as the obvious model for his protagonist also provided a framework within which Welles addressed a number of important social and political issues, creating considerable controversy but also gaining considerable attention for his message.

*Citizen Kane* is the fictional biography of Charles Foster Kane, "the greatest newspaper tycoon of this or any other generation," with Welles delivering a dazzling performance in the lead role. It begins in the aftermath of Kane's death, with a cut to newsreel footage covering the highlights of Kane's career. The remainder of the film is structured around the efforts of Jerry Thompson (William Alland), a reporter for a picture magazine, to gather information for a retrospective story on Kane's life. In particular, Thompson seeks an innovative angle from which to address the story, hoping to find it through discovery of the meaning of Kane's dying word, "Rosebud." Thompson interviews a number of Kane's former acquaintances, including nightclub singer Susan Alexander Kane, the magnate's second wife (played by Dorothy Comingore); Mr. Bernstein, one of the principal managers of Kane's business enterprises (played by Everett Sloane); and Jedediah Leland, Kane's longtime friend and sometime employee (played by Joseph Cotton). Thompson also uncovers considerable details about Kane's early life from reading the manuscript of a diary left by Wall Street banker Walter Payton Thatcher (played by George Coulouris).

Kane's rise to wealth and fame begins in his childhood in Colorado, when his formerly impoverished mother inherits some land on which immensely rich deposits of gold are discovered. His mother then sends him to New York to live under the tutelage of Thatcher and thus presumably to have a better life away from his abusive father. Kane grows up with all of his material needs more than met, attending the best schools and learning the ways of the rich. He also grows up without affection or tenderness and will continue throughout his life to have difficulty regarding other people as anything other than either competitors or commodities. At age twenty-five, he gains official control of his already huge financial empire, formerly held in trust by Thatcher, whom Kane resents and despises. Kane shows little concern for most of his holdings, but does take a strong interest in the New York *Inquirer*, a small newspaper he finds that he owns. He takes personal control of the paper and builds it into a major force in the New York media, aided by Bernstein and Leland. Kane becomes a more and more prominent figure as his media empire expands across the country, crusading against trusts and governmental corruption. However, he also shows a certain ruthlessness, and there are hints that he may have virtually orchestrated the Spanish-American War as a media event to give his papers something sensational to cover.

Kane marries Emily Norton (Ruth Warrick), niece of a U.S. president, and begins a political career of his own, campaigning for governor of

New York in 1916 as a "fighting liberal" opposed to the corrupt political machine of Boss Jim Gettys (Ray Collins). The campaign goes well, and Kane seems destined for political success until he meets and begins an affair with Susan Alexander, finding irresistible her down-to-earth humanity and apparent attraction to him for himself rather than his wealth. But the affair is discovered and exposed by Gettys, ending both Kane's gubernatorial bid and his marriage. Kane then marries Susan and sets about attempting to make her into a successful opera star, thereby presumably validating his attraction for her. He spends huge sums of money, going so far as to build a new multimillion-dollar opera house in New York for Susan to perform in. But she simply lacks the talent, and her career becomes an object of derision.

Kane, after a momentary setback in which the Depression seriously damages his fortune, continues to build his wealth but begins to retreat from the limelight, constructing "Xanadu," an elaborate private retreat in Florida, and stocking it with "the loot of the world." He and Susan retreat to Xanadu while the estate is still under construction, but he spends little time with her there, leaving her to her own devices, which largely consist of working jigsaw puzzles. These puzzles, like the earlier newsreels, function as one of the film's numerous self-referential images. Susan eventually leaves, concluding that Kane is incapable of love and that he is growing increasingly to resent her role in his life. Kane, in a bravura scene, then goes berserk and wrecks her room, in the process finding and pocketing a child's snow globe that reminds him of his Colorado childhood. He keeps the globe with him until his death, living his last years in almost total isolation while watching his empire decline around him. By the time Thompson comes to Xanadu as part of his research, the never-completed palace is already beginning to decay. Thompson learns relatively little while he is there, but we the viewers learn the secret of "Rosebud" when we see workmen, clearing the estate of rubble, toss an old child's sled bearing that name into the furnace.

This last scene adds a touch of pathos, but in general Welles presents Kane's story in a mode free of sentimentality, though he does humanize the central character, thus producing a certain amount of sympathy for a man who himself has little sympathy for anyone else. But Kane's story is not merely a personal one. It comments in important ways on the rise of the modern American media and on the dehumanizing and alienating consequences of capitalism, whatever its material benefits. Indeed, Kane is an allegorical figure of modern American society, a fact apprehended in Welles's use during filming of working titles such as "American" and "John Citizen, U.S.A." Among other things, Welles's portrayal of Kane has an antifascist slant (Kane is shown in one shot rubbing elbows with Hitler), producing a warning that the tendencies of the American media and American capitalism might, if left unchecked, lead in the direction of fascism. The film thus makes an important political statement even if it is now best remembered for its technical innovations. *Screenplay:* Herman J. Mankiewicz and Orson Welles. *Selected bibliography:* Bazin; Bordwell; Callow; Denning; Higham (*Films*); Higham (*Orson Welles*); James Howard; Maland ("Memories"); Mulvey; Naremore (*Magic*); Schatz (*Boom*); David Thomson (*Rosebud*).

*THE DEVIL AND MISS JONES:* DIR. SAM WOOD (1941). *The Devil and Miss Jones* is a romantic comedy that details the education of the eponymous "devil," magnate J. P. Merrick, "the richest man in the world," played by Charles Coburn, who won an Academy Award nomination for best supporting actor for the role. In particular, Merrick learns to understand and sympathize with the "little people" who work for him in his business enterprises. As the film begins, the workers at Neeley's Department Store have conducted a major protest against the store's unfair management practices, burning an effigy of Merrick in the street outside the store. Merrick, whose holdings are so extensive that he had not even realized that he owned the store, decides to investigate, going under cover to root out and remove the instigators of this protest, whom he regards as evil subversives. Posing as "Thomas Higgins," Merrick gets himself hired to work as a salesman in the shoe department and then experiences a series of revelations about the lives of the workers in his employ. He is constantly tormented by Hooper, the abusive manager of the shoe department, while also learning, to his surprise, that the store employs a variety of detectives, hired shoppers, and other operatives to spy on the employees. Meanwhile, he comes to understand and appreciate the goodness and humanity of the workers, especially the eponymous Mary Jones (Jean Arthur). He even comes, to a certain extent, to admire and respect union organizer Joe O'Brien, Mary's boyfriend (Robert Cummings).

In a series of scenes, including an extended comic outing to a crowded Coney Island, Merrick, formerly insulated from real life by his wealth, comes for the first time into contact with the lives of "real" people. He even becomes romantically involved with Elizabeth Ellis (Spring Byington), a saleslady in the shoe department, though he is concerned when she announces that she could never marry a rich man for fear she was unconsciously marrying him for his money. Events finally culminate in a highly comic scene in which O'Brien, Mary, and Elizabeth, still not realizing Merrick's identity, negotiate with the store's board of directors and are stunned by the deference shown Merrick by the various board members. These negotiations, of course, lead to the recognition of the union and the cessation of unfair management practices at the store. All, in fact, live happily ever after. The film ends as Merrick marries Elizabeth and O'Brien marries Mary. All sail away (along with numerous other employees of the store, presumably at Merrick's expense) on a cruise ship as the employees lovingly salute Merrick's generosity, singing "For He's a Jolly Good Fellow."

At times, *The Devil and Miss Jones* comes close to making some genuine political points, as when Merrick, separated from his party, is arrested at Coney Island on suspicion of being a thief and a vagrant. But Merrick is rescued when O'Brien comes to the station and begins demanding his rights, reciting the Constitution. What might have been an important commentary on the class-oriented nature of justice then descends into unrealistic farce as the police sergeant orders both Merrick and O'Brien released simply because O'Brien's speechifying is such a nuisance. Similarly, the store management is clearly shown as unfair, while the union is presented in a positive light, though O'Brien's demands for justice are presented as comic, while it is the billionaire Merrick who is the real hero of the piece. *The Devil and Miss Jones* is thus a post-Depression fantasy that ultimately endorses the capitalist system, arguing that all will be well if only better communication can be established between the rich and the poor. *Screenplay:* Norman Krasna.

*HIGH SIERRA:* DIR. RAOUL WALSH (1941). *High Sierra* is historically important for a number reasons. For one thing, it provides a sort of bridge between the gangster films of the early 1930s and the films noirs of the 1940s and 1950s. For another, it was the film in which Humphrey Bogart established once and for all the tough-guy-with-a-heart-of-gold persona that would make him one of the major figures in American cinema for the next twenty years. The film was also an important landmark for screenwriter John Huston, who soon afterward turned to directing his own films. Despite such anticipations of the future, *High Sierra* projects a strongly elegiac tone, presenting its protagonist (Bogart) as an aging criminal whom the world has passed by. As Nick Roddick puts it, "it depicts a world where values have slipped and nothing can any longer be relied on" (86). In this sense, though in a displaced way, the film recalls the sense of a loss of the American dream that, according to Michael Denning, pervades American leftist culture in the Popular Front period.

Bogart plays Roy Earle, a notorious but past-his-prime criminal who begins the film by receiving a pardon and a release from the Illinois State Prison. On the outside, he learns that he is expected to participate in a Los Angeles hotel robbery planned by Big Mac (Donald MacBride), the criminal mastermind who was responsible for securing his pardon. But the heist seems doomed from the beginning. When Earle arrives in California he finds that he is expected to work on the job with a gang of young and highly unprofessional criminals. In addition, two of his cohorts, Babe Kozak (Alan Curtis) and Red Hattery (Arthur Kennedy), have picked up a woman, Marie Garson (Ida Lupino). They have not only told her all about the planned robbery, but are meanwhile at each other's throats fighting over her. Earle tries to get rid of her but eventually befriends her and becomes her protector. To top things off, Earle finds that he is adopted by Pard, a mongrel dog who apparently carries a curse, all of his former owners having come to bad ends, a fact Earle learns from Algernon (Willie Best), the film's comic black, presented via blatantly racist stereotypes.

In the meantime, Earle, the son of Indiana farmers, meets a farm family from Ohio who have traveled to California in search of economic opportunity. He becomes smitten with Velma (Joan Leslie), the club-footed granddaughter of the family. He pays for the surgery to correct Velma's club foot, only to find that she is in love with someone else and therefore has no interest in Earle's proposal of marriage. Predictably, the robbery goes badly as well; Earle shoots and kills a policeman during the job, while Red and Babe are killed in the getaway. Louis Mendoza (Cornel Wilde), the final member of the gang, is captured and identifies Earle to the police. Earle manages to make off with half a million dollars in jewels and takes them to Big Mac to exchange them for cash, only to find that Big Mac has died. Earle then goes on the run with Marie and Pard, eventually taking refuge at the top of Mt. Whitney, only to be killed by a police sniper. Marie, accompanied by Pard, walks away in tears, proclaiming that Earle is free at last, thus suggesting the way in which American society refused to allow him any path out of criminal conduct other than death. *Screenplay:* John Huston and W. R. Burnett. *Selected bibliography:* Clarens; Denning; Roddick; Schatz (*Boom*).

**HOW GREEN WAS MY VALLEY: DIR. JOHN FORD (1941).** *How Green Was My Valley* has long been one of the most admired films of the 1940s. The third entry in Ford's trilogy of films about the tribulations of poor and working people (joining *The Grapes of Wrath* and *Tobacco Road*), the film won five Academy Awards, including those for best director and best picture, beating out Orson Welles and *Citizen Kane*. Thomas Schatz describes *How Green Was My Valley* as "Ford's consummate achievement during the prewar years at Fox," and other critics have expressed similar admiration (84). The film, which relates fifty years in the history of a Welsh coal mining valley, does have its virtues, as in its positive figuration of the working-class culture of the valley and in its condemnation of the gradual environmental destruction of the valley by the mine that increasingly dominates it. Meanwhile, the culture of the valley deteriorates as well, but this deterioration is attributed as much to the pernicious effects of union organization as to the growing exploitation of the miners by the mining company. Moreover, the depiction of the miners and their lives is preposterously romantic, sentimental, and unrealistic.

While the film does at times suggest the hardship and danger of mining, we see relatively little in the way of actual work, observing the miners mostly as they traipse to and from the mine, singing in amazingly perfect harmony and looking more like the seven dwarfs than like actual miners. In general, the miners are presented via Orientalist stereotypes, as either comic grotesques (in the mode of *Tobacco Road*) or exotic specimens of a primitive, bygone world.

The film, based on Richard Llewellyn's 1940 novel of the same title, begins as an aging Huw Morgan packs his bags to leave his beloved, but doomed, valley for the last time. The film then reverts to Huw's childhood as he (played by a precocious Roddy McDowall) grows up in the valley in better days. The bulk of the film, and the book, consists of Huw's memories of his time in the valley, memories which are, as the title indicates, highly nostalgic evocations of bygone pastoral days. The valley is as much the central character of the film as is Huw, and the narrative relates both the story of Huw's early life and the history of the valley. But both the book and the film are rather weak as historical accounts, concentrating mostly on evocations of the natural beauties of the valley and on accounts of the private affairs (focusing on love, courtship, and marriage) of the Morgan family. While the narrative does indicate certain pressures of modernity (symbolized by the creeping slag heap that increasingly threatens the valley and eventually leads to Huw's departure) that gradually undermine the traditional life of the valley, the book pays relatively little attention to political analysis of historical events, focusing on Huw's nostalgic memories of what he perceives, from his perspective in the 1930s, as having been better days. Indeed, it is significant that all of the events narrated in the film occur well before the 1930s and far away from America, thus keeping the narrative safely insulated from those highly politicized days.

Producer Darryl Zanuck removed the original screenwriter, Erenst Pascal, from the project because he feared that the film was being "turned into a labor story and a sociological problem story" (Schatz 85). Zanuck's desire to avoid politics is visible throughout the film, in which the principal dramatization of anything approaching class conflict occurs not in battles between the miners and the mine company, but in the prejudice encountered by Huw as the son of a miner when he attends a nearby middle-class school and is tormented by the other students and by a snotty and abusive schoolmaster, Mr. Jonas (Morton Lowry), who at one point beats Huw into unconsciousness. The comic miner, Dai Bando (Rhys Williams), gives Huw boxing lessons so he can defend himself from the other students. Meanwhile, Bando goes to the school and punches out the schoolmaster, after Huw has convinced his brothers not to seek revenge. The book similarly downplays class conflict as a largely personal matter. Indeed, if there is a central political opposition in the book, it is not the class struggle between miners and mine owners but the ethnic one between the Welsh and the English. This opposition, however, is played down in the film, which depicts the Welsh miners devotedly singing "God Save the Queen" in a central scene. Meanwhile, both book and film suggest some of the ways in which the miners were exploited and unfairly treated by the mine owners. Labor activism hovers in the margins of both as well, as Huw's brothers, especially Davy (Richard Fraser), become leaders in the drive to organize an effective union for the local miners. But Huw's father, Gwillym (Donald Crisp), presented as a heroic and admirable figure in both texts, is a militant foe of the union and a strong advocate for the mining company. In one scene, his opposition to a strike draws the ire of his fellow miners, causing Mrs. Morgan (Sara Allgood) to excoriate the strikers as cowards and hypocrites.

The film's principal suggestion of the miners' hardships resides in the periodic accidents that strike the mine, though these are presented as unavoidable facts of mining life, with no suggestion that the accidents may be caused by unsafe conditions due to corner-cutting in the mines. One of Huw's brothers, Ivor (Patric Knowles), is killed in such an accident, after which Huw goes into the mine (and dreams of stepping into Ivor's shoes in other ways as well, given his infatuation with Ivor's widow, Bronwyn). Soon afterward, brothers Ianto (John Loder) and Davy, the mine's two most productive workers, are dismissed because their wages have become too high. They leave the valley to seek work elsewhere, as the family, like the culture it represents, continues to disintegrate. In a final climactic accident, Huw's father is killed by a cave-in, dying in the mine in the boy's arms. (In the book, Huw's father is killed in a cave-in while inspecting the mine for damage during a strike, probably part of the 1910–11 Cambrian Combine Dispute. But this strike is not mentioned in the film.) This heart-wrenching death scene is followed by Mrs. Morgan's claim that Gwillym has reported to her on the glories of heaven, which leads to the film's final nostalgic shot of Huw and his father walking over a green hill in earlier days.

In many ways, the film's most admirable character is Mr. Gruffyd (Walter Pidgeon), the virtuous local parson, who battles against religious hypocrisy, while working to keep religion at the very center of the culture of the valley. Gruffyd is a paragon of moderation, as when he advises the men to go ahead and form their union but to exercise restraint and "responsibility" in doing so. But it is also Gruffyd who identifies the valley's first miners' strike as a sign of the decline of the valley's culture, stating that "something has gone out of this valley that will never be replaced." Gruffyd befriends Huw and also falls in love with Huw's only sister, Angharad (Maureen O'Hara). Angharad loves Gruffyd as well, but she is courted by the son of the mine owner, Mr. Evans and marries him after Gruffyd nobly declares that he is too devoted to his religious work to make a good husband for her. Angharad's subsequent married life is empty and unhappy, while unfounded gossip about a possible adulterous relationship between Angharad and Gruffyd causes the latter the leave the valley to avoid scandal—but only after excoriating the locals for their hypocrisy and after participating in a heroic attempt to rescue Gwillym and the others from the cave-in.

Given the nature of the book, it is not surprising that Welsh critics such as Dai Smith, upset by Llewellyn's romanticized and inaccurate depiction of life in Wales, have strongly criticized the book for its "glamorized nostalgia" and its falsification of Welsh history. Derrick Price summarizes such criticisms well, noting that critics (especially Welsh ones) have "attacked it for its lack of verisimilitude to working class life; for its obfuscation and reactionary analysis of significant historical struggles; for its individualist account of political action; and for its racism and sentimentality" (73). Moreover, Price concludes that these criticisms are largely justified, noting that the text gives us "an account of life in the valleys in which history, memory and political action are stripped of collectivity and presented as the qualities of heroic individuals" (75). Meanwhile, Price notes that *How Green Was My Valley* participates in a long tradition of literary accounts of Wales as a place of nature and romance—a fact that helps to account for Llewellyn's stance in the book but which also makes it all the more important to challenge the "social constructions" of the Welsh past that it helps to promulgate (93). The film merely extends these stereotypes, making them even more romantic and sentimental and producing a nonthreatening view of working-class life for an American audience. It is no accident, of course, that Ford and Zanuck chose to adapt Llewellyn's sentimental novel rather than more realistic, and more radical, accounts of Welsh mining life, such as those in the novels of Harold Heslop or Lewis Jones. *Screenplay:* Philip Dunne. *Selected bibliography:* Gallagher; Derrick Price; Schatz (*Boom*); Dai Smith.

*THE LITTLE FOXES:* DIR. WILLIAM WYLER (1941). Based on screenwriter Hellman's play of the same title, *The Little Foxes* is a tale of capitalist greed in the Deep South. It focuses on the Hubbards, a family of unscrupulous merchants, who have risen from small-time storekeeping to big-time investing in a single generation, largely through cheating their poor customers. The grasping Hubbards, caught up in the birth of the New South, desperately strive to mimic both the capitalist shrewdness of Northern businessman and the aristocratic gentility of their predecessors among the wealthy of the South. As the play opens, brothers Ben and Oscar Hubbard (played by Charles Dingle and Carl Benton Reid) are trying to close a deal with Chicago investor William Marshall (Russell Hicks) to build a new cotton mill in their small Southern town, where the labor is cheap and the cotton, much of it grown on a plantation owned by the Hubbards, is nearby. They envision making a huge fortune from this deal. The only problem is that they lack the funds to meet their end of the investment without the help of their sister, Regina Hubbard Giddens (Bette Davis), and her husband, banker Horace Giddens (Herbert Marshall). Horace, away at a sanitarium in Baltimore to recover from a heart attack, is highly skeptical of the deal, not because he is afraid it will not make money, but because he is sure it will, thus propelling the conniving Hubbards into a position of economic dominance in the community.

Regina sends their daughter, Alexandra (Teresa Wright), to Baltimore to fetch Horace home, where Regina expects to be able to use her feminine wiles to get him to make the investment. But Horace, who is near death and knows it, staunchly refuses; he also supports Alexandra in her effort to resist the family's pressure to make a match with Oscar's oafish son, Leo (Dan Duryea). Alexandra prefers the attentions of crusading reporter David Hewitt (Richard Carlson), of whom her mother and uncles roundly disapprove. In the meantime, Leo, who works in Horace's bank, breaks into Horace's safety deposit box and steals $75,000 in bonds, which he then turns over to his father to make up the necessary funds to close the deal with Marshall. Horace learns of the theft and decides to declare it a loan to the brothers, which they are repay to Regina from the mill's profits, in which she will not otherwise share. He then makes plans to change his will to leave everything except this $75,000 to Alexandra. Eventually, however, Regina's harangues cause Horace to suffer another heart attack before he can either change the will or declare the loan, after which she delays seeking medical help until it is too late to save him. As the film ends, Regina seems to triumph when she forces her brothers to turn over 75 per cent of their interest in the mill to her in return for her silence about the theft of the bonds. However, her victory becomes bittersweet when Alexandra announces her disgust at the behavior of her mother and uncles, then leaves the family home to begin a new life, accompanied by Hewitt, of battling against capitalist exploitation such as that practiced by her family.

Despite appearing at times to be something of a Deep South soap opera, *The Little Foxes* addresses a number of important issues involved in the historical transformation of the American South from a semifeudal, agrarian society to a modern capitalist one. In particular, the film sees this process as part of the global phenomenon of capitalist expansion. The film's view of capitalism is probably best expressed by the servant, Addie (Jessie Grayson), who clearly implies a phenomenon that goes beyond the Hubbards when she notes that "there's people that eats up the whole earth and all the people on it—like in the Bible with the locusts." Indeed, *The Little Foxes* is one of the strongest indictments of capitalism in all of American film, a stance it probably gets away with by its setting in the South, making available the interpretation that only the decadent Southern bourgeoisie, not bourgeoisie in general, are devouring the earth around them like locusts. *Screenplay:* Lillian Hellman, Arthur Kober, Dorothy Parker, and Alan Campbell. *Selected bibliography:* Dick (*Hellman*); Watson.

*THE MALTESE FALCON:* DIR. JOHN HUSTON (1941). *The Maltese Falcon* is the best known (and probably the best) of the various film adaptations of the novels of Dashiell Hammett. Screenwriter/director Huston stays scrupulously close to the original novel, filming it virtually scene by scene (with only a couple of sexually suggestive scenes from the book deleted). The dark subject matter of the book is enhanced in the film by a dark look, complete with exaggerated atmospheric shadows. The film is thus often considered one of the first works of the film noir. The film was Huston's directorial debut; it also helped to establish Humphrey Bogart, via his portrayal of Hammett's rough-but-vulnerable detective, Sam Spade, as a major Hollywood star.

*The Maltese Falcon* begins as a "Miss Wonderly" (played by Mary Astor) comes to Spade's office in San Francisco to hire him to help her find her missing sister, who has supposedly run off with a man by the name of Floyd Thursby. Spade's caddish partner, Miles Archer (Jerome Cowan), agrees to handle the case personally, after wolfishly ogling Miss Wonderly in a manner that makes the nature of his personal interest quite clear. That night, however, Archer is shot and killed while shadowing Thursby. Thursby is shot soon afterward. As Spade begins to investigate the killings (partly because the police seem to suspect him), it soon becomes clear that Miss Wonderly's original story was a ruse. She finally admits that her real name is Brigid O'Shaughnessy and that she is in danger but remains reluctant to explain the nature and source of the danger. Then Joel Cairo (Peter Lorre) comes to Spade's office, and, after a complex encounter in which Cairo is at one point knocked unconscious by Spade, offers Spade $5,000 to help recover a lost statuette of a black bird.

Spade soon realizes that Brigid is the only one who knows the location of the bird. However, his attempt to negotiate a deal between her and Cairo is soon complicated by the arrival of the "fat man," Kasper Gutman (Sydney Greenstreet), who is also seeking the statuette. Gutman, accompanied by his noxious henchman, Wilmer (Elisha Cook, Jr.), finally explains to Spade that the statuette has been enameled over in black, but is actually a jewel-encrusted gold falcon, made in the sixteenth century by the Knights Templar of Malta as a tribute to the Emperor Charles V, The statuette was subsequently been stolen by pirates and then lost for hundreds of years. After a series of complex and suspenseful turns in which each character tries to out-betray all the others, the statuette finally emerges, but turns out to be a fake, apparently substituted for the real bird by the Russian general from whom it was stolen by Thursby, O'Shaughnessy, and Cairo, acting as Gutman's agents. Meanwhile, it becomes clear that Wilmer killed Thursby, as well as Jacobi (Walter Huston), the captain of the ship that brought the statuette in from Hong Kong.

Spade puts the police onto Wilmer, Gutman, and Cairo, and the lot of them are arrested. Meanwhile, Spade has a final confrontation with O'Shaughnessy, with whom he has developed an romantic relationship in the course of the investigation. Spade deduces that it was O'Shaughnessy who killed Archer, hoping Thursby would be blamed and thus eliminated from the picture. She, in turn, pleads her love for Spade and asks him not to tell the police. He admits that he may be in love with her as well but explains that, despite his lack of affection for Archer, it is his duty as a detective not to let the killing of his partner go unpunished. Further, he explains that he, as an individualist who always looks out for number one, is not willing to endanger himself to protect her, whatever his feelings for her may be. He thus turns a deaf ear to her pleas and turns her over to the police as well.

*The Maltese Falcon* is clearly designed primarily for entertainment. For example, the exaggerated lighting effects work well with the equally exaggerated tough-guy dialogue to give the film an almost campy feel that never interferes with the suspense but merely adds to the fun. Nevertheless, the film has considerable depth and numerous possible political implications. For one thing, the film's entire cast of characters is engaged in a furious and ruthless dog-eat-dog pursuit of wealth, as when Gutman at one point agrees to sacrifice Wilmer, who is "like a son" to him, to the police so the others can go free and share the bounty. Placed within the context of the suggestion that selfish concerns supercede personal relationships, Spade's rejection of O'Shaughnessy appears less laudable. In any case, the entire quest motif of the film has potential implications as an allegory of capitalist greed. On the other hand, though the characterization of Spade, who winds up alone and friendless by the end of the film, might be taken as a criticism of the ideology of individualism, it is also the case that the film seems to encourage an admiration for his strength in not letting his emotions (especially for a woman) cloud his judgment. It is certainly the case that the portrayal of Spade's success in escaping O'Shaughnessy's feminine snares is problematic in terms of the film's figuration of gender. Hammett's novel was also the source of two earlier screen adaptations, *The Maltese Falcon* (1931, directed by Roy del Ruth) and *Satan Met a Lady* (1936, directed by William Dieterle). **Screenplay:** John Huston. **Selected bibliography:** Abramson; Gale; Hall;

Krutnik; Luhr; Naremore ("John Huston"); Naremore (*More than Night*); Robert Ray.

*THE SEA WOLF:* **DIR. MICHAEL CURTIZ (1941).** Based on the 1904 novel by the committed socialist writer Jack London, the film version of *The Sea Wolf* maintains the combination of political commentary and seagoing adventure that was central to the original book. Both the film and the novel focus on the oppressive conditions that prevail aboard a sailing ship ruled with an iron hand by a tyrannical captain, Wolf Larsen. The depiction of the relationship between Larsen and his crew makes the ship a microcosm of capitalism, with its antagonistic relation between a dominant and a dominated class. The film picks up additional political resonance from its 1941 context, in which Larsen's Germanic vision of himself as a Nietzschean superman is supplemented by suggestions of Nazism.

As the film begins, Larsen's notorious ship, the *Ghost*, is in its home port of San Francisco, taking on supplies and a new crew in preparation for an upcoming voyage, presumably to hunt seals. Due to the reputation of the ship and its captain (played by Edward G. Robinson), much of the crew has to be shanghaied. However, at least one new crew member, George Leach (John Garfield), comes aboard willingly, as a means of escaping from the police. The ship sails out of the bay in a deep fog, in which a ferry rams into another boat and capsizes. Two of the passengers from the ferry, Humphrey van Weyden and Ruth Webster (Alexander Knox and Ida Lupino) are taken aboard the *Ghost*. Van Weyden is a successful novelist, who demands to be taken back to San Francisco but is impressed into service aboard the *Ghost* as a cabin boy. Webster, herself a prison escapee, is near death and is taken to a cabin below the deck to be treated by the ship's doctor, Louis Prescott (Gene Lockhart).

Much of the film involves the growing tension between Larsen, a radical individualist, and his crew of rogues, who begin to develop a certain solidarity, despite their tendency, encouraged by Larsen, to pick out and torment the weaker and vulnerable crewmen. However, Larsen, himself a closet intellectual whose personal hero is Milton's Satan, adopts the scholarly van Weyden as his personal favorite so that he will have someone with whom to conduct intellectual conversations. Larsen's colossal ego, meanwhile, is fed by the idea of having van Weyden write a book about him. Eventually, Webster recovers after Prescott gives her a successful transfusion, using blood supplied by Leach. This success gives Prescott, a former surgeon who has descended into a haze of alcoholism, a new sense of pride in his skills as a physician, but his resurgence is immediately undercut when Larsen humiliates him in front of the men, driving him to commit suicide.

Leach, employing what is essentially a rhetoric of proletarian revolution, leads the men in a rebellion, throwing Larsen overboard. The captain, however, manages to get back aboard and regain control of the ship. Cooky (Barry Fitzgerald), the ship's conniving cook, supplies Larsen with a list of all of those who participated in the mutiny, Larsen, however, takes no action against the rebels, instead regaining their obedience by promising them lucrative bounty from the ship's mission, which is piracy, in which they will steal seal skins from other ships rather than hunting seals themselves. Larsen also admits that there is a certain danger in their mission because the *Ghost* is begin pursued by Larsen's own brother, captain of the *Macedonia*, who disapproves of Larsen's piracy. Larsen then identifies Cooky as the informer, and the men retaliate by throwing the man overboard, though he is eventually taken back onto the ship as sharks circle him.

Later, when Larsen has one of his periodic attacks of headaches and blindness, Leach, Webster, van Weyden, and another crewman, Johnson (Stanley Ridges), escape in one of the ship's boats, only to find that Larsen has replaced most of the boat's water supply with vinegar. In one of the film's central utopian moments, Johnson throws himself into the sea, sacrificing himself so that there will be more water for the others. Lost in the fog, the boat again comes upon the *Ghost*, which is now sinking and apparently abandoned after an attack by the *Macedonia*. They board the ship looking for food and water and find that Larsen, nearly blind, is still aboard. Larsen locks Leach in a storeroom, which the others are unable to open. Van Weyden manages to get the key from Larsen so that Leach can be freed, but Larsen shoots van Weyden in the process. As the film ends, Larsen and the dying Van Weyden go down with the ship, while Leach and Webster, now in love, approach an island in the boat.

Called an "unusual mixture of *film noir* and sea adventure" by Sidney Rozenzweig, *The Sea Wolf* is an effective film that vividly evokes its shipboard setting while telling an engaging story and making important thematic points (159). Though still consistent with London's original intention of portraying the crew of the *Ghost* as a proletarian collective in opposition to their domineering boss, the film version of *The Sea Wolf* clearly partakes of the political climate of the Popular Front. Its crewmen represent a diverse group with a variety of interests, yet they ultimately band together to confront the threat represented by the protofascist Larsen. The 1941 film is generally recognized as the best of the several screen adaptations of the London novel. *Screenplay:* Robert Rossen. *Selected bibliography:* Flinn and Davis; Rosenzweig; Susan Ward; Whittemore and Cecchettini.

*TOBACCO ROAD:* **DIR. JOHN FORD (1941).** Based directly on Jack Kirkland's long-running Broadway play and indirectly on Erskine

Caldwell's 1932 novel, both of the same title, *Tobacco Road* relates the comic misadventures of the Lesters, a family of Georgia tenant farmers, during the Depression. Like the original book, the film attempts to create sympathy for the impoverished Lesters, descendants of a once-prominent planting family. But the film is a substantially bowdlerized version of Caldwell's novel that employs conventional slapstick comedy in the place of the bawdy, and often black, folk humor of the original, thus becoming a sort of early version of the television comedy *The Beverly Hillbillies*. The film also lacks most of the social commentary of the book. For example, the racism of the Lesters is an important motif in the book but is entirely absent from the film, in which race is never mentioned. Jeeter Lester (played in the film by Charley Grapewin, who starred in the role on Broadway) is the central character in both versions. In both cases, Jeeter is a somewhat shiftless character who dreams of planting cotton on his depleted land but never does anything about it. In the book, however, he has no choice because economic conditions make the planting of a crop impossible, especially after wealthy Captain John Harmon, owner of the land the Lesters live on, abandons the area and takes no further interest in the plight of his former tenants. Economics are also central to the film, the plot of which (in a motif absent from the book) is principally driven by Jeeter's attempts to raise the money to pay the rent on his house and farm, which have been taken over by a bank that threatens to evict the family so they can institute modern scientific farming methods in an attempt to restore the land to profitability. In the film, however, Captain Tim Harmon, Captain John's kindly son (played by Dana Andrews), returns to the area and pays Jeeter's rent, though he himself has fallen on hard times. He also gives Jeeter money for seed and fertilizer, thus presenting the upper classes in a favorable light and making Jeeter's continuing poverty a result of his own lower-class laziness.

The more grotesque and gothic elements of the book are missing entirely from the sanitized film version, even though the film features most of the same characters and many of the same events as the book. In the book, Ellie May, the Lesters' eighteen-year-old daughter, remains unmarried because her harelip makes her unattractive to men; in the film, Ellie May (played by Gene Tierney) is attractive indeed, and needs only a little washing to make her an absolute beauty. Much of the action of the book occurs when fundamentalist preacher-woman Sister Bessie Rice marries the Lesters' sixteen-year-old son, Dude, then buys him a new car in which he drives about the countryside, crashing into everything in sight. Most of these events (except for Dude's final accident, in which he runs over and kills his grandmother) are reproduced reasonably faithfully in the film, except that the film version of Dude (played by William Tracy) is twenty. Moreover, in the book Sister Bessie has a congenital defect that leaves her effectively without a nose, while the film's Bessie (played by Marjorie Rambeau) is physically normal. Finally, the book ends as Jeeter and his wife, Ada (Elizabeth Patterson), have been burned to death in their sleep after a fire he sets to clear his fields spreads to the house. In the film, their rent having been paid, the Lesters presumably live happily ever after. The last scene closes as Jeeter drifts off for a peaceful nap on his porch, his old hound dog at his side.

The Lesters have a certain exuberance even in the film, but in general they are treated as comic buffoons who lack the almost Rabelaisian dimensions of the originals. Dude, for example, seems to be a complete mental defective in the film. All in all, the film threatens simply to promulgate cultural stereotypes about the ignorance and stupidity of rural Southerners. The same, in fact, can be said for the book, but the book also has important roots in Southern folk cultural traditions that are lacking in the film. The film thus manages to maintain most of the negative characteristics of the book, while omitting most of the potentially positive ones. *Screenplay:* Nunnally Johnson. *Selected bibliography:* Gallagher; William Howard.

*CASABLANCA:* DIR. MICHAEL CURTIZ (1942). Described by Robert Ray as "Classic Hollywood's most representative film," *Casablanca* is certainly one of the best known and most beloved films in American cinema history. It is also a pointedly political drama that clearly grows directly out of the ideology of the Popular Front of the late 1930s. As Michael Denning notes, *Casablanca* was to be the "most enduring" of antifascist thrillers (others included films such as *Hangmen Also Die* and *The Fallen Sparrow*) produced during World War II (378). Described by Thomas Schatz as "Hollywood's seminal wartime 'conversion narrative'," the film can be seen as the story of cynical American Rick Blaine's recognition of the importance of fighting against fascism, though many have seen it more as the story of Blaine's ill-fated love for Norwegian refugee Ilsa Lund (203). It is certainly the case that the film is built around the love triangle of Rick (Humphrey Bogart), Ilsa (Ingrid Bergman), and Czech anti-Nazi activist Victor Laszlo (Paul Henreid), the film's makers apparently feeling that such a structure would appeal to American audiences. Nevertheless, the film is an antifascist work that at least gestures toward an endorsement of the notion that the fight against fascism transcends personal concerns. As Rick says, in one of the film's numerous widely quoted lines, "The problems of three little people don't amount to a hill of beans in this crazy world." This "crazy world," of course, is one in which fascist armies are advancing across Europe; what does count in such a world is the fight to stop this advance, a point made clear when Rick, in the film's famous last scene, makes the personal sacrifice of sending his beloved Ilsa off with Laszlo so that she can support him in his important work against the Nazis.

*Casablanca* is set in December 1941, so that Rick joins the fight against fascism in precisely the same month that the United States joined the war against Germany. Casablanca is a crucial gathering point for refugees who have fled European fascism and hope to move on to America, portrayed throughout the film in glowing terms. The city is ruled by the ostensibly neutral regime of "Unoccupied France," but it is also clear that the French regime remains in power at the whim of the German Nazis, whom they must continually placate. Two German couriers have just been killed in the desert and robbed of important papers, including two valuable letters of transit that will enable the bearers to leave Casablanca and go on to America. Rick has landed in Casablanca after fleeing Paris in the wake of the Nazi advance on the French capital. He runs the Café Américain and avoids commitment to either side in the conflicts that are sweeping Europe, having been driven to bitter misogynist cynicism by Ilsa's sudden and unexplained breakup of the torrid relationship they had shared for a few weeks in Paris. There are, however, clear signs that Rick is really a "sentimentalist" beneath his tough exterior, and we quickly learn that he has a long history of antifascist activity, including running guns to the Ethiopians to aid their fight against the 1935 Italian invasion and personally taking part in the republican fight against Franco's Spanish fascists in 1936. Moreover, his complete neutrality comes into question early on when he agrees to accept and hold the stolen letters of transit for Ugarte (Peter Lorre), apparently the man who killed the couriers.

Ugarte is subsequently arrested by the French authorities (as representatives of the Gestapo look on), then killed while in custody. In the meantime, Rick's bitterness boils into hatred when he sees Ilsa suddenly walk into his bar accompanied by Laszlo, a famous antifascist fighter who has escaped from a concentration camp and then evaded Nazi pursuit all over Europe. Ilsa is surprised to see Rick as well, and soon attempts to explain to him why she had to leave him in Paris. We eventually learn the whole story. She has for some time been married to the much older Laszlo, who acted as a sort of mentor figure for her when she first came to Paris. At the time of her affair with Rick in Paris, she had thought Laszlo dead; she had then broken off the affair after learning that her husband was still alive. It becomes clear that her feelings for Laszlo consist primarily of respect and admiration, while her true passion is for Rick. With the Germans determined to see to it that Laszlo never leaves Casablanca alive, Ilsa offers to stay with Rick in Casablanca if he will only give one of the letters of transit to Laszlo so that he can escape Casablanca. Rick, however, decides that Ilsa is an important support for Laszlo in his work. He then executes a complex plan that leads to the escape of both Laszlo and Ilsa, while Rick is left behind to take the heat, which will apparently be considerable, especially after he kills the Gestapo's Major Strasser (Conrad Veidt) at the airport in the obligatory movie gunfight. All ends well, however, as French police Captain Louis Renault (Claude Rains), depicted throughout as apolitical and self-serving (if charmingly jocular), suddenly shows his own heart of gold by ordering his men to "round up the usual suspects" in the killing of Strasser, even though he witnessed the shooting and knows Rick is the killer. Renault then arranges to flee Casablanca with Rick so that both of them can join the Free French forces gathered in Brazzaville.

As Robert Ray has discussed, *Casablanca* is in many ways a classic American work that shows considerable tensions in its attempt to tell its antifascist World War II story by reworking motifs derived from traditional American culture, such as *Huckleberry Finn* and movie westerns (89–112). The Casablanca of the film is, for example, a clear displacement of the typical Western frontier town. Ray has also appropriately questioned the film's treatment of gender, and it is not finally clear whether Rick has really made a sacrifice in sending Ilsa away or whether he is simply escaping from her female clutches so that he can go away with Renault into an all-male world of rugged adventure in darkest Africa. In this and other ways, the politics of the film are far from radical. The film is careful, for example, to portray Laszlo's battle against the Nazis as a moral, rather than political one. Laszlo's politics (which would probably, in the real world, be communist) are never specified. Meanwhile, the United States, with the help of heroic individuals such as Laszlo, is depicted as the principal obstacle to the Nazi advance, even though, in 1942, the Nazis had been virtually unopposed in Europe for more than a year by anyone except the Soviet Red Army, which ultimately played the key role in the Nazi defeat. Still, *Casablanca* is an interesting illustration of the way in which the romantic and individualist conventions of Hollywood film adapted to the exigencies of the war in ways that were very much in the line with the politics of the Popular Front. *Screenplay:* Julius Epstein, Philip Epstein, and Howard Koch. *Selected bibliography:* Denning; Robert Ray; Randy Roberts; Schatz (*Boom*).

*THE GLASS KEY:* DIR. STUART HEISLER (1942). The principal connection of *The Glass Key* to American leftist culture would appear to lie in the fact that it is an adaptation of the 1931 novel by Dashiell Hammett, a writer whose own leftist sympathies were clear. Otherwise, the film is fairly straightforward hard-boiled detective fare. The film takes place in an unidentified small city, where protagonist Ed Beaumont (played by Alan Ladd with notable stoicism) is the chief lieutenant to Paul Madvig (Brian Donlevy), a shady, but powerful, local political boss. As the film begins, Madvig has decided, against Beaumont's warnings that it will mean trouble, to back reform candidate Ralph Henry in the upcoming gubernatorial election, largely because Madvig is in love with Henry's daughter, Janet (Veronica Lake), whom he hopes to marry. Tough though he may be, Madvig is just a big, loveable lug when it comes to Janet, which impairs not only his judgment, but the film, which in this sense suffers considerably in relation to the book (in which Madvig is a much more believable crime boss who still loves Janet but is apparently interested in her largely because of the social standing and connections a marriage to her would convey on him).

Among other things, Madvig's support for Henry draws the ire of rival crime boss Nick Varna (Joseph Calleia), who runs a series of local gambling joints that might be put out of business by Henry's reformist regime. The central plot strand, however, revolves around the murder of Henry's profligate son, Taylor (Richard Denning), early in the film. The evidence seems to point to Madvig as the killer, especially after it is revealed that Madvig's younger sister, Opal (Bonita Granville), had been having an affair with Taylor over the strenuous objections of her brother. Beaumont works to clear Madvig's name and to find the real killer, though Madvig seems oddly uninterested in clearing himself, preferring instead to rely on his political connections to avert prosecution. In the process, Beaumont becomes entangled in the battle between Varna and Madvig, leading to some of the film's most memorable scenes, in which Varna's henchman, Jeff (William Bendix), sadistically (and homoerotically) pounds Beaumont practically into a pulp. One almost senses, meanwhile, that Beaumont rather enjoys his encounters with Jeff, however painful, which enhances the homoeroticism of the relationship.

Eventually, there is so much evidence pointing to Madvig that he is arrested despite his political clout. Beaumont, however, doggedly pursues the real killer, even after Madvig confesses to him that he killed Taylor Henry. Finally, Beaumont concludes that Ralph Henry is the real killer, then tricks Henry into confessing by convincing the police to arrest Janet for the crime. Meanwhile, passion smolders between Beaumont and Janet, who asks him to take her with him when he prepares to leave town at the end of the film. The inscrutable Beaumont agrees (though with a lack of enthusiasm that is not surprising, given his hostility toward women throughout the film), and they kiss, just as Madvig walks in and observes the scene. In the book, this encounter leads to a troubling and emotionally charged conclusion in which Madvig rushes from the room, justifiably feeling betrayed both by his best girl and his best friend. In the film, however, the good-natured Madvig gives the couple his blessing and wishes them a happy married life (however hard that is to imagine for this couple), thus stripping the ending of its emotional force, but providing the obligatory Hollywood conclusion.

*The Glass Key* makes many of the same points about the seamy side of American life as the film noir, of which it might be considered an early example, though its lighting, however dim, does not achieve the expressionist atmospheric effects of the classic film noir. For example, the film takes for granted that political activity is corrupt and that elections are decided not by a free-thinking citizenry, but by the machinations of behind-the-scenes bosses. The thoroughly repressed Beaumont, meanwhile, might be read as a classic figure of the alienated individual in capitalist society. In any case, Ladd's portrayal of Beaumont as totally amoral and lacking in affect is truly disturbing, and the film's overall cynical vision certainly stands in sharp contrast to most representations of American society in the films of the war years. Hammett's novel was also the basis of a 1935 film (directed by Frank Tuttle, with more lighting and less cynicism) of the same title. *Screenplay:* Jonathan Latimer. *Selected bibliography:* Everson; Naremore (*More than Night*); Porfirio ("No Way Out"); Scher; Schrader.

*KEEPER OF THE FLAME:* **DIR. GEORGE CUKOR (1942).** *Keeper of the Flame* was conceived by leftist screenwriter Donald Ogden Steward as the definitive Hollywood antifascist statement. It features an investigative reporter, Steven O'Malley (Spencer Tracy), who sets out to write a memorial piece on Robert Forrest, a prominent and much-admired American who recently died in an auto accident. In the process, however, O'Malley, already suspicious that Forrest's public image might have been manufactured, uncovers much more than he bargained for. Eventually winning the cooperation of Forrest's initially reticent widow, Christine (Katharine Hepburn), O'Malley discovers that Forrest's Forward America Association was in fact a right-wing organization funded by a handful of wealthy, power-hungry patrons, who hoped to parlay hatred and fear of labor unions and ethnic minorities into a fascist takeover of America. "They painted it red, white, and blue, and called it Americanism," explains the widow. Christine also confesses that she acted to thwart her husband's evil plans by intentionally failing to warn him that a bridge was out, thus leading to the accident that caused his death. Having made these confessions, she burns the retreat that contains evidence of the association's activities, dying in the flames. O'Malley, however, survives to write the story and to warn America of the danger of fascists in our midst.

One of the least commercially successful of the Tracy-Hepburn collaborations, *Keeper of the Flame* is a good example of the antifascist propaganda films that were produced in America during World War II, while Stewart is a good example of the new prominence that these films brought to leftist screenwriters, whose political commitment and sophistication was well suited to the making of antifascist statements. The film, however, was relatively unusual in its clear suggestion of the sometimes sinister motivations of the rich and in its interrogation of the use of the clichés of Americanism for the promotion of fascist ideas. Meanwhile,

Stewart, like other prominent leftist writers of the 1940s, had his career come to a screeching halt amid the anticommunist purges that swept Hollywood in the postwar years. Stewart had eighteen screenwriting credits between 1937 and 1949, then never had another. However, he occasionally worked without credit after relocating to London in 1947. *Screenplay:* Donald Ogden Stewart. *Selected bibliography:* Neve (*Film*); Stewart.

*THE MAGNIFICENT AMBERSONS:* DIR. ORSON WELLES (1942). Based on the Booth Tarkington novel of the same title, *The Magnificent Ambersons* is a historical narrative that chronicles the impact of modern capitalism on midlands America. In particular, the film traces the decline and fall of a single prominent family in a "midland town" (perhaps Indianapolis), dramatizing in the process the passing of an older, more refined, and more genteel way of life. The film begins in 1873, when the Ambersons are rising to the height of their glory. Major Amberson (played by Richard Bennett) is the wealthiest man in the small, quiet town, where he has just built a magnificent mansion, viewed with admiration, and even awe, by all. By the end of the film, the remaining Ambersons have become poor, and the mansion is in decay and has been lost by the family. The quiet town has become a thriving industrial city, "heaving and spreading," but also developing the attendant modern problems, including, crime, noise, and pollution. Modern capitalism thus brings new people, new industries, and a new way of life to the town, but it is a way of life in which much of value has been lost.

Soon after the beginning of the film, the Major's daughter, Isabel, the town beauty, marries Wilbur Minafer after a stormy but aborted courtship with Eugene Morgan (Joseph Cotton), to whom she is greatly attracted but whose antics strike her as too undignified to allow him entry to the Amberson family. Wilbur and Isabel have a son, George Amberson Minafer, who is so spoiled as a child that he terrorizes the entire town. The film then jumps ahead to the beginning years of the twentieth century, when George returns to town from his Ivy League college for Christmas break. During the break, he meets Morgan, now a widower, who has recently returned (after a long absence) to the town in order to pursue the commercial development of his recent invention, a new kind of "horseless carriage." George also meets Morgan's daughter, Lucy (Anne Baxter), with whom he is immediately taken. The personal story line continues as George pays suit to Lucy, Wilbur dies, and Morgan renews his old courtship of Isabel. But the jealous George (egged on by his maiden aunt, Fanny Minafer, played by Agnes Moorehead) interferes, partly for Oedipal reasons and partly because he finds Morgan's active participation in business and industry vulgar. The courtship between Morgan and Isabel comes to naught, and Isabel and George go abroad together with no plans ever to return. Eventually, with Isabel in poor health, they do return. She dies soon afterward (before Morgan can see her), and her father, the Major, dies soon after that. George and Fanny are left to their own resources, inheriting essentially nothing. George, despite his long resistance to joining the world of commerce, is forced to seek work in a dynamite factory because the dangerous work there pays more than he can make anywhere else. But he is seriously injured in an auto accident before this plan can be realized. The film then ends as Morgan visits George in the hospital and learns that George will fully recover. He forgives George for the latter's interference in his courtship of Isabel, feeling that by doing so he is being true to her memory.

This rather contrived (and silly) upbeat ending was tacked on without Welles's knowledge or permission. Indeed, audience testing and other commercial factors led RKO Studios to make numerous changes to the film, including paring it down to 88 minutes in length from Welles's original 148 minute version. These changes, documented by Robert Carringer, greatly compromised the film. But the version that was released is still powerful, remaining one of the most important film commentaries on the dramatic process of modernization (chronicled in great detail in William Leach's *Land of Desire*) that transformed American society in the early decades of the twentieth century. Indeed, the soap-opera-like personal story of the Ambersons and the other characters is merely a device for the presentation of the real story, that of capitalist modernization and the consequent destruction of an older way of life. The film presents this historical change with obvious skepticism. On the other hand, *The Magnificent Ambersons* is in no way a nostalgic call for a return to former days, though it is certainly the case that Welles's original version of the film was much darker and more pessimistic in its portrayal of the consequences of capitalism.

Morgan (interestingly, the film's central capitalist, but also the film's most positive character) expresses the film's attitude toward modernization most directly in a speech in which he responds to George's complaints about the intrusive impact of the automobile (appropriately, the film's central metaphor for modernity) on the life of the town. Morgan grants George's point, going beyond him to argue that the automobile will entirely transform the texture of American life and even the nature of human beings. Morgan also acknowledges his own ambivalence about this transformation and its spiritual costs. But he concludes that progress is inevitable and that the best course is to make the most of it rather than to cling to outmoded ways of life. Thus, though the film (especially as released by RKO) certainly contains no overt Marxist rhetoric or images, it is thoroughly consistent with both the Marxist acceptance of capitalist modernity as a natural and inevitable historical process and the Marxist critique of capitalist modernity as a dehumanizing phenomenon that needs to be overcome in the continuing forward movement to socialism. *Screenplay:* Orson Welles. *Selected bibliography:* Callow; Carringer; Denning; Higham (*Films*); Higham (*Orson Welles*); James Howard; Leach; Naremore (*Magic*); David Thomson (*Rosebud*).

*NATIVE LAND:* DIR. LEO HURWITZ AND PAUL STRAND (1942). The culmination of five years of effort and the ultimate achievement of the independent leftist film company, Frontier Films, *Native Land* is in many ways the central example of Popular Front cultural production in American film. The film was made in response to a clear wave of reaction that was sweeping America in the middle and late 1930s; this wave of reaction attempted to undo not only much of the legacy of the New Deal, but also the important gains made by labor, under the leadership of the Congress of Industrial Organizations (CIO), during the 1930s. Defending the New Deal and, especially, organized labor, the film employs a distinctive political strategy that is highly typical of the Popular Front. On the one hand, the film's makers carefully present themselves as modern-day proponents of Jeffersonian democracy; they associate themselves and the point of view they represent with a tradition of American democracy that begins with settlers coming to the New World in search of freedom in the sixteenth century, finds its most important defining moment in the American Revolution and the founding of the new republic, and is then continued by subsequent leaders such as Abraham Lincoln. On the other hand, *Native Land* carefully associates reactionary antilabor forces with fascist assaults on this American democratic tradition, thus aligning the film's project with the war against fascism then raging in Europe while aligning American reactionaries with the enemy powers in that war.

The film begins with on-screen text noting that the American people have had to fight long and hard to gain and preserve their freedom and that, in recent years, this freedom has once again been threatened by "the fascist-minded on our own soil." The narration, read by Paul Robeson, then begins with a brief history of America, highlighted by the settling of the continent by courageous and determined pioneers, the founding of a nation in the American Revolution, the defense of that nation in the Civil War, and finally by the rise of that nation to its present wealth and power via the industrial revolution and modernization. The fight for freedom was integral to all of these developments, Robeson reminds us, and concepts such as liberty and justice and equality were "built into bridges and dynamos and concrete cities."

The film then presents a series of three brief segments based on real instances of the violation of liberty in recent American history. In the first of these segments (based on events in Custer, Michigan, in September

1934), Fred Hill (played by Fred Johnson), a Michigan farmer, speaks up at a farmer's meeting and is murdered the next day on his own farm by a carload of mysterious, suited men. In the second segment (based on an occurrence in Cleveland in the spring of 1936), a union organizer is found murdered by a cleaning woman (Amelia Romano), who comes to clean his room. Then, in the final introductory segment (based on events in Fort Smith, Arkansas, in the summer of 1936), a meeting of black and white sharecroppers is broken up by deputized thugs. Two sharecroppers, one black and one white (Louis Grant and Housely Stevens), try to escape into the woods together but are hunted down and brutally murdered.

Having provided these powerful reminders of the violence that has been used in recent years against Americans who were simply trying to exercise their lawful rights, the film (which was at first tentatively titled *Labor Spy*) proceeds into its main narrative, a story of labor espionage in which the forces of capital attempt to infiltrate, and then destroy, a labor union. In the film, a spy, Harry Carlisle (Howard Da Silva), ingratiates himself with the union through the clever artifice of exposing another spy, planted there specifically for that purpose. After the union's headquarters are broken into, Carlisle is given the union's crucial membership book for safekeeping. Realizing the enormity of the damage to the union should this book fall into the wrong hands, Carlisle hesitates to turn it over to his bosses but is finally coerced into doing so. He then fakes injuries and convinces the union that the book was taken by force. The ramifications are swift and severe, as the union members are systematically fired from their jobs, then blacklisted, a phenomenon, the film notes, that is occurring all over America.

The film then shifts to a broader depiction of the nationwide effort to suppress union activity. An independent grocer in Memphis is run out of town for supporting unions; a politician in Tampa who opposes the Ku Klux Klan in city elections is abducted and brutally beaten; another union organizer is murdered; a peaceful demonstration in Brooklyn is attacked by police. But the film also depicts the efforts of right-thinking Americans to resist this wave of terror. This resistance leads to a congressional investigation in which the concentrated antilabor effort is revealed as a genuine conspiracy against American liberty, "directed by a handful of fascist-minded corporations." Participants in the conspiracy go on the defensive and destroy their records, making it impossible to determine the true extent of their efforts. But it becomes clear that private armies of criminals have been mobilized in a massive assault on American freedom, and, in particular, on organized labor.

In the next scene, those who have fought for freedom are honored on Memorial Day 1937. In Chicago, as part of the observance of the holiday, 2,000 people participate in a peaceful and legal march toward the Republic Steel Plant. They are attacked by the police. Several of them are killed, shot in the back in "an act of fascism. ... The act of a desperate minority." With this final reminder that this minority is still at work to suppress liberty, the film then ends with a sort of manifesto of the Popular Front, a final exhortation to continue America's 300-year fight for freedom by opposing this minority and thus fighting for the liberties guaranteed by the Bill of Rights, plus "the rights of all Americas, of every creed and color, to a job, a home, adequate food and medical care, the right to bargain collectively, to act for the greatest good of the greatest number, the right to live at peace, unthreatened, threatening no one."

Made on an extremely tight budget and with mostly amateur actors (of the cast, only Da Silva, later blacklisted after his uncooperative testimony before HUAC, had a substantial film career), *Native Land* is a moving film that makes a compelling argument for its seemingly unobjectionable political program, while at the same time demonstrating that the simple liberties it promotes have important enemies in American society. The film received numerous enthusiastic reviews on its initial release but was hampered by the reluctance even of the Communist Party to support its critique of American capital, considered highly controversial in the midst World War II, despite its antifascist message. The film, of course, began in a very different climate in 1937. Ironically, Hurwitz apparently received the proof print of the film from the laboratory the day after the bombing of Pearl Harbor (Klein and Klein 6). The film's project nevertheless remained relevant, and seems even more vital today, given the subsequent demise of organized labor as a force in American social and political life, a demise that can partly be attributed to the ultimate success of the antilabor conspiracies described in the film. That the film should fail to carry the day in its battle to promote unionism as the key to American liberty is a tribute to the power of the capitalist forces that were arrayed against the union movement. That the film was made at all and that it turned out to be the powerful and effective document that it is should be taken as a tribute to the dedication and tenacity of its makers, as well as to the fundamental justice of the cause for which they argued in vain. *Screenplay:* David Wolff (Ben Maddow), Leo Hurwitz, and Paul Strand. *Selected bibliography:* Alexander; Barsam; Klein and Klein; Rollins ("Ideology"); Charles Wolfe.

*THIS GUN FOR HIRE:* **DIR. FRANK TUTTLE (1942).** An excellent example of the development of film noir as a vehicle for pro-American propaganda during World War II, *This Gun for Hire* is also important in cinema history as the film that launched newcomer Alan Ladd, in the role of hired killer Philip Raven, on the road to stardom. The film (which was remade in 1957 as *Short Cut to Hell*, with James Cagney directing) is in many ways a fairly straightforward suspense thriller. It begins in San

Francisco as Raven, has been hired as a killer by a man (played by Laird
Cregar) calling himself Johnson (but who is really Willard Gates, an
executive of Nitro Chemical Corporation of Los Angeles). Raven carries
out his mission, killing a man who has been blackmailing Gates's boss,
Alvin Brewster, president of Nitro Chemical (played by Tully Marshall).
Gates then pays Raven in marked bills that have been reported stolen in
a payroll robbery at Nitro Chemical, planning thereby to see that Raven
is taken by the police, tying up loose ends. Raven, however, is more
resourceful than Gates realizes. He eludes capture, makes his way to Los
Angeles, learns the true identities of Brewster and Gates, and kills them
both before being shot and killed by police.

This main plot is enriched and complicated by a number of developments along the way. For one thing, Raven becomes personally (but not
romantically) involved with Ellen Graham (Veronica Lake), a club singer
and musician who also happens to be the fiancée of Michael Crane
(Robert Preston), the police detective assigned to track down Raven. At
first forced to help Raven at gunpoint, Graham (who is meanwhile
supplying information to a Senate committee in their investigation of
Nitro Chemical), begins to feel sympathy for Raven and ends up helping
him of her own free will. Raven, who has experienced little human
warmth in his life (a fact that helps Ladd to play the character as sympathetic, while at the same time sinister), is genuinely touched by Graham's kindness. In the meantime, in the film's war-related twist, it is
revealed that Brewster and Gates were originally being blackmailed
because they have sold a new secret formula for poison gas to the Japanese, identifying the unsavory pair as traitors to the war effort and at the
same time delivering a warning against such treachery.

Perhaps the most interesting aspect of *This Gun for Hire* involves its
adaptation, by screenwriters Albert Maltz and W. R. Burnett, from
Graham Greene's 1936 novel, *A Gun for Sale*. The thriller aspects of the
novel are transferred to the film cleverly and relatively faithfully, with
the changes necessary to move the setting from Britain in the mid-1930s
to California early in World War II. Other changes occur for obvious
reasons of film decorum, as when the harelip that disfigures Raven in the
book is replaced by a broken wrist, thus allowing the handsome Ladd to
play a more attractive character. What is remarkable, however, is the
smooth way in which Greene's antiwar novel has been transformed into
a piece of prowar propaganda. In the novel, Raven does not kill a black-
mailer, but instead assassinates a socialist minister in the Czech government, a move that is intended by Raven's employer (Sir Marcus, the
chairman of Midland Steel) to provoke a political crisis that will lead to
all-out war—and to increased profits for Midland Steel. The book thus
includes powerful criticisms of the unscrupulous operations of Western
capitalism, warning its readers against the kinds of prowar enthusiasms

that capital might like to inspire. In the film, of course, it is not capitalism, but simply the individual villains Brewster and Gates who are to blame; meanwhile, the war effort itself is endorsed as a necessary battle against the kinds of evil such villains represent. *Screenplay:* Albert Maltz and W. R. Burnett. *Selected bibliography:* Adamson; Falk; Melada; Naremore (*More than Night*); Silver and Ward.

*WOMAN OF THE YEAR:* DIR. GEORGE STEVENS (1942). While containing virtually nothing in the way of overtly leftist political commentary (except for the obligatory passing allusion to the Spanish Civil War), *Woman of the Year* was co-written by left-leaning screenwriter Ring Lardner, Jr., who later became one of the Hollywood Ten. Indeed, the screenplay won an Academy Award. Moreover, in its depiction of protagonist Tess Harding (Katharine Hepburn) as a strong and independent career woman, the film, for its time, is especially progressive in its gender politics. Although the film ultimately suggests that Tess can find total fulfillment only if she has a happy marriage, it also suggests that she will continue her career through this marriage, neither marriage nor career being sufficient in itself to fulfill her needs. *Woman of the Year* helped to establish Hepburn as the prototypical "strong woman" of American film and to establish Hepburn and co-star Spencer Tracy as one of America's most successful film duos for the next three decades, both on and off the screen.

In the film, Tess, the daughter of a diplomat, is a nationally prominent journalist for the *New York Chronicle*. Her advice on important matters of state, during the crucial period of World War II, is valued and sought after not only by her everyday readers, but by the high and mighty in Washington. Her counterpart in the film, Sam Craig (Tracy, in his first of many films with Hepburn), also works for the *Chronicle* and is also successful, but as a sportswriter whose work seems relatively trivial compared to that of Tess. As the film begins, the cultured and refined Tess becomes involved in a feud with the gruff and down-to-earth Sam after she makes a comment during an interview suggesting that baseball is an unimportant diversion that should perhaps be put aside for the duration of the war. For Sam, of course, baseball lies at the very heart of what we are fighting to defend in the war. Tess and Sam are, in fact, the original odd couple, but romance instantly blooms when they get together.

A wedding soon follows, though it is clear that trouble lurks in the way Tess's work continually gets in the way of their relationship. Their wedding night is interrupted when a Yugoslav diplomat, newly escaped from the Gestapo, shows up on Tess's doorstep with his entourage. In retaliation, Sam phones up bar owner and ex-boxer Pinkie Peters (William Bendix) and has Pinkie come over with the gang from the bar to join the fray, resulting in some hilarious moments of culture clash. Indeed, the cultural differences between Tess and Sam, which are essentially class-based, are important throughout the film. The emphasis, however, is on gender, and the most striking aspect of the film is its continual reversal of gender roles, with Sam having to vie with Tess's career for her attention. Their marriage finally on the rocks due to such difficulties, she resolves to change her ways. However, Sam realizes, after an extended scene of high comedy in which Tess attempts to prepare his breakfast, but clearly has no idea how, that Tess will never be happy as a little wife and mother. The two then agree to a compromise in which she will continue to pursue her career but will pay more attention to Sam and his needs. *Screenplay:* Ring Lardner, Jr., and Michael Kanin. *Selected bibliography:* Britton.

*ACTION IN THE NORTH ATLANTIC:* DIR. LLOYD BACON (1943). Scripted by leftist screenwriter John Howard Lawson (who also wrote the screenplays for the World War II films *Sahara* and *Counter-Attack*), *Action in the North Atlantic* is a high-action war film that celebrates the contribution of the Merchant Marine to the Allied effort in World War II. It begins aboard the *Northern Star*, a Merchant Marine tanker that is carrying oil from the United States to England to fuel the fight against the German Nazis. The seasoned, but still idealistic, captain of the tanker is Steve Jarvis (Raymond Massey); its first mate is Joe Rossi (Humphrey Bogart); and its crew is a tough, but loveable, gang of veteran seaman, supplemented by Robert Parker (Dick Hogan), a cadet from the Merchant Marine Academy. Torpedoed by a Nazi U-boat, the *Northern Star* sinks. Most of the crew escapes on a boat, which is then rammed by the sub. The survivors make their way aboard a raft and drift for eleven days, when they are finally rescued.

Back stateside, the men get a break to recover from their ordeal. Jarvis spends the time with his loyal wife (Ruth Gordon), while Rossie meets and marries a bar singer (Julie Bishop). But both men, understanding the importance of the war effort (which is emphasized in dialogue liberally sprinkled with patriotic exhortations), eagerly go back to sea when they are given a new ship. Both of them, plus most of their original crew, are assigned to the *Seawitch*, a new liberty ship that becomes part of a huge international convoy of ships from different nations, all carrying supplies to the Russian allies. On the way, the convoy is attacked by a group of German submarines. Most of the subs are destroyed, but the convoy is scattered. The *Seawitch* is separated from the rest of the convoy and is dogged by the last remaining sub, which turns out to be the same one that sank the *Northern Star*.

Jarvis, Rossi, and their brave crew battle the sub, which they eventually sink; they also beat off an attack by German fighter planes, though

Jarvis is wounded and eight men, including Parker, are killed. Eventually, they make their way to Murmansk, where they are greeted by cries of "*tovarish!*" from a crowd of grateful Russians, including dockworkers, who are mostly women because the men are all off fighting the Nazis. As one of the crewmen explains to another, *tovarish* "means comrade. That's good." The film is thus careful to make clear the important contribution being made by the Soviets to the war effort and to emphasize the anti-Nazi solidarity of Russians and Americans. Mostly, however, the film is pro-Allied propaganda pure and simple, with very little in the way of specifically leftist political statement. It ends with a voiceover (imitating the voice of Franklin Roosevelt) that proclaims the Allied determination to win a "complete and final victory." *Screenplay:* John Howard Lawson. *Selected bibliography:* Carr; Dick (*Radical Innocence*); Koppes and Black.

*DESTINATION TOKYO:* **DIR. DELMER DAVES (1943).** A standard example of Hollywood wartime fare, *Destination Tokyo* combines action and adventure with pro-American and anti-Japanese propaganda, making clear not only the heroism of America's fighting men, but also the presumed righteousness of their cause. The film begins in Washington, D.C., as top-level strategists complete plans for the secret mission that will provide the material of the film. This mission begins as the crew of the submarine *Copperfin* set sail from San Francisco on Christmas Eve. The sub's commander, Captain Cassidy (Cary Grant), writes a sentimental letter of farewell to his wife and kids before he leaves, making clear his sense that he is going away to defend them and their way of life. In the meantime, a shipboard Christmas celebration again emphasizes the American values that the men are fighting for. Such scenes emphasize traditional American values throughout the film, though extensive treatment of the dynamics of the relationship among the men of the crew potentially suggests the value of group efforts in a way that evades the traditional individualism of American war films.

Once at sea, Cassidy opens his sealed orders, which, for some unexplained reason, direct him to take the *Copperfin* to the Aleutians, where they are to pick up Lt. Raymond (John Ridgely), a meteorologist, then deliver him all the way to Tokyo for a secret reconnaissance of the Japanese weather and defense systems in preparations for the upcoming bombing of the city. Raymond is successfully retrieved, though the *Cooperfin* is attacked by two Japanese planes, both of which are shot down. One of the pilots parachutes into the cold water, after which the Americans gallantly try to save him. However, as he is being pulled aboard the sub by one of the men, Mike (Tom Tully), he treacherously pulls out a knife and stabs Mike in the back, killing him. The Americans then cut the pilot to ribbons with machine-gun fire. Mike is buried at sea, while Cassidy tries to explain the pilot's action to his men, pointing out that, in Japanese culture, young boys are trained to be bloodthirsty killers from a very early age. Moreover, we learn, young girls are typically sold to factories or even into prostitution because "the Japs don't understand the love we have for our women." As if these racist and sexist remarks were not bad enough, the original version of the film included a later extended sequence in which Cassidy writes another letter home, describing in detail the racial tendency of Germans and Japanese to be nogood killers, as opposed to the inherent tendency of Chinese and Russians (both allies of the Americans) to be dependable and virtuous. This latter passage has been excised from prints (and videos) available from the 1970s onward, presumably because of the negative racist criticisms of the Japanese and Germans, though perhaps also because of the positive descriptions of the Russians and Chinese. In any case, this excision disguises the extent to which American anti-Japanese propaganda during the war relied on racist sentiments.

The rest of the mission proceeds in a fairly predictable fashion. With great difficulty and with numerous close calls, the *Copperfin* slips into a highly fortified Tokyo Bay, then puts Raymond, along with two crew members, Wolf (John Garfield) and Sparks (John Forsythe), ashore. They get the information required, then narrowly escape a Japanese patrol and get back aboard the *Copperfin*, which successfully slips back out of the bay. The bombing of Tokyo is highly successful, provoking more racist remarks to the effect that there should be many happy Japanese in Tokyo, given that the Japanese are always happy to die for their emperor. The *Copperfin* manages to torpedo a Japanese aircraft carrier but is then subjected to an extended depth-charge assault. They finally manage to sink the destroyer that is pursuing them, then sail peacefully back to San Francisco, where Cassidy's wife and kids greet them at the dock. The sentimental, schmaltzy, and sexist presentations of American culture, combined with the ugly, racist descriptions of the Japanese, hardly make this film a proud moment in the history of American cinema. But it remains a representative example of World War II propaganda efforts. *Screenplay:* Albert Maltz and Delmer Daves. *Selected bibliography:* Neve (*Film*); Polan.

*THE FALLEN SPARROW:* **DIR. RICHARD WALLACE (1943).** *The Fallen Sparrow* is a film noir thriller informed by antifascist politics and containing echoes of support for the Republican cause in the Spanish Civil War. John Garfield, himself a supporter of the Spanish Republicans, was loaned by Warner Brothers to RKO specifically to play the lead role of Kit McKittrick, a veteran of the Lincoln Brigades who has recently escaped and returned to America after being held in Spain in a fascist prison for two years, well past the end of the Civil War. As the last surviving member of a brigade that had been especially effective during the war, McKittrick is despised by the fascists. They cannot kill him, however, because he is the only one who knows the location of the brigade's hidden battle standard, which the fascists have sworn to destroy because of its significance as a symbol of the antifascist fight for freedom. In prison, McKittrick has been repeatedly tortured and interrogated but has refused to reveal the location of the banner, and it later turns out that the fascists have intentionally allowed him to escape in the hope that he would lead them to it.

As the film begins, McKittrick is traveling by train to New York, where his friend Louis Lepetino, who helped arrange his escape from Spain, has just been killed under suspicious circumstances. Although the death has been officially ruled an accident, McKittrick is convinced that Lepetino was murdered by fascist agents, and he immediately sets about gathering evidence to try to find the killers. But, as McKittrick pursues the fascists, the fascists pursue McKittrick and the banner. Garfield dominates the film with his performance as an idealist determined to thwart the fascists but deeply troubled by flashbacks from his years in prison. In the meantime, he encounters a cast of characters that includes Maureen O'Hara as Toni Donne, a femme fatale in the employ of the fascists; Walter Slezak as "Dr. Skaas," a prominent Norwegian historian who has presumably fled to the United States to escape the fascist occupation of his own country; and Hugh Beaumont as Otto Skaas, the doctor's nephew. With the aid of the able Inspector Tobin of the New York Police, McKittrick manages to overcome fascist nefariousness, his own emotional traumas, and his romantic attraction to Donne. He ascertains that both Dr. Skaas and his nephew are impostors, Nazi agents who have replaced the Norwegian originals. He also learns that Otto murdered Lepetino and that Dr. Skaas murdered McKittrick's friend, Ab Parker, a State Department employee who was on the trail of the Nazi spy ring of which the Skaases are key members. McKittrick shoots and kills Dr. Skaas, and the spy ring is broken. As the film ends, Toni Donne is taken away by police, still protesting her innocence. The message seems to be a warning that not all fascists are sinister-looking and sounding foreigners such as Skaas: some, like O'Hara's Donne, are, at least on the surface, attractive indeed.

*The Fallen Sparrow* is in many ways a typical example of the antifascist films that arose in America during World War II and the years immediately afterward. In general, it depicts the opposition between America and fascism as one of good versus evil, without any particular political overtones. Even McKittrick's support for the Spanish Republicans is essentially apolitical; he has several opportunities in the film to explain the motivation for his work in Spain, which he describes largely as a quest for adventure. On the other hand, McKittrick's idealism is clear, and there is at least one politically suggestive moment near the end of the film when he explains that the banner he has given so much to protect is important because he believes it will someday fly again over a new brigade. He thus indicates that the values defended by the Republicans in Spain (without official American support) still live, even if the fascists are for the moment triumphant there. In general, however, the film is essentially a work of pro-American propaganda that does little or nothing to question the efficacy of American capitalism as an alternative to fascism. *Screenplay:* Warren Duff. *Selected bibliography:* Denning.

*HANGMEN ALSO DIE:* **DIR. FRITZ LANG (1943).** Based on events surrounding the 1942 assassination of Reinhard Heydrich, the German "Reichsprotektor" of Nazi-occupied Czechoslovakia, *Hangmen Also Die* is in this sense a companion piece to Douglas Sirk's confused but powerful film, *Hitler's Madman*, also released in 1943. Lang's film is notable as an leading example of the anti-Nazi films of the World War II years and as one of the films that established a close connection between anti-Nazi politics and the techniques of the film noir. It is also notable as the only film produced from a screenplay substantially authored by playwright Bertolt Brecht during his abortive career in Hollywood. On the other hand, Brecht was not given screenwriting credit (which went to veteran screenwriter John Wexley) when the film was originally released, largely because of serious creative differences with Lang during the making of the film over what Brecht saw as Lang's determination to sensationalize the story into a typical Hollywood thriller. Among other things, both Brecht and Wexley felt that Lang was systematically eliminating the film's critique of antisemitism in order to avoid controversy. In the original, Brecht was credited only for coauthoring the story with Lang. In a bit of poetic justice, however, the videotape of the film is now distributed, by Kino Video, in packaging that identifies Brecht as the sole author.

The film is fairly typical Hollywood fare, but residual elements still remain that may indicated Brecht's influence, as in an early scene that emphasizes the support of the Czech people for the Soviet Union in its battle against the German invaders. As the film gets underway, Heydrich is assassinated by Dr. Franticek Svoboda (played by Brian Donlevy), working for the Czech underground resistance. In historical actuality, Heydrich was apparently killed by British agents, but this motif allows the film to place its focus on the underground, which is in many ways (and was even more so in Brecht's original conception) the collective protagonist of the film. Lang employs a number of devices to ensure that his American audience will sympathize with the Czechs, including the simple but effective device of having all the German characters speak either in German or in heavily accented English, while the Czech characters (played by American actors) speak perfect American English. The film involves three different interwoven stories. One involves the efforts of Svoboda (whose surname means "freedom" in Czech), with the help of the underground and of upstanding Czechs such as Professor Stepan Novotny (Walter Brennan) and his family, to evade capture by the Nazis. Another follows the Novotny family, including the growing involvement of daughter Mascha Novotny (Anna Lee) with Svoboda and the imprisonment of Professor Novotny (and numerous others) as hostages by the Germans in an effort to pressure the Czech people into informing against the assassin. The third story involves the infiltration of the Czech underground by German agent Emil Czaka (Gene Lockhart) and the subsequent efforts of the underground to do away with Czaka, whose collaboration with the Germans has been discovered.

As the film proceeds, the three strands of the story converge. The Nazis begin executing hostages on a regular schedule but are still unable to force the Czech people to cooperate with them in their pursuit of Svoboda. Svoboda wants to surrender to end these executions but is convinced by the underground that his surrender would do more harm than good. Professor Novotny, apparently on the verge of execution, dictates to Mascha a letter of farewell to his son young son, Beda, in which he envisions the coming of a better future when liberty will at last have been won. This utopian vision, which includes some potentially socialist undertones, probably shows the hand of Brecht. Eventually, the Czechs concoct a complex plot in which they implicate Czaka both in the assassination of Heydrich and in the murder of Gestapo Inspector Alois Gruber, who is killed by Svoboda and two comrades because he is the only man who can provide an alibi for Czaka. Czaka is arrested and shot by the Germans, Svoboda is cleared, and Professor Novotny and the other remaining hostages are released. These developments are presented with considerable suspense, enhanced by the dark, shadow-haunted look of the film, though the ultimate resolution seems a bit too neat and easy. This difficulty is overcome, however, in a final scene in which it is revealed that the Germans are perfectly aware that Czaka was not Heydrich's assassin but have simply decided to pretend that he was so that they can declare the case solved and avoid admitting the extent to which the Czechs are working to resist German rule. *Screenplay:* John Wexley and Bertolt Brecht (uncredited). *Selected bibliography:* Grimm and Schmidt; Hayman; Humphries; Shindler; Teuchert.

*HITLER'S CHILDREN:* **DIR. EDWARD DMYTRYK (1943).** Based on the anti-Nazi book *Education for Death: The Making of the Nazi* (1941) by Gregor Ziemer, *Hitler's Children* begins with a shot of a book burning in which Ziemer's text is among the volumes being destroyed. The remainder of the film continues this focus on the suppression of free expression under the Nazi regime, while placing considerable emphasis on the brutality and inhumanity of the Nazis as a whole. Colin Shindler calls the film "chief among the most successful demonstrations" of the art of anti-Nazi propaganda in American films of the World War II period. The film was, in fact, a great commercial success, partly, as Shindler argues, because "the juxtaposition of explicitly sadistic scenes (at last by 1943 standards) and a high moral indignation satisfied the latent (and not so latent) sado-masochistic inclinations of the audience and the obligatory outrage of the censors" (66).

It would, of course, be difficult to overstate the brutality of Nazism, and *Hitler's Children* greatly understates the outrages that had been occurring in Nazi Germany for nearly ten years by the time the film was released. There are, for example, no mention of the persecution (and attempted extermination) of Jews and communists, perhaps out of fear that many in the audience might endorse such actions. Instead, the film focuses on the brainwashing of German youth to convince them to put their devotion of Hitler above their own individualistic concerns. Moreover, the film's principal victim of the Nazis is an American girl, Anna Müller (played with suitable innocence by Bonita Granville), who is declared a German citizen by virtue of her Germanic heritage, then taken by force from an American school in Germany and placed in a German labor camp. Some of the film's most striking images, in fact, occur early on in the depicted contrasts between this American school and a neighboring German school. In the co-educational American school, the happy students pursue their own interests, dress according to their taste, and call their kindly instructor, Nicky Nichols (Kent Smith), by his first name. In the all-male German school, on the other hand, the students wear uniforms and are indoctrinated by their tyrannical schoolmaster, Dr. Schmidt (Erford Gage), with Nazi doctrine.

Most of the film concerns Nichols's efforts to retrieve Anna from the camp, in the course of which he continually runs across Gestapo officer Karl Bruner (Tim Holt), a former student in Schmidt's school and a former friend of Anna, in one of the few cases of friendly contact between the schools. Bruner is basically decent (perhaps because he was born in America), but he offers little help to Nichols, who has little success. Eventually, however, Anna escapes on her own, only to be apprehended and sentenced to be flogged in front of the entire camp, then forceably sterilized so that she cannot pass her penchant for "crime" on to future generations. The lurid scene of an innocent young American girl being flogged by evil Nazis was, of course, one of the film's most successful in terms of propaganda; it was a box-office success as well, and the scene was shamelessly played up in promotions for the film. Mercifully, Bruner intercedes after only two lashes, an action that causes him to be sentenced to death. He is given a show trial, which is supposed to culminate in his heartfelt confession, to be broadcast nationwide.

Instead, however, he denounces Nazism and extols its enemies, after which he is shot down. Anna, also present in the courtroom, attempts to rush to his side and is shot down as well. The film then ends as Nichols, forced to leave the country, prepares to mount a plane so that he can return home and report on his experience with Nazism through the 1930s.

The decision to focus on an American girl and on the Nazis' transgressions against the sanctity of the family were no doubt effective from a propaganda point of view. In so doing, however, the film ignores more germane phenomena such as the Holocaust. In some cases, moreover, the film stoops to blatant misrepresentations. For example, in its consistent attempt to depicts Nazism as an enemy of Christianity, it portrays a courageous Catholic bishop as the only German in the film willing openly to speak out against the Nazis. The film thus ignores the strong and enthusiastic support given the Nazis by the Catholic Church, as well as the Nazis' extensive use, with the Church's complicity, of religion as a tool of power. Such crucial historical facts are not mere quibbles, but *Hitler's Children* is not intended as history. It is intended to generate animosity toward Nazi Germany, and in that it succeeded quite well. For this and other services to the American war effort, director Dmytryk was called before HUAC, then ultimately sentenced to prison as a member of the Hollywood Ten. *Screenplay:* Emmet Lavery. *Selected bibliography:* Dick (*Radical Innocence*); Shindler; Ziemer.

*MISSION TO MOSCOW:* **DIR. MICHAEL CURTIZ (1943).** Based on the memoirs of Joseph E. Davies, American ambassador to Moscow from 1936 to 1938, and made at the request of the Roosevelt administration as part of an effort to shore up support for America's Soviet allies in World War II, *Mission to Moscow* stands, along with such contemporaneous films as *Song of Russia* (1943) and *The North Star* (1943), as a marker of a unique moment in American history, before the political climate of the Cold War would make such pro-Soviet works impossible. Paul Buhle describes the film as "outright Common Front propaganda" (110). The film, in fact, came under considerable criticism for its positive portrayal of the Soviet Union, which led critics, as Schatz notes, to complain that the film should have been entitled "Submission to Moscow" (276). It is thus not surprising, however ironic, that many of the film's principals (especially screenwriter Howard Koch, a protegé of Orson Welles) would, in fact, come under suspicion—largely for their participation in this project, despite its direct endorsement and encouragement by the U.S. Government—for having unAmerican sympathies during the anticommunist purges that swept Hollywood in the years after World War II. The film, as its politics became an embarrassment, was later disavowed by Warner Brothers, then buried and largely forgotten, even though it is a fine entertainment that ranks well with the other work of its director Michael Curtiz (best known for *Casablanca*), a master of the Hollywood commercial film. *Mission to Moscow* features a huge cast of major Hollywood stars and was nominated for the New York Film Critic's Circle Award for best film of 1943.

Davies himself (played by Walter Huston) is the principal character of the film, which follows him in a semi-documentary style as he travels for Roosevelt to Moscow in the years leading up to American involvement in World War II in an attempt to determine the reliability of the Soviets as allies in the possible upcoming war. Given that, by 1943, the Soviets had borne the brunt of the battle against the Nazis for two years while the Americans and British played secondary roles, the very premise seems to overestimate the American role in the war and certainly serves as an emblem of American arrogance. But the Soviet Union comes off very well in the film, which is, of course, the whole point, though it is also the case that the film's makers were forced carefully to avoid any specific ideological endorsement of communism, presenting instead a Soviet Union that would be, according to a contemporary review by James Agee "eminently approvable by the Institute of Good Housekeeping" (cited in Halliwell 738). Davies is much impressed by the support shown by the Soviet people both for the war against fascism and for the Stalinist regime. He finds that the Soviets, under Stalin's leadership, are making great social and economic progress, even concluding that the show trials of 1937 were justified as part of the effort of the Soviets to defend the integrity of their nation against foreign enemies.

Such findings, of course, were not controversial at the time, when the U.S. and the Soviet Union were allies, but they would later become untenable when the American line shifted to a portrayal of Stalin as a fiendish monster who held power through sheer terror and intimidation. Neither vision of Stalinism is, of course, completely accurate, while the contrast between the two shows the extent to which American film has long been dominated not by realism and veracity, but by the propagandistic requirements of current government or corporate policy. The essential disappearance of *Mission to Moscow* after World War II also makes a telling comment on the workings of censorship in America. Significantly, the most extensive critical discussion of the film, that by Culbert, is really little more than an anti-Soviet diatribe. ***Screenplay:*** Howard Koch. ***Selected bibliography:*** Buhle; Christensen; Culbert; Halliwell; Schatz (*Boom*); Shindler.

***FOR WHOM THE BELL TOLLS: DIR. SAM WOOD (1943).*** Based on Ernest Hemingway's novel of the same title, *For Whom the Bell Tolls* was one of the major American films of 1943, the biggest box-office hit of that year. The film garnered nine Academy Award nominations, though it won only one Oscar, to Katina Paxinou for best supporting actress. It was written by leftist screenwriter Dudley Nichols, one of the founders, in the late 1930s, of the antifascist Motion Picture Artists Committee. Yet the final product is an excellent example of the purging of political content from American cinema. It deals directly with the Spanish Civil War, one of the major leftist causes of the late 1930s, but it does so in a mode almost entirely devoid of political commentary, treating the war simply as a setting in which protagonist Robert Jordan (played by laconic right-winger Gary Cooper) can have heroic and romantic adventures, battling against dangerous, but ill-defined, foes and pursuing romance with the innocent Spanish girl, Maria (played by Ingrid Berman).

The actual plot of the film follows that of the novel quite closely. Jordan, a Spanish instructor at the University of Montana, has come to Spain to fight for the Loyalist cause, subsequently becoming a demolitions expert. The book covers three days in May 1937, during which Jordan has been sent to a remote mountainous region to blow up a bridge and thereby impede the movements of fascist troops in response to a planned attack in the area by a Loyalist army commanded by the Soviet General Golz (Leo Bulgakov). Jordan is met by the aged and wily guide Anselmo (Vladimir Sokoloff) and taken to the headquarters of a local guerrilla band, ostensibly commanded by Pablo (Akim Tamiroff), but now really led by Pablo's wife, Pilar (Paxinou); Pablo, shattered by his experience in the war, is merely a shell of his former self. Most of the novel involves the interactions among Jordan and the guerrillas as the time for the attack and the bombing of the bridge approaches. Jordan meets and falls in love with Maria (played by Bergman with no attempt at a Spanish accent), who is still recovering from the horrifying experience of seeing her parents killed by fascists, then being gang raped and thrown in a fascist prison. The attack on the bridge is complicated by Pablo's unreliability and by the fact that the fascists, perhaps tipped off about the attack, suddenly begin to move large numbers of troops into the area.

Jordan sends Andrés (Eric Feldary), one of the guerrillas, to warn Golz of the fascist troop movements so that the Loyalist attack can be canceled. The messenger makes his way to the Loyalist lines but then encounters a nightmare of bureaucracy and confusion that continually delays his delivery of the message. By the time the message is finally delivered to Golz, it is too late to call off the attack, which will presumably be a debacle. Meanwhile, back in the mountains, Jordan manages to blow the bridge, though several of his comrades, including Anselmo, are killed in the effort. As the band tries to make its escape, fascist artillery fire knocks Jordan from his horse, and the horse falls on him. Left with a badly broken leg that makes it impossible for him to travel, Jordan bids a tearful farewell to Maria and sends her on with the band, while he stays behind to cover their retreat by holding off the fascists as long as he can, knowing it will mean certain death for him.

*For Whom the Bell Tolls* is a powerful novel that effectively conveys many aspects of Jordan's experience and of his reaction to that experience. It is, however, a very weak historical novel in that it explains very little of the background of the civil war and does essentially nothing to explain what is at stake, other than occasional reminders that the fascists must be defeated at all costs. The film does even less, focusing on Jordan's stoic heroism and on his romance with Maria, with virtually no indication of the nature of the war in which he is involved, apparently at least partly because Franco's fascist regime and the Catholic Church, which strongly supported Franco, both pressured the film's producers to avoid any direct criticism of Franco. Thus, the words "civil war" are never used at all, and the word "fascist" is mentioned only once in the entire film, in a scene in which Jordan, asked by one of the guerrillas why he is in Spain, attempts to explain his motivation but associates fascism with Hitler and Mussolini, not Franco: "A man fights for what he believes in, Fernando. It's not only Spain fighting here, is it? It's Germany and Italy on one side, and Russia on the other, and the Spanish people right in the middle of it all. The Nazis and fascists are just as much against democracy as they are against the communists. And they're using your country as a proving ground for their new war machinery, their tanks and dive bombers, and stuff like that, so they can get the jump on the democracies and knock off England and France and my country before we get armed and ready to fight."

In short, Jordan's politics are those of the Popular Front opposition to fascism. The film does, then, portray the Spanish Civil War as a forerunner to World War II, almost becoming a World War II film, which is not surprisingly given that the film appeared in the midst of the latter war. Like Hemingway's novel, however, the film does not mention that the Loyalist cause could have been saved (and the fascist advance in Europe halted) by intervention on the part of the British and American governments, which stood idly by as the fascists swept across Spain with support from Italy and Germany. (Nichols worked a statement toward that effect into the script, but the line never made it into the film.) Instead, both the film and the book seem to attribute the Loyalist defeat to their own lack of organization and discipline, while doing little to interrogate the historical roots of the Loyalist disarray. Positive aspects of the Loyalist cause, meanwhile, are attributed to the personal characteristics of individual heroes such as Jordan. Hemingway's novel was given a generally negative reception from the American Left, especially among veterans of the Lincoln Brigades, who felt that their experience in Spain had been significantly misrepresented and that the book had greatly distorted the terms of the war. Such criticisms apply doubly for the film, which took Hemingway's already problematic novel and stripped it of its most interesting content, bending over backwards to avoid any real engagement with the political foundations of the conflict in Spain. As Paramount studio chief Adolph Zukor reportedly put it, in an inadvertently telling indictment of the American film industry, they were just trying to make "a great picture, without political significance. We are not for or against anybody" (Agee 49). *Screenplay:* Dudley Nichols. *Selected bibliography:* Agee; Monteath; Myers; Sanderson.

*THE NORTH STAR:* DIR. LEWIS MILESTONE (1943). *The North Star* joins such films as *Mission to Moscow* (1943) and *Counter-Attack* (1945) as explicitly pro-Soviet films produced in America during World War II to further popular support for America's Soviet allies. The film is striking not only for its depiction of the heroism of the Russians in battling against their German invaders, but also in is positive depiction of Soviet life in the days prior to the invasion. It begins with a series of scenes of daily life in a Ukrainian village in the summer of 1941, emphasizing the village's strong sense of community and collective effort. These scenes also emphasize the happiness of the villagers, who are depicted as being very much like Americans, only happier in their communal life, dancing, singing, and generally enjoying their lives. Central figures include the young lovers Damian and Marina (Farley Granger and Anne Baxter), Kolya (Dana Andrews), an officer in the Soviet air force, and Dr. Kurin (Walter Huston), a famous pathologist who has chosen to live and work in the village.

All of this happiness is then disrupted when the German Nazis invade the Soviet Union. The young men of the village go into the hills to form a guerrilla force, while the women, children, and old men stay behind to torch the village and its fields so that they cannot be used by the approaching Germans. Unfortunately, the Germans arrive more quickly than expected and are able to put out the fires and occupy the village. They proceed to terrorize the villagers, among other things rounding up the children so that they can be drained of their blood, which is then to be used by the German army for transfusions.

Although short of weapons, the guerrillas mount an attack on the village, led by the village chairman, Rodion Pavlov (Dean Jagger). With this attack already underway, a shipment of arms arrives, assuring the guerrilla victory. The Germans are routed and driven from the village, and the villagers begin to rebuild their former lives, though many of them have been killed or crippled in the heroic battle against the Germans. The film was nominated for six Academy Awards, though it won none. It also drew the later attention of HUAC investigators, who charged many of the participants with engaging in communist propaganda, even though the film was made at the request of the U.S. government. *Screenplay:* Lillian Hellman. *Selected bibliography:* Christensen; Koppes and Black; Sayre.

*SAHARA:* DIR. ZOLTAN KORDA (1943). Co-written by leftist screenwriter John Howard Lawson and director Korda, *Sahara* exemplifies the Popular Front effort to present a united opposition to fascism during World War II. The film's suspenseful plot begins in the wake of a Nazi rout that has left an American tank commander, Sergeant Joe Gunn (Humphrey Bogart), stranded in the Libyan desert with his disabled tank and two of his men. The Americans, nearly surrounded, manage to get the tank running again and head off into the desert, hoping to make contact with an Allied force so that they can resume the fight. All they find, however, is the remnant of a British hospital corps, whose patients have been killed in a Nazi bombing attack. The groups join forces (under Gunn's command, though the British are led by a captain, played by Richard Nugent) and continue the effort to get to the British lines. Soon, however, they have to turn their attention to finding water, which they manage to do with the help of a Sudanese guide, Sergeant-Major Tambul (Rex Ingram), whom they have also come across in the desert.

The well, however, is almost depleted, though they manage to get enough water to avert the immediate crisis. Another crisis looms, however, as they discover a German battalion approaching across the desert. They resolve to dig in and fight to the end, hoping to make a contribution to the war effort by delaying the German advance as long as possible, even though it will mean almost certain death for the defenders. They battle heroically but are gradually killed off, one by one, leaving only Gunn and Britisher Ozzie Bates (Patrick O'Moore) to defend the well. But, just as all seems lost, the Germans, desperate for water and not realizing there are only two defenders remaining, accept Gunn's offer to surrender their weapons in return for water, which is now (almost miraculously) available because German bombs have reopened the well. As British reinforcements arrive, they discover Gunn and Bates rolling across the desert in the tank, with dozens of German prisoners marching before them. Meanwhile, the British have stopped the German advance at the crucial battle of El Alamein, with the absence of the German battalion captured by Gunn clearly a factor in the British success.

*Sahara* is unabashed pro-Allies, anti-Nazi propaganda, though it presents its message within an adventure-story framework that is designed to be highly entertaining as well. There is little in the way of overt ideology in the film, which presents the Allies as good and the Nazis as evil in unambiguous, black-and-white terms. There are, however, numerous subtle ideological messages. One of Gunn's men, for example, states that he has been fighting the fascists since 1936, in Spain, thus providing the ubiquitous reference to the Spanish Civil War that serves almost as a secret handshake to identify anti-Nazi films with leftist origins. Indeed, *Sahara*'s origins are genuinely leftist: the film is essentially a remake of *The Thirteen*, a 1937 Soviet film about heroic Red Army men in the Kara-kum desert (Carr 84). The most striking aspect of the film is the international solidarity shown by the makeshift force led by Gunn, which includes not only Americans and Englishmen, but one man each from France, Ireland, South Africa, and the Sudan. Despite Gunn's tough-guy leadership (and Bogart's role as star), this effort is clearly collective rather than individual. Race is also an important issue in the film. Although the Sudanese is the only nonwhite in the group, his portrayal as capable, knowledgeable, and heroic (quite unusual at the time in an American film) constitutes part of an antiracist message designed to counter the German mythology of a master race. This motif also has important messages for an American audience. Meanwhile, some of the film's most overtly political messages are delivered by Giuseppe (J. Carrol Naish), an Italian prisoner captured by Tambul and taken along with the group. Giuseppe disavows fascism as a kind of lunacy and suggests, in a confrontation with a German prisoner they are also holding, that the Italians are far less devoted to fascism than are the Germans, who are thus demonized. Giuseppe, we learn, has a cousin who works in a steel mill in Pittsburgh, and it is clear that his characterization is meant as a nod to the Italian-American population, part of the film's vision of a multiethnic front against fascism. *Screenplay:* John Howard Lawson and Zoltan Korda. *Selected bibliography:* Carr; Noble; Schatz (*Boom*).

*SONG OF RUSSIA:* **DIR. GREGORY RATOFF (1943).** *Song of Russia* joins films such as *Mission to Moscow* and *The North Star* (both released in 1943) as attempts by the American cinema to drum up popular support for America's Soviet allies during World War II. In the film, Robert Taylor plays John Meredith, a prominent American symphony conductor on a tour of the Soviet Union just before the outbreak of World War II. While there, Meredith falls in love with a young Russian pianist, Nadya Stepanova (Susan Peters), who seems to be intentionally portrayed as being as much like American women as possible, thus establishing the fact that Americans and Russians are really very much alike. "You could be an American girl," Meredith at one point tells her, apparently meaning that as the highest possible praise. In the film, Nadya helps introduce Meredith to her country, which is portrayed in a very positive light. The two are then married, only to have their honeymoon interrupted by the June 1941 Nazi invasion of the Soviet Union. Nadya joins the Soviet resistance, which heroically and patriotically battles against the invaders

Archconservative Louis B. Mayer, whose MGM studios made the film, claimed it was "about Russians, not communists," and efforts were apparently made (by Taylor, among others) to ensure that the film avoided any open praise for communism, confining its valorization to good American values like courage and patriotism. The film even begins with a scene in which Meredith conducts his orchestra in "The Star Spangled Banner." As Ceplair and Englund put it, the film "managed to avoid an intelligent or in-depth treatment of any of the problems involved in the building of a socialist society and the contradictions of an alliance between a capitalist and a Communist country" (311). Still, *Song of Russia* became a key object of the HUAC inquiries into "communist subversion" in Hollywood, especially after the right-wing writer Ayn Rand, in her own testimony before the committee, identified the film as an example of procommunist propaganda because it showed smiling Russian children. Taylor appeared before the committee as a friendly witness and assured them that he had "objected strenuously" to taking part in the project. Partly because of their participation in *Song of Russia*, screenwriters Richard Collins and Paul Jarrico were both blacklisted. Collins, however, was reinstated after naming names (including Jarrico's) in 1951. Director Ratoff, himself of Russian Jewish descent, chose to go abroad, continuing his directorial career after the war in the United Kingdom. *Screenplay:* Richard Collins and Paul Jarrico. *Selected bibliography:* Caute (*Great Fear*); Ceplair and Englund; Navasky; Shindler.

*TENDER COMRADE:* **DIR. EDWARD DMYTRYK (1943).** *Tender Comrade* tells the story of four World War II army wives, left behind to do their bit on the home front by working in a defense plant while their husbands go off to war. The central figure is Jo Jones (played by Ginger Rogers), whose husband, Chris, pays her a one-night visit at the beginning of the film, just before going overseas to join the war. Much of the film consists of flashbacks that together narrate the courtship and early marriage of Chris and Jo, who have known each other since they were children in the idyllic small American town of Shale City. Among other things, these flashbacks explain the nature of the American way of life, thus presumably showing what the husbands are fighting to protect. Shale City, ironically, was also the home town of Joe Bonham, the protagonist of screenwriter Trumbo's 1939 antiwar novel, *Johnny Got His Gun*. But *Tender Comrade* is very much a prowar piece that, in the course of telling its story, counsels its audience to obey ration laws, support the Allies, and do everything in their power to help our boys defend the cause of freedom.

Early in the film, Jo and three of her co-workers, Barbara Thomas (Ruth Hussey), Helen Stacey (Patricia Collinge), and Doris Dombrowski (Kim Hunter) all decide to go in together to rent a furnished house that will be much nice than the meager apartments they can afford separately. "We could run the joint like a democracy," declares Jo, "on a share and share alike basis." They soon discover, however, that the big, old house they rent demands considerable care, so they add a fifth member to their group, Manya Badenheimer (Mady Christians), another U.S. army wife, who becomes their housekeeper because she is a German citizen (though a staunch foe of the Nazis) and therefore is not allowed to work in the defense plant.

Jo, meanwhile, discovers that she is pregnant and later gives birth to a son, Chris, Jr. Then, amid a celebration as Doris's husband pays her a visit (on which they will finally be able to consummate their marriage, which occurred just before he was shipped out), Jo receives a telegram informing her that Chris, Sr., has been killed in battle. The film then ends with Jo's long, tearful speech to her uncomprehending infant son, explaining to him that his father died in a fight to make the world a better place and that he has a responsibility to carry on that legacy in his own life.

This last scene is only one of many sentimental moments that occur in the film, which leaves no stone unturned in its effort to generate emotional support for the American way of life and for the war currently being waged in defense of that way of life. This syrupy-sweet film is thus an excellent example of the strategic use of sentimentalism in support of patriotic propaganda. Indeed, Trumbo and Dmytryk trot out every possible cliché of Americanism, especially in the pie-baking Rogers's almost bizarrely all-American dialogue (Chris is a "big lug," and Jo's favorite adjective is "darned") and costuming (lots of lace and gingham). It is ironic, then, that this film was later accused—by Rogers's mother, no less—of conveying communist messages because it showed the central characters sharing their resources and working together for the common good. Indeed, the film became a central exhibit in the later persecution of both Trumbo and Dmytryk by HUAC, leading to convictions and prison terms for both for their "un-American activities." **Screenplay:** Dalton Trumbo. **Selected bibliography:** Dick (*Radical Innocence*); Renov.

*WATCH ON THE RHINE:* **DIR. HERMAN SHUMLIN (1943).** Based on the 1941 play of the same title by Lillian Hellman (and scripted for the screen by Hellman and Dashiell Hammett), *Watch on the Rhine* is a central example of the anti-Nazi thrillers produced in Hollywood during and just after World War II. The film received considerable attention, garnering five Academy Award nominations, including a win for best actor for Paul Lukas in the lead role of Kurt Müller (which he has also performed in the play on Broadway), a courageous anti-Nazi underground resistance leader. The action of the film is set in April 1940, before American involvement in the war against Germany. Indeed, the play was first performed before that involvement as well, so it is clear that one function of the play was to encourage American action against the Nazis, though the film (released in the midst of the war) is designed simply as support for actions that were already underway, emphasizing the need to oppose the Nazis by any means necessary. In particular, the film, like the play, not only emphasizes the evils of fascism but carefully aligns Müller and his underground with American interests, most obviously by giving Müller an American wife, Sarah Müller, née Farrelly (played by Bette Davis), who staunchly supports his battle against the Nazis.

The film begins as Müller, Sarah, and their three children return to America (where Sarah has not been for seventeen years), partly so that Müller, ailing from serious wounds suffered fighting against the fascists in the Spanish Civil War, can have some time to recuperate. They go to stay with Sarah's wealthy mother, Fanny Farrelly (played by Lucile Watson), the widow of a U.S. Supreme Court justice. The precocious and amazingly well-disciplined Müller children, reared in hardship on the run from the Nazis all over Europe, are amazed at the amenities offered by the Farrelly mansion. All, however, is not well in the house. Also staying in the mansion as houseguests are Teck de Brancovis (George Coulouris), an exiled Rumanian count, and his wife, Marthe (Geraldine Fitzgerald), the daughter of a close friend of Fanny Farrelly. The count, longing to return to Rumania, where the German Nazis already have considerable influence, hopes to ingratiate himself with the Germans in order to be able to do so.

De Brancovis discovers evidence of Müller's involvement in the underground and threatens to release that information to the Germans unless Müller pays him $10,000 from the funds he has collected for the support of the resistance. Müller staunchly refuses, saying that the money is not his to give (and suspecting that de Brancovis will inform against him even if the money is paid). Müller, meanwhile, is about to return to Germany to try to free his recently imprisoned comrade, the resistance hero Max Freidank. Although he is relatively safe in America, Müller will almost certainly be killed on his return to Germany if de Brancovis identifies him to the Nazis. Therefore, in a scene that caused considerable controversy at the time, Müller is forced to kill de Brancovis to keep him quiet. He then returns to Germany on his rescue mission. Since the Production Code in effect in Hollywood at the time dictated that anyone committing a murder in a film had to pay for the crime, the film then ends with a coda, set several months later, in which Sarah speaks with her eldest son, Joshua (Donald Buka) about the fact that Müller seems to have disappeared without a trace. Joshua vows to go to Germany to try to rescue his father, or at least to continue the fight, as soon as he reaches the age of eighteen, which will occur in a few months. Sarah at first vetoes the idea, then tearfully endorses it, knowing that the fight against the Nazis transcends personal concerns.

Although principally a thriller that doubles as American prowar propaganda, *Watch on the Rhine* manages to make a few leftist points along the way, as in a utopian speech by Sarah that envisions history as a dialectical battle that ultimately progresses toward a better day. Müller expresses a similar idea in his farewell speech to Joshua, in which he identifies his goal as bringing an end to a world in which some men are rich while others go hungry. Indeed, though it is never suggested openly in the film, given Müller's dedicated battle against the Nazis (and given his participation in the war in Spain), the chances are very good that he is meant to be perceived, at least by the initiated, as a communist. Indeed, Hellman modeled Müller after Otto Katz, a member of the German Communist Party who served in the 1930s as a representative of the Comintern in America, where he helped raise funds for anti-Nazi activities (Ceplair and Englund 106). Ironically (given that it was essentially a piece of pro-American propaganda), the film's subtle leftist cues probably contributed to both Hammett and Hellman being called before the House Un-American Activities Committee, where both were uncooperative witnesses. Hammett was subsequently imprisoned and blacklisted, receiving no screen credits after 1947; Hellman was blacklisted, receiving no screen credits between 1946 and 1961. Hellman recounts this experience in her memoir of the McCarthyite purge of Hollywood, *Scoundrel Time*. **Screenplay:** Dashiell Hammett and Lillian Hellman. **Selected bibliography:** Ceplair and Englund; Hellman (*Scoundrel Time*); Patraka.

***DOUBLE INDEMNITY*: DIR. BILLY WILDER (1944).** *Double Indemnity* is one of the defining works of the film noir. All the elements of that genre are present in the film: shadowy lighting and extreme camera angles reinforce the brooding atmosphere, while a tough, cynical antihero (who nevertheless has a soft spot) seeks ill-gotten gain while working both with and against a slinky femme fatale. The film is also notable for its snappy, rapid-fire dialogue, co-written by Raymond Chandler and director Wilder, from the novel by James M. Cain. As R. Barton Palmer notes, the film is remarkable both for its combination of European and American points of view and for the way its look, dialogue, and soundtrack work smoothly together to present a darkly cynical vision of the corrupt nature of modern society. James Agee, in an early review, noted that the film is "soaked in and shot through with money and the coolly intricate amorality of money" (119). In *Double Indemnity*, corruption and violence reside in every aspect of American life, while the general tone of the film suggests the anxiety that pervaded American society at the time. The contrast between the film's cynical vision and the usual rosy view of Hollywood fare may account for the fact that, while *Double Indemnity* was nominated for seven Academy Awards, including best picture, it won none.

In *Double Indemnity*, the antihero is insurance salesman Walter Neff (Fred MacMurray), who doubles as the narrator. The dangerous dame is unhappy suburban wife Phyllis Dietrichson (Barbara Stanwyck). Neff and Phyllis first meet when he makes a sales call at the Dietrichson home. When Neff's sexual fascination with her (and her ankle bracelet) becomes obvious, Phyllis tries to enlist him in a plan to take out a generous life insurance policy on her husband (Tom Powers) and then murder him. Neff, however, knows the formidable investigative powers of his company's claims manager, Barton Keyes (Edward G. Robinson). He therefore believes that they will never get away with the murder and resists the plan. Nevertheless, he becomes involved in an affair with Phyllis and eventually concocts what seems to be a foolproof plan for the murder.

Neff and Phyllis conspire to take out a $50,000 accidental death insurance policy on Dietrichson without the latter's knowledge. The policy includes a double indemnity clause that doubles the payoff should Dietrichson be killed in an accident involving a train. Then they kill Dietrichson, who has recently suffered a broken leg, by breaking his neck. Neff then boards a train posing as Dietrichson, walking on crutches. He then leaps from the back of the train. Phyllis drives up to meet him, and they deposit the crutches and Dietrichson's body on the track, making it look as if he had been killed in falling from the train.

Smooth though this plan may be, the wily and naturally suspicious Keyes immediately smells a rat and begins to investigate the case closely. In the meantime, Neff and Phyllis have to stay away from each other until the heat is off. Neff, however, learns that Phyllis is apparently seeing another man, Nino Zachette (Byron Barr), during this time. This discovery, combined with the growing pressure created by Keyes's investigation, begins to drive a wedge between Neff and Phyllis. In the meantime, however, Phyllis's involvement with Zachette leads Keyes to conclude that Zachette was Phyllis's co-conspirator in the killing of Dietrichson. Neff has a final violent confrontation with Phyllis, who shoots him in the shoulder. He takes the gun away from her and shoots her. Neff plans to pin her killing on Zachette, but then has an attack of conscience and staggers, wounded, back to the insurance company office, where he records a detailed confession on the office dictaphone. This confession provides the narrative framework for the entire film, which occurs in flashback as the confession proceeds. As the film draws to a close, Keyes shows up at the office and learns the whole story, calling an ambulance as Neff collapses, unconscious. *Double Indemnity* makes its criminals seem rather sympathetic, especially as their principal antagonist is a large, impersonal insurance company. However, they are ultimately no match for this corporate entity, which triumphs in the end. *Screenplay:* Raymond Chandler and Billy Wilder. *Selected bibliography:* Agee; Neve (*Film*); Naremore (*More than Night*); Palmer (*Hollywood's Dark Cinema*); Silver and Ward; Willett.

*LAURA:* **DIR. OTTO PREMINGER (1944).** Adapted from Vera Caspary's 1943 mystery novel by the same title, *Laura* is a stylish thriller widely considered to be one of the leading examples of American film noir. Caspary, a member of the Communist Party during the 1930s, maintained leftist sympathies well through the writing of *Laura*, though leftist politics are present in the book (and even more in the film) in only the most subtle and oblique ways. As the film begins, we learn that the title character, Laura Hunt (played by Gene Tierney), has apparently just been murdered. The majority of the film involves the efforts of tough-but-tender New York detective Mark McPherson (Dana Andrews) to investigate the killing, supplemented by flashbacks that introduce the viewer to the kind and beautiful Laura and help to establish the nature of her relationships with various other characters, most of them suspects in the crime. These include the pompous newspaper columnist and radio commentator Waldo Lydecker (played with great aplomb by Clifton Webb), the now-impoverished socialite Shelby Carpenter (Vincent Price), and Laura's wealthy aunt, Ann Treadwell (Judith Anderson). The wealthy Lydecker is a friend of Laura who had helped her, through his numerous connections, to get started in the advertising business, where she had been a great success, rising to become an executive in the firm of Bullitt and Company. Although much older than Laura, Lydecker clearly had romantic designs on her, and it is eventually revealed that he has systematically interfered in her relationships with other men, breaking up most of them. Laura's relationship with Carpenter, to whom Laura had been engaged to be married, appears to have been an exception, though Carpenter is a gigolo and ne'er-do-well who hardly seems suitable for the talented and intelligent Laura. Carpenter appears to be the principal suspect through most of the film, largely because, as he puts it, "I'm a natural suspect, just because I'm not the conventional type." Treadwell, who has been having an affair with Carpenter on the side, is a natural suspect as well.

In the process of his investigation, McPherson, his tough exterior notwithstanding, becomes more and more fascinated with Laura, seeming to fall in love with the portrait of her that hangs in her apartment, where the brutal killing, via a shotgun blast to the face, took place. Then, as he sits in the apartment asleep in a chair, he is suddenly awakened when Laura herself returns, having spent the last few days at her country house reconsidering her upcoming marriage to Carpenter. From that point on, things develop rather rapidly. It becomes clear that the murdered woman was Diane Redfern, a model for Bullitt and Company, who had also been having an affair with Carpenter and had been installed by him in Laura's apartment in her absence. McPherson rapidly puts two and two together and soon deduces that Lydecker had killed Refern out of jealousy, thinking that she was Laura. The film then ends after a tense final scene in which Lydecker nearly kills Laura after all, but is instead himself killed as McPherson and other policemen burst in with guns blazing.

In terms of politics, *Laura* does virtually nothing with its opportunity to critique the advertising industry. The book, incidentally, does more, especially in its depiction (absent in the film) of the way Redfern becomes involved in the advertising business, and in the circles that led to her death, through her fascination with the images she observes in popular magazines. Moreover, we learn in the book, but not in the film, that Redfern (real name Jennie Swoboda) was of Central European extraction and had formerly worked in the silk mills of Paterson, New Jersey, site of the famous strike. The only real working-class character who appears in the film, Laura's faithful maid, Bessie, is treated rather condescendingly, as almost petlike in her devotion and loyalty to Laura. Nevertheless, it is the wealthy Lydecker who turns out to be the murderer, while the other upper-class characters, Carpenter and Treadwell, are depicted as decadent and devoid of morals. Among the characters, only Laura, who worked her way up to the top from relatively humble beginnings, and McPherson, a figure of authority but not of wealth or social standing, are presented as admirable. Indeed, Lydecker's final speech to Laura, in which he describes his class-based disgust at her budding relationship with McPherson, helps to establish class as an issue in the film, aligning the idle rich with evil and more common working people with virtue. *Screenplay:* Jerry Cady, Jay Dratler, Samuel Hoffenstein, Ring Lardner, Jr., and Elizabeth Reinhardt. *Selected bibliography:* Denning; Naremore (*More than Night*); Silver and Ward.

*MURDER, MY SWEET:* DIR. EDWARD DMYTRYK (1944). An excellent adaptation of the Raymond Chandler novel, *Farewell, My Lovely* (under which title the film was released in the United Kingdom), *Murder, My Sweet* helped to establish the film noir as a dominant genre in American film. Dick Powell stars as hard-boiled detective Philip Marlowe, hired by ex-con Moose Molloy (Mike Mazurki) to find his missing girlfriend, Velma Valento (Claire Trevor). In the meantime, Marlowe is hired by Mrs. Grayle, young wife of a wealthy, but old and ailing husband (Miles Mander), to find a valuable stolen jade necklace. Marlowe then moves from the seedy world in which he has been unsuccessfully seeking Velma to the Grayles' posh upper-class world, in the meantime becoming romantically interested in Ann Grayle (Anne Shirley), Grayle's daughter by a previous marriage. Eventually, however, the two worlds begin to converge, and Marlowe realizes that Mrs. Grayle is, in fact, Velma. Marlowe arranges a meeting among the principals involved in both cases, resulting in a shootout in which Moose, Mrs. Grayle, and Mr. Grayle are all killed. Marlowe is himself hurt in the fracas, then arrested by police, but eventually cleared by Ann's testimony. As the film ends, Marlowe and Ann ride away together in a cab, kissing. The plot is thus resolved, though in this film the plot is secondary. It is the film noir look that dominates, especially in some intermediate sequences when Marlowe has been drugged by the minions of the evil Jules Amthor (Otto Kruger), who is also seeking the necklace (which Velma/Mrs. Grayle turns out to have had all along), leading to some bizarre hallucinations.

*Murder, My Sweet* is generally considered Dmytryk's best film. Described by Silver and Ward as "one of the quintessential noir films," *Murder, My Sweet* exemplifies the expressionist lighting, odd camera angles, and generally sinister atmosphere that are central to the genre (192). Powell's performance meshes perfectly with the film's noir look and establishes one of the screen's central images of the hard-boiled detective. Together, the film's look and subject matter combine to create a disturbing vision of the dark side of capitalist society, many elements of which are clearly designed as antifascist commentary. On the other hand, the film's dialogue between the world of Moose Molloy and that of the Grayles suggests a broader critique of the class differences upon which capitalist society is built. The film's political implications thus justify Mike Davis's description of film noir as a genre that approaches "a kind of Marxist *cinema manqué*, a shrewdly oblique strategy for an otherwise subversive realism" (41). *Screenplay:* John Paxton. *Selected bibliography:* Davis; Dick (*Radical Innocence*); Dmytryk; Lester D. Friedman; Palmer (*Hollywood's Dark Cinema*); Silver and Ward; Telotte.

*WILSON:* **DIR. HENRY KING (1944).** *Wilson* was a lavish, big-budget production, intended by producer Darryl F. Zanuck to be a major commercial and critical success. It was, in fact, a disappointment at the box office, though it received reasonably good reviews. It also received ten Academy Award nominations, winning four, but losing in the important categories of best picture and best director, much to the frustration of Zanuck. *Wilson* is, in many ways, an impressive production, with elaborate sets and costumes that help to establish the film's historical setting. It is, however, rather ponderous and slow-moving as it traces the career of Woodrow Wilson (played by Alexander Knox) from 1909, when he left the presidency of Princeton University to enter politics, subsequently experiencing a meteoric rise that saw him become the governor of New Jersey in 1910 and the President of the United States in 1913. The film traces, though rather superficially, his presidential career, as he introduces a number of reforms while struggling to keep the United States out of World War I. Re-elected in 1916 on a platform of staying out of the war, he nevertheless takes the U.S. into the war in 1917 under circumstances that are, according to the film, beyond his control, forced by German provocations. The latter parts of the film are devoted to Wilson's central role in the peace negotiations that followed World War I, focusing especially on his devotion to the concept of the League of Nations, a concept that failed partly because the United States never entered the league. As a result of this refusal, Wilson leaves office at the end of the film a broken and defeated man, nearing death.

*Wilson* is weak as a historical epic, spending more time on the protagonist's private life than on the crucial historical events in which he was centrally involved. In fact, it is really not a historical film at all, but a hagiography of Wilson. It provides very little in the way of genuine explanations of the historical events it describes, while presenting only Wilson's side of the various issues it discusses. As a result, Wilson in the film always looks good, while his critics and opponents either appear evil or do not appear at all. Most important, *Wilson* almost entirely elides the very real controversy that surrounded Wilson's reversal of policy on the U.S. participation in World War I. It dismisses criticism of the move as not worthy of consideration and leaves out altogether the important critique of that move on the Left, a critique that is captured in capsule form in the satirical biographical sketch of Wilson included in John Dos Passos's *1919*, which depicts Wilson as a tool of big business.

There is, however, a political message in the film, which in a number of subtle ways depicts Wilson as the predecessor of Franklin Roosevelt, so that its celebration of Wilson can be taken as an expression of support for Roosevelt's New Deal. Roosevelt's opponents, in fact, complained that the film was propaganda in support of Roosevelt's fourth term. Most centrally, the film's depiction of the controversy over the League of Nations represents a clear plea for the U.S. to learn from that episode and to pursue a more enlightened policy in support of world peace after World War II, which at the time of the film's release had turned strongly in favor of the Allies and already seemed to be nearing its final phases. In retrospect, the film can be read as a warning against precisely the antagonistic policies that led to the Cold War. This warning, of course, was not heeded, and the main result of the film was simply an increase in both popular and scholarly interest in Wilson and his administration. *Screenplay:* Lamar Trotti. *Selected bibliography:* Bailey; Knock; Koppes and Black.

*CORNERED:* DIR. EDWARD DMYTRYK (1945). *Cornered* is, in many ways, a typical example of the antifascist thrillers that were popular in American film during and just after World War II. It is also a founding work of the film noir. The plot is structured around a combined manhunt and whodunit in which Laurence Gerard (played by Dick Powell), a Royal Canadian Air Force flier and former prisoner of war, attempts to track down Marcel Jarnac (Luther Adler), a Nazi collaborator in the French Vichy regime, because Jarnac betrayed Gerard's French war bride to the Nazis, leading to her death. Jarnac is reported to be dead, but Gerard believes those reports to be fabricated. He tracks Jarnac through Switzerland and on to Argentina, where he finds not only numerous Nazis, but also an underground group of Nazi hunters (some of whom he at first mistakes for Nazis). Gerard's hunt is complicated by the fact that he has no idea what Jarnac looks like, so that any of the suspicious characters he meets along the way might potentially be the man he seeks. The complications increase further when Gerard finds himself drawn to Jarnac's wife (Micheline Cheirel), who, oddly enough, has also never seen Jarnac, whom she married in absentia as a means of escaping France, where life had become difficult for her because of her father's former collaboration with the Nazis. After several false leads (and tense moments), Gerard finally encounters Jarnac. In a classic noir scene, they talk, while Jarnac remains obscured in shadow, still a man of mystery. Eventually, Gerard and Jarnac fight; Gerard blacks out during the fight, then awakes to find that he has beaten the evil Jarnac to death. In the meantime, Gerard also recovers important documents revealing the workings of the Nazi operation in Argentina.

In his recantation of his former communist affiliations before HUAC on April 25, 1951, Dmytryk claimed that his decision to leave the Communist Party was partly actuated by his squabbles with fellow communists Adrian Scott (the producer), John Wexley (who worked on a treatment on which the screenplay was based), and John Howard Lawson (to whom Wexley appealed for support in his battles with Dmytryk) during the making of the film. The controversy largely arose over Paxton's deletions of Wexley's indications of cooperation between vestigial Nazis and international capital and over a line spoken by Jarnac at the end of the film in which his fascist viewpoint might be interpreted as similar to communism, its ideological opposite. Part of the confusion arose because the ideology of fascism is never really specified in the film, which largely presents fascism as a moral, rather than ideological evil. As a result, virtually any ideology that one wished to demonize could be plugged into the slot occupied by fascism in the film, as in, fact, communism would soon be in the upcoming purges that swept Hollywood, sending Dmytryk, Lawson, and Scott to prison as members of the Hollywood Ten. *Screenplay:* John Paxton, from a story by John Wexley. *Selected bibliography:* Ceplair and Englund; Dick (*Radical Innocence*); Dmytryk; Lester D. Friedman; Silver and Ward.

*COUNTER-ATTACK:* **DIR. ZOLTAN KORDA (1945).** *Counter-Attack* joins the earlier *Sahara* and *Action in the North Atlantic* (both released in 1943) to comprise a trilogy of World War II films scripted by leftist screenwriter John Howard Lawson. All three of these films are striking in their emphasis on collective, rather than individual, action as the key to success in the war. *Counter-Attack,* meanwhile, is in some ways the most clearly leftist of the three. Based on a play of the same title by leftist writers Janet and Philip Stevenson, which is itself based on the Soviet play *Robyeta* by Ilya Vershinin and Mikhail Ruderman, *Counter-Attack* is the only American war film to focus on the Eastern Front and on the battles of the Soviet Red Army against the Soviet Union's Nazi invaders. Thom Anderson calls *Counter-Attack* the "most radical" of all of Hollywood's pro-Soviet wartime productions, arguing that it is as much communist propaganda as is *Battleship Potemkin* (167). Dorothy Jones, on the other hand, finds very little in the way of communist propaganda in the film, which was surely intended as a contribution to the American war effort (212).

In truth, *Counter-Attack* has very little to do with communism, but instead merely presents its Soviet characters as courageous and virtuous and as embodying very much the same values as the American soldiers in Lawson's other war films. Though beginning with several minutes of furious action of a battle between the Russians and Germans, the film quickly settles into a psychological drama centering on Alexei Kulkov (Paul Muni), an ordinary Russian soldier who is trapped behind the German lines in the cellar of a bombed-out factory building, along with a female partisan, Lisa Elenko (Marguerite Chapman). The Russians wait to be rescued, meanwhile trying to maintain control of seven German soldiers whom they have taken prisoner. One of the Germans, Ernemann (Harro Meller), is an officer who turns out to have crucial information about the German defenses. Muni and Meller are both impressive in their enactment of the subsequent battle of wits and wills between Kulkov and Ernemann, each of whom divulges valuable secrets in order to convince the other to do likewise. At one point, Kulkov nearly falls asleep, and the Germans manage to get his rifle and wound Elenko. Kulkov regains his weapon, and, though desperate for sleep, manages to hold out, with the help of one of the Germans, Stillman (Rudolph Anders), who despises Hitler and is in the war against his will. In the end, a Russian party comes to the rescue, during which Kulkov, first thinking they are Germans, shoots and kills Ernemann to prevent him from passing on the information he has garnered from Kulkov. Kulkov, meanwhile, falls asleep and is carried off on a stretcher but will presumably convey valuable information to his Soviet comrades. *Screenplay:* John Howard Lawson. *Selected bibliography:* Thom Anderson; Carr; Jones.

**DETOUR: DIR. EDGAR G. ULMER (1945).** Shot in a few days on a shoestring budget, *Detour* has nevertheless become something of a cult classic, especially among fans of film noir. The film begins as the protagonist, Al Roberts (Tom Neal), looking seedy and very much worse for the wear, hitchhikes the back roads of America, stopping off at a roadside diner. There, he hears a love song playing on the juke box, which triggers a chain of memories that explains how he got to this point and that provides the actual narrative of the film. This narrative begins in New York, where Roberts works as a piano player in a cheap club. His fiancée, Sue Harvey (Claudia Drake), works in the club as a singer but dreams of bigger and better things. Toward that end, she decides to go away to Hollywood to try to become a star. Roberts, skeptical of the whole idea, stays behind. In Hollywood, Sue finds that stardom is not so easy to come by and ends up working as a waitress. Learning of this, Roberts decides to travel across the country to marry her: if they are both going to have to struggle to get by, they might as well do it together.

Roberts, however, has no cash for the trip, triggering a speech about the evils of money—or at least of the lack of it. He decides to hitchhike, and things look up when he is picked up by Charles Haskell (Edmund MacDonald), who offers him a ride all the way through to Los Angeles. But good luck never lasts long in this dark and brooding film. The mysterious Haskell, who spends most of the time popping pills or describing the origins of his various scars, suddenly dies along the way. Convinced he will be blamed for Haskell's death, Roberts decides to hide the body and continue on in the car. Realizing that he cannot get far without money, he reluctantly takes Haskell's wallet, which contains $768 and identification that will allow him to pose as Haskell.

Roberts manages to reach California, where he picks up an attractive, but embittered woman hitchhiker, who tells him to call her Vera. Vera soon becomes Roberts's worst nightmare, attempting to exploit him in her own effort to achieve the American dream. As luck would have it, she had earlier hitched a ride with Haskell (and given him some of his scars). She accuses Roberts of murdering Haskell, then threatens to tell the police if Roberts does not do as she says. He then becomes her virtual prisoner as they make their way to Los Angeles, where they learn that Haskell's wealthy father is nearing death. Knowing that Haskell had been estranged from his family for more than fifteen years, Vera concocts a plan for Roberts to go on pretending to be Haskell so that he can claim the inheritance when the father dies. When Roberts refuses to cooperate, Vera decides to call the police. Roberts then accidentally strangles her with the phone cord in the subsequent altercation. Knowing that he will certainly be blamed for this death, Roberts gives up his dream of marrying Sue and goes on the lam, hitchhiking across America (and thus into the opening scene of the film), waiting for the moment when he will be picked up by police.

R. Barton Palmer calls *Detour* "undoubtedly the finest example of a purely noir thriller," noting that in it "the ordinary social optimism of the Hollywood film is entirely overthrown in favor of a despairing view of American life" (108). The contrast between the film's bleak vision and the typically bright vision of America presented by Hollywood is indeed striking, and in ways with numerous social and political implications. For example, Roberts depicts himself as the victim of blind fate and pure bad luck, but it is also clear that his main misfortune is simply a lack of cash, thus suggesting that the American dream, which so thoroughly fails to materialize in this film, is only available to those who can make the payments. The emphasis on luck and fate, in turn, suggests that those who can make these payments cannot necessarily do so because of their own hard work or ability, except perhaps their ability to exploit others. *Screenplay:* Martin Goldsmith. *Selected bibliography:* Buhle; Neve (*Film*); Naremore (*More than Night*); Palmer (*Hollywood's Dark Cinema*).

*OBJECTIVE, BURMA!:* **DIR. RAOUL WALSH (1945).** *Objective, Burma!* is a rousing combat drama, filled with action and suspense, as well as mythic structures. However, it contains little in the way of leftist politics, despite the participation of leftist writers Lester Cole and Alvah Bessie. In some ways, it is still one of the best war films made in America during World War II, partly because it is relatively free of the patriotic clichés that tend to dominate such films. The film does, however, characterize the Japanese as thoroughly "evil," and audiences are encouraged to hate them. Indeed, one character, a British war correspondent (played by Henry Hull), at one point declares that the Japanese are degenerate savages who should be wiped off the face of the earth. Bessie and Cole protested against this scene, arguing that Japanese brutality should be associated with the ideology of fascism, not with the racial savagery of the Japanese (Koppes and Black 263). They were, however, overruled. The Japanese are also frequently referred to as "monkeys," but they are at least depicted as formidable and capable opponents for the Americans.

The film begins as the Allied forces, training in India, prepare for an all-out invasion in the effort to retake Burma, a British colony recently occupied by the Japanese. As a preliminary, a force of American para-troopers, commanded by Major Charlie Nelson (Errol Flynn, in one of his less obnoxious performances), are dropped into the interior of Burma on a mission to destroy a Japanese radar post in the midst of the jungle. Finding and destroying the post, however, turns out to be the easy part of the mission. Having accomplished that goal without a single casualty, the Americans discover that they are cut off by the Japanese and cannot be retrieved by plane as originally planned. Instead, they are forced to try get out of Burma on foot, struggling through 150 miles of dense jungle, much of it heavily patrolled by the Japanese. Supplies are peri-odically dropped to them by the Allies along the way, but conditions are still incredibly arduous. Moreover, after the Americans split into two groups, one group is ambushed by the Japanese. Those who are not killed in this original assault are then taken to a Burmese village for questioning, where they are horribly tortured to death. The discovery of their mutilated bodies triggers the war correspondent's denunciation of the Japanese.

Finally, the Americans make it to the location specified by Allied headquarters, but find themselves seemingly in the middle of nowhere. Meanwhile, they have to beat off another furious Japanese assault after they arrive. Then, the American-led Allied invasion begins, and Nelson, accompanied by the handful of survivors from his original force of more than fifty, is rescued by the invading troops, flown back to India in a glider. The film ends as the invasion begins, though a final on-screen message announces that, while this particular narrative has reached its conclusion, "this story ... will end only when the evil forces of Japan are totally destroyed."

*Objective, Burma!* was highly successful in the U.S., though it caused a scandal in Great Britain for its emphasis on Americans to the almost total exclusion of the British, which was especially problematic given that the Allied forces in Burma consisted almost entirely of British troops. The film won three Academy Award nominations, including one to Bessie for best original story, though the final film bore little resemblance to Bessie's treatment, while the story was not really original, but was adapted from a nonfiction book entitled *Merrill's Marauders*. In fact, after Bessie was given the book (for which Warner Brothers had not paid for screen rights) and directed to adapt it, changing the British to Americans, both he and Cole objected that this was essentially plagiarism. Again, the studio ignored their protests. *Screenplay:* Ranald McDougall, Lester Cole, and Alvah Bessie (story). *Selected bibliography:* Cole (*Hollywood Red*); Koppes and Black; Robert Ray.

## THE STORY OF G.I. JOE: DIR. WILLIAM WELLMAN (1945).

In some ways, *The Story of G.I. Joe* is a fairly straightforward, though unusually realistic, example of the World War II film, designed both to entertain and to drum up enthusiasm for the American war effort. On the other hand, the film was not released until the war in Europe was over, and its late placement perhaps shows in its unglamorous treatment of combat, emphasizing not the heroism of its soldiers but their weariness and daily hardships. Based on the reports of legendary war correspondent Ernie Pyle (especially his 1943 book, *Here Is Your War*) and featuring Pyle (played by Burgess Meredith) as the central character, the film details the grueling effect of extended combat service on a platoon of American soldiers the Italian campaign. Led by Lieutenant Walker (Robert Mitchum) and accompanied by Pyle, the platoon slowly advances, experiencing both danger and boredom but very little in the way of glory.

British audiences reacted negatively to *The Story of G.I. Joe*, which, as the title implies, focuses on American soldiers. In fact, the film omits all reference to the contribution made by British combatants in the North African and Italian campaigns. In the U.S., however, the film was successful enough to win four Academy Award nominations, including to Mitchum for best supporting actor and to the three screenwriters (two of whom, Endore and Stevenson, were prominent figures on the American cultural Left) for best screenplay. While some felt the film's depiction of war was so grim as to make it an antiwar movie, James Agee declared it a "tragic and eternal work of art" precisely because of its unflinching portrayal of the realities of combat (174). Pyle never saw the film; moving on to cover the war in the Pacific, he was killed there in the last months of the war. *Screenplay:* Leopold Atlas, Guy Endore, and Philip Stevenson. *Selected bibliography:* Agee; Pyle; Shindler.

*THE BEST YEARS OF OUR LIVES:* DIR. WILLIAM WYLER (1946). Specifically marketed by producer Samuel Goldwyn as a "great" film, *The Best Years of Our Lives* was an expensive project that many expected to be a box office disaster. Instead, it went on to become one of the biggest grossing pictures in American film history to that time. It also received considerable critical acclaim, eventually winning six Academy Awards, including those in such major prestige categories as best picture, best director, best actor (Fredric March), and best screenplay. In addition, handless veteran Harold Russell won a special Academy Award as a supporting actor for bringing hope to disabled servicemen, while Goldwyn won the Thalberg Award as the industry's top producer for the year. The film, with its central theme of the readjustment of returning servicemen to civilian society, clearly struck a chord with American audiences and critics in the immediate aftermath of World War II, especially as it treats this theme sensitively, intelligently, and (by the standards of American film of the time) realistically.

*The Best Years of Our Lives* begins as Air Force Captain Fred Derry (Dana Andrews), Army Sergeant Al Stephenson (March), and Navy sailor Homer Parrish (Russell), all previously unacquainted, separately try to make their ways back to their home town of Boone City after demobilization. The film begins with an ominous warning of the problems that may be facing these veterans, as Derry finds himself unable to get aboard a commercial flight, while a wealthy businessman, carrying golf clubs, gets first-class service. Eventually, the three veterans are able to catch a ride on a military bomber that happens to be headed for an airbase near Boone City. On the flight, the three become friends, introducing themselves to each other and to the audience. Derry is a young man from a working-class background who has achieved unaccustomed status as an officer (and decorated hero) in the war. He was married only days before he went overseas and is eager to become acquainted with his new wife, whom he really hardly knows. Stephenson is a middle-aged banker with a wife, a grown daughter, and a teenage son. Parrish is a young man returning home with considerable trepidation, wondering how he will be greeted by his family and his sweetheart now that both of his hands have been lost in the war, replaced by mechanical hooks.

When they reach Boone City, each of the three has his own individual problems adjusting to civilian society. Derry finds that his war record carries little weight in the postwar world; expecting to find a good job, he is able to find employment only as a lowly paid counter clerk in a drug store. In the meantime, tensions grow in his fledgling marriage as his fun-loving wife, Marie (Virginia Mayo), begins to realize that the civilian Derry is a far less romantic figure than the dashing military officer she married. Parrish's problems predictably revolve around his lost hands. His family and his sweetheart, Wilma (Cathy O'Donnell), struggle to be understanding and make him feel comfortable, but clearly feel awkward around him. For his own part, Parrish grows increasingly bitter and withdrawn, rejecting their pity, but with it their compassion. Stephenson seems to have the best situation of all; he returns to a stable and loving family and also to economic prosperity. In fact, he not only gets back his job in the bank, but is promoted to vice president in charge of small loans in anticipation that many of the small-loan customers will be returning GI's with whom Stephenson will be able to deal in an especially informed manner.

As the film proceeds, however, Stephenson finds that his comfortable position makes him feel guilty given the problems of other ex-servicemen. Moreover, he has conflicts with the bank when they discourage him from being so trusting and generous in approving loans. He also comes into conflict with Derry when the latter, growing increasingly estranged from his wife, falls in love with Stephenson's daughter, Peggy (Teresa Wright), who returns his feelings. Parrish remains withdrawn, though he begins to develop his ability to deal with others through the good offices of his uncle, Butch Engle (Hoagy Carmichael). Eventually, all seems to work out well. The film ends at the wedding of Parrish and Wilma, at which Derry, now having been left by his wife, agrees to share his life with Peggy, who ends the film in his arms.

Among other things, the scene at this final wedding obscures and simplifies certain problems and issues, such as the class differences among the three returning veterans. Left-leaning critics were quick to point out the superficiality of the film's social analysis, and it is certainly the case that there is very little in the way of genuine political statement in the film. The only vaguely leftist moment occurs when an obnoxious customer in the drug store where Derry works complains that the American war effort was misdirected and that we should have been fighting the Russians instead of the Germans. The man is then quickly silenced when he first scuffles with Parrish and is then knocked through a glass counter by Derry. If this problem is thus solved quickly, it is also the case that the more significant problems the film details in relation to the three veterans seem to be solved rather too easily as well.

There are, however, unanswered questions that remain, giving the ending of the film an edge that is lacking in the typical fairy tale conclusions of Hollywood films. *The Best Years of Our Lives* makes it clear that Parrish's missing hands will continue to diminish the quality of his life, however devoted and understanding Wilma might be. It is also clear that Derry and Peggy will have a long struggle against both social and economic problems, though he has recently gotten a better, and highly symbolic, job working for a company that recycles military aircraft into prefabricated housing. Stephenson, successful banker though he may be, remains unsettled and is clearly developing a drinking problem. He thus stands, at the end of the film, as a nagging reminder that all is not right with the American dream in the wake of the war and as an anticipation of the coming wave of increasing alienation that will sweep the American populace in the decades after the war. *Screenplay:* Robert E. Sherwood. *Selected bibliography:* Martin A. Jackson; Polonsky; Robert Ray; Schatz (*Boom*); Warshow (*Immediate Experience*).

*CLOAK AND DAGGER:* DIR. FRITZ LANG (1946). When the OSS (Office of Strategic Services, predecessor to the CIA) realizes that they lack the technical expertise to interpret much of the technical information that is coming in via their intelligence gathering in support of the Allied side in World War II, they turn for help to American physics professor Alvah Jesper (Gary Cooper). Jesper is at first reluctant to join the intelligence agency, complaining that there seems to be plenty of government funding available to support the war effort, but little for peacetime research such as finding a cure for cancer. But, when he learns that respected physicist Katerin Loder (Helene Thimig) has defected from Germany and is now in Switzerland, he agrees to go there to meet with her on behalf of the OSS. When he does meet her, he learns that the Nazis have threatened to begin executing prisoners unless she goes to go to Italy to work on nuclear weapons research with Italian physicist Giovanni Polda (Vladimir Sokoloff). Jesper suggests that she go to Italy but serve as an Allied spy there. Before she can do so, she is kidnapped by the Nazis, who have identified Jesper as a probable enemy agent. Jesper, meanwhile, is contacted by an American woman, Ann Dawson (Marjorie Hoshelle), working as a Nazi agent. Jesper outsmarts Dawson and manages to get her to reveal the location of the house where Loder is being held, but Loder is shot and killed when Allied agents go there to rescue her.

Recognizing the potential danger of the Nazi nuclear weapons program, Jesper himself goes to Italy to contact Polda. Aided by Allied agents headed by an agent whose code name is "Pinkie" (played by Robert Alda), Jesper discovers that Polda passionately hates the Italian fascists and their German Nazi backers but is working for them because they are holding his daughter hostage. Polda agrees to defect to the Allies if they can first get his daughter out safely. While that plan is being carried out, Jesper hides out with Gina (Lilli Palmer), an Italian woman working as an agent of the Allies. The two experience a series of narrow escapes from fascists as the obligatory Hollywood romance blooms between them. In the end, it turns out that Polda's daughter has been dead for months. Pinkie, meanwhile, is killed holding off a fascist assault while Jesper, Polda, and Gina escape to a waiting plane. Jesper bids a tearful farewell to Gina, who stays behind to continue the fight. He promises that he will return for her as soon as conditions make it possible.

Lang and the screenwriters of *Cloak and Dagger* had hoped to include a strong statement against nuclear weapons in the film, but that statement was nixed by the studio, which allowed only Jesper's initial speech about the value of peacetime research. As a result, the film is rather conventional Hollywood fare, with little in the way of real political statement. Its indictment of fascism is clear, but somewhat taken for granted. The main political position it supports is good old-fashioned American patriotism. *Screenplay:* Albert Maltz and Ring Lardner, Jr. *Selected bibliography:* Humphries; McGilligan; Ott; Sayre.

*FROM THIS DAY FORWARD:* DIR. JOHN BERRY (1946). *From This Day Forward* was the first film directed by Berry, a promising young director who would go on to become a leading practitioner of what Thom Anderson has identified as film gris. However, Berry's career in Hollywood would soon be cut short when he was identified as a communist by Edward Dmytryk and other witnesses testifying before HUAC. Berry subsequently directed a brief film entitled *The Hollywood Ten* (1951), produced to raise money for the legal defense of those being persecuted by HUAC. He then moved to Europe and continued his career there, returning to work in the United States only in the 1970s.

*From This Day Forward* is based on the novel *All Brides Are Beautiful* (1931), by Thomas Bell. It deals with the travails of an ordinary married couple amid the economic hardships of the Depression. The film occasionally gestures toward a realistic depiction of the lives of Bill and Susan Cummings (played by Mark Stevens and Joan Fontaine), and some of its commentary on their plight has a potential political charge. Bill, for example, has returned from military service only to find that the society he had gone away to defend offers him little in the way of appreciation or reward. Instead, he struggles to make a life with Susan amid crushing poverty. Most of the story is told via flashbacks that narrate the beginnings of their courtship, his draft into the army, and his hassles with government employment centers after his return. In the end, however, all is well, despite the Depression. Their love allows them to overcome the various obstacles placed in their way, giving the film a romantic, but entirely unrealistic happy ending. The film thus lacks the political bite of the original novel, in which, among other things, Bill is not an army veteran, but a committed communist, whose politics are an important part of his life. The book, incidentally, also ends on an optimistic note — by looking forward to a proletarian revolution, a far cry from the entirely private resolution offered by the film. *Screenplay:* Garson Kanin, Edith Sommer, Hugo Butler, and Charles Schnee. *Selected bibliography:* Thom Anderson; Neve (*Film*).

*NOTORIOUS:* **DIR. ALFRED HITCHCOCK (1946).** *Notorious* is Hitchcock's contribution to the spate of anti-Nazi thrillers that was produced during and just after World War II. It begins just after the end of the war in a courtroom in Florida, where German-American John Huberman is being sentenced to twenty years in prison for treason for conspiring with the German Nazis against the United States. The focus then shifts to Huberman's daughter, Alicia (Ingrid Bergman), a jet-setter of notorious reputation. American agent T. R. Devlin (Cary Grant) is assigned to keep Alicia under surveillance and, having ascertained her loyalty to the U.S., to try to enlist her in an effort to root out a ring of Nazi agents known to be operating in Brazil. Devlin succeeds in recruiting Alicia, and the two of them go together to Rio de Janeiro to begin the mission. They also begin a torrid love affair, only to learn after their arrival in Brazil that it will be Alicia's mission to seduce Alexander Sebastian (Claude Rains), a key member of the Nazi ring, who also happens to be an old friend of Alicia's father and to have formerly been in love with Alicia.

Alicia agrees to take the assignment, though the nature of it breeds considerable tension between her and Devlin, who is furiously jealous of Sebastian and highly suspicious of Alicia's quick success in winning the Nazi's confidence. Sebastian and Alicia are soon married, giving her almost unlimited access to Sebastian's home, the headquarters of the Nazi group. She wins the complete confidence (and devotion) of Sebastian, though she is faced with the resentment of Sebastian's sinister mother (Mme. Leopoldine Konstantin). Alicia is able to convince Sebastian to host a large party at the house, to which Devlin (of whom Sebastian is likewise jealous) is invited. During the party, Alicia manages to slip Devlin into Sebastian's top-secret wine cellar. There, Devlin discovers wine bottles filled with what turns out to be uranium ore, providing the key that eventually allows the American agents of the film to track down an entire uranium smuggling operation being run by the Nazis, presumably toward the eventual development of nuclear weapons for use in a Nazi comeback.

Sebastian, however, discovers that Devlin has been in the cellar and realizes that Alicia has helped him, concluding that she is an American agent. He and his evil mother then concoct a plot slowly to poison Alicia, making her death seem due to natural causes and thus making it unnecessary to reveal to the other Nazis Sebastian's gullibility in allowing himself to be seduced by the American. Devlin, too jealous to stand the sight of Alicia with Sebastian any longer, asks for a transfer to Spain, but first has one last meeting with Alicia. In the meeting, she seems seriously ill. He realizes she may be in danger and returns to the house, where Alicia has discovered the poisoning plot, but is now too weak to get out of bed. Devlin locates her and helps her up, but is confronted by Sebastian and his mother before he can get her out of the house. Threatening to reveal her mission to the other Nazis, who emerge from a meeting in a room in the house, Devlin convinces Sebastian to help him and Alicia to his car, telling the other Nazis that they are taking her to the hospital. Devlin then pushes Sebastian away from the car and makes off with Alicia, knowing that the other Nazis will put two and two together and take a quick vengeance on Sebastian. Devlin thus ensures that Sebastian will get his just deserts for his Nazi activity, though it is clear that Devlin's real motive is to take revenge on Sebastian for his marriage to Alicia.

The Nazis of *Notorious* are suitably ruthless and dangerous, though there is little to indicate that the Americans of the film are any less so. Indeed, the dark atmosphere of the film has as much to do with the characterization of Devlin as with that of the Nazis. Obsessed with Alicia's checkered past, Devlin is consistently cruel in reminding her of it, while Alicia is revealed as an unhappy and fundamentally innocent woman desperate for affection and acceptance. Until she is finally revealed as an American agent, she gets more of both from Sebastian than from Devlin, contributing to the film's sense of moral ambiguity, a sense somewhat in the mode of the film noir, with which the film has much in common. *Notorious* is a classic instance of Hitchcockian suspense, but this ambiguity makes it weak as an anti-Nazi film. *Screenplay:* Ben Hecht. *Selected bibliography:* Beebe; Robert A. Harris; Spoto.

### *THE POSTMAN ALWAYS RINGS TWICE:* **DIR. TAY GARNETT (1946).**
Based on the novel by James M. Cain, *The Postman Always Rings Twice*, is a classic example of the film noir in terms of its plot, though the visual style of the film is less distinctive in terms of mood lighting and odd camera angles than many examples of the film noir. With its emphasis on steamy adulterous sexuality, the film was also something of a milestone in the easing of censorship in American film. Indeed, the central tensions of the film arise from the torrid sexual energies that immediately arise

when restless drifter Frank Chambers (played by John Garfield, in a powerful performance) stops at a California roadside diner and catches his first glimpse of sultry Cora Smith (Lana Turner), the wife of Nick Smith (Cecil Kellaway), the diner's owner and manager. The eventual result is a plot by Cora and Frank to kill Nick in a fake automobile accident so they can be together. The plan seems to work, only later to have Cora killed in a real automobile accident, after which Frank is wrongly convicted and executed for her murder. Apparently it is impossible, in modern America, for individuals to beat the system. As James Agee puts it, the film "represents the Law as an invincibly corrupt and terrifying force before which mere victims, whether innocent or guilty, can only stand helpless and aghast" (199).

Taken with Cora, Frank accepts Nick's offer of a job as an all-around handyman at the diner and the filling station that is attached to it. He then sets about seducing Cora, who is clearly interested in his attentions, despite her initial efforts to appear cool. Obviously unsatisfied by her physical relationship with her older husband, whom she married for his money, Cora soon succumbs to Frank's advances, and the two become lovers. At one point, they consider running away together, but Cora, having already spent several unromantic years with Nick just for material gain, is unwilling to give up the relative financial comfort that life with him offers. So they eventually decide to kill Nick in order to inherit his assets, which turn out to be even more lucrative than they realized when they learn that he had recently taken out a new $10,000 accidental death insurance policy.

Unfortunately, the existence of this new insurance policy also makes his death look more suspicious, leading District Attorney Kyle Sackett (Leon Ames) to charge Cora with murder in Nick's death. Lacking hard evidence, Sackett attempts to play Cora and Frank off against one another to get a confession. However, he is outsmarted by Cora's wily lawyer, Arthur Keats (Hume Cronyn). As a result of Keats's legal maneuvers, Cora is convicted of manslaughter, rather than murder, and is given only a suspended sentence. The way appears to be clear for Cora and Frank to be together, but tensions triggered by Sackett's strategies continue to plague the couple. Then Cora announces that she is pregnant, and she and Frank appear to have a full reconciliation during an outing at the beach in which she intentionally nearly drowns, just to see whether he will save her or take advantage of the opportunity to be rid of her. Save her he does, and the two drive back to the diner seemingly again very much in love.

However, fate has one final cruel twist in store for the couple when they become involved in another car crash. Cora is killed in the crash, and Frank is convicted of her murder. Sackett visits Frank in his cell shortly before his execution and informs him that he knows he is innocent of Cora's death, but that he believes he deserves to die for the killing of Nick. Even Frank sees the logic and appears to accept his approaching execution as poetic justice. As is often the case in the film noir, the law turns out to be just as devious as the criminals, but far more powerful. That Frank is ultimately undone because of his attraction to a woman of questionable virtue is also typical film noir fare, though in this case the woman has a soft side and seems genuinely to be seeking love, even if she is not willing to give up financial security in order to get it. The film's indictment of the corrupt materialism of modern capitalist society is thus made especially clear. *Screenplay:* Harry Ruskin and Niven Busch. *Selected bibliography:* Agee; Leff and Simmons; Silver and Ward.

*THE STRANGER:* DIR. ORSON WELLES (1946). *The Stranger* is probably the most conventional (and thus the most commercially successful) of Welles' s films, largely because of changes dictated by producer Sam Spiegel of International Pictures, the film's production company. Nevertheless, the film displays the distinctively offbeat touch that is Welles's trademark. Indeed, despite its apparent conventionality, André Bazin still finds *The Stranger* perhaps "the most demented work" of Welles's career (91). Most of the film takes place in the pastoral college town of Harper, Connecticut, which seems just enough like the ideal American community to make that association clear, yet at the same time seems just artificial enough to be troubling and to suggest something bogus in American ideals. James Naremore notes Welles's ironic presentation of the town as being "as if Norman Rockwell were being retouched by Charles Addams" (124).

As the film begins, notorious Nazi Franz Kindler (played by Welles), the architect of the Final Solution, has escaped captivity in the wake of World War II and has made his way to Harper, where he has quickly established himself as respected college professor Charles Rankin, a leading local citizen and the husband of Mary née Longstreet (Loretta Young), the daughter of a state supreme court justice. Agent Wilson (Edward G. Robinson), a war crimes investigator, is on Kindler's trail, which has gone cold. He thus concocts a plan to allow Kindler's former lieutnenant, Konrad Meinike (Konstantin Shayne), to escape as well, hoping Meinike will lead him to Kindler.

Meinike does makes his way to Harper, where Wilson follows him, posing as an antique dealer. But Wilson again loses the trail after Kindler murders Meinike, the only person who can identify him. Tensions build in a rather Hitchcockian manner, enhanced by carefully constructed film noir shadows that give the ideal New England town a weirdly sinister look that perfectly complements Welles's portrayal of Kindler/Rankin. Importantly, Wilson begins to suspect Rankin after a key scene in which the latter attempts to cover himself by railing against Germans, arguing that they should all be exterminated because of their fundamental inability to comprehend concepts such as equality and justice. Reminded that Marx was German (thus implying that Marx was a leading proponent of equality and justice), Rankin immediately responds that Marx was not German, but Jewish. Suspecting that only a Nazi would produce such a response, Wilson focuses his subsequent efforts on Rankin, eventually leading to a spectacular climax in which Kindler, who has long devoted himself to the repair of the clock in the town's central church steeple, dies by falling from the tower after being impaled on a sword borne by a figure of an avenging angel attached to the clock. If nothing else, Kindler is thus saved from the lynch mob that has gathered in the square, the town's kindly citizens having suddenly been moved to murderous frenzy.

Even if a bit overdone, this ending is rich in symbolic suggestiveness, as is the entire film. Michael Denning characterizes *The Stranger* as the third volume of Welles's "U.S.A. trilogy" (the others are *Citizen Kane* and *The Magnificent Ambersons*), which as a whole bemoans the loss of the post-Civil War American dream amid the rampant commodification of modern capitalist America. For Denning, then, the small New England town of *The Stranger* is an image of what he calls the "Lincoln republic," its unwitting adoption of an escaped Nazi as a leading citizen suggesting the attraction to fascism that constitutes the dark side of modern American society (387). In retrospect, the film's subtle suggestion that there may be hidden and unrecognizable Nazis lurking among us also acts as an ironic anticipation of the similar vision that would soon be applied to communist amid the Cold-War hysteria of America in the decade after the war. *Screenplay:* Anthony Veiller, John Huston (uncredited), and Orson Welles (uncredited). *Selected bibliography:* Bazin; Denning; Higham (*Films*); Higham (*Orson Welles*); Naremore (*Magic*).

*THE BIG CLOCK:* **DIR. JOHN FARROW (1947).** Based upon Kenneth Fearing's 1946 novel of the same title, *The Big Clock* is one of the classic examples of the film noir thriller. Fearing's novel (together with this first film adaptation) also provided the inspiration for the 1987 Kevin Costner vehicle, *No Way Out*. The Farrow film maintains much of the political commentary of the Fearing book and even supplements it in significant ways. The film thus represents an important extension of the work of Fearing, who was one of the leading American leftist poets of the 1930s. Beginning in the 1940s, he wrote a series of detective novels that continued many of the themes of his earlier poetry. The most successful of these was *The Big Clock*, which effectively combines a compelling detective-story plot with a number of important satirical observations about modern American society. It thus serves as one of the better examples in American culture of the use of popular fiction to convey leftist ideas.

As in the original book, the central character of the film version of *The Big Clock* is George Stroud (played by Ray Milland), who works as the editor of *Crimeways* magazine, which covers notorious crimes, often leading to the capture of the perpetrators. Stroud is so devoted to his job that his wife, Georgette (Maureen O'Sullivan), complains that he is married more to the magazine than to her. The magazine is part of the publishing empire of Janoth Enterprises, headed by Earl Janoth (Charles Laughton). The egomaniacal and dictatorial Janoth is obsessed with time, parceling out all his activities to the nearest minute. He is thus a slave to time, despite his extensive power as a wealthy publisher, and he illustrates (better in the film than in the book) the regimentation of behavior under capitalism. Janoth is involved in an affair with beautiful Pauline York (Rita Johnson), who also becomes briefly involved with Stroud, though the latter is unaware that Pauline is Janoth's mistress. The detective-story plot of the film is initiated when Janoth arrives at Pauline's apartment building just as Stroud, whom Janoth sees in the distance but does not recognize, is leaving. The jealous Janoth follows Pauline up to her apartment and questions her about the departing man, whom she identifies as "Jefferson Randolph" to avoid revealing her involvement with Stroud. The two argue, and Janoth flies into a rage and strikes Pauline with a sundial, killing her. He then goes to the apartment of his friend and chief lieutenant, Steve Hagen (George Macready) and confesses the crime, planning to go from there to the police. Hagen coolly convinces him to keep quiet and promises to help cover up Janoth's involvement in the murder. The key problem, however, is the departing man, who can place Janoth at the scene of the crime. Hagen enlists Stroud, the company's expert on detective work, to find "Randolph," claiming that the man committed the murder. Stroud immediately realizes that he is seeking himself, but the net nevertheless begins to close about him. Surviving a couple of close calls, Stroud is able to avoid detection long enough to put together a series of clues that seems to point to Hagen as the killer. In response, Hagen identifies Janoth as the killer. Already crumbling beneath the stress of the entire experience, Janoth becomes unhinged and shoots Hagen, then attempts to run away, but falls down an elevator shaft and is killed.

Aside from its obvious suggestion (supplemented by the atmosphere created by the film's classic noir look) of unscrupulous, even criminal, activity at the highest levels of corporate America, *The Big Clock* makes a number of important satirical comments about modern American society. In the book, the title metaphor refers to Stroud's personal belief that every aspect of life is ordered as if run by a big clock "to which one automatically adjusts his entire life." But the film, in keeping with its more literal use of the metaphor, features an actual big clock inside the Janoth building. Described as the "most accurate and most unique privately owned clock in the world," the big clock features a futuristic digital display and is connected to all of the other clocks in the building so that they can be precisely synchronized. Such images actually make the film more effective than the book in its treatment of the motif of regimentation by time. However, the book is more effective in its satire of the commodification of modern American culture, a phenomenon Fearing had observed firsthand in his own earlier work as a publicity and editorial writer, including work for such publications as The *New York Times* and *Newsweek*. *Screenplay:* Jonathan Latimer. *Selected bibliography:* Andrew Anderson; Barnard; Fearing; Ryley; Silver and Ward.

*BODY AND SOUL:* **DIR. ROBERT ROSSEN (1947).** *Body and Soul* is considered by many to be the definitive boxing movie, the work that established prizefighters as central figures (complete with an array of obvious allegorical resonances) in American film. Boxing, in many ways, is a perfect allegory for capitalism, as Bertolt Brecht pointed out as early as 1923 in the introduction to his play, *In the Jungle of Cities*, loosely based on Upton Sinclair's *The Jungle* (Ewen 115–16). *Body and Soul* takes excellent advantage of these allegorical opportunities. The film begins as its protagonist, the Jewish prizefighter and world champion Charley Davis (played by John Garfield) is on the eve of a major title defense against challenger Jack Marlowe (Artie Dorrell). Davis is distraught, however, because of the sudden death of his trainer, Ben Chaplin (Canada Lee), due to complications arising from injuries sustained in his own earlier boxing career, including the bout in which Davis took the world title from him. Moreover, he is also upset because Roberts (Lloyd Gough), a gangster who dominates the New York fight scene and who is largely responsible for Chaplin's death, has fixed the fight, and Charley is supposed to lose. Most of the film is then a retrospective of Charley's career leading up to this night, beginning with his days as a local amateur champion on New York's East Side and with his first meeting with artist/designer Peg Born (Lilli Palmer), the love of his life.

Charley is the son of poor Jewish parents who run a small candy store on the East Side, but Mr. Davis is soon killed in an explosion that occurs when gangsters bomb a speakeasy next to the candy store. The Depression is in full swing, and times are hard. The fiercely proud Charley, despite the objections of his mother (played by Anne Revere), decides to become a professional fighter so that the family will not have to undergo the indignity (to him) of going on relief. Charley cuts a deal with Quinn, a somewhat shady fight promoter and, accompanied by his sidekick from the neighborhood, Shorty Polaski (Joseph Pevney), quickly rises to the top and his title bout with Chaplin. The money pours in (and out), and Charley is clearly losing touch with his humble roots. Shorty remains more down to earth, warning Peg that Quinn and Roberts have converted Charley into a "money machine" and that they are "cutting him up a million ways." In this sense, of course, Charley is little different from any other worker under capitalism.

Charley, not knowing that Chaplin is already seriously hurt, agrees to a deal giving Roberts fifty percent of his future earnings in return for a title shot. Roberts, meanwhile, assures Chaplin and his handlers that Charley knows about the injury and will take it easy in the fight. Charley, of course, fights his usual fight, and Chaplin is nearly killed. Shorty learns about the entire deal, and tells Charley, complaining later to Peg that Charley is "not just a kid who can fight. He's money. And people want money so bad they make it stink." Shorty is soon afterward assaulted by one of Roberts's thugs, then staggers into the path of an oncoming car and is killed. Peg insists that Charley give up fighting at once, then breaks off the engagement when he refuses. He also becomes involved in an affair with Alice, a gold-digging club singer who was formerly involved with Quinn. She encourages him to spend wildly, and he gets more and more in debt to Roberts, setting up the final situation in which he is forced to agree to throw the fight with Marlowe.

Charley, assured that Marlowe will play along, performs lackadaisically in the title fight and appears to be going along with the fix. In the late rounds, however, Marlowe mounts a furious assault, and Charley realizes that he, like Ben, has been double-crossed by Roberts. Infuriated, he charges into the ring in the last round and knocks Marlowe out, retaining the title but obviously ending his boxing career. Peg greets him at ringside and the two are reunited, walking off together into the night, though with the clear threat of retaliation from Roberts and his thugs hanging in the air. "What can they do," Charley asks, "kill me? Everybody dies." Director Rossen, incidentally, had originally favored a more pessimistic ending in which Charley is killed by mobsters, falling into a barrel of garbage; Rossen was convinced by screenwriter Abraham Polonsky to use the more affirmative (if ambiguous) ending.

More than most fight pictures, *Body and Soul* makes clear, especially through Shorty's comments on the commodification of Charley, its use of the sport of boxing as a metaphor for capitalism, where each individual must fight to get ahead, yet finds that his or her best efforts are often thwarted by larger economic forces. Thom Anderson describes *Body and Soul* as the first *film gris*, a genre similar in look to *film noir*, but with greater social and psychological realism (186). It was also the first film produced by the independent production company formed by Garfield and producer Bob Roberts to give Garfield greater freedom (both political and artistic) in the projects he could pursue. Indeed, Anderson sees Garfield as the dominant figure in the *film gris* genre (184). Garfield's leftist politics are well known, of course, and Anderson describes the makers of films in this genre as being in general "Browderite Communists and left-liberals," who began, after the gruesome end of World War II in the nuclear bombings of Japan, to understand "the unreality of the American dream" (187). They then expressed this insight in their films. For Anderson, *Body and Soul* joins the later *film gris*, *Force of Evil* (also starring Garfield and directed by Polonsky), as "an autopsy of capitalism" that offers "a critique of capitalism in the guise of an exposé of crime" (186–87). *Screenplay:* Abraham Polonsky. *Selected bibliography:* Thom Anderson; Denning; Frederic Ewen; Neve (*Film*).

*CROSSFIRE:* **DIR. EDWARD DMYTRYK (1947).** Released just before *Gentleman's Agreement*, which deals with a similar theme, *Crossfire* was the first postwar film to treat the theme of American antisemitism. It was thus a marker of Hollywood's new willingness to tackle difficult social issues in the postwar years. On the other hand, the film is actually based on a novel by Richard Brooks that explores the issue of homophobia, telling the story of a homosexual who is beaten to death by his fellow Marines because of his sexual orientation. RKO found that issue too hot to handle and so converted the homosexual of the novel into a Jew.

The film, shot entirely in a dark, brooding, film noir style, begins with the murder, though we see only shadows and therefore cannot identify the killer. The film then proceeds as police detective Captain Finlay (Robert Young) attempts to unravel the mystery of the murder, which seems particularly perplexing because none of the major suspects appeared to know the victim, Joseph Samuels (Sam Levene), whom they all had apparently just met on the night of the killing. These suspects are a group of army war veterans who are in the process of being mustered out into civilian society after the war. They include Montgomery (Robert Ryan), Bowers (Steve Brodie), and Mitchell (George Cooper), with suspicion initially focusing on the latter. Army sergeant Peter Keeley (Robert Mitchum) soon becomes involved as well, helping Finlay to solve the mystery, which deepens when Bowers is also found murdered, apparently to keep him quiet.

Eventually, it becomes clear that Montgomery, figured not only as a particularly hateful anti-Semite, but as a sort of protofascist, is the killer and that he brutally murdered the congenial Samuels purely out of his hatred of Jews. He then murdered Bowers, his best friend, to prevent him from revealing Montgomery's role in the earlier crime. Keeley and another soldier help Finlay concoct a plan to entrap Montgomery and establish his guilt. The plan works, but Montgomery escapes and runs away into the darkened street, where he is shot down by Finlay. *Crossfire* is a reasonably effective detective thriller that nevertheless makes clear the message that the defeat of Nazi Germany has eradicated neither antisemitism nor fascism and that right-thinking Americans need to remain vigilant against these tendencies in our own society. The picture was a commercial and critical success—which did not stop government anticommunist witch hunters from moving in on director Dmytryk and producer Adrian Scott soon after it was released. Both became members of the Hollywood Ten and served jail terms, though Dmytryk later recanted and thus was able to resume his career relatively soon. *Screenplay:* John Paxton. *Selected bibliography:* Christensen; Dmytryk; Leff; Muller; Naremore (*More Than Night*); Neve (*Film*); Silver and Ward.

*GENTLEMAN'S AGREEMENT:* DIR. ELIA KAZAN (1947). Often regarded as Hollywood's first significant attack on antisemitism, a subject that was avoided even in the anti-Nazi propaganda films of the war years, *Gentleman's Agreement* was a major commercial and critical success, winning three Academy Awards (and a total of eight nominations), including the prestigious ones for best picture and best director. In the film, Gregory Peck plays Phil Green, a successful magazine writer who has just moved to New York with his mother (Anne Revere) and his son, Tommy (Dean Stockwell), to take a position writing for *Smith's Weekly*, a liberal magazine. His first assignment is to do a series of articles on antisemitism in America, an assignment of which he is at first highly skeptical, especially as his new editor, John Minify (Albert Dekker), insists that he find a new and compelling angle on the story. At last, however, Green discovers the angle: he pretends to be Jewish and then observes the treatment he receives as a result.

In the course of the film, Green receives a number of slights because of his Jewishness, some subtle and some not so subtle. He discovers that antisemitisim is far more prevalent than he had ever realized, especially in veiled forms. He also discovers some of the genuine pain that is caused by this antisemitism, as when Tommy is insulted by other boys, who refuse to play with him because they think he is Jewish. Green even discovers that his new (blonde) secretary at *Smith's*, herself a Jew, has changed her name to hide the fact and is prejudiced against "kikey" Jews that she is afraid will give highly assimilated Jews like herself a bad name. In the meantime, the entire experiment is complicated when Green meets and falls in love with Kathy Lacy (Dorothy McGuire), Minify's niece. Kathy, who quickly agrees to marry Green, is aware that he is not really Jewish, though she seems troubled by the fact that everyone else will think he is. Her discomfort causes serious problems in the relationship and eventually leads to a breakup when he concludes that she is antisemitic.

In the meantime, Green's old friend, Dave Goldman (John Garfield), comes to town and adds his special insights, as a real Jew, to Green's research. More experienced with various forms of antisemitism than Green, Goldman realizes that Kathy is not really antisemitic, but has simply not had the courage to stand up to those who are. He points out to her that it is not enough to be against antisemitism, but that one must fight against it in practice. She sees the error of her ways and agrees to rent a cottage she owns to Goldman and his family, though she knows it is in a neighborhood where there is a "gentleman's agreement" to keep out Jews. Further, she assures Goldman she will stand by him and actively oppose any in the neighborhood who object to his moving in. In the end, Green's series is published to much acclaim, while he and Kathy are reunited.

For its time, *Gentleman's Agreement* was a particularly hard-hitting attack on antisemitism in America. However, the film continues to adhere to a number of romantic conventions, sometimes in a rather artificial manner, as in the sudden dismissal of the evidence that Kathy is antisemitic and in the final reunion of the lovers. Moreover, the ease with which the trouble between Green and Kathy is resolved tends to suggest that antisemitism and other forms of bigotry are easier to overcome than they really are; the film also tends to suggest that the solution to bigotry is to eliminate difference altogether and make all Americans the same. Nevertheless, the film at least makes clear not only that antisemitism is evil, but that it is widely practiced at all levels and in every aspect of American society, at great cost not only to Jews, but to the stated principles of American democracy. The fact that the film was accused by some of being communist propaganda indicates not only the extremism and paranoia of many on the Right, but the extent to which the American Left had identified itself by World War II with opposition to racism and bigotry. *Screenplay:* Moss Hart. *Selected bibliography:* Crowdus (*Political Companion*); Neve (*Film*); Sayre.

*MONSIEUR VERDOUX:* DIR. CHARLES CHAPLIN (1947). *Monsieur Verdoux* is, on the surface, a black comedy of manners, punctuated with scenes of Chaplinesque farce. However, it makes a number of crucial political points and marks the continuing evolution of Chaplin as an overtly political artist. The film's story line is simple. Henri Verdoux (Chaplin), a French bank teller who has worked loyally for the same bank for more than thirty years, suddenly, in 1930, finds himself unemployed due to the Depression. Fifty years old and with his opportunities limited by the collapse of the French economy, Verdoux concludes that he must turn to crime in order to be able to support his young son, Peter (Allison Roddan), and crippled wife, Mona (Mady Correll). He becomes a "Bluebeard," leading multiple lives in which he marries a series of well-off women around the country, milks them for whatever funds he can, then murders them when it becomes more profitable to get them out of the way. Much of the plot concerns his comically unsuccessful attempts to murder one of his current wives, Annabella Bonheur (Martha Raye), whose name indicates the astonishing luck with which she continually avoids being killed. At the same time, he is also involved in the courtship of Marie Grosnay (Isobel Elsom), whom he has marked out as his next wife/victim. An important subplot involves Verdoux's meeting with a destitute young woman (Marilyn Nash), a refugee from Belgium, whom he picks up on the street, panning to use her as an experimental subject on whom to test a lethal new poison he has developed. His theory is that her life is so bleak she would be better off dead. However, after she expresses her love of life, he takes pity on her and cancels the experiment, giving her money and encouragement instead.

Verdoux uses the money obtained from his various marriages to invest in the stock market, but eventually loses everything when the market crashes. In the meantime, his wife and son both die, and he is left in despair. He again meets the Belgian refugee, now living in luxury through her association with a wealthy munitions manufacturer, with the clear implication that the munitions industry is one of the few that continues to thrive through the Depression and with the more subtle implication that the buildup toward World War II may have been an intentional attempt to stimulate that industry. From this point on, the film reads almost like a dark parody of the final stages of Stendhal's *The Red and the Black*. Verdoux is captured, tried, and convicted of multiple murder. As he is sentenced to death, Verdoux makes a speech (somewhat reminiscent of, but darker than that of the barber at the end of Chaplin's 1940 film *The Great Dictator*) declaring that, by the standards of the world in this year of 1937, he is an amateur as a mass murderer. Later, as he awaits execution, having refused to appeal for clemency, he reemphasizes this point to a reporter who comes to interview him, noting, in Brechtian fashion, that robbery and murder are the "way of business" in the modern world, where "one murder makes a villain, millions a hero." As the film ends, he is led away to the guillotine, while fascism raises its ugly head across Europe, especially in Spain, where the Western democracies do nothing to avert the victory of Franco and the subsequent beginning of world war.

Many of the political points made by *Monsieur Verdoux*, as in the plot's demonstration of the instability of capitalism or in Verdoux's eqation between capitalism and crime, are rather clear. Some points, however, are more subtle. As Charles Maland points out, for example, the film is important (and highly unusual, as American films go) in its disavowal of individual agency and its endorsement of "the conception that larger social and economic forces, particularly economic depression and war, determine the fates of individual people" (233). Thus, no matter how reliable Verdoux is as a bank clerk, no matter how clever he is as a criminal, he is never really in charge of his own fate. The point, however, is not that human beings do not make history, but that individuals do not. It does not rule out successful collective action. Under the current competition-based social system, Verdoux can help his wife and child only by harming others, and then only temporarily. But collective action might lead to systematic changes that would provide more permanent and stable solutions to social ills.

Although some have seen Verdoux's multiple killings of women as a misogynist motif, perhaps growing out of some of Chaplin's own bad experiences, it is also possible to read Verdoux's criminal career in a more positive way as a deconstruction of romantic myths that have traditionally served to shore up social and economic exploitation of women and others. Verdoux' s experience suggests, among other things, that, under the system of capitalism, individuals, in order to survive, are forced to treat others as economic objects rather than fellow human beings. Ironically, Verdoux kills his wives out of devotion to his wife. His continuing devotion to his child and his original wife (combined with his love of cats and other helpless creatures) suggests the extent to which sentimentality is used in bourgeois society to justify all manner of atrocities, including mass murder. The Nazis, after all, were famed for their love of sentimental music and kindness to animals.

Michael Denning argues that *Modern Times* (1936), *The Great Dictator* (1940), and *Monsieur Verdoux* are Chaplin's "Popular Front classics" (92). If so, the latter occupies a special position by virtue of being released after World War II, as the Cold War was getting underway and destroying the antifascist alliances of the previous few years. Indeed, the setting of the film in the 1930s might at first glance appear to be anachronistic, it doing little good by 1947 to warn against the rise of fascism in Spain. On the other hand, the temporal setting of the film can be taken as a calculated attempt to warn audiences that the conditions that made fascism possible still exist and antifascist vigilance should therefore not be relaxed. As Maland notes, Chaplin seems to have regarded the alliance between the West and the Soviet Union during World War II as an extremely encouraging development (239). One might, then, read *Monsieur Verdoux* as a plea to continue that alliance and as an early outcry against the Manichean oppositions of the Cold War. In any case, though less known than the first two installments of Chaplin's Popular Front trilogy, *Monsieur Verdoux* is an extremely rich and complex work the full implications of which are worth pondering at great length. *Screenplay:* Charles Chaplin (based on an idea by Orson Welles). *Selected bibliography:* Denning; Flom; Maland (*Chaplin*); Wallach.

**THE WEB: DIR. MICHAEL GORDON (1947).** An interesting example of the postwar crime drama, *The Web* has numerous political implications. It features Vincent Price as Andrew Colby, an international corporate tycoon who is willing to employ any means necessary to increase his wealth, brutally stepping on anyone who gets in his way. As he explains at one point in the film, "All my life I've worked for only one thing—money, and the power that goes with it." He encounters lawyer Bob Regan (Edmond O'Brien) when the latter attempts to sue one of Colby's enterprises for damages when their negligence causes damage to the pushcart of Regan's immigrant client. Amused, Colby agrees to pay the damages, then hires Regan as his bodyguard, claiming that an ex-busines associate, fresh out of prison, has threatened to kill him. Regan quickly realizes that Colby is involved in activities that are not only unscrupulous, but illegal. Then, with the help of the tough police detective, Lieutenant Damico (William Bendix), Regan tricks Colby into revealing himself as a killer.

*The Web* contains no explicit political commentary, but its treatment of Colby suggests that his villainy is par for the course among corporate moguls. In this sense, the contrast between the evil of the wealthy Colby and the virtue of Regan, with his working-class background and sympathies, is crucial to the film's message. Finally, the portrayal of personal relationships among those involved in Colby's enterprises as based on ruthless economic competition makes a potentially significant comment about the alienation of personal relations under capitalism. *Screenplay:* William Bowers and Bertram Millhauser. *Selected bibliography:* Neve (*Film*).

*THE BOY WITH GREEN HAIR:* **DIR. JOSEPH LOSEY (1948).** *The Boy with Green Hair* was the first major feature directed by Losey, a director with strong roots in American leftist culture, going back to his participation in the Brechtian "Living Newspaper" stage production of the 1930s. The film is essentially an antiracist and antiwar parable that critiques the persecution of those who happen to look different from the norm. The boy of the title is twelve-year-old Peter (Dean Stockwell), a orphan who has been shunted from one relative to another, and is being being raised in a small town by an old man who likes to be called "Gramp" (Pat O'Brien), a singing waiter whom the boy regards with great admiration. When the sensitive Peter sees posters depicting emaciated war orphans, he becomes powerfully upset, especially after a fellow student notes that Peter (who is unaware that his parents are dead) is also an orphan. Soon afterward, Peter takes a bath, then finds as he dries his hair that it has somehow turned green. Predictably, the green-haired Peter is regarded with suspicion and hostility by most of the townspeople. Frustrated, he runs away but reluctantly returns after having a dream in which a group of war orphans asks him to use his green hair to convey a warning against war. His message, however, is not well received, and, eventually, Gramp finally gives in to pressure from the neighbors and convinces Peter to shave his head. The boy then runs away again and winds up in a police station, where the film begins, the previous action to be related in flashback.

Brian Neve, describing the film as "a strange mixture of aesthetic experiment, social protest and studio sentiment," notes that the film's uncompromising antiwar stance was viewed as controversial enough that its makers were subjected to considerable pressure to moderate the film's message, which caused them to add scenes that suggest the need for preparedness (100–101). Ironically, these attempts to squelch the film's message mirror the attempts of the townspeople of the film to silence Peter, while at the same time marking the early stages of the wave of repression that was beginning to sweep America and that would eventually drive Losey and screenwriter Ben Barzman from the country. In any case, the antiwar message of the resultant film, which can be taken as an early-Cold War plea for mutual understanding between the United States and the Soviet Union, is clear despite these efforts at censorship. *Screenplay:* Ben Barzman and Alfred Lewis Levitt. *Selected bibliography:* Caute (*Joseph Losey*); Ciment; Hirsch; Neve (*Film*); Palmer and Riley.

*FORCE OF EVIL:* **DIR. ABRAHAM POLONSKY (1948).** *Force of Evil* is a compelling and intelligent gangster film that uses its portrayal of organized crime to comment on the workings of capitalism as a whole. Indeed, spurred partly by the recent advocacy of Martin Scorsese, the film has come to be regarded as a classic work of the American cinema. It is also a highly political work. Beginning with its opening shot of Wall Street, the film continually suggests that the New York crime syndicate run by mob boss Ben Tucker (played by Roy Roberts) is operated very much in the fashion of any big business under capitalism. (This point is made even more clearly in Ira Wolfert's 1943 novel, *Tucker's People*, on which the film is based.) As one of the film's characters puts it when another character accuses him of being a gangster, "What do you mean gangsters? It's business." Brian Neve concludes that both *Force of Evil* and the 1947 *Body and Soul*, for which Polonsky wrote the screenplay, "suggest [Polonsky's] Marxist thinking, about the nature of capitalism" (135–36).

As *Force of Evil* begins, Tucker is planning to fix the numbers on the next day as part of a move to eliminate his competition in the numbers rackets, taking over the remaining numbers "banks" as part of a "combination" that will dominate the business. Meanwhile, Tucker has engaged Wall Street lawyer Joe Morse (John Garfield) in an effort to have the numbers racket legalized, so that he can run it as a legitimate business. Morse is, in fact, the dominant figure in the film, even though he is a relatively minor character in the Wolfert novel, where he is simply a lieutenant to Tucker and not an established lawyer. The emphasis on Morse, who is also attempting to fend off the efforts of a special prosecutor, Hall, to shut down the rackets altogether, allows Garfield to dominate the film with a rousing performance in which he delivers his lines in a unique, stylized, rhythmic fashion reminiscent of blank verse. Such dialogue perfectly complements the brooding look of the film to produce a finely integrated commentary on the dark side of American capitalism.

Legitimate lawyer though he may be, Morse is not above temptation, and he hopes to cash in big on Tucker's takeover of the numbers racket. The problem is that Joe's brother, Leo (Thomas Gomez), who largely raised him, runs one of the banks that is threatened by Tucker's move. Eventually, Joe manages to convince the reluctant Leo to go along with Tucker, cutting a deal that leaves Leo's operation as the number one bank in the combination. In the process, Joe applies pressure by engineering a police raid on Leo's bank, which drives Leo's bookkeeper, Freddy Bauer (Howland Chamberlin), to near hysteria. In the meantime, Joe meets Leo's innocent young secretary, Doris Lowry (Beatrice Pearson), and develops an interest in her.

The developing relationship between Joe and Doris (whose innocence serves as a counterpoint to the corruption of the other characters) provides a romantic subplot to the remainder of the film, which involves increasing suspense as various forces come to bear on Leo's operation. Bauer, forced to stay on though he wishes to quit, triggers additional police raids to try to put the bank out of business. Hall continues his investigations, tapping the phones of Tucker and Joe. In addition, Tucker's former partner, the less "respectable" Ficco, is determined to horn in on Tucker's numbers operation. These events culminate in the kidnapping of Leo by Ficco's thugs, with the collaboration of Bauer, who is nevertheless killed by the thugs.

Joe, realizing that things are getting out of hand, decides to take whatever cash he can get his hands on and skip town, inviting Doris to go with him. First, however, he has to try to rescue Leo, not knowing that the stress of the kidnapping has already caused the ailing Leo to die of a heart attack. Joe bursts into Tucker's home, where Tucker is making a deal with Ficco. Ficco informs Joe of Leo's death and tells him where the body has been dumped. Joe secretly takes Tucker's phone off the hook, hoping Hall's investigators will listen in on the conversation as it proceeds. When Tucker realizes this, a gun battle ensues. Tucker and Ficco are both killed. Joe then goes, accompanied by Doris, down to the waterfront to find Leo's body, while Garfield's voiceover informs us that Joe will now cooperate with Hall to try to end the kind of corruption that led to his brother's death.

In the book, Joe is arrested and hangs himself in jail, while Tucker skips town with a huge sum of cash. The numbers racket goes on, run by Ficco. The book is thus considerably darker than the film, which nevertheless has a brooding and ominous quality. Thom Anderson describes *Force of Evil* as a leading example of the leftist genre that Anderson calls *film gris*, a genre similar in look to *film noir*, but with greater social and psychological realism (186). It was also the only film to be directed by

Polonsky (who had written the screenplay for Garfield's earlier *film gris*, *Body and Soul*) before he ran afoul of the House Un-American Activities Committee (HUAC) and was blacklisted. He received no further screen credits from 1951 to 1968, when he wrote the screenplay for *Madigan*, a police drama starring Richard Widmark and Henry Fonda. Polonsky did, however, continue to work during the period of the blacklist. For example, he wrote the screenplay for the 1959 film *Odds Against Tomorrow*, on which the leftist novelist John O. Killens fronted for him as the credited screenwriter. In addition, Polonsky was fronted on numerous episodes of the television series *You Are There*, and he wrote and published novels, including *The World Above* (1951, perhaps his most politically radical novel) and *A Season of Fear* (1956). *Screenplay:* Abraham Polonsky and Ira Wolfert. *Selected bibliography:* Thom Anderson; Denning; Naremore (*More than Night*); Neve (*Film*).

*THE LADY FROM SHANGHAI:* **DIR. ORSON WELLES (1948).** Based on Sherwood King's novel, *If I Die Before I Wake*, *The Lady from Shanghai* is a complex thriller with sinister undertones that well illustrate the brooding atmosphere of the film noir. The film also well illustrates the subtle, subterranean politics that often inform works of that genre. Like many films noirs, the film depicts its wealthy characters as decadent to the point of downright evil. Indeed, the machinations of the film's upper-class characters (and, by extension, of the bourgeoisie as a whole) are compared through much of the film to the central metaphor of a school of sharks turning on each other and devouring each other in a frenzy of competition. The decadent rich are contrasted to the film's virtuous working-class protagonist, the seaman Michael O'Hara (Welles). More interested in preserving his personal integrity than in pursuing wealth, O'Hara also has vaguely specified leftist political inclinations. At one point, he is described in a newspaper report as a "notorious waterfront agitator." And, while this report may, given its context, be an example of inflated journalistic sensationalism, it is also revealed in the course of the film that O'Hara had spent time in Spain fighting against Franco and was imprisoned there for a year after the fascist takeover. *The Lady from Shanghai* thus displays the antifascist politics of many films noirs, while at the same time commenting on the American ideology of competition in ways that tend ultimately to link that ideology to fascism.

In the beginning of the film, O'Hara encounters the beautiful Elsa "Rosalie" Bannister (played by Rita Hayworth, Welles's wife from 1943 to 1947, and still so when the film was made, in 1946) when he saves her from an attack by robbers. He learns that she is the daughter of White Russian aristocrats and that she grew up in China after her family was forced to flee Russia in the wake of the Bolshevik Revolution. He eventually also learns that she is the wife of famed trial lawyer Arthur Bannister

(Everett Sloane), who meanwhile hires O'Hara to join the crew of his yacht, on which he and Elsa are about to set sail from New York on a cruise in the Caribbean, through the Panama Canal, and up the coast to San Francisco, where they live. On the way, they stop off in Acapulco, where Welles manages to work in some extremely vague passing commentary on American imperialism in Latin America. Meanwhile, O'Hara inadvertently becomes entangled in the corrupt affairs of the Bannisters, partly because of his sexual attraction to Elsa, and partly out of a chivalrous desire to rescue the young woman from her much older, crippled (perhaps by polio) husband, who seems to be holding her in the marriage through some sort of coercion. O'Hara also becomes caught up in the designs of Bannister and his vile law partner, George Grisby (Glenn Anders), both of whom hope to use Bannister for their own purposes.

From this point, the plot becomes rather complicated, but is in any case largely a pretext designed to allow Welles to set up his opposition between the virtue of O'Hara, the working-class leftist, and the evil of the film's bourgeoisie, Bannister and Grisby, and its Russian aristocrat (and enemy of the Bolsheviks), Elsa. The remainder of the film involves the mutual efforts of Grisby and the two Bannisters, like the school of crazed sharks, to kill each other off, using O'Hara either to do the dirty work or to take the blame. (Among other things, Grisby concocts a complex scheme in which he claims to want to fake his own murder so he can disappear to a South Sea island where he will be safe from the threat of nuclear warfare.) Eventually, Grisby is murdered, leading to O'Hara's arrest and trial for the crime and for the killing of Sid Broome (Ted de Corsia), Bannister's hired detective, who had actually been shot by Grisby. O'Hara is defended (halfheartedly) in court by Bannister, who admits to his client just as the jury is coming in that he hopes to lose the case and thus abort any romantic relationship between O'Hara and Elsa. But, before the verdict can be announced, O'Hara manages to escape, eventually winding up in an abandoned amusement park. There, in the film's most famous scene, he meets Elsa in the park's house of mirrors. As she confesses to being Grisby's killer, Bannister arrives there as well. In a bizarre shootout, the two spouses kill each other amid shattering mirrors bearing their own reflections. O'Hara, however, survives and finds that he is in the clear because Bannister has already informed the district attorney that it was in fact Elsa who killed Grisby. O'Hara walks away, leaving Elsa dying on the floor.

Mark Graham argues that *The Lady from Shanghai* is ultimately meaningless, a sort of elaborate joke, "wonderful celebration of the incomprehensible and the absurd" (162). Nothing, however, could be farther from the truth. James Naremore, for example, is closer to the mark when he agrees that the dialogue and imagery of the film are rather zany but concludes that there is a great deal of meaning in this zaniness, especially in the way it serves to parody and mock the lack of meaning in most Hollywood films (127). In any case, *The Lady from Shanghai* is an offbeat thriller to say the least. It is also an excellent example of the complex methods that had to be used by filmmakers who wished, in the late 1940s, just as McCarthyism was kicking into gear, to make leftist political statements. Indeed, if many viewers found the film hopelessly confusing, that may have been precisely the point. Amid this confusion, Welles manages to make political points that he might otherwise never have been able to get away with. *Screenplay:* Orson Welles. *Selected bibliography:* Bazin; Callow; Mark Graham; Higham (*Films*); Higham (*Orson Welles*); Naremore (*Magic*); Naremore (*More Than Night*).

*THE QUIET ONE:* **DIR. SIDNEY MEYERS (1948).** Directed by Sidney Meyers, a veteran of Frontier Films, the Film and Photo Leagues, and other leftist filmmaking activities, *The Quiet One* is a socially committed documentary that carries on the 1930s tradition of leftist documentaries. Rather than employ standard documentary footage, the film uses a technique of dramatic re-enactment to tell the story of a slum boy from New York, emphasizing the emotional damage wrought on children by a life of poverty. The boy, Donald Peters (played by Donald Thompson), is a student a the Wiltwyck School in Esopus, New York, a special school established to try to help New York children "who have reacted with grave disturbance of personality to neglect in their homes and in their community." The film indicates the source of Donald's emotional difficulties in his dysfunctional childhood, then demonstrates that social programs such as those conducted at the school can make a real contribution to the correction of these difficulties. *The Quiet One* is thus partly a plea for support for programs such as the Wiltwyck School. At the same time, it is clear from the film that the real problem (and thus the real solution) lies in the social and economic conditions that maim the lives of slum children in the first place.

As the film opens, Donald is emotionally crippled, so withdrawn that the teachers and counselors of the school are unable to reach him. The film then dramatizes Donald's earlier life in an effort to explain how he got in this condition. Unwelcome in the home of his mother and stepfather, Donald lives with his grandmother, a woman who tries to meet his physical needs but offers little in the way of affection or emotional sustenance. Indeed, frustrated with the boy's behavior, she often beats him, driving him even further into emotional desolation. Adrift and hopeless, Donald finally winds up at the Wiltwyck School.

The film then shifts to a dramatization of the process through which Donald finally begins to make progress at the school, largely through establishing an emotional connection to Clarence (played by Clarence Cooper), one of the counselors at the school. Donald remains emotionally fragile and vulnerable, but eventually, after an episode in which he runs away from the school, he is nearly hit by a train. This experience triggers an emotional catharsis that allows him to come to grips with the memories of his tormented past. He returns to the school, where he begins to open up and make friends. The narrator, a psychiatrist who works at the school (played by Meyers, though the narration is actually spoken by Gary Merrill), expresses the hope that they will now be able to help Donald cope with the world and his future. The film then ends with a final reminder of the number of children who live maimed lives, desperately needing the kind of help Donald has been fortunate enough to get at the school. *The Quiet One* is an effective film that won Academy Award nominations for best documentary feature and best screenplay. *Screenplay:* Helen Levitt, Janice Loeb, Sidney Meyers, and James Agee (commentary and dialogue). *Selected bibliography:* Barnouw; Barsam; Griffith.

*THEY LIVE BY NIGHT:* DIR. NICHOLAS RAY (1948). Based on Edward Anderson's novel, *Thieves Like Us* (1937), *They Life by Night* is a Depression-era tale of lovers on the run from the law. It thus echoes such films as *You Only Live Once* (1937), while anticipating such films as *Bonnie and Clyde* (1967). The film opens, even before the credits, with a shot of the kissing lovers, Bowie and Keechie (played by Farley Granger and Cathy O'Donnell), accompanied by the ominous caption, "This boy … this girl … were never properly introduced to this world of ours." This motif of lovers out of step with the reality of the social world continues throughout the film, which then proceeds, after the credits, to the sudden contrast of an impressive overhead shot (one of the first scenes ever filmed from a helicopter) of a frantic chase scene in which police pursue a car carrying Bowie and two hardened criminals. These criminals, Chicamaw (Howard Da Silva) and T-Dub (Jay C. Flippen) have escaped from prison accompanied by the relatively naïve Bowie, whom they also take along as they begin a crime spree.

When Bowie is hurt in an auto accident, he goes into hiding to recover and is nursed back to health by Keechie, who comes upon him while he recovers. The two of them fall in love and marry, determined to get beyond his checkered past. However, Chicamaw and T-Dub coerce Bowie into joining them in still another robbery, which goes badly. T-Dub is killed during the hold-up, and Chicamaw and Bowie part in anger soon afterward. Chicamaw is subsequently tracked down and killed by police, while Bowie is turned in by T-Dub's sister, Mattie (Helen Craig), hoping to win her own husband's release from prison. Bowie is brutally gunned down, leaving Keechie devastated, though he at least leaves her a final letter declaring his undying love.

*They Live By Night* is effective in its presentation of the powerful social forces that entrap Bowie and Keechie; it also emphasizes the Depression-era economic conditions that make these forces all the more insurmountable. On the other hand, it does little to suggest an alternative to the inhuman system it describes, contrasting the uncaring nature of the legal and economic system of Depression-era America only with the moments of private bliss shared by the lovers. The film makes it clear that these private moments can never overcome the impersonal social forces that surround the lovers. The film was remade by Robert Altman in 1972 under Anderson's original title and in a mode somewhat more in keeping with the mood of the novel. *Screenplay:* Charles Schnee and Nicholas Ray. *Selected bibliography:* Clarens; Geoff; Nicholas Ray; Silver and Ward.

*THE TREASURE OF THE SIERRA MADRE:* DIR. JOHN HUSTON (1948). Based on the 1927 novel by the mysterious B. Traven, *The Treasure of the Sierra Madre* is a rousing adventure story that at the same time makes telling and powerful statements about capitalist greed. Indeed, given the political climate in America in 1948, the film sticks remarkably close to the book in terms of plot and even political stance, though the film's maker were pressured by Warner Brothers to mute the latter. The film was highly successful with both audiences and critics, winning an Academy Award nomination for best picture; director Huston was given the Academy Award for best director and best screenplay for the film.

The plot of *The Treasure of the Sierra Madre* is quite simple and straightforward. Having failed to win at the lottery, down-and-out American Fred C. Dobbs (Humphrey Bogart) finds himself begging in the streets of the Mexican port town of Tampico. Along with another American, the good-hearted Curtin (Tim Holt), he gets a job on the construction of an oil derrick. They work in brutal heat, only to be cheated out of their pay. Eventually they meet up with the experienced prospector Howard (Walter Huston), and the three decide to try their luck at prospecting for gold in the nearby mountains. The wily old Howard warns them early on of the seduction of gold, which produces a lust for more that is almost impossible to satisfy but that will drive men to any extreme in the attempt. He also issues one of the film's most trenchant (and most Marxist) economic statements early on when he explains that gold, not being particularly useful in itself, is as valuable as it is because of "the amount of human labor that went into the finding and the getting of it."

Indeed, one of the major points of the film is to show the amount of human labor involved in the mining of gold, thus demystifying romantic myths about the get-rich-quick nature of prospecting while at the same time substantiating Marx's labor theory of value. The three protagonists struggle against inhospitable natural surroundings and with the back-breaking labor required to extract gold from the remote mountain where they go to prospect. Howard's experience stands them in good stead, however, and (despite the tensions and mutual distrust that grow among the three of them, especially on the part of Dobbs) they manage after months of labor to gather a substantial amount of gold in the form of sandlike grains. The three weather the intrusion of a fourth prospector and an attack by bandits, then eventually set out to return to civilization in order to cash in their gold.

On the way, Howard revives a young Indian boy who is comatose after a near drowning, and the Indians insist that he stay with them for a while so that they can show their gratitude. Dobbs and Curtin continue on, taking Howard's share of the gold with them. Curtin is appalled when Dobbs suggests that the two of them abscond with Howard's share, and Dobbs's greed eventually drives him to mental instability. He overpowers and shoots Curtin, leaving him for dead. Dobbs then goes on alone but is soon accosted by the bandits, who kill him and take the gold-laden burros. They mistake the gold for sand and simply scatter it on the ground, taking the burros and other supplies with them to a nearby town to sell. There, they are recognized as robbers, captured, and summarily executed by Mexican soldiers after being forced to dig their own graves.

Curtin, meanwhile, revives and is reunited with Howard, now living in tranquility in the Indian village. Although Curtin is still weak from his wound, the two set out, accompanied by Indians, in search of Dobbs and the gold. The two of them make their way to the town and recover their burros, only to learn that the gold dust has been lost, blown away in a windstorm. Howard decides to remain among the Indians, where he is now a revered medicine man. Curtin heads north to Texas and whatever further adventures fortune brings.

*Treasure* is a highly successful and entertaining adventure film that also treats a number of important issues in an intelligent way. These issues are very strongly social and political, and many of them are addressed from a perspective with strongly leftist intonations, though certainly in a muted form. For example, the disintegration of Dobbs's personality beneath the pressure of greed can be seen as a comment on human nature but also as a powerful allegory of the damaging effect on the human psyche of a capitalist civilization based on the quest for monetary gain. Indeed, the alienation caused by capitalism is a central theme of *Treasure*, which opposes the fragmentation of social relations under capitalist society to the communal nature of traditional Mexican Indian societies, which function as the text's principal utopian image. **Screenplay:** John Huston. **Selected bibliography:** Brill (*John Huston's Filmmaking*); Engell; Kaminsky; McCarty (*Films of John Huston*).

*CHAMPION:* DIR. MARK ROBSON (1949). *Champion* begins as world middleweight boxing champion Midge Kelly (played by Kirk Douglas, in a role that won him an Oscar nomination and made him a star), enters a crowded arena to defend his title. A ringside announcer proclaims the compelling nature of Midge's personal story, which most of the rest of film, in an extended flashback, then proceeds to tell. The flashback begins as Midge and his crippled brother, Connie (Arthur Kennedy), ride the rails cross-country, traveling from their Chicago home to Los Angeles, where they have supposedly bought part interest in a diner. On the way, Midge substitutes for an injured fighter in a bout in Kansas City. Having no ring experience, Midge is no match for his opponent, Johnny Dunne (John Day), though he shows considerable toughness, drawing the attention of fight manager Tommy Haley (Paul Stewart). He is also cheated by the promoter out of most of his promised pay, a recurring theme in his life.

When the Kellys arrive in Los Angeles, they discover that they have been swindled in the diner deal, but the diner's true owner takes them on as hired help. Midge soon strikes up a relationship with the owner's daughter, Emma (Ruth Roman), which eventually leads to a shotgun wedding at the insistence of her father (Harry Shannon). Midge and a reluctant Connie (who is in love with Emma) skip out immediately after the wedding. Midge looks up Haley, who agrees to train him. Then, after an extended period of grueling preparation, Midge finally has his first real professional fight, which he wins by a knockout, showing a savage killer instinct. From this point on, Midge rises rapidly through the middleweight ranks, eventually getting a fight in New York against Dunne, who is now the top contender for the title. The fight, however, has been fixed by the mob that controls the New York fight game. Midge is supposed to lose, clearing the way for Dunne to fight for the title. Instead, Midge knocks out Dunne in the first round, after which Midge, Connie, and Haley are all beaten up by thugs. Midge is then blacklisted and finds it impossible to get another fight in New York.

Midge eventually makes a deal to play ball with the mob, dumping Tommy as his manager and signing with the mob-connected Jerome Harris (Luis Van Rooten) instead. Connie returns to Chicago, where he lives with their mother and Emma, who comes to join them and who soon plans to divorce Midge and marry Connie. In the process, Midge strikes up a relationship with Grace Diamond (Marilyn Maxwell), the blonde gold digger who accompanied Dunne on his rise to the top, then dropped him as soon as he lost to Midge. Grace is clearly a sort of female counterpart to Midge: both market their bodies for profit and ruthlessly exploit those they encounter in the process.

With his new mob connections, Midge quickly rises to the top and captures the world title. Along the way, he dumps Grace and becomes involved with Harris's young wife, Palmer (Lola Albright), whom he drops as well after Harris offers him a handsome bribe. The film then returns to its starting point, as Midge enters the ring to defend his title against Dunne, who has now come back from the injuries suffered in his earlier fight with Midge. After a furious bout in which Dunne seems to have the upper hand, Midge wins by a knockout in a final burst of the fury that has always fueled his success as a boxer. Soon after the fight, however, Midge falls dead of a brain hemorrhage. Connie gives reporters a final statement praising Midge, then walks away with Emma.

The fight scenes of *Champion* lack the realism of those seen in *The Set-Up*, released in the same year, but the film is compelling in its depiction of the character of Midge within the cutthroat environment of the fight game and of American capitalism as a whole. The film clearly suggests that Midge's amoral ruthlessness is a direct result of his experience with capitalist society, which he sees as his real opponent in the ring. As he puts it, "No fat belly with a big cigar is gonna make a monkey outta me. I can beat 'em." In particular, *Champion* makes clear the background of extreme poverty that has made Midge willing to do anything necessary to get ahead. At times, the film also calls attention to its use of the fight game as a metaphor for capitalism, as when Midge declares that boxing is just like any other business, "only the blood shows." **Screenplay:** Carl Foreman. **Selected bibliography:** Neve (*Film*); Recchia ("Setting").

*HOME OF THE BRAVE:* DIR. MARK ROBSON (1949). *Home of the Brave* deals with a reconnaissance mission carried out by a group of American GI's on a Japanese-held island in the Pacific, just prior to the invasion of that island by American forces. It is, however, far more than a mere combat film. Its real subject is racism, in both the American military and American society as a whole. As the film begins, Peter Moss (James Edwards), an African American soldier, is being treated in a military field hospital, where the doctor concludes that the paralysis of Moss's legs has psychological, rather than physical, causes. He questions Moss, gradually piecing together the background of his ailment in the reconnaissance mission and in his life before the military. Most of the rest of the film narrates that mission in flashback.

As the mission begins, young Major Robinson asks three of his men, Mingo (Frank Lovejoy), Finch (Lloyd Bridges), and T. J. (Steve Brodie), to volunteer to accompany him on the mission, which will also include a surveyor from the engineering corps. Finch is delighted to learn that the surveyor is Moss, his old schoolmate and friend. However, T. J., a bigot, is disgusted to learn that Moss is black. He is bothered by class prejudices as well; having been a business executive in civilian life, he finds it demeaning to take orders as a mere corporal in the army, especially from someone as young as Robinson. Nevertheless, all of the men, including T.

J., agree to go on the mission. They are put ashore on the island, then make their way through the thick jungle, taking photographs and preparing maps as they go. All goes well until the survey is nearly complete and they begin to pack up to go home. Then Mingo is wounded by a Japanese sniper. Finch and Moss frantically scramble to gather the maps, in the heat of which Finch nearly makes a racist remark. Finch is then also shot, and Moss is forced to leave him behind in order to take the maps to the beach. Moss and the others hear Finch's screams as the Japanese find and torture him. Moss eventually makes his way back and finds a mutilated Finch crawling through the jungle. Finch dies in Moss's arms, triggering Moss's paralysis, apparently as a result of his guilt over feeling momentarily glad when Finch was shot.

Pursued by Japanese, the others manage to carry Moss back to the beach and get safely aboard the boat that has come to pick them up. Back at the American base, Mingo has to have his arm amputated, while Moss is treated for his paralysis. Eventually, the doctor convinces Moss that all soldiers feel that momentary gladness when someone else is shot, simply out of relief that they themselves have not been hit. Moreover, he helps Moss to understand that his guilt is rooted in feelings of inadequacy caused by a lifetime of racial insults but not by any fault of his own. Eventually, Moss regains the use of his legs. He and Mingo are sent back stateside, where they agree to go into business together as the owners of a restaurant and bar, something Moss had originally planned to do with Finch.

For its time, *Home of the Brave* is a powerful indictment of racism, especially in its dramatization of the suffering caused by racial bigotry and intolerance. On the other hand, the emphasis on Moss's personal traumas tends to make the problem seem more a question of individual neurosis than social inequity. Indeed, Roffman and Purdy conclude that the emphasis on Moss's oversensitivity makes the problem seem "as much his own fault as that of racist America" (246). The film is also weakened by a truly awful soundtrack and by a certain amount of overacting, while the final alliance between Mingo and Moss provides an overly easy solution to the serious social problems the film has exposed. Nevertheless, given the overt anti-Japanese racism of so many World War II films, the use of the war film genre to make a statement against racism should be regarded as an important development. *Screenplay:* Carl Foreman. *Selected bibliography:* Neve (*Film*); Roffman and Purdy; Sayre; Shindler.

*KNOCK ON ANY DOOR:* **DIR. NICHOLAS RAY (1949).** Based on Willard Motley's 1947 novel of the same title, *Knock on Any Door* narrates the decline of a young Italian-American, Nick Romano (played by John Derek), into juvenile delinquency and crime. Nick is a sort of Jim Stark without money, and *Knock on Any Door* can, to an extent, be seen as a forerunner of Ray's 1955 *Rebel Without a Cause*. Much of Motley's book is devoted to a detailed narration of Nick's childhood and adolescence, making clear that Nick's criminality is a result not of a natural proclivity to crime but of his dehumanizing and impoverished environment. Both the book and the film indict a system of justice and social services that seems designed not to help Nick rehabilitate himself but instead to push him into more and more serious crimes. The book, however, is a sort of anti-bildungsroman that narrates the decline and degradation of Nick, its protagonist, while the film is primarily a courtroom drama dealing with Nick's trial for murder after a policeman is gunned down in the opening scene.

Nick's lawyer, Andrew Morton (Humphrey Bogart) emerges as the central figure in the film, though he is a minor character in the book. (In fact, the film's Morton is a composite of the book's Morton and another character, Grant Holloway, a writer interested in juvenile justice reform.) Most of what we learn about Nick's background in the film is supplied through flashback segments that illustrates the arguments made by Morton to the court on Nick's behalf. Morton has a special sympathy for Nick, partly because Morton himself came from a similarly underprivileged background. But Morton also befriends Nick out of a sense of guilt; Nick's slide into crime began after his father was wrongly convicted of manslaughter and sent to prison, where he died of a heart attack. That conviction occurred because Morton, who was supposed to defend Mr. Romano, was too busy working on the will of a rich client and thus turned the case over to his partner, who bungled the defense.

Morton now works for a prestigious law firm, where, early in the film, he is offered a partnership if only he will refuse to defend Nick in the murder case, which might generate publicity detrimental to the firm. But the upright Morton takes the case nevertheless and soon becomes convinced of Nick's innocence. As the trial proceeds, Morton seems to be winning the case, partly because two of Nick's friends supply alibis and partly because Morton is able to demonstrate that the prosecution, led by District Attorney Kerman (George Macready), has been bribing and threatening witnesses to convince them to testify against Nick. (The film, however, omits the book's demonstration that Nick had been viciously beaten by the police after his arrest in an unsuccessful attempt to extract a confession.)

Morton is also a master at jury manipulation, and his narration of Nick's troubled past clearly draws sympathy from the jury. For example, they (and we) learn that Nick and his best friend had been sent to a gruesome reform school during adolescence and that the friend died there as a direct effect of inhuman punishment. Describing the school as an "island of outrage," Morton argues that such experiences "degrade and brutalize," that they "twist a kid, and turn him." Morton also argues that Nick has tried very hard to go straight, but has been continually thwarted by the society around him. Moreover, his latest descent into criminality has been triggered by the suicide of his young wife, Emma (Allene Roberts), who had been the one positive influence in his young life.

Emma, in fact, is Nick's one soft spot, a fact Kerman takes advantage of when he questions Nick on the stand. Nick seems about to escape the cross-examination unscathed, but, when Kerman asks about Emma's suicide, Nick loses his composure and ends up confessing to the shooting of the policeman. Despite feeling betrayed by Nick's former protestations of innocence, Morton makes a final heart-rending plea for mercy, declaring that "Nick Romano is guilty, but so are we, and so is that precious thing called society." Judge Drake (Barry Kelley) claims to be greatly moved, but rules that the law dictates a death sentence, which he delivers. As the film ends, Nick is taken away by guards as Morton wistfully looks on, having committed himself to spend the rest of his life working to help kids like Nick.

All of these circumstances combine to generate considerable sympathy for Nick, even though Derek makes the character particularly unattractive. Indeed, that is part of the point, as the film seeks to show how environment has molded Nick into an almost psychopathic figure. However, it is also the case that the film's (and the book's) most remembered line is Nick's motto, "Live fast, die young, and leave a good-looking corpse," which tends to detract from the pathos of his characterization. In any case, the obvious point of the film is that we need to reform the juvenile justice system and to work in other ways to provide better opportunities for poor kids like Nick, lest our neglect come back to haunt us. However, as Dana Polan notes, the film has larger implications as well. Placing the film within the context of postwar anxieties about rising rates of juvenile delinquency, Polan also suggests that it reflects anxieties about the future in general. The film's ultimate, nightmarish, message, he argues, is that "one's children don't reflect back one's place in the world but, rather, show it coming to a farcical or unbearable point of no return" (246). At the same time, the film, more than the book, has its reassuring aspects, especially in the portrayal of Morton, who has had the same disadvantages as Nick, but has become a successful and productive member of society, presumably by virtue of his own strength of character. There are, of course, ethnic differences between Morton and Nick, but the film makes nothing of these. On the other hand, the generational difference between Morton and Nick tends to suggest that the social problems to which both have been exposed are getting worse with time. Motley's book was followed by a sequel, the 1958 *Let No Man Write My Epitaph*, which became a Bogart film in 1960. ***Screenplay:*** Daniel Taradash and John Monks, Jr. *Selected bibliography:* Andrew; Blaine; Eisenschitz; Geoff; Neve (*Film*); Polan; Nicholas Ray.

*THE LAWLESS:* DIR. JOSEPH LOSEY (1949). Made on a tiny budget (and over the objections of the Breen Office that its subject matter was too critical of America and its people), *The Lawless* is nonetheless a reasonably successful thriller that manages to tell a compelling and suspenseful story while also making some trenchant comments about economic and racial oppression in America. The film centrally addresses the persecution and exploitation of immigrant fruit pickers in California, revolving around a racial disturbance at a dance, after which a young Mexican-American of Aztec ancestry, Paul Rodriguez (played by Lalo Rios), strikes a policeman by mistake, then panics and escapes by stealing a car. Arrested, Rodriguez again escapes when the police car carrying him crashes and burns. While he is on the run, he is wrongfully accused of assaulting a white girl. The press sensationalizes these events, but, when newspaperman Larry Wilder (Macdonald Carey) reports on the case in a manner that is perceived as sympathetic to Rodriguez, a white mob breaks into and wrecks the newspaper office, planning then to go after Rodriguez. Wilder, however, shows up and excoriates the mob, shaming them into submission, especially after they realize that a crusading woman reporter, Sunny Garcia (Gail Russell), was nearly killed in the attack on the newspaper.

There is, in *The Lawless*, a certain critique of the rich, particularly of the unscrupulous fruit growers who employ, and exploit, the migrant pickers. Moreover, the film carefully points out the class difference between Paul and his poor family and the well-to-do family of Joe Ferguson (John Sands), one of Paul's white tormentors. On the other hand, the film's depiction of racially motivated mob violence is strongly critical of the ordinary American masses, potentially suggesting a dark side in the American character similar to that which led to the rise of Nazism in Germany. Although relatively realistic, *The Lawless* employs a number of expressionistic effects to create an atmosphere of sinister threat. Losey would soon experience this threat firsthand. Blacklisted in Hollywood after failing to respond to a call to testify before HUAC in 1951, Losey moved to Britain, where he directed a number of important films over the next three decades. *Screenplay:* Geoffrey Homes (Daniel Mainwaring). *Selected bibliography:* Caute (*Joseph Losey*); Ciment; Hirsch; Neve (*Film*); Palmer and Riley.

*PINKY:* DIR. ELIA KAZAN (1949). Considered daring in its time, *Pinky* is a racial problem film that traces the experiences of African American Patricia Johnson (Jeanne Crain), who is called Pinky because of her extremely light skin. Actually, the film does not reveal Pinky's exact racial background, except for the fact that her grandmother, Dysey Johnson (Ethel Waters) is black. But Pinky is clearly regarded as black within the racist context of the small Southern town in which she and Dysey live, and her white appearance generally seems only to stir up hostility from the town's white population. To some extent, the fact that Pinky looks entirely white, but is treated as black, demonstrates the absurdity of racial prejudice. At the same time, the film seems to regard Pinky as entirely black despite her white appearance, presenting her decision not to continue to pass for white as a matter of accepting her true identity, even though it is rather obvious that she has at least as much white blood as black. In any case, the basic premise of the film could have worked perfectly well with a genuinely black female protagonist, but apparently the makers of the film did not feel that, in 1949, they could successfully make a film with such a protagonist. As Roffman and Purdy put it, the casting of ultra-white actress Jeanne Crain as Pinky "makes her blackness acceptable without forcing us to confront it" (248–49).

As the film begins, Pinky returns home to the South after several years in Boston, where she has completed nursing school and become a professional nurse. She soon reveals to Dysey that, while in Boston, she passed for white, evoking rage and shame in her grandmother. We also learn that Pinky became romantically involved with a white doctor, Tom Adams (William Lundigan), though the relationship is now on the skids due to her confession of her racial background. Back in the South, Pinky, accustomed to living as a white woman in Boston, finds the racial prejudice that she encounters extremely oppressive, and she soon decides to return to the North, especially after Adams shows up generously to announce that he can now cope with her racial background and that he still wants to marry her.

Meanwhile, old Miss Em (Ethel Barrymore), a white woman who still lives in a plantation house built by slaves, has a heart attack and hovers near death. With no other trained nurses available, Pinky reluctantly agrees to nurse the cantankerous old woman as a favor to Dysey, who is devoted to Miss Em, whom she has known all her life. Pinky sticks with Miss Em until her death, and the two gradually grow fond of each other. Shortly before her death, Miss Em drafts a new will leaving her house and land to Pinky. Miss Em's horrendous, greedy relatives contest the will in court, but, surprisingly, justice prevails, and Pinky, with the aid of her lawyer, Judge Walker (Basil Ruysdael), wins the case. Afterward, she breaks off her engagement with Adams once and for all, realizing that he will never overcome his ambivalence about her race. She then converts Miss Em's old house into a clinic and nursery school for black children, knowing that Miss Em would have been pleased to see the house put to such good use. The film thus ultimately accepts the reality of segregation in the South and does nothing to challenge that situation. *Screenplay:* Philip Dunne and Dudley Nichols. *Selected bibliography:* Kazan; Neve (*Film*); Roffman and Purdy.

*SALT TO THE DEVIL:* DIR. EDWARD DMYTRYK (1949). An adaptation of Pietro di Donato's 1939 proletarian novel, *Christ in Concrete, Salt to the Devil* (originally released in the United Kingdom as *Give Us This Day*) features a director, screenwriter (Ben Barzman), and star (Sam Wanamaker), all of whom were working in exile in Britain after their blacklisting in America as a result of the HUAC-inspired anticommunist purges of Hollywood. Di Donato's novel, written in a highly experimental mode that relies greatly on symbolism and stream-of-consciousness, would not appear to be a good candidate for adaptation to the screen. But Barzman and Dmytryk were reasonably successful in their adaptation, maintaining the central situation and much of the plot of at least the first section of the novel, adopting some of its central images, and producing a film the overall impact of which is at least recognizably similar to that of the novel.

The plot of the film is fairly simple and indeed is greatly condensed from that of the book. Geremio (Wanamaker), a poor Italian immigrant, works in construction, while he and his wife, Annunziata (Lea Padovani), dream of saving enough money to be able to buy their own home. Unfortunately, their plans are thwarted when the Depression hits and Geremio's subsequent unemployment makes it necessary for the family to spend their meager savings just to survive. Desperate, Geremio accepts a dangerous job in an unsafe workplace, then falls into a wet slab of concrete and is entombed within it. The film then ends with an ironic twist in which the insurance settlement received by Annunziata is just enough to buy the home of which she has so long dreamed, though the dream, without Geremio to share it, will be an empty one.

This ending is far different from that the similar episode in the book, in which the unscrupulous contractor, Murdin (played in the film by Sidney James), falsely claims that the accident was Geremio's fault, and the insurance company therefore refuses to pay any compensation to Geremio's survivors. Meanwhile, the film elides the role played by Geremio's son, Paul, who is actually the most important character in the book, thus also omitting the book's most overtly leftist episode, Paul's final rejection of Catholicism in favor of radical political activism. Compared to the book's, then, the film's political stance is rather muted, though the film does at least have the virtue of treating manual labor as an honorable undertaking. Peter Bondarella, in fact, argues that "in no other American film of the period is the dignity of manual labor so strongly underlined" (231). There are also moments when the film seeks to emphasize the communal spirit of its immigrant workers, in opposition to the individualism encouraged by American capitalism. In one episode, for example, Murdin offers a reward to the bricklayer who can work fastest, but his five men decide to work as a team and split the reward rather than working against one another. Seen by Bondarella as an example of the American film noir that nevertheless owes a great deal to Italian neorealism, *Salt to the Devil* is an interesting and ambitious film despite its obviously low budget. **Screenplay:** Ben Barzman. **Selected bibliography:** Bondarella; Gardaphé; Neve (*Film*).

*THE SET-UP:* **DIR. ROBERT WISE (1949).** *The Set-Up* is a dark and pessimistic, but gripping, fight drama that contains some of the most realistic boxing scenes ever put on film. The narrative develops in real time as the seventy-two-minute film presents seventy-two minutes in the life of over-the-hill boxer Bill "Stoker" Thompson (Robert Ryan). Indeed, periodic shots of clocks during the film emphasize this effect by indicating how much time has passed. During these minutes, Stoker prepares for a boxing match, hoping, as he always does, somehow to land one magical punch that will propel him to victory, break his string of defeats, and put him back on the road to financial success. What he does not know is that his seedy manager, Tiny (George Tobias), has accepted fifty dollars from local gangster "Little Boy" (Alan Baxter) in return for his assurances that Stoker will throw the fight. Tiny knows that Stoker would never go along with the deal but assumes that Stoker will lose anyway, as he typically does.

The film includes a telling behind-the-scenes look at the fight game as Stoker prepares for his fight along with other boxers in the dilapidated dressing room at the arena in which the night's fights are being held. Boxing is presented as a realm of broken dreams, where young men go with high hopes of fame and fortune, only to end up, except for a chosen few, physically beaten and financially exploited. In this sense, as in so many boxing films, the presentation of boxing in *The Set-Up* can be taken as an allegory of capitalism, in which official rhetoric inspires dreams of universal upward mobility, while physical reality produces frustration and exploitation. In boxing, as in capitalism, the success of one comes at the expense of the failure of others, while the entire system is organized such that those who perform the actual labor profit from it less than those who manipulate them from behind the scenes. Similarly, Stoker's dream of landing the punch that will bring him success at last parallels typical dreams of a "big break" amid capitalist competition. But the film does not emphasize such allegorical points. Indeed, it focuses on a direct and realistic treatment of boxing, and Stoker's actual four-round bout takes up more than eighteen minutes of the film's total time.

Stoker puts up such a furious fight that Tiny has to inform him, after the third round, that the fight has been fixed. But this knowledge only infuriates Stoker, who fights all the more fiercely in the final round, knocking out his opponent, Tiger Nelson (Hal Fieberling), shortly before the scheduled end of the fight. Retribution is swift and predictable: after the fight, Little Boy and his thugs trap Stoker in an alley, beating him mercilessly. Then they crush his right hand with a brick, so that he will never be able to fight again. He staggers into the alley and collapses on the street, directly in front of a club called "Dreamland." His wife, Julie (Audrey Totter), who was unable to watch the fight because she was tired of seeing him take beatings, rushes to his side. She assures him that it is for the best that he will be unable to fight again, but it is also clear that fighting is crucial to his identity and that his subsequent life will be difficult indeed. *Screenplay:* Art Cohn. *Selected bibliography:* Neve (*Film*); Silver and Ward.

*THE THIRD MAN:* **DIR. CAROL REED (1949).** Set in occupied Vienna just after the end of World War II, *The Third Man* is an intensely atmospheric film that effectively uses its setting to enhance the air of evil and corruption that pervades the entire piece. The war-torn Vienna of the film is in many ways the central character. Shot mostly at night and largely in ruins, the former imperial capital of Austria-Hungary is, in fact, depicted as a broken shadow of its former splendid self, and in more ways than one. Not only has it been extensively damaged by the war, but it is also steeped in decadence, clearly a city in moral as well as physical ruin, a kind of specter of the feudal past struggling to cope with the capitalist present.

Capitalism is, in many ways, at the core of the film. In the opening scenes, we are introduced to a Vienna in which the supply of almost all commodities relies on black market distribution and in which almost all of the citizens participate in the black market. A shot of a floating corpse, however, reminds us of the potential fate of those who dabble in this market and helps to set the tone for the entire film. The actual plot of the film then begins as American novelist Holly Martins (played by Joseph Cotten), a writer of pulp Westerns, comes to Vienna to assume a job offered him there doing publicity work for a "medical charity" run by his old friend, Harry Lime (Orson Welles). On his arrival, however, he is told that Lime has just been killed in a street accident. When Martins attends the burial, he meets the British military policeman Major Calloway (Trevor Howard), who informs him that Lime had been the mastermind behind the blackest of black market schemes. Lime and his ring, Calloway claims, were stealing penicillin from local hospitals, then diluting it and selling it at huge profits on the black market. But the diluted drug was ineffectual, resulting in horrible suffering and gruesome deaths for those who were treated with it.

Martins, a sort of American naif abroad, is at first incredulous and decides to seek evidence of Lime's innocence. In the process, he meets (and eventually falls in love with) Lime's former girlfriend, the beautiful Anna Schmidt (Alida Valli). He also meets a weirdly sinister cast of Lime's former associates in Vienna, including Baron Kurtz (wonderfully played by Ernst Deutsch as a sort of degenerate vampire and figure of the decline of the European aristocracy), Dr. Winkel (played by Erich Ponto in a clearly Naziesque mode), and the sleazy Rumanian Popescu (Siegfried Breuer). The more evidence Martins collects (especially from the porter of the building in which Lime had lived), the more suspicious appear the circumstances surrounding Lime's death. Then the porter is killed, and Martins becomes convinced that Lime was murdered. In the meantime, however, Calloway has convinced him that Lime really was trafficking in tainted penicillin, so he concludes that the murder represented a kind of justice.

Unable to get Anna (who is still mourning Harry's death) to respond to his advances, Martins decides to leave Vienna. Then comes the film's most memorable moment, as Martins spots a figure apparently watching him from a darkened doorway. Martins approaches the doorway, complaining loudly about being under constant surveillance, causing a neighbor to turn on a light, which falls perfectly on the cherubic-sinister face of Welles/Lime, illuminated pure white against the black background of the doorway. But Lime runs away and seems to vanish into nowhere, leaving the befuddled Martins alone in the street. Martins reports the sighting to Calloway, who exhumes Lime's coffin, finding in it the body of a local hospital orderly who had been involved in Lime's scheme. Martins manages to meet with Lime, who informs him that he is hiding out in the Soviet sector of the city, protected by the Russians in return for their cooperation.

After this meeting, Martins decides not to help the British police capture Lime. However, the Russians have by now discovered (apparently from Lime) that Anna is not Austrian, but Czech, and they plan (for reasons unspecified in the film, which seems to assume that Russians simply do such things as a matter of course) to force her to return to Soviet-occupied Czechoslovakia. That, presumably, would be a fate worse than death, so Martins finally agrees to cooperate with Calloway in return for the latter's promise to help Anna escape from the Russians. Martins arranges a meeting with Lime, and Calloway stakes out the meeting, leading to the film's memorable chase sequence through the sewers beneath the city (which oddly seem better lighted and certainly in better repair than the streets and buildings above), resulting finally in Lime's shooting death at the hands of Martins. The film then repeats Lime's burial, after which Calloway is to take Martins to the airport to return to America. Instead, however, Martins stays behind to try to help

Anna, leaving both their futures uncertain as they stand together against the receding background of a lane lined by severely trimmed, leafless trees.

*The Third Man* is, properly speaking, a British film, made by a British company with a British screenwriter and director. Moreover, it is decidedly British in its outlook, presenting the British Calloway as a paragon of virtue and capability, while Americans are either bumbling innocents or vicious capitalists, Austrians are decadent blood-suckers, and Russians are so obviously horrid that their evils need not be specified. On the other hand, *The Third Man* is in many ways a quintessential example of the film noir, that decidedly American genre, with its detective-story plot amid an air of decadence and evil, dark and brooding look, weird shadows cast by expressionist lighting, and out-of-kilter camera angles. The film does, however, go beyond the typical film noir in its modernist techniques, especially in its haunting sound track of mostly cheerful zither music, completely out of whack with the look and content of the film. This disjunction creates a sort of Brechtian alienation effect that greatly enhances the film's pervasive (and bizarre) air of a world out of joint.

Still, the film has strong connections with the culture of the American Left. For one thing, Lime's evil black market scheme can obviously be taken as a comment on the especially predatory nature of American capitalism (which turns out in this film to have roughly the same moral content, or lack thereof, as Russian communism, as opposed to the genuine morality of British culture). Similarly, the film's depiction of the pulp novels produced by Martins can be taken as a comment on the debased nature of American culture, a comment enhanced when Martins attempts to give a lecture before a British-run cultural group in Vienna, where he demonstrates that he is virtually illiterate and knows essentially nothing about literature. Finally, Welles's role in the project (and he dominates the film, despite not appearing until it is two-thirds over) can be taken as a signal of his endorsement of the film's criticisms of American culture. It is worth recalling that Welles's participation in *The Third Man* marked the beginning of a self-imposed exile of several years, during which Welles remained in Europe to escape not only the Hollywood studio system, but the congressional witch-hunts of the time. *Screenplay:* Graham Greene. ***Selected bibliography:*** Bazin; Gomez; Glen K. Man; Moss; Naremore (*Magic*); Naremore (*More than Night*); Van Wert.

*THE ASPHALT JUNGLE:* **DIR. JOHN HUSTON (1950).** *The Asphalt Jungle* is a classic crime drama, one of the defining works of that genre. It combines an effective film noir look with a taut and suspenseful plot, while at the same time making some important observations about modern capitalist society. As the title indicates, the film portrays the modern city as a jungle, drawing upon a literary tradition that dates back to such illustrious predecessors as Upton Sinclair and Bertolt Brecht. In particular, *The Asphalt Jungle* suggests that crime and violence pervade every aspect of modern urban society—on both sides of the law. At the same time, the film explores the link between crime and capitalist acquisitiveness in a particularly insightful manner. This social analysis leads Thom Anderson to consider the film an example of the film gris (183). It gained four Academy Award nominations, including best director and best screenplay, but it won no awards, perhaps because of its dark message. *The Asphalt Jungle* was widely criticized for its sympathetic treatment of its criminal characters, who are generally presented as far more virtuous than the film's solid citizens.

The film begins as criminal mastermind Erwin "Doc" Riedenschneider (Sam Jaffe), fresh out of prison, immediately begins to carry out an elaborate jewel robbery that he had first planned seven years earlier, just before his imprisonment. He goes about the operation in an extremely professional manner, suggesting clear parallels between the workings of crime and the workings of everyday American business. For example, his first step is to secure investment capital, which he seeks, using the bookie Cobby (Marc Lawrence) as a middle-man, from respected attorney Alonzo Emmerich (Louis Calhern). Emmerich also agrees to help with the marketing of the stolen jewels. Meanwhile, Doc hires a crew of professional specialists, including safecracker Louis Ciavelli (Anthony Caruso), getaway driver Gus Ninissi (James Whitmore), and gunman Dix Handley (Sterling Hayden).

This carefully assembled group is presented in a largely positive light. Doc is cold and calculating, in many ways a typical example of the negative image of intellectuals (especially German intellectuals) in postwar America. Even his human side, which surfaces primarily in his irresistible attraction to young girls, has a sinister aspect. At the same time, he is not really evil; he abhors violence and steals only from the rich. Louis, meanwhile, is a skilled professional who commits crimes only because of his devotion to his family, and Gus is a warmhearted hunchback who helps out unfortunates and loves cats. Dix is in many ways the central character. Not the brightest guy in the world, he shows evidence of genuine kindness and commits crimes largely to further his dream of recovering his family's lost farm back in Kentucky. In short, the film's actual "workers" are upright and sympathetic, while the only really evil characters are the corrupt bourgeois Emmerich, the criminal capitalist Cobby, and the corrupt cop, Lieutenant Ditrich (Barry Kelley).

The robbery seems to go off well until alarms unexpectedly sound, drawing the police. Doc and his gang still manage to secure the jewels and to make their getaway, though Louis is seriously wounded by a gunshot (in a freak accident) in the process. Meanwhile, the gang is double-crossed by Emmerich, who turns out to be desperate for cash due to his profligate lifestyle, which among other things involves the keeping of an expensive mistress, Angela Phinlay (played by Marilyn Monroe, in a small role that clearly shows evidence of her future star quality). Emmerich unsuccessfully attempts to steal the jewels for himself; in the process, Emmerich's henchman, Bob Brannom (Brad Dexter), is shot and killed by Dix, who is in turn wounded by Brannom. Doc then suggests that, with the heat on, Emmerich should try to make a deal with the insurance company for the return of the jewels at a discount price, no questions asked.

The insurance company agrees to pay $250,000 for the return of the jewels. Unfortunately, the police are closing in, and the whole plan seems to be collapsing, especially when the police identify Doc as their principal suspect. Eventually, Cobby spills his guts to the police, who begin to round up the gang. Retribution is swift. Gus and Ditrich join Cobby in jail; Emmerich shoots himself to avoid arrest; Louis dies of his wound. Doc seems on the verge of escape when he manages to find a German cab driver who agrees to take him to Cleveland. However, on the way out of town they stop for food at a roadside diner, where Doc becomes fascinated by a teenage girl dancing to the jukebox and ends up lingering so long that police arrive and arrest him. Dix, though weakening from loss of blood, manages to drive all the way back to Kentucky, accompanied by his faithful moll, Doll Conovan (Jean Hagen). He then staggers onto his family's old farm and drops dead on the land he loved, surrounded by horses. The film is then wrapped up as Police Commissioner Hardy (John McIntire) talks with reporters and explains all of the recent developments as typical episodes in modern city life. *Screenplay:* Ben Maddow and John Huston. *Selected bibliography:* **Thom** Anderson; Brill (*John Huston's Filmmaking*); Clarens; Kaminsky; McCarty (*Films of John Huston*); Naremore (*More than Night*); Neve (*Film*); Porfirio ("Whatever Happened"); Silver and Ward.

*BROKEN ARROW:* **DIR. DELMER DAVES (1950).** *Broken Arrow* was one of the few American films to attempt to treat Native American culture with sensitivity and respect, triggering a whole series of relatively sympathetic "Indian" movies, as well as spinning off into a radio serial and television series of its own. Based loosely on actual historical events, the film begins as the Apaches of Arizona are involved in an all-out war against the white soldiers and settlers who have invaded their lands. Tom Jeffords (James Stewart), a white pioneer, is prospecting in the wilderness when he comes upon an Apache boy who has been wounded by soldiers. Jeffords nurses the boy back to health, in the process coming to realize that Apaches are people and not crazed, subhuman savages. He therefore sets about studying the Apache culture and language, which eventually allows him to establish a close friendship with Cochise (Jeff Chandler), the chief of the Apaches.

Knowing of this friendship, General Howard (Basil Rusdael), the agent in charge of local Indian affairs, convinces Jeffords to help him establish a peace treaty with Cochise and the Apaches. The treaty is approved, though some Apaches, led by Geronimo, dissent, carrying on their guerrilla campaign against white intrusions into Indian lands. Meanwhile, a gang of white Apache haters, led by rancher Ben Slade (Will Geer), ambushes Cochise, Jeffords, and a group of Apaches, killing Sonseeahray (Debra Paget), the young Apache woman who has become the wife of Jeffords. Furious, Jeffords vows revenge, but Chochise insists on continuing to abide by the terms of the treaty. The local whites, appalled by the murderous attack, round up the culprits and bring them to justice, thus solidifying the peace.

Cochise is presented in the film as a dignified and statesmanlike figure, and the film as a whole attempts a sympathetic representation of Apache culture, even if this representation remains trapped within certain Hollywood stereotypes, ultimately endowing the Apaches with what are essentially white, bourgeois virtues. In historical reality, incidentally, Jeffords really did help negotiate a peace with Chochise in 1872. Jeffords then became the Indian agent for the new Apache reservation that was established in that treaty. However, Chochise died in 1874, after which the U.S. government broke the treaty and removed the Apaches to a different reservation, their original land having become too valuable. The film, perhaps not surprisingly, leaves out this development. Moreover, it limits its sympathy for Apaches to the cooperative Cochise, depicting the more recalcitrant Geronimo in an extremely negative light. Although the screenplay for *Broken Arrow* was originally credited to Michael Blankfort, screenwriting credit has now been restored to the then-blacklisted Albert Maltz, for whom Blankfort served as a front. *Screenplay:* Albert Maltz. *Selected bibliography:* Biskind (*Seeing*); Neve (*Film*); Michael Walker ("Westerns").

*HE RAN ALL THE WAY:* **DIR. JOHN BERRY (1951).** *He Ran All the Way* is a compelling crime drama that was the last film of important leftist actor John Garfield, described by Thom Anderson as the embodiment in American film of the Jewish working class (184). Anderson considers the film one of the leading examples of the film gris, a genre that for him conveys some of the same critique of the American dream as the film noir, but with greater social and psychological realism. The film features Garfied as Nick Robey, a small-time hood, who carries out a payroll robbery with his friend, Al Molin (Norman Lloyd). The robbery goes badly, and the thieves panic, leading to a shootout. Both Molin and a guard are wounded. Robey flees with the stolen money to a nearby swimming pool, where he meets Peg Dobbs (Shelley Winters), who takes him home with her and introduces him to her working-class parents and younger brother. Later, Robey again panics and takes the family hostage at gunpoint. When he learns that the wounded guard has died, he tries to use the hostages to escape but is eventually shot down by Peg in order to save her father (Wallace Ford).

Garfield, in his final film, dominates the film with his affecting portrayal of a man on the run, feeling surrounded and threatened by forces larger than himself. Eddie Muller, in fact, considers this Garfield's finest performance (32). The dynamic of Robey's relationship with the Dobbs family is particularly interesting as he almost desperately seeks to be accepted by them but is ultimately unable to trust them or to feel like one of them. Robey thus becomes an allegorical representative of the alienated capitalist subject, making *He Ran All the Way* an even more direct criticism of capitalism than most films of its genre. This aspect of the film may show the influence of leftist screenwriters Endore and Butler, who were aided in their work by an uncredited (and blacklisted) Dalton Trumbo. *Screenplay:* Guy Endore and Hugo Butler. *Selected bibliography:* Thom Anderson; Muller; Neve (*Film*); Silver and Ward.

*I CAN GET IT FOR YOU WHOLESALE:* **DIR. MICHAEL GORDON (1951).** Susan Hayward plays Harriet Boyd, a model in a dress house in New York, who hopes someday to become a big-time designer. Toward that end, she starts her own company, taking with her Teddy Sherman (Dan Daily) and Cooper (Sam Jaffe), two key employees of her old firm. As they pool their resources to get the new company going, Sherman falls in love with Boyd, who is in the meantime considering an exclusive deal to design and manufacture evening gowns for a ritzy department store, represented by Noble (George Sanders). Sherman opposes the deal, feeling they should concentrate on making inexpensive dresses for ordinary women rather than catering to the rich. The independent-minded Boyd, who is rather ruthlessly devoted to the success of the business, secretly makes the deal with Noble anyway, but Sherman and Cooper refuse to go along, and their company goes bankrupt. Boyd decides to go away to Europe with Noble, but he realizes she is only going with him to get revenge on Sherman. Living up to his name, Noble cancels the trip and suggests that she make her peace with Sherman instead. Boyd returns to Sherman, and the film ends as he takes her into his arms, presumably the first step toward rebuilding both their romance and their business, though there are certainly still issues to be resolved.

Although concentrating, Hollywood style, on romance, *I Can Get It for You Wholesale* does pay significant attention to the world of business in a way that is highly critical of the capitalist dedication to making profit, rather than providing service. Given this, perhaps it is not surprising that both director Gordon and screenwriter Polonsky were soon to be black-listed as a result of the HUAC hearings. Meanwhile, the film is, for its time, quite forward-looking in its treatment of gender, even if that aspect of the film ultimately conflicts with its critique of capitalism. Thus, Boyd is depicted as a woman who initially puts aside her budding romance with Sherman in favor of a single-minded devotion to business, but the film ultimately condemns this devotion, while returning her to the arms of Sherman, her true love. *Screenplay:* Abraham Polonsky and Vera Caspary. *Selected bibliography:* Buhl; Neve (*Film*).

*NATIVE SON:* **DIR. PIERRE CHENAL (1951).** *Native Son* is a low-budget adaptation of Richard Wright's powerful 1940 novel of the same title, featuring Wright in the central role of Bigger Thomas. Wright, at forty-two, was more than twice the age of the character in the book, though Bigger's age is boosted to twenty-five in the film. Nevertheless, Wright's performance is not awful and remains perhaps the most interesting reason to see the film, which is otherwise so heavily bowdlerized that it loses most of the visceral power of the book. The film also lacks the book's leftist political power, opting to avoid the book's communist perspective and indeed avoiding any mention of communism whatsoever.

As the film begins, Bigger, a bitter young black man from the South Side of Chicago, is hired as a live-in chauffeur for the Daltons, a wealthy white family. On his very first night on the job, he is assigned to drive their daughter, Mary (Jean Wallace), to the college where she attends classes. Once in the car, however, Mary orders Bigger to drive her downtown to pick up her boyfriend, Jan Erlone (Jean Michael), identified only as a member of an "outfit" that is associated with unions. Jan and Mary ask Bigger about his life and get him to drive them to the South Side, where they visit a club where Bigger's girlfriend, Bessie Mears (Gloria Madison), is debuting as a lounge singer. By the time Bigger gets Mary home, she is so drunk he has to carry her to her room. When Mary's blind mother (Ruth Roberts) comes into the room, Bigger panics and stifles Mary with a pillow so she will not reveal her drunkenness. Too late, he realizes he has suffocated her, then carries her body to the basement and disposes of it in the furnace.

After an investigation in which Bigger attempts to cover himself by making it look as if Mary has been kidnapped by Erlone, Bigger is finally implicated in Mary's death. He goes on the run and, in the process, murders Bessie, whom he wrongly thinks has betrayed him to police. He is then captured, taken to jail, and tried for murder. The film almost totally omits the efforts of the communist lawyer, Max (Don Dean), to save Bigger, efforts that are the political center of the book. It also omits the prosecution's groundless charges that Bigger had raped Mary before killing her. In the end, Bigger is predictably convicted and sentenced to death. *Screenplay:* Pierre Chenal and Richard Wright. *Selected bibliography:* Burks; Jerry W. Ward, Jr.

*A PLACE IN THE SUN:* DIR. GEORGE STEVENS (1951). A loose adaptation of Theodore Dreiser's *An American Tragedy* (1925), *A Place in the Sun* is a fine Hollywood film. Technically well made, it features fine acting performances and tells an effective and compelling story. Unfortunately, this story is not the one told by Dreiser's novel, which emphasizes the tendency of American capitalist society to create dreams and expectations that can never be fulfilled within the strict class structure that informs that society. The political commentary of the book is, in fact, almost entirely absent from the film. As George Barbarow puts it, Dreiser's "indictment of a social and economic system" is reduced in the film to the Holywood cliché that "crime doesn't pay" (290). But even crime is not the focus of the film, which is little more than a conventional tale of doomed love, detailing a passionate but troubled romance between George Eastman (Montgomery Clift) and Angela Vickers (Elizabeth Taylor).

Granted, class differences play a role in the difficulties that face this relationship. George is a poor relation trying to work his way up in a company owned by his wealthy uncle, Charles Eastman (Herbert Heyes); Angela is the daughter of wealthy friends of Charles. In point of fact, however, George surmounts these class difficulties relatively easily. He seems headed not only for success in the business, but also wins the love of Angela. He passionately returns this love but shows few signs of the way in which his counterpart in the book, Clyde Griffiths, falls in love with his version of Angela largely because of her class position, viewing her as a sort of commodity that can serve as a sign of his commercial success.

The romance between George and Angela (in this sense closely paralleling the book) is complicated by George's previous involvement with a poor woman who works in his uncle's factory and who announces that she is pregnant by him. In the film, this woman, Alice Tripp (Shelley Winters), is a somewhat annoying and pathetic figure, babbling endlessly and at times seeming almost villainous in her demands that the alienated and confused George marry her. In any case, she is clearly no match for the charming and dazzlingly beautiful Angela. Unlike the book, however, the film downplays the class difference between the two women, treating the situation simply as an ill-fated love triangle in which George meets his true love too late.

Desperate, George decides to murder Alice by drowning her in isolated Loon Lake. He takes her out in a boat, then loses his nerve and is unable to kill her. She ends up falling in and drowning by accident.

Circumstantial evidence nevertheless points to murder, and George is soon arrested for the crime. He is tried and convicted, then sentenced to death. Angela, faithful to the end, pays him one last visit on death row and declares her undying love one last time before their final farewell. George is then taken away to the electric chair as the film ends. He thinks of Angela as he makes the walk.

As Nora Sayre notes, Dreiser joined the Communist Party shortly before his death in 1945, which may explain the film's attempt to strip away the "social analysis" of his novel within the oppressive political climate of the Cold War. She argues, however, that Clift's performance, despite the "defanging of Dreiser," conveys one of the most effective portrayals of alienation in 1950s film (130). Shortly after filming, Anne Revere, who plays George's mother, Hannah Eastman, was identified as a communist by Larry Parks in testimony before HUAC. Most of her major scenes were subsequently edited out of the film, and she was blacklisted, never appearing in another film. *Screenplay:* Michael Wilson and Harry Brown. *Selected bibliography:* Barbarow; Neve (*Film*); Sayre.

*THE PROWLER:* **DIR. JOSEPH LOSEY (1951).** Reportedly Losey's favorite among his five American films, *The Prowler* is a dark in brooding piece that, in terms of both atmosphere and plot, is a classic example of film noir, though Thom Anderson classifies it as a film gris because of its important element of social commentary (183). The central character is Los Angeles police patrolman Webb Garwood (Van Heflin), who responds with partner Bud Crocker (John Maxwell) to a report of a prowler at the home of Susan Gilvray (Evelyn Keyes), the wife of William Gilvray (Emerson Treacy), a late-night commentator at a local radio station. No prowler is found, but Garwood becomes interested in Susan. He later returns and strikes up an acquaintance with her, learning that her husband's will provides her with a small fortune in the event of his death. He also learns that he and she are from the same home town (Terre Haute) but that she was from a well-to-do family, while his family was poor. This sense of class difference centrally informs Garwood's attitude toward Susan, which is compounded of sexual attraction, hostility, and greed. Having long dreamed of retiring from the force and owning his own motel, he seduces Susan and then kills her husband, hoping to get at the inheritance.

Garwood arranges to make Gilvray's death look like a justifiable shooting in the line of duty. Both a coroner's inquest and Susan accept Garwood's story, though she still seems to have her doubts. Nevertheless, she soon marries Garwood. They use her inheritance to buy a motel in Las Vegas, fulfilling Garwood's dream. Then Susan discovers she has been pregnant since before her husband's death, even though her husband was sterile. Afraid that the pregnancy will point toward his guilt in

Gilvray's death, Garwood moves Susan to a deserted ghost town to have the baby, which he plans to deliver himself. When complications arise, Garwood brings in a doctor, to whom he blurts out a confession of the murder. Susan realizes that Garwood plans to kill the doctor after the successful delivery of the baby. She helps the doctor escape. He then calls the police, who arrive and shoot down a fleeing Garwood in a scene that ironically repeats Garwood's earlier shooting of Gilvray.

*The Prowler* is dominated by Heflin's impressive performance as a jittery sociopath, a performance that is central to the dark and disturbing tone of the film as a whole. However, sociopath though he may be, Garwood is in many ways the all-American boy in pursuit of all-American dreams. His ruthlessness in that pursuit and the superficial nature of the dreams constitute a potentially powerful critique of the American way, as does the suggestion that frustration due to his working-class origins has contributed to Garwood's bitterness and cynicism. Still, the film's social commentary is somewhat muted by the fact that Garwood comes off as too pathological to be a representative figure. David Caute thus grants that "Losey and Trumbo intended an exposure of America petty-bourgeois materialism" but concludes that in the process they "lost their way in melodrama" (92). *Screenplay:* Dalton Trumbo (uncredited) and Hugo Butler. *Selected bibliography:* Thom Anderson; Caute (*Joseph Losey*); Ciment; Hirsch; Neve (*Film*); Palmer and Riley; Silver and Ward.

*TRY AND GET ME:* **DIR. CY ENDFIELD (1951).** Originally released as *The Sound of Fury, Try and Get Me* is a dark thriller based on an actual 1933 kidnapping and murder that occurred in San Jose, California. In the film, Howard Tyler (Frank Lovejoy) is a down-and-out war veteran who finds himself unable, amid the emergent consumer capitalism of the 1920s, to provide his family with the sorts of commodities that the society around them encourages them to expect to have. Eventually, as the Depression gets under way, he teams up with hardened criminal Jerry Slocum (Lloyd Bridges) to commit a series of robberies in order to get the money he feels he needs in order to live a decent life. The stakes are soon raised when Tyler and Slocum turn to kidnapping, taking captive Donald Miller, the town's richest young man. Unfortunately, this plan goes badly awry when Slocum unnecessarily kills Miller (partly out of class-based resentment), causing an outcry of outrage among the local citizenry.

Tyler, cracking under the strain, finds that his marriage to wife Judy (Kathleen Ryan) is disintegrating, further contributing to the total collapse of his once-hopeful existence. The two kidnappers are eventually captured, then find the jail surrounded by an ugly lynch mob, consisting largely of clean-cut, all-American types, who have been stirred to fanaticism by a series of inflammatory newspaper articles by local journalist Gil Stanton (Richard Carlson). The mob gradually gets more and more out of control and eventually breaks into the jail. They reach the two prisoners and savagely beat them to death in what Thom Anderson calls "the most unrelenting and disturbing scene of mob violence I have ever seen in a Hollywood movie" (188).

Through tracing the life experiences of Tyler, *Try and Get Me* presents a virtually documentary exposition on the social causes of crime. The dark look of the film combines with this subject matter to suggest the tradition of the film noir, though the film's obvious social consciousness, including its commentary on the dark aspects of class, consumerism and the media in American society, makes it an excellent example of the film gris, as discussed by Anderson. Anderson sums up the message of the film: "If the American dream could go this far wrong, the dream was empty to begin with (188). *Screenplay:* Jo Pagano. *Selected bibliography:* Thom Anderson; Naremore (*More than Night*); Neve (*Film*); Silver and Ward.

*HIGH NOON:* DIR. FRED ZINNEMANN (1952). One of the classic Westerns of all time, *High Noon* includes the requisite good guys, bad guys, and gunplay, but it also explores a number of ethical and political issues, giving it a depth sometimes lacking in the genre. The action takes place in the town of Hadleyville (perhaps recalling Mark Twain's Hadleyburg, bastion of bourgeois corruption and conformity), a formerly wild and dangerous town that Marshal Will Kane (Gary Cooper) has tamed, making it a good place to live and raise a family. One of his major accomplishments in this regard was the arrest and conviction, for murder, of local badman Frank Miller (Ian McDonald), sent away to state prison five years earlier. But, as the film begins, Miller has just inexplicably been pardoned and is now headed back to Hadleyville to seek revenge on Kane; Miller is due to arrive on the noon train, thus the title of the film. But Hadleyville has been peaceful for so long that most of Kane's deputies have been let go, and most of the townspeople have grown comfortable and complacent. The town is thus ill equipped to deal with the threat posed by Miller and his allies, who come to town and gather at the train depot to await his arrival.

To complicate matters, Kane is being married on this very day, and his new wife, Amy (Grace Kelly) is a Quaker, who abhors violence in any form, causing Kane to resign as marshal so he can pursue a peaceful life as a storekeeper. At the urging of the townspeople, Kane and Amy head out of town immediately, but then Kane concludes that he must go back to await Miller, both because he does not want to leave the town unprotected and because his sense of personal honor will not allow him to flee from the danger represented by Miller. Kane arrives back in Hadleyville and dons his badge and gun at 10:50, seventy minutes before the arrival of the train and seventy minutes before the end of the film, which thereafter proceeds virtually in real time. Amy issues an ultimatum and then prepares to leave town alone when Kane insists on staying.

Kane spends much of the remaining time attempting to recruit deputies among the townspeople, only to find that none of them are willing to stand by his side in the upcoming confrontation with Miller and his fellow gunmen. He therefore stands alone, though Amy experiences a last-minute change of heart and rushes to his side. After Miller arrives, Kane conducts a running gun battle with the four outlaws through the streets of the town, picking them off one by one. Finally, Miller takes Amy hostage. She knocks Miller off balance, and Kane shoots him down, ending the battle. Kane and Amy then resume their original trip out of town without a word to the townspeople, Kane tossing his badge with disgust into the dusty street.

Although Amy eventually stands by her man, she functions through much of the film as the classic example of the stereotypical confining woman who tames a man and limits his ability to pursue masculine adventure. There is, however, one strong and independent woman in the film, in the person of Helen Ramirez (Katy Jurado), a beautiful Mexican woman who is the former lover of both Kane and Miller and the current lover of Pell. But she is far more than a passive love object, despite her stunning beauty. Among other things, she is a successful businesswoman, though in this role she has had to struggle against prejudice on the basis of her gender and her ethnic origins. She is also a strong and courageous woman. In the end, fed up with the smug townspeople and the masculine posturing of Kane, Miller, and others, she leaves town in disgust. That the makers of the film decided to make this character a Mexican woman (whose exotic sexuality remains untamed by the various men in her life) is worthy of further contemplation, especially given that the good (and blonde) American girl remains passive when it really counts, despite her attempts at domesticating Kane.

Viewed as a straightforward Western, *High Noon*, with its individualist hero and its disdain for the masses who inhabit the town, hardly seems like a leftist film. However, it is generally recognized that the film also functions as a leftist allegory about the anticommunist purges sweeping Hollywood, with Kane functioning as the rare individual who stands up against persecution, while all around him are taking the easy road and giving in. As Biskind puts it, "once the Millers were equated with HUAC or McCarthy, the craven townies became friendly witnesses." He then quotes writer Carl Foreman to the effect that the film was about "Hollywood and no other place but Hollywood" (Biskind 48). One could even argue that Miller's resurgence after his earlier defeat by Kane associates HUAC and McCarthy with the fascism that had been presumably defeated a few years earlier in World War II. *Screenplay:* Carl Foreman. *Selected bibliography:* Biskind (*Seeing*); Christensen; McReynolds and Lips; Neve (*Film*); Joanna E. Rapf; Sayre; Tompkins.

*VIVA ZAPATA!:* **DIR. ELIA KAZAN (1952).** *Viva Zapata!* is a biopic detailing the participation of agrarian revolutionary leader Emiliano Zapata in the Mexican Revolution. It thus follows in the footsteps of such Hollywood fare as *Viva Villa!* (1934) and *Juarez* (1939). Like its predecessors, *Viva Villa!* is willing to play fast and loose with history in the interest of a good story, and the story told in the film is, in fact, a good one, though it is not always historically accurate and certainly does little to explain the real issues involved in the events it describes. As entertainment, *Viva Villa!* is a not a bad movie at all. Marlon Brando's performance in the title role is strong, and he actually makes a convincing Mexican—as opposed, say, to the ludicrous performance given by Charlton Heston in Orson Welles's *Touch of Evil.* But Brando's performance may be part of the problem with the film. which focuses on romanticizing its individual hero while paying little attention to the real character of the Mexican Revolution as a mass movement. Indeed, the film, which Kazan later characterized as anticommunist in his infamous HUAC testimony, is strongly antirevolutionary. It portrays Zapata's actions as heroic and his cause, to the extent it is explained at all, as just. But it suggests that violent revolution cannot possibly lead to positive social change, but can only breed additional violence. Meanwhile, the film's critique of the Mexican Revolution can quite easily be read as an oblique commentary on the Russian Revolution. Zapata, of course, had no real counterpart among the Bolsheviks, who were led by intellectuals, not peasants, from which point of view it might be significant that the film's most evil character is the intellectual Fernando Aguirre (Joseph Wiseman), who constantly changes sides as the tide of power shifts, ultimately playing a central role in Zapata's death.

The film begins in Mexico City as Zapata leads a delegation of peasant farmers from his home state of Morelos to complain to President Porfirio Diaz (Fay Roope) that their farmlands are being confiscated by a local estate. Diaz offers little help but marks down the name of Zapata as a potential troublemaker. When the peasants try to take matters into their own hands, they are attacked by heavily armed troops. Zapata and his followers are driven into hiding in the mountains, but Zapata soon emerges to try to pursue a respectable life so that he can marry Josefa Espejo (Jean Peters), the daughter of a local luminary (Florenz Ames). The marriage will, eventually, take place, but first Zapata runs afoul of the law and then joins the revolutionary movement headed by Francisco Madero (Harold Gordon), who commissions Zapata a general in the revolutionary army. Zapata's forces win a series of victories over federal troops in southern Mexico, contributing significantly to the victory of the revolution.

In this film, however, that victory is hardly good news. Those who gain power through violence are, in Kazan's vision, doomed to continue their violent ways in a quest for still more power. The virtuous peasant generals Pancho Villa (Alan Reed) and Zapata soon return to their agrarian homelands, while more sinister and power-hungry leaders (possibly figures of Stalin) gain control of the federal government in Mexico City. Soon Zapata finds himself once again at the head of a rebel army doing battle against federal troops. Eventually, the government forces manage to lure Zapata into an ambush and cut him to ribbons with gunfire, ending his life, but not his legend. In fact, the local peasants, always in search of a strong, charismatic leader (despite Zapata's own advice that they should think of themselves as their own leaders), continue to hope that he still lives in the mountains and will return when they need him.

*Viva Zapata!* involves a number of subplots, most them conveying invidious stereotypes. Josefa, for example, is the confining woman whose sexuality acts as a trap that might potentially lure a strong male into domestic confinement. Similarly, revolutionary journalist Aguirre acts as the prototype of the cold-hearted leftist intellectual who is willing to commit any level of perfidy in his quest for raw power. Such stereotypes add to the basic political conservatism of the film, a stance that probably helped it to gain five Academy Award nominations, though the only award actually won was given to Anthony Quinn for best supporting actor as Zapata's Rabelaisian brother, Eufemio. *Screenplay:* John Steinbeck. *Selected bibliography:* Biskind ("Ripping Off Zapata"); Braudy; Brunk; Butler; Christensen; Millon; Neve (*Film*); Reed; Vanderwood ("American Cold Warrior"); Womack.

*APACHE:* **DIR. ROBERT ALDRICH (1954).** *Apache* details the ongoing rebellion of renegade Apache warrior Massai (Burt Lancaster), who continues his fight against white domination by conducting a one-man guerrilla war against the U.S. Army, even after Geronimo and his followers have been defeated (in 1886) and shipped off to Florida. The film is highly sympathetic to the plight of Massai and to that extent has its heart in the right place. Unfortunately, the film entirely romanticizes Massai's individualist rebellion, which runs entirely counter to the nature of Native American societies. In an apparent nod to the film-going public, the film also yields to convention and provides a sentimental romantic subplot involving the developing love between Massai and Nalinle (Jean Peters), daughter of the alcoholic chief who succeeds Geronimo as the leader of the local Apaches.

Among other things, the film bizarrely suggests that, if Native Americans will only adopt white ways, then they will be treated entirely as equals. Massai's love for Nalinle tempers his hatred for whites, and he eventually agrees to give up his warlike ways in order to grow corn with Nalinle in the mountains, thereby replicating the agricultural success he has observed among the Cherokees during an earlier trip through Oklahoma. This motif may derive from the fact that Geronimo eventually became a prosperous farmer in Oklahoma. Massai is not allowed this luxury, however, and the white forces, led by Al Sieber (John McIntire), eventually track him to his mountain home, melodramatically arriving just as Nalinle goes into childbirth. After a furious battle, Massai gets the drop on Sieber, but then lets him go when he hears the nearby first cries of his newborn son. In a rather silly ending that was imposed on director Aldrich by United Artists, Massai drops his weapon and walks slowly off to join his family. Sieber lets him go, understanding that Massai's days as a rebel are over. Recognizing that Massai's domestication announces the final taming of the West (and the victory of bourgeois routinization over romantic adventure), Sieber nostalgically longs for the good old days. "This was the only war we had," he sadly notes. "And we ain't likely to find another." *Screenplay:* James R. Webb. *Selected bibliography:* Biskind (*Seeing*); Silver; Umland.

*BROKEN LANCE:* **DIR. EDWARD DMYTRYK (1954).** *Broken Lance* begins as Joe Devereaux (Robert Wagner), the youngest son of cattle baron Matt Devereaux (Spencer Tracy), returns home after three years in prison. Most of the remainder of the film narrates, via an extended flashback, the events that led to Joe's imprisonment and to the fact that he returns home vowing revenge against his three older half-brothers, Ben, Mike, and Denny (Richard Widmark, Hugh O'Brian, and Earl Holliman). These events begin when Matt discovers that a copper mine that is operating on his ranch is polluting a stream and poisoning his cattle. Enraged, Matt and his sons go to the mine to demand that this practice be stopped. Instead, the mine manager orders his men to attack them, but they are saved when a ranch foreman suddenly appears leading a contingent of the Devereaux ranch hands, who rout the miners and destroy the mining facility. This destruction leads to legal charges being placed against Matt Devereaux by the mining company. The governor (E. G. Marshall), a close associate of Devereaux, refuses to intercede on Matt's behalf unless the latter will order Joe (who is half Comanche) to stay away from the governor's daughter, Barbara (Jean Peters). Matt refuses and is thus left vulnerable. In the subsequent legal wranglings, Joe ends up taking the rap for his father and going to prison, but only because his brothers refuse to participate in a deal that would have kept Joe out of prison.

This treachery begins a series of betrayals in which the three older Devereaux brothers, led by Ben, eventually drive Matt to his grave. Joe, greatly devoted to his father, thus returns from prison with revenge in his heart. Joe's mother, a Comanche princess (Katy Jurado), convinces him not to take action against his brothers, but then Ben kidnaps Joe and takes him into the mountains to kill him. Joe is saved at the last moment when old Two Moons (Eduard Franz), Matt's longtime right-hand man, appears and shoots Ben instead. In the end, Joe goes away with Barbara, presumably to live happily ever after.

Within the confines of this rather simple plot, *Broken Lance* addresses a number of issues, the most obvious of which is its condemnation of racism. As a half-breed, Joe has experienced racial prejudice all his life, even from his own older brothers, whose mother was white. Peter Biskind argues that the film's treatment of prejudice against Native Americans is a covert commentary on the treatment of African Americans (240). The film also comments on the routinization of the West via its critique of the ruthless inhumanity of modern capitalism, in the form of the copper mine and the oil wells that gradually encroach on the land Devereaux so loves. On the other hand, the film fails to point out that Devereaux is a rich capitalist and that, despite his seemingly benevolent attitude toward Native Americans, his huge ranch has been carved out of territory formerly owned by Native Americans. *Screenplay:* Richard Murphy. *Selected bibliography:* Biskind (*Seeing*); Dmytryk.

*ON THE WATERFRONT:* **DIR. ELIA KAZAN (1954).** *On the Waterfont* details the scene on a New Jersey waterfront, where most of the longshoremen who keep the docks running live and work under miserable conditions. However, the film focuses its critique of these conditions not on the shipping companies who employ the workers but on the local longshoremen's union, headed by gangster Johnny Friendly (Lee J. Cobb), which is so corrupt that the longshoremen have no real union representation. Friendly and his minions rule the entire waterfront, exploiting both the workers and the shipping companies for their own profit. Marlon Brando probably deserved the best actor Oscar he won for his performance in the film, but in general the film is a highly overrated compilation of Hollywood stereotypes, though it admittedly harnesses these stereotypes in a fairly effective way.

As *On the Waterfront* begins, the longshoremen's union is being investigated by the State Crime Commission, presented in the book as a force for righteousness. The investigation is made difficult by the reluctance of anyone on the waterfront to testify against Friendly, but young Joey Doyle, an agitator for union reform, has agreed to cooperate with the commission. Friendly orders his lieutenant, Charley Malloy (Rod Steiger), to take care of Doyle, and Charley engages his brother, Terry

(Brando), an ex-boxer who "could have been a contender" had he not been mismanaged, to lure Doyle to a rooftop from which he is thrown to his death. Terry, not having realized that Doyle was to be killed, is seriously disturbed by this development but takes no immediate action. Most of the rest of the book involves the efforts, initiated by Joey's pure-as-the-driven-snow sister, Katie (Eva Marie Saint), an innocent convent-educated college student, to bring Joey's killers to justice and thus break Friendly's hold on the waterfront. Initially, Katie gets little support, but the dedicated efforts of Father Barry (Karl Malden), a local priest, eventually convince one of the longshoremen, "Kayo" Dugan (Pat Henning), to testify before the Crime Commission. Dugan makes a statement before the commission but is quickly killed by Friendly's thugs. Concerned by Terry's lack of loyalty, Friendly orders his death as well, and Charley is killed for protecting his brother. Furious, Terry plans to kill Friendly, but Barry convinces him instead to testify before the commission, and his testimony is instrumental in initiating the cleanup of the union, just as, presumably, the testimony of Kazan and Schulberg before HUAC helped in the "cleanup" of Hollywood.

In its concern for the exploitation of workers, *Waterfront* clearly participates in a central concern of the Left. However, its presentation of a corrupt union as the principal villain in this exploitation leaves largely unexamined the role of the shipping companies, even though the profits of these companies from this exploitation are acknowledged in the film to be far greater than those realized by the corrupt officials of the union. Positive figures such Katie Doyle and Terry Malloy are, in their separate ways, political naïfs who have no understanding of the role played by the capitalist system in the exploitation of workers. Their perspective helps to reduce the film to a simple opposition between good and evil.

Widely promoted as a daring and hard-hitting exposé of labor-union corruption, *On the Waterfront* is, in fact, a shameless bit of self-promotion and opportunism that rides the tide of antiunion sentiment in the 1950s while providing a rationale for the friendly testimony of Kazan and Schulberg before HUAC. As Daniel Bell notes, the East Coast dockworkers unions were indeed well known for their corruption in the 1950s. Yet the West Coast unions, led by such figures as Harry Bridges, were known for their courageous defiance of capitalist exploitation and their strong advocacy of the rights of their members. If Kazan and Schulberg had wanted to be courageous, they could have told the story of Bridges and other admirable leftist union leaders. But their decision to focus on unions as forces of evil (and on government informers as battlers for justice) provided a much easier and more lucrative road to Hollywood success. *Screenplay:* Budd Schulberg. *Selected bibliography:* Bell; Biskind (*Seeing*); Hey; Neve ("The 1950s"); Quart and Auster; Sayre; Stead.

*SALT OF THE EARTH:* DIR. HERBERT BIBERMAN (1954). *Salt of the Earth* was the first and only film produced by Independent Producers Corporation, a group of leftist filmmakers organized specifically to try to find a way to make socially responsible cinema within the repressive climate that was sweeping Hollywood in the McCarthy years. Aided by funding from the International Union of Mine, Mill, and Smelter Workers, director Biberman, producer Paul Jarrico, and writer Michael Wilson were able to produce a remarkable film that is important in American film history for a number of reasons. For one thing, *Salt of the Earth*, despite its low budget and mostly amateur actors, is a genuinely fine film, a compelling piece of social drama that makes important political points while telling an engaging story built around convincing and genuinely human characters. The social history of the film is also important. Made by a strongly committed group of filmmakers who were not beholden to any Hollywood studios or other interests within the capitalist establishment, *Salt of the Earth* may be the purest example of leftist film in the entire history of the American cinema, though it is hardly extreme. At the same time, the reaction of the capitalist establishment to the film was also significant. Furious efforts were made to suppress the film, and the filmmakers were hounded by HUAC, the FBI, and the CIA during the making of the film. After the film was completed, theaters all over the country, reacting to government and corporate pressure, refused to show the film. The film thus reached only a very limited audience, though it was rediscovered in the 1960s, finally going into general release in 1965.

*Salt of the Earth* deals with the efforts of Mexican-American zinc miners in New Mexico to battle against the exploitative practices of their employer, Delaware Zinc, Inc., thereby hoping to achieve better working and living conditions. In addition to the obvious emphasis on class, the film also deals centrally with the unfair treatment of the miners and their families on the basis of ethnicity. In particular, the company pursues a carefully planned program of ethnic discrimination, treating Anglo miners far better than Mexican ones, thereby hoping to win the loyalty and obedience of the Anglo miners, who are still exploited despite this preferential treatment. *Salt of the Earth* is also particularly strong in its treatment of gender; the wives of the miners play a crucial role in their fight for justice, while the miners, in the process, learn important lessons about their own tendency toward gender-based discrimination.

The film focuses in particular on Mexican-American miner Ramon Quintero (impressively played by Juan Chacon, an actual miner) and his wife, Esperanza (played by Rosaura Revueltas, a professional Mexican actress who was driven out of the United States as the film neared completion, subsequently to be blacklisted in Mexico). However, this focus is far different from that of the typical Hollywood film; the emphasis is not on the private problems of the Quinteros as unique individuals, but on their representative problems as members of a larger community. As the film proceeds, ethnic discrimination and unsafe working conditions finally drive the Mexican miners to declare s strike, with the support of the International Union of Mine, Mill, and Smelter Workers. They are also supported by many of the Anglo miners, who stand beside their Mexican brothers. Though the men are reluctant to get their wives involved, the women eventually provide important support to the picket line, bringing food, drink, and supplies to the men as they picket the entrances to the mine and try to keep out scabs.

The company, supported by the sheriff (played by blacklisted actor Will Geer) and his armed thugs, makes every effort to break the picket line. At one point, they arrest Ramon, beat him so badly that he has to be hospitalized for a week, then take him to jail for a month. While he is in jail, Esperanza gives birth to their third child. Finally, the company gets a court injunction ordering the miners to cease picketing. Having little choice, the men agree to obey the order; however, as the order mentions only striking miners, it does not apply to their wives. The women therefore replace the men on the picket line and keep the strike going, despite the continuing efforts of the company to intimidate them. At one point, the leaders of the women are taken to jail. Esperanza is among them, taking her baby with her, though Ramon eventually takes the child home with him. The picket line holds, however, as women from miles around rush in to fill the spots left by the arrested women. Soon, the women in the jail mount such a protest that the sheriff releases them just to get rid of them. In the meantime, however, Ramon and the other husbands of the jailed women are forced to do the domestic chores normally done by their wives, thus learning better to appreciate the difficulty of the work their women do.

Nevertheless, when the women are released, tensions flare between Esperanza and Ramon, who is feeling threatened by her newfound strength and independence. In response, Esperanza delivers what is probably the central political statement in the film, noting that the mine company's oppression of Ramon is driving him to oppress her in turn, but that a better response would be to work to do away with oppression altogether rather than simply passing it along. Ramon is at first unconvinced by her arguments. Tired of the domestic routine, he and several other men decide to go away on a hunting trip after the women are released. Ramon, however, soon realizes that he has been wrong to resent Esperanza's efforts in support of the strike. He leads the men back home, where they find that sheriff's deputies, in a further attempt to break the strike by intimidating its leaders, are evicting the Quinteros from their company-owned housing. In a classic scene of leftist activism, an angry crowd of workers and wives from miles around gathers at the house and forces the deputies to abandon the eviction. A company official, looking on, concludes that the company had better settle the strike "for the present." The miners and their families thus win at least a temporary victory, thanks to the solidarity they have shown in standing together against the company and its official supporters. Ramon thanks the crowd for their help, acknowledging them as "sisters and brothers." Esperanza, meanwhile, envisions a day when such localized efforts will lead to a better world in which her children, "the salt of the earth," will inherit it.

*Salt of the Earth* is impressively lucid in its delineation of the central labor struggle within the larger context of the capitalist system. It is also highly effective in its depiction of the role played by gender and ethnicity within that system. It avoids clichés, presenting the miners and their families as realistic human beings who are neither romanticized nor heroicized. This realism is also aided by the film's basis in fact, the struggle of Mexican-American miners in the Southwest having been among the most important labor struggles of the 1950s. These same struggles, for example, are the subject of Philip Stevenson's impressive series of four proletarian novels collectively entitled *The Seed*, published during the period 1954–1961, under the pseudonym Lars Lawrence. *Screenplay:* Michael Wilson. *Selected bibliography:* Biberman; Cargill; Christensen; McCarthy; Tom Miller; Morris; Neve (*Film*); Lillian S. Robinson; Rosenfelt; Stead.

## *MR. ARKADIN (CONFIDENTIAL REPORT)*: DIR. ORSON WELLES

**(1955).** *Mr. Arkadin* opens in the seedy world of the Naples waterfront as a man named Bracco (Grégoire Aslan) is knifed to death on the docks. On the scene are American adventurer Guy Van Stratten (Robert Arden) and his stripper girlfriend Mily (Patricia Medina). The dying Bracco manages to whisper to Mily some information about the mysterious and fabulously wealthy Gregory Arkadin (Welles), information that will presumably make Van Stratten and Mily rich. Van Stratten seeks out the elusive Arkadin, in the process becoming fascinated with Arkadin's daughter, Raina (Paola Mori). Eventually, Arkadin reveals to Van Stratten that he suffers from amnesia and can remember nothing that happened before the winter of 1927, when he suddenly found himself in Zürich with 200,000 Swiss francs in his pocket. He then hires Van Stratten to try to uncover the story of his past before that point.

Arkadin explains to Van Stratten that he is about to undergo an intelligence investigation in connection with his attempt to get a big defense contract from the U.S. government and that he wants to find out if there is anything in his distant past that might interfere with the approval of the contract. It soon becomes obvious, however, that Arkadin is trying to hide his checkered past from Raina, of whom he is obsessively protective. Meanwhile, Van Stratten, aided by Mily, travels about the world digging up details of Arkadin's dim past, in the process meeting a colorful gallery of Wellesian grotesques. In this sense, the basic structure of *Mr. Arkadin* closely resembles that of *Citizen Kane*, though *Arkadin* should probably be viewed as a sort of burlesque of *Kane* rather than a simple reiteration. Van Stratten eventually discovers that Arkadin acquired the 200,000 francs (which he later parlayed into a vast fortune through shrewd, and sometimes shady, business deals) in connection with his involvement in a white slavery ring centered in Warsaw.

The plot takes a dark turn when Van Stratten discovers that the people he has been interviewing in connection with Arkadin's early activities are being murdered one by one. Eventually, Mily is murdered as well, and Van Stratten realizes that he will be next, as Arkadin attempts to cover his tracks and prevent Raina from learning the truth about his background. Van Stratten decides that his only chance is to flee to Arkadin's castle in Spain and to tell the story to Raina before Arkadin can kill him. Arkadin charters a private plane and flies to Barcelona alone, only to learn as he approaches the coast that Van Stratten has gotten there before him. Concluding that his attempt to shield Raina from the truth cannot succeed, Arkadin leaps from the plane to his death, leaving his empty plane flying on automatic pilot.

André Bazin identifies the mysterious and powerful international arms dealer Basil Zaharoff as the model for Arkadin, but it is clear that the story of Arkadin can be read as a parable about capitalism as a whole (117). Arkadin's various dealings, which involve prostitution, defense contracts, and financial transactions with Nazis, read almost like a list of the characteristic crimes of modern capitalism, crimes which, tellingly, have taken Arkadin not to prison but to a position of great power and influence. The Baroness Nagel (Suzanne Flon), one of those who holds clues to Arkadin's past, expresses one of the film's central political points when she explains to Arkadin that few criminals have any real money because "those who make real money aren't counted as criminals. It's a class distinction." Indeed, the film, like the plays of Brecht and much other leftist literature, suggests the fundamentally criminal (and ruthless) nature of capitalist financial manipulations. *Screenplay:* Orson Welles. *Selected bibliography:* Bazin; Higham (*Films*); Higham (*Orson Welles*); Naremore (*Magic*).

*REBEL WITHOUT A CAUSE:* DIR. NICHOLAS RAY (1955). One of the most enduringly famous films of American film history, *Rebel Without a Cause* is one of the leading expressions of the youthful alienation of the 1950s. Its central character, Jim Stark, is the prototype of the troubled and radically alienated teen; its star, James Dean, killed in a car crash just before the film was released, remains an American cultural icon, sym-

bolizing the same youthful alienation. The film is, in fact, entirely dominated by Dean's performance, even though, ironically, both the major
supporting actors (Natalie Wood as Judy, Jim's eventual girlfriend, and
Sal Mineo as Plato, Jim's adoring, but doomed sidekick) received Oscar
nominations, whereas Dean did not.

The plot of the film is simple and serves primarily as a framework for
Dean's grimacing expressions of teen anguish. It opens as Jim has just
moved to town with his wealthy parents (played by Jim Backus and Ann
Doran), who hope to escape the disgrace that his behavior brought them
in their former community. In the first scene, Jim is dragged into the
police station, charged with public drunkenness. Judy is also there,
having been picked up on suspicion of prostitution as she walked the
early-morning streets after a confrontation with her distant father, played
by William Hopper. Jim and Judy soon establish a relationship of sorts,
though she is the girlfriend of Buzz Gunderson (Corey Allen), leader of a
prominent gang at Dawson High School, where Jim begins classes,
determined to stay out of trouble. As the new kid in school, Jim quickly
becomes an object of the gang's abuse. When he stands up to them, he
becomes the object of the adoration of Plato, a sensitive teen so alienated
from his fellow students and so neglected by his wealthy, but preoccupied, parents that he has recently been arrested for killing a litter of
puppies in a desperate bid for attention.

In a relationship with clear homoerotic resonances, Jim immediately
becomes a sort of surrogate father for Plato, while sparks fly between Jim
and Judy as well. Challenged to prove his manhood, Jim feels forced to
accept Buzz's invitation to compete in a "chickie run," in which he and
Buzz drive stolen cars toward the edge of a precipice, seeing who can
wait longer before bailing out of the car, thus demonstrating greater
courage. Jim gets out safely, but Buzz gets his leather jacket caught on
the handle of his car and goes over the cliff to his death. Jim is overcome
with guilt and attempts to confess his involvement in the death to the
police but is ignored. He then strikes up a relationship with Judy (who
seems rather unaffected by Buzz's death), while at the same time being
targeted for further abuse by Buzz's old gang, who apparently blame
him for Buzz's death. In an interesting extended scene that becomes a
grotesque parody of American upper-class life, Jim and Judy hang out in
an old, abandoned mansion, their romance blooming and their alienation
fading. Plato joins them there as well, and the three develop a weird
family dynamic, with Plato as the child and Jim and Judy as the parents,
while they cavort among the ruins of American affluence.

When the gang arrives at the mansion to torment Jim, Plato shoots
one of them, triggering a chain of events that eventually leaves him holed
up in the nearby Griffith Observatory, surrounded by police. Jim desperately attempts to save his young friend and manages secretly to unload

Plato's gun. Still, when Plato rushes out of the observatory with the gun, he is shot and killed by police, who do not realize the gun is unloaded. Jim is distraught, but he still has Judy, and in the meantime seems on the verge of a new and better relationship with his father, who comes to his aid.

In many ways, *Rebel Without a Cause* is a key sign of the demise of American leftist culture, a sign of the Cold War turn from the class-based politics of the 1930s to the individual cries of existential despair that passed for "politics" the 1950s. Jim's radical alienation is ostensibly attributed not to the consequences of capitalism but to his poor relationship with his father, arising from the sniveling father's continual submission to Jim's domineering mother, which presumably offers Jim a poor role model and leaves the boy's own masculinity threatened. The troubles in Judy's relationship with her parents are similarly Oedipal, deriving from her father's refusal to show affection as a way of avoiding the obvious sexual sparks that fly between him and his daughter. Yet director Nicholas Ray (working through the 1950s, protected from the blacklist through his personal sponsorship by Howard Hughes) had extensive associations on the Left. Michael Denning, in fact, sees Ray's cinema as a central example of the continuing vitality in postwar America of the Popular Front culture of the late 1930s. He notes, for example, that the roots of Ray's work can be found in activities such as his central involvement (along with Joseph Losey) in the Federal Writers' Project's Living Newspaper, a leftist theatrical group inspired largely by the work of legendary Soviet director Vsevolod Meyerhold (367–69). *Rebel Without a Cause*, as Paul Buhle points out, was made with famed leftist playwright and screenwriter Clifford Odets on the set acting as an advisor. The film works in a number of political points, and its portrayal of the spiritual emptiness of the upper-class American milieu from which Jim Stark emerges is a scathing indictment of capitalist materialism, even if this indictment is submerged within the film's focus on generational, rather than class, conflict. *Screenplay:* Stewart Stern. *Selected bibliography:* Buhle ("Hollywood Left"); Blaine; Castiglia; Denning; Eisenschitz; Geoff; Nicholas Ray; Rosenbaum; Simmons.

*THE MAN WITH THE GOLDEN ARM:* DIR. OTTO PREMINGER (1956). Although considerably sanitized in comparison with the novel by Nelson Algren on which it was based, *The Man with the Golden Arm* was considered highly controversial when it was first released, largely because its frank (if superficial) treatment of drug addiction was unprecedented in American film at the time. The film focuses on Frankie Machine (real name Majcinek in the novel, though that is not specified in the film), a Chicago card dealer renowned for his skill at the table, which has earned him the nickname "The Man with the Golden Arm." As the film begins, Frankie (played by Frank Sinatra) has just returned from six months of incarceration in a government hospital, where he was treated for a heroine addiction. Determined to stay clean of drugs and go straight, Frankie has taken up the drums while in the hospital and has found that he has a genuine talent for the instrument. He therefore has high hopes of pursuing a career as a drummer, thus allowing him to leave his former life as a dealer in illegal card games.

Unfortunately, virtually every aspect of Frankie's life conspires against the successful realization of his plans. His old boss, Schwiefka (Robert Strauss), immediately begins to pressure him to return to work for him. At the same time, his old drug dealer, Louie (Darren McGavin), pressures him to return to his old drug habit. Meanwhile, his wife, Zosch (Eleanor Parker), is so insecure that she is afraid he will leave her if he succeeds in his new life. She therefore does everything in her power to impede him, a project that succeeds largely because of his sense of guilt over an automobile accident three years earlier that has ostensibly left her crippled, confined to a wheelchair. This sense of responsibility keeps him with Zosch despite her attempts to undermine his plans and despite his in love for Molly (Kim Novak), a B-girl who lives downstairs in the same building as Zosch and Frankie.

All of these pressures and difficulties combine to thwart Frankie's ambition to be a drummer and to drive him back to drug addiction. In the meantime, the audience learns that Zosch is not crippled at all but is merely faking her disability in order to keep Frankie with her. When the unscrupulous Louie learns her secret, she has a scuffle with him in which he is knocked through a railing, falling to his death. Frankie, always on the local police's list of usual suspects, is immediately tabbed as the killer. He goes into hiding in Molly's apartment, where, with her help, he succeeds in surviving a difficult cold-turkey withdrawal, once again getting his system cleansed of drugs. He goes back upstairs to Zosch to tell her he is leaving town to get away from all of the pressures that had driven him back to drugs. In response, she becomes so agitated that she leaps out of bed and runs after him, just as the police arrive to arrest him for the murder of Louie. Frankie stares at her, stunned, while police inspector Bednar (Emile Meyer) puts two and two together and realizes that Zosch is the real killer. She runs from the police and ends up leaping to her death. In the aftermath, Frankie and Molly walk away toward the beginning of their new life together.

Numerous aspects of Algren's novel were modified for the film, the most striking of which is that, in the novel, Frankie winds up hanging himself rather than living happily ever after. The conventional Hollywood ending of the film clearly tends to reduce the potency of its social commentary, but its points about Frankie's difficulties are nevertheless made. In addition to the obvious focus on drug addiction, the film clearly

shows that individuals in certain social and economic positions are faced
with mighty obstacles in their quest to live better lives. The film thus
suggests that the American dream is not equally available to all. Moreover, the American dream is called into question since equal access is a
major component of the dream. *Screenplay:* Walter Newman and Lewis
Meltzer. *Selected bibliography:* Frischauer; Pratley; Radell; Robert C.
Rosen; Sayre.

*STORM CENTER:* DIR. DANIEL TARADASH (1956). *Storm Center* is
one of the more direct and overt of the criticisms of McCarthyism that
appeared in American film of the 1950s, as opposed to films such as *High
Noon* (1952), which left itself available to anti-McCarthyism interpretations, but muted them through its wild west setting. At the same time, in
its depiction of a potentially sinister side to small-town America, *Storm
Center* looks back to films such as Fritz Lang's *Fury* (1937). Bette Davis
plays Alicia Hull, a small-town librarian who has devoted most of her
life to work in the town library and to using it to further the educational
development of the town's children. When the town council, caught up
in a wave of anticommunist hysteria, demands that a book entitled *The
Communist Dream* be removed from the shelves because of its political
content, Hull at first complies, then returns the book to the shelves,
feeling that its removal was a violation of her personal integrity and the
principles of American democracy. She is immediately fired, despite her
long service, and replaced by her friend and former assistant, Martha
Lockridge (Kim Hunter). The town judge, Robert Ellerbe (Paul Kelly),
believes that Hull has been unfairly treated and calls a town meeting to
discuss the issue. The move backfires, however, when Paul Duncan
(Brian Keith), Lockridge's boyfriend, seizes the opportunity to further his
own political ambitions by denouncing Hull as a dangerous communist,
winning the sympathy of the townspeople.

To this point, *Storm Center* is a fairly realistic account of the climate of
fear and suspicion that reigned in America in the 1950s. Unfortunately,
the film takes a series of unlikely turns that undermine its political message. When Hull is ostracized by most of the townspeople after the
hearing, one of the children she has befriended, Freddie Slater (Kevin
Coughlin), is so incensed that he sets fire to the library. As the townspeople watch the building burn, they suddenly realize the error of their
ways and reinstate Hull to her former position so that she can supervise
the building of a new library, which will presumably pursue more
democratic policies in its choice of books. This easy resolution thus
weakens the film's message and elides the fact that individuals such as
Hull did, in fact, lose their jobs all over America during the 1950s, few of
them recovering their positions so easily. *Storm Center* is thus ultimately
far less successful as a critique of communism than Charlie Chaplin's

near-contemporary *A King in New York*. *Screenplay:* Daniel Taradash and Elick Moll. *Selected bibliography:* Christensen; Crowdus (*Political Companion*); Neve (*Film*); Sayre.

*EDGE OF THE CITY:* DIR. MARTIN RITT (1957). *Edge of the City* was the first directorial credit for the formerly blacklisted Ritt. It is a dark tale of urban life in America that explores the difficulty of interracial friendship in a fundamentally racist society. John Cassavetes is Axel North, an army deserter without a friend in the world, a lonely outcast who is estranged from his family because they blame him for the accidental death of his brother. When he gets a job working in a railway yard in New York, however, he is befriended by an easy-going black fellow worker, Tommy Tyler (Sidney Poitier). For a time, this friendship gives North a new lease on life, but *Edge of the City* is far from a heart-warming tale of interracial friendship. Both Tyler and North are tormented by the sadistic Charles Malik (Jack Warden), the yard's racist union representative. Eventually Malik kills Tyler in a vicious fight with grappling hooks, afterward claiming that the death was an accident. North, a witness, is hesitant to report the killing to the police because he is afraid he will be identified as a deserter in the course of the investigation. After a talk with Tyler's widow (Ruby Dee), North takes matters into his own hands in a final fight with Malik, whom he chokes into unconsciousness. He then telephones his parents and is surprised to find that they want him to come home.

Somewhat reminiscent of Elia Kazan's *On the Waterfront* (1954), *Edge of the City* is indicative of the suspicion of labor unions that had permeated American society by the 1950s. In North's reluctance to cooperate with the police, however, Ritt's film is diametrically opposed to the open endorsement of informing that is central to the Kazan film. Meanwhile, though the treatment of Tyler is a bit idealized, *Edge of the City* represented an important step forward in the evolution of serious roles for black characters in American film. Ritt would continue this trend with later films such as *The Great White Hope* (1970) and *Sounder* (1972). *Screenplay:* Robert Alan Arthur. *Selected bibliography:* Crowdus (*Political Companion*); Carlton Jackson; Whitaker.

*A FACE IN THE CROWD:* DIR. ELIA KAZAN (1957). *A Face in the Crowd* is a powerful indictment of contemporary popular culture, with a number of political implications. It begins in the Tomahawk County Jail in Pickett, Arkansas, where a Sarah Lawrence-educated local radio reporter, Marcia Jeffries (played by Patricia Neal), comes to interview the prisoners for her program, "A Face in the Crowd," which features interviews with ordinary people on the street. In the jail, she encounters Larry "Lonesome" Rhodes (Andy Griffith), a colorful, guitar-toting prisoner, who agrees to perform on her program in return for an early release from jail. Rhodes is an immediate hit with his folksy blues singing, billed as representing the viewpoint of "outcasts, hoboes, and nobodies." Jeffries convinces Rhodes to become regular performer on the station, and he quickly becomes a local celebrity.

Rhodes soon graduates to a television program in Memphis after negotiating a shrewd deal with the station there. He is again a great success, and his career as a media star is launched. Rhodes is, from the start, a savvy performer, who knows very well how to parlay his apparent naivete into media success. He soon has his own network television show, on which he hawks a patent medicine that supposedly increases sexual potency, in the grand tradition of American conmen. Rhodes begins to exert considerable personal influence around the country, eventually becoming involved in politics, viewing himself as a king-maker. However, he gets in over his head in his subsequent association with the powerful supporters of a right-wing senator ("the last of the isolationists"), who are not content to let him be the tail that wags the dog. Out of touch with his roots, Rhodes becomes increasingly alienated, bitter, and cynical about his own success. Jeffries, who accompanies him on his rise to fame, is very much aware of his growing megalomania and of his tendency to chase other women, such as the adoring young Arkansas majorette Betty Lou Fleckum (Lee Remick), whom Rhodes displays semi-nude on his program as a sort of trophy. It is Jeffries who eventually destroys the phenomenon that she helped to create, by leaving a microphone open when Rhodes thinks it is off, thereby inducing him unknowingly to broadcast his true feelings over the air. He is left only with his beloved proto-postmodern applause machine to keep him company and respond to his talents.

Rhodes is, for Brian Neve, a compound of various figures, including Will Rogers and Walter Winchell (197). Michael Denning, on the other hand, sees him as a combination of Woody Guthrie and Elvis Presley. In addition, Denning describes *A Face in the Crowd* as "a straightforward Popular Front satire on the mass media" in which the "classic depression concerns with radio demagogues and native fascists fuse with the Cold War panic over mass culture" (469). Kazan later claimed that the film "anticipated Ronald Reagan" (566). Screenwriter Budd Schulberg, meanwhile, once claimed that the characterization of Rhodes was in part a comment on Joseph McCarthy's use of the media in his own rise to power (Sayre 166). It is certainly true that the film shows considerable suspicion of connections between right-wing politics and popular culture, though neither Kazan nor Schulberg, notorious informers both, was in the strongest position for a critique of McCarthy. In any case, the film clearly resonates with the work of leftist critics of Western popular culture, such as Max Horkheimer and Theodor Adorno. *A Face in the*

*Crowd* is, however, far less effective as a satire of contemporary American culture than Charlie Chaplin's far less known *A King in New York*, also released in 1957. Rhodes is, from one point of view, a man of the people who is corrupted by big business interests, but it is also the case that Rhodes is a shrewdly amoral character who, from the very beginning, knows what he wants and is willing to do anything to get it. In this sense, he may still be a prototype of the right-wing demagogue. But the success of his folksy populism suggests an elitist contempt for mass taste that mirrors Rhodes's own. In truth, he is no Guthrie or Presley, and his singing, which is more like yelling, is pretty awful. The dramatic success of the obnoxious Rhodes is never very believable, and Schulberg and Kazan surely underestimate both the ability of American popular culture to produce genuinely seductive images and the taste of the American people (questionable though it may be). Kazan, at least, should know better, having participated in the making of *People of the Cumberlands* in 1938. But perhaps the difference between the visions of southern folk culture in *People of the Cumberlands* and *A Face in the Crowd* can be taken as a marker of the general decline of Kazan's vision over the two decades that separate the two films. *Screenplay:* Budd Schulberg. *Selected bibliography:* Denning; Kazan; Neve (*Film*); Quart; Sayre.

*A KING IN NEW YORK:* **DIR. CHARLES CHAPLIN (1957).** Although made in Britain (during Chaplin's political exile from the United States) and not released in the U.S. until 1975, *A King in New York* remains one of the leading film commentaries on the American culture of the 1950s. Though the film was released five years after Chaplin was driven back to Europe by political persecution in America and three years after Joseph McCarthy was censured by the Senate and thus passed the peak of his power, the anticommunist hysteria that the film critiques was still very much in force in 1957. Moreover, the film's commentary on American anticommunism is supplemented by a scathing, almost Nabokovian, critique of American popular culture, which suggests that McCarthyism was not a short-term aberration from the American way, but a quintessentially American phenomenon, part and parcel of the consumerist culture of America as a whole. The film, which carries numerous autobiographical resonances and can be read as Chaplin's direct response to his shoddy treatment by American authorities in the midst of the anticommunist purges, is Chaplin's most overt and most radical political critique of American society.

    *A King in New York* begins with an on-screen caption announcing that "One of the minor annoyances of modern life is a revolution." It then proceeds to show scenes of a revolution underway in the European country of Estrovia, though the revolutionaries, largely in business dress, are clearly depicted as bourgeois rather than middle-class. King Shahdov

(Chaplin), the country's monarch, flees to America in the wake of the revolution, taking with him the contents of his country's treasury. He is not, however, out for personal gain but hopes to use the money to finance his long-term dream of creating a utopian society based on the wealth made possible by cheap and abundant nuclear power, produced by plants that he himself has designed. Soon after Shahdov arrives in America, however, his former prime minister, Voudel (Jerry Desmonde) absconds to South America with the funds, leaving Shahdov, accompanied by his loyal aide, Jaume, penniless in New York.

The early scenes of the king's stay in New York primarily concern his attempts to deal with the constant barrage of American popular culture with which he finds himself bombarded wherever he turns. Rock-and-roll music and women's magazines are among the satirized forms, though the most powerful commentary is reserved for film and television. These scenes include a particularly effective one in which Shahdov and Jaume attend a film but leave in disgust after viewing the coming attractions, a series of parodies of trailers for films of various current American genres, including a tale of gender confusion, a Western, and a film noir. The comment on the current state of American film is clear. Even more powerful is the film's critique of television, as Shahdov finds followed everywhere by Orwellian telescreens. There is even a screen (complete with windshield wiper) in the shower in his hotel room. As in Orwell, the telescreens work both ways, suggesting the element of surveillance that pervades American society. The king attends a dinner party to which he has been lured by the seductive Ann Kay (Dawn Addams), only to learn later that the entire party has been broadcast, Candid Camera-like, on television via a hidden camera for the television show "Ann Kay's Real-Life Surprise Party."

At first, the king is horrified to learn that his conversation at the party (during which he was induced to perform the to-be-or-not-to-be soliloquy from *Hamlet*) has been broadcast. However, the show is a big hit, and the king (in a clear comment on the fascination of American culture with European royalty) is soon showered with offers to appear on other programs and, especially, to endorse various commercial products. At first, he resists such offers, feeling them vulgar and beneath his dignity. However, when there proves to be no market for his nuclear power plans in America (the Americans already have plans of their own), the king is desperate for cash. He eventually begins to accept the offers and soon becomes, despite his incompetent performances, a successful media star. Image, after all, is everything, and he is, after all, a king. In the meantime, apparently in the process of a divorce from his wife (with whom he had made a merely political marriage), he attempts to become romantically involved with Ann Kay, though she resists his advances, preferring to act as his agent and to keep their relationship on a professional, if friendly, basis.

Trying to learn more about America, the king visits a progressive school and encounters there a precocious young man, Rupert Macabee (played by Chaplin's son, Michael), in the act of reading Karl Marx. Rupert makes an impassioned radical speech against oppression and authority of all kinds, engaging in, and clearly winning, a debate with the king when the latter tries to claim that, in a democracy like America, authority is not a bad thing but merely the will of the people. Rupert warns the king that, should he attempt to test the system, he will find that freedom in America has strict limits indeed. Eventually, Rupert runs away from the school to avoid questioning by federal authorities, who are investigating his parents, suspected communists, for HUAC. The king finds the boy on the street and takes him in, befriending him. While with the king, the boy decides to admit that he is a communist, not because he necessarily accepts communist views, but because he feels that American society forces everyone to accept some label or other, much in the mode of brand names. Again, image is everything. In the meantime, the boy's parents refuse to name names before the committee and are imprisoned on charges of contempt of Congress. Rupert is re-trieved by federal marshalls, and the king, because of his involvement with the boy, is himself called to testify before HUAC, as Chaplin had once been.

Despite some riotously funny comic mishaps (in which, among other things, the king inadvertently sprays the committee with a fire hose), the king goes over well in the committee hearings, suggesting the vacuous-ness of the hearings, which clearly parallels the emptiness of American popular culture. Shahdov, as a king, already has a convenient label and is cleared of all suspicion of communist sympathies. But, in the film's most powerful comment on the human consequences of the HUAC investigations, Rupert does not fare so well. Browbeaten by federal authorities who entice him to cooperate by offering freedom for his imprisoned parents, the boy eventually agrees to name names. When the king again encounters him, he is a broken shell of his former combative self, torn by guilt over his testimony. The king, having had enough of America and on the way to a reconciliation with his wife, is about to return to Europe but assures Rupert that he hopes soon to have him and his parents over for a visit, though the schoolmaster hints that there may be "complications" to such an arrangement, suggesting that the boy and his parents, because of their political affiliations, may not be allowed to travel abroad. In the end, the king flies to Europe to stay, having de-clared that "it's too crazy" in America.

The initial American critical response to *A King in New York* was, pre-dictably, negative. Moreover, as Charles Maland notes, American reviews often went out of their way to emphasize, not entirely accurately, that foreign reviews of the film had been negative as well (321–25). Indeed, David Robinson, reviewing British reaction to the film, concludes that "the British press was largely favourable and at worst respectful" (158–61). The film remains one of Chaplin's least known and appreciated works, but, viewed on its own terms, it is a powerful piece of satire, one of the best film commentaries on both McCarthyism and popular culture. It is, in fact, the best film commentary on the relationship between these two phenomena. *Screenplay:* Charles Chaplin. *Selected bibliography:* Flom; Maland (*Chaplin*); David Robinson.

*NO DOWN PAYMENT:* DIR. MARTIN RITT (1957). *No Down Payment* is a social drama that explores the consequences of the flight to the suburbs that was a central fact of middle-class American life in the 1950s. At times, however, the film seems in danger of becoming a mere soap opera. Set in a new California subdivision known as "Sunrise Hills," the film focuses on four couples as they seek the American dream only to find that life in the suburbs has its own social problems, including the alienating effect of living amid row after row of identical houses, making it difficult for any of them to seem like a real home. Also central to the film are the financial pressures brought about when many of the inhabitants overextend themselves in buying their new homes and now must struggle to make their mortgage payments.

The couples include electronics engineer David Martin (Jeffrey Hunter) and his flirtatious wife, Jean (Patricia Owens); used-car salesman Jerry Flagg (Tony Randall) and his wife, Isabelle (Sheree North); gas-station manager Troy Boone (Cameron Mitchell) and his wife, Leola (Joanne Woodward); and hardware-store manager Herman Kreitzer (Pat Hingle) and his wife, Betty (Barbara Rush). All of these individuals have their particular problems, though all of the husbands struggle to make enough money to meet their mortgage payments and all of the wives remain primarily in the domestic sphere. The film explores each of the four stories essentially in parallel, though they sometimes come into contact at key points amid the episodic and somewhat fragmented flow of the narrative. Flagg is a man with big plans and high hopes, but they never seem to pan out in reality, causing him to take to drink and causing Isabelle to threaten divorce. Kreitzer is a responsible straight shooter whose hardware business is quite successful, though he runs into difficulty when he tries to arrange for his assistant, Iko (Aki Aleong) to move into Sunrise Hills. Because Iko is Japanese American, some of the residents, including Betty Kreitzer, strenuously object to having him live among them. Ex-serviceman Boone is a decorated war veteran who has found civilian society rather unappreciative of his contribution to the war effort. Frustrated and embittered by the lack of opportunity open to him, he gets drunk and, in a scene that was highly controversial at the time, rapes Jean Martin, leading David Martin to confront him the next day as he works under his car. During the confrontation, Boone becomes upset and accidentally knocks the jack from under the car, which falls on him and kills him, providing the dramatic climax of the film.

While *No Down Payment* is certainly critical of the ethos of middle-class suburbia, it is not overtly leftist. Indeed, it ends as most of the characters attend a church service, suggesting that religion might eventually provide the sense of community that has otherwise been missing from their lives. Nevertheless, rumors about the film caused Ritt to be subpoenaed by HUAC even before the film was made. The subpoena was never served because HUAC's agents were unable to locate Ritt. Asked by the head of Twentieth Century Fox to appear before HUAC voluntarily, Ritt refused, appalled by the very existence of HUAC and angry at his own earlier blacklisting from television. He went on to complete the film and many more, becoming one of the first to defeat the efforts of HUAC to interfere in his film career. *Screenplay:* Philip Yordan. *Selected bibliography:* Carlton Jackson.

*PATHS OF GLORY:* **DIR. STANLEY KUBRICK (1957).** A commercial flop that received relatively little attention when it was first released (except to be banned in France), *Paths of Glory* has, over the years, come to be regarded as a classic cinematic statement against the brutality and absurdity of war. The film captures much of the horror and senselessness of World War I trench warfare, in which thousands of men were killed and maimed in pointless efforts to capture a few yards of worthless ground, yards that would in any case likely be lost in a future counter-offensive. It also captures the stupidity of a military bureaucracy that can command men to make such useless sacrifices in the name of empty platitudes such as glory, duty, and patriotism.

The film centers around a French offensive on the "Ant Hill," a heavily fortified hill held by the Germans. At the urging of his superior, General Broulard (Adolphe Menjou), French General Mireau (George Macready) agrees to undertake the perilous assault on the hill in the hope of enhancing his reputation and receiving a promotion. Both Mireau and Broulard know that the French losses will be huge, but, in a clear display of class-based imperiousness, they do not really regard the men beneath them as fully human. Indeed, Peter Biskind describes the film's critique of the military bureaucracy as "veiled class warfare" (92). Mireau assigns the assault to a battalion commanded by Colonel Dax (Kirk Douglas), despite Dax's protestations that the assault is insane. Dax leads his men out of their trenches into the battle-scarred No Man's Land that separates them from the German lines, but heavy German fire soon makes it clear that the assault is hopeless. The last wave of Dax's men refuses even to leave their trenches, causing Broulard, who looks on from a safe distance, to order his artillery to open fire on the reluctant men. Fortunately, Captain Nichols (Harold Benedict), the commander of the artillery, refuses the order, just as the survivors from the first wave scurry back into their own trenches.

Refusing to admit that the assault on the hill was an error in judgment on the part of Generals Broulard and Mireau, the military bureaucracy decides to blame the fiasco on the cowardice and insubordination of Dax's men, despite the latter's furious protests. Eventually, it is decided that one man from each company involved in the assault will be assigned to stand trial for cowardice under fire as an example to the others. Of these three men, Private Arnaud (Joseph Turkel) is selected by drawing lots, Private Ferol (Timothy Carey) is designated because his captain believes him a "social undesirable," and Corporal Paris (Ralph Meeker) is designated because he has witnessed his lieutenant in an act of cowardice and betrayal, so that the lieutenant wants to get rid of him.

Dax, a famous trial lawyer in civilian life, valiantly defends the men at their court martial, but it is clear that the proceeding is merely a formality. The men are summarily convicted and sentenced to death by firing squad, despite Dax's best efforts. After some touching scenes of the three doomed men awaiting execution, the film presents this execution in a moving sunrise scene that makes clear the insanity of the entire process. Yet Mireau and Broulard later congratulate each other over a sumptuous breakfast, declaring the execution a glorious and splendid demonstration of French military discipline. Then Broulard, aware of Mireau's order to the artillery to fire on the French trenches, calmly informs Mireau that he is being relieved of his command. The pompous Broulard then offers Mireau's command to Dax, who angrily rejects the offer, calling Broulard a "degenerate, sadistic old man."

Dax storms back to his quarters, but on the way overhears a ruckus in a café, where drunken French soldiers are tormenting a captured German girl, demanding that she sing for their entertainment. For a second, Dax wonders if the imperious attitude of Mireau and Broulard toward ordinary French soldiers might be justified. But then the girl begins to a sing a sentimental song that touches the hearts of the men, even though they cannot understand the words. Soon they are humming along, with tears running down their cheeks. Heartened by this display of humanity, Dax goes on his way, reaffirmed in his faith in his men, who do indeed remain human, despite the inhumanity of war. *Screenplay:* Stanley Kubrick, Jim Thompson, and Calder Willingham. *Selected bibliography:* Biskind (*Seeing*); Falsetto; Sayre; White.

*TIME WITHOUT PITY:* DIR. JOSEPH LOSEY (1957). Made in England after both director Losey and screenwriter Barzman fled there from political persecution in the United States, *Time Without Pity* is a thriller whose main political message seems to be a demonstration of the pitfalls of capital punishment. In the film's first scene, shown even before the credits, we see Jenny Cole (Christina Lubicz) being murdered by Robert Stanford (Leo McKern). Then, as the film proceeds, we quickly learn that young Alec Graham (Alec McGowan) has been wrongly convicted of the murder and sentenced to death. Indeed, Alec is to be executed within twenty-four hours when we first meet him as his father, novelist David Graham (Michael Redgrave), visits him in prison. The elder Graham has just returned from treatment in Europe for alcoholism and was away during Alec's trial. Indeed, he has been away during most of the key moments in Alec's life, as we learn when the son complains, during the visit, of his father's negligence.

Convinced of his son's innocence, David Graham begins a frantic attempt to find the real killer before Alec is executed. In the process, he meets Stanford, the owner of the apartment in which Jenny was killed. Stanford is a prominent automobile manufacturer who is currently involved in the testing of a new model. A self-made man, Stanford serves as a sort of image of capitalist ruthlessness, a man whose obvious obsession with power and control is enacted both in his business dealings and in his affairs with young women, including Jenny. Indeed, Graham eventually realizes that Stanford killed Jenny, though he is unable to prove it. Growing desperate as the time of Alec's execution draws near, Graham induces Stanford to kill him and thus to reveal his murderous impulses. Stanford's wife and adult son rush in just after the shooting, then phone the police to turn in Stanford for the murder of both Jenny and Graham. Alec is saved at the expense of his father's death.

Some of the film's developments are overly predictable; others are inexplicable. Nevertheless, Redgrave's performance is extremely effective as the distraught father whose lack of professional success has driven him to alcohol and to neglecting his family. Serving as an interesting counterpart to Graham, Stanford is a man who has been estranged from his family by his immersion in his successful business. In both cases, the economic demands of capitalist society are suggested as a powerful force for individual alienation, even from one's own family. Meanwhile, that Alec is nearly executed for a crime he did not commit makes a strong statement against capital punishment, supplemented by a scene in which Graham attends a parliamentary committee hearing on the advisability of outlawing capital punishment. *Screenplay:* Ben Barzman. *Selected bibliography:* Caute (*Joseph Losey*); Hirsch.

**THE DEFIANT ONES: DIR. STANLEY KRAMER (1958).** A critical and commercial success, *The Defiant Ones* is a leading example of the attempt of American film in the 1950s to begin to come to grips with the reality of racism in America. Among other things, it is important in American film history as the film that established Sidney Poitier as a major star of the American cinema. As the film begins, Poitier plays Noah Cullen, an African American convict, who is being transferred by truck to a different prison. As a sort of cruel joke, he has been chained to a bigoted white prisoner, John Jackson (Tony Curtis). When the prison truck wrecks, the two escape and flee through the woods, still chained together. Much of the film relates their struggle to make their way across the countryside with the authorities in hot pursuit. Along the way, they find that, because of the chains, they must continually work together in order to survive. They also gradually begin to appreciate each other as human beings who have a great deal in common. For example, though white, Jackson comes from an impoverished background and has suffered considerable humiliation in his life at the hands of upper-class whites.

The two make their way to a turpentine manufacturing camp where Cullen once worked. There, they break into the company store seeking food and tools with which to remove the chains. They are discovered and flee, knocking one of their pursuers unconscious. Captured, they are nearly lynched, causing Jackson frantically to protest that he cannot be lynched because he is white. Eventually, they are saved by the intervention of Big Sam (Lon Chaney, Jr.), who helps them escape because, as a former convict himself, he can sympathize with their plight. Eventually, they make their way to a farmhouse, where a white woman (Cara Williams) lives with her son (Kevin Coughlin). There, they get food and are able to remove the chains.

Jackson, ill from an infection caused by the rubbing of the manacle on his wrist, recuperates and strikes up a relationship with the woman, who begs him to take her away with him. Finally, he agrees to drive south with her in her car. She gives Cullen instructions on how to reach a nearby railroad so that he can hop a train headed north. After Cullen leaves, however, she admits to Jackson that she has directed Cullen into a swamp, where he will probably be lost forever (and thus unable to tell the authorities about them if captured). Furious, Jackson knocks the woman aside and rushes off to warn Cullen; the boy takes a shot at him as he leaves and wounds him in the shoulder. Jackson, weak from his recent illness and from his new wound, is on the verge of collapse by the time he locates Cullen. Nevertheless, they manage to get out of the swamp and find the railroad. Jackson, however, is too weak to hop the passing train; Cullen, refusing to leave his friend behind, fails to get aboard the train as well. The two sit in exhaustion as Sheriff Max Muller (Theodore Bikel) approaches to recapture them.

The film's metaphoric dramatization of blacks and whites being joined together in American society is a bit obvious, and it is certainly the case that *The Defiant Ones* does very little to examine the root causes of racial prejudice or to propose anything but the most banal of solutions to the problem. Nevertheless, the film makes its points about the evils of racism fairly effectively, and the basic simplicity of the film's conception is in many ways an asset. At the same time, the film presents racism in an extremely unthreatening manner, and the nobly sacrificial Cullen certainly appears as a rather unthreatening African American—which may account for the fact that the film was able to win wide acceptance, including nine Academy Award nominations and two awards. One award was for best screenplay, shared by Harold Jacob Smith and blacklisted screenwriter Nedrick Young, who used the pseudonym "Nathan Douglas." Much of the effectiveness of the film can be attributed to the fine performances of both Poitier and Curtis, which lend a certain genuineness to the developing relationship between Jackson and Cullen. *Screenplay:* Nedrick Young and Harold Jacob Smith. *Selected bibliography:* Ellison; Sayre; Spoto (*Stanley Kramer*).

*THE NAKED AND THE DEAD:* **DIR. RAOUL WALSH (1958).** Although touted in its own promotions as a daring film, *The Naked and the Dead* is a seriously bowdlerized version of the 1948 Norman Mailer novel on which it is based. *The Naked and the Dead*, Mailer's first novel, is still widely regarded as one of the finest novels to have come out of World War II. The film, however, lacks most of the elements that make the book so effective, settling for a fairly banal "war is hell" message. It was, in fact, described by Mailer as "one of the worst movies ever made" (187). The film does seriously dilute the book's critique of the American war machine, a critique that, among other things, suggested that the American military establishment was driven by neofascist impulses that made it irrelevant who actually won the war. What is particularly disappointing is the film's failure to convey the strong sense of class that informs the novel and its critique of American society. In particular, the film completely fails to capture the way in which the book suggests that the war functions as a microcosm of the antagonistic social relations that prevail under capitalism, while it presents the army as a microcosm of American capitalist society.

Both the film and the book deal with the assault on a fictional Japanese-held island in the Pacific by a large American force under the command of General Edward Cummings (played in the film by Raymond Massey). Both the book and the film focus in particular on a single Intelligence and Reconnaissance platoon, the members of which represent a cross section of large elements of American society. It is necessarily, however, an all-male microcosm, and most of the characters tend to think of women with hostility, lust, or a combination of the two. The film omits most of the book's "Time Capsule" segments that relate their backgrounds of the men in the platoon before joining the army, settling for a single flashback in which Sergeant Croft (Aldo Ray) discovers his wife cheating on him, thus presumably explaining his hostile attitude toward men and his viciousness in general. The sadistic Croft coldly murders Japanese prisoners and plucks the gold teeth from the mouths of dead Japanese, hoping eventually to accumulate a fortune in gold. The film does not, however, detail the backgrounds of the rest of the men, paying special attention to their class origins, in the way the book does. Meanwhile, the film seems to suggest that Croft's brutality can be blamed on his cheating wife, while the book makes Croft a product of certain dark impulses in American capitalist society as a whole.

Cummings's left-liberal aide, Lieutenant Robert Hearn (Cliff Robertson) is the central figure through most of the story. He is depicted relatively sympathetically, as a sort of foil to Cummings. In what is perhaps the film's most overt political statement, he responds to Cummings's cold treatment of his men as pawns in the chess game of war by suggesting that Cummings commands his forces very much the way Hearn's wealthy father manages the factory he owns—by treating the workers like part of the factory machinery. Near the end of the book, Hearn is placed in command of the recon platoon as a punishment for his insubordination in resisting Cummings's domination. Hearn then leads the men on a dangerous patrol to the back side of the island to establish an observation post atop Mt. Tanaka and to scout out a possible rout for a rear assault on the Japanese. The final segment of the film is devoted to this mission, which turns out to be entirely pointless. The men make their way through difficult and dangerous terrain. On the way, one man dies of snakebite and another is killed by Japanese fire. Eventually Hearn is seriously wounded when Croft, who greatly resents Hearn's presence, intentionally decides not to inform him that there is a Japanese patrol ahead. Hearn is then carried back to the beach on a stretcher by three of the men. In the film, he is eventually rescued, though in the book he dies. The main body of the patrol continues up Mt. Anaka, where one of them, the Jewish Roth (Joey Bishop), falls to his death after being taunted by Croft's antisemitic insults, though Croft's antisemitism is considerably toned down in the film relative to the book. Eventually, Croft himself is killed, and the others return to the beach without ever reaching the summit. Meanwhile, the American assault on the island succeeds by sheer luck, making the entire work of the patrol meaningless. *Screenplay:* Denis Sanders and Terry Sanders. *Selected bibliography:* Biskind (*Seeing*); Koppes and Black; Mailer.

*NEVER STEAL ANYTHING SMALL:* **DIR. CHARLES LEDERER (1958).** *Never Steal Anything Small* opens to the strains of a song that begins "Steal a hundred dollars and they put you in stir. Steal a hundred million, they address you as sir." These lyrics, together with the film's

Brechtian title, seem to offer considerable promise that the film will be a critique of the unscrupulous workings of capitalism. In addition, an argument presented early in the film that criminals are vital to the workings of the American system seems to promise a potential Foucaultian exploration of America as a carceral society. Neither promise is fulfilled. Indeed, the film is essentially a musical comedy with no serious agenda whatsoever. Meanwhile, its treatment of corruption in organized labor as something that can be taken for granted, part of the *On the Waterfront* syndrome that swept American culture in the 1950s, shows the extent to which labor unions had been discredited in the popular imagination by that time.

The film centers on Jake MacIllaney (James Cagney), a small-time crook who employs every manner of foul play in order to get himself elected president of Local 26 of the United Stevedores Union. In the process, he gets arrested for extortion, employing young Dan Cabot (Roger Smith) as his lawyer. He also becomes smitten with Cabot's wife, Linda (Shirley Jones), prompting him to attempt to frame Dan on a theft charge so that he can have Linda for himself. In the end, however, MacIllaney takes the rap, claiming he committed the theft "for the men," a ploy he hopes will help him in his bid to unseat the union president, the mobster Pinelli (Nehemiah Persoff). The ploy works, but MacIllaney's crusade against the mob (and, presumably, for social justice) is little short of ludicrous, as is the film itself. *Screenplay:* Charles Lederer. *Selected bibliography:* Zaniello.

*TOUCH OF EVIL:* DIR. ORSON WELLES (1958). Widely acknowledged as a classic of the American cinema, *Touch of Evil* is perhaps the single most representative film of Welles's career. It epitomizes his ability to push the boundaries of genre, twisting and extending conventions in such a way as to produce recognizable genre films that at the same time question the premises of the genre to which they belong. As James Naremore puts it, *Touch of Evil* is the Welles film in which "all his strengths — the showman, the political satirist, the obsessed romantic, the moral philosopher, the surrealist — are somehow merged" (146). On the surface, *Touch of Evil* is a film noir, but it pushes the typical film noir lighting effects to an almost absurd extreme, thereby conducting a self-reflexive and self-parodic inquiry into the thematic use of darkness and shadow in the film noir. The plot that accompanies this lighting also resembles that of the typical film noir, but again to an extent that spills over into parody. It is almost as if Welles constructed the film from a sort of film noir tool kit, making sure that all the elements were there but putting them together with twine and bailing wire that remain clearly visible.

One story about the origin of *Touch of Evil* is that the film began when producer Albert Zugsmith dared Welles to try to make a good film out of the worst script Zugsmith could find (Naremore 148). True or not, the story certainly provides an interesting gloss on the resulting film, which seems to try to raise cheesiness to an art form. It begins as a mysterious figure plants a bomb in the trunk of a car. An impressive overhead tracking shot then follows the car as it drives through a Mexican border town, crosses the border into America, then suddenly explodes, obliterating the occupants of the car, who include wealthy contractor Rudy Linnekar and a blonde bimbo (Joi Lansing). Among other things, this opening shot calls attention to its own virtuosity, announcing the film's reflexivity. In the meantime, a couple walks the same route and are soon identified as newlyweds Miguel "Mike" Vargas and Susan Vargas (played by Charlton Heston and Janet Leigh). Vargas is a prominent crimebuster with "nearly cabinet status" in the Mexican government; Susan is an American woman who seems to regard all Mexicans as potential rapists, presumably (though not certainly) with the exception of her husband, whom she insists on calling "Mike" and who, fortunately, speaks perfect American English without a trace of an accent. Dressed throughout the film in either tight sweaters or lingerie, Leigh prefigures her upcoming role in *Psycho* (1960) by stumbling through the film as a prototypical white-woman victim, surrounded by sleazy, swarthy tormentors. Meanwhile, Heston ostensibly plays the straight man amid the film's gallery of grotesques, yet Vargas is in many ways the oddest character of the lot. For one thing, he is an absurdly unconvincing Mexican whose lack of accent is compensated for by ludicrous skin-darkening makeup and a thin moustache so fake-looking it would make Groucho Marx's look real. For another, Vargas speaks almost entirely in pompous clichés, delivered with a hokey breathless passion that sounds for all the world like a bad comedian doing impressions of Heston. Interestingly, in his interview with James Delson, Heston seems to have no idea that he cut such a ridiculous figure in the film, also speaking in clichés as he fields Delson's compliments and calls his own performance in the film "as satisfying creatively as anything I've ever done" (70).

While Vargas is the film's "hero," the real central figure in the film is the corrupt American police captain, Hank Quinlan (Welles), who first arrives on the scene to investigate the car bombing. Quinlan is a literally larger than life figure; the swollen Welles limps and mumbles his way through the film with his rumpled clothing supplemented by stubble and a putty nose, looking as disreputable as possible. As the bizarre Mexican gypsy Tanya (played by Marlene Dietrich with no attempt to hide her German accent) tells him when she sees him, apparently for the first time in years, "You're a mess, honey." The wise and wearily tolerant Tanya has no particular role in the plot, but she functions, among other things, as a counterpoint to the innocently bitchy Susan, just as Quinlan is contrasted with Vargas. Tanya, however, is a far more attractive figure than Susan, while, in one of the film's many ironies, the grotesque Quinlan (partly due to Welles's superb performance) is not only more interesting, but far more believable than the upright, repressed Vargas. Among other things, Quinlan serves as an allusion to Welles's recent casting as a fat racist in films such as *Man in the Shadow* (1957) and *The Long Hot Summer* (1958), though the film provides its own explanation for Quinlan's condition. He has supposedly deteriorated to this state due to his despair over the unsolved murder of his wife, years earlier, apparently the only area murder in recent history that has gone unsolved. It turns out, however, that Quinlan's technique for solving murders is to deduce the identity of the culprit through intuition, then to plant evidence to ensure that the designated culprit will be convicted. The murder of his wife, then, may have gone unsolved because, for once, he wanted to make sure he captured the real perpetrator. Of course, it is possible that Quinlan murdered her himself, but this interpretation seems inconsistent with the oddly sympathetic presentation of Quinlan in much of the film.

The final major character is the Mexican gangster Joe Grandi (Akim Tamiroff), whose brother is being prosecuted by Vargas and who is attempting (when not wrestling with his recalcitrant hairpiece) to gain some sort of leverage with which to undermine that prosecution. These major characters are also supplemented by minor characters, such as Grandi's gang and Quinlan's lieutenants, though many of the secondary characters are included less for their roles in the plot than to increase the overall surreal atmosphere. Particularly memorable is Dennis Weaver as the hysterical (in more ways than one) "night man" of the deserted motel (owned by Grandi) where Susan is inexplicably stashed during much of the film, there to be terrorized by Grandi's gang. There are also a number of brief cameo appearances by a diverse crew that includes Merecedes McCambridge, Zsa Zsa Gabor, Ray Collins, and old-time Wellesian, Joseph Cotton.

With such a cast of characters, it almost goes without saying that the plot is largely beside the point. Quinlan quickly concludes that a Mexican worker, Manolo Sanchez (Victor Millan), is the killer, especially after it becomes clear that Sanchez had been recently fired from Linnekar's construction firm because he was involved with Linnekar's daughter, Marcia (Joanna Moore). Sanchez and Marcia turn out to have been secretly married, but that doesn't stop Quinlan, with the help of long-time crony Pete Menzies (Joseph Calleia), from planting evidence that will connect Sanchez with the crime. Vargas, however, catches them in the act, then spends the remainder of the film trying to prove that Quinlan has framed Sanchez. Quinlan, meanwhile, responds by conspiring with Grandi to discredit Vargas, principally by framing Susan as a junkie (and faking her gang rape), with the implications that Vargas has been using his official position to obtain drugs for his and her use. The stakes are raised when Quinlan murders Grandi and attempts to associate Susan with the killing. Feeling that Quinlan has gone too far, Menzies helps Vargas get the evidence he needs against Quinlan, leading to a shootout in which Menzies and Quinlan shoot and kill each other. Vargas then drives away with Susan, while Schwartz (Mort Mills), an investigator from the district attorney's office, arrives to announce that Sanchez apparently really was the killer. That leaves Tanya, who for some reason also appears at the scene, to deliver Quinlan's epitaph as he lies in a pool of filthy, stagnant water: "He was some kind of a man. What does it matter what you say about people?"

*Touch of Evil* makes a number of thematic political points. In addition to its obvious critique of official corruption and police racism, it undermines racist stereotypes through its characterization (the corrupt policeman is American, the virtuous one Mexican) and through constant shifts in setting back and forth across the border, creating deliberate confusion as to which side is which. Confusion is, in fact, the principal theme of the film, which powerfully undermines the tendency toward clear polar oppositions that were central to the Western Cold War rhetoric of the 1950s. The corrupt Quinlan makes no money from his corruption and is apparently usually correct in his intuition; the virtuous Vargas admits to compromising his ethics to be able to get along with "the machine." The film also challenges the easy moral distinctions that were often made in American films of the 1950s, and *Touch of Evil* is very much a film about film. The same might be said of the film noir in general, of course, but *Touch of Evil* goes farther, also questioning the premises of the film noir, thereby producing a warning against the degeneration of the genre into conventionality. **Screenplay:** Orson Welles. **Selected bibliography:** Bazin; Cowie ("Study"); Delson; Denning; Munby; Naremore (*Magic*); Naremore (*More than Night*); Nericcio; Stubbs; Welles, Bogdanovich, and Rosenbaum.

*INHERIT THE WIND:* **DIR. STANLEY KRAMER (1960).** Adapted by Harold Jacob Smith and the blacklisted Ned Young (writing as Nathan E. Douglas) from the play of the same title by Robert E. Lee, *Inherit the Wind* is a courtroom drama based on the famous 1925 "monkey trial" of schoolteacher John Scopes, charged with a criminal offense for teaching Darwin's theory of evolution in a public school in Dayton, Tennessee. The trial was a landmark battle in American legal history, a titanic clash between the near-legendary figures of William Jennings Bryan, brought in as a special prosecutor, and Clarence Darrow, brought in to defend Scopes. More important, Darrow sought to defend what he saw as crucial constitutional issues raised by the case, including separation of church and state and freedom of thought and speech. The film version, transplanted to the fictional town of Hillsboro, makes clear these issues, though it emphasizes the personal battle between the lawyers, represented here as the aging warhorses Henry Drummond (Darrow, played by Spencer Tracy) and Matthew Harrison Brady (Bryan, played by Fredric March). The third major figure in the film is journalist E. K. Hornbeck (Gene Kelly) of the Baltimore *Herald*, who fills the role played in the original trial by the Baltimore *Sun*'s H. L. Mencken, a near legendary figure in his own right.

The Scopes figure, Bertram Cates (Dick York) is actually a relatively minor character, though his staunch integrity (which may explain the otherwise inexplicable fact, as a matter of principle, that he spends the entire trial in jail rather than free on bail) is crucial to the film's presentation of the trial, which makes it quite clear that the defense stands for liberty and modernity, while the prosecution stands for ignorance and religious bigotry of near-medieval proportions. This is especially clear in the depiction of the town's religious leader, the fanatical Reverend Jeremiah Brown (Claude Akins), who, among other things, threatens to disown his adult daughter, Rachel (Donna Anderson), who, in a fictional subplot introduced for purposes of the film, remains loyal to Cates, her fiancé. In the courtroom scenes, Brady's scowling style helps to establish him as a villain, though one who is as much pathetic as evil. Tracy plays Drummond with his typical gruff charm, establishing him as the defender of right, even though the odds are clearly stacked against him in the small-town trial. In many ways, however, it is Kelly's Hornbeck who (in appropriate Menckenesque fashion) gets the best , if most cynical, lines, as when he quips, modifying Marx and Engels while observing an anti-Cates mob demonstrating in the streets of Hillsboro, "Hooligans of the world, unite. You've got nothing to burn but your intellectuals."

Predictably, Drummond loses the case, though Cates is merely sentenced to a \$100 fine, which Drummond plans to appeal. (The conviction of the historical Scope was later overturned by the state supreme court.) In the process, however, Drummond makes the entire town of Hillsboro, and particularly his former friend and ally Brady, look ridiculous. Brady, in fact, gradually becomes unhinged, especially after Drummond calls him to the stand to testify on questions of biblical scripture, revealing ambiguities and inconsistencies in the Bible that make Brady's demand for literal interpretation appear preposterous. As the trial comes to a close, a near-hysterical Brady is attempting to make one final speech but is ignored by those present, causing him, somewhat melodramatically, to drop dead on the spot. (The historical Bryan died in his sleep five days after the trial, during which he was called to the stand and ridiculed by Darrow.) The film then ends with an unfortunate, sentimental coda in which Drummond complains to Hornbeck of his cynicism and refusal to honor the memory of Brady, whom the latter still characterizes as a "bible beating bunko artist." Drummond then exits, carrying copies of both the bible and Darwin's *The Origin of Species* tucked under his arm as the "Battle Hymn of the Republic" is sung in the background.

This ending moderates the message of the film and seems designed as a guard against criticism that the film is antireligious or radical in any other way. If nothing else, however, the film, by heroicizing the Darrow figure, helped to preserve the popular memory of one of the most important figures in American legal history, and one who was often associated with radical causes. Darrow, for example, first became widely known for his much-admired 1894 defense of Eugene Debs and others who had been arrested in connection with the Pullman strike of that year. Darrow devoted most of the remainder of his long career to the defense of the downtrodden and persecuted, many of them political radicals. Among numerous prominent cases were his successful defense in the murder trial of Big Bill Haywood in 1906 and his controversial defense of the McNamara brothers in the Los Angeles *Times* dynamiting case (1911). Darrow was a particular opponent of capital punishment, defending more than 100 persons charged with murder, none of whom were ever sentenced to death. The McNamara case was the subject of the 1911 silent film *A Martyr to His Cause*, while Darrow played himself (defending a socialist politician framed by capitalist opponents) in the 1913 silent *From Dusk to Dawn*. Darrow also appeared as himself in the 1931 pro-evolution documentary, *The Mystery of Life*. His defense in the "thrill" murder trial of Leopold and Loeb (1924) was the basis of the film 1959 *Compulsion*, in which Orson Welles played the role of Jonathan Wilk, the film's Darrow figure. *Inherit the Wind* was remade as a television movie of the same title in 1989, with Jason Robards and Kirk Douglas as Drummond and Brady, respectively. Darrow's career was the basis of the 1991 American Playhouse television docudrama, *Darrow*, with Kevin Spacey in the title role. **Screenplay:** Nathan E. Douglas (Ned Young) and Harold Jacob Smith. **Selected bibliography:** Darrow; De Camp; Gurko; Scopes; Irving Stone.

**SPARTACUS: DIR. STANLEY KUBRICK (1960).** *Spartacus* was based on a 1951 novel by leftist writer Howard Fast, written mostly while Fast was in prison for his leftist political beliefs. The film shows clear traces of its leftist origins. Both the film and the novel are based on a famous rebellion, ending in 71 B.C., in which the gladiator Spartacus led a rebel army composed of slaves and other gladiators in a two-year war against the power of Rome. While ultimately unsuccessful, this rebellion would long stand as a source of inspiration for the Left, as when the communist rebels who nearly took control of the German government under the leadership of Rosa Luxemburg and Karl Liebknecht in 1919 referred to themselves as "Spartacists." Moreover, like the novel, the film clearly suggests parallels between Roman slavery and American slavery, while also indicating parallels between the Roman exploitation of slave labor and the exploitation of proletarians in modern capitalist America.

Nevertheless, *Spartacus* is not really a radical film. For one thing, it was an extremely expensive film that had to seek a mass audience in order to recover the cost of the film. In its attempt to attract and please such an audience, it mutes its political message, while making a number of concessions to the conventions of Hollywood cinema. Spartacus (played by Kirk Douglas, who was also the film's executive producer) espouses a personal ideology that sounds suspiciously similar to Jeffersonian democracy, while the film pays an excessive amount of attention to Hollywood motifs such as Spartacus's romance with the former slave Varinia (Jean Simmons). In addition, the film, a genuine epic with a consistent tone of grandeur, sometimes seems to get carried away with its own status as gorgeous spectacle. But the very splendor of the film makes it unique among left-leaning works of the American cinema, which have seldom had access to the budgets required to produce such a grand epic.

The film begins as Spartacus and other slaves work in the mines of Libya, providing a potential link to modern proletarian culture, in which miners are often central figures. Spartacus's rebelliousness leads him to be sentenced to death, a fate from which he is saved when he is purchased by Lentulus Batiatus (Peter Ustinov) for training as a gladiator. The film details this training in considerable detail. In the midst of the training, Spartacus is offered Varinia as a sexual favor. He declines, feeling that the two of them are being mated like animals. The two begin to develop a bond. Then, a group of Romans, including powerful Roman patrician Marcus Licinius Crassus (Laurence Olivier), arrives at the training camp and asks to be entertained by some gladiatorial fights to the death. Chosen to participate in one contest, Spartacus is rendered helpless by his opponent, an Ethiopian. However, the Ehtiopian refuses to kill Spartacus and instead rushes the Roman onlookers, whereupon he is killed. His body is hung up as a warning to the other gladiators. Meanwhile, Crassus purchases Varinia and sends her away to Rome.

When the trainer Marcellus (Charles McGraw) taunts Spartacus concerning Varinia, Spartacus becomes furious and kills him, triggering a full-scale revolt among the gladiators. Soon, Spartacus leads the gladiators into the surrounding countryside, freeing slaves as they go and thus building a burgeoning army. Varinia is among the first slaves liberated by the rebels, joining Spartacus as his wife and soon becoming pregnant. They camp on Vesuvius for military training, then conceive a plan to march across Italy to the port city of Brundisium, where they hope to bribe pirates to take them away from the peninsula and out of the immediate reach of Roman power. Meanwhile, back in Rome, the Senate debates a response to the revolt, which becomes the center of a power struggle between Crassus and Gracchus (Charles Laughton), who counters Crassus's haughty patricianism with a belief that real political power resides in the masses of common people. Spartacus's army begins its march, winning a series of surprising victories over the Roman armies that are sent to stop them. As the slave army nears Brundisium, Gracchus attempts to arrange for their safe passage with the pirates, hoping to get them out of Italy and thereby remove any opportunity for Crassus to make political capital out of their defeat. Crassus outmaneuvers him, however, and arranges for the pirates to betray the rebels, while two Roman armies converge on Brundisium. Spartacus has no choice but to turn north and march on Rome in a desperate last-ditch fight for freedom.

Crassus, now the first consul of Rome and commander-in-chief of the Roman armies, meets the advancing slave army with a vastly superior force, defeating them in a decisive battle that destroys Spartacus's army once and for all. Crassus searches among the dead and the prisoners, hoping to identify Spartacus. In the process, he locates Varinia and her newborn infant son lying alive amid the carnage. He sends the two of them back to his house in Rome. Finally, he offers a reprieve from crucifixion for all of the prisoners if they will identify Spartacus. Spartacus comes forward and cries, "I am Spartacus!" But then another voice cries out the same, and eventually all of the prisoners proclaim themselves to be Spartacus, serving the double function of defeating Crassus's desires and making the point that, in a very real sense, they all *are* Spartacus, the symbol of their collective effort. Frustrated, Crassus orders them all crucified, saving a few for gladiatorial contests; soon the Appian Way is lined with the bodies of 6,000 crucified rebels hanging on crosses.

Spartacus is crucified as well, following a last emotional scene in which he kills the young former slave Antoninus (Tony Curtis) in a gladiatorial battle to save Antoninus from the agony of being crucified. Antoninus dies in his arms. Meanwhile, Gracchus, continuing his opposition to Crassus, arranges for Batiatus to rescue Varinia and her son. Using the power invested in him as a senator, Gracchus grants articles of freedom to Varinia and the infant, then bribes Batiatus to take them away to safety. Gracchus then prepares to commit suicide, knowing that Crassus's soldiers will soon be coming for him. On the way out of Rome, Varinia sees Spartacus hanging on the cross, still alive. She can do little but bid him a tearful farewell and wish him a hasty death, but she is at least able to show him his son and to announce that his son is free.

*Spartacus* obeyed the conventions of Hollywood film well enough to win six Academy Award nominations and three Academy Awards. The screenplay for the film was written by blacklisted screenwriter Dalton Trumbo, making it one of the first films significantly to defy the blacklist, in that sense following hard on the heels of Otto Preminger's *Exodus*, for which Trumbo was also given screenwriting credit. In point of fact, Trumbo got on extremely poorly with director Kubrick and found working on the film a far from liberating experience. The film was rereleased in a significantly abridged form in 1967 but restored to its original length in 1991. Indeed, one scene cut from the original, in which Crassus makes homoerotic suggestions to Antoninus, then his slave, was added in the 1991 restoration. *Screenplay:* Dalton Trumbo. *Selected bibliography:* Duncan Cooper; Dick (*Radical Innocence*); Hark; Jeffrey P. Smith.

*THE CHILDREN'S HOUR:* **DIR. WILLIAM WYLER (1961).** *The Children's Hour* is a relatively faithful, if somewhat lethargic, adaptation of Lillian Hellman's play by the same title, first brought to the screen by Wyler and Hellman in a substantially bowdlerized version as *These Three* in 1936. The film focuses on the Wright-Dobie School for Girls, which headmistresses Karen Wright (Audrey Hepburn) and Martha Dobie (Shirley MacLaine) have worked long and hard to make a success. Their efforts are starting to pay off, and the boarding school is just beginning to turn a profit, which among other things allows Wright to begin to make concrete her long-delayed plan to wed local physician Dr. Joe Cardin (James Garner). Dobie and Wright are quite close, and Dobie seems rather jealous of the match between Wright and Cardin, a fact pointed out to her by her eccentric aunt, Lily Mortar (Miriam Hopkins), in a moment of anger when Lily is asked to leave the school, where she has been teaching. Some girls overhear the conversation, which is then conveyed to the other girls. One of the girls, Mary Tilford (Karen Balkin) is an inveterate liar, who resents the frequent punishments she receives for her mendacity. Finally, in revenge, she repeats to her wealthy grandmother, Mrs. Amelia Tilford (Fay Bainter), the rumor about Dobie's jealousy, significantly elaborating on it to imply that a full-blown lesbian love affair is taking place between the schoolmistresses on the school grounds.

Shocked, Mrs. Tilford spreads the rumor among the parents of the other children, all of whom are subsequently removed from the school. When Wright and Dobie realize what has happened, they confront Mrs. Tilford, but Mary sticks to her story, backed up by another girl, Rosalie Wells (Veronica Cartwright), whom Mary bullies into confirming the tale. With the school ruined, Wright and Dobie file a libel suit against Mrs. Tilford, but lose when Aunt Lily refuses to return to town to testify on behalf of her niece. Cardin is dismissed from the hospital where he works because of the scandal, and the engagement between Cardin and Wright is broken off when she realizes that he has been having doubts about the truth of the rumors, though he has been supportive throughout. All of these events lead Dobie to reevaluate her own feelings; she concludes that she does, in fact, have feelings for Wright that go beyond mere friendship. Horrified at her feelings and the trouble they have caused, she hangs herself. The film then ends as Wright silently and proudly walks away from the site of Dobie's burial, passing by Cardin and a group of the townspeople whose prying judgmental attitudes have driven Dobie to her death.

One of the first American films to deal with lesbianism in a sympathetic manner, *The Children's Hour* marked a lightening of the heavy-handed censorship that had forced *These Three* to elide the issue of lesbianism altogether. It also marked the effective return of Hellman from the HUAC-inspired blacklist that had left her without screen credits for the previous fifteen years. *Screenplay:* John Michael Hayes and Lillian Hellman. *Selected bibliography:* Dick (*Hellman*); Erhart; Hellman (*Scoundrel Time*); Titus.

*THE HUSTLER:* DIR. ROBERT ROSSEN (1961). *The Hustler* follows the career of pool shark Fast Eddie Felson (Paul Newman), in the process presenting the game of high-stakes pool as an allegory of capitalist competition, much in the mode of the boxing film genre of which this film is clearly an offshoot. Felson is a tough individualist who, despite his considerable talents, finds it difficult to make a living in his chosen field without capital supplied by others, who then demand the lion's share of the value produced by his labor. He is thus the quintessential image of the worker under capitalism. He is also a typical early 1960s film protagonist, a nonheroic hero whose marginal social status suggests the growing feeling of anxiety about the American dream that gripped American society during that period. The role propelled Newman to stardom, and the film proved that director Rossen, who had directed the 1947 boxing classic *Body and Soul*, still had the touch.

As the film begins, Felson works his way across the country with his partner, Charlie Burns (Myron McCormick), picking up traveling money by hustling in dingy small-town pool rooms along the way. Finally, they arrive in New York City, where Felson hopes to challenge the legendary Minnesota Fats (Jackie Gleason), partly for the cash, but mostly just to determine once and for all who is America's greatest shooter of pool. Felson does manage to get a game with Fats and even beats him for a while, but the marathon struggle gradually goes against Felson, who become drunk and exhausted by the end of the contest. When it is all over, Felson is beaten and flat broke.

Felson breaks up with Burns and decides to go it alone. In the meantime, he strikes up a romantic relationship with Sarah Packard (Piper Laurie), an alcoholic cripple who is treated as an outcast by her wealthy family. Given their joint emotional baggage, the relationship is a troubled one, though they stick together as Felson returns to small-time hustling, hoping eventually to accumulate a stake that will allow him to challenge Minnesota Fats to a return match. The road back, however, is a difficult one. Caught in the act of hustling, Felson is beaten up by thugs, who break both his thumbs, leaving him unable to play pool for an extended period.

Meanwhile, Bert Gordon (George C. Scott), a ruthless and unscrupulous gambler, warns Felson that he will never be able to make it alone. In one of the film's most overt commentaries on capitalism, Gordon offers to put up a stake (capital) and to set up games (provide a job) for Felson, in return for which he wants 75 percent of Felson's winnings. Recognizing the analogy to capitalism immediately, Felson rejects the offer and responds, "Who do you think you are, General Motors?" Eventually, however, Felson is forced to give in and to join forces with Gordon, who sets up a private game for him with James Findley (Murray Hamilton), a rich, Southern gentleman in Louisville.

Felson, Packard, and Gordon travel to Louisville for the game. They go to a decadent party at Findley's mansion, and Packard begins to realize that Gordon is leading Felson down the road to perdition. Felson, however, ignores her warnings and goes on with the game. Findley turns out to be a tough competitor, especially as he insists on playing formal billiards rather than the straight pool Felson is accustomed to. Gradually, however, Felson masters the new game and gets the upper hand, winning a total of $12,000, of which $9,000 is to go to Gordon.

Felson, upset by the whole experience, decides to walk back to the hotel. By the time he gets there, Packard has been seduced by Gordon and has subsequently committed suicide, with hints that she has sacrificed herself in a desperate bid to get Felson to turn away from Gordon. Turn away he does. Back in New York, Felson again goes it alone, using his $3,000 from the game in Louisville to challenge Minnesota Fats to a new game. This time, Felson wins, while the jealous Gordon greedily looks on. Afterward Gordon demands half of Felson's winnings, then threatens violence when Felson refuses. Finally, Gordon withdraws the threat but warns Felson that, if he continues to refuse to cooperate, he will never play high-stakes pool again. He will, in short, be blacklisted, a favorite technique used by capitalist enterprises against recalcitrant workers (or capitalist moviemakers against recalcitrant screenwriters and directors). *Screenplay:* Sidney Carroll and Robert Rossen. *Selected bibliography:* Neve (*Film*); Wood.

*A RAISIN IN THE SUN:* **DIR. DANIEL PETRIE (1961).** An effective adaptation of Lorraine Hansberry's successful Broadway stage play of the same title, *A Raisin in the Sun* is important not only for its thematic treatment of a number of social issues, but also because, with its excellent all-black cast, it portrays African Americans as ordinary human beings, not as the marginal (and sometimes grotesque) characters they had usually been in American film. Described by Michael Denning as a "classic 'late' Popular Front production," the film focuses on the Youngers, a three-generation family of African Americans who live together in a cramped Chicago apartment. The inhabitants of the apartment include the family matriarch, Lena Younger (Claudia McNeil), and her two children, son Walter Lee (Sidney Poitier) and daughter Beneatha (Diana Sands). Also living in the apartment are Walter Lee's wife, Ruth (Ruby Dee), and son, Travis (Stephen Perry).

As the film begins, Lena's husband, Walter, Sr., has recently died after a life of grueling work in support of his family. The family is about to receive a $10,000 life insurance check, which Lena plans to use to purchase a house for the family and to help Beneatha get through medical school. Walter Lee, who works as a chauffeur, wants to use the money to go into business with two of his friends, who hope to open a liquor store. He sees this business opportunity as his only chance to become more than a servant and to live a dignified life within the racist context of America. Lena, however, is an extremely religious woman who disapproves of liquor and therefore refuses to support him in this activity. In the meantime, the film also conveys a great deal of the texture of the lives of the Youngers and of African Americans as a whole. For example, we meet two of Beneatha's suitors, including George Murchison (Louis Gossett, Jr.), a member of the black bourgeoisie, and Joseph Asagai (Ivan Dixon), a student from Nigeria.

When the check arrives, Lena ignores Walter Lee's strident pleas and puts $3,500 of the money down on a house—in a white neighborhood. She then places the remaining $6,500 in the care of Walter Lee to show that she trusts him to handle that much money. She instructs him to put $3,000 in a savings account for Beneatha's education and to place the remaining $3,500 in a checking account which he is to use to manage the family's expenses. Instead, Walter Lee gives the entire $6,500 to his friend, Willie Harris (Roy E. Glenn, Sr.), for the liquor store. Harris promptly skips town with the money, leaving the Youngers penniless. In the meantime, a citizens' group from the white neighborhood into which they are about to move sends a representative to try to buy back the house and thus prevent an African American family from coming into the neighborhood.

Crushed by the loss of the insurance money, Walter Lee argues that they should take the offer. However, in the film's emotional climax, Walter Lee reverses himself when the representative arrives to close the deal and explains that his family has too much pride and dignity to accept such an offer. As the film closes, the family prepares to move into the new house, and Lena bids farewell to the apartment where she has lived since she was a newlywed. *Screenplay:* Lorraine Hansberry. *Selected bibliography:* Denning; Reid.

*DR. STRANGELOVE OR: HOW I LEARNED TO STOP WORRYING AND LOVE THE BOMB:* **DIR. STANLEY KUBRICK (1963).** Based on the novel *Red Alert* (1958) by Peter George, *Dr. Strangelove* is an absurdist satire of the ideology of the Cold War arms race. *Dr. Strangelove* became a cult favorite of the 1960s youth movement and was one of the classics of American culture of the 1960s, even though, strictly speaking, it is a British film, produced at London's Hawk Studios. The film is so representative, in fact, that historian Margot Henriksen entitled her own study of the ideology of Cold War America *Dr. Strangelove's America.* The premise of the film is simple: both the United States and the Soviet Union are so caught up in the arms race that they pursue insane courses that make nuclear holocaust almost inevitable. Indeed, the film's crisis is triggered by literal insanity, that of General Jack D. Ripper (played with appropriately grim lunacy by Sterling Hayden), commander of Burpelson Air Force Base and of a wing of the Strategic Air Command's fleet of B-52 nuclear bombers. Unhinged by his extreme anticommunist paranoia (which leads him to believe that communist conspiracies are seeking to "sap and impurify all of our precious bodily fluids" through techniques such as fluoridation of water), Ripper orders his bombers to attack the Soviet Union, thereby triggering the labyrinthine security procedures that make it almost impossible to recall such an order.

Most of the film involves the efforts of the American government to recall the attack and thus avert the inevitable Russian retaliation. Much of it is set in the memorable war room, where President Merkin Muffley (played by Peter Sellers, who also plays Dr. Strangelove and Group Captain Lionel Mandrake, a British exchange officer serving as Ripper's aide) convenes a meeting of his chief strategic advisors in an attempt to deal with the crisis. Chief among these advisors are General Buck Turgidson (played by George C. Scott and so named for both his phallic exploits and his penchant for inflated rhetorical posturing) and the zanily sinister Strangelove, whose continuing loyalty to his former Nazi bosses becomes increasingly obvious in the course of the film. When all attempts to avert the attack seem to be failing, Turgidson suggests an all-out assault while the United States still has the element of surprise on its side. Muffley, however, opts to warn the Russians, apologetically explaining the situation to Soviet Premier Dimitri Kissov in terms that make launching a nuclear strike seem like nothing more than a sort of social faux pas. The Americans then learn to their horror that the Russians, as a deterrent to precisely such attacks, have installed a Doomsday Machine that will be automatically triggered by any nuclear blast over the Soviet Union, enveloping the planet in a cloud of radioactive dust and destroying all life.

Ripper, the only man who knows the code that can cancel the attack order, commits suicide to avoid revealing it. Fortunately, however, Mandrake manages to deduce the code, but before he can deliver it to the president, he is taken captive by Army Colonel "Bat" Guano (Keenan Wynn), who suspects that he, as a foreigner, is a commie "prevert." Finally, after a comic scene in which he has to convince Guano to break open a Coke machine (with warnings of potential retribution from the Coca Cola Company) to get change to use a pay phone, Mandrake calls the president and gives him the information so the attack can be averted. In the meantime, one of the bombers, commanded by Major J. T. "King" Kong (Slim Pickens), has been damaged by antiaircraft missiles and is unable to receive the command to avert the attack. The crew struggles to keep the plane aloft and manages to reach a potential target, only to find that the damage from the missile has also caused the bomb doors to jam. Kong crawls down into the bomb bay and manages to open the doors and release the weapon, dropping out of the plane astride the bomb and, in one of the most memorable scenes in modern film, riding it bronco-style, waving his cowboy hat and whooping it up as the bomb falls to earth.

The screen then goes white as the bomb hits, which might have been the best ending, dramatically, for the film. However, Kubrick tacks on an additional scene that makes some important thematic points. In the scene, Strangelove, while involved in a comic wrestling match with his bionic right arm, which seems intent on shooting upward in a Nazi salute, concocts a plan for preserving civilization by founding colonies at the bottom of mine shafts, safe from the radioactive cloud. Among other things, this plan suggests the amazing resilience of fascism. In addition, Strangelove suggests that, in order to facilitate repopulation, the new colonies should include ten women for every man and that, in order to encourage the men to do their reproductive duty, these women should be chosen for their "stimulating sexual characteristics." Turgidson's gleeful reaction to this plan reveals the true nature of his personality. Meanwhile, the scene ends as both the Americans and the Russian ambassador, called to the war room as part of the effort to avert the crisis, begin to get concerned about a possible "mine shaft gap," suggesting that the two sides have still failed to learn their lesson about the folly of such competition. The film then ends with a sequence of shots of nuclear explosions and mushroom clouds, with sentimental music (Vera Lynn's "We'll Meet Again") playing in the background.

In many ways, *Dr. Strangelove* is weak as a political film. In particular, it does nothing to examine the historical and political background of the Cold War, depicting it essentially as an ego contest between American madmen and Russian madmen. In particular, it characterizes the Cold War as a phallic contest driven by erotic energies, with macho generals on both sides trying to establish their greater manhood by proving that they have the bigger and more effective weapons. Strangelove (so memorable in Sellers's portrayal, despite the fact that he is actually onscreen a surprisingly short time) may be the book's most potent political image. His crucial presence as the president's chief strategic advisor in the Cold War (emphasized through the titling of the film) tends to align the American position with that of the German Nazis, suggesting that Cold War America has followed in Hitler's footsteps in attempting to exterminate the Soviet Union and all it represents. If nothing else, this motif calls attention to the willingness of the United States to align itself with repressive right-wing regimes around the world in the effort to win support in the battle against communism. In addition, the film can, as Charles Maland notes, be read as a powerful critique of the "Ideology of Liberal Consensus" that was the dominant paradigm of American political life in the late 1950s and early 1960s. Still, the primary political orientation of the film is not procommunist, or even anti-American, but antimilitary, with the Soviet military leaders being at least as insane as the Americans in their blind pursuit of nuclear superiority. *Screenplay:* Terry Southern, Stanley Kubrick, and Peter George. *Selected bibliography:* Henriksen; Kagan (*Kubrick*); Maland ("*Dr. Stangelove*"); Suid; Gary K. Wolfe.

*HUD:* **DIR. MARTIN RITT (1963).** Based on the Larry McMurtry novel, *Horseman Pass By* (1961), *Hud* is an anti-Western featuring Paul Newman as Hud Bannon, its antihero. The 34-year-old Hud has long been at odds with his prickly and somewhat domineering father, Homer Bannon (played by Melvyn Douglas); this battle only exacerbates Hud's penchant for hard drinking, hard driving (of his pink Cadillac), and hard pursuit of numerous married women in the area. Hud and Homer live together on the family ranch with the family's housekeeper, Alma (played by Patricia Neal in a role that won her an Academy Award for best supporting actress), and Hud's 17-year-old nephew, Lon (played by Brandon de Wilde). Lon's father, Norman, Hud's brother, was killed in the year of the boy's birth in an automobile accident in which Hud, then himself 17, was driving while intoxicated, thus increasing tensions between Hud and Homer.

Most of the film has to do with establishing Hud's character and his relationship with the other major characters in the film. He is a sort of rebel mostly without a cause, other than cynical self-interest and the rather Oedipal attempt to behave in ways of which he knows his father will not approve. It is clear that Hud's hell-raising grows more out of bitterness and alienation than any enjoyment it might bring him. Also of central interest is the relationship of Lon to Hud, a sort of hero worship against which Homer warns the boy. In one of the film's more interesting political moments, the old man declares that the direction of the country is largely determined by the nature of the "men we admire," thus providing a warning against the prominence in American popular culture of the late 1950s and 1960s, of alienated loners such as Hud. The sexually charged relationship between Hud and Alma (formerly married, apparently slightly older than Hud, and definitely wise in the ways of the world) is also important. Hud pursues her constantly, but Alma, though she is extremely attracted to him, resists his advances, knowing he is just playing games. She finally leaves the ranch (and town) after Hud, in a drunken fury after a row with his father, attempts to rape her.

The main plot line of *Hud* revolves around the discovery, early in the film, that one of the Bannon calves has died, probably of foot-and-mouth disease. Hud wants to sell off the ranch's stock as quickly as possible, before word gets out, but Homer insists on taking a more honorable route. Rather than risk infecting the herds of his neighbors, he waits as the government completes tests on his herd. When the tests come back positive, the whole herd has to be destroyed, and with it the fruits of Homer's lifelong labors on the ranch. Hud's resistance to the government's involvement in the entire affair shows another aspect of his (not necessarily admirable) individualist rebellion against authority, potentially providing an oblique critique of the general demonization of government in Western Cold War rhetoric (where big government is essentially equated with Stalinism). Indeed, *Hud* differs sharply from many contemporary films in that the government here (especially the government veterinarian, played by Whit Bissell) clearly plays a sympathetic role, while the rebellious individual plays an unscrupulous one. *Hud* also differs from most 1960s generation-gap narratives in that the father figure is clearly more admirable than Hud, however old-fashioned Homer might be and however charming Hud (and the charismatic Newman) might be. Hud's opposition to government intervention on the ranch can also be taken as a critique of the regimentation and routinization of life under capitalism, though Hud shows another dark side of his character when he decides to use this same routinization in his own interest, hiring a lawyer to have Homer declared incompetent so Hud can gain control of the failing ranch and convert it into oil fields—something Homer, the dedicated cattleman, has vehemently resisted as a modernizing desecration of the land and his traditional way of life. This final image of Hud's capitalist ruthlessness culminates in Homer's death after the old man falls from a horse and lacks the will to fight to overcome his injuries. The idealistic Lon, disillusioned with Hud at last, packs his things and goes away. As the film ends, Hud is indeed in control of the ranch, but (appropriately, given his character) finds himself completely alone there, the master of a one-man domain. *Screenplay:* Harriet Frank, Jr. and Irving Ravetch. *Selected bibliography:* Carlton Jackson.

*THE PROFESSIONALS:* DIR. RICHARD BROOKS (1966). Set during the latter part of the Mexican Revolution, *The Professionals* features four highly skilled experts who are nevertheless rapidly becoming anachronisms in the face of the increasing capitalist modernization and routinization of the West. Indeed, in one of the film's numerous contradictions, their own professionalism and specialization is a sign of this modernization and of the waning of the world to which they have become accustomed. The experts, led by Henry Rico Farden (Lee Marvin), include demolitions expert (and lovable rogue) Bill Dolworth (Burt Lancaster), expert tracker (and inscrutable nonwhite) Jacob Sharp (Woody Strode), and horse specialist Hans Ehrengard (Robert Ryan), the conscience of the group. As the film begins, the four are hired by American millionaire J. W. Grant (Ralph Bellamy) to retrieve his young wife, Maria (Claudia Cardinale), whom he claims has been kidnapped by Mexican bandit Jesus Raza (Jack Palance). Offered $10,000 each for the safe return of Mrs. Grant, the professionals accept the mission, though two of them, Farden and Dolworth, had formerly spent years fighting side by side with Raza in Pancho Villa's revolutionary army. They therefore know that Raza is not a bandit, but a skilled military leader of committed revolutionary forces. Nevertheless, they believe Grant's story and go after Maria, blasting Raza's compound with dynamite to create a diversion, then literally plucking the woman from the arms of Captain Raza, only to learn that she had not been kidnapped at all, but had in fact gone willingly with Raza, with whom she has been in love since childhood, when he was a stable boy working on her father's ranch. Grant, in fact, is the real kidnapper, having appropriated Maria along with her father's ranch and numerous other Mexican resources as part of his unscrupulous business operations in northern Mexico.

But the $10,000 reward is irresistible, especially for experts whose skills are rapidly becoming obsolete. The four therefore take Maria back to the United States. Raza follows; in the course of the pursuit, the professionals kill many of Raza's followers, who are differentiated from Farden's group by their relative lack of professionalism. By the time they rendezvous with Grant north of the border, the professionals have been joined by a wounded Raza, whom Grant orders killed. But Farden and Dolworth know that Grant is the real villain, and enough is enough. They hold off Grant and his thugs and allow Maria to return to Mexico with Raza to rejoin the revolution. They thus forfeit their payment but gain the satisfaction of doing the right thing, thus adhering to the most important tenet of their code as professionals, while also fulfilling the letter of their charge to save Maria from a kidnapper.

In its positive figuration of the revolutionary Raza, *The Professionals* significantly deviated from conventional Hollywood representations of Mexicans as sleazy bandits, though the portrayal of the rich capitalist Grant as a ruthless villain had by then become something of a cliché of its own. Many saw the film's portrayals of the incursions of Americans into Mexico, where they are opposed by local guerrillas, as a reference to the American involvement in Vietnam, and the film is certainly critical of the neocolonial rape of northern Mexico (and of Maria) by the evil Grant. The film is far from radical, however, and tends, despite its positive portrayal of Raza, to suggest that revolutions can never be expected to work permanent positive change. *Screenplay:* Richard Brooks. *Selected bibliography:* Neve (*Film*); Robbins; Wright.

*BONNIE AND CLYDE:* **DIR. ARTHUR PENN (1967).** Set in the early 1930s, *Bonnie and Clyde* tells the story of Depression-era outlaws Clyde Barrow and Bonnie Parker (played by Warren Beatty and Faye Dunaway), and thus recalls such earlier films as Fritz Lang's *You Only Live Once* (1937) and Nicholas Ray's *They Live by Night* (1948). But *Bonnie and Clyde* is very much a film of the 1960s, and its antiestablishment tone derives less from the economic hardships of the Depression than prevailing cultural attitudes at the time the film was made. Indeed, while numerous aspects of the film carefully place it in its proper historical context (as when they attend a screening of *Gold Diggers of 1933*), the film is shot in richly splendid colors that seem more suggestive of 1960s affluence than 1930s poverty. In the film, Bonnie and Clyde are portrayed as largely sympathetic figures, their crimes almost taking on the aspect of a Robin Hood-like quest for social justice through robbery. But they are mostly presented simply as two young people in love, battling against the restraints placed on their pursuit of pleasure by society and its authoritarian rules. The film's success in reflecting the mores of late-1960s American society can be seen in its tremendous take at the box office. In addition, the film appealed to contemporary critical taste well enough to gain ten Academy Award nominations, including most of the major categories, though it won only two awards, in the categories of best supporting actress (Estelle Parsons) and best cinematography.

The film begins as Clyde, freshly out of prison on an armed-robbery charge, meets Bonnie in the dusty Texas town of West Dallas, then takes her away from her boring life as a waitress to join him in a more exciting life of crime. The film establishes a positive view of their crimes in an early scene in which the two take refuge in an abandoned farmhouse that has been claimed by a local bank in a foreclosure. The two then help the dispossessed farmer shoot up the house (and the bank sign in front of it), clearly marking banks as enemies of the poor, while Bonnie and Clyde are identified as defenders of the poor and enemies of the rich. After an ignominious beginning, in which Bonnie and Clyde are portrayed as bumbling amateurs rather than professional criminals, the two finally manage to conduct a successful series of robberies and to become notorious bandits. Their gang is soon joined by young mechanic C. W. Moss (Michael J. Pollard), then by Clyde's brother, Buck (Gene Hackman), accompanied by his frumpy and hysterical wife, Blanche (Parsons).

The gang spends far more time in the film fleeing from police than committing actual robberies, and it soon becomes clear that their exploits have been greatly exaggerated by the press, with the result that they become central targets of law enforcement from Texas to Missouri. But they also become heroes to the poor and disenfranchised, who sometimes come to their aid in helping them evade police, who are depicted as bloodthirsty killers determined to murder the gang.. Eventually, after a series of near escapes, Buck is shot and killed, while Blanche is captured. C. W. takes Bonnie and Clyde (both of whom are wounded) to refuge in the home of C. W.'s father, Ivan Moss (Dub Taylor), where they begin to recuperate from their wounds. But the elder Moss turns them in to the police in return for lenient treatment for his son. Moss then sets up an ambush in which Bonnie and Clyde are shot to ribbons by deputies in a slow-motion "ballet of death," one of the most memorable scenes of 1960s cinema—and one of the most violent scenes in American film to that time.

*Bonnie and Clyde* violates a number of the conventions of the Hollywood commercial film, especially in its complex mixture of different moods and genres. In this sense, it is reminiscent of the work of French New Wave directors such as Jean-Luc Godard and François Truffaut, each of whom contributed to the development of the project and was at one time or another considered as a possible director for the film. Indeed, Robert Ray calls *Bonnie and Clyde* a sort of "pastiche of New Wave effects" (289). Ultimately, the film's flaunting of Hollywood convention reinforces its antiauthoritarianism and is to that extent effective. On the other hand, the film at times seems overly taken with its own stylistic play, which may enhance its overt celebration of nonconformism, but which tends to diminish its latent anticapitalist message. *Screenplay:* Ben Barzman. *Selected bibliography:* Clarens; Lawson; Joyce Miller; Milner; Murray; Robert Ray.

*THE GRADUATE:* DIR. MIKE NICHOLS (1967). One of the definitive American films of the late 1960s, *The Graduate* is a sort of bildungsroman (or perhaps bildungsfilm) that depicts the efforts of new college graduate Ben Braddock (Dustin Hoffman) to come to grips with the emptiness and moral vacuity of the materialist society represented by his parents and their wealthy friends. Having been a star student in a prestigious Eastern university, Braddock returns after graduation to his posh suburban home in Southern California, only to find himself without direction or motivation, seeing the bourgeois activities of his parents and their circle as pointless and meaningless. When Mrs. Robinson (Anne Bancroft), wife of the partner and best friend of Ben's father, attempts to seduce Ben early in the film, he is shocked, appalled, and terrified, barely escaping her feminine clutches in a bravura display of comic acting on the part of Hoffman. Eventually, however, boredom overcomes shock, and Ben begins an affair with Mrs. Robinson after all, though it is a relationship totally devoid of human contact, in which the participants remain thoroughly alienated from one another.

The plot takes a turn when Ben falls in love with the Robinson daughter, Elaine (Katharine Ross), whom Mrs. Robinson has forbidden him to see. When Ben decides that he wants to marry Elaine, Mrs. Robinson takes extreme steps to break up the relationship, first claiming she had been raped by Ben, then revealing her relationship with Ben to Mr. Robinson (Murray Hamilton). Eventually, the Robinsons arrange for Elaine to marry her pervious suitor, Carl Smith (Brian Avery), to keep her away from Ben. But a desperate Ben finds his way to the church just as the ceremony is being concluded and manages to make off with Elaine after fighting off the families and wedding guests with a large crucifix. In the end, Ben and Elaine ride away on a bus, true love presumably having triumphed over the false values of their parents, though it is not clear exactly what Ben and Elaine will do next.

Embraced by young audiences as a celebration of their youth-based rebellion against the hypocrisy and conformity of their parents, *The Graduate* is actually an extremely safe film that keeps its rebellion within safe, bourgeois limits. After all, Ben will now marry the girl his parents have always wanted him to marry, staying safely within his class. He will presumably now settle down to a serious career in order to support his new family. Indeed, director Nichols has stated that he sees Ben and Elaine following very much in the footsteps of their parents. *Screenplay:* Calder Willingham and Buck Henry. *Selected bibliography:* Fairchild; Robert Ray; Ryan and Kellner.

*GUESS WHO'S COMING TO DINNER:* **DIR. STANLEY KRAMER (1967).** When first released in 1967, *Guess Who's Coming to Dinner* was considered to be controversial and daring, though it is largely silly and safe, which may account for its ten Academy Award nominations, including best picture. On the other hand, the film won only two awards, including one given to Katharine Hepburn for best actress. Supposedly a dramatization of America's racial tensions, the film is primarily about the reactions of Matt Drayton and wife Christina (Spencer Tracy and Hepburn) to the sudden announcement that their daughter, Joanna (Katharine Houghton), has decided to marry an African American, Dr.

John Prentice (Sidney Poitier), whom she met ten days earlier during a vacation in Hawaii. The Draytons are liberals who have always taught their daughter to abhor racism, but they presumably experience a crisis when they are forced to come to terms with the fact that she has taken their teachings literally. Prentice's black parents eventually appear as well. Both fathers frown on the planned marriage while both mothers find it wonderfully romantic, especially given that John and Joanna are so obviously, and so passionately, in love. The mothers, of course, win out (once Matt Drayton recalls what it was like to be young and in love), and all is well in the end.

As if the stereotypical gender-based reactions of the parents (practical fathers versus starry-eyed mothers) were not bad enough, the film shows no awareness that the entire relationship of John and Joanna is preposterous for reasons that have little to do with race. Not only have John and Joanna known each other only a short time, but they have not even slept together, because the super-virtuous John has refused to do so—no wild black man threatening to rape white women here. Moreover, John makes matters more ridiculous by bizarrely insisting that he will not marry Joanna unless her parents give their unqualified approval. In addition, John is a world-famous physician, highly renowned and respected for his work in tropical medicine, while the twenty-three-year-old Joanna appears to have no profession and has no personal qualities to recommend her other than the fact that she is a pretty little thing who is always happy. The two, in short, hardly seem well matched, and the film almost seems to imply that pretty young white girls are such valuable sexual commodities that any black man, even the superhuman John, would be lucky indeed to have one for his own. In any case, it is hardly radical to suggest that John, with all his accomplishments, is good enough to marry Joanna, whatever his race. It also helps that John is safely nonmilitant and has virtually no racial consciousness, declaring that he does not think of himself as a black man, but simply as a man. Ultimately, the film, however well meaning, does very little to explore the very serious racial issues that plague American society. It is also predictable and almost unbelievably slow-moving, though the fact that it ever made such a splash certainly makes a telling comment about American society. *Screenplay:* William Rose. *Selected bibliography:* Christensen; Spoto (*Stanley Kramer*).

*PLANET OF THE APES:* **DIR. FRANKLIN J. SCHAFFNER (1968).** One of the true classics of science-fiction cinema, *Planet of the Apes* combines an imaginative plot with trenchant, though slightly clumsy, social commentary. The film was co-written by the formerly blacklisted Michael Wilson, who had earlier written the leftist classic, *Salt of the Earth*. In *Planet of the Apes*, George Taylor (Charlton Heston) leads a group of

American astronauts on a mission of interstellar exploration. Placed in suspended animation so they can survive the long journey, they awake after landing on a strange planet. The clock on their ship informs them that the year is 3978, 2,000 years after their departure from earth, and they estimate that they are more than 300 light years from home. The air of the earthlike planet proves perfectly breathable, though the landscape is arid and barren. Eventually, the astronauts make their way to an area in which vegetation grows. There, they encounter a group of the planet's inhabitants, who seem surprisingly human, except that they are quite primitive and seem entirely mute.

This group, along with the three astronauts, is suddenly attacked by a group of armed apes on horseback. Indeed, on this planet apes are the ruling intelligent species, while humans are considered to be loathsome, untamable, subsimian beasts. One of the astronauts, Dodge (Jeff Burton), is killed in the attack, while Taylor and the other astronaut, Landon (Robert Gunner), are captured along with the indigenous humans, who are being rounded up for scientific experiments. Taylor, however, is shot in the throat, causing him to lose the ability to speak (and thus sparing the audience from Heston's overacting for an extended portion of the film). Taylor thus has considerable difficulty communicating with the apes (who, oddly enough, speak English), though he is finally able to convince Cornelius (Roddy McDowall), a sympathetic scientist, and Zira (Kim Hunter), an animal psychologist, that he is intelligent. They, however, have considerable trouble convincing ape officialdom, including their superior, Dr. Zaius (Maurice Evans), of this fact, even after Taylor regains his voice.

Zaius, it turns out, is intentionally suppressing evidence of Taylor's intelligence. He has, in fact, already had a lobotomy performed on Landon and plans to do the same to Taylor. Taylor, however, escapes, along with Zira, Cornelius, and Nova (Linda Harrison), a human woman native to the planet. They travel to the "forbidden zone," where Cornelius has previously uncovered evidence of an ancient civilization predating that of the apes by thousands of years. They are followed there by Zaius and a troop of armed apes, who seek to suppress Cornelius's research as heresy against the official ape religion, which denies the existence of such ancient civilizations.

Taylor takes Zaius hostage and is able to secure his escape, along with Nova. Zira and Cornelius stay behind with the other apes, who seal the cave to destroy the evidence found by Cornelius. It turns out that Zaius is already aware of the existence of the ancient civilization, which fell through its own self-destructive tendencies, and he wants to ensure that these tendencies will not be renewed in the current civilization. Taylor and Nova, meanwhile, travel in search of a refuge where they can live free of persecution by the apes. They come upon the ruins of the Statue of Liberty protruding from the sand, and suddenly it becomes clear to Taylor—and the audience—that this planet is, in fact, earth in the year 3978. The earlier civilization that destroyed itself was Taylor's and our own.

*Planet of the Apes* makes a number of obvious points about the dangers of nuclear war, which was surely the form of this destruction. It also critiques persecution and oppression in the treatment of humans by apes on this future world. This critique is most obviously aimed at racism, but it can also be taken as a comment on class-based oppression as well. In addition, the seemingly blind opposition of the apes to any new ideas can be taken as a negative comment on religion, or even as a comment on paranoid movements such as McCarthyism. At the same time, this blind fear of the new turns out to have a rational basis in the fear of repeating the nuclear holocaust of the past, somewhat muting the critique. The film is also problematic in its treatment of gender, especially in the presentation of Nova, beautiful, submissive, and entirely mute, as a sort of ideal sex object. *Screenplay:* Michael Wilson and Rod Serling. *Selected bibliography:* Greene.

*BUTCH CASSIDY AND THE SUNDANCE KID:* DIR. GEORGE ROY HILL (1969). *Butch Cassidy and the Sundance Kid*, which became the most financially successful Western in history, was probably the central work in the spate of revisionary Westerns that appeared at the end of the 1960s and beginning of the 1970s, substantially renewing the genre. Like many of these Westerns, *Butch Cassidy* is set at the end of the nineteenth century and thus at a time when capitalist modernization is leading to the closing of the frontier and to the waning of the Wild West world of which outlaws such as Butch and Sundance, presented in the film as charming and lovable rogues, were a central part. Based on actual historical events, the film comments not only on the closing of the American frontier, but on the subsequent turn of America to new imperial frontiers. In particular, the Spanish-American war provides the background for much of the film's events, helping to place the action in 1898, while also placing the experiences of Butch and Sundance within the context of the emergence of the United States as a global imperial power.

*Butch Cassidy* opens as Butch (Paul Newman) sadly inspects a new modern bank that not only lacks the charm and beauty of earlier banks, but also features a variety of high-tech security devices designed to foil robbers such as himself. This opening scene sets the stage for the remainder of the film, in which Butch and Sundance (Robert Redford) continually find that the modern world is passing them by. Butch continually worries that they are "over the hill," while the forces of law and order that oppose them are increasingly efficient and professional. When Butch, Sundance, and their "Hole-in-the-Wall Gang" rob a train, they find that the Union Pacific Railroad has hired a special force to hunt them down, led by a legendary lawman, Joe Lefors, and an expert Indian tracker, Lord Baltimore. This force pursues Butch and Sundance relentlessly, despite their best efforts at evasion, causing the pair continually (and admiringly) to ask each other, "Who are those guys?" Eventually, the outlaws find themselves trapped on a ledge at the edge of a steep river canyon, after which, in a famous scene, they leap into the water, escaping their pursuers at last.

Butch and Sundance recognize, however, that the handwriting is on the wall for them in the United States. They thus decide to travel, with Sundance's lover (and Butch's good buddy), Etta Place (Katharine Ross), to Bolivia, which they hope will still have some of the wildness they once enjoyed in North America. Bolivia also has numerous lucrative payrolls associated with the emergent mining industry there, just waiting to be robbed. After some fumbling attempts at bank robbery and an abortive attempt at going straight, the pair eventually settles into a successful series of robberies in Bolivia. Etta, however, returns to the States, feeling that the two are headed for certain doom as their notoriety grows, especially after it appears that Lefors has come to Bolivia to continue the chase. She is, of course, correct, and the two soon find themselves surrounded by Bolivian lawmen in a final, fatal shootout. Trapped, they discuss a possible flight to Australia, but it is clear that, amid the increasing globalization of capitalist modernization, there is essentially nowhere they can go where they will not already be anachronisms. The film ends as Butch and Sundance rush from their hiding place with guns blazing, hoping to shoot their way to freedom, but not realizing that the police who surround them have been reinforced by hundreds of troops from the Bolivian army, thus making the situation hopeless. In the twentieth century, rebellious individuals like Butch and Sundance cannot hope to succeed against the overwhelming social, economic, and political forces that are arrayed against them.

In this sense, the story of Butch and Sundance is largely a tragic one, though, in keeping with the film's generally light tone, Hill chooses to eschew the violent terminal scenes of near-contemporary films such as *The Wild Bunch* (1969) or *Bonnie and Clyde* (1967). *Butch Cassidy* thus ends with a freeze frame of the two outlaws charging forth, indicating their final demise only in the gunfire of the film's continuing soundtrack. The audience is thus invited to remember the outlaws as they once were, though in a nostalgic mode that makes it clear that their once carefree lifestyle, so free of the regimentation of modern bourgeois routine, is no longer available as the twentieth century proceeds. It is tempting to read the conclusion of the story of Butch and Sundance as a veiled reference to the death of famed revolutionary Che Guevara in Bolivia in 1967. But the political message of the film, despite the vague tone of 1960s rebelliousness and of protest against the waning of the West, is ultimately conservative, or at least pessimistic, depicting opposition to capitalist modernization as a hopeless, whimsical, and unrealistic quest. *Screenplay:* William Goldman. *Selected bibliography:* Deer; Robert Ray; Ryan and Kellner; Steckmesser; Wright.

*EASY RIDER:* **DIR. DENNIS HOPPER (1969).** One of the quintessential cinematic statements of the 1960s counterculture, *Easy Rider* follows two hippie bikers, Billy and Wyatt (Dennis Hopper and Peter Fonda), as they make their way from Los Angeles to New Orleans to attend the Mardi Gras in search of maximum grooviness. On the way, they are treated with great hospitality in a desert commune but encounter considerable hostility on the part of middle America and are, among other things, forced repeatedly to camp out because no motel will allow them in. In Texas, they playfully join a Main Street parade and are promptly thrown in jail, where they appear in danger of considerable abuse until they are rescued by their cellmate, George Hanson (Jack Nicholson), who happens to be a civil rights attorney and the son of a prominent local businessman.

Hanson then decides to join Billy and Wyatt on the road to the Mardi Gras, along the way sharing with them his offbeat philosophy, while they share with him their considerable supply of drugs. In the film's most overt critique of capitalism, Hanson explains to Billy that the hostility he and Wyatt have encountered along the road arises from the fact that they represent a kind of freedom ordinary Americans can never know. "It's real hard to be free," he declares, "when you are bought and sold in the marketplace." On the trip, Hanson himself begins to experience real freedom for the first time, but it is cut short when local rednecks attack the camp one night and beat all three travelers savagely, killing Hanson. Billy and Wyatt bid Hanson farewell and continue on to New Orleans, where they have some fine food, visit a fancy whorehouse, and attend the Mardi Gras, which turns out to be something of an anticlimax. They drop acid with two hookers (Karen Black and Toni Basil) in a cemetery, then go back on the road. Soon afterward, however, the film reaches a grim climax when two rednecks in a pickup truck blast them with a shotgun, killing them both.

*Easy Rider* made Nicholson a star and proved that the counterculture could be big box office, partly because it also helped to demonstrate that the counterculture of the 1960s was no ultimate threat to the American capitalist system. Indeed, in both its ending and Wyatt's conclusion shortly before that "we blew it," the film issued one of the first verdicts on the failure of the counterculture to work any real change in America. It is, in short, not nearly as subversive as it might first appear. Ryan and Kellner thus see the film as a central demonstration of the "ambivalent ideology of sixties individualism" that is ultimately "aimed toward an ideal of freedom that is highly traditional" (23). *Screenplay:* Peter Fonda, Dennis Hopper, and Terry Southern. *Selected bibliography:* Biskind (*Easy Riders*); Burns; Christensen; James; Leibman; Murphy and Harder; Robert Ray; Ryan and Kellner.

*MEDIUM COOL:* **DIR. HASKELL WEXLER (1969).** Set in Chicago just before and during the 1968 Democratic National Convention, *Medium Cool* explores American society's fascination with violence and the complicity of the media in that fascination. With the recent assassinations of Martin Luther King and Robert Kennedy as background, the film builds toward the Chicago police riots that erupted during the convention. It particularly notes the way in which the antiestablishment demonstrators who gathered in Chicago for the convention relied upon media coverage to keep official violence in check, only to find that the presence of the media seemed to spur the police to even greater levels of brutality. Combining documentary footage with a fictional narrative, much of the film has a highly authentic look, enhanced by actual police harassment of Wexler and his crew while they were filming.

The film focuses on television news reporter/cameraman John Cassellis (Robert Forster) as he travels about Chicago, accompanied by his sound man, Gus (Peter Bonerz), in search of stories that will interest a television audience that seems interested only in the sensational and the violent. Cassellis is, initially, completely disengaged from the material he covers, interested only in getting a good piece of film. His cynicism is established in the opening scene as he films the victim of a car crash, calling an ambulance only after he completes filming. Then he meets Eileen Horton (Verna Bloom), a young woman freshly arrived in Chicago from the hills of West Virginia. Cassellis's relationship with Eileen and her thirteen-year-old son, Harold (Harold Blankenship), seems to bring a certain amount of authentic humanity into his formerly superficial life. He also begins to realize the political irresponsibility of his former attitude toward his work, but this new turn is short-lived.

As the convention begins, with Cassellis inside the hall covering the event, Harold disappears into the confusion- and violence-filled streets. Eileen searches frantically for him and is eventually joined by Cassellis. The film then abruptly ends as the car in which they are driving crashes, killing Eileen and seriously injuring Cassellis. This crash seems pointless at first, except perhaps to provide a rather gratuitous echo of the film's beginning. But the camera then pulls back to reveal a cameraman filming the accident, then slowly turning his camera on the audience of the film. The implication is clear: this cataclysmic ending, however seemingly gratuitous, is precisely the sort of ending demanded by American audiences in their lust for violence. This media-fed lust has also fueled the viciousness of the Chicago police riots, a phenomenon that points toward potentially even more dire consequences in the future. *Screenplay:* Haskell Wexler. *Selected bibliography:* Adair; Christensen; James; Muse; Ryan and Kellner.

*SLAVES:* DIR. HERBERT BIBERMAN (1969). Described by Thom Anderson as "the only intelligent Marxist film ever produced by a Hollywood studio," *Slaves* was the product of a late-1960s liberalization in Hollywood attitudes, an attitude that allowed Biberman to return to directing after fifteen years as a persona non grata in Hollywood (180). Blacklisted in the 1950s, Biberman remained anathema to Hollywood even beyond the blacklist, partly because of his central participation in the making of 1954 independent film classic *Salt of the Earth*, a film that openly defied the blacklist and Hollywood censorship. *Slaves* combines Biberman's traditional leftist perspective with sensibilities deriving from the civil rights movement of the 1960s not only to criticize the extent to which slavery was central to the building of the American nation, but to point out the fundamental economic basis of slavery. It also points out the extent to which women slaves were used by their masters for sexual purposes, a motif that had long been repressed in historical accounts of slavery and that would receive substantial acknowledgement in American culture only with the advent of Toni Morrison's 1987 novel *Beloved*. Unfortunately, the film treats this sexual material somewhat awkwardly, sometimes giving an otherwise intelligent and insightful film a rather melodramatic air. Well received in Europe, the film was a critical and commercial failure in the U.S., where its political points struck a little too close to home.

*Slaves* stars Ossie Davis, a former victim of the blacklist, as Luke, a Kentucky slave who is sold, along with two others, to Nathan MacKay (Stephen Boyd), a plantation owner in Mississippi. MacKay is an educated man who has decorated his plantation house with artifacts from African culture. But this seeming respect for African art does not extend to Africans themselves, and MacKay treats his slaves with considerable brutality. When MacKay allows a slave woman to die in childbirth rather than call a doctor for her, Luke decides to raise the infant girl as his own. Eventually, Luke is killed for helping the baby girl escape from the plantation, along with Cassy (Dionne Warwick), MacKay's much-abused black mistress. The killing of Luke then galvanizes the other slaves on the plantation into an all-out revolt. They set fire to the cotton fields, creating a diversion that allows Cassy, the infant, and another slave woman to escape safely. *Screenplay:* Herbert Biberman, John O. Killens, and Alida Sherman. *Selected bibliography:* Thom Anderson; Dick (*Radical Innocence*).

*TELL THEM WILLIE BOY IS HERE*: DIR. ABRAHAM POLONSKY
**(1969).** *Tell Them Willie Boy Is Here* was the first film to be directed by the
blacklisted Polonsky since *Force of Evil* in 1947. It was also one of a number of left-leaning anti-Westerns to be produced in Hollywood in the late
1960s and early 1970s. As Brian Neve notes, the film's sensibilities are
clearly those of the late 1960s, reflecting a "general disaffection with the
war in Vietnam, and a strong emotional commitment to minority causes"
(236).

The film seeks to reverse a number of stereotypes of the Western
genre. Its sympathies are clearly with Willie Boy (Robert Blake), the title
character, a Paiute Indian, who runs afoul of an uncaring white legal
system that has no respect for Native Americans and their customs.
Moreover, the film is an ambitious one that clearly seeks (not entirely
successfully) to suggest Willie Boy's particular victimization as a sort of
allegory of the Native American experience as a whole: despite his
individual ability, he stands no chance against the mighty forces of
modernization that are arrayed against him. Set in 1909, the film treats
modernizations as a central theme, indicating the closing and taming of
the frontier that is central to so many "waning of the West" films.

Early in *Tell Them Willie Boy Is Here*, Willie Boy continues his courtship of Lola (Katharine Ross), a young Paiute woman, whose father,
Mike (Mikel Angel), has forbidden the relationship. When a rifle-toting
Mike catches Willie Boy and Lola making love in a grove, Willie Boy kills
Mike in self-defense. According to Paiute custom, this settles the matter
and makes Lola Willie Boy's wife. But both Willie Boy and Lola know
that the white man's law will not see it this way, so they flee together into
the wilderness. They are quickly pursued by a posse that includes Ray
Calvert (Barry Sullivan), an old Indian fighter who is only too anxious to
get another crack at killing Indians, as in the old days. The leader of the
posse, however, is Sheriff Christopher Cooper (Robert Redford), who
actually becomes the central figure in the film as it proceeds. Cooper has
nothing against Native Americans and would clearly rather not be
involved. Cooper is also distracted by his strange and somewhat sadistic
relationship with Indian agent Liz Arnold (Susan Clark), a well-educated
Eastern liberal with an M.D. from Johns Hopkins. Arnold is sympathetic,
though condescending, to the Paiutes, but her sympathies are worth very
little to Willie Boy and Lola.

Cooper's life is further complicated when he is called away from the
manhunt to help provide security for an upcoming visit to the area by
President Taft, one of the film's central images of the intrusion of modernity into the West. Eventually, Willie Boy's flight triggers wild (and
unfounded) rumors that the Paiutes hope to begin a full-scale rebellion
by killing Taft when he visits. Cooper is thus forced to renew his hunt for
Willie Boy to try to calm the volatile situation. Cooper closes in on Willie

Boy's camp, only to find Lola dead from a fresh gunshot wound, possibly self-inflicted. Cooper continues his pursuit, finally shooting Willie Boy when the latter threatens him with a rifle that turns out not to have been loaded. Cooper realizes that Willie Boy preferred death to captivity; he turns Willie Boy's body over to the Paiutes for a traditional cremation, infuriating some of the local white officials, who insist that the body is needed for evidence. Cooper angrily replies that they will get no trophies from him, then leaves them digging through the embers of Willie Boy's funeral pyre. *Screenplay:* Abraham Polonsky. *Selected bibliography:* Christensen; Neve (*Film*).

*THEY SHOOT HORSES, DON'T THEY?:* **DIR. SYDNEY POLLACK (1969).** Based on Horace McCoy's 1935 novel of the same title, *They Shoot Horses, Don't They?* is one of contemporary American culture's best-known evocations of the specific economic conditions of the Depression-era 1930s. Meanwhile, in its focus on spectacle and in its treatment of the Hollywood dream factory, the film, like McCoy's novel and like the novels of Nathanael West, with which McCoy's work is often compared, also seems to suggest that the roots of the postmodernist culture of the late twentieth century were already present in the 1930s. Edmund Wilson set the tone for sociological readings of the novel in an essay written in 1940 when he described its subject as "the miserable situation of movie-struck young men and women who starve and degrade themselves in Hollywood." Further, he noted that the novel is worth reading if only for its vivid documentation of "those dance marathons that were among the more grisly symptoms of the depression" (*A Literary Chronicle* 217). Both comments hold for the film as well, though the film uses its Depression-era setting to suggest a commentary upon the political situation in America in the late 1960s as well.

The plot of the film follows that of McCoy's novel fairly closely. As it begins, the cynical and hard-boiled Gloria Beatty (Jane Fonda) is about to enter a marathon dance contest in the hope of winning the $1,500 grand prize. When she loses her original partner to illness, she teams up with Robert Syverton (Michael Sarrazin), a passerby with no real enthusiasm for the contest. The contest is a parable of the cruel realities of capitalist competition, especially in an age of scarcity. As the master of ceremonies, Rocky (Gig Young), announces as the contest begins, "One couple, and only one, will waltz out of here, over broken bodies and broken dreams, carrying the grand prize." Young is perfect as the unscrupulous Rocky and in fact won an Academy Award for best supporting actor for the role. (The film garnered a total of nine Academy Award nominations, though only Young won.) The prize money is a powerful inducement in the midst of the Depression. The contest and its promoters also dangle the possibility that the contestants will be discovered by Hollywood talent scouts, thus providing an additional motivation to suffer the excruciating agony of the grueling contest, which goes on, day after day, week after week, with only brief intervals for food and rest. Both Robert and Gloria hope to get into the movies, though the Hollywood motif is enacted in particularly vivid form through the character of Alice LeBlanc (Susannah York), a would-be Jean Harlow type whose broken dreams eventually drive her to a nervous breakdown in the course of the contest.

Other contestants include the aging World War I veteran, Harry Klein (Red Buttons), and a farmer (Bruce Dern) and his pregnant wife (Bonnie Bedelia). The bodies, minds, and clothing of all of the contestants gradually deteriorate as the contest goes on, though some of them win sponsorships from companies who supply fresh clothing bearing their advertisements, reinforcing the interpretation of the contest as an allegory of capitalism. Most of the narrative concerns the experiences of the bitter and cynical Gloria and the still idealistic Robert as they struggle to survive the grueling and dehumanizing contest. It also traces the growing bond between the two partners, even though for a time they switch partners after Robert has sex with Alice during a break. The competitors struggle on bravely, though the contest brings out the worst in many of them. Harry eventually dies when his heart gives out during one of the periodic "derbies," in which the contestants race-walk furiously around the perimeter of the dance floor in an attempt to avoid elimination. Alice has her breakdown immediately afterward. Sarrazin and (especially) Fonda deliver impressive and convincing performances in the central roles, and the film as a whole is effective in its presentation of the cruelty of the contest and its suggestion of the economic conditions that would drive people to submit to such cruelty.

Gloria discovers during an encounter with Rocky that the winners of the contest will be billed for expenses, thus greatly reducing the actual amount of the prize money. Realizing that all of the suffering has been for essentially nothing, Gloria decides to leave the contest. She and Robert go out onto the pier outside the building in which the contest is being held. There, fed up with life, she takes out a gun and begs Robert to shoot her. He complies, and she is free at last; the contest, however, goes on. Robert, meanwhile is arrested and taken away. In McCoy's novel, the story of the dance marathon is narrated by Robert in a retrospective mode as he sits in court awaiting his death sentence. The film attempts to mimic this effect through the insertion of periodic brief flashforward segments showing scenes, without explanation, of Robert's arrest, incarceration, and trial. In both cases, there is a suggestion of inevitability in the characters' ultimate fates, which have already been determined even as the narrative is underway.

The dance marathon in *They Shoot Horses* can clearly be interpreted as an allegory of American capitalism, and the description of this contest provides a powerful critique of the dehumanizing consequences of a capitalist system in which individuals are driven to compete with one another for economic resources. Unfortunately, neither the film nor the book offers any alternative to the capitalist system. Thus, as Thomas Sturak points out, though the book can be read as a scathing indictment of the American system, it propounds no particular "political program or ethical system" — other than the notion that "life should have some dignity" (148). This lack of a clear political perspective tends to support readers who see the book as a commentary on the inevitable nature of human life. Paul Warshow nicely summarizes the specific social commentary of McCoy's book when he notes that, while it can clearly be interpreted as a broad allegory of human existence and as a critique of human society in general, it also serves (more so than Pollack's film, which Warshow nevertheless greatly prefers over the novel) as a particular critique of "a particular kind of fraudulent society — specifically American capitalistic society — which promises its citizens the advantages a society is supposed to offer, but does not keep its promise" (37). *Screenplay:* James Poe and Robert E. Thompson. *Selected bibliography:* Sturak; Warshow; Edmund Wilson.

*TWO MULES FOR SISTER SARA:* **DIR. DON SIEGEL (1969).** *Two Mules for Sister Sara* is set during the Juarez-led rebellion against French imperial rule in Mexico in the 1860s. However, despite the participation of formerly blacklisted leftist screenwriter Albert Maltz, the film is weak on politics and historical background, doing very little to explain the terms of the rebellion, other than vaguely to hint that the Juaristas are the good guys and the French the bad guys. It is left to the viewer to understand that the French are bad because of their imperialist intervention in Mexico — and perhaps to infer a connection between the French presence in Mexico in the 1860s and the American presence in Vietnam a hundred years later.

In typical Hollywood fashion, *Two Mules for Sister Sara* relies on sex and violence for its effect. Most of the violence is perpetrated by the protagonist, Hogan, played by Clint Eastwood via his usual Western persona of the laconic loner with a mysterious past. The sex inheres primarily in the tension between Hogan and Sister Sara (Shirley MacLaine), who poses as a Catholic nun through most of the film, revealing late in the film that she is actually a prostitute and thus enabling this tension to be consummated. Both Eastwood and MacLaine deliver strong performances, but the film as a whole suffers from its failure to establish any rational ideological basis for the fight against the French and from its sometimes outrageously masculinist perspective, which MacLaine's feisty character is unable to overcome. Nevertheless, *Two Mules for Sister Sara* has some virtue, if only in its refusal to assume that

Latin American revolutionaries must by definition be crazed felons. Indeed, the only actual Juarista we see at any length in the film, Colonel Beltran (Manolo Fabregas), is presented very positively, at least on the masculinist terms of this film—which means that he is tough, strong, and brave, able to stand toe-to-toe with Hogan in a contest of male egos.

The film begins as Hogan, an American mercenary who has come to Mexico to work for the Juaristas (purely for monetary gain), discovers Sister Sara, about to be raped by three desperadoes in the Mexican desert. He kills the desperadoes and then helps Sara elude the French army, hoping that her inside knowledge of the town of Chihuahua will help him in his quest to aid the Juaristas in attacking the French garrison in that town. After a series of adventures in which Hogan is frequently puzzled by Sara's un-nunlike behavior, they finally join the Juarista forces commanded by Beltran and do indeed succeed in overcoming the French garrison in Chihuahua. In the meantime, Hogan learns that Sara is actually a prostitute (with a heart of gold) who has become devoted to the Juarista cause, largely because of her firsthand observations of the evils of the French. Armed with this knowledge, Hogan is at last able to act on the strong sexual attraction he has felt for Sara ever since first seeing her, near-naked and on the verge of rape, in the desert. He then rides off into the distance, carrying his share of the loot from Chihuahua, with Sara trailing dutifully behind, apparently tamed by Hogans's masculine power. *Screenplay:* Albert Maltz. *Selected bibliography:* Dick (*Radical Innocence*).

*THE WILD BUNCH:* **DIR. SAM PECKINPAH (1969).** Perhaps the ultimate waning-of-the-West film, *The Wild Bunch* details the adventures of an over-the-hill gang of outlaws as they struggle to score one last major heist before fading into retirement in the face of rapid capitalist modernization and routinization in the early twentieth-century West. As the film begins, the gang, led by the aging Pike Bishop (William Holden), rides into a dusty Texas town disguised as cavalrymen. As they ride in, the film interposes shots of children playing on the edge of town by torturing a scorpion they have placed in the middle of a swarming colony of red ants. The scene is thus symbolically set for both the film's critique of the violence in American society and its treatment of the gang as dangerous scorpions who are nevertheless to be overwhelmed by the teeming ants of modernity.

The gang proceeds to rob the town's bank, which they expect to contain a large railroad payroll. But the railroad anticipates the robbery and ambushes the gang, killing several of them. Those who escape flee to Mexico, where they discover that the bags of "gold" they took from the bank contain nothing but metal washers. Meanwhile, the railroad's hired bounty hunters, led by Deke Thornton (Robert Ryan), a former friend and associate of Bishop, pursue the gang to Mexico, which is in the midst of postrevolutionary violence. Northern Mexico is in a particularly chaotic state, with Pancho Villa and his followers battling against the forces of the evil General Victoriano Huerta, who has betrayed the revolution and replaced Francisco Madero as the new president of Mexico.

Eventually, the gang goes to the town of Agua Verde, where they are hired by Mexican General Mapache (Emilio Fernandez), a follower of Huerta, to go back into Texas to rob a trainload of guns and ammunition from the U.S. Army. The robbery succeeds, despite the fact that the railroad has planned another ambush, loading the train not only with Thornton and his scruffy bounty hunters, but with soldiers. The gang then flees back to Mexico with the bounty hunters in pursuit. Meanwhile, Bishop agrees to give one case of the stolen rifles to Angel (Jaime Sanchez), the gang's only Mexican member, who wants to pass the rifles on to guerrilla fighters from his village. These guerrillas, who are treated very positively in the text, do not appear to be aligned with Villa, but are fighting their own battle for justice. Unfortunately, Mapache discovers the appropriation of the rifles and takes Angel captive, torturing him mercilessly. Eventually, all of the gang members are killed in an incredibly violent scene in which they battle against two hundred of Mapache's well-armed troops in an attempt to free Angel, though Angel is killed by mapache early in the battle.

In the aftermath of this bloody scene, Thornton and his bounty hunters ride into town. The bounty hunters take the bodies of the gang with them and head back toward Texas, but Thornton decides to stay behind in Mexico. Soon afterward, the bounty hunters are themselves killed by Angel's guerrillas, who then ride into town, accompanied by Sykes (Edmond O'Brien), the only remaining member of Bishop's gang and an old associate of both Bishop and Thornton. With the American West rapidly becoming "civilized," both Thornton and Sykes are anachronisms there. Both decide to stay in Mexico and join the guerrillas, thus continuing to experience some of the old adventure of the once-wild West.

*The Wild Bunch* is sprinkled with signs of the modernization of the West, most of which have sinister implications. Perhaps the most striking of these is Mapache's shiny automobile, which he uses to drag Angel through the streets of Agua Verde. Also important is the deadly machine gun that the gang acquires in the train robbery and then uses to annihilate dozens of Mapache's soldiers in Agua Verde. Such high-tech weapons make warfare impersonal and nonheroic, challenging the conventions of the Western and anticipating the mechanized carnage of World War I, which is about to start during the time frame of the film. Meanwhile, the incursions of such American weaponry into Mexico has been taken by some critics as an allusion to events underway in Vietnam at the time the film was made, though the link to Vietnam is less clear than in such films as *Little Big Man* (1970), *Soldier Blue* (1970), or *Ulzana's Raid* (1972). In any case, *The Wild Bunch*, famed for its spectacular and bloody violence, should be read not as a glorification of violence, but as a criticism of the increasingly violent nature of the modern world. However, its seeming presentation of the old days of the outlaw West, where individual heroism reigned supreme, as a utopian alternative to modernity is highly questionable. *Screenplay:* Walon Green and Sam Peckinpah. *Selected bibliography:* Allison Graham; Robert Ray; Ryan and Kellner; Tompkins; Torry.

**LITTLE BIG MAN: DIR. ARTHUR PENN (1970).** Based on the novel by Thomas Berger, *Little Big Man* parodies and revises the Western genre, reversing many of its conventions, while at the same time challenging mainstream versions of American history. In particular, the film represents the nineteenth-century conflict between Native Americans and white settlers at least partly from the point of view of the Native Americans, making the whites, or at least certain leaders among them, the real villains of history. The film also had a particular contemporary significance via the clear way in which it paralleled the genocidal white American assault on Native Americans to the imperialist American assault then underway in Vietnam. It was, in fact, one of the most effective of the numerous anti-Vietnam Westerns of the time, a subgenre that included *The Professionals* (1966); *The Wild Bunch* (1969), *Soldier Blue* (1970), *Two Mules for Sister Sara* (1970), and *Ulzana's Raid* (1972).

The film begins as 121-year-old Jack Crabb (Dustin Hoffman) is interviewed by a researcher (William Hickey) seeking information about Native American cultures. Crabb then sets the scholar straight about a number of aspects of American history via his account of his own first-hand experience, an account that occupies the remainder of the film. Crabb's rather picaresque narrative begins when he is ten years old, accompanying his family as they migrate westward across the Great Plains. Their party is attacked by a group of Pawnee warriors and all are killed except Jack and his sister, Caroline (Carol Androsky), who escape by hiding from the attackers. They are later collected by a Cheyenne brave who comes on the scene. This brave, Shadow that Comes in Sight (Ruben Moreno), takes the two of them back to the Cheyenne camp, though Caroline soon escapes after apparently being disappointed when the Cheyenne make no attempt to rape her. Jack then stays with the Cheyenne and is raised as one of them, growing to be a brave under the tutelage of Chief Old Lodge Skins (Chief Dan George) and taking the name Little Big Man.

The Cheyenne culture is depicted as sophisticated and humane, far more in tune with nature than the rapacious white culture that is currently threatening their traditional way of life. But Jack's idyllic life among the Cheyenne comes to an abrupt end when he is captured during a battle with white soldiers, then put in the care of the fanatical Rev. Silas Pendrake (Thayer David). Pendrake is suitably ludicrous as the self-righteous preacher who uses his hatred of sin as an excuse to administer sadistic beatings to Jack. However, Mrs. Pendrake (Faye Dunaway), the reverend's young, beautiful wife, is different a matter altogether. Not only does she attempt to protect Jack from the preacher's beatings, but she also administers her own particular brand of Christian kindness, which largely consists of seeking every possible opportunity to fondle his smooth, young body in ways that reveal a decidedly sinful intent.

Not surprisingly, Jack develops an adolescent crush on Mrs. Pendrake, only to be disillusioned when he observes her in flagrante with a storekeeper. He runs away and joins up with Allardyce T. Meriweather (Martin Balsam), a traveling snake-oil salesman and forerunner of American consumer capitalism. Unfortunately, Meriweather soon runs afoul of an angry mob of townspeople, who discover that his elixir is less than wholesome, then tar and feather both Meriweather and his young assistant. It is only then that the leader of the mob, Caroline, realizes that Jack is her long lost brother. Jack goes to live with Caroline, becomes a gunfighter, and experiences a series of cultural transfers in which he moves back and forth between life in the white world, depicted as hypocritical and dishonest (in the mode of Pendrake and Meriweather), and in the Cheyenne world, depicted as sensible and virtuous (epitomized by Old Lodge Skins). Along the way, Jack meets up with General George Armstrong Custer (Richard Mulligan), portrayed as a murderous and pompous fool, willing to commit any level of murder and mayhem to further his own political ambitions.

In a key scene, the Cheyenne camp along the Washita River, on land promised them in perpetuity by the U.S. government. But (in an actual historical episode), the camp is attacked by Custer's troops, who brutally murder men, women, children, and even horses in a gruesome massacre that is presented in a way that clearly suggests the recently revealed My Lai massacre in Vietnam. Little Big Man and Old Lodge Skins escape, but the former's four wives and infant son are slaughtered. After a number of other adventures, however, Jack gets his revenge when, working as a scout, he helps maneuver Custer into the battle of Little Big Horn, where the general and his troops are slaughtered. Jack then returns to live among the Cheyenne, where Old Lodge Skins, old and blind, is nearing death, while recognizing that the Cheyenne way of life, in the face of the white onslaught, is dying as well. Old Jack then wraps up his story, sending the researcher away feeling that he now understands American history in a whole new way.

Clearly, the defeat of the Cheyenne also amounts to the defeat of idealistic visions of what America might have been. *Little Big Man* is a serious film that shows modern American as a corrupt society built on conquest and genocide, thus providing the historical background to the American involvement in Vietnam, which thereby becomes not an aberration, but a mere extension of tendencies that have been central to the American way from the very beginning. Noting that the film's political critique is far sharper than that of the original novel, Mark Bezanson argues that the film turns "Berger's amoral saga of the West into a vehicle of moral protest against the United States' imperial adventure on the Far Eastern Frontier" (281). At the same time, the film makes its points without being smug or sanctimonious. It is, in fact, highly irreverent, mixing its basically tragic tale with episodes of good-natured humor. In that sense, its political critique is very much in the spirit of the 1960s. *Screenplay:* Calder Willingham. *Selected bibliography:* Bezanson; Michael Klein; Neve (*Film*); Robert Ray; Turner.

*M*A*S*H:* DIR. ROBERT ALTMAN (1970). Written by former Hollywood Ten member Ring Lardner, Jr., *M*A*S*H* is one of the most successful films to be scripted by a formerly blacklisted screenwriter. Lardner, in fact, won an Academy Award for his adaptation of the screenplay from the novel by Richard Hooker. The film was also the first major success for director Altman, propelling him into a major career. *M*A*S*H* is in many ways the quintessential cinematic expression of the political mood that swept America in the 1960s and early 1970s, later becoming a legendary television series that ran from 1972 to 1983. Although set in the Korean War, the film's mockery of war as an absurd exercise in futility appealed in particularly direct ways to a generation of young people galvanized into political action by opposition to the war in Vietnam. Further, the irreverence shown toward authority by its major characters, who continually flaunt military discipline and get away with it, provided vicarious pleasure for an audience that had grown increasingly suspicious of authority. In this sense, *M*A*S*H* clearly appealed far more to the sensibilities of its contemporary audience than did more somber antiwar films such as *Johnny Got His Gun* (1971), rooted as it was in the politics of the 1930s.

The film has no real plot, but is simply a series of episodes detailing daily life in the 4077th M.A.S.H. unit (Mobile Army Surgical Hospital), operating only three miles from the front during the Korean War. Many of the surgical scenes are powerfully realistic, making a strong statement about the inglorious carnage of war. But the prevailing mood is comic, beginning with the opening scene in which Captain Hawkeye Pierce (Donald Sutherland), newly arrived in Korea, steals a jeep to drive out to his unit, taking with him another new surgeon, Captain Duke Forrest

(Tom Skerritt). The two are soon joined by heart surgeon Captain Trapper John McIntyre (Elliott Gould), and together the three of them proceed to wreak havoc on the base with their antiauthoritarian antics. All, of course, are highly skilled surgeons, which is one reason their behavior is tolerated, though it is also the case that their commanding officer, Colonel Henry Blake (Roger Bowen), is preoccupied with other matters, such as seducing nurses. Their principal opposition comes from their fellow surgeon, Major Frank Burns (Robert Duvall), a sanctimonious religious fanatic, and head nurse Major Margaret Houlihan (Sally Kellerman), a career army nurse who is obsessed with regular army discipline.

Burns and Houlihan, of course, function primarily as butts for the film's humor. They are certainly no match for Pierce, McIntyre, and their supporters, who outsmart and make fools of them at every turn. In one episode, a microphone is placed under Houlihan's bed so that her lovemaking with the holier-than-thou Burns (who has a wife and kids back home) can be broadcast over the camp's public address system. In the aftermath, Burns is driven to distraction and taken away in a straightjacket. Houlihan, now saddled with the nickname "Hot Lips," remains behind to continue the fight and to be tormented by Pierce and his allies until she finally gives in by the end of the film and joins the fun. Pierce and McIntyre are at their antiauthoritarian best on an outing in Tokyo, where they are called so that McIntyre can perform surgery on the son of a congressman, but where they spend most of their time in various extracurricular activities, which they get away with by drugging a stodgy colonel and then photographing him in various compromising positions in a geisha house. Other major episodes include an elaborate mock suicide and funeral for the camp dentist, "Painless Pole" Waldowski (John Schuck), who decides that he wants to die after concluding that he is gay, despite his reputation as a womanizer with immense phallic endowments. The ceremony is concluded, however, when Waldowski is resurrected by the good offices of nurse Lieutenant "Dish" Schneider (Jo Ann Pflug) and returns to his former self. In the final major episode, the unit fields a football team for a challenge match against General Hammond (G. Wood) and his unit. Hammond fields a team laced with professional footballers, but the M.A.S.H. unit responds by acquiring a ringer of its own, in the person of ex-49er Oliver "Spearchucker" Jones (Fred Williamson). The medical unit also employs certain special skills, such as incapacitating the opponents' star player with drugs, and the upshot is that they win the game (and their extensive bets) on a trick play as the gun sounds to end the contest.

In the final scene, Pierce and Forrest complete their tours of duty and are ordered home, departing by again absconding with the same jeep in which they arrived. The film then ends as the camp's public address announcer, who has broadcast descriptions of various World War II movies being shown on the base throughout the film, describes the film we have just seen, thus announcing an explicit dialogue between *M*A*S*H* and more conventional war films. But this dialogue is implicit throughout, and the film is clearly intended as an interrogation not only of war and war films, but of the elements of American society (especially American popular culture, with its core of violence) that might make that society particularly prone to involvement in warfare. In this sense, the film is a direct, and potentially subversive, investigation of the background of the U.S. involvement in Vietnam. Of course, the conflicts in Korea and Vietnam were both offshoots of the Cold War in which American military force was brought to bear to prevent the spread of communism, but *M*A*S*H* does not really address the specific ideologies involved in either conflict. In any case, the film's politics, like much of the oppositional politics of the 1960s, are hardly procommunist, but thoroughly bourgeois, celebrating the victories of rebellious individuals over a bureaucracy-ridden authority. **Screenplay:** Ring Lardner, Jr. **Selected bibliography:** Budd and Steinman; Dick (*Radical Innocence*); Feineman; Kagan (*American Skeptic*); Keyssar; Plecki.

*THE MOLLY MAGUIRES:* DIR. MARTIN RITT (1970). The Molly Maguires were a secret organization of Irish coal miners who operated in Pennsylvania in the 1860s and 1870s, employing a variety of means in an attempt to resist the exploitation and brutalization of the miners by the coal companies and their lackeys in the local governments. Although reviled by the coal companies as terrorists and murderers, the Molly Maguires have often been seen as heroic fighters for social and economic justice and as the forerunners of modern trade unions. The film takes a fairly positive view of their activities, though it still treats them as dangerous and violent and does little to establish the justice of their cause.

In the film, the Molly Maguires are led by Irish American miner Jack Kehoe (Sean Connery), though much of the focus is on James McParlan (Richard Harris), a detective working for the Pinkerton agency who, as James McKenna, infiltrates the Molly Maguires in an attempt to learn about their operation and identify their members. Kehoe suspects McParlan/McKenna from the very beginning, but the detective manages to gain the confidence of the miners. He also gains the affections of Mary Raines (Samantha Eggar), the houskeeper at his lodgings, with whom he pursues a romance that forms an important subplot in the film.

Although historical accounts have disagreed as to the actual extent to which the Molly Maguires participated in the violence that was attributed to them, in the film they are depicted as guilty of the crimes with which they are charged and of which they are convicted, based largely on the testimony of McParlan/McKenna. As a result, the questionable legal proceedings in which they were convicted seem less questionable in the film, even if the final execution of Kehoe and the other miners is treated as tragic. The film fails to give any real explanation of the gruesome conditions that had caused the Molly Maguires to be organized in the first place. McParlan/McKenna, meanwhile, is treated with surprising sympathy in the film, especially given that, in historical reality, his testimony led to the hanging of twenty miners. In addition, the detective moved on from there to spearhead Pinkerton's efforts to frame Big Bill Heywood for murder by arranging false testimony against him. *The Molly Maguires* is extremely weak as a political film, ultimately reducing to a dramatic confrontation among individuals who operate out of personal principles rather than participation in a larger cause. *Screenplay:* Walter Bernstein. *Selected bibliography:* Bimba; Broehl; Carlton Jackson; Lewis; Palladino; Zaniello.

*SOLDIER BLUE:* **DIR. RALPH NELSON (1970).** *Soldier Blue* is an anti-Western that reverses many of the conventions of the Western genre, emphasizing the savagery of white American civilization in its imperialist expansion into the West, destroying Native American cultures along the way. Actually, the film begins with an attack by a Cheyenne war party on a detachment of the U.S. Cavalry, headed for Fort Reunion, Colorado, to deliver the payroll for the fort's men and to deliver a young woman, Cresta Marybelle Lee (Candice Bergen), to her intended groom, a lieutenant at the fort. The detachment is wiped out in the Cheyenne attack, though at least the fight is a fair one of warrior against soldier. Cresta and Private Honus Gant (Peter Strauss) are the only survivors; Most of the film then details their efforts to struggle through the American wilderness to get back to civilization, encountering substantial hardships (and falling in love) along the way.

Honus is somewhat taken aback to learn that Cresta had formerly lived among the Cheyenne as the wife of Chief Spotted Wolf (Jorge Rivero). He is also surprised at her positive descriptions of Cheyenne culture and at her insistence that the real atrocities in the West are being perpetrated not by Native Americans but by the white settlers and soldiers who are slaughtering Native Americans in order to take their land. To drive this point home, the film then ends with the dramatization of an actual historical event, in which a large detachment of U.S. Cavalry attacked a peaceful Cheyenne village at Sand Creek, Colorado, destroying the village and killing over 500 of its inhabitants, including numerous women and children. Cresta tries to warn the Cheyenne of the impending attack, while Honus tries to convince the cavalry, commanded by the almost cartoonishly murderous Colonel Iverson (John Anderson), to allow the Cheyenne peacefully to surrender. But both their efforts are in vain, and a horrific massacre, depicted in graphic and gory detail, ensues.

*Soldier Blue* is a sometimes clumsy effort that suffers from lackluster performances by both Bergen and Strauss. At the same time, the film does gain a certain visceral power from the fact that the brutality it depicts in the Sand Creek Massacre is based on historical reality. The film also gains in complexity through its subversive dialogue with the Western genre and through the fairly obvious way in which it parallels the destruction of Native American culture with the destructive impact of the then-contemporary American intervention in Vietnam. In this, it joins a number of other anti-Vietnam War Westerns of the time, including *The Professionals* (1966); *The Wild Bunch* (1969), *Little Big Man* (1970), *Two Mules for Sister Sara* (1970), and *Ulzana's Raid* (1972). **Screenplay:** John Gay. **Selected bibliography:** Adair; Michael Klein; Muse.

*JOHNNY GOT HIS GUN:* DIR. DALTON TRUMBO (1971). The film version of *Johnny Got His Gun* represents the culmination of a long-term effort on the part of the veteran screenwriter (and Hollywood Ten member) Trumbo to bring his classic 1939 antiwar novel to the screen. The film is a relatively true adaptation of the book, as one might expect given Trumbo's central involvement in both. The book had already become one of the most widely and enthusiastically read novels of the 1960s, as an entire new generation of readers, stirred to antiwar sentiments by the ongoing conflict in Vietnam, found in the book an eloquent expression of their own feelings. The 1994 Citadel Press edition of the book reflects this phenomenon, including an introduction by anti-Vietnam War activist Ron Kovic, who expresses his strong identification with the book's protagonist, calling the book "the most revolutionary, searing document against war and injustice ever written" (xvii). The film, which features important antiwar activists such as Donald Sutherland, is in a sense the culmination of the rebirth of the novel as a statement against the American involvement in Vietnam, though in retrospect it fails to capture the spirit of the anti-Vietnam resistance as effectively as, say, *M\*A\*S\*H*.

The film begins with newsreel footage from World War I, accompanied by the opening credits and martial music. A bomb explosion then leads to a blank screen and the beginning of the story proper, which essentially takes place inside the head of its protagonist, Joe Bonham (played by Timothy Bottoms), who awakes in a hospital after being severely wounded in battle in World War I. Much of the early part of the film deals with his gradual recognition of the horrifying extent of his wounds, which have led to the loss of both arms and both legs and to the obliteration of his face, leaving him with no eyes, ears, nose, or mouth. He is, in short, almost entirely cut off from the world, buried alive, as it were, inside the remains of his body. Meanwhile, the authorities keep him locked away in a utility room, believing him to be a mindless piece of meat, but hoping to learn something from his case that will be useful in the treatment of future war casualties.

Joe struggles to maintain some sense of humanity, trying to learn to sense what is happening around him, to keep track of time, and to pass that time by indulging in various fantasies (such as conversations with a cynical Christ, played by Sutherland) and memories of his past, which together, through a series of flashback segments, unveil the story of his life up to the moment of his mutilation. The film contrasts the richness of Joe's mental existence, which is shown in color, with the poverty of his physical world, which is shown in black and white. Desperate to establish a connection between the two worlds, Joe conceives a plan to try to communicate with his new and more compassionate nurse (Diane Varsi) by tapping out signals in Morse code via movements of his head. The attempt succeeds, and the nurse brings in a team of doctors, who ask Joe what he wants. He frantically searches for an answer, knowing there is virtually nothing he can do in his condition. Finally, he asks that he be put on public display, partly so that admission charges can be used to pay for his care, but primarily so that those viewing him can become aware of the brutal realities of war. When this request is refused, Joe asks to be killed, and his nurse is sent away after she attempts to comply with his request. Joe is then left alone, endlessly tapping out a cry for help.

Although it shared the Grand Prize of the Jury at the 1971 Cannes Film Festival, the film ultimately fails to achieve the horrifying power of the book, perhaps partly due to its low budget. The film ends with an on-screen display of statistics of war casualties and the motto, a reference to the famous antiwar poem by Wilfred Owen, "DULCE ET DECORUM EST PRO PATRIA MORI." The antiwar statement of the film is thus abundantly clear, especially given the context of its 1971 release date. On the other hand, the book ends with a much more specific and powerful political statement as Joe muses on the possibility of a future in which the masses of common people who traditionally have to fight wars will realize once and for all that those wars are not being fought to their advantage. In an outpouring of class-based anger, Joe envisions a day when the "little people" who "make bread and cloth and guns" will refuse to fight, except perhaps to turn their guns on the "lying thieving sons-of-bitches" who have traditionally manipulated the working class into fighting their wars for them (307). In this day, Joe warns, if anyone dies in war, "it will be you—you who urge us on to battle you who incite us against ourselves you who would have one cobbler kill another cobbler you who would have one man who works kill another man who works you who would have one human being who wants only to live kill another human being who wants only to live" (308). Indeed, the principal difference between the content of the book and that of the film is the film's almost complete omission of the class-based politics that are central to the book, perhaps reflecting the change in the political climate from 1939, when class was still the central preoccupation of the American Left, to 1971, when class had been effectively suppressed as a category of social analysis in America, even on the Left. *Screenplay:* Dalton Trumbo. *Selected bibliography:* Dick (*Radical Innocence*); Kovic (Introduction); Trumbo (*Johnny*).

*McCABE AND MRS. MILLER:* DIR. ROBERT ALTMAN (1971). *McCabe and Mrs. Miller* was one of a number of anti-Westerns produced in the late 1960s and early 1970s. The film undercuts a number of conventional representations of the heroic taming of the West, presenting that taming more as a gradual process of capitalist routinization than as a romantic adventure. The film is thus a central example of director Altman's trademark technique of working within conventional genres while undermining them in subtle ways. For example, the film contains its fair share of the requisite Western gunplay, but in a decidedly nonheroic mode. In addition, though set in the great Northwest, the film has an oddly claustrophobic look and is shot primarily in dark, low-ceilinged interiors, suggesting the way in which modernity is closing in on the Western frontier. By placing the film in 1901, Altman does not necessarily demonstrate that the West was never romantic, but simply that, by the beginning of the twentieth century, there is no longer a place for romance in an America increasingly dominated by capitalist expansion. There is, in fact, an elegiac tone to the entire film, very effectively enhanced by the sense of loss embodied in the Leonard Cohen ballads that constitute the major part of the musical soundtrack.

*McCabe and Mrs. Miller* focuses on John McCabe (Warren Beatty), a gambling drifter of mysterious origins who arrives in the cold, muddy frontier town of Presbyterian Church, somewhere in the wild Northwest. McCabe is in search not of adventure, but of profit, and he quickly parlays his winnings in a local poker game into a burgeoning one-man service industry. Based on the central capitalist premise of supply and demand, McCabe focuses his efforts on meeting the needs of the town's rough-and-tumble miners, concentrating his investments in a complex of establishments that offer gambling, prostitution, and liquor. This marketing strategy is a good one, and McCabe has considerable success, though his own limited education and imagination keep his enterprise relatively small. Then Mrs. Constance Miller (Julie Christie), an experienced cockney madam, arrives in town and becomes McCabe's partner, using her professional background and ambitious imagination to prod McCabe into modernizing and expanding his business.

The two partners make a formidable combination, and their business thrives. They are also clearly attracted to one another, but their personal chemistry never really has a chance to develop. Their relationship remains primarily a professional one. Soon, however, their joint enterprise is so successful that it draws the attention of Harrison and Shaughnessy, Inc., the large corporation that operates the area's mines. The corporation sends representatives to Presbyterian Church to try to buy out McCabe, who, trying to act like a proper businessman, rejects their initial offers in an attempt to obtain a better price for his business. Mrs. Miller warns him that Harrison and Shaughnessy are ruthless and that rejecting their offer could be highly dangerous, but McCabe continues to hold out. To his surprise, the company abruptly breaks off negotiations and sends a team of hired killers to town to remove him from the picture. Though there are hints in the film that McCabe might formerly have been a gunfighter, he seems hardly heroic in his efforts to evade the killers. Still, he eventually manages to shoot and kill all three of them, but in the process he is mortally wounded. This outcome, of course, is entirely appropriate: both the individual entrepreneur McCabe and these gun-slingers are anachronisms in the modern West. The film then closes as McCabe lies dead in the snow, while Mrs. Miller lies inside their estab-lishment, staring hopelessly into the void. *Screenplay:* Robert Altman and Brian McKay. *Selected bibliography:* Kagan (*American Skeptic*); Keyssar; Glenn Man; Merrill; O'Brien; Plecki; Robert Ray.

*THE ASSASSINATION OF TROTSKY:* DIR. JOSEPH LOSEY (1972). *The Assassination of Trotsky* is a rather strange film in which Losey attempts (with the help of a script by offbeat British novelist Nicholas Mosley) to detail the final days leading up to the 1940 assassination of Leon Trotsky in Mexico City. Much of the film simply shows Trotsky (played by a woefully miscast Richard Burton) going about his daily work, which consists mostly of producing anti-Stalinist propaganda. But the film also focuses a great deal on the mysterious assassin (played by Alain Delon), who floats through the film, donning a series of identities, meeting with a variety of personages, and generally acting sinister. Eventually, this assassin (sometimes known as Frank Jacson, sometimes as Jacques Monard) manages to gain entry to Trotsky's heavily guarded compound, with the help of his lover, Gita (Romy Schneider), who works for Trot-sky. On his first visit to Trotsky's study, he claims to seek Trotsky's commentary on a political essay he has written, then watches as Trotsky corrects the essay like a schoolmaster. On his second visit, he shows Trotsky the revised essay, then buries an ice axe in the head of the old revolutionary. Jacson/Monard is beaten by Trotsky's guards (most of whom are Americans), then turned over to police. Trotsky is rushed to the hospital, where he dies.

The film is extremely slow and sometimes a bit heavy-handed in try-ing to establish an atmosphere. In one interminable scene, for example, the killing of a bull at a bullfight is shown in great detail, apparently as a precursor to the killing of Trotsky. Meanwhile, the film only hints at the political issues at stake in Trotsky's career, though it does at least make clear his continuing devotion to Marxism, despite his antagonism toward Stalin. Another virtue of the film is its refusal to speculate. Rather than attribute Trotsky's killing directly to the orders of Stalin, as many have, though without evidence, the film simply leaves the identity of the killer and of the agents with whom he works as an unsolved puzzle. Still, what might have been a sweeping historical epic becomes mostly a disappointing exercise in French New Wave technique. *Screenplay:* Nicholas Mosley. *Selected bibliography:* Caute (*Joseph Losey*); Ciment; Hirsch.

**BOXCAR BERTHA: DIR. MARTIN SCORSESE (1972).** *Boxcar Bertha,* the first feature-length film directed by Scorsese, is a Depression-era tale based on the 1935 autobiography of Boxcar Bertha Thomson. A Roger Corman production, the film seems to take every opportunity to display spectacular violence or to unveil the pneumatic young body of its star, Barbara Hershey. Still, Scorsese shows directorial promise through some interesting camera work and (considering the low budget) excellent period detail. The film joins such near-contemporary productions as *Bonnie and Clyde* (1967) and *Thieves Like Us* (1974) in portraying 1930s protagonists who are driven to crime by the harsh economic conditions of the Depression. At times, in fact, it gestures beyond these other films in its suggestions of the importance of union activity (and antiunion activity) to the social context of the 1930s, with its sympathies clearly on the side of the unions. Unfortunately, it never really pursues these suggestions and ultimately collapses into a fairly conventional crime drama.

 *Boxcar Bertha* begins as Bertha's father, a crop duster, is killed in the crash of his small plane. The teenage Bertha (Hershey) is left alone in the world and begins to ride the rails, in the process of which she strikes up a relationship with Big Bill Shelley (David Carradine), a radical railway union organizer. As Bertha continues her travels, she takes up with Rake Brown (Barry Primus), a Northern gambler now working in the South. Brown is accused of cheating during a card game, resulting in an altercation in which Bertha shoots and kills a prominent attorney. She and Brown thus go on the run, hopping a freight car in which they again meet up with Shelley, Bertha's true love. Deputies attack the boxcar as it pulls into Memphis. Bertha escapes, but Shelley, Brown, and the others are arrested and taken to jail, where Shelley, a notorious "Bolshevik," is badly beaten.

 In jail, Shelley meets up with his old friend, Von Morton (Bernie Casey). Shelley, Morton, and Brown all end up working on the chain gang together but are rescued when Bertha helps them escape. Despite Shelley's uneasiness about being regarded as a common criminal, the four then go on a crime spree aimed specifically at the Reader Railroad, an

Arkansas company notorious for its antiunion stance. They garner considerable loot, though Shelley turns his proceeds over to the railway
union, which decidedly disapproves of his criminal activity. Eventually,
however, they are trapped in an ambush set up by the railroad and its
hired detectives, including the murderous McIvers (Victor Argo and
David Osterhout), two brothers who float through the entire film. Bertha
again escapes, but Brown is killed, and Morton and Shelley are sent back
to prison.

Again on her own, Bertha finds work in a brothel, where she stays
until she again meets up with Morton, who informs her that Shelley has
again escaped from prison. Morton takes her to see Shelley, who is
greatly aged and worn from his latest prison term. As the two lovers
reunite, the McIvers and other hired thugs of the railway again attack. In
a surprisingly powerful scene, they beat Shelley viciously, then nail him,
still alive and conscious, to the side of a boxcar so that his body can be
carried about the countryside as a warning to others. Morton returns
with a shotgun and kills all of the detectives and thugs, splattering lots of
blood, but it is too late to save Shelley. The train pulls away with Shelley
crucified (and looking extremely Christlike) on the side. Bertha, anticipating her role as Mary Magdalene in Scorsese's *The Last Temptation of
Christ* (1988), weeps as Shelley is pulled away into the distance. Indeed,
there is a direct link between the two films. Scorsese apparently became
interested in making *Last Temptation* when Hershey gave him a copy of
the Nikos Kazantzakis novel on the set of *Boxcar Bertha* (Biskind 406).
*Screenplay:* Joyce H. Corrington and John William Corrington. *Selected
bibliography:* Biskind (*Easy Riders*); Doel; Lawrence S. Friedman; Kelly;
Boxcar Bertha Thomson; Zaniello.

*THE GODFATHER:* DIR. FRANCIS FORD COPPOLA (1972). Widely
recognized as one of the greatest of all American films, *The Godfather*,
together with its two sequels, comprises one of the most respected,
admired, and beloved sequences in American film history. This original
won the Academy Awards for best picture and best adapted screenplay,
while star Marlon Brando won the Oscar for best actor. The film combines an engaging narrative, impressive acting performances, and thematic richness to produce a work that is both compelling and thought-
provoking. Its story of the operations of the Corleone family add to an
already rich tradition of American gangster films, while making especially clear that this organized crime family of Italian immigrants is a
quintessentially American phenomenon, pursuing the American dream
in ways that are paradigmatic of modern capitalist society.

*The Godfather* begins just after the end of World War II with the elaborate wedding of Connie Corleone (Talia Shire), daughter of Don Vito
Corleone (Brando), to Carlo Rizzi (Gianni Russo), a small-time hood. This

grand communal festival speaks volumes about the traditional family values represented by the Corleone syndicate under the leadership of the aging, and old-fashioned, Vito. But it also announces the beginning of the deterioration of family traditions. Many of the attendees are show business personalities and others who represent a more modern era in American society. One of these is Vito's youngest son, Michael (Al Pacino), an Ivy League graduate and recent war hero, who arrives still wearing his military uniform, indicating his complete interpellation into American society. Michael is accompanied to the wedding by his WASP girlfriend, Kay Adams (Diane Keaton), a further sign of his assimilation.

It is, of course, part of the secret of the popular success of the film (which, by 1974, had grossed more than any other film in history) that it gradually shifts its focus to Michael, the individualist American, and away from Vito, the communalist Italian. The family hopes to keep Michael free of their criminal operations so that he can spearhead their future plans to move into legitimate businesses, suggesting the Americanization of the entire clan enterprise. In the same way, Michael's adopted brother, Tom Hagen (Robert Duvall), has been educated as a lawyer so that he can help out with the family's legal problems. Both cases show the strain placed on the Corleones as they continue to attempt to base their operations on family connections, while also modernizing and becoming more businesslike.

Soon after the wedding, the traditional operations of the Corleone clan face a specific threat when drug dealer Virgil Sollozzo (Al Lettieri), backed by the rival Tattaglia family, attempts to enlist the support of the Corleones in a major expansion of his drug operations. Vito, feeling that drugs are a dirty business the involvement in which might jeopardize the important political contacts he has cultivated for years, declines the offer. As a result, Sollozzo and the Tattaglias decide it is best to remove the Corleones from the scene altogether, launching a gang war in which Vito is seriously wounded in an assassination attempt. Michael, incensed by the attack on his father (and by his own abuse at the hands of a New York police captain who is in league with the Tattaglias), takes the lead in seeking revenge, personally killing both Sollozzo and the police captain (Sterling Hayden). He is then forced to flee to Sicily until things cool down, leaving his hotheaded older brother, Santino (James Caan), in charge of the family business while Vito continues to recuperate.

In the meantime, the war goes on. Santino ("Sonny" to his family and friends) is killed in an ambush that Carlo Rizzi helps to set up. An assassination attempt is also made on Michael in Sicily. He escapes, but the young bride he has taken there is killed. Michael returns to America with vengeance in his heart, taking over the management of the family when Vito retires. But Michael is no hothead, and he bides his time, meanwhile marrying Kay, starting a family, and gradually preparing to move the family business to the more lucrative setting of Las Vegas, where huge amounts of money can be made in relatively legal ways. Finally, on the eve of the move, the time is right, and Michael, in one of the sequence's many overt examples of fantasy fulfillment, arranges a carefully coordinated bloodbath in which all of the family's major enemies (including Carlo) are killed virtually simultaneously. The family then prepares to head for Las Vegas and to begin their new era of more efficient and businesslike management.

*The Godfather* seeks in numerous ways to suggest parallels between the operations of organized crime and of capitalist business in general. Its gangsters continually refer to themselves as businessmen, once pointing out that their goal is pure profit, because "after all, we're not communists." Indeed, *The Godfather* may make this point more effectively than any other American film. On the other hand, as Fredric Jameson has pointed out, there is a real danger that this parallel will simply displace criticisms that should rightly be directed at capitalist business, instead attributing the negative effects of the capitalist system to criminal aberrations from that system. "The function of the Mafia narrative," Jameson notes, "is indeed to encourage the conviction that the deterioration of daily life in the United States today is an ethical rather than economic matter, connected not with profit, but rather 'merely' with dishonesty, and with some omnipresent moral corruption whose ultimate mythic source lies in the pure Evil of the Mafiosi themselves" (32). At the same time, however, Jameson also notes that *The Godfather* counters this tendency by presenting the Corleones in a relatively positive light, as men of dignity and principle who tend, if anything, to resist, if unsuccessfully, corruption by the conditions they find around them. Moreover, the representation of the Corleone family as quite literally a *family* before its appropriation by capitalist modernization suggests a utopian vision of an older and more humane form of social organization that is no longer available in contemporary America. *Screenplay:* Mario Puzo and Francis Ford Coppola. *Selected bibliography:* Biskind (*Easy Riders*); Biskind (Godfather *Companion*); Clarens; Cowie (*Coppola*); Cowie (Godfather *Book*); Ferraro; Jameson (*Signatures*); Lebo; Papke; Robert Ray.

*SOUNDER:* DIR. MARTIN RITT (1972). An adaptation of William H. Armstrong's Newbery Award-winning novel of the same title, *Sounder* tells the story of a struggling family of black sharecroppers in Depression-era Louisiana. The success with which it tells this story (the film won four Academy Award nominations, though no Oscars) made the film a landmark in the representation of African Americans in the American cinema. *Sounder* is essentially a somewhat sentimental tale of family togetherness in the face of social and economic hardship. It focuses on the Morgan family, which includes parents Nathan Lee and

Rebecca (Paul Winfield and Cicely Tyson), as well as their three children. The title character, however, is the family dog, who accompanies Nathan Lee and eldest son David Lee (Kevin Hooks) as they attempt to supplement the family's meager supply of food by hunting raccoons and opossums in the woods around the shack in which they live.

Driven to near desperation by the hunger of his family, Nathan Lee steals some food and is soon arrested by the local sheriff and two deputies, one of whom, out of sheer meanness, shoots Sounder in the process. The dog limps off into the woods, apparently to die, only to reappear weeks later, essentially healed. Nathan Lee is given a summary trial and sentenced to a year at hard labor in a brutal prison camp, while the rest of the family struggles against all odds to get by in his absence. David Lee, accompanied by Sounder, attempts to visit his father in the camp, but is instead beaten by a guard. The injured boy comes upon a school where a black teacher, Camille Johnson (Janet MacLachlan), teaches black students to be proud of their heritage. Miss Johnson tends David Lee's wounds and introduces him to such figures as Harriet Tubman, Crispus Attucks, and W.E.B. Du Bois.

In a dramatic scene, Nathan Lee finally returns from the camp after having been crippled by a dynamite blast. Nevertheless, he works to make it possible for David Lee to return to Miss Johnson's school to continue his education so that he might someday "beat the life they got all laid out for you in this place." Like the children's book on which it is based, *Sounder* is rather juvenile in tone, but it effectively portrays the hardships faced by poor Southern blacks, as well as the courage and humanity with which they work to overcome these hardships. *Screenplay:* Lonnie Elder III. *Selected bibliography:* Carlton Jackson; Rutherford.

**ULZANA'S RAID: DIR. ROBERT ALDRICH (1972).** *Ulzana's Raid* was one of an entire family of late-1960s and early 1970s Westerns that commented, indirectly on the American involvement in Vietnam. Other films in this family include *The Professionals* (1966), *The Wild Bunch* (1969), *Little Big Man* (1970), *Soldier Blue* (1970), and *Two Mules for Sister Sara* (1970). On the surface, *Ulzana's Raid* is a fairly simple and straightforward Western. It begins as Ulzana (Joaquin Martinez) leads a band of renegade Apaches as they break out of an Arizona reservation and begin to terrorize the local white settlers. Most of the plot then involves the attempts of the U.S. Army to track down and apprehend the renegades. In particular, young Lieutenant DeBuin (Bruce Davison), a naïve officer newly arrived from back East, is assigned to lead a detail of cavalry on this mission, accompanied by the Apache scout Ke-Ni-Tay (Jorge Luke) and McIntosh, a wily old Indian fighter (Burt Lancaster).

Predictably, the Apaches commit various atrocities while at large but are eventually tracked down and killed by the cavalry detachment. Along the way, however, the film addresses a number of issues (most of them relevant to the Vietnam experience) in ways that differ substantially from those found in the typical Western. Indeed, the film functions as a sort of anti-Western that questions many of the conventional premises of the genre. While the film seems overly fascinated with presenting atrocities committed by the Apaches against whites (presumably paralleling communist atrocities in Vietnam), it at least tries to take a sort of cultural relativist approach. In particular, it suggests that what might seem like crazed savagery from the point of view of Western Enlightenment culture might be perfectly sensible and well motivated from the point of view of Apache culture. In a situation with obvious parallels to Vietnam, DeBuin's inability to comprehend Apache culture leaves him in pursuit of a mysterious and elusive enemy that seems able to outwit him at every turn, were it not for the expert help of McIntosh and Ke-Ni-Tay. DeBuin's difficulties can be taken as a comment on the Ugly American syndrome as a whole, as Americans blunder about the Third World in complete ignorance of the cultures they are encountering. Indeed, though the obvious referent is Vietnam, it is also the case that the Vietnamese analogy breaks down to some extent given that communism itself has roots in the Western Enlightenment and is not nearly as foreign to the West as, say, Native American culture is. *Screenplay:* Alan Sharp. *Selected bibliography:* Muse; Pye.

*THE LONG GOODBYE:* **DIR. ROBERT ALTMAN (1973).** *The Long Goodbye*, like many of Altman's films, operates within a standard genre (the film noir detective story) but twists the conventions of that genre just enough to make the film both a legitimate example of the genre and a parody of the genre. The later aspect of the film gains special energy from the fact that the film is based on a novel by Raymond Chandler, the quintessential creator of detective stories. It focuses on detective Philip Marlowe, the quintessential Chandler detective. But Altman's Marlowe, as played by Elliott Gould in an almost Brechtian example of intentional miscasting, has little in common with Chandler's tough, hard-boiled, and efficient original. Altman's Marlowe, in fact, is something of a lovable bungler. He has a soft spot for cats, does not get the girl, and never wins a fight. Moreover, in a surprising twist, he ends the film by shooting down his best friend in cold blood. Meanwhile, *The Long Goodbye* is anachronistically set not in the 1930s, but the early 1970s, giving the entire film an off-kilter feel. Finally, the film, which both begins and ends with "Hooray for Hollywood" playing in the background, also satirizes Hollywood and its values, making the film a sort of forerunner of Altman's later Hollywood satire, *The Player* (1992).

The film begins as Marlowe's friend, Terry Lennox (Jim Bouton), comes to Marlowe and asks him to drive him to Tijuana. Marlowe complies, then learns that Lennox has been implicated in the murder of his wife. Convinced of Lennox's innocence, he spends most of the film trying to find the real killer. In the process, he encounters the requisite dangerous blonde, in the person of Eileen Wade (Nina van Pallandt). He also encounters Eileen's husband, Roger Wade, a broken-down, alcoholic writer, wonderfully played by old time film noir star Sterling Hayden. Marlowe also encounters gangster Marty Augustine (Mark Rydell), who is trying to recover the $350,000 that Lennox was holding for him. Augustine is convinced that Marlowe either has the money or knows where it is, so the detective is repeatedly manhandled (and once nearly castrated) by Augustine's thugs, including one played by a young Arnold Schwarzenegger (in the days when he was still credited as Arnold Strong).

Marlowe manages to keep his genitals when the money is returned at the last moment. Meanwhile, he has concluded, based largely on information supplied by Eileen, that Roger Wade killed Mrs. Lennox, with whom the writer was having an affair. Marlowe does not realize until the end of the film that he has been duped, that Lennox was having an affair with Eileen, and that Lennox did, in fact, kill his wife as originally charged. In the meantime, Wade conveniently commits suicide, and the wealthy Eileen heads to Mexico to join Lennox. By the time Marlowe realizes what has happened, the two lovers are living it up in high style. Infuriated by the betrayal of his friendship and by Lennox's escape from justice, Marlowe goes to Tijuana, confronts Lennox, and coldly shoots him down. He walks away as Eileen drives up in her Jeep, not realizing what has happened. This ending seems a bit improbable, but that may be the point; it can effectively be read as a parodic comment on Hollywood's insistence that closure be obtained by bringing criminals to justice, by any means necessary. *Screenplay:* Leigh Brackett. *Selected bibliography:* Ferncase; Kagan (*American Skeptic*); Keyssar; Naremore (*More than Night*); O'Brien; Silver and Ward.

*THE WAY WE WERE:* **DIR. SYDNEY POLLACK (1973).** *The Way We Were* aspires to be a meditation on America's loss of innocence and idealism from the 1930s to the 1950s, though it is ultimately dominated by the sentimental love story between the characters played by its big-name stars. Barbra Streisand plays Katie Morosky, an idealistic Jew; Robert Redford is Hubbell Gardner, a more practical WASP. They meet in college in the late 1930s, when she is the president of the campus chapter of the Young Communist League, campaigning against fascism and for world peace. Hubbell, on the other hand, is devoted to shallow and superficial socializing with his WASP friends, most of whom treat

Katie as a joke. However, he clearly finds something attractive about Katie's idealism, while Katie, an aspiring writer, is attracted to Hubbell for his obvious writing talent.

This attraction leads nowhere during college, and World War II soon intervenes in their lives. They meet again during the war, when Hubbell is a dashing naval officer and Katie works for the Office of War Information producing radio broadcasts in support of the war effort. He is drunk, and she takes him to her apartment, where he passes out. During the night, they make love, though he has no memory of the experience the next morning. Near the end of the war, they meet again, she still harboring a crush and he still with no memory of their previous encounter. She reveals that she has read and admired (with reservations) his only published novel, and eventually they begin a relationship, though the differences in their social backgrounds and political attitudes continue to cause problems and tensions.

After the war, Hubbell and Katie marry and move to California, where he works as a screenwriter, battling against the commodification of his writing. Katie, meanwhile, becomes a housewife but rejoins the political fight when she goes to Washington to protest the HUAC investigations. While she is away, Hubbell begins an affair with an exgirlfriend. Katie is pregnant, but the marriage soon ends, more out of their very different reactions to the HUAC probes than out of Hubbell's adultery. As the film ends, the two meet again in New York, years later. He has now completely sold out and is writing trash for television. She remains idealistic and is campaigning for nuclear disarmament when they meet. Hubbell shakes his head as Katie gathers her pamphlets, calling out, "You never give up, do you?"

*The Way We Were* clearly presents Katie's idealism as morally superior to Hubbell's sell-out. At the same time, her attitude is consistently presented as somewhat simplistic, unrealistic, and serious to the point of sanctimony. The relatively positive treatment of Katie's radical politics is a clear step forward for Hollywood film. But Katie never seems like a real radical, and her politics are safely contained within her perfectly conventional appearance, lifestyle, and devotion to true love. She is, as Hubbell puts it, a "nice, Jewish girl" despite it all. Indeed, her politics seem largely beside the point, more related to a temperamental incompatibility with Hubbell than any genuine radicalism. *The Way We Were* is ultimately about neither politics nor history but about the star-crossed love affair between its mismatched lovers. Indeed, the political content of the film (especially its treatment of the HUAC investigations and subsequent Hollywood purges) was intentionally toned down, apparently with an eye toward better box office. *Screenplay:* Arthur Laurents. *Selected bibliography:* Christensen; Robert Ray.

*CHINATOWN:* DIR. ROMAN POLANSKI (1974). *Chinatown*, despite being shot in color, is in many ways a classic film noir, combining a complex detective story plot with a general air of corruption and a darkly claustrophobic look and atmosphere. In many ways, the protagonist, J. J. Gittes (Jack Nicholson), is a paradigmatic film noir detective, willing to bend the rules but ultimately sincere in his quest for the truth. Similarly, the central female character, Evelyn Mulwray (Faye Dunaway), is the quintessential film noir femme fatale, seductive, but seemingly dangerous, largely because of her mysterious past. In some ways, however, *Chinatown* is even darker than the typical film noir. Gittes succeeds in solving the film's mystery, but he is no match for the mighty forces that are arrayed against him, powerless to prevent the realization of the complex, evil plot that his investigation uncovers. Ultimately, the film becomes a confrontation between Gittes as a lone, ultimately righteous individual, and capitalist modernization, embodied in the central villain, Noah Cross (played by film noir pioneer John Huston), but also pictured as an inexorable historical force. This force is far too much for Gittes, whose final helplessness and even ridiculousness is emphasized in the way he goes through most of the second half of the film with a huge, almost comical, bandage on his nose after a thug (Polanski) slits one of his nostrils open with a knife, with the memorable warning that nosey people have a tendency to lose their noses.

The film is set in 1937 and employs exquisite period detail to make that setting clear. In addition, it is based on actual Los Angeles water scandals dating back to the first decade of this century. Nevertheless, *Chinatown* is very much a film of the 1970s, both in its underlying ecological concerns and in its cynicism about the possibility of opposing the ruthless and greedy quest for profit that constitutes the context of the film. As Ryan and Kellner note, the film was at the center of a revival in film noir in the mid-1970s, a revival they relate to "the emerging reality of political liberalism—that it was powerless against the entrenched economic power blocs of the country" (83). One of the most highly praised films of the 1970s, *Chinatown* garnered eleven Academy Award nominations but won only one Oscar, for Robert Towne's screenplay.

Gittes begins the film as an unwilling dupe, hired by a woman posing as Evelyn Mulwray to gather evidence of an extramarital affair on the part of Evelyn's husband, Hollis Mulwray (Darrell Zwerling), the chief engineer of the Los Angeles city water system. This evidence is then leaked to the press in an attempt to discredit Mulwray, who is involved in a bitter political battle because of his opposition to the construction of a new dam near the city. Soon afterward, Mulwray is murdered, while the young woman with whom Gittes had spotted him disappears. Gittes is meanwhile hired by the real Evelyn Mulwray to find out what happened to her husband, then is subsequently retained by Cross (Evelyn's father and Hollis Mulwray's former business partner) to find the missing woman, presumably so that Cross can help her out of deference to Mulwray's affection for her.

Gittes's subsequent investigation reveals that Mulwray had been killed by Cross because he had discovered, and opposed, an intricate scheme involving the city's water system. Indeed, Gittes, who becomes romantically involved with Evelyn, is able to ascertain the exact nature of the plot, which is part of a complex scheme to ensure that the proposed dam will be built. The perpetrators of this scheme, led by Cross, have meanwhile plotted to acquire large amounts of land in a valley north of the city. They then plan to divert the water made available by the new dam to the irrigation of this valley, vastly increasing the value of the land there and leading to huge profits for themselves at the expense of the taxpayers of Los Angeles. Gittes also discovers (in his famous daughter … sister … daughter … sister interrogation of Evelyn) that the missing woman, Katherine, is both the daughter and the sister of Evelyn Mulwray, the product of an earlier incestuous liaison between Cross and his teenage daughter.

Through most of the film, Chinatown functions simply as a (somewhat Orientalist) metaphor for mystery and corruption, but Gittes's investigation culminates in the only scene of the film that actually occurs in Chinatown, a final confrontation involving most of the final characters. In this scene, it becomes clear that Gittes's investigation will go for naught because the wealthy Cross "owns the police." Cross openly flaunts this fact in front of a helpless Gittes. Meanwhile, when Evelyn tries to escape with Katherine to keep her away from Cross, the police shoot and kill Evelyn. In the end, police lieutenant Lou Escobar (Perry Lopez), a former colleague of Gittes in the L. A. police department, sends Gittes home and advises him to forget the entire matter. Cross, with the power of his immense wealth behind him, is left to do as he will, with Katherine, the taxpayers' money, the L. A. water supply, and anything else he wants. *Screenplay:* Robert Towne. *Selected bibliography:* Belton; Biskind (*Easy Riders*); Cawelti; Naremore (*More than Night*); Robert Ray; Ryan and Kellner.

## *THE GODFATHER, PART II:* DIR. FRANCIS FORD COPPOLA (1974).

One of the most successful sequels in American film history, *The Godfather, Part II*, was, for many, at least as good as its predecessor. Like the original *Godfather*, *Part II* won the Academy Award for best picture and best adapted screenplay. It also won four other Oscars, including best director to Coppola and best supporting actor to Robert De Niro; it was nominated in five more categories. *Part II* includes two different narrative segments. The principal segment is a direct sequel to the original *Godfather*, following the efforts of Michael Corleone (Al Pacino) to manage and extend the increasingly "legitimate" business empire of the Corleone family. The secondary segment is a prequel to the original, detailing the early years of Don Vito Corleone (De Niro) as he comes to America and gradually establishes himself in organized crime. This secondary segment adds an air of historical authenticity to the entire *Godfather* sequence, while also enhancing its narration of the growth of the Corleone family within the context of the growth of American capitalism as a whole.

In the secondary segment, young Vito is orphaned in Sicily when both parents are killed by Don Ciccio, a local Mafia lord. He comes alone to America in 1901 as a nine-year-old boy, makes his way through Ellis Island, and somehow manages to survive to adulthood, when he struggles to make a life for himself and his family in an ethnic Italian neighborhood of New York. Eventually, however, he runs afoul of Don Fanucci, the local Mafia chief, eventually eliminating Fanucci and taking his place. Vito's courage and resourcefulness help him to establish himself as a growing power in organized crime. Later, he returns to Sicily and kills Don Ciccio as well, before to returning to America to build the empire that exists at the beginning of the original *Godfather*.

In the principal narrative segment, Michael puts more and more of the family resources into legal operations in the hotels of Las Vegas and Reno, though he is willing to employ bribery, intimidation, and a number of other techniques when necessary to further the success of those operations. He also becomes involved in a complex battle against his enemies in the underworld, while facing the continual deterioration of his once-close family. Much of the film is essentially a suspense-thriller in which Michael outwits and defeats his enemies, while also evading the attempts of a Senate committee to implicate him in its investigations of organized crime. He succeeds in these efforts, eventually eliminating the aged Hyman Roth (Lee Strasberg), last of the old dons of his father's generation, and clearing the way for his new, more modern techniques of operation. He does not, however, succeed in restoring the former closeness of the family. As the film draws to a close, he is estranged from his wife Kay (Diane Keaton) and has ordered the death of his older brother, Fredo (John Cazale), whom he has discovered to be in league with Roth. Michael himself grows increasingly suspicious and seems to trust no one, even his loyal lawyer and stepbrother, Tom Hagen (Robert Duvall). In the final scene of this segment, Michael sits alone, lost in thought and alienated from everyone around him. The film then closes with a contrasting scene from 1941, as Don Vito celebrates his birthday, with all of his children and other family members together to share the moment.

*The Godfather, Part II,* is significantly enhanced by one sequence in the principal narrative segment, in which Michael and Roth go to Cuba to discuss the expansion of their operations on the island. They meet with officials of Batista's government, which they find extremely receptive to their efforts and to the efforts of the other American businessmen (representing a variety of large, "legitimate" corporations) who attend the same meeting, emphasizing not only the American neocolonial exploitation of Cuba, but also the similarity between the operations of organized crime and ordinary American capitalism. These plans go awry, however, as Castro's rebels march into Havana, forcing both Batista and the Americans to flee. Fredric Jameson describes this event as "the climactic end moment of the historical development" of the film, "when American business, and with it American imperialism, meet that supreme ultimate obstacle to their internal dynamism and structurally necessary expansion which is the Cuban Revolution" (34). *Part II* thus proposes, as a potential alternative to the alienating capitalist modernization represented by Michael Corleone, not only the older system of social relations represented by his father, but the newer system represented by socialism. The second part of the *Godfather* sequence is thus far stronger in its political content than is the first, though both of these parts can easily be read as mere "gangster" films, leaving audiences the option of ignoring the political content altogether. *Screenplay:* Francis Ford Coppola and Mario Puzo. *Selected bibliography:* Biskind (*Easy Riders*); Biskind (Godfather *Companion*); Clarens; Cowie (*Coppola*); Cowie (Godfather *Book*); Ferraro; Jameson (*Signatures*); Lebo; Papke; Robert Ray.

*THIEVES LIKE US:* **DIR. ROBERT ALTMAN (1974).** Based on Edward Anderson's 1937 novel of the same title, *Thieves Like Us* is much more faithful to this original than was Nicholas Ray's 1948 film noir version, *They Live by Night.* The Altman film follows the Anderson novel almost exactly in plot, the major change being that the film takes place in Mississippi, while the book takes place in Oklahoma and Texas. The film begins as T. W. Masefield (called T-Dub, played by Bert Remsen), Elmo Mobley (or Chicamaw, played by John Schuck), and Bowie Bowers (Keith Carradine) escape from a Mississippi prison. T-Dub and Chicamaw are experienced criminals, specializing in bank robbery. Although serving a life sentence for murder, the younger Bowie is actually rather innocent, his one crime having been committed almost as an accident. The three take refuge at the home of Chicamaw's cousin, Dee Mobley, who owns a small-town filling station. There, Bowie meets Dee's daughter, Keechie (Shelley Duvall), who seems to resent their presence but soon begins to warm up to Bowie.

The three escapees soon begin a series of successful bank robberies, leading to increasing press coverage of their exploits. Identified and with rewards on their heads, the three proceed cautiously and decide to lie low for a while. Bowie, however, is involved in an automobile accident. Chicamaw shoots and kills two policemen who come to the scene to investigate the accident, then drives on with the injured Bowie, eventually leaving him at Dee's filling station to recuperate. Keechie tends Bowie's wounds, and romance blooms between the two of them. They make love for the first time as an enactment of *Romeo and Juliet* plays on the radio. They rent a remote lakeside cottage and set up housekeeping. Bowie, meanwhile, attends a prearranged rendezvous in Yazoo City with T-Dub and Chicamaw, after which they pull still another bank robbery. Bowie then heads back to rejoin Keechie but hears on the radio that, in the aftermath of the robbery, T-Dub has been shot and killed by police, while Chicamaw has been captured.

Chicamaw is sent to the Mississippi State Penitentiary, causing Bowie to contemplate breaking him out. Bowie and Keechie meanwhile consider moving to Mexico. They travel to the town of Pickens, where T-Dub's sister-in-law Mattie (Louise Fletcher) now owns a motor court, bought for her by T-Dub from his robbery money in recognition of her loyalty to her husband, his brother, who is currently in prison. Posing as a sheriff, Bowie does indeed manage to get Chicamaw out of prison. The two argue after Chicamaw unnecessarily kills a hostage, then makes disparaging remarks about Keechie. Bowie puts Chicamaw out on the side of the road. He then returns once more to Keechie, who has by this time has discovered that she is pregnant. Soon after his arrival, however, police appear and surround their rented cabin, having been tipped off by Mattie, who hopes thereby to get her husband out of prison. Bowie and the cabin are shot to bits as a horrified Keechie looks on. The film then ends as the pregnant Keechie takes a train to Fort Worth to try to start a new life, while a speech by famed 1930s right-wing radio commentator Father Coughlin plays in the background on the train station radio.

This speech by the right-wing Coughlin helps to emphasize the film's subtle suggestion that the crimes committed by Bowie, T-Dub, and Chicamaw tell us more about certain dark tendencies in American society than about the criminal proclivities of the thieves themselves. In addition, radio programs such as *Gangbusters* and *The Shadow* frequently sound in the background in the film, suggesting a fascination with violence and criminality in American culture as a whole. *Thieves Like Us* emphasizes in a fairly obvious way that, in Depression-era America, people like Bowie and Keechie, no matter how basically good, have few opportunities to build the kind of life advertised as the American dream. The film lacks the book's repeated emphasis on the fact that the robberies being pulled by Bowie, T-Dub, and Chicamaw are no more dishonest, and often no more violent, than the day-to-day activities of American business and professional people, but it does at least gesture in this direction. **Screenplay:** Calder Willingham, Joan Tewkesbury, and Robert Altman. **Selected bibliography:** Clarens; Feineman; Kagan (*American Skeptic*), Keyssar, Plecki.

*THE DAY OF THE LOCUST:* DIR. JOHN SCHLESINGER (1975). *The Day of the Locust* is a surprisingly effective adaptation of Nathanael West's 1939 novel of the same title, a novel that seems unpromising as the basis of a film, both because of its own postmodern qualities and because of its strong critique of the Hollywood film industry. Schlesinger's film continues this critique, at the same time bringing to life the strange cast of characters through which West (drawing upon his own experience as a Hollywood screenwriter in the late 1930s) enacted his vision of the dream factory of Hollywood as the epitome of American consumer culture, in all of its bogus glory. Set, significantly, against the background of the Depression, both film and book depict Hollywood as a factory for the production of prefabricated dreams and thus as a central means through which the desires of the American public can be manipulated by unscrupulous magnates. Importantly, however, the thoroughly commodified nature of these dreams implies that the desires associated with them can never be fulfilled with any level of satisfaction. Thus, *The Day of the Locust* depicts Hollywood as a giant dumping ground upon which broken dreams can be discarded to make way for the ever newer dreams constantly being turned out by the American Culture Industry.

The film stars William Atherton as artist Tod Hackett, an aspiring Yale-educated painter who has been brought to Hollywood to work as a set and costume designer for a film studio. While there, he falls in love with Faye Greener (Karen Black), a beautiful but untalented would-be starlet who has thus far been able to find work only as an extra. Faye is both a product and a victim of the Hollywood dream factory. A walking object of commodified desire, she is unable to experience any genuine emotions but instead treats every situation in her life as if it were a scene in a movie. The venal Faye encourages but evades Tod's attentions and instead goes to live, as a purely "business arrangement," with Homer Simpson (Donald Sutherland), a former bookkeeper from the Midwest who has retired early to California for his health. Faye, disappointed by her own lack of success in the film industry, takes out her frustrations on Simpson and treats him with great cruelty, inviting potential rivals (including a cowboy from Arizona and a young Mexican) to live in Simpson's garage. Eventually, she leaves Simpson after a drunken party at which her admirers fight over her. The various segments of the plot converge in a final apocalyptic scene during which a crowd gathered for a movie première turns to bloody mob violence after the distraught Simpson goes berserk and murders Adore (Jackie Earle Haley), a child film star of ambiguous gender, who has been taunting him. Simpson is then set upon by the crowd, which begins mindlessly to attack and destroy everything in sight. Tod vainly attempts to save Simpson, then is overwhelmed by a sense that the scene is enacting a painting he has been working on through much of the film. In the aftermath of the riot, Tod leaves Hollywood.

*The Day of the Locust* indicts not only the film industry, but all of Los Angeles, as a land of duplicity and inauthenticity. Both are, in fact, part of a nightmare realm dominated by images of commodified sex and violence and inhabited by grotesquely dehumanized victims of the American dream factory. Moreover, this characterization becomes not a bizarre deviation from the norm of American life but the ultimate expression of it. Indeed, *The Day of the Locust* depicts Hollywood as the epitome of an American capitalist system that generates desire through the presentation of beautiful images, then drives individuals to violence and despair when they discover that these desires can never be realized. *Screenplay:* Waldo Salt. *Selected bibliography:* Barnard; Raban; Jerome E. Rapf.

*NASHVILLE:* DIR. ROBERT ALTMAN (1975). *Nashville,* widely considered one of the most important American films of the 1970s, is an impressive satire that uses a critical examination of Nashville's country music industry to comment on the violence, greed, apathy, and rampant commodification that Altman sees as characteristic of 1970s American society as a whole. The film focuses on the activities of twenty-four different major characters, most of them involved in the music business, carefully weaving their separate stories into a coherent fabric. It is essentially a slice of Nashville life, following the various characters during several days of relatively normal activity toward the film's conclusion, in which most of them come together during a free concert being held in Nashville's Centennial Park to promote the presidential campaign of third-party candidate Hall Phillip Walker, a populist with no coherent political philosophy other than dissatisfaction with the status quo.

As a result of this structure, which is surprisingly effective, *Nashville* is really more a series of character sketches than a narrative. Many of the characters are successful country music performers, some of whom can be related to actual country stars, though it is probably better to see them as representing types rather than specific individuals. These country stars include the cynical, corrupt, and self-promoting Haven Hamilton (Henry Gibson); the frail, earnest Barbara Jean (Ronee Blakley); the ambitious and back-biting Connie White (Karen Black); and the black man made good, Tommy Brown (Timothy Brown). There are also would-be stars, including Albuquerque (Barbara Harris), who has some talent, but cannot seem to get a chance to use it, and Sueleen Gay (Gwen Welles), who has no talent whatsoever and is eventually reduced to stripping before an audience of leering businessmen (played largely by members of the actual Nashville Chamber of Commerce) in order to get a forum in which to sing. Altman also indicates the way in which, by the mid-1970s, the Nashville music industry was already extending its scope beyond traditional country music. He thus includes Tom, Bill, and Mary, a trio of pop-folk singers, who are recording in Nashville. The three form a romantic triangle as well, with Tom (Keith Carradine) regularly bedding Mary (Christina Raines), who is the wife of Bill (Allan Nicholls). Tom seduces every other woman he can get his hands on as well, including Opal (Geraldine Chaplin), an absurd British radio journalist who has come to report on the Nashville scene for the BBC, and Linnea Reese (Lily Tomlin), a formerly virtuous suburban wife and would-be gospel singer.

The principal narrative thread that holds most of the individual stories together involves the efforts of political consultants John Triplette (Michael Murphy) and Linnea's husband, Delbert Reese (Ned Beatty), to recruit various performers for Walker's Centennial Park concert. They have considerable success and manage to recruit even such major stars as Haven Hamilton and Barbara Jean, though none of the performers have any real commitment to Walker's candidacy. Instead, Hamilton sees the concert as an opportunity for self-promotion, while Barbara Jean's unscrupulous manager-husband, Barnett (Allen Garfield), sees it as a chance for his wife to re-establish her stardom after a recent nervous breakdown. The concert is performed on the steps of one of Nashville's most bizarre landmarks, the Parthenon, a postmodern simulacrum, full-scale and completely restored, of the Parthenon of Athens. Hamilton and Barbara Jean open the concert beneath a huge American flag, only to be interrupted when Kenny Fraiser (David Hayward), a mysterious figure who has floated through the entire film, emerges from the audience and shoots both performers, apparently killing Barbara Jean. The two victims are rushed off the stage, and momentary chaos ensues. Tellingly, however, the concert goes on without missing a beat. Albuquerque, seizing her opportunity, grabs the mike and launches into a bluesy rendition of the film's theme song, "It Don't Worry Me." The performance is highly successful. She is soon joined by a gospel choir on hand for the concert, while the audience claps and sings along, demonstrating the "waning of affect" that Fredric Jameson sees as principal characteristic of postmodern society. They are, in fact, almost entirely unaffected by the shootings, which have, after all, become common events in mid-1970s America.

*Nashville* is a compelling film that has an almost documentary quality, partly because it includes so many actual musical performances by its actors, who in general both wrote and performed their own songs. Some of the songs are highly successful, and Carradine's "I'm Easy" became a major hit and won an Oscar for best original song. However, many in Nashville found the film unrealistic and were understandably upset by Altman's characterizations of the country music industry, which are certainly exaggerated. But exaggeration is the typical mode of satire.

Moreover, the target of the satire in *Nashville* is not country music, but the destruction of country music by the country music industry. It is a film not about the tawdriness of Southern culture, but about the ways in which modern American capitalism has conscripted country music, removing it from its authentic folk roots and making it just another thoroughly commodified capitalist enterprise. Subsequent events in the history of country music, which is now virtually indistinguishable from mainstream pop music except that its practitioners occasionally wear cowboy hats, have proved Altman's point. The Nashville music industry now flourishes, in terms of profits, as never before. But there is little connection between the rough-hewn old-style country music of Hank Snow or Loretta Lynn and the high-tech electric blues of Travis Tritt and Wynonna or the slickly produced pop megahits of Garth Brooks and Shania Twain. **Screenplay:** Joan Tewkesbury. **Selected bibliography:** Baker; Christensen; Feineman; Kagan (*American Skeptic*); Keyssar; O'Brien; Plecki; Ryan and Kellner.

*ONE FLEW OVER THE CUCKOO'S NEST:* DIR. MILOS FORMAN (1975). Highlighted by Jack Nicholson's bravura performance as the rebellious McMurphy and Louise Fletcher's cold-hearted turn as the sinister Nurse Ratched, *One Flew Over the Cuckoo's Nest* is one of the most memorable films of the 1970s. The film begins as McMurphy, by feigning insanity, manages to get himself transferred from a prison work detail to a mental hospital. But, in what might almost be a direct enactment of Michel Foucault's comments on the carceral nature of institutions such as hospitals, McMurphy finds that conditions in the hospital are even more oppressive than those in the prison. Placed in a ward under the supervision of Nurse Ratched, McMurphy finds that every aspect of his life and the lives of the other inmates of the ward is closely supervised and regulated. In response, he intentionally antagonizes the nurse, leading at one point to his pacification through electroshocks to his brain.

McMurphy's subversion of Nurse Ratched's authority is thus rather ineffectual, though he does manage to trigger the beginnings of independent thought in some of the other previously submissive patients, including the huge and powerful Native American, Chief Bromden (Will Sampson), previously thought incapable of lucid human communication. McMurphy's activities culminate in the wild Christmas party he organizes in the ward in the absence of Nurse Ratched, complete with booze and women brought in from the outside. When Nurse Ratched returns the next morning, she finds the ward littered with the detritus of the party, including hungover patients. She also discovers Billy Bibbit (Brad Dourif), a young man crippled more by shyness and his domineering mother than by any sort of insanity, in flagrante with one of the women.

When the nurse announces that she is going to inform Billy's mother, he becomes frantic and kills himself. In response, McMurphy attacks Nurse Ratched and nearly chokes her to death before an orderly intervenes. McMurphy is taken away, and, in the next scene, the ward has returned to its former peaceful state, though the patients are still wondering what happened to McMurphy. That night, McMurphy is brought back to the ward, a lobotomized vegetable. Chief Bromden, realizing what has happened, suffocates McMurphy with a pillow to end his suffering. He then breaks out of the hospital and escapes into the night.

The antiauthoritarian orientation of *One Flew Over the Cuckoo's Nest* is abundantly clear, though the criticism is aimed less at capitalism and class society than at any sort of institutional authority that would seem to repress sexuality or other "natural" impulses. The film thus grows out of the political climate of the 1960s and was indeed based on a novel by Ken Kesey, one of the high priests of the 1960s counterculture. But, countercultural tendencies aside, the film was popular with mainstream audiences and critics, winning five Academy Awards, including best picture, best director, best adapted screenplay, best actor (Nicholson), and best actress (Fletcher). As Ryan and Kellner note, much of the film's popularity can be attributed to its focus on a central, rebellious, male protagonist, in high Hollywood style (24). *Screenplay:* Lawrence Hauben and Bo Goldman. *Selected bibliography:* Billingsley and Palmer; Foucault; Robert Ray; Ryan and Kellner; Safer; Slater; Zubizarreta.

*SHAMPOO:* **DIR. HAL ASHBY (1975).** *Shampoo* features Warren Beatty as George Roundy, a Beverly Hills hairdresser, who uses his job to meet an endless stream of women and thus to provide fodder for his boundless sexual appetites. As he explains late in the film, "I fucked them all. That's what I do. That's why I went to beauty school." But the action of the film occurs on the day of Richard Nixon's first election to the presidency in November 1968, thus setting Roundy's 1960s-style promiscuity against a looming turn toward conservatism in America. Indeed, the entire film is structured around this opposition between a conservative Republican desire to get down to business and a hedonistic desire to pursue pure physical pleasure.

The contrast between these two groups is dramatized in the opposed election night parties that provide the centerpiece of the film. The Republicans gather in tuxedoes at a fancy restaurant, cheering returns that show Nixon in the lead, while watching Spiro Agnews's pompous televised moralizing, a moralizing the post-Watergate audience of the film already knows to be hypocritical. At the other party, a younger, but still obviously affluent, group cavorts in a cascade of sex and drugs, oblivious to the election returns and their ominous implications. But, as it turns out, the Republicans are just as hedonistic as their free-spirited critics, while the free spirits are not only political irresponsible, but, deep down, are just as materialistic as the Republicans. Thus, while *Shampoo* is certainly critical of the hypocrisy and greed of American business, it is equally critical of that strand in 1960s politics that tended to employ drug-taking and sexual permissiveness as a form of political protest, a form that, in *Shampoo*, is figured as pointless, ineffectual, and hypocritical in its own right.

The film's political opposition is to some extent personified in the contrast between Roundy and the other main male character, Lester Carr (Jack Warden), a rich Republican businessman. However, the opposition ultimately collapses amid a flurry of sexual activity and confusion. Roundy has a semi-steady relationship with Jill (Goldie Hawn), an aspiring actress, but is having an affair with Felicia Carr (Lee Grant), Lester's wife. In the meantime, he pursues sexual liaisons with virtually every woman he meets, including Lorna (Carrie Fisher), the teenage daughter of Lester and Felicia. Lester, on the other hand, is in the midst of an affair with Jackie Shawn (Julie Christie), the ex-mistress of Roundy. Lester thus shares Roundy's sexual adventurousness, if on a smaller scale. Roundy, on a smaller scale, shares Lester's desire to succeed in business.

Indeed, many of the film's plot complications occur because Roundy is lobbying Lester for a business loan so that he can start his own salon. It is through his suit of Lester that Roundy renews his acquaintance with Jackie. Thus, while pursuing the loan from Lester, Roundy is nailing (his word) both Lester's wife and his mistress, at the same time allaying Lester's suspicions by pretending to be gay. In the process, however, Roundy concludes that he truly loves Jackie and wants to settle down with her. The film appears headed toward a typical Hollywood conclusion as he tearfully proposes marriage. But *Shampoo* is no typical Hollywood romance. Jackie declines the offer because she already has a proposal from Lester, who has broken up with Felicia. Money triumphs over love, or at least sex, and the film ends as Jackie goes away with Lester in his Rolls, while the lonely Roundy sadly looks on from the hills above. This ending, of course, does more than challenge Hollywood stereotypes. As Ryan and Kellner nicely put it, "The failure of romance is associated with the success of conservative capitalism and the undermining of human relationships" (153). In addition, the film's ending figures the inadequacy of sex as a weapon against capitalism, thus suggesting the political impotence of 1960s-style sexual subversion. *Screenplay:* Robert Towne and Warren Beatty. *Selected bibliography:* Biskind (*Easy Riders*); Christensen; Leibman; Ryan and Kellner.

**BOUND FOR GLORY: DIR. HAL ASHBY (1976).** *Bound for Glory* narrates the rise of folk singer Woody Guthrie (played by David Carradine), beginning in 1936 in the dying dust-bowl town of Pampa, Texas, and ending as he heads for New York and fame. In between, the film, loosely based on Guthrie's 1943 memoir of the same title, presents a cross-section of America during the Depression, as Guthrie, an itinerant farm worker, faith healer, and sign painter, rides the rails to California looking for work picking fruit. Along the way, the film presents some fine land-scapes, contributing to cinematographer Haskell Wexler's winning of an Academy Award for the film. Agricultural work in California, Guthrie finds, is poorly paid and hard to come by, but he does get his start in show business, singing on a local radio program that stars country singer Ozark Bule (Ronny Cox). Bule also introduces Guthrie to the plight of California's migrant farm workers, whom he is helping to form a union to resist the brutal exploitation they have been suffering at the hands of large farming interests. Guthrie's political consciousness is quickly galvanized by the plight of the farm workers, and he becomes involved in the union effort as well. This new political commitment is sometimes an obstacle to Guthrie's burgeoning singing career, as he continually resists the pressure to make his music more commercial and less politi-cal. But his faith in and devotion to common working people is also central to what makes his music special as an expression of the point of view of the poor and disenfranchised. As the film ends, Guthrie decides to forego lucrative commercial opportunities in Los Angeles and instead goes back on the road, heading for New York, where there are, after all, "people and unions" and thus an audience for his music.

Clearly influenced by *The Grapes of Wrath*, *Bound for Glory* puts more emphasis on the plight of the California farm workers than does Guth-rie's memoir, which spreads its emphasis over his wanderings around the country, meeting all sorts of poor people who help to inspire his radical politics and to whom his music will ultimately give a voice. Meanwhile, it is clearly the evolution of Guthrie's music that provides the real center of the film. At that, the film focuses on Guthrie's best-known songs, including the title track and the classic "This Land Is Your Land," leaving out some of his more radical music, such as those con-tained on the album *Ballads of Sacco and Vanzetti*, recorded somewhat later than the period covered by the film, just after World War II. The film also pays far too much attention to Guthrie's personal relationships, such as his troubled marriage to his wife, Mary (Melinda Dillon), and his courtship of a rich woman, Pauline (Gail Strickland). Such experiences, the detailed narration of which may account for the 147-minute length of a film that narrates only a small portion of Guthrie's career, are not, of course, what makes Guthrie special; apparently director Ashby felt that such material would humanize Guthrie and increase the interest of audiences accustomed to films that focus on personal relationships. Still, the film would surely have profited by paying more attention to Guthrie's music and politics and less to his personal life. *Screenplay:* Robert Getchell. *Selected bibliography:* Guthrie (*Born to Win*); Guthrie (*Bound for Glory*); Hampton; Joe Klein; Yates; Yurchenco and Guthrie.

*BUFFALO BILL AND THE INDIANS, OR SITTING BULL'S HISTORY LESSON:* DIR. ROBERT ALTMAN (1976). Released in July 1976, in the midst of the Bicentennial celebrations, *Buffalo Bill and the Indians* is one of the most radical assaults on the mythology of America in all of American film. Focusing on the show "Buffalo Bill's Wild West," an extravagant staging of the mythology of the American West that was one of America's most successful show-business phenomena before the advent of the film industry, the film demonstrates the element of theater and spectacle that was central to the mythologization not only of the West, but of America as a whole. Buffalo Bill is presented in the film as pompous, preening, and self-absorbed, so obsessed with his own image that he is beginning to lose the ability to distinguish between reality and his own intentionally fabricated images. Bill, played at just the right pitch by Paul Newman, is a drunk who has only one drink a day (in a huge schooner) and a womanizer who consorts only with opera singers, thus enhancing the air of theatricality that already surrounds him. Even Bill's famous long hair is fake, as is, one suspects, much of the patriotic rhetoric with which he seeks to present himself as the quintessential American hero — as a sort of allegorical representative of the American national identity. Given his allegorical status, the implications of Bill's fabricated image are huge. As one of his admirers suggests, "It's a man like that made this country what it is today."

Set in 1885, when Buffalo Bill's Wild West, founded in 1883, was just hitting its stride, the film devotes a great deal of its time to scenes from the show, which is rousing entertainment, but which also represents an extremely staged and stylized version of the West, despite its claims to historical authenticity. As the film begins, the famous Sioux chief, Sitting Bull (Frank Kaquitts), is about to join the show, as he in fact did for a period during 1885 and 1886. Much of the film is structured around an opposition between Buffalo Bill, as charlatan and simulacrum, and Sitting Bull, a genuine hero, whose quiet dignity stands in sharp contrast to the superficial showmanship of Buffalo Bill. By extension, the traditional culture of the Sioux is suggested as an authentic alternative to the fabricated and commodified culture of modern America. Sitting Bull, as it turns out, has joined the show not in quest of wealth or fame, but as an attempt to help his people, of whom only a little over one hundred remain after recent massacres at the hands of the American military. For one thing, he hopes to use his income from the show to provide blankets and other needed supplies to his people. For another, he hopes to parlay his participation in the show into an audience with U.S. President Grover

Cleveland (Pat McCormick), to whom he hopes to plead the case of his people.

Not surprisingly, tensions immediately flare between Bill and Sitting Bull, who objects to the show's falsification of history and in particular to Bill's plan to restage the massacre of General Custer and his men at Little Big Horn as a case of cowardly betrayal on the part of the Sioux. Sitting Bull, instead, suggests an authentic restaging of a massacre of the inhabitants of a peaceful Sioux village by the U.S. Cavalry. Moreover, as if Bill did not have enough problems, writer Ned Buntline (Burt Lancaster), whose dime novels were primarily responsible for creating the myth of Buffalo Bill in the first place, shows up at the camp and refuses to leave when Bill, not wishing to be reminded of the origins of his myth, tries to get rid of him. Buntline plays a marginal, but crucial, role in the film, providing commentary that indicates the manufactured nature of Bill's celebrity and, by extension, American celebrity as whole. As he tells Bill when he finally agrees to leave, late in the film, "It was the thrill of my life to have invented you."

Finally, Bill agrees to let Sitting Bull participate in the show by simply riding his pony alone about the arena, assuming that such a no-frills performance will lead audiences to jeer and humiliate the proud chief. Instead, Sitting Bull's regal presence wins the day, and the crowd cheers him wildly, confounding Bill, who looks on. Sitting Bull then turns out to be prescient as well, as President Cleveland, in the midst of a honeymoon trip, arrives with his new bride and asks for a command performance of the show. But the president is a pompous buffoon with a tendency to spouting empty platitudes of the kind favored by Bill. Cleveland refuses even to hear Sitting Bull's request, rejecting it as impossible to meet even without knowing what it is.

Soon afterward, word comes that Sitting Bull has been found dead. (In reality, Sitting Bull was assassinated in 1890, several years after leaving the show.) That night, Bill sees a vision of the chief and tries to explain and justify himself to the apparition; clearly, there is a level at which Bill understands the complete inauthenticity of his image and everything it represents. Nevertheless, the show goes on. The next day, Bill adds a new routine in which he easily defeats Sitting Bull, now played by his former interpreter, William Halsey (Will Sampson), in hand-to-hand combat. The crowd cheers wildly at this allegorization of genocide, and the film ends with a close-up of Bill/Newman, with blue eyes shining and perfect teeth gleaming, a perfect vision of the star as con man.

*Buffalo Bill and the Indians* was largely shunned by audiences and bashed by critics, with Daniel O'Brien's description of it as "a dull disappointment, a failed attempt to add a note of subversion to the patriotic celebrations of America's Bicentennial year" being a typical critical judgment (69–70). It is, however, a riotously funny and highly entertaining piece that nevertheless makes a number of crucial points about the mythologization of the American past and the founding of the American national identity on the Madison Avenue-like conversion of genocide into heroism. The choice of Buffalo Bill and his show as the focal point for this message was perfect, though many audiences in 1976 were probably unaware of the extent to which Bill, in his heyday, really did come to be known as the embodiment of the American national identity. Moreover, as Richard Slotkin notes, Bill's image referred not just to the past, but to the future, setting the stage for the conquest of the West in the nineteenth century to serve as the paradigm for American imperialist expansion around the globe in the twentieth century. *Screenplay:* Robert Altman and Alan Rudolph. *Selected bibliography:* Feineman; Kagan (*American Skeptic*); Keyssar; O'Brien; Russell (*Lives*); Russell (*Wild West*); Self; Slotkin.

*THE FRONT:* **DIR. MARTIN RITT (1976).** Although enlivened by numerous comic moments, *The Front* is a poignant and powerful story of the McCarthyite blacklists that blighted the American entertainment industry in the 1950s. Woody Allen is entirely convincing in the lead role of Howard Prince, an underachieving schlemiel who finally gets his chance at success when successful television writer Alfred Miller (Michael Murphy), a friend and former schoolmate, asks Prince to front for him so that he can continue to sell scripts even though he has just been blacklisted as a communist sympathizer. Prince agrees, and the arrangement is so successful that he soon begins to front for other blacklisted writers as well, making a good living from his 10 per cent cut of their fees. He also begins a romantic relationship with beautiful television producer Florence Barrett (Andrea Marcovicci), so that all in all his prospects look bright. In the meantime, comedian Hecky Brown (played by Zero Mostel, blacklisted in 1950) is fired from the television show for which Prince "writes," on evidence of minor involvement by Brown in communist activities (apparently in an attempt to seduce a woman who was a communist). However, Brown is given a chance to redeem himself by spying on Prince, and, his once thriving career now in ruins, he agrees to do so, though with great misgivings.

As the film nears its conclusion, Prince is called to testify in a private executive session before a subcommittee of the House Un-American Activities Committee (HUAC). The network urges him to cooperate, assuring him that the committee merely wants a pro forma statement of his loyalty to America and opposition to communism. By this time, political pressure has also forced Barrett to leave the show, and Prince, though apolitical, is growing increasingly offended by the intrusions of the committee into the lives of innocent Americans. Nevertheless, he is tempted to cooperate with the committee to a point, if only to protect the writers for whom he is fronting. Then, as the time for Prince's testimony nears, Brown commits suicide, as did real-life performer Philip Loeb (blacklisted for such atrocious activities as signing a petition to end segregation in professional baseball), on whom the character of Brown is partly based (Navasky 341). Prince then goes before the committee determined to defeat their questioning with clever evasions, but their insistence that he name names (including that of Brown) makes him furious. He denounces the committee's activities, tells them to go fuck themselves, and angrily leaves the room. In the final scene, he is being taken to prison for contempt, a hero to Barrett and to a crowd of demonstrators who are protesting on his behalf.

*The Front* is convincing in its presentation of the destruction of the lives of innocent Americans during the McCarthyite purges. It is also convincing in its portrayal of the political climate of fear and intimidation that allowed such destruction to continue for years, despite its obvious injustice and illegality. The film is particularly good in its portrayal of the activities of HUAC as a pure quest for power, with the attempt to defend America against communism as a mere pretext. Of course, much of the authenticity of the film probably arises from the fact that many of its principals were themselves victims of the blacklist, including director-producer Ritt and screenwriter Walter Bernstein, who was also the author of an important 1996 memoir about the blacklist. In addition to Mostel, cast members Herschel Bernardi, Lloyd Gough, and Joshua Shelley were also blacklist victims. *Screenplay:* Walter Bernstein. *Selected bibliography:* Walter Bernstein; Bessie; Caute (*Great Fear*); Ceplair and Englund; Navasky.

*HARLAN COUNTY, U.S.A.:* **DIR. BARBARA KOPPLE (1976).** *Harlan County, U.S.A.* is a powerful and compelling documentary that was deservedly awarded the Oscar for best documentary feature of 1976. Using footage of events as they actually occurred, the film documents a 1973–74 strike of Harlan County, Kentucky, coal miners against the Brookside Mine and its parent company, Duke Power Company, triggered when the mining company refused to honor a national contract between the United Mine Workers Union (UMW) and the Bituminous Coal Operators Association (BCOA). The film effectively shows the courage and determination of the striking miners as they stand together to resist attempts of the company to break the strike by bringing in scabs to work the mine and armed thugs to intimidate the picketers. It also shows the background of the strike, making it clear that the miners have legitimate grievances, while also detailing the tradition of labor struggles in Eastern Kentucky, a tradition that goes back to the famous and violent coal miners' strike of the early 1930s, when the area came to be known as

"Bloody Harlan." The film follows in the footsteps of the leftist docu- mentaries of the 1930s and makes an important contribution to the working-class culture of America.

Particularly important in the strike is the support given by the women of the community, as miners' wives, mothers, sisters, and girlfriends provide not only moral, but physical support, standing firm on the picket lines despite being assaulted by thugs and even fired on by machine guns. Meanwhile, the company steadfastly refuses to negotiate in good faith, forcing the union to increase the pressure by expanding the protest beyond Harlan, picketing Wall Street to encourage investors to avoid Duke Power Company stock. This effort draws national attention to the strike, and at one point miners from hundreds of miles around come to Harlan in a major demonstration of support. Veterans of the strike of the 1930s lend their support as well, including Florence Reese, who partici- pates in a rally, singing the famous union song "Which Side Are You On?" that she composed in support of the earlier strike. Eventually, company attempts at intimidation lead to the shooting death of a pick- eter, after which the company, with national attention focused on the killing, is finally forced to reach an agreement with the union, ending the strike, which has at this point lasted more than a year.

Reese's song, part of a soundtrack that includes a number of local la- bor songs, helps to create a sense of the folk culture of Eastern Kentucky and of the participation of this culture in the lives of the miners. It also helps, as the title indicates, the reinforce the clear sense of class struggle that informs the strike. The film then ends with a sort of prologue that reminds viewers that a single successful strike can hardly end this class struggle. The national contract that the Brookside Mine finally accepts soon expires, and the UMW, under its new reform-minded president, Arnold Miller, is forced to call a national strike in an effort to get a new contract. Another strike occurs in 1975 to protest company violations of that new contract, and still another strike occurs in 1976, as the film is being prepared for distribution, to protest court interference in labor- management relations in the coal industry. The miners fight on in their quest for social and economic justice, while the companies fight on in their quest for higher profits. Director Kopple extended her documenta- tion of this struggle into the meatpacking industry in the 1992 film, *American Dream*. **Screenplay:** Barbara Kopple. **Selected bibliography:** Lynda Ann Ewen; Fred Harris; Hevener; Rosenthal; Scott; Zaniello.

**HOLLYWOOD ON TRIAL: DIR. DAVID HELPERN, JR. (1976).** *Holly- wood on Trial* is an effective documentary that details the HUAC investi- gations of Hollywood in the late 1940s and 1950s, as well as the blacklists that followed these inquiries. The film begins by establishing the back- ground of the purges in the labor activism of the 1930s, a phenomenon that included the unionization of most trades in Hollywood. It thus becomes clear that the HUAC hearings, like much of the anticommunist hysteria of the post-World War II years, were at least partly motivated by a desire on the part of American business to undo the gains made by organized labor in the 1930s and during World War II.

Most of the film focuses on the Hollywood Ten (Alvah Bessie, Herbert Biberman, Lester Cole, Edward Dmytryk, Ring Lardner, Jr., Howard Lawson, Albert Maltz, Samuel Ornitz, Adrian Scott, and Dalton Trumbo), including extensive footage from their actual uncooperative appearances before the committee in 1947, appearances that eventually led to their arrest, imprisonment, and blacklisting. The film also includes later interviews with many of the ten, including Bessie, Cole, Dmytryk, Lardner, Maltz, and Trumbo, who look back on their experience of persecution, imprisonment, and blacklisting, as the film seeks to explore the human price paid by these individuals for their resistance to the illegal inquiries of the committee. Dmytryk, of course, paid the smallest price, avoiding the blacklist by repudiating the Left after his prison term. But the other members of the ten remained officially unemployable for years

The film also details the opportunistic reaction of Hollywood's right wing to the climate of fear and intimidation provoked by the HUAC investigations and the subsequent blacklist. For example, the film includes footage from preposterous anticommunist films such as *The Red Menace* (1949), produced by Hollywood to demonstrate a repudiation of the leftist inclinations with which the film industry was being charged. In this sense, the film's principal villain is Ronald Reagan, whose various filmed comments endorsing the purges and blacklist reveal a genius for making ludicrous, but sinister and self-serving, statements that far predated the Reagan presidency. *Screenplay:* Arnie Reisman. *Selected bibliography:* Caute (*Great Fear*); Ceplair and Englund; Dick (*Radical Innocence*); Navasky.

**NETWORK: DIR. SIDNEY LUMET (1976).** *Network* is a scathing and viciously cynical commentary on the debased and thoroughly commodified nature of American culture in the postmodern era of late capitalism. Anticipating the tabloidization of the news that has become an increasingly obvious feature of American television programming in the 1990s, the film focuses on the willingness of a television network to stoop to any level of exploitation in the interest of higher ratings. At the same time, it conducts a thorough critique of the global capitalist system of which this unscrupulous network is merely a symptom.

The film begins as long-time network news anchor Howard Beale (Peter Finch) is fired from the United Broadcasting System (UBS) because of falling ratings. He then goes on the air, announces his "retirement," and informs his audience that he plans to commit suicide on the air during his last broadcast, one week thence. Network officials are horrified, but he is given a chance to go back on the air the next night to issue a more dignified farewell. Instead, he announces that he just "ran out of bullshit" and decided to start being honest with his audience for a change. To the surprise of network executives, this approach seems to be a great success with the viewing audience, and ratings begin to rise. Beale is allowed to stay on the air as a regular commentator, railing against the sad state of American civilization and adopting the slogan, which becomes a national catch-phrase, "I'm as mad as hell, and I'm not going to take it any more!"

Ratings soar, especially after programming executive Diana Christensen (Faye Dunaway) takes over the production of the news show, converting it into increasingly tawdry entertainment. Max Schumacher (William Holden), president of the news division of UBS and a long-time friend of Beale, who has clearly become insane, protests this exploitation of Beale and the general commodification of the news. As a result, Schumacher is fired, and UBS continues to cash in on Beale's increasingly insane ravings, which become the top-rated act on television. Then Beale goes too far and rails against a deal in which the parent company of UBS is about to be acquired by Saudi Arabian oil interests, injecting badly needed capital into the company. He declares the deal a threat to American democracy and urges his audience to write to the White House in protest.

Beale is then called on the carpet by Arthur Jensen (Ned Beatty), chairman of the board of the parent corporation. Jensen, in thundering tones, lectures Beale on the new world of global capitalism, which he describes as the "multinational dominion of dollars" in which "there is no America. There is no democracy. There is only IBM and ITT and AT&T, and Dupont, Dow, Union Carbide, and Exxon." "The world," he tells Beale, "is a business," in which only profit matters and in which nations and ideologies are irrelevant. The deranged Beale treats Jensen's diatribe as a sort of message from God, then goes back on the air preaching the gospel of global capitalism. Audiences find his arguments that we are now in a postnational and postindividualist age depressing, and ratings plummet. When Jensen insists that Beale be left on the air to deliver this message regardless of ratings, ruthless UBS chief Frank Hackett (Robert Duvall) conspires with Christensen to have Beale assassinated on the air by members of the Ecumenical Liberation Army (ELA), an ultraleftist terrorist group that UBS has already appropriated, turning their activities into a weekly television series.

In addition to this main plot, the film also features the obligatory romantic subplot, though its presentation of the romance between Christensen and Schumacher hardly conforms to the conventions of Hollywood romance. Despite their professional disagreements, Schumacher, aging in search of one last burst of passion before he recedes into old age, falls in love with the cold-blooded Christensen, who for her part seems incapable of real passion. Predictably, their relationship soon collapses, and Schumacher returns to his wife, but not before he delivers an assessment of Christensen that is also an indictment of the late capitalist culture of which she is a product. "You're television incarnate," he tells her. "Indifferent to suffering, insensitive to joy. All of life is reduced to the common rubble of banality. ... You even shatter the sensations of time and space into split seconds and instant replays."

In many ways, *Network*'s indictment of global capitalist society provides a striking anticipation of the more theoretically coherent discussions of late capitalism and postmodernism in the work of Marxist critic Fredric Jameson, though the UBS appropriation of the ELA and of communist Laureen Hobbs (Marlene Warfield) cynically suggests that the ability of capitalism to conscript any and all opposition for its own purposes goes beyond even that attributed to it by Jameson, who considers socialism the one point of view that cannot be appropriated by capitalism. Interestingly, the film is a perfect example of the appropriative power of capitalism. *Network* is a powerful critique of the dehumanizing consequences of late capitalism and of the complicity of the media and popular culture in that phenomenon. Yet the film was produced by a large corporation (MGM) and was a major critical and commercial hit, winning four Oscars and being nominated for six others. It thus, if inadvertently, demonstrated the ability of capitalism to turn a profit even from the criticism of capitalism. *Screenplay:* Paddy Chayefsky. *Selected bibliography:* Christensen; Jameson (*Postmodernism*); Ryan and Kellner.

*TAXI DRIVER:* DIR. MARTIN SCORSESE (1976). Although highly controversial for what some saw as a celebration of violence (especially after it apparently played a central role in inspiring John Hinckley to attempt to assassinate President Ronald Reagan in 1981), *Taxi Driver* is a much respected film that made major Hollywood figures of director Scorsese and star Robert De Niro. A study in alienation that recalls the earlier tradition of the film noir, *Taxi Driver* follows Vietnam vet Travis Bickle (De Niro) as he becomes an all-night taxi driver in an attempt to deal with his insomnia. In this job, he sees the New York streets at their worst, increasing his sense of disgust at the world around him. Through Bickle's eyes, we see the dark side of contemporary society, meeting a variety of capitalism's outcasts, misfits, and losers. Eventually, Bickle turns to violence as an expression of his growing rage, but, tellingly, he receives nothing but accolades from the society around him for this conduct.

Early in the film, Bickle spots Betsy (Cybill Shepherd), a young woman who works as a volunteer in the New York campaign office of presidential candidate Charles Palantine (Leonard Harris). Beautiful, blonde, and seemingly ethereal, Betsy seems to Bickle an island of purity in the sea of filth that he sees around him. Expressing his fascination, he is able to get her to agree to go out to a movie with him. Unfortunately, the only movies he ever attends are porno films, and when he takes Betsy to one of these, she is revolted and bolts out of the theater. He tries to resume the courtship, but she rebuffs his further advances.

In the meantime, Bickle repeatedly encounters Iris (Jodie Foster), a twelve-year-old prostitute, whom he resolves to save from the filth into which she has descended. He also acquires a collection of handguns and begins to train himself for some vaguely defined mission of violence. Still fascinated with Betsy, he seems headed for an assassination attempt on Palantine, perhaps as a misguided way of seeking Betsy's attention. But, discouraged by the Secret Service agents that surround Palantine, Bickle goes instead to Iris's neighborhood and begins a campaign of vengeance against her pimp, Sport (Harvey Keitel), and others involved in Iris's degradation. Although badly wounded, Bickle kills a total of three men in an orgy of bloody violence.

The film then jumps forward in time to the aftermath of this scene, when Bickle has recovered from his wounds and has been declared a hero in the press for his murder of the three small-time criminals. He is also a hero to Iris's parents, who have recovered their daughter as a direct consequence of the publicity surrounding the killings. In the final scene, Bickle, back at work, picks up Betsy, who now seems rather fascinated with him. But he takes her home and then drives away without even collecting a fare.

Although some felt that *Taxi Driver* endorsed its protagonist's campaign of vengeance as far more effectual than the political platitudes of Palantine, the film is fairly clear in its identification of Bickle as insane and in its suggestion that his killing of three neighborhood thugs will hardly work the kind of fundamental change he seems to be seeking. Meanwhile, in shifting the focus of Bickle's violence from Palantine to Sport, the film suddenly shifts genres, becoming not a political thriller, but a parody of right-wing celebrations of heroic individual vengeance against criminals as a means of securing law-and-order. As Robert Ray notes, the film ultimately repudiates the American "myth of regeneration through violence" (358). It is also critical of the media for celebrating Bickle's insane murders. Finally, in identifying Bickle as a veteran of Vietnam, the film suggests that the Vietnam war was enabled by this same, insane American fascination with violence as a solution to social problems. **Screenplay:** Paul Schrader. **Selected bibliography:** Biskind (*Easy Riders*); Christensen; Corrigan; Lawrence S. Freidman; Kelly;

Naremore (*More than Night*); Palmer (*Hollywood's Dark Cinema*); Robert Ray.

*UNION MAIDS:* **DIR. JAMES KLEIN, MILES MOGLESCU, AND JULIA REICHERT (1976).** Based on the account in Alice and Staughton Lynd's *Rank and File: Personal Histories by Working-Class Organizers*, *Union Maids* is a highly successful documentary that details the careers, focusing on the 1930s, of radical Chicago Congress of Industrial Organizations (CIO) union organizers Kate Hyndman, Stella Nowicki, and Sylvia Woods. Both Hyndman and Nowicki were open communists, though the importance of the Communist Party to these women (and to the CIO as a whole) is elided in the film. The radical devotion of all three women to union activism as a tool of fundamental social and economic change does come through in the film, however.

The documentary consists largely of interviews with the three women, supplemented by actual footage of the historical events they describe in their reminiscences of their lives and work. The result is an important account of the contributions of women to the labor movement of the 1930s, as well as a vivid picture of Chicago in that decade. We learn a great deal about the individual backgrounds of the three women. Hyndman grew up on a farm in Michigan and moved from there to work in the stockyards of Chicago, seeking the opportunity to move beyond conventional gender roles; Nowicki, daughter of a Garveyite black nationalist, also worked in the Chicago stockyards; and Woods, originally from New Orleans, worked in a large commercial laundry in Chicago, where she helped the black and white workers get together to organize a union. But the film also conveys the awareness of the three women that their work as individuals was part of a larger phenomenon and that their true constituency was the working class as a whole.

While there is, predictably, an almost eulogistic tone in the treatment of the bygone days of the 1930s, all three women remain committed to the work they had begun in that decade. Hyndman, for example, remains convinced that the work they did led to important changes that continue to the current day of the film. Woods optimistically sees the continuation of her work from the 1930s in the contemporary work of the women's movement of the 1970s, though she is also aware that the women's movement has sometimes tended to ignore the special problems of working women and issues of class in general. All in all, the stories of these obviously admirable women help to present 1930s radical labor activism in a very positive light. The film is an effective exercise in oral history that received considerable attention, eventually gaining an Academy Award nomination for best documentary feature. *Selected bibliography:* Benson and Strom; Lynd and Lynd; Rosenthal; Zaniello.

*JULIA:* DIR. FRED ZINNEMANN (1977). Based on an episode from Lillian Hellman's book of reminiscences, *Pentimento* (1977), *Julia* details the long-time friendship of Hellman (played by Jane Fonda) and the title character (played by Vanessa Redgrave). At the same time, the film also chronicles Hellman's early efforts as a playwright, while touching on her romantic involvement with novelist Dashiell Hammet (played by a Jason Robards, who unfortunately looks far older than the forty or so that Hammet was at the time of most of the chronicled events). Hellman and Julia are close childhood friends, and the film, which cuts back and forth between the past and the present (in the 1930s), details many of their early moments together. Eventually, Julia goes off to medical school, first at Oxford, then in Vienna, where she plans to study with Freud. Hellman, meanwhile, stays in America and works on her writing, with the encouragement and sometimes rather blunt criticism of Hammett.

Events take a dramatic turn when Julia, who has become a committed socialist despite her wealthy background, is attacked by Nazi thugs in Vienna, losing a leg as a result of her injuries. Hellman, at the time working on her writing in Paris, visits Julia in the hospital in Vienna, but her injured friend then suddenly disappears without a trace. In the subsequent years, Julia's whereabouts remain a mystery: she has gone underground to fight against the Nazis. Hellman does receives an occasional communication from her, however, meanwhile enjoying the successful run of her first play on Broadway. Then, when Hellman is again in Paris, this time on her way for a visit to the Soviet Union to observe the theater there, Hellman is contacted by Johann (Maximilian Schell), an agent working with Julia's underground group. Johann gives Hellman $50,000, which she agrees, though with considerable trepidation, to deliver to Berlin for the use of anti-Nazi resistance forces there. She successfully reaches Berlin, where she meets Julia herself and hands over the money. She also learns that Julia has a baby and agrees to let Julia send the baby to her in America for its own safety.

Hellman goes on to Moscow, where she receives word that Julia has been murdered by Nazis in Frankfurt. She returns to London, where Julia's body has been sent for burial, then conducts an extensive search in an attempt to locate Julia's baby. The search is in vain, however, and the baby must be given up for lost as all-out war erupts on the continent. *Julia* is a touching film that effectively evokes much of the atmosphere of the 1930s, though its characterization of Hellman as a political naif who lacks both the courage and the commitment of her friend Julia is somewhat misleading. The film was welcomed by most feminists, especially for its portrayal of Julia, but Ryan and Kellner are right to point out that the film, through its use of "woozy flashbacks, hazy tones, and a lace-fringed emotionality in the voice-over narration," inscribed its feminine characters "within the dominant representational code for women" (143).

*Julia* was nominated for eleven Academy Awards, winning for best adapted screenplay, while Robards and Redgrave both won Oscars for their performances in supporting roles. *Screenplay:* Alvin Sargent. *Selected bibliography:* Christensen; Hellman (*Pentimento*); McCreadie; Ryan and Kellner.

*BLUE COLLAR:* DIR. PAUL SCHRADER (1978). Although not particularly leftist in its politics, *Blue Collar* is unusual among American films in the extent to which it focuses on working-class experience, especially in the actual workplace. It also suggests that members of the working class are often exploited by powerful forces in a society that does not appreciate their contributions to it. Unfortunately, the film continues what was by then a well-established Hollywood trend by identifying the labor union that represents the workers as the most important of the forces that exploit them. It thus promulgates the insidious false impression that workers would be far better off without union representation at all. Moreover, by focusing on auto workers, the film clearly aims its indictment of unions at the United Auto Workers (UAW), though the union of the film is called the "AAW." *Blue Collar* thus labels as corrupt and ineffectual what was (and still is) one of the best-run and most successful labor unions in America.

In the film, Zeke Brown (Richard Pryor), Jerry Bartowski (Harvey Keitel), and Smokey James (Yaphet Kotto) are three buddies who work at the Checker Cab plant in Detroit. All are plagued by money troubles, and all are frustrated by the refusal of their union to represent them adequately. They thus conceive a plan to break into the safe at union headquarters, thus solving their financial woes while at the same time striking back at the union for its lack of attention to their needs. They manage to carry out the crime but come away with little cash. They do, however, wind up with an incriminating ledger that records illegal loans of union funds to various individuals in Las Vegas and elsewhere. They then decide to use the information in this book to blackmail the union.

Predictably, the three soon find that they are in over their heads. The union quickly discovers their identities, putting them all in mortal danger. Brown decides to accept a job from the union as the shop steward at their plant, both for his own protection and out of a belief that he can really change things. James, on the other hand, is murdered in a fake industrial accident. Bartowski, seeing no alternative, decides to talk to John Burrows (Cliff De Young), an FBI agent who is investigating corruption in the union. As the film ends, Brown and Bartowski are at each other's throats, each accusing the other of selling out. A voiceover then reminds us of James's earlier statement that the powers that be will do anything necessary to foster dissension within the working class. But, however powerful the potential implications of this final statement about the importance of working-class solidarity, *Blue Collar* fails adequately to explore the issues toward which it gestures. Peter Stead thus describes it as "a film that could have achieved greatness but which settled for routine entertainment" (225). *Screenplay:* Paul Schrader and Leonard Schrader. *Selected bibliography:* Christensen; Puette; Stead; Zaniello.

*COMING HOME:* **DIR. HAL ASHBY (1978).** *Coming Home* was a critical and commercial success that was nominated for eight Academy Awards, winning three, including a best actor award to Jon Voight and best actress award to Jane Fonda, who was thus forgiven for her political activities during the Vietnam War and invited back home to Hollywood. Although *Coming Home* lost the best picture Oscar to *The Deer Hunter*, it is a much finer film that at least attempts to establish a coherent political orientation, namely, one that is is antiwar, profeminist, and suspicious of the motivations of the U.S. government.

Unfortunately, however, *Coming Home* still fails to explore the real historical background of the American involvement in Vietnam, settling for a couple of vague suggestions of admiration for the courage and determination of the Vietnamese communists (without any mention of their political ideology) and for a demonstration of the high cost of the pointless war in terms of its impact on the minds and bodies of the American soldiers who served there. Although still the definitive movie of returning from Vietnam, *Coming Home* is limited by the fact that the returning veterans it follows are in unusual situations and have little or no chance of resuming their former lives. As a result, the film says little about the difficulties suffered by the hundreds of thousands of veterans who returned home physically and psychological whole enough that they could at least attempt to rejoin American society.

As the film begins, Marine Captain Bob Hyde (Bruce Dern) is being sent for a tour of duty in Vietnam, where he is anxious to go in order to fight for his country. He leaves behind his devoted and subservient wife, Sally (Jane Fonda), who struggles to cope with his absence by becoming a volunteer worker in a veterans hospital. She is joined by her friend, Viola Munson (Penelope Mitford), whose brother, Bill (Robert Carradine), is a patient in the hospital's psychiatric ward, having suffered a breakdown as a result of his experiences in Vietnam. Among other patients, Sally meets Luke Martin (Jon Voight), a Marine sergeant paralyzed from the waist down as a result of wounds suffered in Vietnam.

Consumed by horrible memories of atrocities committed by American forces in Vietnam and by the feeling that his loss was for nothing, Luke is an angry and bitter young man who gradually gets back in touch with his humanity through his growing friendship with Sally. Sally, living on her own for the first time in her life and experiencing great personal growth, especially within the political context of the late 1960s, returns his feelings of friendship. In the meantime, Bill Munson commits suicide, driving Luke to an expression of protest against the war and its effects by chaining himself and his wheelchair to the gates of a Marine recruitment center. Sally gets Luke out of jail, and the two return to his apartment, where they become lovers. The film is, by Hollywood standards, quite daring in its depiction of their lovemaking, which is fulfilling for both of them despite his paralysis. At the same time, Luke remains haunted throughout their ongoing relationship, knowing that Sally will eventually return to her husband when he comes home.

Eventually, Bob does return home, with a minor leg wound. His psychic wounds are, however, more serious. He remains distant and unable emotionally to relate to Sally, even before he discovers her previous affair with Luke. Then, in one of the film's central commentaries on the sinister activities of the U.S. government, Bob is informed of this affair by FBI agents, who have had Luke under surveillance since his arrest at the recruitment center. There are some tense moments during which Bob, clearly unstable, seems on the verge of murdering Luke, or Sally, or both. In the end, however, he kills himself. Unable to cope with civilian life, he strips off his Marine dress uniform on the beach and then swims away into the ocean, in a scene that is intercut with shots of Luke making an impassioned antiwar speech to a group of high school students. Luke thus finds, through his political activity, the meaning Bob no longer has in his life. Sally, meanwhile, will presumably survive as well, having learned important lessons about her validity as a human being apart from her marriage to Bob. *Screenplay:* Waldo Salt and Robert C. Jones, from a story by Nancy Dowd. *Selected bibliography:* Adair; Anderegg ("Hollywood and Vietnam"); Jeffords; Martin; Muse; Selig.

*THE DEER HUNTER:* DIR. MICHAEL CIMINO (1978). If Cimino's much maligned *Heaven's Gate* is not really quite as bad as its critical response would indicate, then *The Deer Hunter*, which received so much praise and so many awards, is not nearly as good as that praise would suggest. In many ways, it is a truly awful film, in which Cimino touches on a large number of important issues without really making a statement about any of them. He also displays a genuine gift for packing the film with huge amounts of material, yet still having it move at a snail's pace. The film's biggest shortcoming is its Orientalist treatment of Vietnam, depicted as an exotic land of debased pleasures, while the Vietnamese are depicted as crazed savages capable of unlimited cruelty and perversion. On the other hand, some have seen the film's focus on working-class Americans as a virtue, and it is this class emphasis that links the film to the interests of the American Left. However, the film treats the working class as unremittingly masculine (and white), while depicting working-class males mostly as drunken louts who get their pleasure primarily from drinking beer, killing animals, and beating up women.

*The Deer Hunter* begins in the steel mill town of Clairton, Pennsylvania, as three millworkers, Michael (Robert De Niro), Nick (Christopher Walken), and Steven (John Savage), prepare to depart for military service in Vietnam. The film's first segment focuses on the working-class culture of this community, beginning with scenes of camaraderie among the millworkers as they drink beer and play pool after the end of their shift. Then follows a long segment that shows the wedding ceremony and reception for Steven and his financée, Angela (Rutanya Alda). This segment again gestures toward a portrayal of the communal values of this working-class community of Slavic immigrants, but nevertheless seems largely pointless. Steven and Angela (who, we learn, is pregnant by another man) then go away for a brief honeymoon, while Mike and Nick, accompanied by friends Stan (John Cazale), John (George Dzundza), and Axel (Chuck Aspegren), go into the mountains for one last hunting trip together. Mike, who approaches deer hunting with a sort of religious reverence, bags a buck, and the five friends return to town in a drunken revel, with the deer strapped on the hood of the car.

The film then suddenly cuts to a scene of battle in Vietnam. Mike, Nick, and Steven, are all captured by the Viet Cong, who are depicted as brutal savages, taking great pleasure in devising exotic methods to torture and terrorize their prisoners. They especially enjoy forcing their prisoners to play Russian roulette, a technique that causes Steven to suffer a breakdown. However, when Mike and Nick join the game, they, as superior Americans, easily outwit and, Rambo-like, blow away their captors. They then escape, taking Steven with them, though the latter is seriously hurt in the process and ends up having to have both legs amputated. Back in Saigon, Nick recovers in a military hospital, then goes into the streets, seeking out the city's savage underworld, which, among other things, features clubs in which Russian roulette is played as a sport.

In the third segment of the film, Mike, a decorated war hero, returns to Clairton to much fanfare, most of which he attempts to avoid. Nick has gone AWOL and remained in the Saigon underworld, while Steven is in a veterans' hospital, avoiding all of his old acquaintances, including Angela. Mike becomes lovers with Nick's old girlfriend, Linda (Meryl Streep). But, with the American evacuation of Saigon underway in anticipation of the upcoming communist victory, Mike returns to Saigon to try to reclaim Nick, who has been sending money to Steven on a regular basis. The money, we discover, has been won in the Russian roulette game, in which he is a regular participant. Mike manages to locate him, only to watch him blow his brains out as his luck finally runs out in the gruesome game. The film then cuts to Nick's funeral back in Clairton, after which his friends gather to drink, toasting Nick and inanely singing "God Bless America," as the film finally, and mercifully, comes to a close in one final outburst of stupidity.

Needless to say, the film's depiction of the Vietnamese as either savage killers or passive victims has been widely criticized as an Orientalist fantasy designed to make Americans look and feel superior. In addition, the totally fabricated emphasis on the fascination of the Vietnamese with Russian roulette attempts to tap into Cold War stereotypes about savage communists to reinforce its racist stereotypes about Orientals. The participants in the game even wear red headbands, as if the anticommunist suggestions were not clear enough. As Timothy Corrigan puts it, *The Deer Hunter* "captures the way the Vietnam War is often understood today only through the exaggerations, distortions, and incoherencies that impede any accurate historical representation of that war" (14–15). Indeed, the film is, as Gilbert Adair notes, "a before-and-after advertisement for the USA" (89). As such, it is not only an insult to the people of Vietnam but a sad comment on American society, which seems able, on the evidence of this film, to promote itself only through racist diatribes against others. It says little for (but a lot about) the American film industry that *The Deer Hunter* was nominated for nine Academy Awards and won five, including those for best picture and best director. *Screenplay:* Deric Washburn. *Selected bibliography:* Adair; Corrigan; Hellmann; Michael Klein; Muse.

*GO TELL THE SPARTANS:* **DIR. TED POST (1978).** Although lacking the budget and hype of big-time Vietnam films such as *Apocalypse Now* or *The Deer Hunter*, *Go Tell the Spartans* is actually a fairly good film that illuminates certain aspects of the war that many of its better known cousins do not. In particular, *Go Tell the Spartans* is set in 1964 when Americans were supposedly serving in Vietnam only as advisors to the South Vietnamese government forces. Yet it suggests that, even at this early date, anyone who bothered to look could see that the Americans had no business in Vietnam and that their involvement there would probably be a disaster. Of course, that point might be easy to make after the fact, when the film was made, though the point still stands. For example, Graham Greene's 1955 novel, *The Quiet American*, had made this point even when it was still primarily the French (though already with American support) who were battling against the Vietnamese communists.

*Go Tell the Spartans* features Burt Lancaster as Major Asa Barker, the salty commander of a group of American military advisors in South Vietnam. Barker seems already to realize that the American presence in Vietnam is ridiculous, as can be seen from his tendency to ignore instructions from his superiors and to file fabricated intelligence reports because he knows the information will be useless, anyway. Early in the film, he is ordered to check out the abandoned hamlet of Muc Wa, site of an old French outpost. He ignores the order and files a false report, a fact of which his superior, General Hamitz (Dolph Sweet) is perfectly aware. Hamitz then orders Barker to send American advisors, along with a detachment of South Vietnamese regular army and militia, to occupy Muc Wa, even though Barker argues that this action could not possibly have any effect except to stir up trouble. But, given a direct and specific order of this kind, he has no choice but to obey, so he sends the force. "Cowboy" (Evan Kim), a fanatical hater of communists, commands the South Vietnamese troops, though he is only a sergeant. The American forces, who are clearly in charge, are headed by Lieutenant Raymond Hamilton (Joe Unger), assisted by Sergeant Oleonowski (Jonathan Goldberg) and Corporal Stephen Courcey (Craig Wasson).

On the way to the outpost, they take a Viet Cong prisoner, whom Cowboy promptly murders when he refuses to talk. Otherwise, they arrive at the outpost without difficulty, noting the inscription on the gate of the old French cemetery, which, quoting the doomed Spartans at the disastrous battle of Thermopylae, translates to "Stranger, when you find us lying here, go tell the Spartans we obeyed their orders." Once they establish control of the outpost, they almost immediately find themselves under attack by the Viet Cong. Hamilton is killed, and Barker is forced to send his right-hand man, Captain Al Olivetti (Marc Singer), to assume command of the outpost. Eventually, Barker goes there by helicopter to evacuate the Americans. Courcey, however, refuses to leave and insists on staying with the South Vietnamese, for whom there is no room on the helicopter. Resigned, Barker stays as well, and together they attempt to lead the South Vietnamese to safety on foot. They are soon overwhelmed by the Viet Cong, however, and most, including Barker, are killed. Courcey survives and staggers homeward as the film ends with the year 1964 emblazoned on the screen as a reminder of the next decade of things to come.

Among other things, Cowboy's nickname indicates the close connection of this film to the genre of the Western, with Muc Wa playing the part of the frontier outpost and the Viet Cong playing the part of the Indians. This generic mix potentially suggests a link between the genocidal extermination of Native Americans and the American assault on Vietnam. But this film makes little overt political commentary and settles mostly for a suggestion of the absurdity and hopelessness of the American involvement in support of a South Vietnamese government that is clearly unworthy of support. Cowboy's viciousness is only one characteristic of American's South Vietnamese allies in this film; they are also corrupt, undisciplined, and incompetent. Most of the American advisors are not much better, and it is quite clear that the American/South Vietnamese alliance, like the Spartans at Thermopylae, is doomed to destruction in the war. *Screenplay:* Wendell Mayes. *Selected bibliography:* Adair; Berg; Muse; Tony Williams.

*APOCALYPSE NOW:* DIR. FRANCIS FORD COPPOLA (1979). One of the most anticipated films in American cinema history, *Apocalypse Now* was initially regarded by many as a disappointment. It was nominated for Academy Awards, including best picture and best director, but won none. Over time, however, the film has come to be widely regarded as a classic. All in all, *Apocalypse Now* is probably the finest of the many films that have been made about the Vietnam War. Drawing upon Joseph Conrad's *Heart of Darkness* for its basic atmosphere and plot structure, the film is an impressive and intelligent work of cinematic art, using all of the visual and auditory resources of the medium to create a brooding atmosphere of insanity, terror, and darkness. Meanwhile, the connection to Conrad helps to initiate a number of other intertextual dialogues as well, with predecessor texts ranging from T. S. Eliot, to The Rolling Stones, to the whole genre of the American war movie. *Apocalypse Now* does little to represent the Vietnamese point of view or to explain the background of the conflict, but that is partly the point. The film depicts the American presence in Vietnam as entirely nonsensical, as an absurd exercise in metaphysical evil with little rational motivation behind it. It also effectively uses music and other images from American popular culture to suggest that this evil arises from something deep within American culture, asking viewers therefore to re-examine and re-evaluate their commitment to the American way of life. As such the film probes not only into the dark heart of the Vietnamese jungle, but into the heart of darkness of the American soul.

The film begins with apocalyptic images of explosive destruction, wrought by American helicopters as they bomb the Vietnamese jungle. Then, with the The Doors' "The End" sounding hauntingly in the background, the scene shifts to a Saigon hotel room, where an experienced American military intelligence operative, Captain Willard (Martin Sheen), awaits his next assignment and hovers near the edge of insanity. This scene helps to set the tone of basic insanity that the film sees in the American involvement in Vietnam, a motif that takes an important turn when Willard's assignment finally comes. He is to travel deep into the jungle of Cambodia to locate and assassinate Col. Walter E. Kurtz (Marlon Brando), a Green Beret officer who has supposedly gone insane and begun to use "unsound methods," including the murder of South Vietnamese army officers suspected of complicity with the enemy. From the beginning, Willard sees something suspect about the assignment. Insanity, after all, is the norm in Vietnam. Moreover, Willard thinks to himself, "Charging a man with murder in this place is like handing out speeding tickets at the Indy 500." Perhaps, then, the real danger of Kurtz is not that he violates American policy in Vietnam, but that he reveals the nature of that policy all too clearly.

To reach Kurtz, Willard is to go up the Nung River on a Navy small patrol, manned by a crew that includes its Chief (Albert Hall); Chef (Frederic Forrest), a saucier from New Orleans; Lance (Sam Bottoms), a famous surfer from Southern California, and Mr. Clean (a young Laurence Fishburne), a teenage slum kid from the South Bronx. First, however, they must get into the river, the mouth of which is heavily guarded by enemy forces. This problem is solved with the aid of an Air Cavalry unit commanded by the memorable Lieutenant Colonel Kilgore (Robert Duvall), who has a passionate love for killing and for surfing. He combines the two as his helicopters assault an enemy-controlled village at the mouth of the river, blasting away at the terrified villagers as Wagner's "The Ride of the Valkyries" sounds from a loud-speaker mounted on Kilgore's helicopter. There is something definitely postmodern about this weird musical accompaniment, which converts the attack into sheer spectacle, but the choice of Wagner also potentially links the American assault to the genocidal legacy of German Nazism. Then, as the village is still being subdued, with the help of fighter planes dropping napalm (the smell of which Kilgore loves in the morning), Kilgore tops matters off by ordering Lance and several other surfers in his unit to grab their boards and head out into the water to take advantage of the excellent surfing conditions.

The basic absurdity of this scene combines with the tragic impact of the attack on the people of the village to comprise one of the film's central comments on the nature of the American involvement in Vietnam. The bulk of the film then presents the trip up the river, as the boat moves deeper and deeper into the heart of the dark, menacing jungle, while Willard reads Kurtz's dossier and muses on the object of his quest. In this sense, *Apocalypse Now* parallels Conrad quite closely, providing important reminders of the close historical parallel between the European colonial conquest of Africa in the late nineteenth century and the imperialist assault on Vietnam by American troops a century later. Along the way, Willard and the other men on the boat encounter a variety of scenes that gradually reinforce the film's mood of strangeness and insanity. In one scene that makes a rather obvious statement about the violent and sexist nature of American popular culture, they stop at an American base where Playboy Playmates dance, using guns as obviously phallic props, on stage as part of a U.S.O. show. The show is a great hit, though the reaction of the men suggests a certain amount of misogynist hostility, as when Lance expresses his "approval" of the moves of one of the dancers by yelling, "You fucking bitch!" Eventually, the aroused men rush the stage, and the endangered Playmates have to flee by helicopter, no doubt leaving the soldiers to take out their sexual frustration (and aggression) on the Vietnamese. This comment on American popular culture is reinforced by the film's use of Western popular music and by frequent allusions to Disneyland, Charles Manson, and other icons of American culture, which is thus characterized as spectacularly violent and unreal, much like the war itself.

Later, in one of the film's most horrifying scenes, the boat encounters a Vietnamese sampan coming down the river. They stop the sampan and begin to search it. Then, when a woman on board makes a sudden move to conceal something on the sampan, the Americans open fire, apparently killing all of those on board. The concealed object turns out to be a puppy, and the sampan turns out to be an innocent civilian vessel. They then discover that one woman on the sampan is still alive, and Chief orders his men to take her on board the American boat so she can be taken for medical attention. Willard, unwilling to have his mission interrupted, coldly pulls his pistol and shoots the woman, obviating the need for medical care.

Eventually, they make their way through the various strange scenes that await them and reach Kurtz's compound, the strangest scene of all. Kurtz reigns, godlike, over what is apparently an ancient temple and religious site, accompanied by his loyal Montanyard troops, who apparently regard themselves as his children. Willard and Chef go ashore into the surreal scene, and are greeted by a manic American photojournalist (Dennis Hopper), who attempts to make them understand Kurtz, whom he obviously worships. Willard is taken captive and placed in a cage, where Kurtz later presents him with Chef's head, apparently in an attempt to break his spirit. Willard is later released and allowed free access to Kurtz's quarters.

Kurtz, filmed mostly in low light that both obscures Brando's obesity and emphasizes the dark, mysterious nature of Kurtz, explains his vision to Willard, while meanwhile seeming to spend most of his time reading the poetry of T. S. Eliot, with its hints of cultural and metaphysical crisis. Willard is much taken with Kurtz, but he eventually kills him nevertheless. In a grotesque scene in which the film's generally effective mythic symbolism is a bit overdone and heavy-handed, Willard hacks Kurtz to death with a machete, intercut with scenes of the symbolic slaughter of an ox by Kurtz's "children." Kurtz and Lance then make their way back to the boat and head back down the river, as echoes of Kurtz's whispered last words, "the horror, the horror," echo in the background.

The surreal look, sound, and feel of *Apocalypse Now* might be interpreted as a sort of realism, intended to convey the experience of Vietnam more accurately than any straightforward realistic account could ever do. It is also the case, however, that the film does not attempt conventional realism and so cannot be criticized if all of its events do not seem quite credible. The film, like most American films about Vietnam, focuses on the American experience, but it does at least give some suggestion of the impact of the American presence on the Vietnamese. Some of the descriptions of the Vietnamese communist certainly border on a combination of Orientalist and Cold War stereotypes. When Kurtz expresses his admiration for the ability of the Viet Cong to commit astonishing acts of brutality in the interest of their cause, he suggests a vision of coldly fanatical Oriental communists. He does, however, at least indicate that the Viet Cong are human beings, "filled with love," and that it must require superhuman strength for .them to do some of the things they do. Nevertheless, he avoids the common sense explanation that the Viet Cong were not superhuman, but simply fought with greater resolve than the Americans because they were defending their homes, while the Americans had no idea what they were fighting for. *Screenplay:* John Milius and Francis Ford Coppola, with narration by Michael Herr. *Selected bibliography:* Cahir; Corrigan; Cowie (*Coppola*); Desser; Greiff; Hellmann; Laskowsky; Muse; Tony Williams.

*THE CHINA SYNDROME:* **DIR. JAMES BRIDGES (1979).** *The China Syndrome,* which focuses on a fictional near-disastrous accident in a nuclear power plant, was released in 1979, only weeks before the accident at the Three Mile Island plant in Pennsylvania. As such, the antinuclear message of the film gained a particular currency. However, *The China Syndrome* is really less about nuclear power than about corporate corruption and the willingness of large corporations to endanger the health and safety of the general population in their quest for larger profits. Nevertheless, the film, which essentially descends into a conventional thriller, was widely criticized for its sacrifice of political substance in the interest of entertainment value.

In the film, Jane Fonda plays Kimberly Wells, an ambitious television news personality who does cutesy features on the "California Closeup" segment of the local news on Los Angeles station KXLA. She hopes, however, to move into harder news stories, and she gets her chance when she, cameraman Richard Adams (Michael Douglas), and sound man Hector Salas (Daniel Valdez) are sent to do an innocuous feature at the Ventana Nuclear Power Plant. While they are there, the accident occurs, and disaster is averted only by the quick action of shift supervisor Jack Godell (Jack Lemmon). Adams secretly catches the entire event on film, then the crew rushes back to the station with their exclusive report. The report is squelched by station management, however. Meanwhile, the entire episode is whitewashed by the power company, which is anxious to avoid controversy because they are about to open a new plant and will lose millions should the licensing of that plant be delayed.

The government investigation of the accident is essentially a whitewash as well. Godell, however, conducts his own investigation and discovers that the accident was caused by faulty welds in a crucial pump—welds that, in order to cut costs, were never given the X-ray examinations required by regulations. Worried that these faulty welds will lead to another accident, but unable to get the power company to take any action to correct the problem, Godell conveys proof of the dangerous situation to the news crew, which is still struggling to get their report of the accident out to the public. Salas rushes this information to a hearing on the proposed new plant but is murdered on the way. Godell himself narrowly escapes death. Realizing the extent to which the company is willing to go to cover up the dangerous conditions at the plant, he decides to take desperate measures.

Godell takes over the Ventana plant's control room at gunpoint, then threatens to destroy the plant if he is not allowed to explain the situation to Wells on live television. Wells and the crew are brought in and the broadcast begins, but a SWAT team breaks into the control room and kills Godell before he can fully explain himself. The plant is shut down, nearly causing a pump failure and a consequent catastrophic accident. Nevertheless, the company continues the coverup, announcing that Godell had been insane and that all is well at the plant. Wells, however, knows the truth and puts aside her own ambitions to risk her career by broadcasting a statement by another plant worker supporting Godell's contentions. *Screenplay:* Mike Gray, T. S. Cook, and James Bridges. *Selected bibliography:* Christensen; McMullen; Ryan and Kellner.

*NORMA RAE:* DIR. MARTIN RITT (1979). *Norma Rae* was a commercial and critical success that netted two Academy Awards (including a best actress Oscar to Sally Field) and two other nominations, for best picture and best adapted screenplay. It is thus one of the most prominent films about organized labor in the history of American cinema, probably exceeded only in this sense by the anti-union *On the Waterfront*. But *Norma Rae* is avowedly pro-union. The film appropriately focuses on the Carolina textile industry, which has been the focal point of some of the most bitter labor struggles in American history—and which was involved in such a dispute (at the J. P. Stevens mills in Roanoke Rapids, North Carolina) at the time the film was made. Its sympathies are quite strongly with the textile workers and their attempt to organize, and the film is important for its focus on the title character (played by Field and based on real-life union activist Crystal Lee), thus calling attention to the centrality of women workers in this struggle. On the other hand, *Norma Rae* has a tendency to descend into romantic cliché and to portray its oppositions in terms of good versus evil rather than genuine class struggle.

The film is as much a story of Norma Rae's personal development as of the union movement in the textile mills, and much of the plot involves her growing sense of herself as a mature, responsible, and independent individual. The agent of her transformation is a Jewish northern union organizer, Reuben (Ron Leibman), who comes to town to rally the workers. He encounters considerable opposition but eventually succeeds, largely because Norma Rae sees the value of what he is doing and comes strongly to his aid. Norma Rae's work with Reuben causes her husband, Sonny (Beau Bridges), to become jealous. In the end, however, Sonny and Norma Rae are reconciled, the textile mill is unionized, and the company, which eventually attempts to drive out the union through terror tactics, is forced to give in to many of the union's demands. Norma Rae remains a leader of the local workers, and Reuben moves on to the next town where workers are being exploited due to their lack of collective representation.

In addition to the central focus on gender, *Norma Rae* is strong in its treatment of race—particularly in its recognition of the importance of solidarity between black and white workers, while the company attempts to split the workers along racial lines. The topicality of the film gives it an extra force as well. Finally, while the ultimate focus on the protagonist's private life and feelings weakens *Norma Rae* as a political film, this strategy obviously allowed the film to appeal to American audiences and thus to spread its prolabor message more widely. *Screenplay:* Irving Ravetch and Harriet Frank, Jr. *Selected bibliography:* Benson and Strom; Conway; Carlton Jackson; Leifermann; Stead; Zaniello.

*HEAVEN'S GATE:* **DIR. MICHAEL CIMINO (1980).** Notorious as one of the greatest box office disasters of all time, *Heaven's Gate* is a flawed film that is nevertheless not quite as bad as its reputation would indicate. It is, in fact, almost excellent, marked by near misses in a number of promising areas that might have made it a fine film indeed. For example, the film at least attempts to establish a number of subversive dialogues with the traditional American Western in potentially positive ways that call attention to the economic exploitation involved in the winning of the West, thus challenging the heroicization of that phenomenon in the classic Western. More critical attention should probably have been given to this dialogue, but critics instead have focused on the film's technical problems (its long length and slow pace, its noisy soundtrack that often obscures the dialogue) and on its confused attempts apparently to try to do too much. Even the film's visual effects, though often splendid, could be criticized as perhaps too splendid, serving the purpose of art for art's sake while contributing little to (or even obscuring) the movement of the plot.

Nevertheless, *Heaven's Gate* does at least attempt to address some weighty political and historical issues, something that has not always been true of big-budget Hollywood productions in the last decades of the twentieth century. The film is based on an important moment in American history, the years at the end of the nineteenth-century when settlers (many of them poor immigrants) began to move into the West in large numbers, meeting sometimes violent opposition from the wealthy cattlemen who had for years treated the region as a sort of private kingdom, having cleared it by force of its previously Native American inhabitants. There are many crucial issues at stake in this phenomenon. The class opposition between the rich cattlemen and the poor farmers and miners who attempt to supplant them is obvious, as are the implications of the support given the cattlemen by the state and federal government. Less obvious, however, are the oppositions of larger historical forces in this confrontation. In particular, though all of the power seems to be on the side of the cattlemen, history is on the side of the new settlers who are the predecessors (and the pawns) of a new wave of modernity against which the almost medieval practices of the cattlemen would ultimately prove helpless. Like contemporary immigrants in the 1990s, these immigrants of the 1890s are hated and feared, yet their presence is necessary for the continuing evolution of American capitalism. These are complex issues, and Cimino's attempt to address so many of them may account for what many have seen as the muddled quality of the picture.

*Heaven's Gate* begins with an extended scene showing the 1870 graduation celebration at Harvard College, as the sons of the American elite prepare to go forth and assume places of power in American society. Meanwhile, the beautiful daughters of that elite watch from the wings as the official parts of the ceremony proceed, looking very much like prizes waiting to be claimed by the new graduates. The scene focuses on two of the graduates, James Averill (played by Kris Kristofferson) and William C. Irvine (played by John Hurt), the class orator. There is then a sudden cut to 1890, in Wyoming, where Averill (apparently, by unspecified means, having rebelled against assuming his proper place among the American elite) now works as a federal marshall, devoted to the protection of the numerous poor immigrants who constitute most of the population of Johnson County, his territory. Irvine, now a pathetic drunk broken by the moral compromises he has been forced to accept to stay among the elite, is in Wyoming as well. He is one of the wealthy cattlemen who have long dominated the state and who now, led by the sinister Frank Canton (Sam Waterston), plan to take steps to ensure the continuation of that domination.

We soon learn that the cattlemen, their range rapidly shrinking because of the influx of new settlers, are developing an extreme plan to get rid of the new arrivals, whom they claim are thieves and anarchists. With the support of the state and federal governments (and, indeed, backed up by the U.S. cavalry), they have recruited a private army of hired gunmen, who have been assigned to restore "order" in Johnson County.

In particular, the gunmen have been given a list of 125 leaders among the immigrants who are to be eliminated, though it is also clear that they plan to eliminate anyone else who interferes with the plan. This elimination is entirely legal, thanks to the government's support of the project, but Averill nevertheless refuses to go along with the plan. Instead, he warns the immigrants about the upcoming attack and even supplies them with the hit list. He then prepares to leave the area, but his departure is complicated by his personal relationship with local madam, Ella Watson (Isabelle Huppert), who happens to be on the list, ostensibly for accepting stolen cattle as payment for the services of her establishment. Averill and Watson are apparently in love, but she is reluctant to leave the area, which she now regards as her home and where she has a thriving business. So, instead, she decides to accept a marriage proposal from her long-time suitor, Nate Champion (Christopher Walken), a gun-toting immigrant who has turned coat and joined the private army raised by the cattlemen.

This unlikely love triangle remains a central part of the plot even after the private army arrives in Johnson County. Indeed, for some unexplained reason, one of the first things the hired killers do is attack Watson's brothel, murder all of her prostitutes, and rape her. They presumably plan to kill her as well, but Averill arrives to rescue her before they can do so. Finally realizing the evil with which he has become involved, Champion then withdraws from Canton's army, and thus becomes the object of their next attack, in which he is killed. Watson, meanwhile, informs the locals that the gunmen are at Champion's cabin. She then helps lead a mad horseback charge against the invaders, leading to an extended battle in which the disorganized immigrants are beaten back by their less numerous, but more professional opponents. Averill then joins the fray, helps the settlers get organized, and leads another assault, employing Roman battle techniques that he presumably learned at Harvard. This time the immigrants actually seem to be getting the upper hand, despite the fact that Roman battle techniques are anachronistic and not designed to work against modern weapons. Among other things, Irvine is killed in the battle. Then suddenly the cavalry rides in, led by Canton, and saves the killers, just as in traditional Westerns they typically ride in and save embattled white men and women from the attacks of crazed Indians.

In the next scene, Watson decides to leave with Averill after all, but as they prepare to leave, Canton again arrives with hired thugs and kills Watson and John Bridges (Jeff Bridges), local barman and civic official, who has helped to lead the settlers in their resistance. Averill kills Canton in the shootout and then remains the only major character who is still alive, though the "Johnson County Wars" actually remain unresolved after over three hours of film combat. Cimino then cuts to a final scene, set in 1903, in which Averill, having presumably returned East to reclaim his rightful place in elite society, wanders about his yacht off Newport, Rhode Island, looking miserable, accompanied by a sedentary woman, presumably his new, bourgeois wife.

While Cimino's almost allegorical opposition between evil, rich cattle barons, and poor, oppressed immigrant farmers is abundantly clear, the politics of *Heaven's Gate* are ultimately muddled. Few of the immigrants emerge as vivid characters, and it remains for the wealthy Averill (who is, as another character points out, only pretending to be poor) to lead the fight against the cattlemen and their henchmen, essentially converting the film's class-based oppositions into an almost Oedipal fight of a rogue individualist against the authority that he has rejected in order to go his own way. When immigrants are shown in detail, Cimino fails to explore the implications of their lives. Watson is a central, and mostly sympathetic, character. Yet she herself is an exploitative capitalist, though the film never interrogates the parallel between prostitution and capitalism. Champion is potentially interesting as the figure of the thoroughly Americanized immigrant, but this motif again never quite develops. When the other immigrants are depicted, they typically appear as an inarticulate, almost hysterical mob, jabbering in a Babelian patois of various European languages, but able actually to communicate only when they speak English. We learn little about their backgrounds, seeing only that they are frightened and confused, desperately in need of someone with Averill's education and sophistication to tell them what to do. Thus, though the film has an opportunity to comment on important aspects of the American past (and in ways that obviously resonate with more recent attempts to halt the incursions of immigrants into America), it ultimately collapses beneath its own weight, becoming a gorgeous, but muddled spectacle. *Screenplay:* Michael Cimino. *Selected bibliography:* Crowdus.

*MELVIN AND HOWARD:* DIR. JONATHAN DEMME (1980). Based on actual historical events, *Melvin and Howard* relates the background of the controversial "Mormon will," in which billionaire Howard Hughes purportedly left $156 million to Melvin Dummar, an unknown loser. At the same time, the film details the way in which American society encourages its citizens to dream of luxury and wealth, then typically makes it impossible for those dreams to be fulfilled. The film begins as struggling factory worker Dummar (Paul LeMat) drives through the desert in his battered pickup truck and encounters an old man (Jason Robards), who appears to be a derelict. Dummar gives the old man, who claims to be Hughes, a lift into Las Vegas. Afterward, Dummar largely forgets about the incident and goes about his life, drifting from one job to another and one marriage to another in search of the elusive combination that will make the American dream of material comfort and personal happiness come true. Eventually, Dummar ends up managing a service station in Willard, Utah, where a mysterious man, in the wake of Hughes's death, drops off a document that purports to be Hughes's will. Among other things, the will makes Dummar the beneficiary of a $156 million inheritance. Considerable media attention and litigation ensue, the result of which is that Dummar gets his fifteen minutes of fame but never sees a dime of the inheritance.

Significantly, the loss of this inheritance is only the last of series of disappointments in the life of Dummar. Get-rich-quick schemes such as gambling in Las Vegas predictably fail. Working hard fails as well. In one sequence, Dummar works diligently at his job as a milkman in Glendale, California, eventually winning a television set as milkman of the month. But he finds that the exploitative dairy company for which he works levies so many miscellaneous charges against his salary that he is actually losing money by working for them. Meanwhile, the television set he wins does little more than inundate Dummar and his family with a barrage of images that remind them of all the commodities they are supposed to desire but have failed to acquire.

Things momentarily look up when wife Lynda (Mary Steenburgen) wins $10,000 as a contestant on "Easy Street," the television game show that is the family's favorite viewing. The show requires contestants to perform in a talent contest, for which Lynda tap dances (badly) to the music of The Rolling Stones' "Satisfaction," a routine she perfected during earlier stints dancing in strip joints. But the song, with its theme of desire that can never be fulfilled, is a perfect theme song for the Dummar family's inability to achieve their quest for the American dream. Meanwhile, the $10,000 only encourages Melvin to run up more debts, leaving the family worse off than before and driving Lynda to divorce him for the second time. The "Mormon will" only causes trouble as well, and the implied critique of the ideology of the American dream seems clear. *Screenplay:* Bo Goldman. *Selected bibliography:* Bliss.

*RAGING BULL:* **DIR. MARTIN SCORSESE (1980).** In many ways, *Raging Bull* can be regarded as a sort of culmination of a rich tradition of American boxing films that includes such classics as *The Golden Boy* (1939), *Body and Soul* (1947), *Champion* (1949), and *The Set-Up* (1949). In terms of its technical accomplishment, *Raging Bull* may be the best film of the lot; the fight scenes are extremely realistic (though the blood is sometimes overdone), and the black-and-white cinematography perfectly captures the mood of the piece. The acting is also superb, and Robert De Niro won a richly deserved Academy Award for best actor for his performance as Jake LaMotta, the film's protagonist. At the same time, *Raging Bull* is less politically potent than the earlier films. It vaguely continues their treatment of boxing as a metaphor for American indi-vidualist alienation and competition but fails to explore the economic dimension of this metaphor (and thus to treat boxing specifically as a metaphor for capitalism) in any meaningful way. The film begins with a scene in which LaMotta loses a controversial decision, provoking a riot in the crowd, thus suggesting their propensity to violence and indicating that the brutish LaMotta is very much a product of his social environ-ment. Otherwise, however, the film sticks pretty much to LaMotta's personal story and avoids any real engagement with social issues. Ryan and Kellner find the film an effective exploration of "male pathologies," but the film sometimes seems to revel in the bloody violence that it is presumably intended to critique (154–55).

Based on the autobiography of former middleweight champion La-Motta, *Raging Bull* follows LaMotta's career, beginning in 1941, when he is a promising contender who is continually denied a shot at the title because of his refusal to cooperate with influential mob interests, repre-sented primarily by Tommy Como (Nicholas Colasanto), who runs the local mob in LaMotta's own Bronx neighborhood. Between 1942 and 1945, LaMotta makes something of a career out of fighting against Sugar Ray Robinson (Johnny Barnes), who is also repeatedly denied a shot at the title. LaMotta and Robinson have a series of five memorable bouts in this period, with Robinson winning four. LaMotta finally gets a title fight in 1947 but has to agree to take a dive in order to get it. Finally given a legitimate shot at the title in 1949, he wins by TKO over Frenchman Marcel Cerdan and finally realizes his ambition to be world champion.

In the meantime, the alienated LaMotta has difficulty carrying on any sort of meangiful personal relationship. Early in the film, he falls in love with a fifteen-year-old girl, eventually divorcing his wife and marrying the girl four years later. But his relationship with his new wife, Vickie (Cathy Moriarty), is troubled as well, especially as Jake is insanely jeal-ous. His jealousy finally climaxes when he wrongly concludes that Vickie has been cheating on him with his own brother and manager, Joey (Joe Pesci). LaMotta flies into a rage and beats up both Vickie and Joey. He later convinces Vickie to stay with him despite the incident, though his relationship with Joey is entirely broken off.

Increasingly struggling with his weight and his personal demons, LaMotta soon loses his title to his old nemesis, Robinson. He then retires to Florida with Vickie and their two children and seems to have a rela-tively comfortable life there, where owns his own night club and per-forms monologues for the entertainment of his customers. Unfortunately, some of these customers are underage girls, leading eventually to La-Motta's imprisonment on vice charges. By this time, Vickie, increasingly estranged from her husband, has already divorced him. In the end, however, LaMotta achieves a certain measure of salvation. After he gets out of prison, he returns to New York City (in the mid-1960s), where he performs his club act with some success. He also begins to try to patch things up with Joey, the only person who had ever been really close to him. *Screenplay:* Paul Schrader and Mardik Martin. *Selected bibliography:* Biskind (*Easy Riders*); Librach; Recchia ("Setting"); Ryan and Kellner; Stern.

*RETURN OF THE SECAUCUS SEVEN:* DIR. JOHN SAYLES (1980). *Return of the Secaucus Seven* focuses on a single weekend in the late 1970s, when a group of friends from the 1960s gather for their annual reunion. As such, it obviously anticipates the later, glossier *The Big Chill* (1983), but Sayles's film is much richer and more interesting, despite its low budget. The friends gather at a New England house rented for the summer by Mike (Bruce MacDonald) and Kate (Maggie Renzi), two high-school teachers who have been together as a couple for years. Other members of the Seven present for the weekend are J. T. (Adam LeFevre), an aspiring country music singer; Frances (Maggie Cousineau), a medical student; Jeff (Mark Arnott), a social worker who runs a drug detoxification center; Maura (Karen Trott), an actress; and Irene (Jean Passanante), who works as a speech writer for a U.S. senator. Accompanying Irene is her new boyfriend Chip (Gordon Clapp), who also works for the senator and who is meeting the other members of the group for the first time.

The Seven have complicated, intertwining histories dating back to their college days, including the fact that Jeff and Maura have been lovers for years but break up on the eve of the weekend. But what unites them all, and what initially made them think of themselves as a group, is a late-1960s experience in which they were all arrested in Secaucus while on their way to Washington for an antiwar demonstration. This experience also sets the political tone for the film, which is certainly about friendship, but which is first and foremost about the legacy of 1960s political activism at the end of the 1970s. None of the members of the Seven were leading figures in the political movements of the 1960s, but all were more or less committed to the goals of those movements. Meanwhile, none of them have sold out in the often-described mode; all instead have attempted to live their lives as best they can, while compromising their principles as little as possible.

Jeff is perhaps the most earnest, and most frustrated, of the Seven; he seems to be devoting himself to increasingly lost causes, partly out of a desire to do good, but perhaps also out of a sense that working genuine political change is impossible. Jeff's intensity has led to the breakup with Maura, who is in many ways a more natural match with J. T., who is Jeff's best friend, but who, like Maura, has chosen art as a profession, thereby evading the most stultifying aspects of bourgeois routine. Frances hopes to help people through her medical practice, while Irene clings to the belief that she can work subtle change and thus do good within the system via her work for the senator. Mike and Kate, however, are growing increasingly cynical about their teaching; both are pleased they are seemingly allowed to teach anything they want, including radical history, but both are also becoming aware that they have this freedom because it does not really matter what they teach.

The central scene of the film is a long one in which the central characters gather at a local bar, along with locals Howie (Sayles) and Ron (David Strathairn), former high-school classmates of Mike. The lonely Frances leaves early with Ron for a night of sex at the local hotel, where Howie works as the night clerk. The others drive back to the house but stop when they encounter a dead deer in the road. They stop to examine the deer, which has been shot; they are all then arrested on suspicion of having shot it out of season. Their subsequent experience in the jail brings back memories of the earlier arrest, but they are soon released, as they were the first time as well. They laughingly recall having dubbed themselves the Secaucus Seven in the earlier incident (accompanied by fantasies of making trouble in jail in the mode of the women in *Salt of the Earth*) as a joke. These characters are not desperados or revolutionaries; they are simply decent people trying the make the world a slightly better place.

Ultimately, *Return of the Secaucus Seven* makes clear the failure of 1960s activism to change the world in the ways most of its participants hoped to do. Yet the film is far from an indictment of, or even obituary for, the 1960s. It makes clear that the ideals of the 1960s are not entirely dead and continue to inform the lives of normal people like the Seven, who were not even centrally involved in the movements of the 1960s. Among other things, the film suggests that the idealism of the 1960s continues to provide a rudimentary sense of community among those who had been involved in it and thus might potentially be a valuable resource against the increasingly radical alienation of life under late capitalism. *Screenplay:* John Sayles. *Selected bibliography:* Christensen; Sayles (*Sayles*).

*RAGTIME:* **DIR. MILOS FORMAN (1981).** Although nominated for eight Academy Awards, none of which it won, *Ragtime* is a rather disappointing adaptation of E. L. Doctorow's 1974 novel of the same title, made all the more so by the tantalizing fact that Robert Altman was nearly chosen to direct the adaptation, which would have been perfectly suited for his talents. On the other hand, the novel was a difficult one to bring to the screen in any case, partly because of its structural complexity and partly because its effect depends in a central way on the hauntingly rhythmic style in which Doctorow wrote the book. Doctorow's *Ragtime* can be read as an allegorization of the large and powerful forces that transformed America in the early decades of the twentieth century from a mostly rural provincial backwater to the richest, most powerful, and most industrialized nation on earth. "Its official subject," as Fredric Jameson puts it, "is the transition from a pre-World War I radical and working-class politics (the great strikes) to the technological invention and new commodity production of the 1920s" (22). In this sense, Doctorow's book can be seen as a literary version of historical works such as William Leach's *Land of Desire;* it can also be seen as a sort of postmodern reinscription of Dos Passos's *U.S.A.* trilogy, its major literary predecessor.

The film is less ambitious. While it includes most of the book's major characters and to some extent still allegorizes the early twentieth-century history of America, the film ultimately focuses on the story of African American ragtime musician Coalhouse Walker, Jr. (Howard E. Rollins, Jr.), which is really only a subplot in the book, which focuses at least as much on the parallel stories of a white, bourgeois family and a Jewish immigrant family. These families, represented by the rather allegorical Father (James Olson) and Mother (Mary Steenburgen) in the first case, and Tateh (Mandy Patinkin) and Mameh (Fran Drescher) in the second, are still present in the film but recede into the background of the Coalhouse Walker story.

In both the film and the book, the fictional characters freely interact with a variety of real historical figures, enhancing the sense of authenticity in both. Indeed, a major subplot in both the film and the book deals with the notorious real-life story of Evelyn Nesbit (played in the film by Elizabeth McGovern), who became a famous sex symbol after her husband, millionaire Harry K. Thaw (Robert Joy), murdered prominent architect Stanford White (Norman Mailer) in a fit of jealousy. This story helps establish the atmosphere of early twentieth-century America, as does the contrast between the comfortable suburban lifestyle of the bourgeois family and the urban poverty of the immigrant family, though Tateh eventually manages to carve out a lucrative career in the new Hollywood film industry.

In the film, however, such class issues are secondary to the gender issues surrounding Nesbit and the racism encountered by Walker in his attempt to partake of the burgeoning American dream of the time. When his beloved automobile is ransacked by racists, Walker takes matters into his own hands and starts a full-scale rebellion that is eventually put down when Walker is killed by New York police after he thinks he has struck a deal with Police Commissioner Waldo (James Cagney). The film's focus on this motif seriously hampers its historical authenticity, especially as Walker is really an anachronistic figure from the 1960s, a fact that creates interesting dialogues in the book but is essentially ignored in the film. Nevertheless, the film captures some of the quality of the emerging consumer capitalism of the early decades of the century and some of the book's sense that only a privileged few are able to enjoy the full benefits of this new historical phenomenon. *Screenplay:* Michael Weller. *Selected bibliography:* Christensen; Jameson (*Postmodernism*); Leach.

*REDS:* DIR. WARREN BEATTY (1981). *Reds* is a sumptuous historical epic, which Terry Christensen calls "one of America's most important political films" (180). It centers on the life and career of radical journalist John Reed (played by director Warren Beatty), while at the same time presenting a sort of mini-history of the American Left from the days just before World War I into the early 1920s. It begins as Reed, back home in Portland, Oregon, after his on-the-scene coverage of the Mexican Revolution, meets and is fascinated by Louise Bryant Trullinger (Diane Keaton), the wife of a local dentist, but also an aspiring journalist in her own right. At Reed's urging, Bryant leaves her husband and her bourgeois life and joins him in the bohemian environs of New York's Greenwich Village, where she hopes to find conditions amenable to her writing. There, she meets a varied cast of antiestablishment types, including such figures as the radical feminist Emma Goldman (Maureen Stapleton), the novelist Floyd Dell (Max Wright), and Max Eastman (Edward Herrmann), editor of *The Masses*, the radical journal for which Reed does much of his writing. Many of the actual people who traveled in this circle appear in the film as "witnesses," who share their recollections of Reed and his times in brief segments that are interspersed with the actual narrative. These reminiscences, many of them from old-time leftists, enhance the sense of the film as a recovery of the history of the American Left, while also reminding the audience that Reed was a real person and not a mythical figure.

At first, Bryant is rather overwhelmed by the new world of New York, while feeling neglected by Reed, who devotes much more time to his writing and political activism, especially on behalf of the Industrial Workers of the World (IWW), than to her. Indeed, one of the greatest weaknesses of *Reds* as a political film is its excessive fascination with the private lives and problems of Reed and Bryant, though this focus does contribute to the sense of Reed's reality. In addition, these private lives are intricately interwoven with the public life of a large portion of the American cultural Left, whether in Greenwich Village or on Cape Cod with Eugene O'Neill (Jack Nicholson) and the Provincetown Players.

After working furiously (and vainly) against U.S. involvement in World War I, Reed, accompanied by Bryant (who has returned to Reed after a brief fling with O'Neill), eventually travels to Russia in 1917, in the weeks leading up to the October Revolution. The film depicts many of the events that Reed observed in Russia, struggling to make sense of the momentous developments around him. Reed gathers copious notes, then returns to America, where he writes his masterpiece, *Ten Days that Shook the World* (1919), still widely regarded as the finest firsthand account of the revolution. Bryant lectures in order to support them while he writes. Then, inspired by the high hopes raised by the Russian Revolution, Reed, though really more of a syndicalist than a communist and more of an individualist than a socialist, also becomes heavily involved in attempts to found a viable Communist Party in America after the American Socialist Party refuses to support the Russian Bolsheviks. Sectarian battles send Reed scurrying back to Russia in an attempt to gain the Comintern's official support for his faction, the Communist Labor Party of America. Having failed to get this support, he attempts to return to America, but finds that the new Soviet Union has been surrounded and sealed off by hostile capitalist armies. He is captured and imprisoned in Finland, where he falls ill in jail.

Bryant frantically attempts to locate Reed and eventually undertakes the difficult journey to Finland in an attempt to free him. By the time she finally reaches the jail, however, Lenin and the Bolsheviks have already secured Reed's release and return to the new Soviet state. Reed resumes his work for the new Soviet government, traveling to Baku for a conference intended to inspire revolutionary activity in the Middle East. On the trip, he narrowly escapes an attack by counterrevolutionaries and also falls seriously ill with typhus. By the time he returns to Moscow, in 1920, Bryant has arrived there and greets him at the train station. Unfortunately, he quickly declines and dies in the hospital soon afterward. Reed would be buried in the Kremlin wall, an honored hero of the Soviet people. He was also later honored by American communists, who founded "John Reed Clubs" around the country in the 1930s to promote the development of leftist and proletarian literature.

In some ways, *Reds* is a valiant effort at recovery of the repressed history of the American Left, despite its ultimate concessions to Hollywood convention in its focus on the romantic relationship between Reed and Bryant. *Reds* also adheres to standard Cold War stereotypes in its depiction of the quick descent of the Russian Revolution into bureaucratic totalitarianism, opposed by a heroic Reed, who continues to espouse quintessentially American views celebrating democratic individualism. But the film at least captures some of the early excitement about the revolution as a genuine step toward human freedom, while at the same time depicting the concurrent lack of liberty in the United States, where leftists such as Reed and his circle were being brutally persecuted in the Red Scare of 1917–1921. **Screenplay:** Warren Beatty and Trevor Griffiths. **Selected bibliography:** Christensen; Culbert ("*Reds*"); Hicks; Reed (*Insurgent Mexico*); Reed (*Ten Days*); Rosenstone; Ryan and Kellner.

*THE ATOMIC CAFÉ:* DIR. JAYNE LOADER, KEVIN RAFFERTY, AND PIERCE RAFFERTY (1982). *The Atomic Café* is an interesting compendium of documentary footage from the 1940s and 1950s, beginning with the Manhattan Project and the testing of the first atomic bomb and ending with a sequence of films on what to do in the case of a nuclear attack by the insidious Russians. Along the way, the film makes a number of points about the gruesome consequences of the atomic bombings of the Japanese cities of Hiroshima and Nagasaki, made all the more horrifying by the gleeful proclamations of American triumphalism that followed those bombings. This glee is short-lived, however, as World War II almost immediately gives way to the Cold War, while the American sense of total military superiority is quickly challenged by the Soviet explosion of an experimental atomic bomb in 1949. *The Atomic Café* does a good job of capturing the hysterical anticommunism of the Cold War years, presenting documentary footage ranging from widespread demands that nuclear weapons be deployed in Korea, to the McCarthyite purges of suspected communists in virtually all sectors of American life, to the questionable conviction and execution of the Rosenbergs. The film also includes propaganda footage of American affluence and of American homes being blown apart by Soviet bombs, making the point that our wonderful life is seriously threatened by our evil (and envious) Russian enemies. The final sequences concerning instructions on what to do in the case of an attack seem designed to make such an attack seem inevitable, while at the same time making nuclear warfare thinkable, paving the way for the Americans, the only people to have ever used nuclear weapons, to do so again. Anyone who thinks the Soviets employed outrageous propaganda during the Cold War would do well to look at this footage exposing American propaganda, some of it wildly funny, but all of it chilling and disturbing for what it says about American culture and society. *Selected bibliography:* Barsam; Hixson.

*MISSING:* DIR. CONSTANTIN COSTA-GAVRAS (1982). Based on a true story, *Missing* is set in the aftermath of the bloody U.S.-backed military coup that unseated Salvador Allende, the legally elected socialist president of Chile. The film makes it quite clear that the U.S. government organized the coup in order to head off the growing success of Allende's movement toward socialism in Chile, a movement that seriously threatened the extensive investments of U.S. corporations in Chile. On the other hand, neither Chile nor Allende is mentioned by name in the film, which is simply set in an unnamed South American country, thus providing a suggestion that the events it describes are not unique to Chile but are typical of U.S. interventions all over Latin America. Indeed, as the film ends, many of the covert operatives involved in the coup have already moved on to Bolivia, presumably to pursue covert activities there.

The film centers on American Charles Horman (John Shea), who has moved to Chile with his wife, Beth (Sissy Spacek), to pursue his ambition to be a writer. Just before the present time of the film, Charles has been on a trip with visiting friend Terry Simon (Melanie Mayron) to the oceanside town of Viña del Mar, apparently the place where the coup was organized. Charles and Terry find Viña swarming with American military officers and intelligence agents, who are surprisingly open about discussing their activities, assuming that Charles and Terry, being Americans, will be sympathetic. Charles and Terry then return to the capital in the wake of the coup. There, they encounter a nightmare world of political terror in which roving gangs of soldiers terrorize the citizenry, arresting and executing civilians who seem suspect for any reason.

Beth greets the couple, greatly relieved that they have returned safely. Soon afterward, however, Charles disappears while Beth is away from their house. Neighbors report that he was taken away by soldiers, but Beth's attempts to track him down prove fruitless in the face of official denials that he had ever been arrested. Back in New York, Charles's father, Ed Horman (Jack Lemmon), contacts congressmen, senators, and the state department seeking help, but gets none. Frustrated, Ed travels to Chile to join Beth in the search. Their attempts to work through the U.S. embassy prove futile, and it soon becomes clear that American officials, including Consul Phil Putnam (David Clennon) and the ambassador (Richard Venture) are giving them the run-around.

Ed and Beth continue the search on their own, aided by American reporter Kate Newman (Janice Rule). In the process, Ed and Beth develop a growing mutual respect, though the conservative Ed had never approved of what he saw as the irresponsible, bohemian lifestyle of his son and daughter-in-law. Ed, initially convinced of the righteousness of the U.S., government, learns important political lessons as well as it gradually becomes clear not only that the U.S. had helped to engineer the coup but that American officials had been complicit in the arrest and execution of Charles, apparently because of fear that, as a writer, he would be in a position to reveal what he had learned in Viña.

As the film ends, with the execution confirmed, Ed and Beth prepare to return to New York, with assurances that Charles's body will be shipped there within a few days. On-screen text then informs us that, back in the States, Ed filed suits against a variety of American officials in connection with the death of his son but that all of the suits were eventually dismissed because the U.S. government declared all of the evidence related to the case classified and thus denied the courts access to it. This ending caps the film's critique of the hypocrisy and cynicism of a U.S. government willing to stoop to any level of perfidy, including the murder of American citizens, to prevent the success of a socialist society anywhere in the world, particularly in the Western hemisphere. Of course, the implication that it is somehow more serious to kill Americans than other people is problematic, as is the film's focus on the tribulations of a single North American white family amid a South American landscape littered with the brown bodies of Latin Americans. But *Missing* is extremely effective in its evocation of the atmosphere of terror that reigns in post-Allende Chile, in its indictment of the role of the United States in creating this terror, and in its exploration of personal relationships in a larger political context. As such, it is one of the most powerful political films of recent decades and one of the most trenchant critiques of American Cold War policies ever produced. *Screenplay:* Donald Stewart and Constantin Costa-Gavras. *Selected bibliography:* Crowdus and Rubenstein; Faundez; Hauser; Mihalczyk (*Costa-Gavras*); Petras; Ryan and Kellner.

*THE BALLAD OF GREGORIO CORTEZ:* DIR. ROBERT M. YOUNG (1983). Gregorio Cortez was a turn-of-the century Mexican farmer in Texas who ran afoul of the law because of a linguistic misunderstanding and then became the object of a sensational manhunt that made him something of a folk hero to the Mexican Americans of Texas. His story has been conveyed in a variety of ways, including the well-known *corrido* from which the film takes its title. The film thus has a number of historical sources, though the most important and direct was the book *With His Pistol in His Hand*, by the Chicano novelist and folklorist Américo Paredes, who sings *El Corrido de Gregorio Cortez* in the film's opening. *The Ballad of Gregorio Cortez* is important for its positive, but realistic, treatment of Mexican American history, making the semi-legendary story of Gregorio Cortez a very human one.

As the film begins, Gregorio (Edward James Olmos) and his brother, Romaldo (Pepe Serna), are questioned by Morris (Timothy Scott), an Anglo sheriff, about the recent selling of a stolen horse in the area. Unfortunately, the Cortez brothers speak no English, while the sheriff speaks no Spanish, though he is accompanied by Boone Choate (Tom Bower), who knows just enough Spanish to further the linguistic confusion that surrounds the interview. This confusion eventually leads Morris to draw his gun and shoot Romaldo. Gregorio shoots Morris in return (and in self-defense), while Choate runs away into the surrounding fields. Gregorio takes Romaldo to the home of a friend, where he soon dies. Gregorio takes refuge in the home of another friend, but a posse, led by Sheriff Glover, soon tracks him there. The posse assaults the house in the middle of the night, leading to wild confusion in which Glover and one of the deputies are killed, perhaps by their own men. Gregorio somehow escapes, heading for Mexico.

Gregorio is separately pursued by a group of Texas Rangers and a posse led by Sheriff Frank Fly (James Gammon), Glover's replacement. He eludes his pursuers for eleven days, thus fueling what would become his legend. Eventually, however, he learns that his family is being held in jail, essentially as hostages, and so allows himself to be captured and taken back to trial. The court appoints a reluctant B. R. Abernathy (Barry Corbin) to serve as Gregorio's lawyer. Although Abernathy has to speak to Gregorio through an interpreter, Carlota Muñoz (Rosana DeSoto), he soon realizes what has happened and warms to the defense, despite his initial skepticism. Abernathy's efforts at least save Gregorio from hanging, but he is nevertheless convicted of murder and sentenced to fifty years in prison. He is then nearly lynched by an angry Anglo mob, saved only by the intercession of Fly, who manages to turn the mob away.

The next day, Gregorio's wife and children are finally released from jail. They trail behind Fly and Gregorio as the sheriff takes the prisoner to a waiting train for transportation to the state prison. The film ends as Gregorio bids a touching farewell to his small son, then boards the train. On-screen text then informs us that Gregorio's conviction was reversed on appeal four months later, but that he was continually retried until, on the sixth attempt, the government finally won another conviction for murder, this time accompanied by a life sentence. In 1913, Gregorio was pardoned by the governor of Texas, then finally released after twelve years in prison.

*The Ballad of Gregorio Cortez* neither romanticizes its protagonist nor demonizes his Anglo pursuers. Nevertheless, Olmos plays Gregorio with a quiet dignity that tends to reinforce his status as a Mexican American folk hero, while challenging the kind of negative stereotypes of Mexican Americans that have appeared all too frequently in American film. In the meantime, the story of Gregorio Cortez, with its thematic emphasis on the possible dangers of intercultural miscommunication continues to have a special currency a century after the events dscribed, as the United States becomes an increasingly multicultural society. *Screenplay:* Robert M. Young and Victor Villaseñor. *Selected bibliography:* Berumen; Gutiérrez-Jones; Hoffman; Paredes; David Rosen; Sorell.

*DANIEL:* DIR. SIDNEY LUMET (1983). *Daniel* is an adaptation of E. L. Doctorow's 1971 novel *The Book of Daniel*, which is itself based on the trial and execution of Julius and Ethel Rosenberg at the height of American anticommunist hysteria in the early 1950s. Scripted by Doctorow, the film is a relatively faithful adaptation of the book, though it necessarily loses some of the book's postmodernist experimentalism. Both the film and the novel focus on the attempts of Daniel Isaacson (played in the film by Timothy Hutton), in the late 1960s, to come to grips with a personal past that includes the execution of his parents, Paul and Rochelle

Isaacson (Mandy Patinkin and Lindsay Crouse), for espionage in the 1950s. The Isaacsons are based quite transparently on the Rosenbergs, and their story, presented by Doctorow in an emotionally powerfully and moving fashion (including a graphic description of the execution), addresses one of the most controversial episodes in recent American history. However, Doctorow chooses to fictionalize his presentation extensively, not only changing the names of the principals but also altering a number of the details. However, these alterations are part of the point of both the book and the film, which conduct extensive inquiries into the difficulty of recalling the past accurately.

*The Book of Daniel* is an extremely complex text that involves metafictional commentary on its own composition as well as a meditation on the process of historical reconstruction. The film captures some, but not all, of this flavor by frequenting cut back and forth between scenes set in Daniel's present and at various points in his childhood. In the process, the book, and, to a lesser extent, the film conduct detailed explorations of the entire history of the American Left. For example, the film is punctuated with scenes involving leftist activity in support of the Scottsboro boys, strikes during the Depression, and the Spanish Civil War; one scene shows the Isaacsons caught up in the anticommunist violence of the attack on Paul Robeson's planned 1949 Peekskill concert. Both the book and the film include a number of Daniel's childhood memories of life in his old-left family, with a father who struggles to educate him in the workings of American bourgeois ideology to prevent his appropriation by that ideology. Paul Isaacson thus tries to explain to his son the exploitative policies of the companies with whose advertising the boy is daily bombarded—and even attempts to demonstrate the ideological manipulations that lie behind the baseball and comic books of which the boy is so fond. From the point of view of the 1960s, however, Paul's arguments seem almost quaint, and his style of leftist politics is clearly associated—at least by Daniel—with the thought of an older generation.

In particular, the book, more clearly than the film, presents the execution of the Isaacsons as a sign of the death of the old Left that had risen to prominence in the 1930s, while Daniel and his sister Susan (Amanda Plummer) become involved in a new Left in the 1960s that has lost all sense of connection to older leftist traditions. Both children are scarred not only by the deaths of their parents, but by the death of the old Left in which their parents so strongly believed. As a result, Susan becomes suicidal, while Daniel is angry and bitter, struggling to find a viable sense of connection to something bigger than himself. The film ends on an upbeat note as Daniel, wife Phyllis (Ellen Barkin), and their small child participate in a large peace rally, seeming to come together as a family through their membership in the lager community represented by the demonstrators around them. The book is less optimistic (and more emotionally powerful), but both film and book conduct a searing critique of contemporary American capitalist society that is made all the more effective by the tragic story of the Isaacson family, both generations of which are victims of this society. *Screenplay:* E. L. Doctorow. *Selected bibliography:* Carmichael; Christensen; Meeropol and Meeropol.

*HANNA K.:* DIR. CONSTANTIN COSTA-GAVRAS (1983). Not one of director Costa-Gavras's better efforts, *Hanna K.* is notable only because it is one of the very few Western films to depict Palestinians (usually the objects of abusive stereotyping and Orientalist mockery in American film) in a relatively positive light. However, the film never really explains the Palestinian case and only barely touches on the extent to which Palestinians have suffered as a result of official Israeli attempts to drive them from their ancestral lands, making way for Jewish settlement. Perhaps the most remarkable fact about the film is that such an insipid piece would cause such an uproar of protest when it was first released in the U.S. Indeed, protests against the film were so violent that it was withdrawn from distribution within months of its release, indicating the extent to which it is simply impossible to convey pro-Palestinian views in the American media.

The film details the attempts of Palestinian Mohamed Bakri (played by Selim Bakri) to gain admission to Israel, where he hopes to claim title to a house and property his family has owned for generations. He is repeatedly denied legal entry into the country, then repeatedly arrested when he attempts to enter the country without permission. Eventually his case is taken up by fledgling lawyer Hanna Kaufman (Jill Clayburgh), a Jewish American now living in Israel. Kaufman becomes aware that Selim has a legitimate case and that he has been treated in an unreasonable manner by the Israeli authorities. By extension, the film presumably makes the point that numerous other Palestinians might have legitimate grievances as well, though this point is not really emphasized. Indeed, the focus of the film is on Hanna's personal problems, as she attempts to make some order out of a confused personal life that includes an ongoing relationship with her estranged husband, Frenchman Victor Bonnet (Jean Yanne), and a rather passionless affair with Israeli district attorney Joshué Herzog (Gabriel Byrne), Selim's principal persecutor and the father of Hanna's infant son.

Eventually, Hanna becomes involved with Selim as well, when he is finally allowed to remain in Israel after serving a prison sentence for illegal entry into Israel. Hanna's acceptance of the noble Selim presumably suggests his humanity, as do the repeated scenes of him gently cradling her infant son while serving as her babysitter. On the other hand, such scenes tend merely to suggest that Selim is not like those *other* Palestinians, who are involved in a violent struggle against Israeli appropriation of their homelands. It does essentially nothing to argue that this struggle (and, especially, this violence) might be justified. Ultimately, nothing is resolved in the film, except that Hanna finally decides to divorce Bonnet and to break off her relationship with Herzog once and for all. Her relationship with Selim is left open, but it appears unpromising given the social pressures that Israeli society would place on a Jewish woman involved with a Palestinian man. Moreover, as the film ends, Selim is suspected of terrorist activity and appears on the verge of another arrest. *Screenplay:* Constantin Costa-Gavras and Franco Solinas. *Selected bibliography:* Shaheen.

*SCARFACE:* DIR. BRIAN DePALMA (1983). *Scarface* began when producer Martin Bregman conceived the idea of remaking the 1932 Howard Hawks gangster classic by the same title, transplanted from 1930s Chicago bootlegging to the Florida cocaine trade of the 1980s. From the beginning, Bregman saw Al Pacino in the title role, and it was apparently Pacino who suggested that they get Oliver Stone to write the screenplay. The result, which is dedicated to Hawks and screenwriter Ben Hecht from the earlier film, is a fascinating bit of screen adaptation that follows the original extremely closely (up to the direct transcription of a number of key lines), yet fits in seamlessly with its own contemporary context. Indeed, the smoothness of the adaptation contributes in a crucial way to the central message of the film, placing the cocaine trade in historical context, while also providing a reminder that the dark side of capitalism investigated in the Depression-era film continues to exist, and to thrive, in the Reagan era.

    *Scarface* begins with an on-screen printed prologue that describes the historical 1980 Mariel boat lift, in which American boats were allowed to come to Cuba and bring back 125,000 Cubans to the United States. Many of these were family members of Cubans already in the states, but about 25,000 of them had criminal records. In fact, suggests the prologue, Cuba's Castro took advantage of the event to send "the dregs of his jails" to the U.S. Castro thus transferred a major social problem from the island to the mainland in retaliation for the decades of American economic subjugation of Cuba, providing, among other things, a huge increase in the criminal population of Florida and an immediate boost in the manpower available to the Florida drug trade. Among these "dregs" is Cuban hood Tony Montana (Pacino), who manages to win a place in "Freedomtown," a holding camp for refugees, by claiming to have been a political prisoner in Cuba. Indeed, Montana's continual claims throughout the film to be a dedicated anticommunist provide one of the film's most trenchant political comments, powerfully questioning the motivation of the large right-wing Cuban population in Florida, a group whose political clout has been largely responsible for the senseless ongoing American persecution of Cuba.

This suggestion that anti-Castro Cubans are often involved in drug activity is enhanced when Montana begins his criminal career in America, aided by his friend and lieutenant, Manny Lee (Steven Bauer), by murdering a fellow "refugee" in the camp because of the latter's former support for the Castro regime. This murder, performed at the behest of drug lord Frank Lopez (Robert Loggia), wins Montana and Lee their release from the camp (and green cards). It also wins them an entry into Lopez's organization, just as, in the 1932 film, Tony Camonte and his right-hand man, Guino Rinaldo, won posts in the organization of Johnny Lovo by murdering Big Louis Costillo. After some initial difficulties (including a busted drug buy in which one of Montana's associates is carved up with a chain saw by Columbian drug dealers), Montana rises rapidly to a position of prominence in Lopez's organization. Along the way, he meets and is fascinated by Lopez's mistress, Elvira Hancock (Michelle Pfeiffer), just as Camonte had been fascinated by Lovo's Poppy. Montana also re-establishes contact with his long-estranged mother and sister, Gina (Mary Elizabeth Mastrantonio), who are living in Florida. The mother, disgusted by Montana's criminal activity, wants nothing to do with him, but Gina accepts the money he offers her, and they soon establish a rather incestuous relationship in which Montana attempts to prevent his sister from any involvement with other men, mirroring the relationship between Camonte and his sister, Cesca, in the earlier film.

Eventually, Montana's ambition causes him to exceed the orders given him by Lopez, which, combined with Montana's obvious attraction to Elvira, leads to a rift between Montana and Lopez. Then, again closely following the plot of the 1932 film, Lopez orders Montana killed, but Montana escapes and kills Lopez instead. Montana then goes to claim Elvira as his prize, and they are soon married. The relationship, however, does not go well. Montana is preoccupied with his business, Elvira is bored, and both of them (in the film's principal departure from the Hawks original) become heavily involved in cocaine use, violating a cardinal rule of drug dealing, articulated early in the film: "Don't get high on your own supply." Montana's business, however, is for a time a great success. He and Elvira live in a fabulous, heavily guarded estate, and he founds a series of legitimate businesses to front his drug operation, including Montana Management Company and Montana Realty Company. He finds, however, that the world of legitimate business can be as ruthless and unscrupulous as the world of drug dealing. Gouged by a banker who is helping him to launder his drug money, an angry Montana declares, "Do you know what capitalism is? Get fucked!" "A true capitalist if ever I saw one," Elvira bitterly replies, indicating her husband.

Montana's troubles grow when his organization is infiltrated by police, leading to his arrest. His lawyer informs him that he should be able to beat the drug charges, but that he will almost certainly have to do prison time for tax evasion given the extensive evidence of his money laundering activities. "The fucking country was built on washing money," Montana responds. Bolivian drug lord Alejandro Sosa (Paul Shenar), with whom Montana has had extensive dealings all along, then offers to use his connections in Washington to ensure that Montana does not go to prison, in return for Montana's help in assassinating an anti-drug activist who has recently targeted Sosa's operation. Montana accompanies Sosa's hit man to New York, but then, in a sudden outburst of sentimentality, kills the hit man to prevent him from triggering a bomb that would kill not only the activist, but his wife and children.

This action, predictably, triggers a strong response from Sosa, who sends a veritable army to Florida to execute Montana. Montana, meanwhile, has serious personal problems as well. Elvira has left him, and, when he returns to Florida from New York, he discovers that Gina is living with Lee. In a sequence that closely follows the 1932 original, Montana assumes that Lee, an inveterate skirt chaser, is merely toying with Gina; he goes to the house and guns down Lee. A horrified and tearful Gina embraces the dead man and explains to Montana that she and Lee had been married the day before. Montana takes her back with him to his house, which is immediately besieged by Sosa's army, but only after a scene in which the hysterical Gina offers herself to Montana, daring him to fuck her, while shooting at and wounding him with a pistol. In the subsequent bloody scenes, Gina is shot down by Sosa's executioners, and Montana is eventually killed as well, but only after mowing down dozens of the attackers. In the last scene he falls, riddled with bullets, from a balcony, landing in a pool beneath a sculpture bearing the now-ironic motto, "THE WORLD IS YOURS," which Montana had earlier observed on a blimp bearing a Pan American Airlines advertisement—and which Camonte had admired on a billboard for Cook's Tours in the 1932 film.

The parallels between gangsterism and private enterprise, already present in the 1932 film, are made even more direct in the DePalma version, which also supplements these parallels with scenes involving corrupt politicians and capitalists. Critics such as James Wolcott felt that *Scarface* was perhaps too ambitious, going beyond the usual conventions of the gangster film to attempt an epic of the proportions of the *Godfather* series, but "madder and kinkier ... mounted as if it were a Brechtian epic of power mania run amok—a punk faced *Arturo Ui*." Wolcott's evocation of Brecht, who used American gangsterism as a metaphor for both capitalism and right-wing politics in a number of works, is appropriate. Other critics, such as Pauline Kael, complained that the film's political statements were too overt, but then for many critics virtually any political statement is too overt by definition. *Scarface*, of course, treads particularly controversial ground in its implied critique of right-wing anti-Castro Cubans, a group Stone described in an interview as "the single most dangerous group of guys I've met." They are also a group virtually immune from official political critique for fear that the critics will be perceived as supporting Castro. The film is not entirely successful and sometimes seems to become absorbed in the very violence it seeks to criticize. Moreover, it presents nothing in the way of a workable alternative to the debased violence it sees as reigning in the worlds of crime, business, and politics. But it is a thought-provoking work worthy of serious attention. *Screenplay:* Oliver Stone. *Selected bibliography:* Bogue; Kael; Kagan (*Oliver Stone*); Stone (Interview); Wolcott.

*SEEING RED:* DIR. JAMES KLEIN AND JULIA REICHERT (1983). *Seeing Red* is a fascinating documentary based on Reichert's interviews, in the early 1980s, with a number of individuals who had been active rank-and-file members of the American Communist Party from the 1930s to the 1950s. The film is relatively sympathetic to the political commitment of these individuals, portraying their activity during these decades as a genuine attempt to further the cause of social and economic justice. As such, the film dispels a number of myths about the evil and perfidy of the Communist Party (CP), providing reminders that, for many years, the party was not only a genuine force in American life, but was in fact the principal proponent of a number of crucial issues. As Reichert notes in her narration, the CP was the first major American political group to put central emphasis on opposition to racism and such racist practices as lynchings. In addition, the CP was the first major group to agitate for a number of reforms that would later be taken for granted as part of a democratic society, including social security and unemployment insurance. Finally, the film notes the central participation of the CP in the growth of trade unions in the 1930s.

Most of Reichert's interviewees remember the 1930s with great fondness, as a time when it was possible openly to work for genuine radical change, supported by tens of thousands of fellow communists working for the same agenda. The 1930s were also a time when the CP was in the vanguard of opposition to fascism, leading eventually to the unique period in the first half of the 1940s when the United States and the Soviet Union were aligned as allies against the fascist threat in Europe. Soon after the war, however, anticommunist hysteria swept America, leading to widespread persecution of communists and suspected communists. The party was then further damaged by Nikita Khrushchev's attacks on

Joseph Stalin in 1956, quickly leading to the resignation of 80 percent of the party's membership. At the time of the interviews for the film, however, many of Reichert's subjects remained members of the party, while others remained devoted communists, even if no longer aligned with the CP. There are no retractions, no regrets, and no apologies, only a sense that history is long and that the battle for justice has not yet been entirely lost. The film closes with Pete Seeger singing a song of hope for the future, capturing this sense that there are still battles to be fought. *Selected bibliography:* Caute (*Great Fear*); Healey and Isserman; Isserman; Ottanelli; Shafransky.

*SILKWOOD:* **DIR. MIKE NICHOLS (1983).** Based on a true story, *Silkwood* details the efforts of Karen Silkwood (Meryl Streep) to blow the whistle on the shoddy methods being practiced at the Kerr-McGee nuclear fuel processing plant in Oklahoma in the early 1970s. Silkwood becomes increasingly concerned that the plant is not employing adequate safety measures to protect the workers in this highly hazardous industry. She and the other workers are repeatedly exposed to radiation in the course of her work, while the company continually assures them that the radiation levels they have experienced are within acceptable limits. Meanwhile, Silkwood also discovers that the company is cutting other corners as well, such as altering inspection X-rays of welds in fuel rods, thus possibly allowing the production of faulty rods that could lead to a disastrous nuclear accident. In its focus on the nuclear industry and its special dangers, *Silkwood* is somewhat reminiscent of *The China Syndrome* (1979). However, *Silkwood* is a more complex film that is more realistic than the earlier film in its criticism of corporate America as an impersonal machine bent on making profits, whatever the human cost. Although focusing on the nuclear industry, *Silkwood* is a film, as Christensen puts it, about "workers, women, and unions" (163). It is thus directly relevant to other industries as well.

At the same time, the company works to decertify the union that represents the workers in the plant, thus opening the way to even shoddier treatment. Silkwood responds by becoming a union activist, working both to preserve the union as the official representative of the workers and to encourage the union to take stronger measures to demand safer working conditions. Eventually, the union arranges for Silkwood to meet with a reporter from the *New York Times* so she can present the evidence she has gathered concerning the company's shoddy practices. On the way to the meeting, she is killed in a suspicious automobile accident the cause of which was never determined and about which the film refuses to speculate, though it is clear from the film that the Kerr-McGee Corporation would certainly not be above murder.

Much of the film simply presents Silkwood's ordinary daily activities, thus providing a realistic picture of working-class life. She lives in a modest rented house with her boyfriend, Drew Stephens (Kurt Russell), and her friend, Dolly Pelliker (Cher), who happens to be a lesbian. Both Drew and Dolly also work at the plant. In addition to the details of her domestic existence, we also see Silkwood's interactions with her fellow workers in the plant. At first, there is a great deal of camaraderie in these interactions, though Silkwood's activities eventually lead the other workers, terrified of losing their jobs, to shun her. *Silkwood* documents the willingness of the company to endanger the lives of its employees and of the general population in its quest for higher profits, with the suggestion that it is willing, in extreme cases, even to stoop to murder. But the film also suggests the power of collective action among workers to resist the company's exploitation, a power the company acknowledges in its own attempts to break the union and to foster animosity among the workers. Despite her association with the union, Silkwood's efforts to oppose the company are ultimately those of an individual and thus fail; only by working with her fellow workers could she have hoped to succeed. *Screenplay:* Nora Ephron and Alice Arlen. *Selected bibliography:* Christensen; Rashke; Ryan and Kellner; Zaniello.

*UNDER FIRE:* DIR. ROGER SPOTTISWOODE (1983). *Under Fire* focuses on a group of American journalists who cover the last days of the Somoza dictatorship in Nicaragua in 1979. The central character is world-renowned photojournalist Russell Price (Nick Nolte), who arrives in Nicaragua fresh from covering a civil war in the African country of Chad, thus suggesting that the kind of conflict currently underway in Nicaragua may be part of a larger global phenomenon. Arriving with Price are Claire (Joanna Cassidy), a radio reporter, and Alex Grazier (Gene Hackman), a television reporter. Alex and Claire have been lovers for some time, but break up on the eve of their departure for Nicaragua. Alex soon departs for New York to become a network news anchor, while Claire becomes romantically involved with Price, a long-time friend.

In the midst of all of this, Nicaragua is in the midst of an all-out revolution, and the greatest weakness of the film is its tendency to focus more on the private problems of its American characters than on the revolution. Nevertheless, the film makes it clear that the Somoza (René Enriquez) is a dictator and a murderer and that he maintains his power largely through U.S. support. But this support seems to be flagging in the face of the growing likelihood that the revolution is now unstoppable. At a crucial moment, however, the important rebel leader, Rafael, is killed in battle, a fact that might extend the conflict considerably, by both discouraging the rebels and encouraging the Americans to step up support for

Somoza. The rebels thus try to convince Price, whose observations in Nicaragua have led him to sympathize with their cause, to fake a photograph that supposedly proves that Rafael is still alive. Price, whose motto is, "I don't take sides. I take pictures," hesitates but finally agrees.

The photograph causes such a sensation that Alex returns to Nicaragua, hoping Price can get him an interview with Rafael. When he learns of the faked photograph, he is furious but agrees to continue the deception. Soon afterward, Alex is killed in cold blood by Somoza's soldiers, an act Price captures on film. The photographs of the murder trigger a wave of anti-Somoza outrage in the United States, causing one of the Nicaraguans to complain that the Americans have been oblivious to the deaths of 50,000 Nicaraguans in the fighting but are now up in arms over the death of a single American. "Maybe we should have killed an American journalist fifty years ago," she complains.

In any case, the film ends as the Sandinistas sweep into power, an event that is greeted with considerable celebration by the Nicaraguan people. The film gives few actual historical details, but it nevertheless makes it clear that the Sandinista victory in 1979 was the culmination of a long and heroic struggle by the Nicaraguan people to resist the forces of oppression in their country, forces that were consistently propped up by support from the United States. Actually, U.S. interference in Nicaragua goes well back into the nineteenth century, and U.S. marines landed there as early as 1912 to intervene in a civil war. The Sandinistas took their name from Augusto César Sandino, who led a fight against continuing occupation of Nicaragua by U.S. forces, which were finally withdrawn in 1933. In 1936, Anastasio Somoza seized power in the country. He ruled until his assassination in 1956, despite considerable resistance to his regime in Nicaragua. He was succeeded by first one son, then another, the Somoza of the film. The brutal Somoza regime, because of its opposition to communism, had long received support from the United States. Unfortunately, the Reagan-Bush administration continued to intervene in Nicaragua after the Sandinista victory, sabotaging the nation's economy through a trade embargo, the illegal mining of the nation's principal harbors, and clandestine support for the right-wing Contra armies that repeatedly invaded Nicaragua from neighboring Honduras. The Sandinistas fell from power in a popular election in 1990, and many of their important reforms in education, health care, and land redistribution were curtailed. *Screenplay:* Ron Shelton and Clayton Frohman. *Selected bibliography:* Christensen; Gilbert; Miranda, Morley; Ryan and Kellner; Thomas W. Walker (*Nicaragua*); Thomas W. Walker (*Reagan*); Thomas W. Walker (*Revolution*).

## THE BROTHER FROM ANOTHER PLANET: DIR. JOHN SAYLES (1984). *The Brother from Another Planet* is an allegory that explores the

workings of race and class in urban America, while at the same time parodying big-budget sci-fi special effects pictures, such as the *Star Wars* series. It begins as the Brother, an escaped slave from another planet (where his race is apparently despised not for their black skin, but for their three-toed feet), crash lands his spacecraft on, of all places, Ellis Island. This landing in a sense makes him an emblem of all immigrants who come to America seeking freedom, only to find persecution. But the slavery motif and his own black skin make him a particular figure of the African American experience, as does the setting of most of the film in Harlem.

The Brother, after some initial unfortunate encounters, finally makes his way to Harlem, where at least his skin color does not make him unwelcome. However, he still has other problems, including that he cannot talk or, initially, understand those around him. Eventually, he learns to understand English, though he remains mute. He happens into a neighborhood bar, where the owner, Odell (Steve James), and some of the patrons take pity on him. They help him find lodgings, then one of them, Sam (Tom Wright), a social worker helps him get a job repairing video games, after it is discovered that he has a mysterious ability to commune with machines and to heal their ailments.

Meanwhile, in a sustained effort at cognitive mapping, the Brother wanders about Harlem, trying to make sense of his surroundings. This effort includes one scene that parallels Dante's *Inferno*, as the Brother, under the influence of heroine, wanders through a surrealistic sequence in nighttime Harlem, guided by a Jamaican named Virgil (Sidney Sheriff). The Brother gradually begins to appreciate the totality of Harlem as a community and to understand the extent to which illegal drugs are destroying that community. He tracks much of the local drug supply to Vance (Edward Baran), a white business executive, who simply treats his drug operations as part of his overall capitalist enterprise. The Brother confronts Vance with evidence of the damage his drugs are doing to the youth of Harlem, then kills the businessman by smothering him in his own heroine.

The Brother then goes back out onto the street, where he is at once confronted by the two weird slave catchers from his home planet (played by Sayles and David Strathairn), who have been pursuing him throughout the film, causing one of the patrons of Odell's bar to remark that "white folks get stranger all the time." Indeed, these two black-clad characters provide much of the film's humor (among other things parodying the detectives from the television series *Dragnet*), though they also provide much of its critique of oppressive authority. In the end, however, community triumphs over authority. Fleeing the slave catchers, the Brother runs into an assemblage of various Harlem characters he has encountered through the film. These individuals, in a sudden show of solidarity, defend the Brother from his pursuers, who, confronted by the collective power of this community action, allegorically self-destruct into ashes.

*The Brother from Another Planet* includes a number of inspired, and sometimes hilarious scenes, as when Noreen (Maggie Renzi), a city social worker, repels the slave catchers by demanding that they fill out an avalanche of paperwork before she can give them any information. The film's obvious allegorization of racial discrimination is reinforced by an awareness of class issues as well, as when the Brother continually encounters workers who complain of mistreatment by their bosses, culminating in the characterization of the high-level executive, Vance. All in all, *The Brother from Another Planet* is a typically thoughtful Sayles film, with the director's typical emphasis on community. But it is a bit funnier and more offbeat than most of Sayles's films. *Screenplay:* John Sayles. *Selected bibliography:* Boyd ("But Not the Blackness"); Packer; Sayles (*Sayles*).

*LATINO:* DIR. HASKELL WEXLER (1985). Set in the 1980s, during the period of Sandinista rule in Nicaragua, *Latino* focuses on the illegal clandestine support provided by the Reagan administration to the right-wing Contra guerrillas who repeatedly invaded Nicaragua from Honduras during that decade. The central figure is Green Beret Lieutenant Eddie Guerrero (Robert Beltran), who is sent with a detachment of American forces to provide training and support to the Contras. Guerrero, a Vietnam vet, is devoted to performing his duty, but, in Central America, he develops the gradual suspicion that, in this case, he may be fighting on the wrong side. For one thing, the Contras with whom he works seem to be engaged in a campaign of murder, rape, terror, and torture against innocent civilians in Nicaragua. For another, Guerrero is uncomfortable with the fact that the activities in which he is engaged are being kept a secret from the American people.

In Honduras, Guerrero becomes romantically involved with Marlena (Annette Cardona), a Nicaraguan agronomist working in Honduras. Marlena already sympathizes with her fellow Nicaraguans in the fight against the Contras, and these sympathies expand when her father is killed by the Contras in one of their raids. She helps Guerrero to see that the Sandinistas are attempting to build a genuinely democratic society in Nicaragua but then decides to move back to Nicaragua with her small son, leaving Guerrero behind in Honduras.

The plot of the film culminates in a major Contra assault on the town of El Porvenir, where Marlena is now living and working with the local farmers. Guerrero is among the Americans who participate in the raid, under orders not to carry with them their dog tags or other documents that would identify them as Americans, in the event they are killed or captured. The town and its surrounding fields go up in flames as a result of the attack, but the townspeople manage to defend themselves and beat back the attackers. Guerrero, disgusted with the whole situation, removes his uniform and surrenders, naked, to the Nicaraguans; but he carries with him the dog tags that will provide evidence of the participation of the U.S. military in the raid. Presumably, this evidence (and this film) will help inform the American people of the activities of their government in Nicaragua. Unfortunately, these activities were actually stepped up in 1985, when the Reagan administration, in violation of U.S. and international law, continued its secret support for the Sandinistas, while also declaring a trade embargo against Nicaragua. This intervention, combined with the illegal mining of Nicaragua's harbors in 1984, wrecked the Nicaraguan economy and thus played a major role in the eventual defeat of the Sandinistas in a popular election in 1990. Of course, the effectiveness of the film in preventing this eventuality was limited by the fact that, due to its politics, it received only limited distribution in the U.S. *Screenplay:* Haskell Wexler. *Selected bibliography:* Christensen; Crowdus and Georgakas; Gilbert; Miranda, Morley; Ryan and Kellner; Thomas W. Walker (*Nicaragua*); Thomas W. Walker (*Reagan*); Thomas W. Walker (*Revolution*).

*THE COLOR OF MONEY:* DIR. MARTIN SCORSESE (1986). Twenty-five years after his earlier appearance in *The Hustler* (1961), pool shark Fast Eddie Felson (again played by Paul Newman) returns to the screen. Now working as a liquor salesman and bankroller of younger pool hustlers, Felson discovers small-time hustler Vincent Lauria (Tom Cruise), a raw, but untutored talent who, Felson immediately recognizes, has the talent to be a big winner in the game. Felson takes Lauria, along with Lauria's tough-minded girlfriend, Carmen (Mary Elizabeth Mastrantonio), with him on the road to teach Lauria the finer points of pool hustling and to prepare him for a big upcoming nine-ball tournament to be played in Atlantic City.

Lauria's lack of discipline causes considerable problems on the road, but his talent for the game seems to offer him a promising future. Meanwhile, in the course of mentoring Lauria, Felson renews his own love for the game he was forced to leave twenty-five years earlier after a run-in with powerful gang figure Bert Gordon. He discovers, however, that his skills, both mental and physical, are extremely rusty, a fact that is driven home when he loses a bundle to a small-time hustler (Forest Whitaker). Still, Felson decides to enter the Atlantic City tournament. Armed with a new pair of glasses, he goes on the road alone to hone his skills, sending Lauria and Carmen to Atlantic City without him. In the tournament, both Lauria and Felson win their early matches, then face each other head-to-head in the quarterfinals. Felson wins and feels that he has regained his old touch, only to learn that Lauria lost the game intentionally in order to win a bet. Humiliated, Felson forfeits his semifinal match, then challenges Lauria to a side game to see if he can really beat him in an honest contest. The cocky Lauria agrees, though warning Felson that the older man stands no chance. As the film closes (before the game is played), Felson responds that if does not beat Lauria this time he will beat him soon, because "I'm back."

*The Color of Money* is an entertaining film that effectively continues *The Hustler's* character study of Felson, with Newman again delivering a fine performance. Indeed, Newman won the best actor Oscar for his role in the later film, an honor many thought he deserved for the earlier film. However, *The Color of Money* lacks most of the social commentary of the earlier film. Felson, by backing Lauria in return for 60 percent of Lauria's winnings, to an extent plays the same role for Lauria as Gordon had played for him earlier. Felson, however, seems a benevolent figure, so that his business relationship with Lauria lacks the implied criticism of capitalist exploitation in the earlier film. On the other hand, the later film's depiction of the increased professionalization of the game of pool relative to the earlier film can be taken as a commentary on the growing commodification and routinization of life in late capitalist America. **Screenplay:** Richard Price. **Selected bibliography:** Lawrence S. Friedman; Kelly.

*NATIVE SON:* **DIR. JERROLD FREEMAN (1986).** This second film adaptation of Richard Wright's 1940 novel is slightly slicker and slightly less bowdlerized than the 1951 adaptation, directed by Pierre Chenal. This second adaptation captures most of the plot of the book reasonably well, though it still carefully excludes some of the more troubling material in an apparent attempt to make the protagonist, Bigger Thomas, more sympathetic to the audience. These exclusions contribute to the tepidity of the film, which utterly fails to convey the raw power of Wright's novel. Moreover, the strong leftist political statement of the novel is effaced almost entirely, making the film a story of personal tragedy in which race is involved (and in which communists even appear), but in which there is absolutely no suggestion that the horrors described can be attributed directly to the inequities of the capitalist system.

Bigger (Victor Love) is a young black man who lives with his mother and two siblings in a rat-infested tenement on the South Side of Chicago. Early in the film, he gets an opportunity to become a live-in chauffeur for the Daltons, a wealthy family of white liberals. On his very first night on the job, he is assigned to drive their daughter, Mary (Elizabeth McGovern), to a night class at her college. Once in the car, however, Mary orders Bigger to drive her downtown to the headquarters of the Labor

Defender's Office, a communist organization. There, she meets her boyfriend, Jan Erlone (Matt Dillon), a young working-class communist of whom her parents disapprove. Curious, Jan and Mary go driving with Bigger and try to get him to explain what his life is like. Much to Bigger's discomfort, they go for dinner to his favorite spot on the South Side. By the time Bigger gets Mary home, she is so drunk he has to carry her to her room. When Mary's blind mother (Carroll Baker) comes into the room, Bigger stifles Mary with a pillow so she will not reveal her drunkenness. Too late, he realizes he has suffocated her. He panics and disposes of the body in the basement furnace.

After an investigation in which Bigger attempts to cover himself by making it look as if Mary has been kidnapped by communists, Bigger is finally implicated in Mary's death. He goes on the run but is quickly captured and taken to jail. Jan brings the radical lawyer, Max (John Karlen), to see the terrified and bewildered Bigger, who somewhat reluctantly accepts Max's representation. Bigger is rushed to trial amid sensational press coverage, then quickly convicted and sentenced to death. In keeping with the film's avoidance of leftist political statement, the trial scenes omit almost all of the impassioned radical arguments that are the heart of Max's defense of Bigger in the book. *Screenplay:* Richard Wesley. *Selected bibliography:* Boyd ("Literacy"); Burks; Cripps; Kiuchi; Jerry W. Ward, Jr.

*PLATOON:* **DIR. OLIVER STONE (1986).** The plot and characterization of *Platoon* carry a number of symbolic and allegorical resonances, though the film is probably best known and remembered for its intensely realistic look and sound. This realism is indeed impressive, and the film can at times be emotionally powerful. It is rather weak as a political film, however. For one thing, the film's "grunts" are interested more in simple survival than in political questions. For another, as Clyde Taylor has pointed out, the film's depiction of African American troops does little to challenge Hollywood stereotype. In any case, while *Platoon* as a whole avoids demonizing the Vietnamese communists and acknowledges some of the racist atrocities committed by the American forces, it does very little to examine the underlying causes of the conflict. Indeed, the film is not really about the conflict between the Americans and the Vietnamese communists at all. Instead, it focuses on internal conflicts within the American platoon that is the central focus of the film, treating the enemy forces as simply another in a series of natural obstacles (heat, rain, disease, insects, snakes) that are encountered by the American forces in the jungles of Vietnam. In the process, the American presence in Vietnam seems to be criticized as much for its damage to the natural environment as to the Vietnamese people.

*Platoon* follows a single American infantry platoon in Vietnam through several months in late 1967 and early 1968. As such, it is an episodic work that has little in the way of a continuous plot. It begins as protagonist Chris Taylor (Charlie Sheen) and other new recruits arrive by plane to begin their tours of duty in Vietnam. In an ominous moment that sets the tone for much of the rest of the film, they disembark at an American airbase and are immediately confronted with the sight of bodybags being arranged for shipment back to the states. Taylor, something of a stand-in for writer/director Stone, is a rich kid who has dropped out of college and volunteered for service in Vietnam, partly as a way of rebelling against the bourgeois conformism of his parents, and partly as a sort of social protest against the unfair burden being borne by the poor in the conduct of the war. He finds, however, that the working-class soldiers in his platoon, many of them African Americans, are largely unimpressed by his gesture, which they see as both foolish and pointless. As one of them, King (Keith David), tells him, "The poor are always being fucked over by the rich. Always have, always will."

This consciousness of class remains in the margins throughout *Platoon*, but the film largely becomes a rather simple story of good versus evil. As the naïve Taylor struggles to learn to survive amid the tumultuous confusion of Vietnam, he also gradually becomes aware that the platoon is riven by a conflict between two of its sergeants. Sergeant Barnes (Tom Berenger), badly scarred by his multiple wounds, is a vicious killer, willing to go to any extreme or commit any atrocity to subdue the enemy. His quest to destroy the enemy is at one point explicitly compared to Ahab's quest for the white whale. On the other hand, Sergeant Elias (Willem Dafoe), though himself a highly effective fighting machine, retains a sense of humanity, decency, and compassion, both for his men and for the Vietnamese civilians who continually get caught up in the war. In opposition to Barnes's gung ho patriotism and racist hatred for the Vietnamese, Elias is philosophical about his growing feeling that the Americans are losing the war. "We've been kicking other people's asses for so long, I figure it's time we got ours kicked," he declares.

In one horrifying scene, the platoon invades a village, eventually burning it to the ground. Along the way, amid other atrocities, Barnes pointlessly murders a Vietnamese woman. Elias, who stops Barnes from committing further killings, declares his intention of filing a formal complaint against Barnes when they get back to the base. Soon afterward, however, Elias gets separated from the rest of the platoon during a battle. Barnes goes after him, presumably to save him, but instead shoots him down in cold blood. Elias is not killed, but later struggles to his feet, only to be run down and killed by the enemy, falling to his knees and dying in a scene clearly designed to parallel his death to the crucifixion of Christ—thus foreshadowing Dafoe's later appearance as Christ in

Martin Scorsese's *The Last Temptation of Christ* (1988). Taylor, virtually certain that Barnes is responsible for Elias's death, tries to convince the other men in Elias's squad to take revenge on Barnes, but Barnes faces them down and then pummels Taylor in one-on-one combat. Taylor soon avenges this beating and Elias's death, however. Amid the confusion of a disastrous battle in which the platoon is virtually destroyed, he comes upon a wounded Barnes and coldly finishes him off. Reinforcements eventually arrive to rescue Taylor and the other survivors. Now twice wounded, Taylor is shipped back to the States, unfortunately finishing the film with a lame voiceover in which he declares his intention of drawing upon his experience in Vietnam in order to seek "goodness and meaning" in the rest of his life. As Timothy Corrigan puts it, this final statement produces a "blur" that "borders on nonsense" (43).

*Platoon* does an excellent job of portraying the hardship, confusion, and sheer terror that comprised the texture of day-to-day experience for American soldiers in Vietnam. It was greeted with considerable critical acclaim, largely because of the realism of its portrayal of this experience. Nominated for eight Academy Awards, the film won four, including those in the prestige categories of best picture and best director. *Platoon* was eventually joined by *Born on the Fourth of July* (1989) and *Heaven and Earth* (1993) to complete Stone's important trilogy of films about Vietnam. *Screenplay:* Oliver Stone. *Selected bibliography:* Adair; Bates; Beck; Christopher; Corrigan; Kagan (*Cinema of Oliver Stone*); Kinney; Michael Klein; Lichty and Carroll; Muse; Porteous; Taylor.

*SALVADOR:* **DIR. OLIVER STONE (1986).** Based on the firsthand experiences of journalist Richard Boyle, who co-wrote the screenplay with director Stone, *Salvador* captures the atmosphere of terror and repression that reigned in El Salvador in 1980 and 1981, as right-wing military officers terrorized the people of the country with active support from the United States. The film begins in Los Angeles, where Boyle (played by James Woods) is down on his luck, looking for a chance to make a comeback as a journalist. The unrest in El Salvador seems to offer an opportunity, especially as Boyle already has extensive connections in the country. He thus decides to drive south to El Salvador in his beat-up convertible, hoping to get freelance work covering events there. He is accompanied (reluctantly) by his friend, Dr. Rock (James Belushi), an over-the-hill disk jockey.

Boyle, in openly Orientalist terms, tries to convince Dr. Rock that El Salvador will be a tropical paradise of cheap booze and "the best pussy in the world." Instead, they arrive in a nightmare landscape of terror, violence, and confusion. Immediately arrested on their arrival, they are released because of Boyle's acquaintance with army Colonel Figueroa (Jorge Luke), who hopes the journalist Boyle will make him famous.

Boyle also renews his relationship with his former girlfriend, Maria (Elpidia Carrillo), as he and Dr. Rock try to get their bearings in the new country, where it is initially difficult to tell the good guys from the bad guys. At first, Boyle does not care which is which. He just wants a job and is willing to work with whichever side will give him a scoop. Finally, he begins to lean to the left when he manages to negotiate a deal to visit the leftist rebels hiding in the hills.

In the meantime, the murderous activities of the right-wing government, with official support from the United States, gradually increase Boyle's sympathy with the rebels. Indeed, one of the film's central stories is the gradual awakening of Boyle's consciousness as a result of his experiences in El Salvador. In the midst of all this, Ronald Reagan is elected president of the United States, with concomitant promises of increased American support for the right-wing elements in El Salvador. Convinced that they can now act with impunity, these elements, under the leadership of the sinister Major Max (Tony Plana), step up their campaign of terror, and the country erupts in all-out civil war.

Boyle and another journalist, John Cassady (John Savage), cover the fighting, in which Cassady is killed. Boyle decides to flee the country with Maria and her children, at the same time taking the film shot by Cassady and himself back to America so that people there can get a better picture of what is really going on, with American support, in El Salvador. They are stopped at the border, and Boyle is nearly killed, though he is saved at the last moment through the intervention of the departing U.S. ambassador, Thomas Kelly (Michael Murphy), with hints that the new ambassador, appointed by Reagan, would not have made such a move. Soon afterward, Boyle and his new family reach California, land of freedom, but also of capitalism. Here, he tells Maria, "you can be what you want. Do what you want. As long as you have the money." The film then ends with an ominous commentary on American freedom as Maria and her children are dragged off a bus by immigration agents to be deported back to El Salvador. Boyle, who protests the move, is arrested, never to see Maria again.

This ending is powerful, and the film makes clear the extent to which right-wing terror in El Salvador was promoted by the policies of the United States, especially under Reagan. At the same time, a central motif in its presentation of conditions in El Salvador is confusion, and the film at times suggests, rather ludicrously, that it is difficult to differentiate between the two sides in the conflict. Further, the focus on Boyle is pure Hollywood formula and tends to divert attention from the suffering of the people of El Salvador. *Screenplay:* Oliver Stone and Richard Boyle. *Selected bibliography:* Beaver; Chomsky; Christensen; Kagan (*Cinema of Oliver Stone*); Ryan and Kellner.

*FULL METAL JACKET:* DIR. STANLEY KUBRICK (1987). Although one of the better known films about the war in Vietnam, *Full Metal Jacket* is less about the war than about certain aspects of the culture and ideology of America that enabled the war to occur. For one thing, the film features numerous allusions to previous American war films, especially those involving John Wayne, presented as the epitome of masculine posturing. Popular music is used to particularly good effect throughout the film, as mostly upbeat popular tunes sound in the background of gruesome and horrifying scenes of combat and destruction. The potential implication that American popular culture is entirely consonant with the American involvement in Vietnam is then further reinforced by the film's treatment of media coverage of the war. In one memorable scene, a newsreel crew films a Marine combat unit in Vietnam, while the men pose as if appearing in a movie, perhaps a Western. "We'll let the gooks play the Indians," one of them says, completing the link among American popular culture, the racist war in Vietnam, and the genocidal extermination of Native Americans.

The first forty-five minutes of *Full Metal Jacket* are devoted to the training undergone by a group of new marine recruits in preparation for their service in Vietnam. During this training, the men are subjected to extreme abuse at the hands of their sadistic, foul-mouthed drill instructor, Sergeant Hartman (Lee Ermey). This training is clearly designed to be dehumanizing, part of a process through which the men are transformed from human beings, who might have sympathy for the enemy, to unfeeling killing machines. During this training, a private dubbed "Joker" by Hartman because of his wisecracks emerges as something of a leader among the men. Much of this segment of the film focuses on the particular difficulties suffered by Private Leonard Lawrence (Vincent D'Onofrio). Overweight and not too bright, Lawrence becomes a special target of Hartman, who dubs him "Gomer Pyle" and rides him mercilessly. Hartman even encourages the other trainees to be cruel to Lawrence as well, thus using Lawrence as a tool to stimulate ruthlessness in the others. Ultimately, Lawrence learns all too well the message being delivered by Hartman. On the last night of training, Lawrence literally becomes a killing machine, shooting and killing first Hartman, then himself.

The film then suddenly cuts to Vietnam, where the trainees are now Marines serving in the war. Joker (Mathew Modine) is a reporter for *Stars and Stripes*, charged with the formidable task of putting a good face on the American war effort. Soon after this segment begins, the North Vietnamese and Viet Cong launch their Tet offensive in early 1968, turning the tide of the war against the Americans once and for all. Joker and his photographer, Rafterman (Kevyn Major Howard), are sent into the field in Hue City, where some of the most serious fighting is underway. Joker and Rafterman join a Marine unit that includes "Cowboy" (Arliss Howard), another of the trainees from the first segment of the film. They accompany Cowboy and his fellow Marines as they work their way through the ruined city, trying to clear it of snipers and other enemy troops. Indeed, all of the battle scenes in the film occur in this urban setting, making *Full Metal Jacket* rather unusual among Vietnam war films, which tend to focus on jungle warfare. This decision was motivated partly by historical reality, as Hue City was, in fact, a crucial site of conflict in the Tet offensive. But it is also obviously motivated by the fact that the entire film was shot in England, where jungle settings are hard to come by, to say the least.

Despite this urban setting, the film still captures some of the especially terrifying nature of Vietnam combat, which was so often waged against mysterious and unseen enemies. It also captures much of the cynicism that informed the efforts of the American soldiers in the war. In one scene, the men of the unit view two of their comrades, who have just been killed. "At least," says Rafterman, inanely, "they died for a good cause." Animal Mother (Adam Baldwin), the unit's most ruthless and effective killer, looks at Rafterman in disbelief. "What cause was that?" he asks. "Freedom?" responds Rafterman, tentatively. Animal Mother scoffs, "Flush out your headgear, new guy. You think we waste gooks for freedom? This is a slaughter."

Ultimately, Cowboy is also killed, though the mission is largely successful. Joker and Rafterman survive to report the story, while American troops from around the city stream back toward their base on the banks of the nearby river. In one final bizarre, but telling, comment on the fundamental link between American popular culture and the American war effort in Vietnam, the men, in perfect unison, sing the Mickey Mouse Club theme song as they march along, rifles on their shoulders. The implication is clear. Third World opponents of American imperialism must face not only the formidable physical weaponry of the American military but also the even more formidable psychological weaponry of Disney and other bastions of American popular culture. In this sense, the film presents a powerful critique of American imperialism, though the effectiveness of this critique is ultimately limited by the failure to adequately to explain the link between American culture and American imperialism. The film also presents no points of view other than the American masculine one, and it fails to document the true impact of American imperialism on the people of Vietnam and the Third World. *Screenplay:* Stanley Kubrick, Michael Herr, and Gustav Hasford. *Selected bibliography:* Adair; Corrigan; Doherty ("Full Metal Genre"); Michael Klein; Janet C. Moore; Muse; Pursell; Reaves; Claude J. Smith, Jr.; Stevenson; Tony Williams; Willoquet-Maricondi.

*MATEWAN:* **DIR. JOHN SAYLES (1987).** Although made on a small budget, *Matewan* probably remains Sayles's finest film. Beautifully shot by cinematographer Haskell Wexler, *Matewan* is a work in the tradition of the proletarian culture of the 1930s. Based on the bitter and bloody labor battles that tore through the West Virginia coal fields in the early 1920s, the film focuses on a conflict between the Stone Mountain Coal Company of Matewan, West Virginia, and the coal miners who work for the company. This dispute is clearly presented in terms of class struggle, as the protagonist, the union organizer and ex-Wobbly Joe Kenehan (Chris Cooper), urges the miners to transcend their other differences so they can present a united front against their common class enemy. There are two kinds of people in the world, he tells them, those who work, and those who do not but feed off of those who do. In the end, the conflict turns to violence, as the company sends in hired killers to terrorize the miners, only to find that the miners, supported by local police chief Sid Hatfield (David Strathairn) are willing and able to meet force with force.

As the film begins, in 1920, the Stone Mountain Coal Company announces a cut in the tonnage rate paid to miners for coal. Already angered by the poor working conditions in the local mines, the miners, who have been struggling for some time to organize in the face of violent company opposition, declare a strike. The United Mine Workers Union sends Kenehan to Matewan to help the miners conduct the strike effectively. Although naturally suspicious of outsiders, the miners soon accept his help, and he wins an early victory when he convinces the Italian and African American workers who have been brought in to break the strike to go out as well. He also convinces the original strikers to welcome these new allies, overcoming their racial and ethnic prejudices in the interest of class solidarity. This solidarity is a major theme of the film, as African Americans such as "Few Clothes" Johnson (James Earl Ray) and Italians such as Fausto (Joe Grifasi) become central figures in the strike, while the families of the African Americans, Italians, and longtime West Virginians learn to regard each other as allies rather than enemies.

Nevertheless, the miners face formidable opposition from a coal company that is determined to deny them the right to organize. The company sends two hired thugs from the Baldwin-Felts agency to spearhead the effort to break the strike. These men, Hickey and Griggs (Kevin Tighe and Gordon Clapp), are virtual personifications of evil and would appear exaggerated and cartoon-like were it not for the historical fact that such agents, widely deployed against strikes in the early twentieth century, were in fact willing to stoop to any level of crime in their effort to destroy unions. In fact, Sayles notes in an interview that he had "tone those guys down" relative to the historical record in order to make them believable at all to modern audiences (*Sayles* 127).

Kenehan consistently urges the strikers to employ nonviolent methods, but the company and their hired thugs make it increasingly difficult to stick to such methods. After most of the strikers are evicted from their company-owned housing, they set up a camp in the woods. This camp is then repeatedly attacked by armed gangs hired by the company. In the meantime, individual strikers are harassed, intimidated, and even murdered. Meanwhile, Hickey and Griggs, aided by C. E. Lively (Bob Gunton), a strike leader who is actually a spy for the company, concoct a plot to discredit Kenehan by claiming he is a company agent. As a result, Kenehan is almost killed by the strikers, but he is saved when fifteen-year-old miner (and fledgling Baptist preacher) Danny Radnor (Will Oldham) discovers the plot and cleverly signals it to the miners in one of his sermons.

The strikers stand firm and even manage to spread their strike throughout Mingo County. Desperate, the coal company sends a larger force of Baldwin-Felts agents to Matewan in an undisguised mission to kill the leaders of the strike. Hatfield faces off against more than a dozen hired killers, ordering them out of town. A gun battle ensues, but, to the surprise of the hired guns, the miners appear to support Hatfield. As a result, the Baldwin-Felts men are routed. Most of them, in fact, are killed, including Hickey, who is blown away by Danny's mother, Elma Radnor (Mary McDonnell), the boardinghouse manager Hickey and Griggs have been terrorizing throughout the film.

The miners thus score a victory in this first all-out battle of the West Virginia coal field wars, though Kenehan and several others are killed. Meanwhile, the narrator (an aged Danny looking back from the perspective of the 1980s) informs us that Hatfield was later gunned down by Baldwin-Felts agents. It is clear, though few details are given in the film, that the miners will not win the war that has begun in Matewan. Indeed, as dramatized in Denise Giardina's novel *Storming Heaven* (published in 1987, the same year *Matewan* was released), this war culminated in the Battle of Blair Mountain, a crucial historical event in which thousands of Appalachian coal miners, in the summer of 1921, took up arms to oppose the increasingly brutal and corrupt practices (including the murder of Hatfield) through which they were being exploited by the mining companies and oppressed by the allies of the companies who were running the local governments of the area. In the battle, the miners were defeated by a combined force of sheriff's deputies, company thugs, and the U.S. Army, sent in by President Coolidge to help quell the rebellion and prevent it from spreading among the poor and oppressed of other areas of the country. *Screenplay:* John Sayles. *Selected bibliography:* Giardina; Isaacs; Marat Moore; Packer; Nora Ruth Roberts; Savage; Sayles (*Sayles*); Sayles (*Thinking*); John Alexander Williams.

*WALL STREET:* DIR. OLIVER STONE (1987). *Wall Street* is the definitive film commentary on the culture of greed in 1980s America. Director
Stone, the son of a stockbroker, presents the world of Wall Street as one
of ruthless competition in which unscrupulous predators compete in a
no-holds-barred battle for supremacy for money and power, without
regard for the lives and finances of the small investors, honest brokers,
and company employees whose lives and finances may be ruined along
the way. *Wall Street* is, in fact, a sort of morality play, complete with
allegorical characters who represent particular forces and positions
within the phenomena being described. The protagonist of the film is
Bud Fox (played by Charlie Sheen), a struggling young broker dazzled
by the world of high finance and hoping to get the big break that will
move him to the next level of wealth and power. Like his namesake in
the animal world, Fox is both predator and prey, willing to break the
rules in pursuit of success, but still troubled by the basic sense of fairness
and decency that has been implanted in him by his virtuous father, Carl
(played by Martin Sheen, Charlie's real-life father), a machinist and
union representative for Bluestar Airlines. Carl's influence for the good is
balanced by Bud's admiration for big-time Wall Street shark Gordon
Gekko, played by Michael Douglas in a performance that won him an
Academy Award for best actor.

The basic plot of the film is simple and in many ways strikingly parallel to that of Stone's earlier film, *Platoon* (1986), which also stars Charlie
Sheen as a naif in a brutal world. However, *Wall Street* presents a vivid
depiction of the complex workings of high finance that is both convincing and understandable. It also involves numerous complications and a
certain amount of suspense as the various characters perform high-stakes
financial maneuvers. The persistent Bud manages, early in the film, to
get Gekko's attention and to become Gekko's protegé, bringing him
immediate rewards, including a job promotion, a spectacular new
apartment, and an impressive new girlfirend, the beautiful decorator
Darien Taylor (played by Daryl Hannah). But director Stone is careful to
make it clear that Bud's newfound success is potentially transitory, as
easily lost as won. Taylor, for example, is essentially on loan to Bud from
Gekko, with whom she is also secretly having an affair. Just as ambitious
as Bud, she leaves him as soon as he breaks off his association with
Gekko. This breakup, meanwhile, is fairly predictable, given the kernel
of decency that remains in Bud's character.

Gekko is the embodiment of greed, and indeed one of the film's most
memorable set pieces is Gekko's "greed is good" speech, delivered at a
stockholders' meeting of Teldar Paper, a company he is attempting to
take over with the help of Bud. But Gekko takes over companies not to
run them, but to destroy them. He is a specialist in acquiring companies
through insider trading, then liquidating them, dismantling the compa-

nies he acquires and selling off the pieces, generally to the great detriment of the companies' employees. When Gekko tries to use this strategy on Bluestar, Bud decides he has had enough. He bands together with his father and representatives of the company's other employees and concocts a strategy that saves the airline from Gekko's clutches, causing Gekko to lose a fortune on the deal. This takeover is hardly radical, however. Rather than leaving the airline in the control of its workers, this strategy actually leaves the company in the hands of Gekko's archenemy, the virtuous (and much richer) British billionaire, Sir Larry Wildman (Terence Stamp), a builder and saver of struggling companies. As the film ends, Bluestar is "saved," but Bud is arrested for his earlier unscrupulous dealings (whether in support of Gekko or in opposition to him is unclear). He will apparently go to jail, though Bud cooperates with authorities, wearing a wire to get incriminating evidence against Gekko, who will presumably go to jail as well.

Stone's film is clearly meant to be an indictment of the entire capitalist system, with its ideology of profit at all and any cost. Its indictment of the ruthless machinations of this system is at times powerful and effective. Gekko, on the other hand, is an especially rapacious case, apparently because of feelings of inferiority engendered by his own working-class background, which leaves him with a drive to prove that he is not just as good as, but better than the Ivy-League types who comprise most of his peers in his new role as wealthy financier. It is here that the film's figuration of class is particularly problematic. Despite the presentation of Carl Fox and other representatives of the working class as admirable figures, the characterizations of both Bud and Gekko seem to suggest that working-class individuals fare better when they stay in their place, doing their jobs in workmanlike fashion and leaving high-finance for those who, like Wildman, are born with wealth and can thus handle it with dignity and grace. *Screenplay:* Oliver Stone. *Selected bibliography:* Beaver; Boozer ("*Wall Street*"); Kagan (*Stone*); Kunz (*Films*).

*EIGHT MEN OUT:* DIR. JOHN SAYLES (1988). *Eight Men Out* is a compelling dramatization of the 1919 "Black Sox" scandal, when eight members of the Chicago White Sox were charged with conspiring with gamblers to lose the World Series intentionally. The film does a good job of telling the story and includes some very effective scenes from the actual games of the Series, which the White Sox ultimately lost to the Cincinnati Reds, five games to three. It also brings many of the individual players to life as they struggle with the moral dilemma of participation in the fix. Ultimately, however, *Eight Men Out* is most important for its exploration of the roots of the scandal in the exploitative practices of White Sox owner Charles Comiskey (Clifton James), who makes huge profits from the team but pays the players so poorly that they become fair game for unscrupulous gamblers who offer them a chance at easy money by throwing the Series.

But the gamblers, like Comiskey, are typical capitalists, so it comes as no great surprise that, after losing four of the first five games of the Series, the players find that they are being stiffed by the gamblers, who fail to come up with the promised payoff. The players begin to rebel against the fix, and the Sox win the next two games, including the seventh game, in which pitcher Eddie Cicotte (David Strathairn), a central figure in two of the earlier losses, pitches a masterpiece. The gamblers increase the pressure on the players for the eighth game, threatening to kill the wife of starting pitcher Lefty Williams (James Read) if he does not cooperate. Williams responds by getting bombed in the first inning. He is pulled by manager Kid Gleason (John Mahoney) with the Sox down 4-0; they ultimately lose the game 10-5, ending the series with a Cincinnati victory.

In the aftermath of the Series, sportswriters Ring Lardner (Sayles) and Hugh Fullerton (Studs Terkel), who had noticed suspicious plays throughout the Series, reveal their suspicions in their columns, leading to an investigation. Comiskey frantically struggles to find a way to minimize his losses in the light of the scandal, playing a leading role in the appointment of Judge Kennesaw Mountain Landis (John Anderson) as Commissioner of Baseball for life in an effort to assure fans of the integrity of the game. Meanwhile, Comiskey attempts to protect his investment in his players, negotiating with gambling kingpin Arnold Rothstein (Michael Lerner) to cover up the scandal as much as possible and hiring a team of top lawyers to defend his players in court. These lawyers succeed in winning acquittals for all eight players who are charged with criminal conspiracy in relation to the scandal. However, Landis, to the surprise and chagrin of Comiskey, promptly bans all eight players from Major League baseball for life, even though two of them, Buck Weaver (John Cusack) and "Shoeless" Joe Jackson (D. B. Sweeney), played well in the Series and do not appear to have actually participated in the fix.

*Eight Men Out* is a fine baseball film that doubles as an effective commentary on the exploitation of labor by capital, nicely summed up by Cicotte's lament during the trial that he and the other players are facing possible jail sentences, while Comiskey and the gamblers are in the back room dividing up the profits that the players have earned through their labor and talent. Meanwhile, the film explodes the myth that baseball and America were both pure and innocent before the scandal, and that the corrupt Black Sox players somehow destroyed this innocence. In *Eight Men Out*, the corruption was already there and is in fact inherent to capitalism; the players were the victims of corruption, not the instigators. Sayles has stated that he was influenced by the Watergate scandal in his depiction of the Black Sox controversy. The film also has a particular contemporary relevance as a potential rejoinder to negative fan reaction to recent attempts by baseball players to resist exploitation by owners through collective union actions. *Screenplay:* John Sayles. *Selected bibliography:* Asinof; Dickerson; Edelman; Good; Sayles (*Sayles*).

*THE MILAGRO BEANFIELD WAR:* **DIR. ROBERT REDFORD (1988).** Based on John Nichols's novel of the same title (the first volume of Nichols's New Mexico Trilogy), *The Milagro Beanfield War* retains much of the charm and whimsy of the original. It also sticks quite close to the plot of the novel, differing primarily in the compression that was required to fit Nichols's six-hundred-page plus novel into a film of a reasonable length. The film also definitely mutes the leftist political stance of the original novel, but it is still quite clear in its depiction of the negative impact of capitalist modernization on the small New Mexico town of Milagro, whose poor inhabitants find themselves the victims of considerable economic exploitation at the hands of rich capitalists, such as local land developer Ladd Devine (Richard Bradford), who are supported by the local and state government in the interest of economic growth.

As the film begins, Milagro is a dusty and dying town, though things seem about the improve due to the efforts of Devine to build a dam and create a new lake as part of his plan to construct the Miracle Valley Recreation Area, a huge golfing and vacation complex that should bring significant economic growth to the town. Unfortunately, this growth is sure to drive up taxes to the point that the less fortunate locals, most of whom are subsistence farmers, will be forced to sell out and move elsewhere, thus bringing their generations-long relationship with the town to an end. The real plot of the film begins as local handyman Joe Mondragón (Chick Vennera), frustrated by the current economic situation in the town, begins (at first by accident, then by design) to tap into Indian Creek to irrigate his father's old beanfield, even though decades-old water-use rules deny the use of this water to the area's small farmers, designating it for the use of big landowners like Devine. Devine and his supporters are furious when they hear of this development. It is clear, however, that Mondragón's show of defiance has captured the imagination of many of the locals, and Devine and the local authorities quickly recognize that they need to proceed cautiously in taking action against Joe, for fear of triggering a full-scale revolt among the local citizenry.

Tensions gradually mount as the town squares off into two opposing camps. Ruby Archuleta (Sonia Braga), a tough-but-beautiful local small businesswoman, takes the lead in supporting Joe, dragging semiretired radical lawyer Charlie Bloom (John Heard) reluctantly into the fray as well. Old Amarante Córdova (Carlos Riquelme), a town fixture now in his nineties, is especially adamant in his support of Joe, digging out his ancient revolver to guard the beanfield against potential enemies.

Devine, of course, has the support of the town's wealthier citizens (who will profit from the upcoming development), supplemented by the support of the state police and the state government in general. The matter even gets the attention of the governor, as various officials in the state capital ponder action, sending sleazy undercover agent Kyril Montana (Christopher Walken) to the area to check out the situation and help suppress the rebellion begun by Joe and his supporters. Local sheriff Bernabé Montoya (Ruben Blades) is officially aligned with Devine as well, but he has considerable sympathy for Joe and his side and acts through most of the film as a sort of mediator, attempting to prevent the situation from erupting in murderous violence.

Violence does occur, however. Joe is beaten up by thugs, and someone fires a shot through the window of his house. Devine, meanwhile, finds himself the object of a variety of guerrilla actions that are clearly designed to frighten him into leaving Joe alone. Ruby, Joe, Bloom, and their group seem to be gaining momentum despite the odds that are against them, only to have the situation undergo a sudden change when Joe becomes involved in an altercation with Amarante in which the old man is shot and seriously wounded. Although the shooting was accidental and anyway in self-defense, Joe, knowing that the authorities are looking for any opportunity to take revenge on him for his irrigation project, flees into the mountains.

Montana leads a posse into the mountains in pursuit of Joe, but to no avail, especially after Horse Thief Shorty (James Gammon), one of Devine's own henchmen, helps Joe to escape. Eventually, Joe returns to town, leading to a potentially explosive situation in which he is arrested by police, only to have his supporters gather with guns and demand his release. Montoya arrives to defuse the situation, announcing that Amarante is recovering and refuses to press charges. Joe is released. Meanwhile, this collective (armed) effort on the part of Joe's supporters has implications that reach all the way to the capital, where the governor orders that the development of the Miracle Valley Recreation Area be put on hold, given that it seems to be causing more trouble than it is worth. The people of Milagro celebrate their victory, while Devine fumes at his defeat. *Screenplay:* David S. Ward and John Nichols. *Selected bibliography:* Bruce-Novoa; Zaniello.

*TALK RADIO:* **DIR. OLIVER STONE (1988).** Based on a play by star Eric Bogosian that was largely inspired by the real-life story of murdered Denver talk-show host Alan Berg, *Talk Radio* details the life of a Dallas radio talk-show host while at the same time producing a powerful commentary on the entire phenomenon of talk radio and the social conditions that give rise to this phenomenon. The host, Barry Champlain (Bogosian), is an acerbic, abrasive, smart-mouthed Jew who makes a living by insulting his callers and listeners, virtually begging for the kinds of hostile, antisemitic calls that give his show most of its charge. There are plenty of such calls, suggesting the high level of anger, frustration, and bigotry that inform the attitudes of the general population. That Berg was murdered by neo-Nazis gives this aspect of the film a particularly chilling quality.

Many of Champlain's viewers clearly call out of sheer loneliness, desperate to talk to someone, even if that someone taunts and belittles them. The film thus also identifies loneliness and alienation as widespread problems in American society. Champlain is a radically alienated figure who seems unable to sustain lasting personal relationships. The show thus provides a sort of therapy for him as well as his audience. On the other hand, Champlain is clearly interested less in helping his listeners than in exploiting them. His show and, by extension, the media as a whole, thus becomes a central object of the film's critique.

Tellingly, Champlain's show is a big hit. It is, in fact, being seriously considered for national distribution, though the huge media conglomerate that seems about to pick up the show is a bit concerned that Champlain's shock tactics sometimes go a bit too far. The film demonstrates the engaging quality of the show by spending most of its time simply showing Champlain at work in his studio, thus implicating the film's audience in the same phenomena as Champlain's audience. Of course, Bogosian's high-octane performance is crucial here, and it takes quite a feat of acting to make such an unpleasant character so engaging. Part of this engagement arises the sense of doom that pervades the piece, and it comes as no surprise when the film comes to a sudden and abrupt end when an irate listener shoots and kills Champlain in the station parking lot after a broadcast. Nevertheless, the ending is powerful, adding a particularly visceral charge to the film's depiction of the anger, violence, and frustration that pervade modern American society and that the media help to propagate by pandering to these proclivities in their audiences.

Unfortunately, the film does not indicate the motivations of Champlain's killer, who is not identified as a neo-Nazi (or anything else). Meanwhile, the film's indictment of modern American society is powerful, but it never really explores the sources of the ills it identifies in American society other than suggesting that the media make these ills worse in their quest for profit. This quest, of course, is part of a larger capitalist system that is the real source of the problem, but this point is never made in the film. Nor does the film take any real advantage of its opportunity to identify the distanced and antagonistic relations between Champlain and his audience as typical of social relations under the system of modern capitalism. *Screenplay:* Eric Bogosian and Oliver Stone. *Selected bibliography:* Beaver; Kagan (*Cinema of Oliver Stone*); Kunz (*Films*); Kunz ("Talk Radio").

*BORN ON THE FOURTH OF JULY:* DIR. OLIVER STONE (1989). *Born on the Fourth of July* is the second installment of director Stone's Vietnam trilogy, following *Platoon* (1986) and preceding *Heaven and Earth* (1993). Like *Platoon, Born on the Fourth of July* was a considerable critical and commercial success. It was nominated for eight Academy Awards, winning two, including Stone's second award for best director. The film is based on the autobiography of Ron Kovic, a disabled Vietnam war veteran who eventually became an important antiwar activist—and who helped write the screenplay. In fact, *Born on the Fourth of July* is very much Kovic's personal story, to the point that it actually has very little to do with the war in Vietnam, focusing instead on the personal crisis encountered by Kovic after his return from Vietnam, paralyzed from the mid-chest down due to a bullet wound. The film handles this story in a powerful and dramatic way, but its treatment of Kovic's transformation from gung ho Marine to antiwar activist and radical critic of the U.S. government is extremely weak. The film does have its interesting moments, however, as in the use of actors such as Tom Berenger and Willem Dafoe as supporting performers, thus implying allusions to earlier Vietnam war films such as Stanley Kubrick's *Full Metal Jacket* (1987), somewhat in the same way that Stone's casting of Charlie Sheen in *Platoon* evokes images of Martin Sheen in *Apocalypse Now*.

*Born on the Fourth of July* begins on July 4, 1956, which happens to be Kovic's tenth birthday. It shows him and his family and friends participating in an all-American July 4 celebration in their home town of Massapequa, Long Island. This scene helps to establish the background that would eventually lead Kovic to accept the rhetoric of Americanism to the hilt, and the film's most powerful political statement is its clear suggestion, through the narration of Kovic's subsequent experiences, that this rhetoric is misleading and dishonest. Indeed, the film makes some potentially very dark comments about the dishonest (and even murderous) nature of American culture and the contribution of that culture to the debacle in Vietnam. Unfortunately, most of these comments are left as vague suggestions and are not sufficiently explained.

Kovic joins the Marines at the end of his high school years, apparently genuinely convinced that he is going away to defend the American way of life against a serious communist threat. The situation in Vietnam, however, is not nearly so clear-cut, as Kovic dramatically discovers during one confusing day of combat in which he and his squad accidentally kill a number of innocent Vietnamese women and children, followed by a hasty retreat in which Kovic shoots and kills one of his own men. Only months later, Kovic receives his own paralyzing wound, as a bullet severs his spinal cord.

When the paralyzed Kovic finds himself being treated in a squalid, rat-infested veterans' hospital that is short of both doctors and equipment, he begins to suspect that the government for which he so proudly fought has sold him a bill of goods. Nevertheless, he remains a dedicated patriot and proponent of the war, disgusted by the antiwar protestors he sees on television and indeed finds all around him when he returns home to Massapequa. Eventually, betrayed by the government he served and unappreciated by the people he thought he was defending, Kovic sinks into self-pity and becomes a drunk, a descent powerfully captured in Tom Cruise's performance as Kovic. Kovic winds up in a bizarre Mexican seaside resort staffed by hookers who cater to the sexual needs of crippled Vietnam veterans. There, he finally hits bottom. However, he begins to work his way back when he returns to America and pays a call on the parents of the American solider he accidentally shot in Vietnam.

Then, without explanation, Kovic suddenly becomes an antiwar activist, leading a group of disabled veterans at the 1972 Republican National Conventional, where Richard Nixon is being renominated for his second term. Kovic and the other demonstrators are treated rudely, harangued by crazed Republicans and beaten by brutal police, in total disregard of the sacrifice made by these veterans in their military service. Then, there is a sudden cut to the 1976 Democratic National Convention, where Kovic, now a famous activist, is an honored invited speaker on the conventional platform. Unfortunately, the film does nothing to explain the developments that led to this turn in Kovic's fortunes, and the film closes with a conventional Hollywood happy ending, with Kovic approaching the speaker's podium in his wheelchair, with the strains of "It's a Grand Old Flag" sounding in the background. *Screenplay:* Oliver Stone and Ron Kovic. *Selected bibliography:* Doherty ("Witness"); Kagan (*Cinema of Oliver Stone*); Kovic; Muse.

*CASUALTIES OF WAR:* **DIR. BRIAN DE PALMA (1989).** *Casualties of War* follows hard on the heels of Oliver Stone's *Platoon* (1986) and Stanley Kubrick's *Full Metal Jacket* (1987) to join the parade of films about the Vietnam War made by major American directors in the late 1980s. Based on a real incident in the war, as reported in a 1969 article by Daniel Lang in *New Yorker* magazine, *Casualties of War* focuses on the abduction, rape, and murder of an innocent Vietnamese girl by a patrol of American soldiers. In so doing, it addresses many of the issues and concerns that have been central to film treatment of the war, including the dehumanizing effect of the war on American soldiers, the brutal (and usually racist) treatment of the Vietnamese by their American invaders, and the element of sexual aggression that resides in all wars but seemed to become particularly obvious and brutal in this one. *Casualties of War* can thus be taken as a statement about the horrors of war in general, though it functions most specifically as a critique of the American presence in Vietnam, for which rape and murder are effective metaphors. On the other hand, the film, while presumably sympathetic to the plight of the raped Vietnamese girl, focuses primarily on the anguish of an American G.I. who refuses to participate in the rape. It does nothing to challenge the disturbing tendency of American Vietnam War films to treat Vietnamese women as little more than passive objects for male sexual desire — and aggression.

The patrol is commanded by Sergeant Meserve (Sean Penn), still only twenty years old, but a grizzled veteran of Vietnam, slated to return home in less than a month. The other members of the patrol include the vicious racist Corporal Clark (Don Harvey) and three privates, the gullible Hatcher (John C. Reilly), the radio operator Diaz (John Leguizamo), and the innocent new recruit Eriksson (Michael J. Fox). Ordered out on a mission to look for Viet Cong tunnels, Meserve, frustrated by not being able to visit town (or a brothel) on his last leave, decides to take a detour to a village to abduct a girl for the sexual gratification of himself and his men. At first, Eriksson is convinced that Meserve is only kidding, but then watches in horror as Meserve and the others actually go to a village and abduct a girl.

They take the girl with them through the bush for several miles, treating her roughly on the way and obviously living out a fantasy of male power, a fantasy in which the film sometimes seems almost complicit. Eriksson and Diaz privately agree between themselves that they will not participate in the serial rape of the girl, but Diaz gives in to the pressure applied by the others, leaving Eriksson as the only one who refuses. Meserve verbally abuses him and accuses him of being a homosexual, then sends him off to stand sentry duty. There, he hears the girl's screams as the other four callously rape her in sequence.

Later, Eriksson tries to comfort the girl, who speaks no English and is therefore unable to represent her position to Eriksson or to the audience. No subtitles or other devices are used. Eriksson, meanwhile, misses an opportunity to help her escape. Then, he goes along as the others take the girl, injured, traumatized, and seriously ill, along with them on a planned ambush of some Viet Cong forces spotted in the area. When she is unable to control her coughing, and thus threatens to give away their position, Clark, on Meserve's orders, brutally stabs her and leaves her for dead. She is nevertheless able to struggle to her feet and attempt to stagger away. The others see her and open fire, finishing her off in the midst of the battle with the Viet Cong.

When they get back to base, Eriksson reports the kidnapping, rape, and murder to a lieutenant and a captain, both of whom do nothing and advise him to keep his mouth shut. That night, Clark attempts to murder Eriksson with a hand grenade, but fails. Finally, Eriksson tells his story to a sympathetic chaplain (Sam Robards), who helps him convince the army to conduct an official inquiry. The four other members of the patrol are all convicted at a court martial and receive prison sentences ranging from eight years for Diaz to life for Clark, though Hatcher's conviction is later reversed on a technicality. Meserve, who spearheaded the entire crime, oddly receives only a twelve-year sentence. Eriksson returns to civilian life, still haunted by the memories of it all, still disturbed whenever he sees a young woman who looks Vietnamese. *Screenplay:* Philip Dunne and Dudley Nichols. *Selected bibliography:* Kazan; Neve (*Film*); Roffman and Purdy; Tony Williams.

*FELLOW TRAVELLER:* DIR. PHILIP SAVILLE (1989). Set primarily in 1954, *Fellow Traveller* focuses on the experience of a left-wing screenwriter to dramatize the impact of the McCarthyite anticommunist purges on Hollywood. The central character, Asa Kaufman (Ron Silver), is a successful screenwriter and former member of the Communist Party, who flees to England to avoid a HUAC subpoena, having already refused attempts of FBI investigators to convince him to identify other leftists working in Hollywood. In London, Kaufman manages to land work writing scripts for a children's television series based on the legend of Robin Hood, though he has to hire a washed-up British writer to front for him because his visa does not allow him legally to work in Britain.

Kaufman adjusts, though with some difficulty, to this dramatic decline in his professional position, sometimes fantasizing about turning his Robin Hood scripts into commentaries on the repressive conditions prevailing in America. He is eventually joined at the end of the film by his wife and children in London, where they begin to try to build a stable life for themselves. In the meantime, Kaufman's personal traumas are exacerbated when he learns that prominent actor Clifford Byrne (Hart Bochner), a lifelong friend, has committed suicide. Later he discovers that Byrne's suicide followed the actor's decision to cooperate with HUAC and name names. One subplot involves Kaufman's association in London with Sarah Atchison (Imogen Stubbs), Byrne's British former lover, who is now heavily involved in the peace and disarmament movement in London, an activity Kaufman is unable to join because of his own delicate status in Britain. Another subplot refers back to Kaufman's growing psychological stress under the pressures of the repressive climate in Hollywood in the early 1950s, an experience that led him to seek psychoanalysis with Dr. Jerry Leavy (Daniel J. Travanti), a progressive analyst who supposedly sympathizes with left-wing causes. It turns out, however, that Leavy is funneling information gained from sessions with his leftist patients directly to the FBI and that this information was crucial to the identification of both Kaufman and Byrne as targets for investigation. Through this and other motifs, *Fellow Traveller* does a good job of indicating both the pervasiveness of the anticommunist investigations that swept America in the 1950s and the human cost of those investigations. At the same time, the film downplays the real political issues involved, focusing on the private problems of individuals such as Kaufman and Byrne and downplaying the genuine political commitment of many Hollywood leftists. *Screenplay:* Michael Eaton. *Selected bibliography:* Fuller.

*ROGER AND ME:* DIR. MICHAEL MOORE (1989). One of the most successful and widely seen documentary films in recent American history, *Roger and Me* describes the destructive impact of the decision by General Motors Corporation and its chairman Roger Smith to close its eleven plants in Flint , Michigan, the city in which the company was born and grew to be an international corporate juggernaut. The film is striking for its comic tone, as Moore, pretending to be a dim-witted naif, wanders about Flint attempting to gain an understanding of events there. Ultimately, however, it is Smith, not Moore, who turns out to be the buffoon of the piece. Smith and the corporation are depicted as cold and ruthless, interested only in profit and having no sense of loyalty to their employees or their community. Meanwhile, their upper-class supports are shown to be selfish, hypocritical, and entirely out of touch with the reality of everyday life for most Americans. Moore's sympathy is clearly with the workers, though he also critiques the United Auto Workers Union for the ineffectuality of their representation of their members in allowing the destruction of Flint. Indeed, the film was skewered as unfair by both General Motors and the union; it received no Oscar nominations, despite being widely regarded as the finest and most effective documentary since Barbara Kopple's *Harlan County, U.S.A.* (1976).

Moore interviews a number of locals as he seeks to present a picture of conditions in Flint, so depressed after the plant closings that the main industry seems to be evictions, which keep the local sheriff constantly busy. Matters are not exactly helped by a seemingly inept city government that continually wastes tax money on ill-conceived projects to try to kick start the local economy. As the poor of Flint get poorer, the rich, of course, get richer, showing nothing but contempt for the plight of the poor. In one bizarre scene, a wealthy local citizen holds a "Great Gatsby" party at his mansion, hiring unemployed local workers to serve as human statues during the party. In another telling scene, a new jail, built to cope with the rise in crime that naturally accompanies widespread unemployment in the city, is opened by allowing rich couples to spend a night in a cell for $100 each.

Moore tracks the impact of the local economic situation on specific working-class families, at the same time highlighting the lack of concern for the plight of these families from those in official power. Various personages comment on the situation, including President Ronald Reagan, who helpfully, and stupidly, suggests that unemployed auto workers might try to find jobs in Texas. Visiting dignitaries, such as Pat Boone and Anita Bryant, pass through town and are observed spouting empty platitudes about the value of hard work and self-reliance. Such scenes are, of course, as funny as they are tragic, and this is a very funny film. It is also a very angry film, and much of the anger and the humor of *Roger and Me* is focused on Smith, whom Moore pursues throughout the film, hoping for an on-camera interview. But the imperious Smith refuses to talk to the scruffy-looking Moore, who is repeatedly turned away by an array of flunkies and security guards. But this refusal to speak in itself speaks volumes, and Moore manages, even without an interview, effectively to convey Smith's contempt for common people and General Motors's contempt for its workers. *Screenplay:* Michael Moore. *Selected bibliography:* Cohan and Crowdus; Hamper; Orvell; Plantinga; Zaniello.

*DANCES WITH WOLVES:* **DIR. KEVIN COSTNER (1990).** A surprising commercial and critical success that won seven Academy Awards, including best picture and best director, *Dances With Wolves* is a Western notable for the extent to which it focuses on the representation of Native American culture, presumably in a sympathetic light. In particular, the film devotes a great deal of attention to the depiction of the everyday culture of the Lakota Sioux, and was effective enough in this sense that the Sioux made Costner a full member of the tribe. On the other hand, this depiction is rather superficial and consists mostly of an attempt to humanize the Sioux, an attempt that all too often takes the form of making them appear part noble savage and part just plain folks, polite and with a good sense of humor. In addition, other tribes, such as the Pawnee, enemies of the Sioux, are still depicted as bloodthirsty savages without a legitimate point of view.

The film begins near the end of the Civil War, when a seriously wounded Union officer, Lieutenant John W. Dunbar (Costner), disillusioned and suicidal, distinguishes himself by his heroic actions in battle—when he is actually attempting to commit suicide. As a reward, he is given his dream assignment—to be posted to Fort Sedgewick, the most distant outpost occupied by the U.S. Army. When he arrives there, he finds it a deserted ruin, then sets about trying to put the fort in order, building a life for himself in the wilderness in ways that carry strong resonances of the activities of predecessors such as Robinson Crusoe. Alone at the fort, he gradually befriends a lone wolf that approaches the fort, giving rise to his new Sioux name, Dances With Wolves. After some initial problems with cross-cultural communication, he manages to make friends with the local Sioux. The Sioux approach Dunbar amid rampant rumors that a massive invasion of whites will soon come to their country, hoping to get information about this possible invasion; Dunbar gradually comes to respect the Sioux and to regard this invasion as an atrocity.

Most of the film is devoted to Dunbar's attempts to get to know the Sioux and to understand their language and culture. But it is clear that Dunbar's real quest is for his own identity, and the film is ultimately far more about this personal quest than about the Sioux. The film also contains the obligatory Hollywood romantic subplot, as Dunbar falls in love with and eventually marries a member of the tribe, Stand With a Fist (Mary McDonnell), who conveniently turns out to be a white woman living with the Sioux. Meanwhile, the film trots out every conceivable sentimental cliché to show the destructive impact of the arrival of white men in the world of the Sioux: white hunters kill a herd of buffalo for their skins, leaving a lonely calf to bleat over its fallen mother; evil soldiers capture Dunbar and shoot his faithful wolf. To an extent, by depicting the white soldiers who attack the kindly Sioux as vicious, uncivilized, and evil, the film is an interesting reversal of Western stereotypes. But it remains mired in a bevy of stereotypes of its own. *Screenplay:* Michael Blake. *Selected bibliography:* Baird; Bovey; Castillo; Hoffman; Ostwalt; Skerry; Tompkins; Michael Walker (*"Dances"*).

*THE GODFATHER, PART III:* DIR. FRANCIS FORD COPPOLA **(1990).** *The Godfather, Part III,* is a direct sequel to *Part II,* following the continuing efforts of Michael Corleone (Al Pacino) to build the family business into a legitimate capitalist conglomerate, though there is a gap of quite a few years between the narrative time of *Part III* and that of *Part II.* There was also a considerable gap between the making of these two films. *Part III* was made by Coppola reluctantly, after a sixteen-year hiatus in the series, largely because he needed money. This third film does lack some of the magnitude of the earlier ones, though it is still a fine film. It was nominated for seven Academy Awards, including best picture and best director, but won none.

*Part III* begins in 1979, by which time Michael has been largely successful in his efforts to become legitimate. He is now a fabulously wealthy and much-respected philanthropist, and, as the film begins, he is receiving a prestigious honor from the Catholic Church—in return for a $100 million contribution. The film thus continues a long literary tradition of critique of the venality of the Church that goes back to such works as Chaucer's "Pardoner's Tale." This critique does, however, take a particularly modern turn. The Catholic Church emerges in *Part III* as a vast corporate enterprise that is at least as ruthless as the Mafia and as conniving in its quest for profit as the typical large corporation. In this sense, the subtext of the film needs to be understood as the triumph of global capitalism in the late twentieth century, when even the Catholic Church, once the most formidable foe of capitalism worldwide, has now been safely brought into the capitalist fold, operating much like any other large corporation. As Archbishop Gilday (Donal Donnelly), one of the principal villains of the piece, explains of the Church, "This is like any other company in the world."

As the plot unfolds, it turns out that the Vatican Bank has run up a huge deficit through certain illicit dealings and is therefore desperate for cash. Michael offers to make up most of the deficit out of his own funds in return for the Church's support in his efforts to gain control of International Immobiliare, the world's largest real estate holding and development company, a move that will allow the Corleones to become legitimate once and for all. Unfortunately, Michael encounters a number of obstacles to this deal, including the reluctance of his former Mafia connections to let him sever his ties with them. An even larger obstacle occurs when the Pope falls ill and dies before he can approve the deal, followed by the election of a new Pope who may not be as cooperative as the old one.

In the meantime, as in all the *Godfather* films, Michael is also struggling with the deterioration of his family, centered in this installation on the decision of his son, Anthony (Franc D'Ambrosio) to forego all association with the family business and instead pursue a career as an opera singer. Michael reluctantly accepts his son's decision. Mary (Sofia Coppola), his daughter, is interested in the family business but is, after all, only a woman, so Michael turns to Vincent Mancini (Andy Garcia), the illegitimate son of Michael's older brother, Santino, as a possible successor. Much like his father, Vincent is violent and hot-tempered, something of a throwback to the earlier days of the family, but he is also talented and resourceful. Moreover, he is desperate to be accepted as one of the Corleones and wants nothing more than to be involved in the family business in a central way.

Eventually, all of these plot strands come together when the Corleones travel to Sicily, where Anthony is to debut at the Palermo Opera. There, the tired, sick, and aging Michael turns over control of the family to Vincent, making him the new don, though it is certainly unclear that Vincent is equipped to run the family's modern corporate business. But Vincent is very good at old-style Mafia intrigue, which immediately comes in handy when the new don has to deal with a plot, engineered by International Immobiliare and the Vatican Bank, to kill Michael and thus prevent him from gaining control of Immobiliare. The same conspirators also plan to kill the new Pope, who is proving unwilling to go along with the criminal schemes of the Vatican Bank. Following very much in his uncle's footsteps, Vincent engineers a sweeping coup in which all of the principal plotters against the Corleones are killed. He is, however, unable to prevent the murder of the Pope, nor can he prevent the shooting of Mary on the steps of the Palermo Opera by an assassin who is aiming at Michael. The film then ends with a final scene of an ancient Michael, now retired in Sicily, falling to the ground, dead from a fatal attack, much in the mode of his father, Vito, at the end of the original *Godfather*. The family, under Vincent's leadership, goes on, however, leaving the door open for possible future sequels should Coppola once again encounter financial difficulties. **Screenplay:** Mario Puzo and Francis Ford Coppola. **Selected bibliography:** Biskind (*Easy Riders*); Biskind (Godfather *Companion*); Clarens; Cowie (*Coppola*); Cowie (Godfather *Book*); Ferraro; Lebo; Papke.

*GOODFELLAS:* **DIR. MARTIN SCORSESE (1990).** *Goodfellas* builds on a long tradition of American gangster films, yet it also has a distinctive spirit all its own. Bloodier and in many ways darker than the *Godfather* films, it also has much more of a sense of humor than those films, of which it often seems to be a sort of parody. Scorsese's gangsters have more fun than Coppola's, but they also have more mundane problems and generally seem less efficient, less professional, and less powerful. There is also less honor among Scorsese's thieves, who are often squabbling among themselves, though they still experience some of the same sense of community that makes mob life in Coppola seem like a sort of utopian enclave in the midst of capitalist alienation. Much of this difference, of course, can be attributed to class, given that the *Godfather* films focus on the upper echelons of organized crime families such as the Corleones, while Scorsese's gangsters are generally low in the mob hierarchy. As a result, their problems in many ways seem more like those of ordinary people, despite the distinctive nature of their lifestyle, which in some ways appears to be simple capitalism, stripped of much of its usually ideological disguises.

Based on real events described in Nicholas Pileggi's nonfiction book, *Wise-Guy, Goodfellas* focuses on Henry Hill (Ray Liotta), who narrates much of the film in voiceover. The film begins as Hill begins to work for local gangsters early in his teen years, giving him a great sense of importance. "I was a part of something," he explains. I belonged." He quickly discovers that his connections with organized crime get him special treatment everywhere he goes, a phenomenon he attributes to respect, but that is obviously more accurately attributable to fear. The film then follows Hill as he grows into young adulthood, including his courtship of Karen, a young Jewish woman, who is dazzled, though perplexed, by his unusual lifestyle, with its strange hours, aura of danger, and seemingly unlimited income. The two are soon married, and the spirited Karen becomes a central character in the film, often helping Hill in his work, but also vociferously complaining (unlike the submissive wives of the *Godfather* films) when she feels she is being wronged. At one point, she wages a ferociously funny one-woman terror campaign against one of Hill's girlfriends, driving the woman out of his life— though he quickly replaces the girlfriend with another without Karen's knowledge. In this all-male world, women are not only secondary but interchangeable.

Hill's two main cohorts in crime are the volatile Tommy DeVito (Joe Pesci) and Jimmy Conway (Robert De Niro), a locally famous hit man and thief whom Hill grew up idolizing. Pesci, who won a best supporting actor Oscar for the film, delivers a particularly rousing performance as the diminutive gangster whose uncontrollable temper constantly causes trouble for him and everyone around him. Their crimes culminate in the theft of six million dollars in cash from the Lufthansa cargo facility at New York's Idlewild Airport, at the time the largest heist in American history. The focus, however, is not on the crime, but on its aftermath, in which Conway and DeVito begin systematically eliminating most of those involved in the crime as a way of covering their own tracks. Soon afterward, DeVito is executed by the mob in retribution for his earlier killing, in a blind rage, of a Mafia member.

Hill, meanwhile, has for some time been supplementing his income with money gained by dealing drugs that he imports through Pittsburgh, an independent operation that he conducts with the help of Conway and DeVito, but without the knowledge of the local don, Paul Cicero (Paul Sorvino). Hill himself becomes a cokehead, snorting away much of his profit. His drug activities eventually lead to his arrest by federal authorities. Faced with the possibility of a long jail sentence and the even more frightening possibility of being knocked off by Conway to prevent him from testifying, Hill enters the federal witness protection program and turns state's evidence. He gives extensive testimony concerning mob activities in New York, then disappears into suburbia, given a new identity by the feds. The film then ends with the disturbing image of Hill as a typical suburbanite, caught in the stultifying boredom of bourgeois routine, compared to which his former mob activities take on a special aura of romance and adventure. *Screenplay:* Nicholas Pileggi and Martin Scorsese. *Selected bibliography:* Durgnat ("Martin Scorsese"); Lawrence S. Friedman; Kelly; Pileggi.

*THE HANDMAID'S TALE:* DIR. VOLKER SCHLONDORFF (1990). *The Handmaid's Tale* is a reasonably faithful, but essentially lifeless, adaptation of Margaret Atwood's 1985 dystopian novel of the same title. Both the novel and the film are set in the near future, when much of the United States has been taken over by conservative Christian fundamentalists, who have established the totalitarian Republic of Gilead in an attempt to purify the former sinfulness of America. Meanwhile, environmental problems have caused widespread sterility, leading to a program in which young fertile women are conscripted as "handmaids," then farmed out to childless couples to have passionless intercourse with the husbands in an effort to create new progeny. Atwood's novel grew out of frustration with the right-wing turn of Reaganite America, as signaled by events such as the defeat of the Equal Rights Amendment. The film continues this political project, though in muted form, making somewhat less clear the exact targets of its critique. Meanwhile, the film loses the linguistic and thematic complexity of the book without any real compensatory richness that might have been supplied through visual or other resources of the film medium.

In the film, a young woman, Kate (Natasha Richardson), is captured while attempting to flee Gilead with her husband, who is killed in the attempt. Also with them is their young daughter, whose fate remains unknown to her mother. Kate is taken to a training and indoctrination center for handmaids, then passed on to the household of the "Commander" (Robert Duvall, who delivers the film's only fine performance), a high official in the security apparatus of Gilead. The Commander's name is Fred, so Kate is given the name "Offred" to indicate his possession of her. She is then forced to undergo monthly ceremonial intercourse with the Commander, while his wife, the former gospel singer Serena Joy (Faye Dunaway), looks on. Offred is also required to abide by extremely restrictive rules of dress and conduct, any violation of which could lead to punishment by the spectacular public means that this society favors.

But break the rules Offred does, both by having illicit meetings with the Commander (in which they pursue such activities as playing scrabble) and by establishing a clandestine sexual relationship with Nick (Aidan Quinn), the household chauffeur. After several months, Offred has still not conceived, leading Serena Joy to suspect that it is the Commander, not Serena Joy, who is sterile. Serena Joy then arranges for Offred to have sex with Nick, hoping that she will become pregnant and thus supply the child that will serve as a tremendous status symbol for Serena Joy. Offred, of course, gladly complies, meanwhile becoming more and more involved in the activities of an underground rebel group of which Nick is secretly a member. Eventually, at the instigation of the rebels, Offred murders the Commander, then is whisked away to the safety of the rebel-held mountains by Nick and his fellow rebels. As the film ends, she waits there, pregnant by Nick and hoping for the day when sanity can be restored to the world.

*The Handmaid's Tale* makes its feminist points in a clear, if simplistic way. But it fails to convey the book's sense that the outrageous sexual practices of Gilead are not all that far from those of modern America. As a result, the film is not only less complex than the book, but less horrifying. **Screenplay:** Harold Pinter. ***Selected bibliography:*** Baughman; Booker (*Dystopian*); Pamela Cooper; Kirtz.

## *AT PLAY IN THE FIELDS OF THE LORD:* DIR. HECTOR BABENCO (1991). Based on Peter Mathiessen's 1965 National Book Award-winning

novel of the same title, *At Play in the Fields of the Lord* details the destruction of the Niaruna Indians of Amazonia through the combined impact of greedy wealth seekers and Christian missionaries. The film depicts the Niaruna as a peaceful tribe, living in perfect harmony with their environment in the deep rain forest. But this peace is disrupted when Christian missionaries come to the region to convert them, throwing their smoothly functioning society into a state of disarray. The Niaruna are then completely destroyed when it turns out that their lands contain valuable resources that can be exploited by capitalist developers. *At Play in the Fields of the Lord* is a powerful and effective evocation of the destruction of traditional cultures by the global expansion of capitalism and Christianity.

The film opens as two American adventurers, Lewis Moon (Tom Berenger) and Wolf (Tom Waits) land their small plane near an outpost town on the Amazon because they are low on fuel. The local police chief, Commandante Guzman (José Dumont), confiscates their papers but then agrees to return them, along with a fresh supply of fuel, if they will help him in his effort to drive the Niaruna from their traditional land. The two fly over the astonishingly beautiful rain forest to bomb the Niaruna village, but Moon, who is half Cheyenne, has a change of heart when he sees the seemingly harmless Niaruna, then turns back without dropping the bombs.

In the meantime, a family of new Protestant missionaries, including Martin Quarrier (Aidan Quinn), his wife, Hazel (Kathy Bates), and their young son, Billy (Niilo Kivirinta), arrives in the town to prepare to take up the mission to the Niaruna, which has been abandoned by the Catholic Church after the killing of a priest. The Quarriers are greeted in the town by Leslie Huben (John Lithgow), the regional coordinator for their missionary society. The sanctimonious Huben is an obvious hypocrite who has no understanding of or respect for the traditional culture of the Niaruna, whom he regards as savages. Unconcerned about the welfare of the Niaruna, he regards their conversion as a matter of his own professional success. Indeed, he regards this process almost as a game, as can be seen from his frequent reference to the Catholics as "the opposition."

The Quarriers take up residence in the former Catholic mission deep in the rain forest, though they have to rebuild it almost from scratch. Billy adapts well and soon befriends the local Niaruna children, somewhat to the chagrin of his mother, who regards the innocent Niaruna as depraved heathens. Moon, meanwhile, becomes obsessed with the similarities between the Niaruna and his own Native American ancestors. He flies back over the rain forest and parachutes into the Niaruna land. Seeing him drop from the heavens, they believe him to be an emissary from Kisu, the thunder spirit, and welcome him into their tribe. Soon, however, events take a dark turn. Billy falls ills with blackwater fever and dies, triggering an emotional breakdown in his already neu-rotic mother. Moon, meanwhile, has a brief encounter with Andy Huben (Daryl Hannah), Leslie's beautiful young wife. After kissing her, he contracts her flu, then takes it back to the Niaruna, who have no resis-tance to the virus. The flu spreads through the village like a plague, decimating the tribe.

It is revealed that a large deposit of gold has been discovered on the Niaruna land. Guzman is thus anxious to get rid of the Indians to open their land up for prospectors. When he prepares another assault on the Niaruna village, Martin Quarrier hears about the plan and goes into the forest to try to warn the Indians, guided by Uyuyu (José Renato Lana), a young Niaruna convert whom the area's missionaries have long kept as sort of combination servant and trophy. As Martin reaches the village, it is attacked by helicopter and destroyed. In the confusion, Uyuyu, seeking revenge for a long series of indignities, clubs Martin to death. Only a few survivors, including Moon, manage to escape into the jungle. One of the Niaruna, Aeore (S. Yriwana Karaja) attempts to kill Moon for bringing death and destruction to the Niaruna, but he is instead shot by Moon. As he dies, Aeore bitterly declares that Moon is not a Niaruna but a white man. The film ends as Moon ponders this declaration, the village burns, and Leslie Huben, the damage done, declares that the area is clearly unsuitable for further missionary work. *Screenplay:* Jean-Claude Carriere and Hector Babenco.

*CITY OF HOPE:* DIR. JOHN SAYLES (1991). *City of Hope* is an ambi-tious film that attempts to capture a broad cross-section of the texture of urban life in America at the beginning of the 1990s. It features a large cast of characters from a variety of ethnic and economic backgrounds, all of them nevertheless in one way or another connected through their com-mon membership in the community that makes up the unidentified city that is the setting of the film, a city Sayles has described as based on "Albany, Atlanta, East Boston, Hoboken" (Sayles 181). By carefully drawing these interconnections, both through the plot and through the composition of individual shots, Sayles makes the point that all of the citizens of the city, whatever their backgrounds, have a common stake in the city's welfare. Moreover, he manages to do so in such a way that escapes sentimental we're-all-in-this-together clichés of the American melting pot. The fundamental connection among the various citizens of Sayles's fictional city is not sentimental, but political, and they are part of a community not in the sense of camp-fire singalongs, but of the notion of an interrelated totality of social and economic life of the kind empha-sized by Marxist thinker George Lukács in much of his work. From this point of view, the film also implies that the direct connections that exist among the city's inhabitants also extend outward beyond the city and that the fate of the city (or any other individual community) is inextricably involved in the fate of America, or even the world.

As the film begins, an embittered Nick Rinaldi (Vincent Spano) resigns in disgust from the sinecure construction job he has been given as the son of Joe Rinaldi (Tony Lo Bianco), the head contractor on the construction project. Nick resigns both because he finds his do-nothing job demeaning and because of his bitterness toward his father, for whom he blames the death, in Vietnam, of his older brother Tony, pressured by Joe to join the Marines in order to avoid criminal charges in relation to a hit-and-run accident. Out on the street, Nick becomes involved in a plan by two hoods, Bobby and Zip (Jace Alexander and Todd Graff), to rob an appliance and electronics store, with the encouragement of Carl (Sayles), a local loan shark and small-time crime boss. The store, incidentally, is owned by "Mad Anthony" (Josh Mostel), a friend of Joe Rinaldi. Nick also becomes romantically involved with Angela (Barbara Williams), a waitress and part-time college student. Angela is the ex-wife of the insanely jealous Mike Rizzo (Anthony John Denison), a cop who patrols the neighborhood. Among the teachers at Angela's college are Les Pullman (Bill Raymond) and Reesha Himes (Angela Bassett). Reesha is the wife of councilman Winton "Wynn" Himes (Joe Morton), a former professor who is now the main advocate on the city council for the poor black neighborhood in which Joe Rinaldi owns a number of run-down tenements. Pullman, meanwhile, is mugged by two black teenagers, Desmond and Tito (Jojo Smollett and Edward Jay Townsend, Jr.), largely because they are frustrated at being constantly harassed by policemen such as Rizzo. Arrested, they claim that Pullman made homosexual advances to them, triggering a controversy in which Himes and other local black leaders become centrally involved.

Meanwhile, Bobby and Zip burglarize Mad Anthony's store but are apprehended by the night watchman, who happens to be Reesha Himes's brother. Nick, the getaway driver, escapes but is identified as the third member of the gang. In order to get the heat off Nick, Joe finally agrees to a plan, which he has long resisted, to tear down his tenements so that a luxury high-rise, the Galaxy Towers, can be built on the site. First, however, the tenants of Joe's building have to be gotten rid of, a problem quickly solved by the organized crime connections behind the Galaxy Towers project when they set fire to the tenements, leading to the death of a woman and her baby. As a result of Joe's cooperation, the charges against Nick are dropped, but Rizzo, not realizing this, nevertheless tries to arrest him. Nick escapes, but is shot by Rizzo. In the final scene, Joe finds his wounded son back in the half-constructed building where the film began. They have a heart-to-heart talk and are largely reconciled. Then, realizing his son is badly hurt, Joe calls for help, but no one responds except Asteroid (David Strathairn), the neighborhood loony, who spends most of the film wandering about reciting advertising slogans, including his favorite, a sort of mantra that serves as a concise summary of the American dream, "Why settle for less when you can have it all?" Asteroid echoes Joe's cries, simultaneously summarizing the plight of the city's slum dwellers as he screams repeatedly and vainly into the night as the film comes to a close: "Help! We need help!"

The impressive thing about *City of Hope* is that all of these labyrinthine interconnections are related in a manner that is natural, coherent, and not the least bit confusing. Meanwhile, the film is uncompromising in its depiction of the realities of urban life, including poverty, violence, and corruption. City luminaries such as the district attorney and Mayor Baci (Louis Zorich) are just as crooked as the sleazy Carl, while well-meaning characters such as Joe Rinaldi and Wynn Himes find that, despite their best efforts, they can make little headway in overcoming the obstacles that the corrupt system places in their path. Importantly, however, this "system" is not merely that of one decaying city; it is the entire system of American capitalism. In one telling scene, Joe Rinaldi turns to a senior mob boss (Lawrence Tierney) to try to get protection from the corruption of Baci and other members of the city's official administration. He is told, however, that the corruption cannot be helped. "It's not the way our society works, Joe," the old don tells him. "You got something good, first everybody on top of you gets a taste. Then you share what's left with everybody below you." In a parallel scene, Himes turns for advice to a retired black politician (Ray Aranha), identified as one of the first black mayors in a major U.S. city. The ex-mayor describes the frustrations that eventually destroyed his idealism, driving him out of politics and onto the golf course, where he now spends most of his time. The job of a leader, he tells Himes, is not to demonstrate his moral fiber, but to lead, which means "take it to the man every chance you get." When Himes counters that "this is not a fight with white people," the former mayor simply responds, "It's always about that, Wynn."

The mayor is not, however, entirely cynical. Nor is the film. The title of *City of Hope* is not entirely ironic, and the film has its utopian moments, even if it does very little to suggest alternatives to the bleak conditions it describes. Wynn, for example, scores one of his best political victories after the conversation with the old mayor, when his constituents meet to discuss the treatment of boys Desmond and Tito. Wynn, who knows the boy's are lying about Pullman, manages to divert the attention of the meeting to the eviction of the inhabitants of Rinaldi's tenements, subsequently leading his constituents in an angry march of protest into a political fund-raising dinner being hosted by Mayor Baci. Most of the film's positive moments occur on a smaller scale, in one-on-one interactions between individuals, who occasionally make genuine contact. In Sayles's vision, however, these moments are not simply private, because each of the individuals involved is always part of a larger community, and each of these personal connections is a step toward collective consciousness. *Screenplay:* John Sayles. *Selected bibliography:* Crowdus and Quart; Horton; Packer; Nora Ruth Roberts; Sayles (*Sayles*).

*GUILTY BY SUSPICION:* DIR. IRWIN WINKLER (1991). While *The Front* (1976) deals very effectively with blacklisting in the television industry, *Guilty by Suspicion* remains the only major Hollywood film to deal directly with the anticommunist witch hunts and blacklists that struck the film industry in the late 1940s and 1950s. Thus, while some critics have complained that *Guilty by Suspicion* is nothing more than a stale would-be revelation of facts that are already well known, it is clear that Hollywood has never dealt sufficiently with the trauma of the McCarthy era and that much remains to be done. Unfortunately, *Guilty by Suspicion* is a rather flat piece that fails sufficiently to explain the historical background of the events it describes. Instead, in its attempt to dramatize the human suffering caused by the anticommunist purges, it focuses on the personal tragedies of a few individuals, at times becoming a story more of private angst than of public persecution. In addition, the film's focus on the persecution of individuals who were never really communists tends to suggest that it was perfectly acceptable to persecute real communists.

*Guilty by Suspicion* focuses on hotshot director David Merrill (Robert De Niro), who returns to Hollywood after a few months in Paris to find the entire town swept up in anticommunist hysteria. Given that the Hollywood witch hunts had been going on since 1947, the apparent suddenness of this development in not very realistic, but it presumably increases the sense of terror that the film seeks to portray as endemic in the film industry. Merrill discovers that he, having innocently attended a couple of Communist Party meetings more than a decade earlier, has just been named as a communist sympathizer in the testimony of screenwriter Larry Nolan (Chris Cooper). This fact, together with Merrill's own refusal to name close friends, such as screenwriter Bunny Baxter (George Wendt), quickly results in Merrill's exclusion from employment in the film industry, despite his former status as the "golden boy" of powerful producer and studio executive Darryl Zanuck (Ben Piazza).

Hounded by FBI agents, unable to find a job, and virtually friendless, Merrill is eventually forced to take up residence in a small apartment with his ex-wife, Ruth (Annette Bening), and their young son, Paulie (Luke Edwards). As the pressure builds on Merrill to testify, Zanuck offers him the opportunity to direct a major new film if he will only cooperate with the committee. Finally, he agrees, then goes to Washington, only to have a change of heart in the hearing room and lambaste the committee for their sinister inquiries. He is then dragged away from the microphone. Inspired by Merrill's example, Baxter, who had also agreed to testify, simply takes the fifth amendment and refuses to answer any questions. Merrill thus wins a moral victory but is charged with contempt of Congress, facing a possible prison term. The film then ends with on-screen text announcing that "thousands of lives were shattered and hundreds of career destroyed by what came to be known as the Hollywood blacklist." *Screenplay:* Irwin Winkler. *Selected bibliography:* Caute (*Great Fear*); Ceplair and Englund; Navasky.

*JFK:* **DIR. OLIVER STONE (1991).** One of the most controversial films of the 1990s, *JFK* narrates the efforts of New Orleans District Attorney Jim Garrison (Kevin Costner) to demonstrate that the 1963 assassination of President John F. Kennedy was in fact the result of a vast conspiracy involving not only the Mafia and right-wing anti-Castro Cubans, but defense contractors, the FBI, the CIA, virtually the entire American Military Intelligence community, and even Lyndon Johnson. The film, from the casting of likeable nice guy Costner in the central role to the construction of the entire narrative as a dramatization of the conspiracy theory, is clearly sympathetic to Garrison's position, which is only to be expected, given that the script was originally based on Garrison's book, *On the Trail of the Assassins*. Elaborately researched and presented in a documentary style, *JFK* presents a case that was convincing enough to stimulate the U.S. Congress to attempt to reopen the investigation of the assassination, though these efforts essentially came to nothing. The film is also an impressive achievement in storytelling, weaving together a vast amount of information and loosely connected strands into a compelling drama that never wavers during its three-hour-plus run. It was nominated for eight Academy Awards, including best picture and best director, though it won only two, for best cinematography and best film editing.

The film sets up its theory by beginning with a clip of President Dwight Eisenhower's parting warning against the growing power of the "military-industrial complex." The film then establishes that Kennedy, as Eisenhower's successor, ran afoul of this sinister entity through a variety of actions, ranging from his refusal to support an all-out invasion to Cuba to his plan to withdraw all American forces from Vietnam before that conflict ever involved American troops in a major way. The film then turns to the assassination, which seems surrounded by disturbing questions, most of which are quickly dismissed by the Warren Commission, which declares that Lee Harvey Oswald (played in the film by Gary Oldman) acted entirely alone in killing the president, even though this conclusion requires the acceptance of a number of unlikely propositions and the dismissal of a number of seemingly important pieces of evidence.

Convinced that the truth of the assassination is being covered up, Garrison begins his own investigation, justified by the fact that numerous personages connected to the assassination, including Oswald, had New Orleans connections. Garrison encounters considerable opposition, including the bashing of his investigation in the media. His family receives threatening phone calls, and his family life is seriously disrupted as wife Liz (Sissy Spacek) urges him to give up the investigation. Most law enforcement agencies inexplicably refuse to cooperate with this investigation, his tax returns are audited by the IRS, and he is asked to resign from the National Guard. Meanwhile, several potentially important witnesses are killed under suspicious circumstances, and Garrison at one point apparently narrowly escapes an attempt on his life. In the meantime, Martin Luther King and Robert Kennedy are assassinated as well, strengthening Garrison's conviction that sinister forces are afoot in America, perhaps leading toward a fascist takeover of the government.

Garrison pursues his case doggedly, despite the obstacles he encounters, finally bringing an indictment against New Orleans businessman Clay Shaw (Tommy Lee Jones) for conspiracy to kill Kennedy. Garrison presents a seemingly compelling case, though the judge refuses to allow him to introduce some of his most important evidence. Nevertheless, Shaw is acquitted of the charge. Garrison vows to continue the fight, but he would never succeed in proving his case in court, though many of the questions he raised remain unanswered to this day. Seen by many as an irresponsible portrayal of an unproven theory as if it were fact, *JFK* was celebrated by many others as a powerful and important film that stimulated much-needed debate concerning the mysteries that still surround the assassination. On the other hand, some of the film's more ominous implications about the real nature of modern American society have been largely ignored. *Screenplay:* Oliver Stone and Zachary Sklar. *Selected bibliography:* Burgoyne; Kagan (*Cinema of Oliver Stone*); Rogin ("Body"); Sharrett; Simon; Staiger.

*THELMA AND LOUISE:* **DIR. RIDLEY SCOTT (1991).** *Thelma and Louise* tells the story of two female friends from Arkansas who suddenly find themselves on the run from the law, then flee together cross-country, along the way establishing a deep interpersonal bond. As such, the film has a great deal in common with a variety of standard Hollywood forms, including the road film, the buddy film, and the fugitive from justice film. Like most Hollywood hits, *Thelma and Louise* poses very little in the way of an alternative to the current male-dominated capitalist system, and it is certainly not the purpose or effect of the film to recommend Thelma and Louise as role models for a full-scale feminist revolution. Nevertheless, the gendering of the film poses certain problems that clearly go beyond mere Hollywood cliché, as can be seen by the intense level of the controversy and debate that the film triggered.

As the film begins, Louise (Susan Sarandon), a waitress, convinces suburban housewife Thelma (Geena Davis) to accompany her on a camping trip, despite the fact that Thelma knows her husband, Darryl (Christopher McDonald), would never approve of the trip. So Thelma skips out without informing Darryl, giving the trip an aura of transgression from the very beginning. Then Thelma, still apparently seeking transgressive experience, insists that they stop at a bar on the way to the cabin. There, Thelma dances with Harlan (Timothy Carhart), a handsome redneck, who then takes her out to the parking lot and attempts to have sex with her. Thelma does not want to be *that* transgressive, so she refuses, whereupon the furious Harlan attempts to rape her. Louise then appears with the gun Thelma has taken along to fight off "psycho killers" and orders Harlan to let Thelma go. He does, but defiantly mouths off to Louise, who promptly blows him away, displaying a level that we later learn arises from the fact that she was formerly raped.

These examples of sexual violence are clearly portrayed in the film as particularly overt examples of the violence suffered by women like Louise and Thelma every day of their lives. They conclude that they will be charged with murder for sure and go on the run, eventually heading for Mexico. Driving through Oklahoma, they pick up a handsome young cowboy, J. D. (Brad Pitt), who turns out to be a former juvenile delinquent and armed robber. He and Thelma have wild sex (her first sexual experience with anyone other than Darryl), then he promptly takes off with all of the money Louise has withdrawn from her bank account to finance their escape to Mexico. Inspired by J. D.'s robbery stories, Thelma decides to become an armed robber, obviously finding the experience empowering. But J. D. is not exactly the best role model for feminine rebellion, and Thelma's robberies only make matters worse for Thelma and Louise, causing the police and FBI to step up their efforts to apprehend the pair. Eventually, for reasons that are only partly explained in the film, the two fugitives wind up in northern Arizona — not a very good way to get to Mexico from Arkansas, but a good way to get to the Grand Canyon for the film's finale. Along the way, they terrorize a highway patrolman and truck driver and thus presumably gain some level of revenge for the abuse and humiliation they have long suffered at the hands of men. As the police close in, Thelma and Louise, in a final show of solidarity and defiance, decide to drive their convertible over the edge of the canyon to avoid apprehension.

Viewed as a fantasy of female empowerment (and not as a realistic story, from which point of view it is simply dumb), *Thelma and Louise* raises a number of important questions, if nothing else calling attention to the relative unavailability of genuinely effective models of feminine rebellion in modern American society. The film is, however, rather weak in its treatment of class, making essentially no effort to explore the sources of women's oppression in the capitalist economic system. *Screenplay:* Callie Khouri. *Selected bibliography:* Boozer ("Seduction"); Joyce Miller; Lillian S. Robinson; Spelman and Minow.

*AMERICAN DREAM:* DIR. BARBARA KOPPLE (1992). The followup to Kopple's award-winning *Harlan County, U.S.A.* (1976), *American Dream* focuses on the much-publicized labor struggles at the Hormel and Company meatpacking plant in Austin, Minnesota, from 1984 to 1986. Like most documentaries, the film involves numerous interviews with various principals in the case, though it also features extensive on-the-scene footage of events as they take place. While the film might have done more to establish the background and history of such labor disputes, it does acknowledge that the meatpackers are fighting to preserve gains they have won through decades of struggle. It also effectively establishes the context of the Hormel situation in the midst of widespread attempts, led by the Reagan administration, to break labor unions all over America, allowing companies in a variety of industries to backtrack on concessions granted to workers in earlier struggles, thus clearing the way to make higher and higher profits by paying lower and lower wages and benefits.

The Hormel dispute begins in late 1984 when the company announces that it is cutting hourly wages in the Austin plant from $10.69 to $8.25 per hour in order to "stay competitive," despite the fact that the company is making huge profits under the existing wage scale. Benefits are cut accordingly, and, with the elimination of incentive programs, some workers find their paychecks reduced by as much as 50 per cent. The company's contract with the United Food and Commercial Workers International Union (UFCW) is nearing expiration, and the union local decides to adopt an aggressive strategy to oppose these wage and benefit cuts as negotiations for a new contract near. Local president Ray Guyette leads this fight, bringing in media consultant Ray Rogers, who specializes in labor battles. Rogers begins an aggressive media campaign, hoping to shame the company into restoring wages in order to avoid bad publicity, even though the national union, through its representative, Lewie Anderson, urges a more diplomatic approach.

As the film proceeds, the local union thus finds itself at odds with both the company and the national union, and the disagreement between the local and the national union provides a central focus of the film, raising fundamental questions about appropriate labor strategies in the difficult anti-union climate of 1980s America. Both the local and the national union are presented as sincere in their advocacy of the workers' cause, and both agree on the ultimate goals of that advocacy. Their conflict is simply over tactics to be used in the struggle. Anderson's more conciliatory attitude obviously has its problems, but he is a seasoned negotiator, and, in the end, his more conservative approach seems a more accurate assessment of the current situation. Guyette and Rogers are successful in drawing national media attention to the struggle in Austin, but they repeatedly find Hormel unresponsive to their attempts to pressure the company through negative publicity. Eventually, the local votes to strike, despite Anderson's warnings that strikes should be a strategy of last resort, used strategically when they have a good chance of success.

Guyette and Rogers do not recognize, until too late, that conditions are not right for a successful strike in Austin, because the company is in a better position to weather a long strike than are the workers. Hormel keeps the Austin plant running at a reduced level, manned by management personnel and temporary strikebreakers. Attempts by the strikers to shut down the plant are thwarted when the governor calls out the National Guard to keep the plant open. In the meantime, Hormel simply shifts much of the former production of the Austin plant to other facilities. The Austin local attempts to spread their strike to these other plants but with little success. Eventually, with the strike entering its sixth month, Hormel tries to force the strikers to return to work by announcing that they are going to hire permanent replacement workers. Under the circumstances, many workers make the difficult decision to return, but most do not. Finally, in June 1986, the national union steps in, dismisses Guyette and the other elected officers of the local, and reaches an agreement with Hormel on its own terms.

This agreement calls for wages of $10.25 per hour, the same as have been negotiated at Hormel's other plants. It does not, however, call for the rehiring of the replaced strikers, and, as of the release of the film six years later, fewer than 20 per cent of the fired workers had been hired back. Meanwhile, as the last scenes of the film show, widespread unemployment throws the town of Austin into an economic recession, many workers are forced to give up their family homes, and many local businesses are forced to close their doors. As the film closes, we are informed by on-screen text that, in 1989, Hormel leased out half its Austin plant to another company that is paying only $6.60 per hour in wages. Thus, the wages of the workers of Austin continue to fall, while Hormel's profits continue to soar. The American public, its attention called to the Austin situation by extensive media coverage, looks on with apathy. *Selected bibliography:* Crowdus and Porton; Orvell; Rachleff; Zaniello.

**BOB ROBERTS: DIR. TIM ROBBINS (1992).** *Bob Roberts* is a fictional documentary that follows the rise of right-wing folksinger Bob Roberts (Robbins) to fame, fortune, and a seat in the U.S. Senate. The film effectively satirizes the vacuity and hypocrisy of Roberts, a master of the media and pure American demagogue, who spouts moralistic slogans but is willing to stoop to any level of deception, and even murder, in a ruthless quest for wealth and power. In this sense, of course, the film can be taken as a commentary on the Republican right in general, a commentary that gains an especially chilling force in the light of the 1994 "Republican revolution," when right-wing opportunists running on uncannily Roberts-like platforms were swept into Congress and the Senate from districts all over America.

*Bob Roberts* is actually a sort of meta-documentary that follows a film crew that is making a documentary about Roberts. It includes performances of a number of Roberts's songs, many of which are hilarious, highlighted by the music video "Wall Street Rap," which glorifies greed and acquisitiveness via a parody of Bob Dylan's "Subterranean Homesick Blues." Indeed, Roberts consistently parodies Dylan, releasing albums with such titles as "The Free Wheelin' Bob Roberts," "The Times Are Changing Back," and "Bob on Bob." This dialogue with Dylan is part of an overall assault on the values of the counterculture of the 1960s, which Roberts sees as a source of moral decay. He particularly campaigns against drug use, which makes it highly problematic when investigative report Bugs Raplin (Giancarlo Esposito) uncovers evidence that Roberts and his sinister handler, Lukas Hart (Alan Rickman), have been involved in an array of shady deals involving failing savings and loan associations, arms shipments to the Nicaraguan Contras, and the smuggling of drugs into the United States.

This evidence is dismissed by the Roberts camp as the ravings of a crazed radical. It nevertheless seriously hampers Roberts's senatorial election campaign against long-time liberal Senator Brickley Paiste (Gore Vidal), overshadowing Roberts's earlier attempt to discredit Paiste by fabricating evidence of an extramarital affair between Paiste and a teenage campaign worker. Desperate, the Roberts's camp concocts an elaborate scheme in which they fake an assassination attempt on Roberts, claiming that he has been crippled by his gunshot wounds. He thus finishes the campaign in a wheelchair, hoping to gain sympathy. In the meantime, the Roberts campaign attempts to kill two birds with one stone by framing Raplin for the shooting using fabricated evidence. Eventually, Raplin is cleared, thanks to the efforts of his lawyer, Mack Laflin (David Strathairn), but the ploy works, and Roberts is elected.

Soon after the election, Raplin is murdered, supposedly by a right-wing fanatic, but there are hints that the reporter is the victim of a concerted conspiracy. Roberts's supposedly moral supporters gleefully cheer the news of Raplin's death, and the film as a whole is particularly powerful in its depiction of these followers as willing to do anything in the service of their adored leader, with clear echoes of the followers of Hitler in Nazi Germany. There are also ominous hints that the covert dealings in which Roberts and Hart are involved are part of a vast network of such dealings, engineered by a secret government headed by the National Security Council. These hints, endorsed by Paiste, may seem paranoid, but events such as the Iran-Contra affair suggest that they contain more than a grain of truth—and that the American people, evoked in the film through analogy to the frog-in-boiling-water commonplace, have become so inured to such activities that they are perfectly willing to let them continue unopposed. *Bob Roberts* is seemingly effective satire, so much so that more than one critic began to compare Robbins to Orson Welles after the release of the film. But this satire clearly had no impact whatsoever on American voters, ironically demonstrating the apathy of the American populace that is a central theme of the film. *Screenplay:* Tim Robbins. *Selected bibliography:* Alter; Kopkind; Morgan; Travers; Troy; Zebme.

*THE PLAYER:* DIR. ROBERT ALTMAN (1992). Altman's contribution to the grand tradition of Hollywood satires of Hollywood, *The Player* uses a detective story format to lampoon the shallowness, venality, and inauthenticity of the values that drive the Hollywood film industry. In so doing, Altman clearly seeks to use Hollywood as a metaphor for American society as a whole, though the film is less successful in this sense than Altman's earlier use of the country music industry in *Nashville* (1975). *The Player* is notable for its numerous Hollywood inside jokes and cameo appearances by prominent Hollywood stars, both of which lend an air of authenticity to the satire, which is strong but not bitter. This lampoon of the film industry is, in fact, infused with a clear affection for film, from the elaborate opening allusion to the famous crane shot at the beginning of *Touch of Evil* (1958), to the film posters that constantly pop up in the film, to the tendency of most of the principals to speak largely in terms of film allusions.

*The Player* focuses on Griffin Mill (Tim Robbins), an ambitious, but insecure studio executive, who spends half his time hearing pitches from would-be screenwriters for potential films and half his time in political maneuvering to try to undermine those whom he identifies as his competition. Central in this regard is up-and-coming whiz kid Larry Levy (Peter Gallagher), rumored to be on his way to supplanting Mill as the studio's second-in-command. Much of the plot interest is supplied by the anonymous threatening notes that Mill has been receiving for months. Given his style of operation and the nature of his business, in which virtually all pitches have to be turned down, Mill has lots of enemies. He concludes (wrongly, it turns out) that the notes are being sent by screenwriter David Kahane (Vincent D'Onofrio), whom Mill had treated particularly rudely after a recent pitch.

Mill tracks down Kahane and tries to make a deal with him, but they end up fighting in a darkened parking lot. Kahane is killed; Mill takes his wallet to make it look like a robbery, then flees the scene. Much of the rest of the film involves the attempts of the Pasadena police, led by detectives Susan Avery (Whoopi Goldberg) and Paul DeLongpre (Lyle Lovett), to solve the killing, while Mill spends much of his time trying to avoid implication in the crime. In the meantime, however, he calls attention to himself by beginning an affair with artist June Gudmundsdottir (Greta Scacchi), a sexy mystery woman who causes Mill to abandon his long-time girlfriend, story editor Bonnie Sherow (Cynthia Stevenson), the only wholesome and virtuous film-industry employee in the entire film.

In the end, Mill does successfully avoid prosecution. Moreover, in a parody of the required Hollywood happy endings that are satirized throughout the film, he becomes the head of the studio, marries June, and lives happily ever after in a luxurious fairy-tale home. Bonnie, meanwhile, is not only dumped by Mill but fired from the studio after she vehemently protests their perversion (due to poor test-audience results with the original) of a dark, existential drama into a stereotypical bit of optimistic fluff, complete with big-name stars. She is left weeping on the steps of the studio offices, while Mill happily drives his Rolls Royce home to his ideal home and ideal wife. In Hollywood, virtue is not rewarded; it is, in fact, a definite liability. Meanwhile, on his way home, Mill receives a call on his car phone from the sender of the earlier threatening messages, offering him a script for a film, called *The Player*, about an ambitious Hollywood executive who kills a screenwriter he thinks has been threatening him. Mill agrees that it sounds like a good idea for a film, especially if it can have a happy ending. *Screenplay:* Michael Tolkin. *Selected bibliography:* O'Brien; Richolson; Sugg.

*UNFORGIVEN:* DIR. CLINT EASTWOOD (1992). A complex and sophisticated retake on the genre of the Western, *Unforgiven* won four Academy Awards, including best picture and best director. Director Eastwood stars as William Munny, an over-the-hill gunslinger who functions as a revision of many Western protagonists, including Eastwood's own earlier characters, especially the Man with No Name of Sergio Leone's spaghetti Westerns. The film begins in the 1880s in the frontier town of Big Whiskey, Wyoming, as a rowdy cowboy, Quick Mike (David Mucci), becomes enraged by a prostitute's innocent remarks about his genitals, then slashes her face with a knife, while his friend, Davey Bunting (Rob Campbell), holds her down. When the town sheriff, "Little Billie" Daggert (Gene Hackman), punishes the men simply by ordering them to pay the owner of the bordello seven horses in restitution for his damaged property, the other prostitutes in the establishment angrily seek justice by pooling their resources to offer a reward to anyone who will kill the two men.

Hearing of this reward, a young would-be gunfighter, who calls himself The Schofield Kid (Jaimz Woolvett), decides to seek the reward. First, however, he attempts to recruit Munny, retired and working peacefully on his farm thanks to the civilizing influence of his now-deceased wife, to help him kill the men. Munny at first refuses, then comes to Big Whiskey after all, accompanied by his long-time sidekick, Ned Logan (Morgan Freeman). They and the other reward seekers are welcomed with anything but open arms by Daggett, who insists on being the only law in town. He brutally beats Munny as a warning, almost killing him. Nevertheless, Munny recovers and, aided by the Kid, kills the two men. In the meantime, however, Logan has become fed up with the whole enterprise and heads back to Kansas. He is captured, however, then killed when the sadistic Daggett tortures him to death in an attempt to get information about Munny.

To this point, *Unforgiven* is essentially an anti-Western. The brutal violence it portrays is anything but heroic, whether it be Daggett's torture of Logan or the Kid's shooting of Quick Mike as he defecates in an outhouse. Indeed, The Kid is so revolted by this, his first killing, that he swears off violence altogether and swears never to kill again. Meanwhile, the West of the film is organized not according to moral codes but economics, whether it be in the overt treatment of the prostitutes as pieces of property or in the willingness even of the protagonist to kill for a relatively small sum of money. Further, the film makes the point that most Western myths are fictions created by opportunists such as the writer W. W. Beauchamp (Saul Rubinek), who circulates through the film seeking material that he can turn into pulp novels—with a clear suggestion that Western films have served much the same purpose as Beauchamp's books.

Both Munny and Daggett attempt to disabuse Beauchamp of his view of the heroic nature of the West. Munny, however, still has killing to do, in retribution for the death of his friend, and the film suddenly veers into a more conventional Western mode at the end. Munny returns to Big Whiskey and confronts Daggett in the town saloon. Then, in a virtuoso display of gunplay, Munny shoots down Daggett and four deputies before riding out of town to return to his peaceful life. This ending clearly complicates *Unforgiven*'s questioning and challenging of the conventions of the Western genre, though, given the popularity of the film, this ending can be taken as a demonstration that audiences, by demanding and expecting such endings, are complicit in the conventions of the genre. *Screenplay:* David Webb Peoples. *Selected bibliography:* Engel; Grist; Ingrassia; Skerry; Tibbetts; Yacowar.

*HEAVEN AND EARTH:* **DIR. OLIVER STONE (1993).** *Heaven and Earth* is the third entry in Stone's Vietnam trilogy, following *Platoon* (1986) and *Born on the Fourth of July* (1989). This third film failed to gain the attention and acclaim of its predecessors, though it is in many ways the best of the three. If nothing else, based on the autobiographical writings of former Vietnamese villager Le Ly Hayslip, it is one of the few American films about the Vietnam War that makes a legitimate attempt to represent the war from a Vietnamese point of view. The film is particularly powerful in its contrast between the traditional values of Vietnamese peasant society and the lack of values in modern American consumer capitalism. Perhaps for this reason, the film was not a commercial success, nor did it receive the critical acclaim (and multiple Academy Award nominations) of Stone's earlier Vietnam War films.

The film begins as Le Ly is a small child growing up in the South Vietnamese village of Ky La, where life has remained virtually unchanged for a thousand years. This idyllic existence is then suddenly interrupted in the summer of 1953, when French troops invade and destroy the village in an attempt to suppress the anticolonial rebellion then underway. The brave and patient villagers endure this disastrous intrusion and gradually begin to rebuild their traditional lives. In 1963, however, this traditional way of life comes to an end once and for all as the village becomes a site of contestation between the Viet Cong and South Vietnamese government, with their American backers. The Americans and their allies attempt to impose their will and point of view on the village, but most of the villagers remain sympathetic to the Viet Cong, who better understand their way of life and who, they believe, are fighting for the liberation of this and other villages from neocolonial domination by the United States via the puppet government in Saigon. The film is relatively sympathetic to the Viet Cong and the North Vietnamese communists, making clear, among other things, the great respect and admiration with which Ho Chi Minh was viewed by the Vietnamese, North and South, as a result of his heroic leadership in the anticolonial struggle against both the French and the Japanese.

In one horrifying sequence, Le Ly (played by Hiep Thi Le), suspected of complicity with the Viet Cong (which her two brothers have joined), is taken for questioning by the South Vietnamese Army. She is then brutally tortured, while American advisors smugly look on. Eventually, Le Ly's mother (played by Joan Chen), bribes the corrupt South Vietnamese and gains Le Ly's release, but this release immediately makes Le Ly an object of suspicion to the Viet Cong, who subsequently take her for questioning of their own. One of them then rapes her, though he threatens to kill her if she tells anyone, making it clear that the rape is not approved Viet Cong practice. This experience shatters Le Ly's sense of connection with the village once and for all. At the age of eighteen, she moves with her mother to Saigon to try to make a life in the city.

Le Ly manages to gain employment as a servant in the home of a wealthy family. She is soon seduced by the husband of the house, who actually treats her well. Le Ly experiences sexual tenderness for the first time; she also becomes pregnant and is exiled, along with her mother to Da Nang. There, she has the baby, a boy, and struggles to survive, selling on the black market and digging through the garbage on the American base there. Eventually, she meets Marine Sergeant Steve Butler (Tommy Lee Jones), who pays court to the much younger Le Ly, explaining to her that his bad first marriage has taught him that "I need a good Oriental woman." Steve and Le Ly live together essentially as a family, and she soon has a second son. Then, when South Vietnam falls, Steve takes Le Ly and the boys home with him to San Diego.

Steve and Le Ly are officially married and later have a third son. She, meanwhile, meets his quintessentially American family and otherwise attempts to adjust to the new world of America, where material commodities are abundant, but where the people seem spiritually empty, with no connection to tradition. Indeed, the presentation of American consumer society, seen through Le Ly's eyes in contrast to the poverty and destruction that reign in Vietnam, is genuinely horrifying. Steve, meanwhile, is financially strapped by alimony and child support payments arising from his first marriage, though he envisions a coming better future when he can leave the marines and become an international arms dealer. Le Ly, having experienced the destruction that weapons can cause, is horrified by this plan, which anyway falls through after Steve, sinking into anger and desspair, turns to drink and is kicked out of the marines. As Steve grows violent and abusive, Le Ly files for divorce. Distraught and unbalanced, Steve kidnaps and threatens the children, then ends up killing himself.

Meanwhile, drawing on support provided by the local Vietnamese immigrant community, Le Ly becomes a successful restaurant owner. Then, in the film's moving final sequence, Le Ly returns for a visit to Vietnam with her three children. In Saigon, her eldest, Jimmy, meets his father for the first time. They then return to Ky La to visit Le Ly's ailing mother. Bon (Vinh Dang), Le Ly's surviving brother, rejects her for marrying an American, given the destruction wrought in Vietnam (including the death of Le Ly's father and her other brother) by Americans. But Le Ly's mother, nearing death, accepts her daughter with open arms. We are then informed by on-screen text that Le Ly and her boys returned to San Diego, where she continued to work for her homeland by helping to build a series of health clinics there through her support for the East Meets West Foundation.

*Heaven and Earth* is a moving and powerful film, though its presentation of the war in Vietnam as a confrontation between Vietnamese tradition and American modernity somewhat simplifies the reality of the war. After all, the primary confrontation there was between communism and capitalism, both phenomena of modernity. Nevertheless, the film, released in 1993, came at an important time when it helped to counter revisionist histories that were beginning to efface the gruesome reality of the American intervention in Vietnam. As Stone put it, he sought in the film to "respond to, in part, the blind militarism and mindless revisionism of the Vietnam War as typified by a certain odious brand of thinking that has snaked its way into our culture over the past decade or so, in which the conflict is refought in comic book style with a brand new ending ... we win!" (qtd in Kagan 208). *Screenplay:* Oliver Stone. *Selected bibliography:* Doyle; Kagan (*Cinema of Oliver Stone*); Kunz (*Films*).

*IT'S ALL TRUE:* DIR. RICHARD WILSON (1993). *It's All True* is a documentary that combines surviving footage from Orson Welles's unfinished early 1940s film of the same title with supplemental information describing the making of Welles's films and the withdrawal of support by RKO Studios that led to the discontinuation of Welles's original project. That original project, begun partly at the behest of the U.S. government, was to be a documentary presenting Latin American culture in a positive light and thereby serving as a gesture of solidarity between the United States and Latin America in the midst of World War II. When it became apparent that Welles, already in hot water with the studio, was operating according to his own agenda, the project was quickly abandoned, and Welles was never able to get support to complete the film.

Welles, working without a script and soon going well beyond the original plans of RKO and the U.S. government, eventually developed a plan to film three separate documentary segments. The first of these, "My Friend Bonito," centers on the relationship between a Mexican boy and his pet calf; it was never completed and now survives only in a few black-and-white fragments, which are included in the 1993 documentary. The second segment was to focus on the Carnaval in Rio and was originally planned as the centerpiece of the film. Shot in spectacular Technicolor, this segment eventually came to focus on the role of the Samba in the Carnaval. It, too, was never completed, and its scenes of interracial dancing were one of the principal reasons why RKO became disillusioned with the project.

The third, and only complete, segment of the film is entitled "Four Men on a Raft." Based on a true story involving poor fishermen, or *jangadeiros*, in Brazil, this segment was made after RKO had withdrawn most of its support. It was shot with a rudimentary crew, using primitive equipment that included a single, stationary camera, with no sound. Yet Welles was able to capture amazing and impressive footage as the film details daily life in a poor fishing village, enacted by the village's actual inhabitants under Welles's direction. He was also, even without sound, able to capture the simple nobility of the people of the village, as well as the economic hardships that force them to pursue difficult and dangerous work in their quest to survive. The plot takes a turn when one of the fisherman, a recent groom whose wedding had been presented earlier in the film, is drowned after his small fishing raft, or *jangada*, capsizes.

The fishermen decide that enough is enough. Four of them resolve to sail one of the rafts to Rio, 1,600 miles away, to protest their working conditions and to demand more social services from the Brazilian government. The film details their long and arduous journey, following them as they almost miraculously succeed in reaching Rio. The Welles segment then ends as they arrive, while the additional information supplied in the 1993 documentary informs us that the men were greeted as heroes, gaining an audience with Brazil's President Vargas, who promised to meet their demands, though he never followed through on his promises. We also learn that Jacaré, the leader of the four *jangadeiros*, subsequently became a controversial figure in Brazil because of his political activities, which led to rumors that he was a communist. Welles, while filming the story, became the object of similar rumors, which did little to endear him to the right-wing Brazilian government. Finally, we also learn that Jacaré, having survived this astonishing voyage in reality, was ironically drowned during the course of re-enacting it for Welles's cameras.

"Four Men on a Raft" is an impressive piece, somewhat reminiscent of the leftist documentaries of the 1930s, though much more technically accomplished than any of them. It has also been seen as an anticipation of Italian neorealism. Michael Denning, for example, compares it to both Paul Strand's 1937 documentary about Mexican fishermen, *The Wave*, and Luchino Visconti's 1948 neorealist film about Sicilian fishermen, *La Terra Trema* (398). The original *It's All True* might have been an important contribution to American leftist cinema. It was, as Robert Stam notes, animated by a "democratic, anti-racist spirit" that sought to "emphasize not elite individual history but rather collective heroism and creativity" (242). *Screenplay:* Bill Krohn, Richard Wilson, and Myron Meisel. *Selected bibliography:* Benamou; Denning; Stam.

**THE BURNING SEASON: DIR. JOHN FRANKENHEIMER (1994).** Based on the life of Brazilian labor leader and environmentalist activist Chico Mendes (played by Raul Julia), *The Burning Season* parallels the brutal exploitation of Brazilian rubber workers with the destruction of the Amazonian rain forest by unscrupulous capitalist interests. The film begins in 1951, when Mendes, as a boy, observes the horrible murder of a union leader who comes to the forest to help the rubber workers organize a resistance to the practices that have long kept them in poverty and fear. It then cuts to 1983, when the rubber workers face a new danger, the destruction of the rain forest to clear land for cattle for the beef industry. Another union leader, Wilson Pinheiro (Edward James Olmos), is in the area with Regina (Sonia Braga), an ecologist, to help the rubber workers resist the destruction of the forest.

The combination of business and political interests that has conspired to facilitate the burning off of the forest arranges to have Pinheiro assassinated. Mendes, who has been working with Pinheiro, is arrested, beaten, and tortured in an effort to intimidate him. But he assumes Pinheiro's leadership role nevertheless, continuing the fight to save the forest and the livelihoods of the rubber workers by whatever means necessary, though he prefers a nonviolent approach. In the meantime, documentary filmmaker Steven Kaye (Nigel Havers) comes to the area to cover the efforts of Mendes and the rubber workers.

When peaceful resistance is met with brutal violence, Mendes attempts a political solution, running for office but losing in a landslide thanks to the corrupt practices of the forces that oppose him. Kaye, however, records Mendes's efforts and brings international attention to the plight of the forest and the rubber workers. Mendes, much to his own discomfort, becomes a celebrity with his face on T-shirts. He welcomes the support engendered by Kaye's work but begins to suspect that many of his international supporters, especially in North America, are simply trendy tree lovers who have no understanding of the real situation and no genuine sympathy with the rubber workers and other poor Brazilians whose lives are being destroyed along with the forest. Mendes is not opposed to progress, or even necessarily to the destruction of the forest: he simply wants progress to occur in a way that leads to less, not more, exploitation and oppression of the workers he represents.

Back in Brazil, Mendes continues to lead the workers' resistance in the face of increasingly violent practices by the developers and their official supporters. Eventually, in 1988, Mendes, too, is assassinated, but he is famous enough that his death leads to a storm of protest that results in government protection of a portion the rain forest in his memory. Elsewhere, however, capitalist modernization marches on, and the destruction of the forest continues unabated. The film certainly means well in its presentation of Mendes's story, though at times it tends to present development of the Amazon region as an unequivocal evil in a way that is inconsistent with Mendes's own support for development in general. In addition, a final voiceover warning of the environmental dangers of the destruction of the rain forest seems inconsistent with Mendes's devotion not to trees but to workers. *Screenplay:* William Mastrosimone, Michael

Tolkin, and Ron Hutchinson. *Selected bibliography:* Dwyer; Revkin; Shoumatoff; Souza.

*NATURAL BORN KILLERS:* DIR. OLIVER STONE (1994). Oliver Stone's masterpiece, *Natural Born Killers* pulls out all the stops, employing all the resources of American popular culture to produce a scathing indictment of that culture. This is a high risk effort, and the film was excoriated as debased, obscene, and immoral, especially from right-wing Republicans and conservative Christians. It was, for example, singled out by Bob Dole in his 1996 presidential campaign as an example of the negative influence of Hollywood films because of its celebration of grotesque violence. But Dole, who at the same time endorsed the equally violent films of fellow-Republican Arnold Schwarzenegger as wholesome entertainment, admitted that he had not actually seen *Natural Born Killers,* thus epitomizing the extent to which the film's critics so often spoke out of ignorance. The film does indeed include a great deal of horrifying violence, but (unlike the films of Schwarzenegger) it does not endorse violence as a solution to life's problems. In *Natural Born Killers,* the horror is directed at the violence and at the celebration of violence in American popular culture, a celebration of which the film is powerfully critical.

*Natural Born Killers* focuses on young lovers Mickey and Mallory Knox (Woody Harrelson and Juliette Lewis) as they work their way across the American Southwest (down the suggestively numbered Highway 666) on a three-week crime and murder spree. In this sense, the film is the culmination of a cinematic tradition that includes such predecessors as *You Only Live Once* (1939), *They Live by Night* (1948), *Bonnie and Clyde* (1967), and *Badlands* (1973). In a larger sense, *Natural Born Killers* is a culmination of American popular culture as a whole. The film is composed of a dizzying array of fragments, quick-cutting MTV-style from color to black and white, from film to video, and among different film stocks, creating a highly disorienting look and feel that greatly enhances the thematic content. This visual fragmentation, of course, mirrors the fragmentation of contemporary American culture. Further it is supplemented by generic fragmentation; the film is essentially constructed from bits and pieces of parodies of various popular genres, including not only crime and police films but Westerns, cartoons, television commercials, and tabloid journalism. Scenes from a variety of earlier films and television shows often literally play in the background of scenes in *Natural Born Killers,* thus identifying the film's predecessors, while also indicating that contemporary American reality exists only within the context of media images.

The film makes especially good use of popular music, employing a sound track that brilliantly enhances the impact of various scenes. The haunting apocalyptic ballads of Leonard Cohen are particularly effective in this sense. One of the major strategies employed in the sound track involves a careful mixture of contemporary violent rock and rap music with traditional saccharine products from earlier years (such as Patsy Cline's "Back in Baby's Arms"), clearly suggesting that these various musical forms arise from similar impulses in American culture, despite their apparent differences. The film makes similar suggestions through its allusions to 1950s television programs that idealize American life (such as *Leave It to Beaver* and *I Love Lucy*). In particular, such idealized sitcoms are skewered in one of the film's most striking set pieces, the presentation of the initial meeting and courtship of Mickey and Mallory via a parodic television sitcom (entitled "I Love Mallory," complete with laugh tracks), in which the two young people meet, fall in love, then murder her grossly abusive father (Rodney Dangerfield) and wimpy mother (Edie McClurg) before setting off on their crime spree.

Crucial to this spree is the extensive media coverage, which makes cult heroes of the murderous Mickey and Mallory. In particular, notorious television tabloid journalist Wayne Gale (Robert Downey, Jr.) makes Mickey and Mallory the focal point of his program, "American Maniacs," which specializes in mass murders and other sensational crimes. Jack Scagnetti (Tom Sizemore), the police detective who devotes himself to the pursuit of the couple, is a media star (and murderer), and one of the most controversial aspects of the film is its tendency to suggest that the dark impulses that drive Mickey and Mallory are so endemic in American society that they also underlie the activities of the police and prison officials who serve as the film's representatives of official authority.

Eventually, Mickey and Mallory are captured and incarcerated, at which point *Natural Born Killers* becomes a prison film, depicting conditions in the prison, run by deranged warden Dwight McClusky (Tommy Lee Jones) as an especially brutal form of the viciousness that pervades all of American society. McClusky, in fact, plots with Scagnetti to murder Mickey and Mallory in prison, feeling that their demonic presence is somehow stirring the other inmates to violence. Meanwhile, Gale brings his camera crew to the prison for an exclusive live interview with Mickey, to be conducted and broadcast immediately following the Super Bowl.

In the midst of the interview, a riot erupts in the prison. Mickey overpowers his captors and takes Gale and a prison guard hostage. They go to Mallory's cell, where Scagnetti is attempting to rape her before killing her. Scagnetti is killed instead, and the couple, with the aid of the other inmates, manages to escape from the prison (on live television), still holding Gale as a hostage. McClusky is overtaken by the prisoners he has tormented for so long; he is torn to pieces. (Stone was forced to remove a scene of the prisoners displaying McClusky's head on a spike, one of many cuts required to reduce the film's rating from NC-17 to R.) Free in the woods, Mickey and Mallory make a final statement for Gale's camera, then turn the camera on their hostage, videotaping as they blow him to bits with shotguns. The film then cuts to a final brilliant scene in which Mickey and a pregnant Mallory drive in a camper van with their two children, thus further linking the murderous pair with ordinary middle Americans. *Screenplay:* David Veloz, Richard Rutowski, and Oliver Stone. *Selected bibliography:* Barker; Burroughs; Corliss; Hoberman; Kagan (*Cinema of Oliver Stone*); Jon Katz; Kunz (*Films*); Nemecek.

**QUIZ SHOW: DIR. ROBERT REDFORD (1994).** *Quiz Show* appropriately begins with the theme music of "Mack the Knife," from Bertolt Brecht's *Threepenny Opera*, a play that presents capitalism as a form of legalized theft. The film then pursues this capitalism-as-crime theme by exploring the famous television quiz show scandals of the 1950s, in the process narrating not only the destruction of American values by capitalist greed, but the complicity of the media, especially television, in this destruction. Indeed, the film's central message seems to be that television has corrupted American values not only by offering easy opportunities for the unscrupulous, but by creating a population of viewers who are inured to deceit.

Focusing on the NBC game show, "Twenty-One," the film begins as Herbert Stempel (John Turturro), a geeky Jew from Queens, is in the midst of a long winning streak on the show. But Stempel, who "has a face for radio," is too uncharismatic for television, so the show's ratings begin to slip. The show's sponsor then conspires with the producers to ensure that Stempel will be defeated, eventually convincing Stempel to lose intentionally by holding out the promise of future appearances on television. Stempel's anointed replacement is Charles Van Doren (Ralph Fiennes), a handsome WASP, who is far more presentable on television. A Columbia University literature professor, Van Doren, as a member of one of American's most prominent intellectual families, also has a perfect pedigree.

Although he is at first reluctant, Van Doren eventually agrees to cooperate in the fixing of the show, rehearsing beforehand with the producers to ensure that he knows all the answers. He wins large sums of money, becomes an immediate media star, and is surrounding by adoring admirers. Stempel, meanwhile, is forgotten by the network, in response to which he complains to the district attorney about the fixing of the show. A subsequent grand jury investigation produces no results, except that Richard Goodwin (Rob Morrow), a young investigator for a congressional oversight committee, gets word of the potential scandal and decides to check into it. Goodwin, on whose book about the events (and his subsequent work in the Kennedy and Johnson administrations) the screenplay is based, has impeccable credentials. He graduated first in his class at Harvard law school and clerked with Supreme Court Justice Felix Frankfurter, but, as a Jew from a relatively modest background in Brookline, Massachusetts, he cannot match the aristocratic pedigree of Van Doren, whose father is a respected Columbia professor, whose uncle won a Pulitzer Prize, and whose family hangs out with the likes of Edmund Wilson, James Thurber, and Lionel Trilling.

Goodwin is somewhat dazzled by his introduction to America's intellectual elite; he also takes a real liking to Van Doren, complicating matters even more. Nevertheless, Goodwin doggedly pursues his investigation, and his efforts provide most of the narrative thrust of the film, which becomes a sort of detective drama. Eventually, Goodwin accumulates enough evidence to force congressional hearings at which the scandal is revealed, and Van Doren confesses his role in the conspiracy. To Goodwin's disgust, however, the investigation merely implicates individuals such as Van Doren and the show's producers, while never even attempting to determine the involvement of the sponsors or the network, whose president turns out to be a golfing buddy of the congressman who chairs the committee. As Goodwin remarks in disgust, leaving the hearing room, "I thought we were gonna get television. The truth is, television is gonna get us."

This ominous warning is central to the message of the film, which seeks to indict not just the quiz show scandal of the 1950s, but the media as a whole as the culprit in a general decline of American values into cynicism and greed from the 1950s forward. If even someone like Van Doren can be seduced by the gold and glamour of television, then there seems to be little chance to resist its inexorable colonization of the American mind. On the other hand, the fact that these scandals occurred so early in the television age tends to suggest that this tendency predates television and should more properly be located in the phenomenon of capitalism, television thus being merely a particularly effective tool with which capitalism can do its unscrupulous work. *Screenplay:* Paul Attansio. *Selected bibliography:* Kent Anderson; Goodwin; Marc.

*LAST MAN STANDING:* **DIR. WALTER HILL (1996).** Based, according to the opening credits, on "a story by Ryuzo Kikushima and Akira Kurosawa," *Last Man Standing* is essentially a remake of Kurosawa's 1961 Japanese film, *Yojimbo,* which was itself based on Dashiell Hammett's 1929 novel, *Red Harvest,* though Hammett is not mentioned in the credits to the Hill film. The Hill film is only loosely based on either Kurosawa or Hammett and is largely an action vehicle for its star, Bruce Willis. Set during Prohibition, the film begins as Willis's mysterious character (who is unnamed, but calls himself, with obvious irony, "John Smith") drives through Texas on his way to Mexico, apparently on the run from someone or something. He decides to stop off for a brief rest in the dusty West Texas town of Jericho, only to find himself in the midst of a war for control of the town between two rival gangs, one Irish and one Italian, engaged in importing bootleg liquor from Mexico, with the help of the Mexican army and police. "Smith" spends most of the rest of the film playing one gang off against the other (with spectacular, if improbable, success), until both gangs are exterminated. "Smith" makes a healthy contribution to the extermination, spending much of the film with both of his two guns blazing, mowing down bad guys in almost cartoonish scenes of violence.

The only message of this film seems to be that the world is a brutal place in which weak men are annihilated by strong ones, who thereby win the rights to any nearby women, who had better run for their lives or use whatever wits they have to try to make the best possible deal for themselves. This message is reinforced by intentionally flat dialogue and bleak and colorless settings and is summed up by "Smith," who frequently speaks as a narrator, when he describes a prostitute who has just betrayed him to one of the gangs as "just trying to make a living in a world where big fish eat little fish." To this extent, the film resembles Hammett's novel, but it lacks the subtleties of Hammett's critique of capitalism, omitting a corrupt millionaire who is a major figure in *Red Harvest* (and who originally brought the gangs to town to help him defeat an attempt by the IWW to organize the workers in his mines), removing most of the official corruption that occurs in the book safely across the border into Mexico (where such corruption is presumably only to be expected), and even introducing a kindly sheriff (played by Bruce Dern) who helps "Smith" survive, whereas the police chief in *Red Harvest* is just as criminal as the mine owner or the battling gang members. *Last Man Standing* is a bleak film that provides little in the way of either an alternative to or motivation for its bleakness. *Yojimbo* was also largely the basis for Sergio Leone's 1964 spaghetti Western (starring Clint Eastwood), *A Fistful of Dollars*, a somewhat more interesting rendition of Hammett's novel than Hill's. *Screenplay:* Walter Hill.

*LONE STAR:* **DIR. JOHN SAYLES (1996).** *Time* magazine headed its review of *Lone Star* with the declaration that "Adults Can Thank John Sayles for *Lone Star*." Indeed, the film, by the standards of American cinema in the 1990s, is an unusually mature work. It is also a rich and complex work that contains a large number of characters, themes, and plot strands. All, however, are carefully woven together within the context of Frontera, Texas, the small, dusty border town where they all take place. Sayles's evocation of the town, its people, its institutions, and its history approaches the method of totalization associated by Georg Lukács with the greatest historical novels, and though the characters are carefully individuated, they are all "typical" in the Lukácsian sense, and we are never allowed to forget that they are all parts of a larger community and that their individual identities derive not only from their own experiences but from the history of the community as a whole. In Sayles's vision, there is only one community in Frontera, despite the town's complex ethnic mix. In this sense, *Lone Star* is an extremely successful work of historical cinema, though its political vision sometimes seems to collapse into a facile suggestion that people would get along fine if only they were not separated by artificial boundaries constructed by governments and special interests.

The main plot of the film is essentially a detective story that begins when some army men from the nearby base, Fort McKenzie, discover a long-buried body while looking for artifacts in the desert. It soon becomes clear that the body is that of former sheriff Charley Wade (Kris Kristofferson), a brutal and sadistic killer who had ruled Frontera in a reign of terror and corruption until his sudden disappearance in the late 1950s, presumably absconding with public funds. He had been replaced by his deputy, Buddy Deeds (Matthew McConaughey), who was willing to bend the rules in his own right, but who was generally respected as man of integrity. The now-deceased Buddy is, in fact, a local legend in whose shadow the current sheriff, his son, Sam Deeds (Chris Cooper), still operates. As Sam investigates Wade's death, the evidence seems to point more and more to Buddy as the killer, while at the same time suggesting that the killing of Wade was a form of justice and a boon to the entire community.

Sam's investigation becomes a full-scale inquiry into his father's legacy and thus into his own past. Indeed, the film becomes a meditation on the past, on the reliability (or unreliability) of historical accounts, and on the proper relationship between the past and the present. In so doing, the film employs a carefully constructed sequence of flashbacks (featuring especially clever transitions between scenes in the past and in the present) to enact the history of the town. This historical theme is supplemented by a number of subplots and specific scenes, as when we see a debate over the relative emphasis to be given to Anglo and Latino points of view in the teaching of history in the local school. In one important subplot, Sam gradually becomes reacquainted with local schoolteacher Pilar Cruz (Elizabeth Peña), while the audience gradually learns that the two of them had been lovers back in high school, broken up by the interference of his father and her mother. Both of the young lovers had gone on to other relationships, and Sam had left town. However, he is now divorced (from a hysterical rich woman, played in a brief bravura turn by Frances McDormand); he returned to town to run for sheriff, with the support of the local political machine, headed by Mayor Hollis Pogue (Clifton James), a former deputy of Wade and crony of Buddy.

Meanwhile, Pilar's husband, Fernando, has recently died. Sam's investigations of the past include his former relationship with Pilar, and it becomes clear that much of Sam's resentment of his father comes from the break-up of this relationship.

Another important subplot centers on the family of hard-nosed, spit-and-polish Colonel Delmore Payne (Joe Morton), the new commander of Fort McKenzie, which is to be closed in the near future. Like Sam in relation to Buddy, Payne's son, Chet (Eddie Robinson), feels that he is neither able nor willing to follow in his father's footsteps. Colonel Payne, meanwhile, has his own difficulties as the son of local institution Otis "Big O" Payne (Ron Canada), the proprietor of Big O's Bar, the only public facility, other than the local black church, where the town's small African American minority can feel at home. Otis had deserted Delmore and his mother when Delmore was a small child, and Delmore has never forgiven him. This multi-generational relationship plays out (with each of the Paynes gradually learning to be more flexible in trying to understand the point of view of the others) in ways that complement the main story.

Much of *Lone Star* seems like typical movie fare. The detective story main plot and the love story subplot appear, on the surface, particularly conventional, though both are engaging. But, as this film demonstrates in numerous ways, appearances can be deceiving. For one thing, Sam's investigation does not come to the expected conclusion that Buddy was the killer. Instead, it turns out that Pogue, then a deputy, had shot and killed Wade, who was about to shoot down Otis in cold blood. Otis, Buddy, and Pogue then together took the body to the desert and buried it. Sam, however, agrees to keep this fact a secret, though he knows his father will continue to be thought of as the killer. (Actually, given Wade's character, this attribution will probably only enhance Buddy's reputation.) Meanwhile, it also turns out that Buddy had had an affair with Mercedes Cruz, the mother of Pilar and the widow of Eladio Cruz, a young man shot down by Wade. Buddy, in fact, was the biological father of Pilar, thus the concern of Buddy and Mercedes that Pilar and Sam not get together. Such plot twists are, however, natural outgrowths of the story and do not seem contrived for effect.

Mercedes is an interesting character whose story provides another subplot. In the present time of the film, she is a paragon of bourgeois respectability, the owner of a local restaurant who despises "wetbacks" and insists that her Mexican employees, who all (she claims) have green cards, speak English because "this is the United States." It turns out, however, that she had once been an illegal immigrant and that her business was founded with money embezzled from the city by Buddy and Pogue, who attributed the theft to the vanished Wade, then handed the money over to Mercedes as "widow's benefits." But she, like Colonel

Payne, has attempted to escape her past by ignoring it. In the end, how-ever, Colonel Payne decides to try to make contact with his father, while Mercedes comes to grips with her own past by coming to the aid of a young Mexican girl who is injured while crossing the Rio Grande to enter America illegally.

In the final scene, Sam reveals to Pilar that Buddy is her father. How-ever, fiercely in love, Sam and Pilar decide to try to make a life together nevertheless. They agree to make a fresh start and not to let the ghosts of the past ruin their relationship. "All that history," Pilar says, "to hell with it, right? Forget the Alamo." The film ends with this seeming renuncia-tion of history, but it is clear from other events that the message of the film is anything but a fatuous suggestion that the past is unimportant. Among other things, this last line can be taken as a plea not to let past differences (such as ethnic battles between Anglos and Latinos) interfere with relationships in the present. Moreover, in this film (and in life, the film implies), the past is crucial. It is important not to be overwhelmed by the past, but it is fatal not to come to grips with it, because the present can be properly understood only as an outgrowth of the past. Sayles's historical vision seems to be very much in line with Marx's, and the entire film might be effectively glossed by Marx's declaration, in a pas-sage in *The Eighteenth Brumaire* in which he also recommends surmount-ing the past, that "men make their own history, but they do not make it just as they please; they do not make it under circumstances chosen by themselves. ... The tradition of all the dead generations weighs like a nightmare on the brain of the living" (Marx and Engels 595). *Screenplay:* John Sayles. *Selected bibliography:* "Adults"; Felperin; Lukács; Marx and Engels; Packer; Sayles (*Sayles*).

*MEN WITH GUNS:* DIR. JOHN SAYLES (1998). Set in an unnamed Central American country (though partly based on Francisco Goldman's 1992 novel, *The Long Night of White Chickens*, which is set in Guatemala), *Men with Guns* explores the destructive impact of modernity on the lives of Central American Indians. Most specifically, it deals with the violence inflicted upon the Indians by the country's U.S.-backed military and, to a lesser extent, by guerrillas who are fighting against that military. How-ever, the film also explores larger issues, noting the army's claim that its violence is necessary to suppress the guerrillas but suggesting that the real reason for the army violence is to drive the Indians off their tradi-tional land so that, in order to live, they will be forced to hire themselves out as cheap labor for large coffee plantation or other capitalist enter-prises. Meanwhile, the Indians who remain independent of such em-ployment are generally forced to devote themselves to the production of specialized crops for consumption by North Americans and wealthy citizens of their own country, thus rendering themselves unable to produce enough food for their own sustenance.

The plot of the film revolves around a vacation trip by the aging Dr. Humberto Fuentes (Federico Luppi), who decides to venture out of the insulation provided by the modern city in which he lives in order to drive into the mountainous interior of the country to visit some of his former students, who went to work among the Indians two years earlier but have not been heard from since. On the trip, Fuentes experiences one revelation after another, gradually coming to realize that he has lived his life in a cocoon of privilege that has blinded him to the harsh realities of life for the poorer people of his country. He also discovers that his former students have apparently all been killed, mostly by the army, though one was apparently killed by the guerrillas.

Early in his trip, Fuentes acquires a guide, young Conejo (Dan Rivera Gonzalez), a boy who has been orphaned by the killings of his parents by soldiers. The boy helps Fuentes find his way through the alien landscape of the mountains and also serves as his interpreter as most of the Indians they meet do not speak Spanish. Fuentes gradually acquires a collection of others passengers, including Domingo (Damian Delgado) a soldier who has deserted and become a thief; Padre Portillo (Damian Alcazar), a priest whose cowardice has apparently caused many in his Indian congregation to be killed by soldiers; and Graciela (Tania Cruz), a young woman who has become mute after the trauma of being raped by soldiers. Together, they travel into the remote mountains of the country, on the way having several frightening encounters with menacing soldiers. At a roadblock, Portillo is arrested and taken away. The others continue, eventually seeking a village, Cerca de Cielo, which is rumored to be a sort of paradise and where Fuentes still hopes to find one of his students.

As the journey gradually shifts to a search for Cerca de Cielo, it takes on increasingly allegorical resonances, reminiscent not only of the Spanish conquistadors' search for El Dorado but of a number of literary precedents. *The Pilgrim's Progress* (in which the protagonist flees the City of Destruction, then picks up various companions on his way to seek the Celestial City) seems an especially important predecessor. The travelers, minus Portillo, continue their search for Cerca de Cielo, going on foot when it becomes impossible to proceed further in Fuentes's Jeep. Climbing up the densely forested mountain, which they think is far from any contact with civilization, they come upon two American tourists (Mandy Patinkin and Kathyrn Grody) examining some ancient Indian ruins. These tourists mean well, and actually seem to know more about the history and culture of the Indians than does Fuentes, but, at the same time, their treatment of Central America as a vacation spot is emblematic of the tendency of the United States to see Latin America as its own domain. As Sayles puts it in an interview, they symbolize the American attitude "Anything that goes on in this hemisphere, we want to control" (Sayles 239).

High on a mountain, the travelers encounter a band of guerrillas, who treat them with respect and camp with them for the night. But the guerrillas, like the army, have never been able to find Cerca de Cielo. Finally, near the peak of the mountain, the travelers find a small hidden village of impoverished Indians, who eke out a meager existence under the cover of the forest. These Indians, almost totally free from contact with the modern world, are able to continue to pursue their traditional way of life, but at a high cost. For one thing, they are unable to grow crops because clearing land would make it possible for the army to find them. For another, they are not totally free of intrusions from the modern world. When the travelers arrive, a woman of the village has been seriously after stepping on a mine dropped into the area by an army helicopter.

Soon after the travelers arrive, Fuentes sits down at the base of a tree and quietly drifts off into death. Domingo, who had been a medic in the army, is convinced by Graciela, despite his initial reluctance to get involved, to take up Fuentes's bag and treat the injured woman. Graciela then walks into a clearing at the peak of the mountain and observes the astonishing natural beauty of the area. This is indeed Cerca de Cielo, and it is indeed a different world. But it is far from a paradise, and modernity—not to mention the U.S.-backed army, still lurks very nearby. Actually, *Men with Guns* fails to indicate this U.S. backing, which is a shortcoming of the film as a political commentary. On the other hand, this failure can be seen as part of the film's overall focus on Latin American, rather than North American characters, a welcome and refreshing departure from most American films about Latin America. *Screenplay:* John Sayles. *Selected bibliography:* "Barbra Streisand's Oscar Snub"; "Director John Sayles"; "John Sayles's *Men with Guns*"; Susan Ryan; Sayles (*Sayles*).

# APPENDIX 1

# Films Listed Alphabetically by Title

*Champion*. Dir. Mark Robson (1949) ... p. 162

*Children Who Labor*. Dir. Ashley Miller (1912) ... p. 7

*The Children's Hour*. Dir. William Wyler (1961) ... p. 217

*The China Syndrome*. Dir. James Bridges (1979) ... p. 292

*Chinatown*. Dir. Roman Polanski (1974) ... p. 260

*Citizen Kane*. Dir. Orson Welles (1941) ... p. 81

*The City*. Dir. Ralph Steiner and Willard Van Dyke (1939) ... p. 67

*City of Hope*. Dir. John Sayles (1991) ... p. 348

*Cloak and Dagger*. Dir. Fritz Lang (1946) ... p. 138

*The Color of Money*. Dir. Martin Scorsese (1986) ... p. 320

*Coming Home*. Dir. Hal Ashby (1978) ... p. 284

*Confessions of a Nazi Spy*. Dir. Anatole Litvak (1939) ... p. 69

*The Contrast*. Dir. Guy Hedlund (1921) ... p. 16

*A Corner in Wheat*. Dir. D. W. Griffith (1909) ... p. 4

*Cornered*. Dir. Edward Dmytryk (1945) ... p. 130

*Counter-Attack*. Dir. Zoltan Korda (1945) ... p. 131

*Crossfire*. Dir. Edward Dmytryk (1947) ... p. 148

*The Crowd*. Dir. King Vidor (1928) ... p. 19

*Dances with Wolves*. Dir. Kevin Costner (1990) ... p. 341

*Daniel*. Dir. Sidney Lumet (1983) ... p. 308

*The Day of the Locust*. Dir. John Schlesinger (1975) ... p. 265

*Dead End*. Dir. William Wyler (1937) ... p. 54

*The Deer Hunter*. Dir. Michael Cimino (1978) ... p. 285

*The Defiant Ones*. Dir. Stanley Kramer (1958) ... p. 205

*Destination Tokyo*. Dir. Delmer Daves (1943) ... p. 109

*Detour*. Dir. Edgar G. Ulmer (1945) ... p. 132

*The Devil and Miss Jones*. Dir. Sam Wood (1941) ... p. 84

*Dr. Strangelove; or, How I Learned to Stop Worrying and Love the Bomb*. Dir. Stanley
    Kubrick (1963) ... p. 221

*Double Indemnity*. Dir. Billy Wilder (1944) ... p. 125

*Duck Soup*. Dir. Leo McCarey (1933) ... p. 32

*Easy Rider*. Dir. Dennis Hopper (1969) ... p. 233

*Edge of the City*. Dir. Martin Ritt (1957) ... p. 197

*Eight Men Out*. Dir. John Sayles (1988) ... p. 331

*A Face in the Crowd*. Dir. Elia Kazan (1957) ... p. 197

*The Fallen Sparrow*. Dir. Richard Wallace (1943) ... p. 110

*Fellow Traveler*. Dir. Philip Saville (1989) ... p. 339

*The Floorwalker*. Dir. Charles Chaplin (1916) ... p. 12

*For Whom the Bell Tolls*. Dir. Sam Wood (1943) ... p. 116

*Force of Evil*. Dir. Abraham Polonsky (1948) ... p. 154

*From Dusk to Dawn*. Dir. Frank E. Wolfe (1913) ... p. 8

*From This Day Forward*. Dir. John Berry (1946) ... p. 139

*The Front*. Dir. Martin Ritt (1976) ... p. 274

*Full Metal Jacket*. Dir. Stanley Kubrick (1987) ... p. 326

*Fury*. Dir. Fritz Lang (1936) ... p. 46

*The Gastonia Textile Strike*. Dir. Sam Brody (1929) ... p. 22

*The General Died at Dawn*. Dir. Lewis Milestone (1936) ... p. 48

*Gentleman's Agreement*. Dir. Elia Kazan (1947) ... p. 149

*The Spanish Earth*. Dir. Joris Ivens (1937) ... p. 61
*Spartacus*. Dir. Stanley Kubrick (1960) ... p. 214
*Storm Center*. Dir. Daniel Taradash (1956) ... p. 196
*The Story of G.I. Joe*. Dir. William Wellman (1945) ... p. 135
*The Stranger*. Dir. Orson Welles (1946) ... p. 143
*The Strike*. Pathé (1904) ... p. 1
*Talk Radio*. Dir. Oliver Stone (1988) ... p. 334
*Taxi Driver*. Dir. Martin Scorsese (1976) ... p. 279
*Tell Them Willie Boy Is Here*. Dir. Abraham Polonsky (1969) ... p. 236
*Tender Comrade*. Dir. Edward Dmytryk (1943) ... p. 122
*Thelma and Louise*. Dir. Ridley Scott (1991) ... p. 353
*These Three*. Dir. William Wyler (1936) ... p. 54
*They Live by Night*. Dir. Nicholas Ray (1948) ... p. 159
*They Shoot Horses, Don't They?* Dir. Sydney Pollack (1969) ... p. 237
*Thieves Like Us*. Dir. Robert Altman (1974) ... p. 263
*The Third Man*. Dir. Carol Reed (1949) ... p. 171
*This Gun for Hire*. Dir. Frank Tuttle (1942) ... p. 105
*Time without Pity*. Dir. Joseph Losey (1957) ... p. 204
*Tobacco Road*. Dir. John Ford (1941) ... p. 94
*Touch of Evil*. Dir. Orson Welles (1958) ... p. 209
*The Treasure of the Sierra Madre*. Dir. John Huston (1948) ... p. 160
*Try and Get Me*. Dir. Cyril Endfield (1951) ... p. 181
*Two Mules for Sister Sara*. Dir. Don Siegel (1969) ... p. 239
*Ulzana's Raid*. Dir. Robert Aldrich (1972) ... p. 256
*Under Fire*. Dir. Roger Spottiswoode (1983) ... p. 316
*Unforgiven*. Dir. Clint Eastwood (1992) ... p. 359
*Union Maids*. Dir. James Klein, Miles Moglescu,
    and Julia Reichert (1976) ... p. 281
*The Unwritten Law*. Lubin (1907) ... p. 3
*Viva Villa!* Dir. Jack Conway (1934) ... p. 45
*Viva Zapata!* Dir. Elia Kazan (1952) ... p. 184
*Wall Street*. Dir. Oliver Stone (1987) ... p. 330
*Watch on the Rhine*. Dir. Herman Shumlin (1943) ... p. 123
*The Way We Were*. Dir. Sydney Pollack (1973) ... p. 258
*The Web*. Dir. Michael Gordon (1947) ... p. 152
*What Is to be Done?* Dir. Joseph Leon Weiss (1914) ... p. 11
*Why?* Éclair (1913) ... p. 9
*Wild Boys of the Road*. Dir. William Wellman (1933) ... p. 37
*The Wild Bunch*. Dir. Sam Peckinpah (1969) ... p. 240
*Wilson*. Dir. Henry King (1944) ... p. 129
*Woman of the Year*. Dir. George Stevens (1942) ... p. 107
*You Only Live Once*. Dir. Fritz Lang (1937) ... p. 63

# APPENDIX 2

# Films Listed Alphabetically by Director

Cimino, Michael. *The Deer Hunter* (1978) ... p. 285
————. *Heaven's Gate* (1980) ... p. 294
Conway, Jack. *Viva Villa!* (1934) ... p. 45
Coppola, Francis Ford. *Apocalypse Now* (1979) ... p. 289
————. *The Godfather* (1972) ... p. 253
————. *The Godfather Part II* (1974) ...261
————. *The Godfather Part III* (1990) ... p. 342
Costa-Gavras, Constantin. *Hanna K.* (1983) ... p. 310
————. *Missing* (1982) ... p. 305
Costner, Kevin. *Dances with Wolves* (1990) ... p. 341
Crosland, Alan. *Massacre* (1934) ... p. 40
Cukor, George. *Keeper of the Flame* (1942) ... p. 100
————. *The Philadelphia Story* (1940) ... p. 78
Curtiz, Michael. *Casablanca* (1942) ... p. 96
————. *Mission to Moscow* (1943) ... p. 113
————. *The Sea Wolf* (1941) ... p. 93
Daves, Delmer. *Broken Arrow* (1950) ... p. 175
————. *Destination Tokyo* (1943) ... p. 109
De Palma, Brian. *Casualties of War* (1989) ... p. 337
————. *Scarface* (1983) ... p. 311
Demme, Jonathan. *Melvin and Howard* (1980) ... p. 297
Dick, Sheldon. *Men and Dust* (1940) ... p. 77
Dieterle, William. *Blockade* (1938) ... p. 65
————. *Juarez* (1939) ... p. 71
Dmytryk, Edward. *Broken Lance* (1954) ... p. 186
————. *Cornered* (1945) ... p. 130
————. *Crossfire* (1947) ... p. 148
————. *Hitler's Children* (1943) ... p. 113
————. *Murder, My Sweet* (1944) ... p. 128
————. *Salt to the Devil* (1949) ... p. 169
————. *Tender Comrade* (1943) ... p. 122
Eastwood, Clint. *Unforgiven* (1992) ... p. 359
Endfield, Cyril. *Try and Get Me* (1951) ... p. 181
Farrow, John. *The Big Clock* (1947) ... p. 144
Ford, John. *The Grapes of Wrath* (1940) ... p. 73
————. *How Green Was My Valley* (1941) ... p. 86
————. *Tobacco Road*. Dir. John Ford (1941) ... p. 94
Forman, Milos. *One Flew over the Cuckoo's Nest* (1975) ... p. 268
————. *Ragtime* (1981) ... p. 301
Frankenheimer, John. *The Burning Season* (1994) ... p. 364
Franklin, Sidney. *The Good Earth* (1937) ... p. 54
Freeman, Jerrold. *Native Son* (1986) ... p. 321
Garnett, Tay. *The Postman Always Rings Twice* (1946) ... p. 141
Gordon, Michael. *I Can Get It for You Wholesale* (1951) ... p. 177
————. *The Web* (1947) ... p. 152
Griffith, D. W. *A Corner in Wheat* (1909) ... p. 4
————. *Intolerance* (1916) ... p. 13

Vidor, King. *The Crowd* (1928) ... p. 19
————. *Our Daily Bread*. Dir. King Vidor (1934) ... p. 42
Wallace, Richard. *The Fallen Sparrow* (1943) ... p. 110
Walsh, Raoul. *High Sierra* (1941) ... p. 85
————. *The Naked and the Dead* (1958) ... p. 207
————. *Objective, Burma!* (1945) ... p. 134
Weiss, Joseph Leon. *What Is to be Done?* (1914) ... p. 11
Welles, Orson. *Citizen Kane*. Dir. Orson Welles (1941) ... p. 81
————. *The Lady from Shanghai* (1948) ... p. 156
————. *The Magnificent Ambersons* (1942) ... p. 101
————. *Mr. Arkadin* (1955) ... p. 191
————. *The Stranger* (1946) ... p. 143
————. *Touch of Evil* (1958) ... p. 209
Wellman, William. *Heroes for Sale* (1933) ... p. 36
————. *The Public Enemy* (1931) ... p. 26
————. *The Story of G.I. Joe* (1945) ... p. 135
————. *Wild Boys of the Road* (1933) ... p. 37
Wexler, Haskell. *Latino* (1985) ... p. 319
————. *Medium Cool* (1969) ... p. 234
Wilder, Billy. *Double Indemnity* (1944) ... p. 125
Wilson, Richard. *It's All True* (1993) ... p. 363
Winkler, Irwin. *Guilty by Suspicion* (1991) ... p. 351
Wise, Robert. *The Set-Up* (1949) ... p. 170
Wolfe, Frank E. *From Dusk to Dawn* (1913) ... p. 8
Wood, Sam. *The Devil and Miss Jones* (1941) ... p. 84
————. *For Whom the Bell Tolls* (1943) ... p. 116
Wyler, William. *The Best Years of Our Lives* (1946) ... p. 136
————. *The Children's Hour* (1961) ... p. 217
————. *Dead End* (1937) ... p. 54
————. *The Little Foxes* (1941) ... p. 89
————. *These Three* (1936) ... p. 54
Young, Robert M. *The Ballad of Gregorio Cortez* (1983) ... p. 307
Zinnemann, Fred. *High Noon* (1952) ... p. 182
————. *Julia* (1977) ... p. 282

Films with unidentified directors

*The Bank Defaulter*. Lubin (1906) ... p. 2
*Labor's Reward*. American Federation of Labor (1925) ... p. 18
*The Long Strike*. Essanay (1911) ... p. 5
*A Martyr to His Cause*. Seely (1911) ... p. 6
*The Mill Girl*. Vitagraph (1907) ... p. 2
*The Mining District*. Pathé (1905) ... p. 1
*The Strike*. Pathé (1904) ... p. 1
*The Unwritten Law*. Lubin (1907) ... p. 3
*Why?* Éclair (1913) ... p. 9

# WORKS CITED

Abramson, Leslie H. "Two Birds of a Feather: Hammett's and Huston's *The Maltese Falcon*." *Literature/Film Quarterly* 16.2 (1988): 112–18.

Adamic, Louis. *Dynamite: The Story of Class Violence in America*. London: Jonathan Cape, 1931.

Adamson, Judith. *Graham Greene and Cinema*. Norman, OK: Pilgrim Books, 1984.

"Adults Can Thank John Sayles for *Lone Star*." *Time* 148.5 (1996): 95.

Agee, James. *Agee on Film*. Vol. 1 of 2. New York: Grosset and Dunlap, 1958.

Alexander, William. *Film on the Left: American Documentary Film from 1931 to 1942*. Princeton, NJ: Princeton UP, 1981.

Alter, Jonathan. "Renaissance Radical." *Vogue* 182.9 (September 1992): 568.

Anderegg, Michael. "Hollywood and Vietnam: John Wayne and Jane Fonda as Discourse." Anderegg. *Inventing Vietnam* 15–32.

Anderegg, Michael, ed. *Inventing Vietnam: The War in Film and Television*. Philadelphia: Temple UP, 1991.

Anderson, Andrew R. *Fear Ruled Them All: Kenneth Fearing's Literature of Corporate Conspiracy*. New York: Lang, 1996.

Anderson, Kent. *Television Fraud: The History and Implications of the Quiz Show Scandals*. Westport, CT: Greenwood P, 1978.

Anderson, Thom. "Red Hollywood." *Literature and the Visual Arts in Contemporary Society*. Ed. Suzanne Ferguson and Barbara Groseclose. Columbus: Ohio State UP, 1985. 141–96.

Andrew, Geoff. *The Films of Nicholas Ray: The Poet of Nightfall*. London: Charles Letts, 1991.

Asinof, Eliot. *Eight Men Out: The Black Sox and the 1919 World Series*. Evanston, IL: Holtzman P, 1963.

Bailey, Thomas A. *Woodrow Wilson and the Lost Peace*. New York: Macmillan, 1944.

Baird, Robert. "Going Indian: Discovery, Adoption, and Renaming toward a 'True American,' from *Deerslayer* to *Dances With Wolves*." *Dressing in Feathers: The Construction of the American Popular Culture*. Ed. S. Elizabeth Baird. Boulder, CO: Westview P, 1996. 195–209.

Baker, Charles A. "Illusion and Reality in *Nashville*." *Studies in the Humanities* 10.2 (1983): 93–98.

Balio, Tino, ed. *Grand Design: Hollywood as a Modern Business Enterprise, 1930–1939*. Berkeley: U of California P, 1995.

Barbarow, George. "Dreiser's Place on the Screen." *Hudson Review* 5 (1952): 290.

"Barbra Streisand's Oscar Snub; John Sayles' *Men With Guns*; Bruce Willis's Bad Hair Day." *Sight and Sound* 7.5 (1997): 4.

Barker, Martin. "Violence." *Sight and Sound* 5.6 (1995): 10–13.

Barnard, Rita. *The Great Depression and the Culture of Abundance: Kenneth Fearing, Nathanael West, and Mass Culture in the 1930s*. Cambridge: Cambridge UP, 1995.

Barnouw, Erik. *Documentary: A History of the Non-Fiction Film*. New York: Oxford UP, 1974.

Barrett, James R. Introduction to *The Jungle* by Upton Sinclair. Urbana: U of Illinois P, 1988. xi–xxxiii.

Barsam, Richard Meran. *Nonfiction Film: A Critical History*. Rev. ed. Bloomington: Indiana UP, 1992.

Bates, Milton J. "Oliver Stone's *Platoon* and the Politics of Romance." *Mosaic* 27.1 (1994):101–21.

Baughman, Cynthia. "*The Handmaid's Tale*." *The Pinter Review* (1990): 92–96.

Bazin, André. *Orson Welles: A Critical View*. Trans. Jonathan Rosenbaum. New York: Harper and Row, 1978.

Beal, Fred E. *Proletarian Journey: New England, Gastonia, Moscow*. New York: Hillman-Curl, 1947.

Beaver, Frank Eugene. *Oliver Stone: Wakeup Cinema*. New York: Twayne, 1994.

Beck, Avent Childreas. "The Christian Allegorical Structure of *Platoon*." *Screening the Sacred: Religion, Myth, and Ideology in Popular American Film*. Ed. Joel W. Martin and Conrad E. Ostwalt, Jr. Boulder, CO: Westview P, 1995. 44–54.

Beebe, John. "The Notorious Postwar Psyche." *Journal of Popular Film and Television* 18.1 (1990): 28–35.

Beja, Morris, ed. *Perspectives on Orson Welles*. New York: G. K. Hall, 1995.

Bell, Daniel. *The End of Ideology: On the Exhaustion of Political Ideas in the Fifties*. New York: Free P, 1962.

Belton, John. "Language, Oedipus, and *Chinatown*." *MLN* 106.5 (1991): 933–50.

Benamou, Catherine Laure. "Orson Welles's Transcultural Cinema: An Historical/textual Reconstruction of the Suspended Film, *It's All True*." Diss. New York U, 1997.

Benson, Edward, and Sharon Hartman Strom. "Crystal Lee, Norma Rae, and All Their Sisters." *Film Library Quarterly* 12.2–3 (1979): 18–23.

Bergan, Ronald. *The Life and Times of the Marx Brothers*. New York: Smithmark, 1992.

Bergman, Andrew. *We're in the Money: Depression America and Its Films*. New York: New York UP, 1971.

Bernardoni, James. *George Cukor: A Critical Study and Filmography*. Jefferson, NC: McFarland, 1985.

Bernstein, Irving. *The Lean Years: A History of the American Worker, 1920–1933*. Boston: Houghton-Mifflin, 1960.

Bernstein, Walter. *Inside Out: A Memoir of the Blacklist*. New York: Knopf, 1996.

Berumen, Frank Javier Garcia. *The Chicano/Hispanic Image in American Film*. New York: Vantage, 1995.

Bessie, Alvah. *Inquisition in Eden*. New York: Macmillan, 1965.

Bezanson, Mark. "Berger and Penn's West: Visions and Revisions." *The Modern American Novel and the Movies*. Ed. Gerald Peary and Roger Shatzkin. New York: Frederick Ungar, 1978. 272–81.

Biberman, Herbert. Salt of the Earth: *The Story of a Film*. Boston: Beacon, 1965.

Billingsley, Ronald G., and James W. Palmer. "Milos Forman's Cuckoo's Nest: Reality Unredeemed." *Studies in the Humanities* 7.1 (1978): 14–18.

Bimba, Anthony. *The Molly Maguires*. 1932. New York: International Publishers, 1970.

Biskind, Peter. *Easy Riders, Raging Bulls: How the Sex-Drugs-and-Rock'n' Roll Generation Saved Hollywood*. New York: Simon and Schuster, 1998.

———. The Godfather *Companion: Everything You Ever Wanted to Know about All Three* Godfather *Films*. New York: HarperPerennial, 1990.

———. "Ripping Off Zapata—Revolution Hollywood Style." *Cineaste* 7.2 (1976): 14.

———. *Seeing Is Believing: How Hollywood Taught Us to Stop Worrying and Love the Fifties*. New York: Pantheon, 1983.

Blaine, Allen. *Nicholas Ray: A Guide to References and Resources*. Boston: G. K. Hall, 1984.

Bliss, Michael. *What Goes Around Comes Around: The Films of Jonathan Demme*. Carbondale: Southern Illinois UP, 1996.

Bluestone, George. *Novels into Film*. Berkeley: U of California P, 1957.

Bogdanovich, Peter. *Frtiz Lang in America*. New York: Praeger, 1969.

Bogue, Ronald. "De Palma's Postmodern *Scarface* and the Simulacrum of Class." *Criticism* 35.1 (1993): 115–30.

Bondarella, Peter. "Edward Dmytryk's *Christ in Concrete* and Italian Neorealism." *Revista di Studi Ango-Americani* 3.4–5 (1984–1985): 227–39.

Bookbinder, Robert. *Classic Gangster Films*. New York: Carol, 1993.

Booker, M. Keith. *The Dystopian Impulse in Modern Literature: Fiction as Social Criticism*. Westport, CT: Greenwood P, 1994.

———. *The Modern American Novel of the Left: A Research Guide*. Westport, CT: Greenwood P, 1999.

———. *The Modern British Novel of the Left: A Research Guide*. Westport, CT: Greenwood P, 1998.

Boozer, Jack. "Seduction and Betrayal in the Heartland: *Thelma & Louise*." *Literature/Film Quarterly* 23.3 (1995): 188–96.

———. "*Wall Street*: The Commodification of Perception." *Journal of Popular Film and Television*. 17.3 (1989): 90–99.

Bordwell, David. "*Citizen Kane*." Beja 90–106.

Bovey, Seth. "Dances with Stereotypes: Western Films and the Myth of the Novel Red Man." *South Dakota Review* 31.1 (1993): 115–22.

Bowser, Eileen. *The Transformation of Cinema, 1907–1915*. Berkeley: U of California P, 1994.

Boyd, Melba. "But Not the Blackness of Space: *The Brother from Another Planet* as Icon from the Underground." *Journal of the Fantastic in the Arts* 2.2 (1989): 95–107.

Boyd, Melba Joyce. "Literacy and the Liberation of Bigger Thomas." *Approaches to Teaching Wright's* Native Son. Ed. James A. Miller. New York: Modern Language Association, 1997. 35–41.

Braudy, Leo. "'No Body's Perfect': Method Acting and 50s Culture." *The Movies: Texts, Receptions, Exposures*. Ed. Laurence Goldstein. Ann Arbor: U of Michigan P, 1996. 275–99.

Brill, Lesley. "Growing up Gangster: *Little Caesar, The Public Enemy*, and the American Dream." *Hollywood: Reflexions sur l'ecran*. Ed. Daniel Royot. Aix-en-Provence, France: U Provence, 1984. 10–22.

———. *John Huston's Filmmaking*. Cambridge: Cambridge UP, 1997.

Britton, Andrew. *Katharine Hepburn: Star as Feminist*. New York: Continuum, 1995.

Broehl, Wayne G. *The Molly Maguires*. Cambridge: Harvard UP, 1964.

Brownlow, Kevin. *Behind the Mask of Innocence*. New York: Knopf, 1990.

Bruce-Novoa, Juan. "There's Many a Slip Between Good Intentions and Script: *The Milagro Beanfield War*." *Post Script* 16.1 (1996): 53–63.

Brunk, Samuel. *Emiliano Zapata: Revolution and Betrayal in Mexico*. Albuquerque: U of New Mexico P, 1995.

Budd, Mike, and Clay Steinman. "*M*A*S*H* Mystified: Capitalization, Dematerialization, Idealization." *Cultural Critique* 10 (1988): 59–75.

Buhle, Mari Jo, Paul Buhle, and Dan Georgakis, eds. *Encyclopedia of the American Left*. Chicago: St. James, 1990.

Buhle, Paul. "The Hollywood Left: Aesthetics and Politics." *New Left Review* 212 (1995): 101–119.

Burgoyne, Robert. "Modernism and the Narrative of nation in *JFK*." *The Persistence of History: Cinema, Television, and the Modern Event*. Ed. Vivian Sobchak. New York: Routledge, 1996. 113–25.

Burks, Ruth Elizabeth. "The Effects of Censorship and Criticism on the Film Adaptations of Richard Wright's *Native Son*." Diss. U of California at Los Angeles, 1993.

Burns, Maggie. "*Easy Rider* and *Deliverance*: Or, The Death of the Sixties." *University of Hartford Studies in Literature* 22.2–3 (1990): 44–58.

Burroughs, Jason. "Is There a Moral to This Story?: The Moral Stance of Oliver Stone and Quentin Tarantino in *Natural Born Killers* and *Pulp Fiction*." *The Image of Violence in Literature, the Media, and Society*. Ed. Will Wright and Steven Kaplan. Pueblo: U of Southern Colorado, 1995. 174–77.

Bush, Gregory W. "Like 'A Drop of Water in the Stream of Life': Moving Images of Mass Man from Griffith to Vidor." *Journal of American Studies* 25.2 (1991): 213–34.

Butler, Jeremy G. "*Viva Zapata!*: HUAC and the Mexican Revolution." *The Steinbeck Question: New Essays in Criticism*. Troy, NY: Whitston, 1993. 239–49.

Cahir, Linda Costanzo. "Narratological Parallels in Joseph Conrad's *Heart of Darkness* and Francis Ford Coppola's *Apocalypse Now*." *Literature/Film Quarterly* 20.3 (1992): 181–87.

Callow, Simon. *Orson Welles*. London: Jonathan Cape, 1995.

Cargill, Jack. "Empire and Opposition: The 'Salt of the Earth' Strike." *Labor in New Mexico*. Ed. Robert Kern. Albuquerque: U of New Mexico P, 1983. 182–267.

Carr, Gary. *The Left Side of Paradise: The Screenwriting of John Howard Lawson*. Ann Arbor, MI: UMI Research P, 1984.

Carringer, Robert L. *The Magnificent Ambersons: A Reconstruction*. Berkeley: U of California P, 1993.

Castiglia, Christopher. "Rebel without a Closet." *Engendering Men: The Question of Male Feminist Criticism*. Ed. Joseph A. Boone. New York: Routledge, 1990. 207–221.

Castillo, Edward D. "*Dances with Wolves*." *Film Quarterly* 44.4 (1991): 14–23.

Caute, David. *The Great Fear: The Anti-Communist Purge under Truman and Eisenhower*. New York: Simon and Schuster, 1978.

———. *Joseph Losey: A Revenge on Life*. New York: Oxford UP, 1994.

Cawelti, John G. "*Chinatown* and Generic Transformation in Recent American Films." *Film Genre Reader II*. Ed. Barry Keith Grant. Austin: U of Texas P, 1995. 227–45.

Ceplair, Larry, and Steven Englund. *The Inquisition in Hollywood*. Rev. ed. Berkeley: U of California P, 1983.

Chomsky, Noam. *What Uncle Sam Really Wants*. Berkeley, CA: Odion, 1992.

Christensen, Terry. *Reel Politics: American Political Movies from Birth of a Nation to Platoon*. London: Basil Blackwell, 1987.

Christopher, Renny. "Negotiating the Viet Nam War through Permeable Genre Borders: *Aliens* as Viet Nam War Film; *Platoon* as Horror Film." *Lit* 5.1 (1994): 53–66.

Ciment, Michel. *Conversations with Losey*. London: Methuen, 1985.

Clarens, Carlos. *Crime Movies*. 1980. New York: Da Capo, 1997.

Clurman, Harold. *The Fervent Years*. New York: Hill and Wang, 1945.

Cohan, Carley, and Gary Crowdus. "Reflections on *Roger & Me*, Michael Moore, and His Critics." *Cineaste* 17.4 (1990): 25–30.

Cole, Lester. *Hollywood Red: The Autobiography of Lester Cole*. Palo Alto, CA: Ramparts P, 1981.

Coleman, Arthur. "Hemingway's *The Spanish Earth*." *The Hemingway Review* 2.1 (1992): 64–67.

Conway, Mimi. *Rise Gonna Rise: A Portrait of Southern Textile Workers*. New York: Anchor, 1979.

Cook, Sylvia. "Gastonia: The Literary Reverberations of the Strike." *Southern Literary Journal* 7.1 (1974): 49–66.

Cooper, Duncan. "*Spartacus*: An Exclusive Report." *Cineaste* 18.3 (1991): 18–37.

Cooper, Pamela. "Sexual Surveillance and Medical Authority in Two Versions of *The Handmaid's Tale*." *Journal of Popular Culture* 28.4 (1995): 49–66.

Corliss, Richard. "Stone Crazy." *Time* 144.9 (August 29, 1994): 66.

Corrigan, Timothy. *A Cinema without Walls: Movies and Culture after Vietnam*. New Brunswick, NJ: Rutgers UP, 1991.

Cowie, Peter. *Coppola*. New York: Scribner, 1990.

———. *The* Godfather *Book*. London: Faber and Faber, 1997.

————. "The Study of Corruption: *Touch of Evil*." Beja 164–70.

Crichton, Kyle. Review of *Modern Times*. *New Masses* (February 1936). Reprinted in *American Film Criticism*. Ed. Stanley Kauffman. New York: Liveright, 1972. 329–31.

Cripps, Thomas. "*Native Son*, Film and Book: A Few Thoughts on a 'Classic.'" *Mississippi Quarterly* 42.4 (1989): 425–27.

Crowdus, Gary, ed. *The Political Companion to American Film*. Chicago: Lakeview P, 1994.

Crowdus, Gary, and Dan Georgakas. "Creating Cinema with a Sense of Urgency: An Interview with Haskell Wexler. *Cineaste* 14.3 (1986): 11–13.

Crowdus, Gary, and Richard Porton. "*American Dream:* An Interview with Barbara Kopple." *Cineaste* 18.4 (1991): 37–38, 41.

Crowdus, Gary, and Leonard Quart. "Where the Hope Is: An Interview with John Sayles." *Cineaste* 18.4 (1991): 4–7, 61.

Crowdus, Gary, and Lenny Rubenstein. "The Missing Dossier." *Cineaste* 12.1 (1982): 30–38.

Culbert, David. "Our Awkward Ally: *Mission to Moscow* (1943)." O'Connor and Jackson 121–45.

————. "*Reds:* Propaganda, Docudrama, and Hollywood." *Labor History* 24 (Winter 1983): 125–30.

Darrow, Clarence. *The Story of My Life*. 1932. New York: Da Capo, 1996.

Davies, Philip, and Brian Neve, eds. *Cinema, Politics and Society in America*. New York: St. Martin's, 1981.

Davis, Mike. *City of Quartz: Excavating the Future of Los Angeles*. New York: Vintage-Random House, 1992.

Davison, Richard Allen. "Frank Norris and the Arts of Social Criticism." *American Literary Realism* 14.1 (1981): 77–89.

DeBauche, Leslie Midkiff. *Reel Patriotism: The Movies and World War I*. Madison: U of Wisconsin P, 1997.

De Camp, L. Sprague. *The Great Monkey Trial*. New York: Doubleday, 1967.

Deer, Harriet A. "The Popular Arts: Suicide and Society in the Sixties." *Youth Suicide Prevention: Lessons from Literature*. Ed. Sara Munson Deats and Lagretta Tallent Lenker. New York: Plenum. 1989. 191–204.

Delson, James. "Heston on Welles." Beja 63–72.

Denning, Michael. *The Cultural Front: The Laboring of American Culture in the Twentieth Century*. London: Verso, 1996.

Desser, David. "'Charlie Don't Surf': Race and Culture in the Vietnam War Films." Anderegg. *Inventing Vietnam* 81–102.

Dick, Bernard F. *Hellman in Hollywood*. Rutherford, NJ: Fairleigh Dickinson UP, 1982.

————. *Radical Innocence: A Critical Study of the Hollywood Ten*. Lexington: U of Kentucky P, 1989.

Dickerson, Gary E. *The Cinema of Baseball: Images of America, 1929–1989*. Westport, CT: Meckler, 1991.

"Director John Sayles Returns With a New Latino-themes movie, *Men With Guns*." *Hispanic* 11.3 (March 1, 1998): 76.

Dittmar, Linda, and Gene Michaud, eds. *From Hanoi to Hollywood: The Vietnam War in American Film.* New Brunswick, NJ: Rutgers UP, 1990.

Dmytryk, Edward. *It's a Hell of a Life, But Not a Bad Living.* New York: Times Books, 1978.

Doel, Frances. "John William Corrington as a Screenwriter." *John William Corrington: Southern Man of Letters.* Ed. William Mills. Conway: U Central Arkansas P, 1994. 134–43.

Doherty, Thomas. "Full Metal Genre: Stanley Kubrick's Vietnam Combat Movie." *Film Quarterly* 42.2 (1988–1989): 24–30.

———. "Witness to War: Oliver Stone, Ron Kovic, and *Born on the Fourth of July.*" Anderegg. *Inventing Vietnam* 251–68.

Doyle, Jeff. "Missed Saigon: Some Recent Film Representations of Vietnam." *Crossing Cultures: Essays on Literature and Culture of the Asia-Pacific.* Ed. Bruce Bennett, et al. London: Skoob, 1996. 91–99.

Draper, Theodore. "Gastonia Revisited." *Social Research* 38 (1971): 3–29.

Drew, William M. *D. W. Griffith's* Intolerance: *Its Genesis and Its Vision.* Hefferson, NC: McFarland, 1986.

Durgnat, Raymond. "Martin Scorsese: Between God and the Goodfellas." *Sight and Sound* 5.6 (1995): 22–25.

Durgnat, Raymond, and Scott Simmon. *King Vidor, American.* Berkeley: U of California P, 1988.

Dwyer, Augusta. *Into the Amazon: Chico Mendes and the Struggle for the Rain Forest.* Toronto: Seal Books, 1990.

Eckert, Charles. "The Anatomy of a Proletarian Film: Warner's *Marked Woman.*" *Film Quarterly* 17 (Winter 1973–1974): 10–24.

Edelman, Rob. *The Great Baseball Films: From* Right Off the Bat *to* A League of Their Own. Secaucus, NJ: Citadel P, 1994.

Eisenschitz, Bernard. *Nicholas Ray: An American Journey.* Trans. Tom Milne. London: Faber and Faber, 1993.

Ellison, Mary. "Blacks in American Film." Davies and Neve 176–94.

Engel, Len. "Rewriting Western Myths in Clint Eastwood's New 'Old Western.'" *Western American Literature* 29.3 (1994): 261–69.

Engell, John. "*The Treasure of the Sierra Madre:* B. Traven, John Huston, and Ideology in Film Adaptation." *Literature/Film Quarterly* 17.4 (1989): 245–52.

Engle, Harrison. "Thirty Years of Social Inquiry." Jacobs 343–60.

Erhart, Julia. "'She Could Hardly Invent Them!' From Epistemological Uncertainty to Discursive Production: Lesbianism in *The Children's Hour.*" *Camera Obscura* 35 (1995): 87–105.

Everson, William K. *American Silent Film.* New York: Oxford UP, 1978.

———. *The Detective in Film.* Secaucus, NJ: Citadel P, 1980.

Ewen, Frederic. *Bertolt Brecht: His Life, His Art, and His Times.* New York: Citadel P, 1969.

Ewen, Lynda Ann. *Which Side Are You On?: The Brookside Mine Strike in Harlan County, Kentucky, 1973–1974.* Chicago: Vanguard, 1979.

Eyles, Allen. *The Complete Films of the Marx Brothers.* Secaucus, NJ: Carol Publishing Group, 1992.

Fairchild, B. H. "'Plastics': *The Graduate* as Film and Novel." *Studies in American Humor* 4.3 (1985): 133–41.

Falk, Quentin. *Travels in Greeneland: The Cinema of Graham Greene.* Rev. ed. London: Quartet, 1990.

Faundez, Julio. *Marxism and Democracy in Chile: From 1932 to the Fall of Allende.* New Haven, CT: Yale UP, 1988.

Fearing, Kenneth. *The Big Clock.* New York: Harcourt, Brace, 1946.

Feineman, Neil. *Persistence of Vision: The Films of Robert Altman.* New York: Arno P, 1978.

Felperin, Leslie. "Walking Alone." *Sight and Sound* 6.9 (1996): 22.

Ferncase, Richard K. "Robert Altman's *The Long Goodbye:* Marlowe in the Me Decade." *Journal of Popular Culture* 25.2 (1991): 87–90.

Ferraro, Thomas J. "Blood in the Marketplace: The Business of Family in the *Godfather* Narratives." *The Invention of Ethnicity.* Ed. Werner Sollors. New York: Oxford UP, 1989. 176–208.

Flinn, Tom, and John Davis. "Warners' War of the Wolf." *The Classic American Novel and the Movies.* Ed. Gerald Peary and Roger Shatzkin. New York: Frederick Unger, 1977. 192–205.

Flom, Eric L. *Chaplin in the Sound Era: An Analysis of the Seven Talkies.* Jefferson, NC: McFarland, 1997.

Foucault, Michel. *Discipline and Punish: The Birth of the Prison.* Trans. Alan Sheridan. New York: Vintage-Random House, 1979.

Friedman, Lawrence S. *The Cinema of Martin Scorsese.* New York: Continuum, 1998.

Friedman, Lester D. "A Very Narrow Path: The Politics of Edward Dmytryk." *Literature/Film Quarterly* 12.4 (1984): 214–24.

Frischauer, Willi. *Behind the Scenes of Otto Preminger: An Unauthorised Biography.* London: Joseph, 1973.

Fuller, Linda K. "The Ideology of the 'Red Scare' Movement: McCarthyism in the Movies." *Beyond the Stars: Themes and Ideologies in American Popular Culture.* Ed. Paul Loukides and Linda K. Fuller. Bowling Green, OH: Popular P, 1996. 229–47.

Gale, Steven H. "*The Maltese Falcon:* Melodrama of Film Noir." *Literature/Film Quarterly* 24.2 (1996): 145–47.

Gallagher, Tag. *John Ford: The Man and His Films.* Berkeley: U of California P, 1986.

Gardaphé, Fred L. Introduction. *Christ in Concrete.* By Pietro di Donato. New York: Signet, 1993. ix–xviii.

Gehring, Wes D. *The Marx Brothers: A Bio-Bibliography.* Westport, CT: Greenwood, 1987.

Geoff, Andrew. *The Films of Nicholas Ray: The Poet of Nightfall.* London: Letts, 1991.

Giardina, Denise. *Storming Heaven.* New York: Ivy, 1987.

Gilbert, Dennis. *Sandinistas: The Party and the Revolution.* New York: Basil Blackwell, 1988.

Goldberg, David J. *A Tale of Three Cities: Labor Protest and Organization in Paterson, Passaic, and Lawrence, 1916–1921.* New Brunswick, NJ: Rutgers UP, 1989.

Gomez, Joseph A. "*The Third Man:* Capturing the Essence of Literary Conception." *Literature/Film Quarterly* 2 (1974): 332–40.

Good, Howard. *Diamonds in the Dark: America, Baseball, and the Movies.* Lanham, MD: Scarecrow P, 1997.

Goodwin, Richard N. *Remembering America: A Voice from the Sixties.* Boston: Little, Brown, 1988.

Gossage, Leslie. "The Artful Propaganda of Ford's *The Grapes of Wrath.*" *New Essays on* The Grapes of Wrath. Ed. David Wyatt. Cambridge: Cambridge UP, 1990. 101–125.

Graham, Allison. "The Final Go-Around: Peckinpah's *Wild Bunch* at the End of the Frontier." *Mosaic* 16.1–2 (1983): 55–70.

Graham, Mark. "The Inaccessibility of *The Lady from Shanghai.*" Beja 146–63.

Greene, Eric. Planet of the Apes *as American Myth: Race and Politics in the Films and Television Series.* Jefferson, NC: McFarland, 1996.

Greiff, Louis K. "Soldier, Sailor, Surfer, Chef: Conrad's Ethics and the Margins of *Apocalypse Now.*" *Literature/Film Quarterly* 20.3 (1992): 188–98.

Griffith, Richard. "Documentary Film since 1939: North and Latin America." Rotha 308–43.

Grimm, Reinhold, and Henry J. Schmidt. "Bertolt Brecht and *Hangmen Also Die.*" *Monatshefte: Für Deutschen Unterricht, Deutsche Sprache und Literatur* 61 (1969): 232–40.

Grist, Leighton. "*Unforgiven.*" *The Book of Westerns.* Ed. Ian Cameron and Douglas Pye. New York: Continuum, 1996. 294–301.

Gunning, Tom. *D. W. Griffith and the Origins of American Narrative Film: The Early Years at Biograph.* Urbana: U of Illinois P, 1991.

Gurko, Miriam. *Clarence Darrow.* New York: Crowell, 1969.

Guthrie, Woody. *Born to Win.* Ed. Robert Shelton. New York: Macmillan, 1965.

———. *Bound for Glory.* New York: E. P. Dutton, 1943.

Gutiérrez-Jones, Carl. "Legislating Languages: *The Ballad of Gregorio Cortez* and the English Language Amendment." *Chicanos and Film: Representation and Resistance.* Ed. Chon A. Noriega. Minneapolis: U of Minnesota P, 1992. 195–206.

Guzmán, Martín Luis. *The Eagle and the Serpent.* New York: Knopf, 1930.

Hagemann, E. R. "*Scarface:* The Art of Hollywood, not 'The Shame of a Nation.'" *Journal of Popular Culture* 18.1 (1984): 30–42.

Hall, Jasmine Yong. "Jameson, Genre, and Gumshoes: *The Maltese Falcon* as Inverted Romance." *The Cunning Craft: Original Essays on Detective Fiction and Contemporary Literary Theory.* Ed. Ronald G. Walker and June M. Frazer. Macomb: Western Illinois UP, 1990. 109–119.

Halliwell, Leslie. *Halliwell's Film Guide.* Ed. John Walker. 8th ed. New York: HarperCollins, 1991.

Hamper, Ben. *Rivethead.* New York: Warner, 1991.

Hampton, Wayne. *Guerilla Minstrels: John Lennon, Joe Hill, Woody Guthrie, Bob Dylan.* Knoxville: U of Tennessee P, 1986.

Hansen, Miriam. "Ambivalences of the 'Mass Ornament': King Vidor's *The Crowd.*" *Qui Parle* 5.2 (1992): 102–19.

Haralovich, Mary Beth. "The Proletarian Woman's Film of the 1930s: Contending with Censorship and Entertainment." *Screen* 31.2 (1990): 172–87.

Hark, Ina Rae. "Animals or Romans: Looking at Masculinity in *Spartacus.*" *Screening the Male: Exploring Masculinities in Hollywood Cinema.* Ed. Steven Cohan and Ina Rae Hark. London: Routledge, 1993. 151–72.

Harris, Fred. "Burning up People to Make Electricity." *Atlantic Monthly* (July 1974): 29–36.

Harris, Robert A. *The Complete Films of Alfred Hitchcock.* Secaucus, NJ: Carol Publishing Group, 1993.

Hauser, Thomas. *The Execution of Charles Horman: An American Sacrifice.* New York: Harcourt Brace Jovanovich, 1978.

Hayman, Ronald. *Brecht: A Biography.* New York: Oxford UP, 1983.

Healey, Dorothy, and Maurice Isserman. *California Red: A Life in the American Communist Party.* Urbana: U of Illinois P, 1993.

Hellman, Lillian. *Pentimento: A Book of Portraits.* Boston: Little, Brown, 1973.

———. *Scoundrel Time.* Boston: Little, Brown, 1976.

Hellmann, John. "Vietnam and the Hollywood Genre Film: Inversions of American Mythology in *The Deer Hunter* and *Apocalypse Now.*" Anderegg. *Inventing Vietnam* 56–80.

Henriksen, Margot A. *Dr. Strangelove's America: Society and Culture in the Atomic Age.* Berkeley: U of California P, 1997.

Hevener, John W. *Which Side Are You On?: The Harlan County Coal Miners, 1931–39.* Urbana: U of Illinois P, 1978.

Hey, Kenneth R. "Ambivalence as a Theme in *On the Waterfront* (1954): An Interdisciplinary Approach to Film Study." Rollins. *Hollywood as Historian: American Film in a Cultural Context* 159–89.

Hicks, Granville. *John Reed: The Making of a Revolutionary.* New York: Macmillan, 1936.

Higham, Charles. *The Films of Orson Welles.* Berkeley: U of California P, 1970.

———. *Orson Welles: The Rise and Fall of an American Genius.* New York: St. Martin's, 1985.

Hirsch, Foster. *Joseph Losey.* Boston: Twayne, 1980.

Hixson, Walter L. *Parting the Curtain: Propaganda, Culture, and the Cold War, 1945–1961.* New York: St. Martin's, 1997.

Hoban, James L., Jr. "Scripting *The Good Earth*: Versions of the Novel for the Screen." *The Several World of Pearl S. Buck.* Ed. Elizabeth Lipscomb, Frances E. Webb, and Peter Conn. Westport, CT: Greenwood, 1994. 127–44.

Hoberman, J. "True Romance." *The Village Voice* 39.35 (August 30, 1994): 41.

Hoffman, Donald. "Whose Home on the Range?: Finding Room for Native Americans, African Americans, and Latino Americans in the Revisionist Western." *MELUS* 22 (Summer 1997): 45–59.

Horak, Jan-Christopher. "Avant-Garde Film." Balio 387–404.

Horkheimer, Max and Theodor W. Adorno. *Dialectic of Enlightenment.* Trans. John Cumming. New York: Seabury P, 1972.

Horton, Robert. "Sayles' New Pitch." *Film Comment* 27.4 (1991): 79.

Howard, James. *The Complete Films of Orson Welles.* New York: Citadel, 1991.

Howard, William L. "Caldwell on Stage and Screen." *The Southern Quarterly* 27.3 (1989): 59–72.

Huff, Theodore. *The Early Work of Charles Chaplin.* 1961. New York: Gordon P, 1978.

———. Intolerance: *The Film by David Wark Griffith, Shot-by-Shot Analysis.* New York: Museum of Modern Art, 1966.

Humphries, Reynold. *Fritz Lang: Genre and Representation in His American Films.* Baltimore, MD: Johns Hopkins UP, 1989.

Ingrassia, Catherine. "Writing the West: Iconic and Literal Truth in *Unforgiven.*" *Literature/Film Quarterly* 26.1 (1998): 53–59.

Isenberg, Michael T. *War on Film: The American Cinema and World War I, 1914–1941.* Rutherford, NJ: Fairleigh Dickinson UP, 1981.

Isserman, Maurice. *Which Side Were You On?: The American Communist Party During the Second World War.* Urbana: U of Illinois P, 1993.

Ivens, Joris. *The Camera and I.* New York: International Publishers, 1969.

Jackson, Carlton. *Picking Up the Tab: The Life and Movies of Martin Ritt.* Bowling Green, OH: Bowling Green State U Popular P, 1994.

Jackson, Martin A. "The Uncertain Peace: *The Best Years of Our Lives.*" O'Connor and Jackson 147–65.

Jacobs, Lewis, ed. *The Documentary Tradition: From Nanook to Woodstock.* New York: Hopkinson and Blake, 1971.

Jaffe, Ira S. "Fighting Words: *City Lights* (1931), *Modern Times* (1936), and *The Great Dictator* (1940)." Rollins. *Hollywood as Historian: American Film in a Cultural Context.* 49–67.

James, David E. *Allegories of Cinema: American Film in the Sixties.* Princeton, NJ: Princeton UP, 1989.

James, David E., and Rick Berg, eds. *The Hidden Foundation: Cinema and the Question of Class.* Minneapolis: U of Minnesota P, 1996.

Jameson, Fredric. *Postmodernism, or, The Cultural Logic of Late Capitalism.* Durham, NC: Duke UP, 1991.

———. *Signatures of the Visible.* New York: Routledge, 1992.

Jeffords, Susan. "Friendly Civilians: Images of Women and the Feminization of the Audience in Vietnam Films." *Wide Angle* 7.4 (1985): 13–22.

Jesionowski, Joyce E. *Thinking in Pictures: Dramatic Structure in D. W. Griffith's Biograph Films.* Berkeley: U of California P, 1987.

"John Sayles's *Men With Guns* is Skillfiul; Absurd Obsession Overcomes John Hurt in *Love and Death on Long Island*; More." *GQ* 68.3 (March 1998): 121.

Jones, Dorothy B. "Communism in the Movies." *Report on Blacklisting.* Vol 1 of 2. Ed. John Cogley. New York: Fund for the Republic, 1956.

Jowett, Garth. "Bullets, Beer, and the Hays Office: *Public Enemy* (1931)." O'Connor and Jackson 57–76.

Kael, Pauline. *State of the Art.* New York: E. P. Dutton, 1985.

Kagan, Norman. *American Skeptic: Robert Altman's Genre-Commentary Films.* Ann Arbor, MI: Pierian P, 1982.

———. *The Cinema of Oliver Stone.* New York: Continuum, 1995.

———. *The Cinema of Stanley Kubrick.* New York: Grove, 1972.

Kaminsky, Stuart M. *John Huston: Maker of Magic*. London: Angus and Robertson, 1978.

Katz, Friedrich. *The Life and Times of Pancho Villa*. Stanford, CA: Stanford UP, 1998.

Katz, Jon. "Natural Born Killjoy." *Wired* 2.12 (December 1994): 126–33.

Kazan, Elia. *A Life*. New York: Knopf, 1988.

Kelly, Mary Pat. *Martin Scorsese: A Journey*. New York: Thunder's Mouth P, 1996.

Kepley, Vance, Jr. "*Intolerance* and the Soviets: A Historical Investigation." *Inside the Film Factory: New Approaches to Russian and Soviet Cinema*. Ed. Richard Taylor and Ian Christie. London: Routledge, 1991. 51–59.

Keyssar, Helene. *Robert Altman's America*. New York: Oxford UP, 1991.

Kinney, Judy Lee. "*Gardens of Stone, Platoon*, and *Hamburger Hill*." Anderegg. *Inventing Vietnam* 153–65.

Kirtz, Mary K. "Teaching Literature through Film: An Interdisciplinary Approach to *Surfacing* and *The Handmaid's Tale*." *Approaches to Teaching Atwood's* The Handmaid's Tale *and Other Works*. Ed. Sharon R. Wilson, Thomas B. Friedman, and Shannon Hengen. New York: Modern Language Association of America, 1996. 140–45.

Kiuchi, Toru. "Richard Wright's *Native Son:* The Film and the Novel." *Motion Pictures and Society*. Ed. Douglas Radcliff-Umstead. Kent, OH: Kent State U, 1990. 62–68.

Klein, Joe. *Woody Guthrie: A Life*. London: Faber, 1981.

Klein, Michael. "Historical Memory, Film, and the Vietnam Era." Dittmar and Michaud 19–40.

Klein, Michael, and Jill Klein. "*Native Land:* An Interview with Leo Hurwitz." *Cineaste* 6.3 (1975): 6.

Kline, Herbert. "Films without Make-Believe." Jacobs 148–57.

Knock, Thomas J. "History with Lightning: The Forgotten Film *Wilson* (1944)." Rollins. *Hollywood as Historian: American Film in a Cultural Context*. 88–108.

Kopkind, Andrew. "A Player Ups the Ante." *Premiere* 6.1 (September 1992): 80.

Koppes, Clayton R., and Gregory D. Black. *Hollywood Goes to War: How Politics, Profits, and Propaganda Shaped World War II Movies*. New Yor: Free P, 1987.

Kovic, Ron. *Born on the Fourth of July*. New York: McGraw-Hill, 1976.

———. Introduction. *Johnny Got His Gun*. By Dalton Trumbo. New York: Citadel P, 1994. vii–xviii.

Krutnik, Christopher. *In a Lonely Street: Film Noir, Genre, Masculinity*. London: Routledge, 1991.

Kunz, Don. "Oliver Stone's *Talk Radio*." *Literature/Film Quarterly* 25.1 (1997): 62–67.

Kunz, Don, ed. *The Films of Oliver Stone*. Lanham, MD: Scarecrow P, 1997.

Langman, Larry. *A Guide to American Crime Films of the Thirties*. Westport, CT: Greenwood, 1995.

Laskowsky, Henry J. "*Heart of Darkness:* A Primer for the Holocaust." *Virginia Quarterly Review* 58.1 (1982): 93–110.

Lawson, John Howard. "Our Film and Theirs: *Grapes of Wrath* and *Bonnie and Clyde*." *American Dialog* 5.2 (1968–69): 30–33.

Leach, William. *Land of Desire: Merchants, Power, and the Rise of a New American Culture.* New York: Vintage-Random House, 1993.

Lebo, Harlan. *The Godfather Legacy.* New York: Simon and Schuster, 1997.

Leff, Leonard J. "Film into Story: The Narrative Scheme of *Crossfire.*" *Literature/Film Quarterly* 12.3 (1984): 171–79.

Leff, Leonard, and Jerrold L. Simmons. *The Dame in the Kimono: Hollywood Censorship and the Production Code from the 1920s to the 1960s.* New York: Anchor Books, 1990.

Leibman, Nina. "Decades and Retrodecades: Historiography in the Case of *Easy Rider* and *Shampoo.*" *The Mid-Atlantic Almanac* 2 (1993): 81–94.

Leifermann, Henry P. *Crystal Lee: A Woman of Inheritance.* New York: Macmillan, 1975.

Leondopoulos, Jordan. *Still the Moving World:* Intolerance, Modernism, and Heart of Darkness. New York: Peter Lang, 1991.

Levy, Emanuel. *George Cukor, Master of Elegance: Hollywood's Legendary Director and His Stars.* New York: Morrow, 1994.

Lewis, Arthur H. *Lament for the Molly Maguires.* New York: Harcourt, Brace, 1964.

Librach, Ronald S. "The Last Temptation in *Mean Streets* and *Raging Bull.*" *Literature/Film Quarterly* 20.1 (1992): 14–24.

Lichty, Lawrence W., and Raymond L. Carroll. "Fragments of War: *Platoon* (1986)." O'Connor and Jackson 273–87.

Long, Priscilla. *Where the Sun Never Shines: A History of America's Bloody Coal Industry.* New York: Paragon, 1989.

Luhr, William. "Tracking *The Maltese Falcon:* Classical Hollywood Narration and Sam Spade." *Close Viewings: An Anthology of Film Criticism.* Ed. Peter Lehman. Tallahassee: Florida State UP, 1990. 7–22.

Lukács, Georg. *The Historical Novel.* Trans. Hannah Mitchell and Stanley Mitchell. Lincoln: U of Nebraska P, 1983.

Lynd, Alice, and Staughton Lynd. *Rank and File: Personal Histories by Working-Class Organizers.* Boston: Beacon, 1973.

Maland, Charles. *Chaplin and American Culture: The Evolution of a Star Image.* Princeton, NJ: Princeton UP, 1989.

———. "*Dr. Strangelove* (1964): Nightmare Comedy and the Ideology of Liberal Consensus." Rollins. *Hollywood as Historian: American Film in a Cultural Context.* 190–210.

———. "Memories and Things Past: History and Two Biographical Flashback Films." *East-West Film Journal* 6.1 (1992): 66–93.

Man, Glenn. "Marginality and Centrality: The Myth of Asia in 1970s Hollywood." *East-West Film Journal* 8.1 (1994): 52–67.

Man, Glenn K. S. "*The Third Man:* Pulp Fiction and Art Film." *Literature/Film Quarterly* 21.3 (1993):171–77.

Marc, David. "Scandal and the Wasp." *Sight and Sound* 5.2 (1995): 10–13.

Martin, Andrew. "Vietnam and Melodramatic Representation." *East-West Film Journal* 4.2 (1990): 54–67.

Marx, Karl, and Frederick Engels. *The Marx-Engels Reader.* Ed. Robert C. Tucker. 2nd ed. New York: Norton, 1978.

McCarty, John. *The Films of John Huston.* Secaucus, NJ: Citadel P, 1987.

———. *Hollywood Gangland: The Movies' Love Affair with the Mob*. New York: St. Martin's, 1993.

McCarthy, Patrick. "*Salt of the Earth:* Convention and Invention of the Domestic Melodrama." *Rendezvoux* 19.1 (1983): 22–32.

McCreadie, Marsha. "'Julia': Memory in *Pentimento* and on Film." *Literature/Film Quarterly* 7 (1979): 260–69.

McDonald, Gerald D. *The Films of Charlie Chaplin*. 2d ed. Secaucus, NJ: Citadel P, 1971.

McElvaine, Robert S. *The Great Depression: America, 1919–1941*. New York: Times Books, 1993.

McGilligan, Patrick. *Fritz Lang: The Nature of the Beast*. London: Faber and Faber, 1997.

McMullen, Wayne J. "*The China Syndrome:* Corruption to the Core." *Literature/Film Quarterly* 23.1 (1995): 55–62.

McReynolds, Douglas J., and Barbara J. Lips. "Taking Care of Things: Evolution in the Treatment of a Western Theme, 1947–1957." *Literature/Film Quarterly* 18.3 (1990): 202–208.

Medhurst, Martin J., and Thomas W. Benson. "*The City:* The Rhetoric of Rhythm." *Communication Monographs* 48.1 (1981): 55–72.

Meeropol. Robert, and Michael Meeropol. *We Are Your Sons: The Legacy of Ethel and Julius Rosenberg*. Boston: Houghton Mifflin, 1975.

Melada, Ivan. "Graham Greene and the Munitions Makers: The Historical Context of *A Gun for Sale*." *Studies in the Novel* 13.3 (1981): 303–21.

Mellencamp, Patricia. "The Sexual Economics of *Gold Diggers of 1933*." *Close Viewings: An Anthology of Film Criticism*. Ed. Peter Lehman. Tallahassee: Florida State UP, 1990. 177–99.

Merrill, Robert. "Altman's *McCabe and Mrs. Miller* as a Classic Western." *New Orleans Review* 17.2 (1990): 79–86.

Meyers, Sidney, and Jay Leyda. "Joris Ivens: Artist in Documentary." Jacobs 158–66.

Michalczyk, John J. *Costa-Gavras: The Political Fiction Film*. Philadelphia: Art Alliance P, 1984.

———. "*The Spanish Earth* and Siercade Teruel: The Human Condition as Political Message." *North Dakota Quarterly* 60.2 (1992): 40–49.

Miller, Joyce. "From *Bonnie and Clyde* to *Thelma and Louise*: The Struggle for Justice in the Cinematic South." *Studies in Popular Culture* 19.2 (1996): 277–86.

Miller, Tom. "Class Reunion: *Salt of the Earth* Revisited." *Cineaste* 13.3 (1984): 31–36.

Millon, Robert P. *Zapata: The Ideology of a Peasant Revolutionary*. 2nd ed. New York: International Publishers, 1995.

Milner, E. R. *The Lives and Times of Bonnie and Clyde*. Carbondale: Southern Illinois UP, 1996.

Mintz, Steven, and Randy Roberts, eds. *Hollywood's America: United States History through Its Films*. St. James, NY: Brandywine P, 1993.

Miranda, Roger. *The Civil War in Nicaragua: Inside the Sandinistas*. New Brunswick, NJ: Transaction Publishers, 1993.

Mistron, Deborah E. "The Role of Pancho Villa in the Mexican and the American Cinema." *Studies in Latin American Popular Culture* 2 (1983): 1–13.

Monteath, Peter. *The Spanish Civil War in Literature, Film, and Art.* Westport, CT: Greenwood, 1994.

Moore, James Tice. "Depression Images: Subsistence Homesteads, 'Production-for-Use,' and King Vidor's *Our Daily Bread.*" *Midwest Quarterly* 26.1 (1984): 24–34.

Moore, Janet C. "For Fighting and for Fun: Kubrick's Complicitous Critique in *Full Metal Jacket.*" *The Velvet Light Trap* 31 (1993): 39–47.

Moore, Marat. "Where the Rubber Meets the Road: John Sayles Talks about His Coal Mining Movie *Matewan.*" *Now and Then* 5.1 (1988): 5–8.

Morgan, Susan. "Tim Robbins." *Interview* 22.8 (August 1992): 66.

Morley, Morris H. *Washington, Somoza, and the Sandinistas: State and Regime in U. S. Policy toward Nicaragua, 1969–1981.* Cambridge: Cambridge UP, 1994.

Morris, Peter. "*Salt of the Earth.*" *Celluloid Power: Social Film Criticism from* The Birth of a Nation *to* Judgment at Nuremburg. Ed. David Platt. Metuchen, NJ: Scarecrow P, 1992. 485–93.

Moss, Robert E. *The Films of Carol Reed.* New York: Columbia UP, 1987.

Muller, Eddie. *Dark City: The Lost World of Film Noir.* New York: St. Martin's, 1998.

Mulvey, Laura. "*Citizen Kane.*" London: British Film Institute, 1992.

Munby, Jonathan. *Public Enemies, Public Heroes: Screening the Gangster from* Little Caesar *to* Touch of Evil. Chicago: U of Chicago P, 1999.

Murphy, Bren Ortega, and Jeffery Scott Harder. "1960s Counterculture and the Legacy of American Myth: A Study of Three Films." *Canadian Review of American Studies* 23.2 (1993): 57–78.

Murray, Lawrence L. "Hollywood, Nihilism, and the Youth Culture of the Sixties: *Bonnie and Clyde* (1967)." O'Connor and Jackson 237–56.

Muscio, Giuliana. *Hollywood's New Deal.* Philadelphia: Temple UP, 1996.

Muse, Eben J. *The Land of Nam: The Vietnam War in American Film.* Lanham, MD: Scarecrow P, 1995.

Musser, Charles. *The Emergence of Cinema: The American Screen to 1907.* Berkeley: U of California P, 1994.

Myers, Jeffrey. "*For Whom the Bell Tolls* as Contemporary History." *The Spanish Civil War in Literature.* Ed. Janet Perez and Wendell Aycock. Lubbock: Texas Tech UP, 1990. 85–109.

Naremore, James. "John Huston and *The Maltese Falcon.*" *Literature/Film Quarterly* 1 (1973): 239–49.

———. *The Magic of Orson Welles.* Dallas: Southern Methodist UP, 1989.

———. *More than Night: Film Noir in Its Contexts.* Berkeley: U of California P, 1998.

Navasky, Victor S. *Naming Names.* New York: Viking, 1980.

Nemecek, Maureen. "From Aesthesia to Anesthesia: Three Decades of Violence in Film." *The Image of Violence in Literature, the Media, and Society.* Ed. Will Wright and Steven Kaplan. Pueblo: U of Southern Colorado, 1995. 168–73.

Nericcio, William Anthony. "Of Mestizos and Half-Breeds: Orson Welles's *Touch of Evil*." *Chicanos and Film: Representation and Resistance.* Ed. Chon A. Noriega. Minneapolis: U of Minnesota P, 1992. 47–58.

Neve, Brian. *Film and Politics in America: A Social Tradition.* London: Routledge, 1992.

———. "The 1950s: The Case of Elia Kazan and *On the Waterfront*." Davies and Neve 97–118.

Noble, Peter. *The Negro in Films.* New York: Arno, 1970.

O'Brien, Daniel. *Robert Altman: Hollywood Survivor.* New York: Continuum, 1995.

O'Connor, John E., and Martin A. Jackson, eds. *American History/American Film: Interpreting the Hollywood Image.* New York: Continuum, 1988.

Orvell, Miles. "Documentary Film and the Power of Interrogation: *American Dream* and *Roger and Me*." *Film Quarterly* 48.2 (1994–95): 10–19.

Ostwalt, Conrad. "*Dances with Wolves*: An American *Heart of Darkness*." *Literature/Film Quarterly* 24.2 (1996): 209–16.

Ott, Frederick W. *The Films of Fritz Lang.* Secaucus, NJ: Citadel P, 1979.

Ottanelli, Fraser M. *The Communist Party of the United States: From the Depression to World War II.* New Brunswick, NJ: Rutgers UP, 1991.

Packer, George. "Decency and Muck: The Visions of John Sayles and Oliver Stone." *Dissent* 44.3 (1997): 105–09.

Palladino, Grace. *Another Civil War: Labor, Capital, and the State in the Anthracite Regions of Pennsylvania, 1840–68.* Urbana: U of illinois P, 1990.

Palmer, James, and Michael Riley. *The Films of Joseph Losey.* Cambridge: Cambridge UP, 1993.

Palmer, R. Barton. "*Film Noir* and the Genre Continuum: Process, Product, and *The Big Clock*." Palmer. *Perspectives on Film Noir.* 141–53.

———. *Hollywood's Dark Cinema: The American Film Noir.* New York: Twayne, 1994.

Palmer, R. Barton, ed. *Perspectives on Film Noir.* New York: G. K. Hall, 1996.

Papke, David Ray. "Myth and Meaning: Francis Ford Coppola and Popular Response to the *Godfather* Trilogy." *Legal Reelism: Movies as Legal Texts.* Ed. John Denvir. Urbana: U of Illinois P, 1996. 1–22.

Paredes, Américo. *"With His Pistol in His Hand": A Border Ballad and Its Hero.* 1958. Austin: U of Texas P, 1971.

Patraka, Vivian M. "Lillian Hellman's *Watch on the Rhine*: Realism, Gender, and Historical Crisis." *Modern Drama* 32.1 (1989): 128–45.

Petras, James F. *The United States and Chile: Imperialism and the Overthrow of the Allende Government.* New York: Monthly Review P, 1975.

Phillips, Gene D. *George Cukor.* Boston: Twayne, 1982.

Pileggi, Nicholas. *Wiseguy: Life in a Mafia Family.* New York: Simon and Schuster, 1985.

Pinchon, Edgcumb. *Viva Villa!: A Recovery of the Real Pancho Villa, Peon, Bandit, Soldier, Patriot.* 1933. New York: Arno P, 1970.

Plantinga, Carl. "Roger and History and Irony and Me." *Michigan Academician* 24.3 (1992): 511–20.

Plecki, Gerard. *Robert Altman.* Boston: Twayne, 1985.

Polan, Dana. *Power and Paranoia: History, Narrative, and the American Cinema, 1940–1950.* New York: Columbia UP, 1986.

Polonsky, Abraham. "*The Best Years of Our Lives:* A Review." *Hollywood Quarterly* 2–3 (April 1947): 257–60.

Porfirio, Robert G. "No Way Out: Existential Motifs in the Film Noir." Palmer. *Perspectives on Film Noir.* 115–128.

——. "Whatever Happened to the Film Noir?: *The Postman Always Rings Twice* (1946–1981)." *Literature/Film Quarterly* 13.2 (1985): 102–111.

Porteous, Katrina. "History Lessons: *Platoon.*" *Vietnam Images: War and Representation.* Ed. Jeffrey Walsh and James Aulich. New York: St. Martin's, 1989. 153–59.

Pratley, Gerald. *The Cinema of Otto Preminger.* New York: Castle Books, 1971.

Price, Derrick. "*How Green Was My Valley:* A Romance of Wales." *The Progress of Romance: The Politics of Popular Fiction.* Ed. Jean Radford. London: Routledge and Kegan Paul, 1986. 73–94.

Price, Theodore. "The Truth about the Bette Davis 1937 Gangster Movie *Marked Woman.*" *Crime in Motion Pictures.* Ed. Douglas Radcliff-Umstead. Kent, OH: Kent State UP, 1986. 24–32.

Puette, William J. *Through Jaundiced Eyes: How the Media View Labor.* Ithaca, NY: ILR P, 1992.

Pursell, Michael. "*Full Metal Jacket:* The Unraveling of Patriarchy." *Literature/Film Quarterly* 16.4 (1988): 218–25.

Pye, Douglas. "*Ulzana's Raid.*" *The Book of Westerns.* Ed. Ian Cameron and Douglas Pye. New York: Continuum, 1996. 262–68

Pyle, Ernie. *Here Is Your War.* New York: Military Heritage P, 1943.

Quart, Leonard. "A Second Look: *A Face in the Crowd.*" *Cineaste* 17.2 (1989): 30–31.

Quart, Leonard, and Albert Auster. *American Film and Society since 1945.* New York: Praeger, 1984.

Raban, Jonathan. "A Surfeit of Commodities: The Novels of Nathanael West." *The Novel and the Nineteen Twenties.* Ed. Malcolm Bradbury and David Palmer. London: Edwin Arnold, 1971.

Rachleff, Peter. *Hard-Pressed in the Heartland: The Hormel Strike and the Future of the Labor Movement.* Boston: South End P, 1993.

Radell, Karen M. "Drugs on Screen: Otto Preminger's *The Man with the Golden Arm* Forces Hollywood to Go Cold Turkey." *Motion Pictures and Society.* Ed. Douglas Radcliff-Umstead. Kent, OH: Kent State U, 1990. 86–91.

Rapf, Jerome E. "'Human Need' in *The Day of the Locust:* Problems of Adaptation." *Literature/Film Quarterly* 9.1 (1981): 22–31.

Rapf, Joanna E. "Myth, Ideology, and Feminism in *High Noon.*" *Journal of Popular Culture* 23.4 (1990): 75–80.

Rashke, Richard. *The Killing of Karen Silkwood.* Boston: Houghton Mifflin, 1981.

Ray, Nicholas. *I Was Interrupted: Nicholas Ray on Making Movies.* Berkeley: U of California P, 1993.

Ray, Robert B. *A Certain Tendency of the Hollywood Cinema, 1930–1980.* Princeton, NJ: Princeton UP, 1985.

Reaves, Gerri. "From Hasford's *The Short-Timers* to Kubrick's *Full Metal Jacket*." *Literature/Film Quarterly* 16.4 (1988): 232–37.

Recchia, Edward J. "Martin Scorsese's *Raging Bull:* In Violence Veritas." *Aethlon* 7.2 (1990): 21–31.

———. "Setting as a Narrative Convention: Locales in the Boxing Film." *Beyond the Stars: Studies in American Popular Film. Volume 4: Locales in American Popular Film.* Ed. Paul Loukides and Linda K. Fuller. Bowling Green, OH: Bowling Green State U Popular P, 1993. 183–203.

Reed, John. *Insurgent Mexico.* 1914. New York: Modern Library, 1995.

———. *Ten Days that Shook the World.* 1919. Harmondsworth: Penguin, 1977.

Reid, Mark A. "*Take a Giant Step, A Raisin in the Sun:* The U.S. Black Family Film." *Jump Cut* 36 (May 1991): 81–88.

Reilly, John M. "Images of Gastonia: A Revolutionary Chapter in American Social Fiction." *The Georgia Review* 28 (1974): 498–517.

Renov, Michael. *Hollywood's Wartime Women: Representation and Ideology.* Ann Arbor, MI: UMI Research P, 1988.

Revkin, Andrew. *The Burning Season: The Murder of Chico Mendes and the Fight for the Amazon Rain Forest.* London: Collins, 1990.

Rhodes, Chip. "Filling the Void: Work and the Modern Subject in King Vidor's *The Crowd*." *Studies in the Humanities* 20.2 (1993): 115–24.

Richolson, Janice. "*The Player:* An Interview with Robert Altman." *Cineaste* 19.2–3 (1992): 61.

Robbins, Bruce. *Secular Vocations: Intellectuals, Professionalism, Culture.* London: Verso, 1993.

Roberts, Nora Ruth. "John Sayles and the Un'Disappearance' of the Working Class: The Vitality of Our History." *Against the Current* 12.4 (1997): 39–42.

Roberts, Randy. "*Casablanca* as Propaganda: You Must Remember This." Mintz and Roberts.

Robinson, David. *The Mirror of Opinion.* Bloomington: Indiana UP, 1984.

Robinson, Lillian S. "Out of the Mine and into the Canyon: Working-Class Feminism, Yesterday and Today." James and Berg 172–92.

Roddick, Nick. *A New Deal in Entertainment.* London: British Film Institute, 1983.

Roffman, Peter, and Jim Purdy. *The Hollywood Social Problem Film: Madness, Despair and Politics from the Depression to the Fifties.* Bloomington: Indiana UP, 1981.

Rogin, Michael. "Body and Soul: *JFK*." *Media Spectacles.* Ed. Marjorie Garber, Jann Matlock, and Rebecca L. Walkowitz. New York: Routledge, 1993. 3–21.

———. "The Great Mother Domesticated: Sexual Difference and Sexual Indifference in D. W. Griffith's *Intolerance*." *Discovering Difference: Contemporary Essays in American Culture.* Ed. Christoph K. Lohmann. Bloomington: Indiana UP, 1993. 148–88.

Rollins, Peter C. "Ideology and Film Rhetoric: Three Documentaries of the New Deal Era." Rollins. *Hollywood as Historian: American Film in a Cultural Context* 32–48.

Rollins, Peter C., ed. *Hollywood as Historian: American Film in a Cultural Context.* Rev. ed. Lexington: UP of Kentucky, 1998.

Rosen, David. "Crossover: Hispanic Specialty Films in the U. S. Movie Market-place." *Chicanos and Film: Representation and Resistance.* Ed. Chon A. Noriega. Minneapolis: U of Minnesota P, 1992. 241–60.

Rosen, Robert C. "*The Man with the Golden Arm:* Anatomy of a Junkie Movie." *The Modern American Novel and the Movies.* Ed. Gerald Peary and Roger Shatzkin. New York: Frederick Ungar, 1978. 189–98.

Rosenbaum, Jonathan. *Movies as Politics.* Berkeley: U of California P, 1997.

Rosenfelt, Deborah Silverton. "Commentary." *Salt of the Earth.* New York: Feminist P, 1978. 93–168.

Rosenstone, Robert. *Romantic Revolutionary: A Biography of John Reed.* New York: Knopf, 1975.

Rosenthal, Alan. *The Documentary Conscience.* Berkeley: U of California P, 1980.

Rosenzweig, Sidney. Casablanca *and Other Major Films of Michael Curtiz.* Ann Arbor, MI: UMI Research P, 1982.

Ross, Steven J. *Working-Class Hollywood: Silent Film and the Shaping of Class in America.* Princeton, NJ: Princeton UP, 1998.

Rotha, Paul. *Documentary Film.* London: Faber and Faber, 1942.

Ruben, Martin. *Showstoppers: Busby Berkeley and the Tradition of Spectacle.* New York: Columbia UP, 1993.

Russell, Don. *The Lives and Legends of Buffalo Bill.* Norman: U of Oklahoma P, 1960.

———. *The Wild West: A History of Wild West Shows.* Fort Worth, TX: Amon Carter Museum, 1961.

Rutherford, Charles S. "A New Dog with an Old Trick: Archetypal Patterns in *Sounder.*" *Movies as Artifacts: Cultural Criticism of Popular Film.* Ed. Michael T. Marsden, John G. Nachbar, and Sam L. Grogg, Jr. Chicago: Nelson-Hall, 1982. 223–29.

Ryan, Michael, and Douglas Kellner. *Camera Politica: The Politics and Ideology of Contemporary Hollywood Film.* Bloomington: Indiana UP, 1988.

Ryan, Susan. "*Men with Guns.*" *Cineaste* 23.3 (1998): 43–44.

Ryley, Robert M. "More than a Thriller: *The Big Clock.*" *Armchair Detective* 16.4 (1983): 354–59.

Safer, Elaine B. "'It's the Truth Even If It Didn't Happen': Ken Kesey's *One Flew over the Cuckoo's Nest.*" *A Casebook on Ken Kesey's* One Flew Over the Cuckoo's Nest. Ed. George J. Searles. Albuquerque: U of New Mexico P, 1992. 151–61.

Said, Edward. *Orientalism.* New York: Vintage-Random House, 1979.

Sanderson, Rena, ed. *Blowing the Bridge: Essays on Hemingway and* For Whom the Bell Tolls. Westport, CT: Greenwood, 1992.

Savage, Lon. *Thunder in the Mountains: The West Virginia Mine War, 1920–21.* Pittsburgh, PA: U of Pittsburgh P, 1990.

Sayles, John. *Sayles on Sayles.* London: Faber and Faber, 1998.

———. *Thinking in Pictures: The Making of the Movie* Matewan. Boston: Houghton Mifflin, 1987.

Sayre, Nora. *Running Time: Films of the Cold War.* New York: Dial, 1982.

Schatz, Thomas. *Boom and Bust: The American Cinema in the 1940s.* New York: Scribner's, 1997.

————. *The Genius of the System: Hollywood Filmmaking in the Studio Era.* New York: Pantheon, 1988.

Scher, Saul N. "*The Glass Key:* The Original and Two Copies." *Literature/Film Quarterly* 12.3 (1984): 147–59.

Schrader, Paul. "Notes on Film Noir." Palmer. *Perspectives on Film Noir.* 99–109.

Scopes, John T. *Center of the Storm: Memoirs of John T. Scopes.* New York: Holt, Rinehart, and Winston, 1967.

Scott, Shaunna L. *Two Sides to Everything: The Cultural Construction of Class Consciousness in Harlan County, Kentucky.* Albany: State U of New York P, 1995.

Self, Robert T. "Author, Text, and Self in *Buffalo Bill and the Indians.*" *Ambiguities in Literature and Film.* Ed. Hans P. Braendlin. Tallahassee: Florida State UP, 1988. 104–16.

Selig, Michael. "Boys Will Be Men: Oedipal Drama in *Coming Home.*" Dittmar and Michaud 189–202.

Shafransky, Renee. "*Seeing Red:* An Interview with James Klein and Julia Reichert." *Cineaste* 13.2 (1984): 24–26.

Shaheen, Jack G. "Screen Images of Palestinians in the 1980s." *Beyond the Stars: Stock Characters in American Popular Film.* Ed. Paul Loukides and Linda K. Fuller. Bowling Green, OH: Popular P, 1990. 49–60.

Sharrett, Christopher. "Conspiracy Theory and Political Murder in America: Oliver Stone's *JFK* and the Facts of the Matter." *The New American Cinema.* Ed. Jon Lewis. Durham, NC: Duke UP, 1998. 217–47.

Shindler, Colin. *Hollywood Goes to War: Films and American Society, 1939–1952.* London: Routledge and Kegan Paul, 1979.

Shoumatoff, Alex. *Murder in the Rain Forest: The Chico Mendes Story.* London: Fourth Estate, 1991.

Silver, Alain. "What Ever Happened to Robert Aldrich? His Life and His Films." New York: Limelight, 1995.

Silver, Alain, and Elizabeth Ward, eds. *Film Noir: An Encyclopedic Reference to the American Style.* 3rd ed. Woodstock, NY: Overlook P, 1992.

Simmons, Jerrold. "The Censoring of *Rebel without a Cause.*" *Journal of Popular Film and Television.* 23.2 (1995): 57–63.

Simon, Art. "The Making of Alert Viewers: The Mixing of Fact and Fiction in *JFK.*" *Cineaste* 19.1 (1992): 14–15. (Part of a special section on *JFK.*)

Skerry, Phillip J. "*Dances With Wolves* and *Unforgiven:* Apocalyptic Postrevisionist Westerns." *Beyond the Stars 5: Themes and Ideologies in American Popular Film.* Ed. Paul Loukides and Linda K. Fuller. Bowling Green, OH: Popular P, 1996. 281–91.

Sklar, Robert. *Movie-Made America: A Social History of American Movies.* New York: Random House, 1975.

Slater, Thomas J. "*One Flew over the Cuckoo's Nest:* A Tale of Two Decades." *Film and Literature: A Comparative Approach to Adaptation.* Ed. Wendell Aycock and Michael Schoenecke. Lubbock: Texas Tech UP, 1988. 45–58.

Sloan, Kay. "A Cinema in Search of Itself: Ideology of the Social Problem Film during the Silent Era." *Cineaste.* 14.2 (1985): 34–56.

Slotkin, Richard. "Buffalo Bill's 'Wild West' and the Mythologization of the American Empire." *Cultures of United States Imperialism.* Ed. Amy Kaplan and Donald E. Pease. Durham, NC: Duke UP, 1993. 164–81.

Smith, Claude J., Jr. "*Full Metal Jacket* and the Beast Within." *Literature/Film Quarterly* 16.4 (1988): 226–31.

Smith, Dai. *Wales! Wales?* London: Allen and Unwin, 1984.

Smith, Jeffrey P. "'A Good Business Proposition': Dalton Trumbo, *Spartacus,* and the End of the Blacklist." *The Velvet Light Trap* 23 (Spring 1989): 75–100

Snyder, Robert L. *Pare Lorentz and the Documentary Film.* Rev. ed. Reno: U of Nevada P, 1994.

Sobchack, Vivian C. "*The Grapes of Wrath* (1940): Thematic Emphasis through Visual Style." Rollins. *Hollywood as Historian: American Film in a Cultural Context.* 68–87.

Sorell, Victor A. "Ethnomusicology, Folklore, and History in the Filmmaker's Art: *The Ballad of Gregorio Cortez.*" *Chicano Cinema: Research, Reviews, and Resources.* Ed. Gary D. Keller. Binghamton, NY: Bilingual P, 1985. 153–58.

Souza, Márcio. *Rain on Fire: Chico Mendes and the End of the Amazon.* London: Viking, 1990.

Spelman, Elizabeth V., and Martha Minow. "Outlaw Women: *Thelma and Louise.*" *Legal Reelism: Movies as Legal Texts.* Ed. John Denvir. Urbana: U of Illinois P, 1996. 161–79.

Spoto, Donald. *The Art of Alfred Hitchcock: Fifty Years of His Films.* Rev. ed. London: Fourth Estate, 1992.

———. *Stanley Kramer, Film Maker.* New York: Putnam, 1978.

Staiger, Janet. "Cinematic Shots: The Narration of Violence." *The Persistence of History: Cinema, Television, and the Modern Event.* Ed. Vivian Sobchak. New York: Routledge, 1996. 39–54.

Stam, Robert. "Orson Welles, Brazil, and the Power of Blackness." Beja 219–44.

Stead, Peter. *Film and the Working Class: The Feature Film in British and American Society.* London: Routledge, 1989.

Steckmesser, Kent L. "The Three Butch Cassidys: History, Hollywood, Folklore." *American Renaissance and American West.* Ed. Christopher S. Durer, et al. Laramie: U of Wyoming, 1982. 149–55.

Stern, Lesley. "Meditation on Violence." *Kiss Me Deadly: Feminism and Cinema for the Moment.* Ed. Laleen Jayamanne. Sydney, Australia: Power, 1995. 252–85.

Stevenson, James A. "Beyond Stephen Crane: *Full Metal Jacket.*" *Literature/Film Quarterly* 16.4 (1988): 236–43.

Stewart, Donald Ogden. *By a Stroke of Luck: An Autobiography.* New York: Paddington, 1975.

Stone, Irving. *Clarence Darrow for the Defense.* Garden City, NY: Doubleday, Doran, 1941.

Stone, Oliver. Interview. *Playboy* (February 1980).

Stubbs, John C. "The Evolution of Orson Welles's *Touch of Evil* from Novel to Film." *Cinema Journal* 24.2 (1985): 19–39.

Sturak, Thomas. "Horace McCoy's Objective Lyricism." *Tough Guy Writers of the Thirties.* Carbondale: Southern Illinois UP, 1968. 137–62.

Sugg, Richard P. "The Role of the Writer in *The Player*: Novel and Film." *Literature/Film Quarterly* 22.1 (1994): 11–15.

Suid, Lawrence. "The Pentagon and Hollywood." O'Connor and Jackson 219–36.

Taylor, Clyde. "The Colonialist Subtext in *Platoon*." Dittmar and Michaud 171–74.

Telotte, J. P. "Effacement and Subjectivity: *Murder, My Sweet*'s Problematic Vision." *Literature/Film Quarterly* 15.4 (1987): 227–36.

Teuchert, Hans Joachim. "Bertolt Brecht's Contributions to the Screenplay of *Hangmen Also Die*." Diss. University of California at San Diego, 1981.

Thompson, Frank T. *William A. Wellman*. Metuchen, NJ: Scarecrow P, 1983.

Thomson, Boxcar Bertha. *Sister of the Road: The Autobiography of Box-Car Bertha*. As told to Ben L. Reitman. New York: Sheridan House, 1937.

Thomson, David. "*All Quiet on the Western Front*." *Movies of the Thirties*. Ed. Ann Lloyd. London: Orbis, 1983.

———. *Rosebud: The Story of Orson Welles*. New York: Knopf, 1996.

Tibbetts, John C. "Clint Eastwood and the Machinery of Violence." *Literature/Film Quarterly* 21.1 (1993): 10–17.

Titus, Mary. "Murdering the Lesbian: Lillian Hellman's *The Children's Hour*." *Tulsa Studies in Women's Literature* 10.2 (1991): 215–32.

Tompkins, Jane. *West of Everything: The Inner Life of Westerns*. New York: Oxford UP, 1992.

Torry, Robert. "Therapeutic Narrative: *The Wild Bunch, Jaws*, and Vietnam." *The Velvet Light Trap* 31 (Spring 1993): 27–38.

Travers, Peter. "*Bob Roberts*." *Rolling Stone* 639 (September 17, 1992): 101.

Troy, Gil. "*Bob Roberts*, Directed by Tim Robbins." *American Historical Review* 98.4 (1993): 1186.

Trumbo, Dalton. *Johnny Got His Gun*. 1939. New York: Citadel P, 1994.

Turner, John W. "*Little Big Man*, the Novel and the Film: A Study of Narrative Structure." *Literature/Film Quarterly* 5 (1977): 154–63.

Umland, Sam. "The Representation of the Native American in the Hollywood Western." *Platte Valley Review* 19.1 (1991): 49–70.

Valleau, Marjorie A. *The Spanish Civil War in American and European Films*. Ann Arbor, MI: UMI Research P, 1982.

Vanderwood, Paul. "An American Cold Warrior: *Viva Zapata!*" O'Connor and Jackson 183–201.

Vanderwood, Paul J., ed. *Juarez*. Madison: U of Wisconsin P, 1983.

Van Wet, William E. "Narrative Structure in *The Third Man*." *Literature/Film Quarterly* 2 (1974): 341–46.

Velde, François R. "On Fritz Lang's *Fury* (1936)." *Stanford French Review* 16.1 (1992): 87–94.

Vidor, King. *A Tree Is a Tree*. 1953. Hollywood, CA: Samuel French, 1989.

Walker, Michael. "*Dances with Wolves*." *The Book of Westerns*. Ed. Ian Cameron and Douglas Pye. New York: Continuum, 1996. 284–93.

———. "The Westerns of Delmer Daves." *The Book of Westerns*. Ed. Ian Cameron and Douglas Pye. New York: Continuum, 1996. 123–60.

Walker, Thomas W. *Nicaragua: The Land of Sandino*. 2d ed. Boulder, CO: Westview P, 1986.

Walker, Thomas W., ed. *Reagan Versus the Sandinistas: The Undeclared War on Nicaragua*. Boulder, CO: Westview P, 1987.

———. *Revolution and Counterrevolution in Nicaragua*. Boulder, CO: Westview P, 1991.

Wallach, George. "Charlie Chaplin's *Monsieur Verdoux* Press Conference." *Film Comment* 5 (Winter 1969): 34–42.

Ward, Jerry W., Jr. "*Native Son*: Six Versions Seeking Interpretation." *Approaches to Teaching Wright's* Native Son. Ed. James A. Miller. New York: Modern Language Association, 1997. 16–21.

Ward, Susan. "Social Philosophy as Best-Seller: Jack London's *The Sea Wolf*." *Western American Literature* 17.4 (1983): 321–32.

Warshow, Paul. *The Immediate Experience*. New York: Atheneum, 1975.

———. "The Unreal McCoy." *The Modern American Novel and the Movies*. Ed. Gerald Peary and Roger Shatzkin. New York: Frederick Ungar, 1978. 29–39.

Watson, Ritchie D., Jr. "Lillian Hellman's *The Little Foxes* and the New South Creed: An Ironic View of Southern History." *Southern Literary Journal* 28.2 (1996): 59–68.

Waugh, Thomas. "'Men Cannot Act in Front of the Camera in the Presence of Death.': Joris Ivens' *The Spanish Earth*." *Cineaste* 12.2–3 (1982–1983): 21–33.

———. "Water, Blood, and War: Documentary Imagery of Spain from the North American Popular Front." *The Spanish Civil War and the Visual Arts*. Ed. Kathleen Vernon. Ithaca, NY: Center for International Studies of Cornell U, 1990. 14–24.

Weales, Gerald. *Canned Goods as Caviar: American Film Comedies of the 1930s*. Chicago: U of Chicago P, 1985.

Weber, Max. *The Protestant Ethic and the Spirit of Capitalism*. Trans. Talcott Parsons. 1930. London: Routledge, 1992.

Weisbord, Albert. *Passaic Reviewed*. San Francisco: Germinal P, 1976.

Weisbord, Vera Buch. *A Radical Life*. Bloomington: Indiana UP, 1977.

Welles, Orson, Peter Bogdanovich, and Jonathan Rosenbaum. *This Is Orson Welles*. New York: HarperCollins, 1992.

Wellman, William A. *A Short Time for Insanity: An Autobiography*. New York: Hawthorn Books, 1974.

Whitaker, Sheila. *The Films of Martin Ritt*. London: British Film Institute, 1972.

White, Susan. "Male Bonding, Hollywood Orientalism, and the Repression of the Feminine in Kubrick's *Full Metal Jacket*." Anderegg. *Inventing Vietnam* 204–30.

Whittemore, Don, and Philip Alan Cecchettini. *Passport to Hollywood: Film Immigrants*. New York: McGraw-Hill, 1976.

Williams, John Alexander. "John Sayles Plays the Preacher." *Appalachian Journal* 15.4 (1988): 344–52.

Williams, Tony. "Narrative Patterns and Mythic Trajectories in Mid-1908s Vietnam Movies." Anderegg. *Inventing Vietnam* 114–39.

Willoquet-Maricondi, Paula. "Full-Metal-Jacketing: Or, Masculinity in the Making." *Cinema Journal* 33.2 (1994): 5–21.

Wilson, Christopher P. "Plotting the Border: John Reed, Pancho Villa, and *Insurgent Mexico*." *Cultures of United States Imperialism*. Ed. Amy Kaplan and Donald E. Pease. Durham, NC: Duke UP, 1993. 340–61.

Wilson, Edmund. *A Literary Chronicle: 1920–1950*. Garden City, NY: Doubleday, 1952.

Winston, Brian. *Claiming the Real: The Griersonian Documentary and Its Legitimations*. London: British Film Institute. 1995.

Wolcott, James. "The Godfather Goes Slumming." *Texas Monthly* (January 1984).

Wolfe, Charles. "The Poetics and Politics of Nonfiction: Documentary Film." Balio 351–86.

Wolfe, Gary K. "*Dr. Strangelove, Red Alert*, and Patterns of Paranoia in the 1950s." *Journal of Popular Film* 5.1 (1976): 57–67.

Womack, John, Jr. *Zapata and the Mexican Revolution*. New York: Knopf, 1971.

Wood, Michael. *America in the Movies; Or, "Santa Maria, It Had Slipped My Mind!"* New York: Basic Books, 1975.

Wright, Will. *Sixguns and Society: A Structural Study of the Western*. Berkeley: U of California P, 1975.

Yacowar, Maurice. "Re-Membering the Western: Eastwood's *Unforgiven*." *Queen's Quarterly* 100.1 (1993): 247–57.

Yates, Janelle. *Woody Guthrie: American Balladeer*. Staten Island, NY: Ward Hill P, 1995.

Yurchenco, Henrietta, and Marjorie Guthrie. *A Mighty Hard Road: The Woody Guthrie Story*. New York: McGraw-Hill, 1970.

Zaniello, Tom. *Working Stiffs, Union Maids, Reds, and Riffraff: An Organized Guide to Films about Labor*. Ithaca, NY: ILR P, 1996.

Zebme, Bill. "Tim Robbins." *Rolling Stone* 642 (October 29, 1992): 54.

Ziemer, Gregor. *Education for Death: The Making of the Nazi*. New York: Oxford UP, 1941.

Zubizarreta, John. "The Disparity of Points of View in *One Flew over the Cuckoo's Nest*." *Literature/Film Quarterly* 22.1 (1994): 62–69.

# INDEX

## About the Author

M. KEITH BOOKER is Professor of English at the University of Arkansas. He is the author of numerous articles and books on modern literature and literary theory, including *Dystopian Literature: A Theory and Research Guide* (1994), *Bakhtin, Stalin, and Modern Russian Fiction: Carnival, Dialogism, and History* (1995), *The Dystopian Impulse in Modern Literature: Fiction as Social Criticism* (1994), and *The Modern British Novel of the Left: A Research Guide* (1998), all available from Greenwood Press.

ISBN 0-313-30980-9

EAN

9 780313 309809

90000>

HARDCOVER BAR CODE